Education and the Courts

Third Edition

Education and the Courts

Third Edition

Richard McManus QC

JORDANS

Published by
Jordan Publishing Limited
21 St Thomas Street
Bristol BS1 6JS

British Library Cataloguing-in-Publication Data

A catalogue record for this book is available from the British Library.

ISBN 978 1 84661 328 9

Typeset by Letterpart Ltd, Reigate, Surrey

Printed in Great Britain by CPI Antony Rowe, Chippenham and Eastbourne

FOREWORD TO THE SECOND EDITION

In the four years that have elapsed since the publication of the first edition, there has been considerable activity both by Parliament and the courts in connection with education. The Human Rights Act 1998 has played a part in this activity but there has been much more. Major Education Acts or amendments to existing Acts have been a feature.

The result is a virtual doubling in length of this book. It remains, however, an invaluable aid both to the lawyer and the non-lawyer alike who wish to discover the relevant law which covers whatever problem they may have. I described the first edition as comprehensive but succinct. I do not, despite the increase in length, resile from that description since it has had to deal with so much more from primary and secondary legislation through ministerial guidance to decisions of the courts.

Richard McManus and those who have helped him with contributions to, or assistance with, parts of this book are all experts in this field. The relevant principles are expounded with admirable clarity. Where there are doubts as to what the law is in any particular area, the author most helpfully indicates his views and is not afraid to criticise decisions of the courts (including my own) which seem to him to be erroneous. A little more use of the first edition of this book might have prevented judges from making decisions in ignorance of prior contrary decisions or the principles which were applicable.

It is still the position that most cases involving education turn on public law principles. There are useful references to authorities drawn from other areas of public law which have relevance to issues which arise in the education field. This is a book which will, I have no doubt, appeal both to those who regularly practise in the field of education and those who may enter it for the first time. All that is necessary is to be found here and found in a thoroughly readable and comprehensible form.

The Hon Mr Justice Collins
Royal Courts of Justice
December 2003

PREFACE TO THE THIRD EDITION

It is now some eight years since the last edition. In that time much has changed. The Law of School Transport has a new statutory framework and those who have statements of special educational needs now not only can litigate pure transport issues in the First-tier Tribunal but also have a right to free transport to the school of their choice even if it is not the nearest suitable school providing this is not prejudicial to the efficient use of resources as a result of the decision of the Court of Appeal in *Dudley MBC v Shurvinton*.

In the field of school organisation Academies now loom large. This has exacerbated the long-standing problems created for local authorities by the discrimination legislation in this field. The Equality Act 2010 has overhauled the law in this area but regrettably no attempt was made to address the problems created by single sex schools and equality duties.

Religion and school dress codes has been a fertile source of litigation. In *R (Begum) v Denbigh High School* the House of Lords held that Ms Begum's rights under Article 9 of the ECHR had not been interfered with when the school did not permit her to wear strict Islamic dress in school, but that in any event the school uniform policy was justified. Further litigation by claimants in the area was largely unsuccessful although this trend seemed to have been halted by Silber J in *R (Watkins-Singh) v Governors of Abderdare High School for Girls*.

In disputes concerning Special Educational Needs the vast majority of litigation now takes place in the First-tier Tribunal. The role of the courts has been much reduced following the introduction of the right of appeal to the Upper Tribunal.

The aim of the book remains, as before, to illustrate the approach of the courts to litigation in this area. I have endeavoured to state the law as at 1 September 2012 although it has been possible to take account of some later changes.

I am indebted to a wide range of people who provided draft Chapters, sometimes in conjunction with each other. They were Anna Biccaregui (Chapters 1 and 4), Heather Emmerson (Chapter 1), Annabel Lee (Chapter 2), Paul Greatorex (Chapter 3), Sarah Hannett (Chapter 4), Saima Hanif (Chapter 5), Jonathan Auburn (Chapter 6), Michelle Pratley (Chapter 6), Jack Anderson (Chapter 7) and Estelle Dehon (Chapters 8 and 9).

Richard McManus QC
October 2012

CONTENTS

TABLE OF CASES

References are to paragraph numbers.

TABLE OF STATUTES

References are to paragraph numbers.

TABLE OF STATUTORY INSTRUMENTS

TABLE OF EU MATERIALS

References are to paragraph numbers.

TABLE OF CODES OF PRACTICE

References are to paragraph numbers.

Chapter 1

SCHOOL TRANSPORT

STANDING TO BRING AN APPLICATION FOR JUDICIAL REVIEW

1.1   It is likely that both the child and the parent have sufficient interest to have standing to bring an application for judicial review of a decision in relation to school transport.[1] It was common in the past for applications to be brought in the name of the child in order to benefit from public funding and avoid the risk of an adverse costs order.[2] In some other areas of education litigation, such as school admissions, the practice of bringing of proceedings in the name of a child to benefit from legal aid funding has been a matter of adverse comment[3] but the view of the Court of Appeal, when granting permission to move for judicial review in the context of a school reorganisation dispute, was that this is not necessarily an abuse of process: *R (on the application of Boulton and Another) v Leeds School Organisation Committee*.[4] When *Boulton* was heard substantively by the High Court, Scott Baker J held[5] that the observations of Kennedy and Ward LJJ in *R v Richmond LBC ex parte JC*,[6] suggesting it was an abuse to bring proceedings in the name of the child to get public funding, were limited to school admission disputes. He nevertheless

---

[1]   Traditionally challenges to decisions of public authorities in relation to transport have been dealt with by way of an application for judicial review. Since the decision of the Court of Appeal in the case of *Dudley Metropolitan Borough Council v Shurvinton & Ors* [2012] EWCA Civ 346, dealt with in paras **1.95–1.97** below, some if not all challenges to transport decisions where a child has a statement of special educational needs may be dealt with by way of an appeal to the First-tier Tribunal.

[2]   For examples of applications brought in the name of the child without adverse judicial comment see *R v London Borough of Havering ex parte K* [1998] ELR 351, *R v Kent County Council ex parte C* [1998] ELR 108, *R (on the application of T) v Leeds City Council* [2002] ELR 91 and *R v Carmarthenshire County Council ex parte White* [2001] ELR 172 (school transport case). Restrictions in public funding for judicial review including education litigation make this an issue of declining importance at present. However, rules on public funding do change from time to time so the present issue may become relevant again if there is a change of political view as to which cases should get legal aid. The difficulty in obtaining legal aid in this area is likely to lead to increasing attempts to obtain protective costs orders. As to these see, for a recent example, *Morgan v Hinton Organics* [2009] EWCA Civ 107 which reviews the relevant authorities.

[3]   See, for example, *R v Hackney ex parte T* [1991] COD 454; *R v Richmond LBC ex parte JC* [2001] ELR 21 and *R (on the application of B and others) v Head Teacher of Alperton Community School* [2001] ELR 359.

[4]   [2002] EWCA Civ 884 at para 7.

[5]   [2003] ELR 67 at para 34.

[6]   [2001] ELR 21 at paras 31 and 68.

went on to say[7] that, at least as far as school reorganisation disputes were concerned, it was ordinarily the parents who had the real and primary interest in bringing the case and it might be an abuse of process to proceed in the name of the child rather than a parent where this was done for the purpose of obtaining public funding and protection against a possible costs order. He held that clear evidence of such abuse would be needed and that it was not present in the case before him. In *Boulton* the evidence of abuse was not present because the applicants were selected at random from a larger group and had it been intended to choose claimants to get public funding there were plenty of parents who were available as they were on state benefits.[8] The Court emphasised that both the parent and the child had standing and the only issue was whether there had been an abuse of process.[9] *Boulton* and *ex parte JC* were referred to by the High Court in *R (Edwards) v The Environment Agency*[10] in considering whether a claim for judicial review in a planning context was an abuse of process. The Court held that it was not because the Legal Services Commission, despite knowledge of the relevant facts, had not withdrawn public funding.[11] The learned Judge however commented that it would be appropriate to refuse permission to move for judicial review in cases in other fields where it could be shown that a claim was brought in a particular person's name solely in order to obtain public funding, or to avoid liability for costs, or was otherwise in all the circumstances an abuse of process.

1.2   There is some anecdotal suggestion that since *Boulton* the Legal Services Commission has been reluctant to provide funding for a child in education related cases.[12] There is no reported case which specifically deals with school transport, but it is certainly strongly arguable that, just as in admissions and school reorganisation cases, it is the parents who have the primary interest in a transport decision, not least because it is usually the parent who has to pay for or provide transport if the local authority (LA) does not. Moreover, it is still the parents who commit the offence under section 444 of the Education Act 1996 (EA 1996) if the pupil does not attend school and it is still a defence if the LA is in breach of its duty to provide transport to the child.[13] Should the issue arise in the future, the courts are likely, therefore, to look carefully at the pre-existing practice and require an explanation for proceedings having been brought in the name of the child rather than the parent. Further, if it is an abuse to bring proceedings in the name of the child to benefit from public funding, it may be easier in many cases than it was in *Boulton* to establish that

---

7   At para 37.
8   [2003] ELR 67 at para 36.
9   See para 35.
10   [2004] 3 All ER 21 at paras 17–19. There were further proceedings in this case which went to the House of Lords where Mr Edwards failed: see [2008] UKHL 22.
11   See para 20. That may be a surprising conclusion on the facts and seemed to involve the learned judge delegating the responsibility for finding an abuse of process to the Legal Services Commission rather than the court determining the issue for itself.
12   See the comments of counsel after judgment was given in *Slough Borough Council v C & Anor* [2004] EWHC 1759 (Admin). Not much weight can be attached to this as Counsel was merely describing his own experience rather than citing a published authority.
13   See the EA 1996, s 444(3B)(a) and (b) as amended.

the only reason the proceedings have been so brought was to obtain that benefit. The simple expedient of making inquiry of the claimants at the commencement of such proceedings and taking the point in the acknowledgement of service should ensure that the factual basis for the issue is before the court. However, whether the court will do anything, once permission has been granted, other than pass adverse comment if there is an abuse, is doubtful.[14] Certainly, if there is prima facie evidence of abuse, attempts should be made pre-trial to get the public funding withdrawn by drawing to the attention of the Legal Services Commission the relevant facts. If public funding is not withdrawn and permission is granted, while it is theoretically possible that the court may decline to grant relief on what is otherwise a well-founded challenge (because relief is discretionary), it is unlikely that it will in fact do so. This is therefore an issue to be resolved before trial if possible.

THE NEED FOR PROMPTNESS IN BRINGING PROCEEDINGS

1.3   Under the provisions of CPR, r 54.5, any application for judicial review should be made promptly and in any event within three months of any decision to refuse to pay for school transport.

1.4   Doubt has been expressed by the House of Lords as to whether the requirement of promptness was sufficiently certain to comply with European Community law and Article 6 of the European Convention on Human Rights (ECHR): see *R (Burkett) v Hammersmith and Fulham London Borough Council*.[15] Lord Steyn,[16] while not deciding the point, simply expressed a doubt as to compliance with European Community law and the law of the ECHR:

> '[There] is at the very least doubt whether the obligation to apply "promptly" is sufficiently certain to comply with European Community law and the European Convention for the Protection of Human Rights and Fundamental Freedoms. It is a matter for consideration whether the requirement of promptitude, read with the three months' limit, is not productive of unnecessary uncertainty and practical difficulty.'

1.5   Lord Hope expressly agreed with Lord Steyn and delivered a speech of his own dealing with the relevance of delay in applications for judicial review in Scotland. He concluded his discussion by saying there was 'much force' in the point that the requirement of promptness without more in the rules was too uncertain to satisfy the requirements of Convention law. Lord Slynn[17] expressly left the point open and decline to comment. Lords Millet and Phillips agreed with the speeches of both Lords Slynn and Steyn.[18]

---

[14]   A court may refuse to grant permission to move for judicial review if it considers that the proceedings have been brought in the name of the child simply to get public funding.
[15]   [2002] UKHL 23, [2002] 1WLR 1593.
[16]   At para 53.
[17]   At para 6.
[18]   At paras 67 and 68.

1.6   The lack of clarity in *Burkett* as to the legality of the promptness requirement in judicial review was unfortunate. All that we had there was dicta, albeit at the highest level, and then only dicta expressing doubts, not concluded views. Whether Lords Millet and Phillips were to be taken as having shared the doubts of Lord Steyn or, as simply not having expressed a view on the point like Lord Slynn, was an open question. It is submitted that the better view was that they had not shared Lord Steyn's doubts because they agreed simply with his reasons for allowing the appeal and what he said about promptness was obiter and not a reason for allowing the appeal.

1.7   Whether Lord Hope was to be taken as entertaining the doubts of Lord Steyn about the legality of 'promptness' from the standpoint of community law was also open to doubt. Although he agreed with Lord Steyn's speech,[19] that was expressly subject to his own observations on, inter alia, promptitude. As is noted in para **1.5** above, his own observations on that issue were limited to a consideration of promptitude from the perspective of Convention jurisprudence. Accordingly it is submitted that the doubts he expressed about the legality of promptness did not extend to the community law context.

1.8   Therefore it is submitted that *Burkett* did not have the effect that the requirement of promptness in CPR, r 54.5 was no longer good law. Nobody in the House of Lords expressly held that requirement infringed either Convention or community law and the majority are not to be taken to have shared the respective doubts expressed by Lords Steyn and Hope. Moreover, *Burkett* did not consider the relevant jurisprudence. The Convention jurisprudence which existed at the time did not support any suggestion that the requirement of promptness was not compliant with the Strasbourg case-law.

1.9   In *Lam v United Kingdom*[20] the European Court of Human Rights had to consider an argument based on the then relevant rule of the Supreme Court, RSC Ord 53, r 4(1), that the refusal of the court to entertain an application for judicial review on the ground that it was not made promptly was a breach of the applicant's Article 6 rights. The court rejected this argument as manifestly ill-founded:

> 'The court is not persuaded that the applicants' other grievances under Art 6.1 disclose a prima facie breach of that provision.
>
> In the first place, their complaint about the interpretation given by the domestic courts to Ord 53, r 4(1) of the Rules of the Supreme Court must be seen in the context of the approach taken to the application of the provision in previous cases. The court notes in this respect that the domestic courts have consistently held that the primary requirement laid down by r 4(1) is that an application must be made "promptly", followed by the secondary provision "… and in any event within three months …". Accordingly, there can be cases where, even though the

---

[19]   At para 55.
[20]   (Unreported), Application No 41671/98.

application for leave was made within the three-month period, leave might be refused because, on the facts, the application was not made promptly. In the court's opinion, and with reference to the instant case, the first instance court and the Court of Appeal both considered that, on the facts, the applicants' leave application had not been made promptly and declined to exercise their discretion to apply the above-mentioned secondary provision.

In so far as the applicants impugn the strictness of the promptness requirement in that it restricted their right of access to a court, the court observes that the requirement was a proportionate measure taken in pursuit of a legitimate aim. The applicants were not denied access to a court *ab initio*. They failed to satisfy a strict procedural requirement which served a public interest purpose, namely the need to avoid prejudice being caused to third parties who may have altered their situation on the strength of administrative decisions.'

1.10 While it is true that nothing in *Lam* expressly deals with whether the requirement of promptness was too uncertain for there to be compliance with Article 6, it is inconceivable that the court would have failed to rule that it was a problem if that was indeed the case. The failure of *Burkett* to make reference to the decision in *Lam* undermines the weight that can be given to the obiter remarks of Lords Steyn and Hope.

1.11 There are four subsequent decisions of the Court of Appeal which have considered the issue of promptness and its compatibility with EC and ECHR law. In *R (on the Application of Boulton & Another) v Leeds School Organisation Committee*,[21] Sedley and Arden LJJ, in the context of an application for permission to apply for judicial review, held at para 8:

'The claim was brought within three months of the decision ... It may be that the application was not prompt, but the remarks of the House [in *Burkett*] at paras 53 and 59–60 have put lower courts on notice that promptness is a tool to be handled now with great care.'

1.12 It is a pity that the Court of Appeal in *Boulton* did not deal with the matter more fully because once they granted permission it was not open to the respondents to raise the question of undue delay at the substantive hearing.[22] Holding that promptness was a tool to be treated with great care, was not the same as saying that the requirement of promptness in CPR 54.5 should be treated as a dead letter, nor, it is submitted, was that what the House of Lords had held in *Burkett*.

1.13 A rather different approach was followed by another division of the Court of Appeal in *R (on the application of Young) v Oxford City Council*.[23]

---

22   *R v Criminal Injuries Compensation Board ex parte A* [1999] 2 AC 330.
23   [2002] EWCA Civ 990, [2003] JPL 232. See also to the same effect the decision of Stanley Burnton J (as he then was) in *R (Elliot) v The Electoral Commission* [2003] EWHC 395 at para 33.

Pill LJ[24] was the only member of the court to deal with *Burkett*; both Potter[25] and Judge LJJ[26] expressly left the point open. Pill LJ, having commented that what Lord Steyn had said was not reasoned in detail and not resolved by the House of Lords, stated as follows:

> 'Unless and until the issue is resolved adversely to the rule, the obligation to file the claim form promptly remains a feature of English law, in my view, and the presence of the word "promptly" in the rule should not be ignored. Those who seek to challenge the lawfulness of planning permissions should not assume, whether as a delaying tactic or for some other reason, they can defer filing their claim form until near the end of the three-month period in the expectation that the word "promptly" in the rule is a dead letter.'

1.14 The issue was addressed directly by the Court of Appeal in *R (Hardy) v Pembrokeshire Country Council*.[27] The appellant challenged the requirement of promptness on the basis that it breached Article 2 and Article 6 of the ECHR. The Court of Appeal rejected this argument on the basis that the requirement of promptitude was sufficiently certain to comply with 'European Law'. This should be interpreted as being confined to ECHR law, as the judgments of the Court of Appeal rely on case-law of the European Court of Human Rights, the argument of the appellant was limited to the ECHR and there is no reference to any EC case-law. The Court of Appeal relied on the decision in *Lam v United Kingdom*.[28]

1.15 The position under EC Law is less clear. The ECJ had considered in *Emmott v Minister for Social Welfare*[29] whether the time limit for bringing judicial review claims in Ireland was consistent with EC law and had implicitly concluded that it was so consistent, holding that States were permitted to lay down reasonable time limits provided they were not framed so as to render virtually impossible the exercise of rights conferred by EC Law, although there was no discussion of whether time limits and the requirements of promptness complied with legal certainty. Other domestic authorities on community law dating from the same period also did not suggest that the requirement of promptness was not compatible with EC Law.[30] However, in *Uniplex (UK) Ltd v NHS Business Services Authority*,[31] the ECJ concluded that a time limit in the context of a challenge to public procurement decisions which required proceedings to be brought 'promptly and in any event within three months'[32] was contrary to EC law as the promptness requirement was insufficiently

---

[24]   At paras 35–40.
[25]   At para 45.
[26]   At para 50.
[27]   [2006] EWCA Civ 240.
[28]   (Unreported) Application No 41671/98. See para **1.9** above.
[29]   Case C-208/90 [1991] ECR 1-4629.
[30]   See for example *R v Customs and Excise Commissioners ex parte Eurotunnel* [1995] CLC at 408B per Balcombe LJ, *R v North West Leicestershire DC ex parte Moses* [2000] EWCA Civ 125, [2000] Env LR 443 and *R v London Borough of Hammersmith and Fulham ex parte CPRE* [2000] Env LR 549, CA.
[31]   [2010] EUECJ C-406/08 [2010] 2 CMLR 1255.
[32]   Set out in the Public Contracts Regulations 2006, Reg 47(7)(b).

predictable. This case has been distinguished by the High Court[33] on the basis that it is limited to construction of Article 1 of Directive 89/665 and has no application to the requirement of promptness in judicial review claims. The matter was then considered again by the Court of Appeal in *R (on the application of Berky) v Newport City Council.*[34] That was also a planning case and the appeal was dismissed on its substantive merits. Accordingly, the consideration of the issue of promptness was obiter and could not resolve the debate. The majority of the Court of Appeal held that the concept of promptness did not satisfy the requirement of certainty under community law and, if the grounds of challenge included a valid community law point, relief could not be refused on any ground on the basis of undue delay.[35] Carnwath LJ, as he then was, held[36] that the requirement of promptness remained extant for purely domestic grounds of challenge. He did not decide whether it remained extant for community law grounds of challenge as he was of the view that this was an uncertain point of law that required a reference to the CJEU.[37] However, he held that even in relation to the community law points he would have refused relief on the grounds of undue delay leading to prejudice both to other interests and to good administration.[38] The current position therefore seems to be that in cases involving, but not confined to, a community law point that is not obviously bad, it will not be possible to refuse to entertain proceedings for judicial review on the grounds that they were not made promptly or to refuse relief in the exercise of the court's discretion on the grounds of undue delay. That is highly unsatisfactory and the need for law reform on the issue is urgent. The legality of a concept of promptness from the perspective of a community law point and the ability of the courts to refuse relief on the grounds of delay where a challenge includes community law points is, however, far from settled. Further litigation to clarify the position seems inevitable.

1.16 In any event, the vast majority of education disputes will not have a material community law or Convention challenge. The right to a fair hearing, which is embraced in Article 6 of the Convention, only applies to the determination of civil rights and obligations or a criminal charge. The long-standing position under Convention law is that rights relating to education do not involve a determination of a civil right or obligation or a criminal charge: *Simpson v UK.*[39]

---

33   *R (Caroll) v Westminster CC* [2010] EWHC 2019, para 39 per Michael Supperstone QC sitting (as he then was) as a Deputy High Court Judge. Some support for this position appears to be advanced by Sir Richard Buxton in *R (on the application of Berky) v Newport City Council* [2012] EWCA Civ 378 at paras 74 and 75.

34   [2012] EWCA Civ 37.

35   See paras 50, 53, 69 and 71–73.

36   See para 43.

37   See para 37.

38   See para 43.

39   (1989) 64 DR 188. The point has been much debated in the national courts following the passing of the Human Rights Act 1998; see Chapter 5 at para **5.137** and *S & Others v London Borough of Brent and others* [2002] EWCA 693, [2002] ELR 556 at para 30 where the Court of Appeal was prepared to make the assumption, which they regarded as tenable, that 'domestic

1.17 Accordingly if an application for permission to apply for judicial review containing a community law point is not made promptly, but within three months, there is a real chance that the court may yet entertain it because of doubts about whether promptness is an EC compliant concept. For other challenges not involving community law points it is more likely permission will be refused on the grounds of lack of promptitude. It is, therefore, prudent to move promptly where this can be done because it is submitted that:

(a) the true reading of the relevant case-law is that promptness is not a non-Convention compliant concept;

(b) in cases involving purely domestic grounds of challenge there is no issue about the legality of a concept of promptness;

(c) a failure to move promptly may mean the court cannot grant any effective relief when it hears the substantive application.

1.18 Dealing with the third of these three points, a failure to apply promptly may result in a refusal by the court to grant anything other than declaratory relief, because by that stage it is too late to grant effective relief (for example, it is academic because the child has left the relevant school or there is a detriment to good administration), Lord Steyn in *Burkett*[40] expressly endorsed (as manifest good sense) the approach of David Pannick QC[41] in *R v Rochdale MBC ex parte B, C and K*:[42]

> 'In my judgment, it is absolutely essential that, if parents are to bring judicial review proceedings in relation to the allocation of places at secondary school for their children, the matter is heard and determined by the court, absent very exceptional circumstances, before the school term starts. This is for obvious reasons relating to the interests of the child concerned, the interests of the school, the interests of the other children at the affected school and, of course, the teachers at that school.'

1.19 At para 53 of his speech in *Burkett*, Lord Steyn went on to say:

> '[In] regard to truly urgent cases the court would in any event in its ultimate discretion or under s 31(6) of the 1981 Act be able to refuse relief where it was appropriate to do so.'

Despite the doubts expressed by the majority of the Court of Appeal in *Berky*[43] as to whether it was appropriate to refuse relief in a case involving a community law challenge on the grounds of undue delay,it must still be the position that the court would not grant relief where no useful purpose would be

---

human rights law' and 'arguably the ECtHR jurisprudence' would regard the right not to be excluded from school as a civil right for Art 6 purposes.

40   At para 19.
41   Sitting as a Deputy High Court Judge.
42   [2000] Ed CR 117.
43   See para **1.15** above.

served by doing so because, for example, as a result of the delay in issuing the proceedings no relief was necessary because the child had left school and no longer needed transport. It is highly unlikely the court would grant any substantive relief in such a case and even declaratory relief may in a particular case serve no useful purpose.

Undue delay in applying for judicial review

1.20 Section 31(6) of the Senior Courts Act 1981[44] provides:

'Where the High Court considers that there has been undue delay in making an application for judicial review, the court may refuse to grant:

(a) leave for the making of the application; or
(b) any relief sought on the application,

if it considers that the granting of the relief sought would be likely to cause substantial hardship to, or substantially prejudice the rights of any person or would be detrimental to good administration.'

1.21 In *R v Criminal Injuries Board ex parte A*[45] the House of Lords considered the approach that should be adopted to this section read with the then current rule of court, RSC Ord 53, r 4, which provided:

'(1) An application for leave to apply for judicial review shall be made promptly and in any event within three months from the date when grounds for the application first arose unless the court considers that there is good reason for extending the period within which the application shall be made.'

1.22 The House of Lords held[46] that the approach to be adopted reading that rule and the Act together was as follows:

'(a) On an ex parte application, leave to apply for judicial review out of time can be refused, deferred to the substantive hearing or given.
(b) Leave may be given if the court considers that good reason for extending the period has been shown. The good reason on an ex parte application is generally to be seen from the standpoint, as here, of the applicant. Thus the reason for the delay here was "the practical difficulties [the applicant's solicitors] have encountered in trying to bring this matter before the court" (counsel for the applicant before Carnwath J). It is possible (though it would be unusual on an ex parte application) that if the court considers that hardship, prejudice or detriment to good administration have been shown, leave may still be refused even if good reason for an extension has been shown.
(c) If leave is given, then an application to set it aside may be made, though as the Court of Appeal stressed, this is not to be encouraged.

---

44 Formerly known as the Supreme Court Act 1981: see Constitutional Reform Act 2005, s 59(5) and para 1 of Sch 11.
45 [1999] 2 AC 330 at 341.
46 At p 341. All their Lordships agreed with Lord Slynn's speech.

(d)   If leave is given, then unless set aside, it does not fall to be reopened at the substantive hearing on the basis that there is no ground for extending time under Ord 53, r 4(1). At the substantive hearing there is no "application for leave to apply for judicial review", leave having already been given.

(e)   Nor in my provisional view, though the matter has not been argued and the question does not arise here, is there a power to refuse "to grant ... leave" at the substantive hearing on the basis of hardship or prejudice or detriment to good administration. The court has already granted leave; it is too late to "refuse" unless the court sets aside the initial grant without a separate application having been made for that to be done. What the court can do under s 31(6) is to refuse to grant relief.

(f)   If the application is adjourned to the substantive hearing, the question under both Ord 53, r 4(1) (good reason for an extension of time) and s 31(6) (hardship, prejudice, detriment, justifying a refusal of leave) may fall for determination.'

1.23   Although *Ex parte A* concerned RSC Ord 53, r 4 and not CPR, r 54.5, it is difficult to see that the change in the wording of the rule will materially affect the practice the courts follow with regard to delay, both in terms of entertaining an application for permission to move for judicial review when not made within the requisite time period and also when deciding what relief, if any, to grant. There is now, however, no power to apply to set aside an order granting permission at the suit of any person who has been served with the claim form by virtue of CPR, r 54.13.

The discretion to refuse relief

1.24   In *Boulton*[47] the Court of Appeal, at para 8, held that the discretion to refuse relief under section 31(6) of the Supreme Court Act 1981 was a tool to be handled with great care and referred back to their own remarks in *Burkett*[48] which they stated had been undisturbed by the House of Lords.[49] Their approach there was to only use what was then section 31(6) of the Supreme Court Act 1981[50] in the rarest cases:

'It is by now clear from experience that it is only in the rare case where the rules are capable of producing one outcome and the Act another that the unfortunate parallelism of these provisions needs to be explored. It is much better in almost every case to proceed as Richards J did here to examine the history of the case in the light of the extant rule, which embraces principles developed over many years by the court to meet each case on its particular facts, and to turn to s 31(6) only where one has to and then with Lord Slynn's guidance[51] to hand.'

---

[47]   [2002] EWCA Civ 884, [2001] Env LR 39.

[48]   [2000] EWCA Civ 321 at para 24.

[49]   For a recent example of how this test has been used in an education context (admissions) see paras 54–86 of *R (on the application of the London Borough of Lambeth) v Lambeth Independent Appeals Panel)* [2012] EWHC 943 (Admin).

[50]   Now known as the Senior Courts Act 1981: see Constitutional Reform Act 2005, s 59(5) and para 1 of Sch 11.

[51]   *R v CICB ex parte A* [1999] 2 AC 330 at 341.

1.25 In *R v Rochdale MBC ex parte Schemet*,[52] Roch J, as he then was, entertained a challenge to an LA transport policy which was outside the three month time-limit because the policy had continuing effect. He followed the unreported Court of Appeal decision in *R v Westminster City Council ex parte Hilditch*,[53] where Nicholls LJ (as he then was) stated:

> 'If the policy is unlawful prima facie it should be discontinued. The mere fact that the policy has been in place for nearly 3 years is not sufficient reason for countenancing its continuing implementation for the indefinite future.'

1.26 In *Schemet*, the court refused to grant certiorari[54] in relation to the out-of-time decisions so as to prevent the education budget for the past being disturbed. It does not necessarily follow that simply because money has been expended the court will hold that there is a detriment to good administration in making a quashing order: see *Burkett*[55] in the Court of Appeal at para 28:

> 'But it does not, in our judgment, follow that the quantum of expenditure can by itself enhance this aspect of a respondent's case. It would distort the ends of justice if the law or practice of the Administrative Court did anything to encourage developers to believe that the more money was poured into a project prior to the formal grant of planning permission, the stronger they could make their resistance to any application for permission to apply for judicial review, however well within the three-month period, on the ground that it was not prompt enough to outweigh the cash investment.'

1.27 Although those remarks were made in the context of expenditure incurred by a developer in reliance upon an apparently valid planning permission, they are not, as a matter of principle, restricted to that context. In *Burkett* the Court of Appeal went on[56] to make some pertinent remarks about the detriment to good administration:

> 'Administration beyond law is bad administration. The courts exist to protect the former as jealously as to stop the latter; but they cannot know which they are dealing with unless they can hear out and decide viable challenges to the legality of administrative acts. This cannot be regarded as a universal rule, since in England and Wales (in contrast to Scotland) not every viable challenge secures permission, but it heavily qualifies the availability of a "good administration" answer to a plea of promptness or an application to enlarge time, and it is doubtless the reason why public authorities rarely consider it appropriate to use it.'

1.28 This does not mean that simply because a public body has acted unlawfully it can never be appropriate to refuse relief on the grounds of the detriment to good administration. If that was correct the discretion to refuse relief under section 31(6)(b) of the Senior Courts Act 1981 would, in fact, be

---

[52]   91 LGR 425 at 436–437.
[53]   (Unreported) 14 June 1990.
[54]   Now known as a quashing order under CPR, r 54.1(2)(d).
[55]   [2000] EWCA Civ 321, [2001] Env LR 39.
[56]   At para 29.

nugatory, but it is not; see, for example, *R v CICB ex parte A*.[57] What it does mean is that it is a factor to be borne in mind when considering the exercise of the discretion under section 31(6), ie that there is a public interest in relief not being refused when a public body has acted unlawfully. How much weight is given to this aspect of the public interest is for the judge, in whom the discretion is vested, to decide.

OVERVIEW OF PROVISIONS RELATING TO SCHOOL TRANSPORT IN ENGLAND UNDER THE EA 1996

1.29 The law on home to school transport is now contained in the EA 1996, following the amendments contained in the Education and Inspections Act 2006 which took effect from April 2007.

1.30 Under the old law, local authorities were under a duty to provide free school transport where the authority considered it necessary for the purpose of facilitating the attendance of pupils at school or the Secretary of State had directed.[58] In effect, local authorities were required to provide free home to school transport in circumstances where parents would otherwise have had a defence to a school truancy prosecution.[59]

1.31 The amendments to the EA 1996 impose a number of mandatory transport duties on local authorities. Local authorities in England must:

(a) provide such travel arrangements as they think necessary for 'eligible' children of compulsory school age for whom no suitable travel arrangements are provided;[60]

(b) prepare and publish for each academic year a 'sustainable modes of travel strategy' and promote the use of sustainable modes of travel;[61]

(c) have regard to the Secretary of State's guidance and publish information about the authority's travel policy and arrangements;[62]

(d) have regard to any parental choice of school based upon the parent's religion or belief,[63] or for a person of sixth form age, that person's choice based on their religion or belief;[64]

---

[57]   [1999] 2 AC 330 at 341 per Lord Slynn.
[58]   EA 1944, s 55(1) and subsequently the EA 1996, s 509(1).
[59]   EA 1944, s 39 and subsequently the EA 1996, s 444. For the linkage under the old law between what became ss 444 and 509 of the EA 1966 see *George v Devon* [1989] AC 573 at 601F and paras **1.29–1.37** of the Second Edition of this book.
[60]   EA 1996, s 508B.
[61]   EA 1996, s 508A.
[62]   EA 1996, s 508D(3).
[63]   EA 1996, s 509AD(1)(a).
[64]   EA 2006, s 509AD(1)(b).

(e) prepare a transport policy statement for each academic year specifying travel arrangements for persons of sixth form age and secure that effect is given to such arrangements.[65]

1.32 The EA 1996 confers a discretionary power on local authorities in England to:

(a) make school travel arrangements as they consider necessary for 'non-eligible' children of compulsory school age;[66]

(b) make a school travel scheme for its area setting out the travel arrangements the authorities consider it appropriate to make;[67] and

(c) provide assistance with travel for nursery education.[68]

1.33 The position in relation to home to school transport in Wales is governed by different provisions[69] and is set out below at paras **1.128–1.144**.

1.34 The Secretary of State has issued statutory guidance in relation to children of compulsory school age: 'Home to School Travel and Transport Guidance' under sections 508A(7) and 508D of the EA 1996. Local authorities in England must have regard to this guidance when discharging their functions under sections 508A, 508B and 508C of the EA 1996. The Secretary of State has also issued statutory guidance in relation to education for persons of sixth form age: '2010 Post-16 Transport Guidance'. Local authorities in England must have regard to this guidance in preparing a statement of transport policy for persons of sixth form age.[70]

CHILDREN OF COMPULSORY SCHOOL AGE IN ENGLAND

Mandatory duty

1.35 Section 508B(1) of the EA 1996 requires an LA in England to provide such travel arrangements as they think necessary in the case of eligible children to whom section 508B(2) applies for the purpose of facilitating the child's attendance at a relevant educational establishment. Such transport arrangements must be provided free of charge in relation to the child.

1.36 The duty in section 508B(1) applies if no travel arrangements relating to travel between his home and school are provided free of charge by any other

---

[65] EA 1996, s 509AA.
[66] EA 1996, s 508C.
[67] EA 1996, s 508E and Sch 35C.
[68] EA 1996, s 509A.
[69] See the Learner Travel (Wales) Measure 2008.
[70] EA 1996, s 509AB(5).

person or such travel arrangements that are provided are not suitable for the purpose of facilitating his attendance at school.

Travel arrangements

1.37 The concept of 'travel arrangements' is a wide one. Section 508B(4) provides that, in relation to an eligible child, it means travel arrangements of any description. That expressly 'includes' the matters set out in sections 508B(4)(a) and (b). Subsection (a) is the provision of transport itself. Subsection (b) sets out three matters which are travel arrangements if those arrangements are made with the consent of the parents. They are the provision of an escort, arrangements for the payment of any person's reasonable travelling expenses and arrangements for the payment of allowances in respect of the use of particular modes of travel. By virtue of section 508B(5), travel arrangements in relation to an eligible child include any arrangements made by the parent providing they are made voluntarily by the parents. Accordingly the LA is not relieved of its duty simply because the parents provide transport to the child in circumstances where the LA have refused to provide transport where they were obliged to do so under section 508B(1). 'Travel arrangements' in relation to an eligible child do not though include arrangements which give rise to additional costs unless there is appropriate protection against those costs.[71]

1.38 The relevant guidance on these provisions is at paragraphs 48 to 51 of 'Home to School Travel and Transport Guidance'. Most of this guidance is self-explanatory and requires no elaboration. However, a subject on which guidance would have been helpful, and is largely absent, is the situation where the LA seeks to discharge its section 508B(1) duty by the provision of an escort. As we have seen, by virtue of section 508B(4)(b) an escort can only be provided if the parents consent. The Act is silent on whether that consent can be withheld unreasonably. This provokes the question whether the parent has an unreasonable right of veto against the provision of an escort. That there should be such a right of veto is unattractive. However, the fact that Parliament could easily have provided consent should not be unreasonably withheld or provided machinery for resolving disputes as to whether such consent had been unreasonably withheld[72] and did neither, suggests that they did intend a parent could have an unreasonable right of veto. On the other hand, pre-existing case-law was to the effect that the parent should do those things which were reasonably practicable to bring about the child's attendance at school.[73] While those remarks were in the context of a discussion of whether the parent should accompany the child to school if that was reasonably practicable, they were not

---

[71] Section 508B(6). As to what are 'additional costs' and what constitutes appropriate protection see s 508B(7).

[72] See for an example of this the Coal Mining Subsistence Act 1991, s 41.

[73] *George v Devon* [1989] AC 573 at 606F per Lord Keith. The rest of their Lordships agreed with his speech.

so confined.[74] Moreover, the absence of any specific machinery in the Act for the LA to determine whether the parent was in breach of his duty to take all reasonable practicable steps to get the child to school is not fatal, because, as appears below, more general provisions in the EA 1996 and the common law would enable the point to be tested. Accordingly, if it is reasonably practicable for an escort to accompany the child to school and the escort is suitable it is probably still the position that the LA is not obliged to make other arrangements for the child's transport to school if the parents refuse the provision of an escort.

1.39 If the contrary view was what was intended by Parliament, that is unfortunate. The provision of an escort may be less expensive for the public authority than the provision of transport and, as the public authority is always obliged to act reasonably, could never be lawfully done unreasonably by the LA. If it is the position that a parent is under no reciprocal obligation to behave reasonably in this context, that is a matter for regret.

Nearest available route

1.40 The question of what has to be taken account of when judging whether a route is available was the subject of two decisions of the House of Lords under the previous statutory framework. In *Essex County Council v Rogers*[75] it was held that, for a route to be available, it had to be reasonably capable of being used by a child accompanied, as necessary, by an adult. A route did not cease to be available because of hazards which would arise if the child was unaccompanied. In *George v Devon CC*,[76] the House of Lords held that the LA was entitled to take into account whether there were any circumstances which prevented it being reasonably practicable for the child to be accompanied.

1.41 The Home to School Travel and Transport Guidance makes reference to children being accompanied where necessary.[77] As is set out above, that requires them to take all reasonably practicable steps to get their child to school. However, if it is not reasonably practicable for the parent to accompany the child to school, for example because of work commitments,[78] the better view is that possible parental accompaniment must be disregarded for the purpose of deciding whether a route is available.

---

[74] *George v Devon* [1989] AC 573 at 606F per Lord Keith. The Guidance refers to this duty at para 85.

[75] [1987] AC 66.

[76] [1989] AC 573.

[77] Paras 46, 47, 81, 82, 84, 85 and 88.

[78] In *George v Devon* [1989] AC 573 at 583B in the Court of Appeal, Lord Donaldson MR was doubtful as to whether an unemployed parent (the child's stepfather) could say it was not reasonably practicable for him to take the child to work because if he did so he might lose an entitlement to unemployment benefit. Although the House of Lords reversed the decision of the Court of Appeal, it seems that they were of the same view as the Court of Appeal on this point because they held that it was open to the LA to conclude that the stepfather was available to accompany the child: see at 607A.

1.42   The LA's duty to act fairly before making a transport decision would enable them to determine whether it was reasonably practicable for the parent to accompany the child and before doing so they should hear what the parent has to say on the matter. If the parent disagreed with the LA's conclusion they could keep the child at home and then seek to argue they were not guilty of the offence under section 444 of the EA 1996 because the LA were not providing suitable transport arrangements. The risk of being prosecuted and convicted may make this an unattractive option for the parent. The matter could also be raised with the Secretary of State under section 496 of the EA 1996[79] and this may be the best option.

1.43   More generally, where there is a dispute between the LA and the parents as to whether the route is available because of safety concerns, judicial review may not be an appropriate means of resolving that issue. In *R v Essex ex parte EB*[80] there was such a dispute. The court refused to grant leave to move for judicial review on the basis that the matter was best resolved by the Secretary of State. In that case, there had been no attempt to resolve the matter by way of complaint to the Secretary of State. It does not follow that the court will invariably refuse to entertain such disputes,[81] although, in general terms, seeking redress from the Secretary of State is likely to be the better course.

The suitability of the travel arrangements

1.44   The question of suitability of the travel arrangements is relevant for two purposes. First, there is no duty on local authorities to provide free school transport where other suitable travel arrangements exist, for example provided by the parents. Secondly, the travel arrangements put in place by an LA must be suitable in order to satisfy the duty under section 508B. The Home to School Travel and Transport Guidance sets out guidance on the meaning of 'suitable' and states that best practice is that travel arrangements must enable an eligible child to reach school without such stress, strain or difficulty that they would be prevented from benefiting from the education so provided.[82] This incorporates the position in *R v Hereford and Worcester County Council ex parte P*,[83] where it was held that proper provision depended on the child's needs and not on what the authority could afford; and that the duty implicitly included a need for transport to be non-stressful.

---

[79]   Transport arrangements relating to young adults and sixth formers have special provisions relating to complaints to the Secretary of State: see the EA 1996, ss 496(5), 508I and 509AE.

[80]   [1997] ELR 327.

[81]   In an unreported decision involving Liverpool City Council, Jackson J granted permission to move for judicial review when the LEA took the view it was safe for a small child to walk in inner city Liverpool without being accompanied by an adult on the basis that this was arguably perverse; *R v Liverpool ex parte Fergusson* (unreported) 16 July 2001. There the parent had, in any event, tried and failed to get the Secretary of State to take action.

[82]   The Guidance provides assistance on the meaning of 'suitable' travel arrangements at paras 52–55.

[83]   [1992] 2 FLR 207.

Eligible child

1.45 Schedule 35B of the EA 1996 sets out the definition of 'eligible child' in paras 2–7 and 9–13.[84] The categories of eligible child are as follows:

(a) Children living within the statutory walking distance who are unable to walk to school[85] by reason of their SEN, disability or mobility problems.[86]

(b) Children living within the statutory walking distance but who are unable to walk to school in safety[87] because of the nature of the route.[88]

(c) Children living outside the statutory walking distance unless suitable arrangements have been made for the child to be registered at a qualifying school nearer their home[89] or the parents have voluntarily made suitable arrangements.[90]

(d) Primary school children from low income families (ie children who qualify for free school meals or whose parents are in receipt of the maximum level of Working Tax Credit)[91] registered at a school more than two miles from their home and no suitable arrangements have been made for them to be registered at a qualifying school nearer their home.[92]

(e) Secondary school children (aged 11–16) from low income families where they are registered at a school which is between two and six miles from home and there are not three or more suitable schools nearer their home.[93]

(f) Secondary school children from low income families who are registered at a school which is between two and 15 miles from home if the parent's

---

[84] EA 1996, para 1 of Sch 35B.

[85] Or a place other than a school where he is receiving education by virtue of arrangements made pursuant to the EA 1996, s 19(1). All of the eligibility provisions apply equally to s19(1) educational arrangements.

[86] Paras 2 and 3 of Sch 35B.

[87] Para 84 of the Home to School Travel and Transport Guidance sets out the factors that should be taken into account by the LA in considering whether the child can reasonably be expected to walk to school given the nature of the route.

[88] Para 4 of Sch 35B.

[89] Where a school is named in Part 4 of a child's statement of SEN, and more than the statutory walking distance from the child's home, the LA cannot refuse to provide transport on the basis that there are closer suitable schools: *R (H) v London Borough of Brent* [2002] ELR 509. An excluded child obliged to attend a place other than their registered school which is outside the statutory walking distance will be treated as an eligible child under para 6: para 8 of Sch 35B.

[90] Paragraphs 6 and 7 of Sch 35B.

[91] Paragraph 14 of Sch 35B.

[92] Paragraphs 9 and 10 of Sch 35B.

[93] Paragraph 11 of Sch 35B.

preference for that school is based on the parent's religion or belief[94] and having regard to that belief there is no suitable qualifying school which is nearer home.[95]

1.46 It will be observed that both in relation to preferences based on religion and in relation to low income families, the definition of 'eligible child' turns in part on the distance between the child's home and the school at which he is registered. So, for example, under paragraph 12 of Schedule 35B the child cannot be an eligible child under that paragraph if he is registered at a qualifying school less than two or more than 15 miles from his home. The Guidance[96] provides an example of a child registered at a school 35 miles away from his home as a result of a faith based preference. The child in that example, the Department advises, would not count as an 'eligible child' under 'these provisions'.

1.47 Again, it is submitted, care should be taken when regard is had to this aspect of the guidance. An LA should be careful not to deny a child free school transport on the basis that the distance criteria in paragraph 12 are not met where the effect of doing so is to render the right of preference illusory. Of course, it should take account of the fact that Parliament has expressly provided that there are distance criteria and so a general policy that reflects those criteria would be appropriate. However, there will be possibly rare cases where the only suitable school for the child having regard to the parent's religious preference is more distant that the fifteen miles provided for in paragraph 12 and that the child will not be able to get to that school unless the LA makes suitable travel arrangements. Not every low income family will be in that position but if the right to express a preference would be rendered illusory, as distinct from difficult to exercise, if the LA did not make travel arrangements for the child then it is probable that it is necessary for the LA to make those arrangements. It is submitted that in such a case a child could be an eligible child under paragraph 6.

1.48 For similar reasons it is submitted that it would be inappropriate to take the view that unless a family counts as a low income family under paragraphs 9 to 14 of Schedule 35B, their income should be disregarded. It is theoretically possible that a family may not count as a low income family under these provisions, either because of the income provisions themselves under paragraph 14, or because of the distance provisions in paragraphs 11 and 13, but to still have an eligible child under paragraph 6 because unless travel arrangements are made for that child the right of preference is rendered not merely difficult to express, but nugatory.

---

[94]   Guidance as to religion or belief in contained Part 5 of the Home to School Travel and Transport Guidance.
[95]   Paragraph 12 of Sch 35B.
[96]   Paragraph 99 'Child C'.

1.49 The statutory walking distance is two miles for children under the age of eight, and three miles for children aged eight or over.[97] Distance is to be measured by reference to the nearest available route.[98]

Qualifying school

1.50 To be eligible for free home to school transport the child must be a registered pupil at a qualifying school. Paragraph 15(2) of Schedule 35B sets out the definition of 'qualifying school'.[99] The School Travel (Pupils with Dual Registration) (England) Regulations 2007[100] provide that where an eligible child is registered at more than one educational establishment (for example at a mainstream and a special school), the relevant educational establishment is whichever he is attending at the relevant time. The Regulations also provide that where a child has no fixed abode 'home to school travel arrangements' means travel from wherever the child is residing at the relevant time to the nearest qualifying school at which he is registered, so far as is reasonably practicable.

Suitability of the school that the LA wishes the child to attend

1.51 There has been considerable judicial discussion of the question of whether it is possible to make 'suitable arrangements' if the qualifying school is unsuitable for the child. Under the old provisions (section 509 considered with section 444(4) of the EA 1996), local authorities had a duty to provide school transport for any child registered at a school that was not within walking distance, unless suitable arrangements had been made by the LA for enabling him to become a registered pupil at a qualifying school nearer to his home. The question was whether the adjective 'suitable' applied solely to the arrangements or also extended to the school.

1.52 This issue was of considerable uncertainty, with conflicting authorities on the point. Presented with these conflicting authorities, the Court of Appeal in *Re S*[101] expressed the view that the adjective 'suitable' governed the arrangements, but not the school, and therefore there was no requirement for the school to be suitable.

1.53 The issue was reconsidered by Collins J in *R v Bedfordshire ex parte WE*.[102] Collins J held that he was bound by the decision of the Court of Appeal in *Ex parte S* to hold that the school did not have to be objectively

---

97 EA 1996, s 444(5). The section uses the metric equivalents.
98 As above.
99 This includes a community, foundation or voluntary school, community or foundation special school, school approved under the EA 1996, s 342, a pupil referral unit, maintained nursery school, city technology college, city college for the technology of the arts or an Academy: para 15(2).
100 SI 2007/1367.
101 [1995] ELR 98.
102 (Unreported) 1 July 1996.

suitable for the arrangements to be suitable, but that had the matter been free from authority, he would have preferred the contrary view. An ex parte application for leave to appeal to the Court of Appeal was refused on the papers by Brooke LJ and, on a renewed application, by the court.[103] Simon Brown LJ dismissed the application for leave to appeal in trenchant terms. He held that it was wrong of Collins J to have criticised the Court of Appeal in *Ex parte S*, not least because it did not arise on the view the learned judge had taken of the other issues in the case. Both Simon Brown LJ and Holman J in *Bedfordshire* seem to have regarded *Ex parte S* as clearly binding.

1.54 The matter was next considered by the High Court in *R v Kent County Council ex parte C*.[104] McCullough J distinguished *Re S* and concluded that an LEA could not properly refuse to provide free transport on the basis that there was a nearer school unless that nearer school was, in its view, suitable. Those remarks are strictly obiter because, on the facts, the court dismissed the challenge to the LEA decision, holding that it was not obliged to provide free school transport to the nearest grammar school because the LEA could lawfully decide that a nearer non-selective school was suitable. Unfortunately, there is no trace in the report of either counsel in that case having referred McCullough J to the Court of Appeal decision in *Bedfordshire* and the decision is inconsistent with *Bedfordshire* and *Dyfed* and, it is submitted, wrongly decided. McCullough J held[105] that *Dyfed* had decided only that it was not for the court to determine whether the school the LEA had allocated the child to was objectively suitable.

1.55 The matter was further considered in *R v Camarthenshire ex parte White*[106] following permission to move for judicial review being granted on appeal by the Court of Appeal.[107] In that case, the child had left a school where she contended she was the victim of bullying and sought to obtain the cost of transport to an alternative school. The LEA refused to pay the cost of transport. Tomlinson J dismissed the application on the basis that the council was entitled to form the view that the bullying that was alleged to have occurred had not taken place and the original school to which the child had been allocated and which she attended was one where she could receive an effective education. Although the case did not, therefore, proceed on the basis that the reference to suitable arrangements in section 444(4)(b) of the EA 1996 meant the school had to be suitable, the test applied by the judge was consistent with such an approach in that he proceeded on the basis that, in order for the LA to lawfully refuse to pay transport to the school the parents had chosen, the school the LA had originally allocated to the child must have been one where the child could have received an effective education. The case, however, is of

---

[103] [1996] EWCA Civ 912.
[104] [1998] ELR 108.
[105] [1998] ELR 108 at 112H–114C.
[106] [2001] ELR 172.
[107] Unreported. The substantive hearing following the grant of permission is reported at [2001] ELR 172.

limited precedent value as it does not make reference to *Dyfed, Essex, Bedfordshire* or *Kent* and, again, there is no trace of the judge having been referred to any of these authorities.

1.56 In *R v Vale of Glamorgan ex parte J*,[108] Elias J followed the approach of McCullough J in the *Kent* case.[109] In that case the applicant, who was of mixed race, was bullied at Albert Primary School because of his ethnic origins. As a result, he was removed by his parents from that school, where there were few children from ethnic minorities, to Ninian Park School, which was a school which was more distant (albeit within walking distance). Ninian Park School had significantly more children from ethnic minority backgrounds. The council refused to pay for transport to Ninian Park School on the ground that it was less than three miles from the child's home and that Albert Primary School was a suitable school for the child to attend. The child brought proceedings for judicial review contending that, on the medical evidence, only a school with 'an appropriate racial mix' was suitable for him and that Albert Primary School did not have that mix. The court held on the evidence that the council could lawfully decide that the child did not need to attend a school with 'an appropriate racial mix' and, accordingly, nearer schools (Stanwell or St Cyres) which did not have a significant number of children from ethnic minorities were nevertheless suitable. Accordingly, it was unnecessary to decide whether or not the alternative schools identified by the LA were suitable, because on the evidence they were. Like *Camarthenshire*, the case is of limited precedent value as it does not make reference to *Dyfed, Essex, Bedfordshire* or *Kent* and, again, there is no trace of the judge having been referred to any of these authorities.

1.57 The *Vale of Glamorgan* case was considered by the Court of Appeal.[110] The court dismissed the appeal on the basis that the LEA had offered a place at a suitable school and it mattered not that that place subsequently became unavailable. In other words, the Court of Appeal applied a test which looked to the suitability of the alternative school the LEA had offered and not simply whether the arrangements the LEA made for the child to attend an alternative school were suitable.[111] Unfortunately, yet again, there is no reference to *Dyfed, Essex, Bedfordshire* or *Kent*, nor is there a trace of the Court of Appeal having been referred to any of these authorities, although one member of the Court of Appeal, Sir Christopher Staughton, had been a party to the decision in *Essex* and can be presumed to have been aware of it.

1.58 More recently, Collins J in *R (on the application of Jones) v Ceredigion County Council*[112] considered whether it is possible for a local education authority to have made suitable arrangements for a child to be a registered pupil at a school if that school would not be educationally suitable for the child concerned. Collins J reviewed a large number of the authorities on this point,

---

[108] [2001] ELR 223.
[109] [1998] ELR 108 at para 13.
[110] [2001] EWCA Civ 593, [2001] ELR 758.
[111] See at para 61.
[112] [2004] EWHC 1376 (Admin).

acknowledging the conflicting views expressed in the Court of Appeal and at first instance. Collins J rejected the argument that McCullough J in *Kent* had regarded the relevant part of *Re S* as obiter when it was ratio and went on to consider section 7 of the EA 1996 which sets out the basic obligation for a child to received efficient full-time education suitable to his age, ability, aptitude and any special educational needs he may have and held that it would be inconsistent with this to make arrangements to register a child at a school that could not provide a suitable education. Collins J concluded that the decision of the Court of Appeal in the *Vale of Glamorgan* case was binding, stating that it was impossible to believe the court had not been aware of and considered the decision in *Re S* and in so doing held that the place offered by the LEA must be at a suitable school.

1.59 Recognising the state of conflict of the authorities on the point, Collins J provided an opportunity for much needed clarification on the issue by a higher court. Collins J certified[113] that the case was suitable for an application to be made direct to the House of Lords for leave to appeal, and, in the event the House of Lords did not give permission to appeal, gave permission to appeal to the Court of Appeal. Two points were sought to be raised before the House of Lords. The first on which permission was sought was that it was not necessary to provide transport if the parent would have a defence to a prosecution under section 444 of the EA 1996. The second on which permission was sought was that it was not necessary for the school the LEA allocated to the child to be suitable for the LEA to make 'suitable arrangements'. Not surprisingly, the House of Lords did not grant permission to appeal on the first issue.[114] They did though grant permission to appeal on the second issue. Unfortunately, the appellants decided they did not want to appeal on the second issue only and withdrew their appeal to the House of Lords. They did though seek to appeal the first issue to the Court of Appeal. The case then became bogged down on the procedural issue as to whether they could do so. It was ultimately decided that they could.[115] It is a great shame that the opportunity was not taken by the council in this case to get the law on suitable arrangements clarified.

1.60 In *R v Leeds County Council*[116] Wilkie J held, obiter, that the school had to be suitable for the arrangements to be suitable, but that the decision as to suitability was for the LEA subject to the usual *Wednesbury* constraints. On the facts it was held that non Jewish schools in Leeds were *Wednesbury* suitable for orthodox Jews who wished to, and did attend orthodox Jewish schools in Manchester.

---

[113] Under the Administration of Justice Act 1969, s 12 it is possible to certify that a case is suitable for applying direct to the House of Lords for permission to appeal if the three conditions therein set out are met.

[114] That issue had been determined by the House of Lords in *George v Devon* [1989] AC 573, which itself affirmed long standing authority to the same effect.

[115] [2005] EWCA Civ 986, [2005] ELR 565 and [2007] UKHL 24.

[116] [2005] EWHC 2495 (Admin) [2006] ELR 25.

1.61 The issue has been considered in Northern Ireland. In *Re SH's Application for Judicial Review*[117] Weatherup J reviewed the English authorities. He held that the balance of authority was to the effect that the school the LEA allocated the child to had to be suitable in order for the LEA to make suitable arrangements for transport. He held that in Northern Ireland because of a Departmental Circular to that effect the same approach should be followed[118] but, that in the absence of the circular he would have reached the same decision.

1.62 None of the above case-law was on the present legislative provisions. However, the concept of suitable arrangements is still present in the legislative scheme: see paragraphs 6 and 9 of Schedule 35B. However, it is to be noted that in other parts of this legislative scheme the concept of suitable qualifying **school** is used.[119] This gives rise to the question whether the different choice of language is deliberate and Parliament intended to distinguish between suitable arrangements and a suitable school.

1.63 It appears that it was not the intention of the Secretary of State. The Guidance[120] in England is, like that in Northern Ireland, to the effect that the nearest qualifying school has to be suitable for the arrangements to be suitable.[121] Although the only obligation on the LA is to 'have regard' to the guidance[122] if the approach that was followed in Northern Ireland is adopted in England, the conflicting case-law can be bypassed. While the duty to have regard to guidance is not the same as a duty to slavishly follow,[123] the reality is that it would be sensible for local authorities to take the same approach as is in the Guidance. Further, there is a clear trend in the most recent case-law to require the alternative school to which the LA wishes to allocate the child to be suitable, at least in the judgment of the LA acting lawfully. The recent case-law that suggests the school has to be suitable does not require that issue to be decided by the court as a matter of objective fact, but merely that the LA has lawfully determined (on traditional *Wednesbury* grounds) that the alternative school is suitable. The change in legislative scheme and new Guidance should not lead to a different approach in future cases.

1.64 As can be seen from the law relating to school admissions, it is unlawful for an LA to allocate children to schools without first giving them the opportunity to express a preference.[124] If, however, it is possible to accede to an expression of parental preference, is it necessary for the LA, in order to avoid any potential duty to provide free school transport, to go through the hypothetical task of examining whether it would have been possible to make

---

[117] [2007] NIQB 39.
[118] See paras 16 and 20.
[119] See paras 11 and 12 of the EA 1996, Sch 35B.
[120] This Guidance is issued under the EA 1996, s 508D.
[121] See para 106.
[122] EA 1996, s 508D(3).
[123] See e g *Watt v Kesteven* [1955] 1 QB 408.
[124] See *R v Rotherham ex parte Clarke* [1998] ELR 152 and see further the discussion in Chapter 5 on school admissions.

suitable arrangements for the child to attend a school within walking distance and, if so, how and at what time? On a strict reading of paragraph 6 of Schedule 35B, arrangements must actually be made. It is highly artificial, however, to make arrangements for the child to attend school A when his parents have applied for him to attend school B and it is possible to accede to his parents' preference. Also, how is account to be taken of the availability of places at school B? If it has capacity for 100 pupils, how many notional allocations can the LA make to it? The answer to these problems seems to be that:

(a)   although no actual arrangements can be made before a preference is expressed, the LA can have a policy that, in general terms, children will be allocated to schools within walking distance subject to parental preference, but that the right of preference would not typically confer an entitlement to free transport to a more distant school;

(b)   once a preference is expressed (for school A) but before it is acceded to, the LA should check whether it is possible to place the child at a nearer school (school B) within walking distance;

(c)   if it is possible to place the child at school B and the preference for school A can be acceded to, then suitable arrangements for attendance at school B have probably been sufficiently made to satisfy paragraph 6 of schedule 35B of the EA 1996;

(d)   if the preference for school A can be acceded to, it should be, but will not carry an entitlement to free school transport with it.

1.65   The decision of the Court of Appeal in *Vale of Glamorgan*[125] has some bearing on this problem. As will be recollected from the discussion above,[126] by the time the case reached the Court of Appeal, the place the LA had offered at Stanwell School was no longer available and the child was attending, apparently happily and as a result of parental preference, Fitzalan High School. It was sought to be contended that the lack of a place at Stanwell meant that the LEA had not made suitable arrangements for the child to attend that school and, accordingly, that the LEA was obliged to pay for the transport to Fitzalan.

1.66   It is perhaps not surprising the Court of Appeal dismissed the challenge. The parent at no stage had wanted the child to go to Stanwell School and had rejected the LEA offer of a place, which was why it had been filled by another pupil. It was clearly, in those circumstances, highly unattractive that the parent should be entitled to complain that the LEA had not made suitable arrangements for the child to attend Stanwell. The Court of Appeal could, therefore, have decided the case that suitable arrangements had been made for

---

[125]   [2001] EWCA 593, [2001] ELR 758.
[126]   See para **1.57** above.

the child to attend Stanwell before the commencement of the new term and it was irrelevant that it was no longer possible to make those arrangements thereafter. In other words, what was crucial for the purposes of section 444 was that arrangements were made for the child to attend a nearer school before the preference for another school was acceded to, and it was not necessary for the LEA to continue to make such arrangements at any later point in time.

1.67 That, however, was not the approach of the Court of Appeal. It held[127] that circumstances could arise where the LEA would be obliged to make arrangements for the child to attend a nearer school after parental preference had been acceded to and, accordingly, at a time outside the normal admissions cycle. The court gave the following example:

> 'It might be, for instance, that a parent was in a financial position to pay for the bus fares to a distant school at the time that the offer of a nearer school was turned down that thereafter his financial circumstances changed and he was no longer in such a position. Suppose he then went to the LEA and explained his predicament yet the Authority, although it was not in a position to offer a place at a nearer suitable school, refused to pay relying on arrangements which it had made previously and which he had then rejected. In such circumstances, unless the Authority made arrangements for the child's transport the child would not be able to get to school. One must not forget that these provisions are primarily enacted for the benefit of children and in circumstances such as those which I have posited it might well be unreasonable for the Authority to refuse to make arrangements for transport to the distant school, at any rate until a place could be found at a suitable school nearer home. If the Authority did not make such arrangements and the child did not attend school but instead prosecuted the parent then the parent would in principle be able to rely on the defence in s 444(4)(b).'

1.68 Accordingly, while in general terms an LA only has to make suitable arrangements for the child to attend a nearer school during the course of the normal admissions cycle, there can be circumstances when it has to reconsider the question of alternative arrangements at a later date. An easy example is where the child moves into the area at a later date. The Court of Appeal was not saying, however, that in every case where a parent applies for free school transport outside the normal admissions cycle the LA will be obliged to consider at that time whether it is in a position to make suitable arrangements for the child to attend a nearer school. If there has been no change of circumstance which impacts on the ability of the child to get to the school of choice, or makes that school no longer suitable, the LEA will be able to rely on the arrangements it made for the child to attend the nearer school at an earlier stage to defeat any entitlement to free transport:[128]

> '[In] the present case ... the Authority were fully entitled to reach the conclusion that it was not necessary to make arrangements for getting J to school and are entitled, as things stand, to adhere to that view. They had offered a place at a suitable school nearby but the parents had, perfectly reasonably, refused to take

---

[127] At para 61. Strictly speaking, this is obiter.
[128] See para 62 per Schiemann LJ.

this place up. The result of the refusal of that offer has not been to deprive the child of his schooling or to lay the parents open to prosecution. On the contrary we understand the child is happy at the school and there is no reason to suppose that he does not attend regularly. In those circumstances it is far from perverse for the Authority to refuse to make transport arrangements.'

1.69 The Guidance deals with these issues at paras 109–110. That provides that the issue of whether there is a suitable alternative school should for the vast majority of cases be determined at the time places are allocated in the normal admissions round. It is also the Department's view that once eligibility has been confirmed on income grounds the LA should consider it met for the entirety of the school year. That is not a direction to local authorities and it is difficult to see why a change of financial circumstance should be taken into account by the LA if the child becomes eligible on the grounds of the parents' income in the middle of the year but not the converse situation.

The impact of parental preference

1.70 Under paragraphs 2, 4, 6, 7, 9, 11, and 12 of Schedule 35B to the EA 1996, the definition of 'eligible child' turns in part on whether suitable arrangements have been made by the LA for the child to become registered at a school nearer his home than the one he is in fact registered at. Sometimes, as is the case with paragraph 6, the child will be registered at a school beyond statutory walking distance yet, if suitable arrangements were made for him to become a registered pupil at a school nearer his home, he ceases to be an eligible child. In other cases, such as paragraph 2, the child will be a registered pupil at a school within walking distance but is still an eligible child unless suitable arrangements are made for him to become a registered pupil at a nearer school. It follows therefore that suitable arrangements for a child to become a registered pupil at a school nearer than that at which he is in fact registered can have the consequence that he is not an eligible child entitled to free transport under section 508B(1).

1.71 Where a child has become registered at a school that is not the nearest one to his home, that will usually be because his parents have successfully exercised a right of preference. The question therefore arises as to whether there can be a duty to make travel arrangements for such a child as a result of the exercise of that preference. This was a question that exercised the courts many times under the previous statutory scheme.

1.72 Under the old law, it was held that there was no duty to provide free school transport when the child was outside the statutory walking distance solely as a result of parental preference: *R v East Sussex County Council ex parte D*.[129] However, the Court of Appeal in *Re C (a minor)*[130] decided that parental preference of a non-religious nature had to be taken into account but

---

[129]   [1991] COD 374. This was followed by Jowitt J in *R v Essex County Council ex parte C* [1994] ELR 54.
[130]   [1994] ELR 273.

was not determinative when deciding what was necessary under section 55(3) of the Education Act 1994 (EA 1994) (subsequently section 509(4) of the EA 1996). The Court of Appeal in *R v Dyfed ex parte S*[131] disapproved of the statement in *Re C* that the school nearer home must be suitable, but did not comment on the issue of parental preference, citing without disapproval May J's decision that parental preference had been taken into account and the LEA's decision was not perverse.

1.73 Section 509AD of the EA 1996, like its predecessor section 509(4), expressly provides that parental preference is a factor to be taken into account if the preference is on the basis of the parent's religion or belief. The provision is restricted to preference based on religious considerations and indicates Parliament's view that the right of preference (outside of the religious field) does not carry the right to free school transport to a preferred school.[132] It is arguable, in light of the scope of section 509AD and the decision of the Court of Appeal in *Essex* that parental preference other than religious preference, does not have to be taken into account when deciding whether to provide free school transport. However, the better view is that expressed in *Re C* namely that parental preference is one factor to be considered, although it is not determinative.

Parental preference and religion or belief

1.74 In exercising any of their functions relating to school travel arrangements under sections 508A, 508B, 508C, 508E, 508F, 509AA and Schedule 35C to the EA 1996, local authorities in England must have regard to any wish of a parent for their child to be provided with education or training at a particular school, where that wish is based on the parent's religion or belief. 'Religion' means any religion, including a lack thereof, and 'belief' means any religious or philosophical belief, including a lack thereof: section 509AD(3).

1.75 The Guidance deals with these issues at paragraphs 97–99 and paragraphs 119–136. While it states that it is for the courts to interpret the meaning of 'religion or belief', the Guidance does give a large number of examples of cases which do, or do not, count as eligible for travel arrangements where preferences have been expressed on religious or other grounds. Most of these examples do not illuminate the question what is a religion or belief (including a lack thereof) as they concern established faiths or well known beliefs which are not faiths, such as atheism. However, there are a few exceptions. It is the Department's view, inter alia, that a belief that a school uniform should not be worn is not a philosophical belief falling within section 509AD(3). Caution should be used when having regard to this Guidance. It is well established that it is not for the courts to determine whether someone's religion or belief does, or does not, require them to manifest it in a

---

[131] [1995] ELR 98].
[132] This point was made expressly by Simon Brown LJ when refusing leave to appeal in *R v Bedfordshire ex parte WE* (unreported), 8 November 1996.

particular way such as the wearing of dress of a particular nature[133] although they are concerned with whether a belief is genuinely held. It is therefore possible that someone will assert a religious belief that no school uniforms should be worn, because for example the uniform that is required by the school is incompatible with the dress required by the religion the person adheres to. Of course a mere objection to school uniform not based on a religion or philosophical belief as that concept is understood[134] is not something that the law protects.

1.76 Both under section 509AD and paragraph 12 of Schedule 35B, attention is directed to the preference for the school in question being based on the parent's belief. The case typically covered by these provisions is where a parent wishes his child to be educated in a school, for example a faith school, where the faith in question is that to which the parent adheres. That type of case creates no legal difficulty, the LA have to have regard to a preference of that nature. However, it has become increasingly common for parents to express a preference for a faith school based on a perception they provide a better education and not based on their own religion. It seems clear that these types of preference are not intended to fall within section 509AD or paragraph 12 of Schedule 35B to the EA 1996. The question therefore arises as to how these preferences are to be addressed by the LA. Do they have to treat them in the same way as preferences that fall within section 509AD and paragraph 12 of Schedule 35B, and if not how are they expected to treat them?

1.77 In order to address that question it is necessary to consider the scope of the various Convention Rights that arise in this field. That is set out in detail in Chapter 10. Because the discussion there is not limited to transport issues, and is a lengthy one, the conclusions on the effect of a preference for a faith school when that is not based on the parent's religion and belief is stated here. It is submitted that to treat differently a parent who expresses a preference for a school not based on his own religion from one who expresses a preference that is based on his religion is prima facie discriminatory. As such it is potentially a breach of Article 14 of the ECHR read with Article 2 of the First Protocol. However, such a decision is not necessarily unlawful. There is clearly a legitimate aim in seeking to accommodate a parent's religious preference when that is based on the school sharing the parent's religion and belief. There is much less legitimacy affording the same accommodation to a parent who does not share the school's religious ethos. Indeed, the effect of providing such an accommodation may be to undermine the legitimate aim of educating children

---

[133]   *R (on the application of Williamson) v Secretary of State for Education and Employment* [2005] UKHL 15 at para 22 per Lord Nicholls.

[134]   For a religion or belief to qualify for protection under Art 9 of the ECHR it has to be consistent with basic standards of human dignity or integrity, relate to matters more than merely trivial, possess an adequate degree of seriousness and importance, be a belief on a fundamental problem, and be coherent in the sense of being intelligible and capable of being understood: see *R (on the application of Williamson) v Secretary of State for Education and Employment* [2005] UKHL 15 at para 23 per Lord Nicholls. While that was expressly in the context of Art 9 of the ECHR and other human rights instruments it is submitted it applies equally to the EA 1996.

in accordance with the parents' religious beliefs because there will be competition for the limited places available. However, that is something that can and is taken into account at the admissions stage by giving priority to those who share the religious ethos of the school. If despite that a child is admitted to the school who does not share its religious ethos, is it lawful to refuse to provide him with travel arrangements that he would have had had he shared that religious ethos? It is submitted that such a refusal may be justified. While the preference of the parent has to be taken into account, it is not determinative and for such a child it may be easier to establish there is a nearer suitable school and hence suitable arrangements can be made under paragraph 6 of Schedule 35B. As we have seen[135] even where the child shares the religious ethos of the school his parents wish him to attend it is possible for a school that does not have that ethos to be suitable for him. Where the parents expresses a preference for a school which does not share his religion or belief there may be more schools the LA can make suitable arrangements for the child to attend which do share his beliefs or lack of them. The effect is that there may be different treatment when one compares the child who shares the school's ethos to one who does not but that such treatment is justified.

Discretion to provide school transport to non-eligible children of compulsory school age

1.78 Under section 508C(1) and (2), local authorities continue to have a discretionary power to make such travel arrangements as they consider necessary, or to pay the whole or part of a child's school travelling expenses in relation to a child who is not an eligible child. As we have seen if a child is an eligible child then the LA is obliged under section 508B to make such travel arrangements as they think necessary for the purpose of facilitating the child's attendance at school. It is entirely possible that a child may in principle be an eligible child, because his parents satisfy the low income provisions in paragraph 14 of Schedule 35B, but fail, for example because of the choice of a school that is more distant that that provided for in paragraph 12 of Schedule 35B, to satisfy all the criteria for eligibility. Such a child is not to be treated as an eligible child. In those circumstances it was plainly the intention of Parliament that there should be a discretion to make school travel arrangement under section 508C(1) and (2).

1.79 The definition of 'travel arrangements' for the purposes of section 508C is similar to that for the purposes of section 508B. Section 508C(4) is identical to section 508B(4) save that the arrangements in section 508C(4) are obviously for a child who is not an eligible child. However sections 508B(5) to (7) have no equivalent in section 508C.

1.80 In exercising their discretion under section 508C, the LA have to have regard to guidance issued by the Secretary of State under section 508D: see section 508D(3). The LA also have to have regard to any wish of the parent for

---

[135] See para **1.60** above.

their child to be provided with education or training at a particular school where that wish is based on the parent's religion or belief: section 509AD(1) and (2). The latter requirement is discussed above. The relevant Guidance is at paragraphs 112–118 of *Home to School Travel and Transport Guidance*. The duty the LA owes under both sections is expressly only to 'have regard to' the parent's wishes. That is a well established statutory formula. It does not mean slavishly follow.[136] An LA is entitled to have regard to other factors such as public expenditure. Nevertheless an LA should normally follow statutory guidance unless there are good reasons not to. A potential good reason would be the need to avoid unreasonable public expenditure. However, the sensible course for an LA that is minded to depart from the guidance when setting its discretionary travel policy is to make express reference to the relevant paragraphs in the guidance and to explain why it has taken a different approach.

1.81 There are a number of areas where the Guidance may be thought to indicate how the LA should approach the exercise of its discretion. That is so in relation to transport to faith schools, transport to institutions providing vocational education, and transport for those from low income families. However, it is not permissible for the Secretary of State to dictate how an LA should exercise its discretion, this should always be borne in mind when considering any particular paragraph in the Guidance.

1.82 In relation to transport to faith schools, the Guidance notes that historically this has been provided by local authorities.[137] The Guidance goes on to state, perhaps optimistically, that local authorities might wish to use their powers under section 508C to continue to exercise this discretion.[138] Further, at paragraph 131 of the Guidance the Secretary of State expresses his hope that long standing travel arrangements are not disturbed and at paragraph 132 he states that such transport arrangements as are necessary to support the parental wishes on the basis of religion and belief should be retained 'wherever possible'. Local authorities may of course wish to continue to exercise their discretion to continue to provide such transport, but they can lawfully determine not to do so because, for example, they can no longer afford it. In those circumstances they can legitimately say that they have followed the Guidance because it was not possible to support the parental wishes because of budgetary constraints.

1.83 As far as those wishing to go to vocational academies is concerned, the Guidance provides, at paragraph 115, that the LA 'should' exercise their discretion to make travel arrangements where the school's catchment area included all, or part of the LA's area if the absence of such arrangements or their cost would have the effect of preventing pupils exercising their rights of preference. Paragraph 115 of the guidance goes on to provide that such travel

---

[136] These principles were established a long time ago, albeit in a different statutory context, in *Watt v Kesteven* [1955] QB 408 at 428–429.
[137] See at para 113.
[138] See at para 114.

arrangements 'should' be provided to pupils from low income families free of charge. While the Secretary of State has no power under section 508D to direct this and accordingly 'should' in this paragraph of the Guidance, cannot be construed as mandatory, an LA that had a discretionary transport policy that rendered nugatory, as distinct from difficult to exercise, any expression of preference would probably be acting unlawfully on general public law principles.[139] Accordingly if there are no means of transport to particular schools for some parents unless the LA provides them, then the LA should make arrangements for transport to such schools. Equally, while in the case of arrangements made under section 508C there is no prohibition on the LA charging unlike under section 508B(1), the LA should not impose a charge where this would defeat an exercise of parental preference. Those principles apply to all preferences and not simply those for vocational education.

1.84 General public law principles mean that the power to make discretionary travel arrangements under section 508C must be exercised reasonably and for a proper purpose. In addition, although local authorities should have a policy they must be careful not to fetter their discretion by failing to consider making exceptions to those policies.

1.85 The LA is entitled to review the exercise of its discretion from time to time. Therefore, where it made a mistake as to the distance of the child's home from school and subsequently discovered that it was less than the relevant distance of three miles, it was entitled to revoke a decision to provide a free bus pass.[140]

The power to charge

1.86 There is a general power to charge for providing transport in the circumstances set out in section 455 of the EA 1996. The transport has to be provided by agreement with the parents: see section 455(2). It is under this section the LA can make a charge for making travel arrangements under section 508C. There are the following prohibitions on charging:

(a) Section 454(3) prohibits the charging for transport which is incidental to the education at the school or is provided to enable him to meet the requirements of a public examination.

(b) Section 509(2) prohibits the charging for transport which the LA is under a duty to provide under section 509(1). Section 509 is now of limited scope in England and is now restricted to persons who are neither children nor of sixth form age.

---

[139] Rendering nugatory statutory rights of preference would be unlawful on the basis of *Padfield v MAFF* [1968] AC 997 as frustrating the policy of the legislation.

[140] *Rootkin v Kent County Council* [1981] 1 WLR 1186, CA.

(c)   Section 509B(1) is the current provision in England that obliges an LA to provide such transport as it is under a mandatory duty to provide to do so free of charge.

(d)   Section 508F is the special case of transport provided to adult learners. There is a prohibition on charging for this under section 508F(4).

(e)   Section 508E(2)(d) and Schedule 35C is the special case of travel schemes. The effect of these provisions is that the power to charge where there is a travel scheme is to be provided for in that scheme. Paragraphs 5–9 of Schedule 35C contain restrictions on the ability to charge under a travel scheme which mirror the restrictions where there is no such scheme.

1.87   The Guidance makes clear though that the Secretary of State believes that low income families who are not entitled to free school transport under section 508B, should not be charged for discretionary transport under section 508C: see paragraphs 117 and 135. By low income families he means those where the children are entitled to free school meals or whose parents are entitled to the maximum level of working tax credit. In relation to children who are not from low income families, paragraph 117 of the Guidance does not steer the LA away from charging, providing the scale of charges is made clear in the school travel policy documents. The charge would, of course, have to be reasonable in the *Wednesbury* sense.

INFORMATION

1.88   The LA is obliged to publish various items of information relating to transport policy. Under the School Information (England) Regulations 2008[141] an LA must publish in a composite prospectus a summary of the LA's sustainable modes of travel strategy, the LA's general arrangements and policies in respect of the making of travel arrangements in accordance with the discharge of their functions under sections 508B and 508C of EA 1996, or where a school travel scheme made by the LA has effect in relation to an admission year, the arrangements made under the scheme. This includes information relating to:

(a)   the provision of free transport;

(b)   the carriage on school buses of pupils for whom free transport is not provided;

(c)   the payment in whole or in part of reasonable travelling expenses;

(d)   the provision of other travel arrangements including escorts;

---

[141]   SI 2008/3093, reg 5 and Sch 2.

(e)   the arrangements for children with special educational needs; and

(f)   the arrangements in respect of transport for pupils to schools for which a pupil's parent has expressed a preference on the grounds of the parent's religion or belief.

Transport in Part 4 of statements of SEN and parental preference

1.89   There are important limitations on the ability of an LA to decide that a school different from that the parents wish the child to attend is suitable where the child has a statement of special educational needs. This was considered by Sedley J in *R v Havering ex parte K*.[142] In that case, following an appeal to the Special Educational Needs Tribunal, the child's statement of special educational needs provided in Part IV that the child was to attend Laleham School in Margate as a weekly boarder, but that the child's mother was to be responsible for providing transport to and from the school at her own expense. In due course, the mother was unable to provide that transport and sought assistance from the LEA. The LEA refused to provide such assistance on the ground that there were three suitable mainstream schools the child could attend other than Laleham. The court held that the LEA was not entitled to make suitable arrangements for the child to attend a school which was not named in the statement.[143] The decision was accordingly quashed on the grounds that immaterial considerations had been taken into account.

1.90   Sedley J's decision in *Havering* is not authority for the proposition that it is never appropriate where a child has a statement of special educational needs naming a particular school for the LA to decide that there are other suitable schools the child can attend which are different from that named in the statement the child in fact attends. He made clear that it was open to an LA to name more than one school in the statement and, if the tribunal agreed more than one school was appropriate, for the tribunal to so specify.[144] In addition he also made clear that if the tribunal's decision that a particular school should be named in the statement was predicated, or dependent, or conditional on the parents' paying the cost of transport, then the parent was bound by that.[145] He held though on the facts that the statement in that particular case was not so predicated and, by contrast the tribunal had held it was the only school that could meet the child's needs.

1.91   In *R v Islington ex parte GA*[146] the child had a statement of special educational needs which named Doucecroft School, but provided that the parents would be responsible for providing transport to and from the school at their own expense. The journeys turned out to be required more frequently than was originally envisaged and detrimental to the mental health of the

---

[142]   [1998] ELR 402.
[143]   See at p 408B-D.
[144]   See at p 404B-C.
[145]   See at pp 408E–409D.
[146]   [2000] EWHC 390.

mother. In those circumstances, the parents looked to the LEA to provide free transport. The LEA refused to do so on the basis that the parents had agreed to be responsible for these costs as recorded in the statement and that there was an alternative appropriate school where the child's needs could be met. Not surprisingly, the court held, following *Havering*, that this was an irrelevant consideration and rendered the decision unlawful.[147]

1.92 Beatson J suggested[148] in *ex parte GA* that this problem could be overcome by naming more than one school in the statement, if in the view of the education authority, more than one school could equally answer the child's needs and that parents could appeal to the tribunal against the naming of the authority's preferred school in the statement.[149] If the tribunal found it to be unsuitable, then the authority would be required to pay the travel costs to the preferred school (if outside the statutory walking distance or necessary for the purposes of section 508B of the 1996 Act). A similar view was also expressed by Michael Supperstone QC, as he then was, sitting as a Deputy High Court Judge, in *R (on the application of H) v London Borough of Brent*.[150]

1.93 This issue was considered further by the Court of Appeal in *R(M) v Sutton Borough Council*.[151] In that case the named school in Part 4 of the statement was the school preferred by the parents, but the statement provided that as that school was further away from the child's home than other schools that could meet the child's needs, the LEA could not accept responsibility for transport costs. The Court of Appeal dismissed the parents' claim for judicial review of the refusal to provide transport to the preferred school, holding that a nomination of the school preferred by the parents on the condition that they agreed to meet all or part of the transport costs was consistent with the statutory provisions, provided that the authority also complied with the obligation to specify the type of school, or if it considered it appropriate to do so, the specific school which it considered to be suitable for the child. It was not

---

[147] [2000] EWHC 390, at paras 27 and 28.

[148] This was obiter dicta as the LA had done not as he suggested. It was, however, well founded being based on the Court of Appeal decision in *Re C* [1994] ELR 273. In that case more than one school was named in Part 4 of the statement. The Court of Appeal held that the LA was not obliged to provide free transport to the parent's preferred school when, as recorded in the statement that preference had been acceded to expressly on the basis that the parents would be responsible for transport thereto and there was a nearer suitable school. Since that decision of the Court of Appeal it has been common for more than one school to be named in Part IV of a statement with wording that the parent's preference is acceded to only the basis they are responsible for the transport costs to their preferred school. It is respectfully submitted that the obiter doubts of Wyn Williams J in *Hill v Bedfordshire County Council* where he noted 'grave reservations about whether the defendant is empowered by any statutory provision to name a school in the statement of special educational needs when it knows and intends that the claimant will, in fact, be educated at a wholly different establishment...' should not be followed.

[149] At para 27.

[150] [2002] ELR 509 at para 34.

[151] [2008] ELR 123.

necessary for it to actually name a specific alternative suitable school in Part 4 of the statement provided it made clear there was, in its opinion such a suitable school.[152]

1.94 More recently this point has been considered by the Upper Tribunal in *MH v Nottinghamshire County Council*.[153] In this case the child's statement stated the local maintained school could meet the child's needs but given the child would attend a more distant alternative school based on parental preference, the parents were responsible for the transport costs. The SENDIST had found both schools were suitable. It then went on to examine the transport costs and concluded that if the cost of funding transport to the preferred school fell on the LA that would be an unreasonable public expenditure. They accordingly dismissed the appeal to them. On a further appeal the Upper Tribunal held that once the SENDIST had concluded that the LA school was suitable, it had no jurisdiction to go further and determine whether the LA should pay the cost of transport to the more distant school preferred by the parents.[154] Because the LA had already given effect to the parents' preference, the issue of prejudice to the efficient use of resources under paragraph 3 of Schedule 27 to the EA 1996 did not arise.[155]

1.95 In *Dudley Metropolitan Borough Council v Shurvington*[156] a three judge Upper Tribunal stated that the decision in *MH v Nottinghamshire* should not be followed. The facts in that case were that the parent wanted to go to a more distant maintained school than that the LA thought was suitable. The LA named both schools in Part IV of the statement and made clear there that the parents could go to their preferred school provided they were responsible for all travelling costs and arrangements. The First-tier Tribunal decided both schools were suitable.[157] They then went on to determine whether it would be an efficient use of resources for the parental preference to be acceded to and concluded that it would not. They accordingly amended the statement to name solely the parent's preferred school.[158] The Upper Tribunal dismissed a further appeal by the LA. They stated the following conclusions:

(a)   It was open to an LA to name more than one school in the statement.[159]

(b)   Transport was non-educational provision.[160]

(c)   If only one school was named in the statement the LA must make arrangements of the child to attend that school.

---

[152]   See at paras 14–19.
[153]   [2009] UKUT 178 (AAC).
[154]   See at paras 14 and 15.
[155]   See at para 17.
[156]   [2011] UKUT 67 (ACC).
[157]   At para 15(d) and (e).
[158]   At para 15(g).
[159]   See para 31.
[160]   See para 32.

(d)   An LA would in those circumstances be in great difficulty in saying it had
      no duty to provide transport to that school under section 508B because it
      could not make arrangements for the child to attend a nearer suitable
      school if it was obliged to make arrangements for the child to attend the
      school named in the statement.

(e)   Where there is no prejudice to the efficient use of resources in the child
      attending the parents' preferred school the tribunal should name only that
      school even if the LA school was suitable.[161]

(f)   Where there was a prejudice to the efficient use of resources if the child
      attended the parents' preferred school but there would not be
      unreasonable public expenditure within the meaning of section 9 of the
      EA 1996 for the child to attend the preferred school, then that school
      alone should be named in the statement.[162]

(g)   If the parents' preferred school had still not been named in the statement
      because giving effect to the preference would be prejudicial to the efficient
      use of resources and involve unreasonable public expenditure if the LA
      paid the transport costs to that school, then the tribunal should still go on
      to consider whether parental preference could be acceded to by making it
      conditional on the parents paying the costs of transport to the school of
      their choice.[163]

1.96 A further appeal to the Court of Appeal was dismissed.[164] Of the seven
points decided by the Upper Tribunal (set out in para **1.95** above) points (a) to
(d) above were not in dispute. The Court of Appeal held that the tribunal had
jurisdiction to hear an appeal where the parents' preferred school was named
subject to a condition they paid the transport costs and upheld the conclusion
of the UT that where there was no prejudice to the efficient use of resources in
the child attending the parents' preferred school, that school alone should be
named. *MH v Nottinghamshire County Council* was overruled. The Court of
Appeal went on to express reservations about the conclusion of the Upper
Tribunal that where was a prejudice to the efficient use of resources parental
preference should still be acceded to unless there was unreasonable public
expenditure.[165]

1.97 It is respectfully submitted that, save for their reservations of the Upper
Tribunal's conclusion that parental preference had to be given effect to if there
was no unreasonable public expenditure, this decision is inconsistent with the
statutory scheme and wrong in principle:

---

[161] See para 40.
[162] See para 42.
[163] See para 43.
[164] *Dudley Metropolitan Borough Council v Shurvinton* [2012] EWCA Civ 346.
[165] See para 47.

(a) It is well established that the jurisdiction of the First-tier Tribunal is statutory and it has no inherent jurisdiction to rule on the funding obligations of the LA.[166] The conclusion of the Court of Appeal that jurisdiction was to be found in section 326(1A)(b) of the EA was a very surprising one because that provision is limited to educational provision and it is well established that transport is non-educational provision. A dispute about who should pay for the cost of transport to the preferred school does not in itself mean that the child will not get education at the preferred school, nor was there any evidence that in the particular case before them that would be the consequence of the LA not paying for transport. Contrary to the Court of Appeal's conclusions the reality of the case was that in a dispute about a transport condition is not a dispute about educational provision but who should pay for the cost of transport. The present provisions on transport postdate the creation of the SENDIST to which the First-tier Tribunal is the statutory successor. It is notable that when Schedule 35B to the EA 1996 was enacted not only did Parliament make the LA the decision maker in accordance with the statutory scheme as to what transport arrangements were necessary, but it also did not give any right of appeal from those decisions to the First-tier Tribunal. The Court of Appeal's decision not only creates a right of appeal where Parliament has chosen not to, but also makes it a full merits appeal rather than control by way of judicial review .

(b) The Court of Appeal applied the test in paragraph 3(3) of Schedule 27 to the EA 1996 in determining who should pay for the cost of transport. That, however, is not the test in Schedule 35B. The test there is, in general terms, one of distance, have suitable arrangements been made for the child to become registered at a nearer school. The decision of the Court of Appeal defeats the provisions of Schedule 35B.

1.98 The decision of the House of Lords in *B v Harrow*[167] established that 'resources' in paragraph 3(3) of Schedule 27 meant the responsible authority's resources. It was argued by the parents in *Harrow* that section 9 of the EA 1996 had a broader construction and that it was possible for section 9 to lead to the result that parental preference should prevail even where there was no prejudice to the efficient use of resources providing that there was no unreasonable public expenditure. That argument was dismissed by Lord Slynn speaking for a unanimous House.[168] Despite this clear ruling a jurisprudence built up based on the misconception that section 9 had not been canvassed in *Harrow* that parental preference under section 9 could outweigh the prejudice to the efficient use of the responsible authority's resources.[169] In *Dudley*, while the CA did not overrule[170] either *O v Lewisham* or *CM v Bexley*, it is doubtful that these

---

[166] See *White and Another v Ealing* [1998] ELR 203 at 220E-F per Dyson J as he then was.
[167] [2000] 1 WLR 223.
[168] See at p 229.
[169] See *O v Lewisham* [2007] EWHC 2130 and *CM v Bexley* [2011] UKUT 215.
[170] The language used at para 47 was that of 'reservations' about the conclusions of the UT on this point.

decisions can now stand. Accordingly a prejudice to the efficient use of the responsible LA's resources should be in itself sufficient to defeat parental preference under section 9 of the EA 1996 regardless of any question of unreasonable public expenditure.

CHILDREN OF SIXTH FORM AGE

1.99 The duty to provide free school transport only applies to children of compulsory school age, however, section 509AA of the EA 1996 requires local authorities to specify what transport and financial support are necessary to facilitate the attendance of persons of sixth form age receiving education or training. A person of sixth form age is defined as a person over compulsory school age, but under the age of 19 or a person who has begun a particular course of education or training at an establishment before attaining the age of 19 and continues to attend that course.[171]

1.100 The Secretary of State has issued guidance under section 509AB(5) which local authorities must have regard to when carrying out their responsibilities in relation to transport arrangements of young people between 16 and 19: '2010 Post-16 Transport Guidance'.

1.101 The duties imposed on local authorities under section 509AA include the duties:

(a)   To prepare a transport policy statement for each academic year specifying the travel arrangements for persons of sixth-form age to facilitate the attendance of those persons receiving education or training at schools or at further education institutions.

(b)   To publish the transport policy statement prior to 31 May[172] in the year in which the academic year in question begins.[173]

(c)   To make and secure that effect is given to the arrangements specified in the transport policy statement.[174]

1.102 The transport policy must specify the arrangements that the LA consider it necessary to make for the provision of financial assistance[175] and any travel concessions for persons of sixth form age[176] and state the arrangements for facilitating the attendance at the educational establishments

---

[171]   EA 1996, s 509AC(1).

[172]   EA 1996, s 509AA(10) as amended by the Apprenticeships, Skills, Children and Learning Act 2009, s 55(2) allows the Secretary of State to change by order the date by which transport policy statements must be published. This commenced on 12 January 2010.

[173]   EA 1996, s 509AA(7).

[174]   EA 1996, s 509AA(7).

[175]   EA 1996, s 509AA(3).

[176]   EA 1996, s 509AA(6).

of disabled persons and persons with learning difficulties.[177] A transport policy statement must not differentiate between types of providers or instructions, for example between schools and further education institutions.[178]

1.103 Sections 509AA and 509AB of the EA 1996 were considered in *R(S) v EduAction (Waltham Forest) and the London Borough of Waltham Forest*.[179] Underhill J emphasised the discretionary nature of the power to provide free school transport for those persons of sixth form age, including children with special education needs.

1.104 Section 509AB(3) of the EA 1996 sets out the matters which an LA must have regard to in making a transport policy statement.[180] These include:

(a) the needs of those for whom it would not be reasonably practicable to attend a particular establishment to receive education or training if no arrangements were made;

(b) the need to secure that persons in their area have reasonable opportunities to choose between different establishments at which education and training is provided;

(c) distance from the learner's home to establishments of education and training;

(d) journey time to access different establishments;

(e) the cost of transport to the establishments in question;

(f) alternative means of facilitating attendance at establishments;

(g) preferences based on religion or belief; and

(h) the need to secure enough suitable education and training is provided to meet the reasonable needs of relevant young adults.[181]

1.105 Section 509AB(6) imposes a duty to consult various bodies in making a transport policy statement, including other local authorities where appropriate and young persons of sixth form age and their parents.[182]

---

[177] EA 1996, s 509AB(1).
[178] EA 1996, s 509AB(2).
[179] [2006] EWHC 3144 (Admin).
[180] See also para 23 of the Post-16 Guidance for detailed discussion of these factors.
[181] Inserted by The Apprenticeships, Skills, Children and Learning Act 2009, s 53. This commenced on 1 April 2010.
[182] EA 1996, s 509AB(6)(ca) (inserted by The Apprenticeships, Skills, Children and Learning Act 2009, s 54).

1.106   Section 509AB(7A) of the EA 1996[183] requires an LA to have regard to the need to provide sufficient information when drawing up the transport policy statement and to consider the need to publish this in good time. Section 509AE of the EA 1996 provides a new power for local authorities to amend and republish their transport policy statements within an academic year in response to complaints or a direction from the Secretary of State. The provision provides that complaints must go through a local complaints process first before they can be considered by the Secretary of State.

Children of sixth form age with special educational needs or disabilities

1.107   Section 509AB(1) requires the transport policy statement to expressly set out the arrangements for facilitating the attendance at educational establishments of disabled persons and persons with learning difficulties. Detailed guidance on this point is set out in the Post-16 Guidance[184] and includes the important points that arrangements cannot be limited to learners who have previously had a statement of SEN and an LA cannot require a learner to use his Disability Living Allowance to support the transport costs to learning.

1.108   The sixth form age transport duties in relation to child with a statement of SEN were considered in *R(A) v North Somerset Council*.[185] In this case the child had been the subject of a statement of SEN and had received transport to and from school until the age of 16. The child was to take up a place at an FE college recommend by Connexions but the nearer college identified in an assessment was rejected by the child. His application for home to college transport was refused by the LA and an appeal to a Transport Panel was dismissed, which concluded that the two colleges provided comparable provision so the additional cost of transport to the preferred college could not be justified. On the application for judicial review, it was held that when considering an individual appeal from a person with learning difficulties or disabilities, particular regard should be paid to those needs, however an LA was not under a duty to provide free transport to the college recommended by the assessment. However, the procedure that had been adopted by the Panel was unfair as it was not made clear to the child what local expertise or knowledge each panel member was relying on in concluding the courses at both colleges were comparable.

TRANSPORT TO EARLY YEARS EDUCATION

1.109   Section 509A confers on local authorities a discretionary power to provide assistance with travel for early years education. The LA must be satisfied that, without such assistance, a child would be prevented from

---

[183]   Inserted by The Apprenticeships, Skills, Children and Learning Act 2009, s 55.
[184]   At paras 27–32.
[185]   [2010] ELR 139.

attending at any premises which are not a school or part of a school but at which relevant early years education is provided, for the purposes of receiving early years education.

1.110 When determining whether or not to exercise its discretion under this provision, an LA may have regard (among other things) to whether it would be reasonable to expect alternative arrangements to be made for the child to receive relevant early years education at any other premises, whether nearer to his home or otherwise.[186] The LA may charge for the provision of transport, but such payments should not exceed the costs to the LA of providing the assistance: section 509A(4).

THE ADULT EDUCATION TRANSPORT DUTY

1.111 Section 508F of the EA 1996 empowers an LA to make arrangements for the provision of transport and otherwise as they consider necessary in relation to adults and relevant young adults. An adult is a person who is neither a child nor of sixth form age, receiving further education or higher education (the latter in establishments maintained by the LA).[187] Relevant young adults are an adult aged under 25 who is subject to a learning difficulty assessment receiving education at institutions outside the further or higher education sector but only when the LA has secured both the provision of education and training at the institution and the provision of boarding accommodation under section 514A of the 1996 Act. These arrangements must be no less favourable than the arrangements made for relevant young adults of the same age for whom the LA secure the provision of education at another institution: section 508F(7) of the 1996 Act. Section 508F provides that such transport must be provided free of charge.

1.112 In considering what arrangements it is necessary to make in relation to relevant young adults, an LA must have regard to its duties in section 15ZA(1) which require an LA to secure enough suitable education and training to meet the reasonable needs of relevant young adults.[188]

1.113 Section 508G requires an LA to prepare a transport policy statement by the end of May in which the relevant academic year begins specifying any transport or other arrangements under section 508F, any payment of travelling expenses to be made and any travel concessions available. Before preparing such a statement, an LA must consult with various persons, to include persons in the LA's area who will be relevant young adults when the arrangements or payments have effect and their parents: section 508G(1).

1.114 Section 508H provides that in undertaking its functions in sections 508F and 508G of the 1996 Act, the LA must have regard to any

---

[186] EA 1996, s 509A(3).
[187] EA 1996, s 508F(9).
[188] EA 1996, s 508F(5).

guidance issued by the Secretary of State. Section 508I deals with complaints about transport arrangements from relevant young adults.

1.115 Local authorities also have a duty under the Education and Skills Act 2008 to encourage, enable and assist the participation of learners with learning difficulties and/or disabilities up to the age of 25 in education and training.

SUSTAINABLE MODES OF TRAVEL STRATEGY

1.116 For each academic year, local authorities must prepare a 'sustainable modes of travel strategy' containing their strategy to promote the use of sustainable modes of travel to meet the school travel needs of their area: section 508A. This strategy should be published and promoted by local authorities. Before doing so, local authorities are particularly required to assess both the school travel needs of their area and the facilities and services for sustainable modes of travel to, from and within their area: 508A(2). In discharging their duties under section 508A, local authorities are required to consult such persons as they consider appropriate: section 508A(9)(a).

1.117 A sustainable mode of travel is one which the LA considers may improve the physical well-being of users and/or the environmental well-being of the whole or part of the local authorities area: section 508A(3).

SCHOOL TRAVEL SCHEMES

1.118 Section 508E and Schedule 35C of the EA 1996 empower local authorities to make school travel schemes. Such schemes set out the LA's policy on providing or arranging transport to and from school and include general arrangements that are made for school travel, the arrangements as regards eligible children and the policy applicable to charging for services provided under the scheme.

1.119 A school travel scheme is not permitted to come into force unless approved by the Secretary of State.[189] In the School Travel Pathfinder Schemes Prospectus and the School Travel (Piloting of Schemes) (England) Regulations 2007 the DfES (as then was) explained that, on a pilot basis, it would approve up to 20 schemes in England. The pilot period continued until 1 August 2012.

1.120 Although sections 508B and 508C do not apply to an LA where a school travel scheme is in force, Schedule 35C virtually replicates the requirement of section 508B to make arrangements for 'eligible children'.

---

[189] EA 1996, para 10(1), Sch 35C.

Discrimination on grounds of disability

1.121 An LA is subject to the requirement not to subject pupils to discrimination on the grounds of their disability, and also subject to the duty to make reasonable adjustments (formerly contained in the Disability Discrimination Act 1995 (DDA 1995), now contained in the Equality Act 2010 (EqA 2010)). The law on discrimination against pupils on grounds of disability and/or special educational needs is set out in detail in Chapter 3.

1.122 The key authority on whether an LA has discriminated against a child in relation to the provision of transport from home to school is *Bedfordshire County Council v Dixon-Wilkinson.*[190] The facts are worthy of some detailed consideration. D, a disabled boy suffered from Asperger's Syndrome. The LA provided free transport for D from home to school on a bus with other children, the return journey commencing at 3pm when the school day finished. D wished to attend an after school club once a week and requested that the LA provide transport at 4:30pm. The LA refused to provide a taxi. On appeal to the Special Educational Needs and Disability Tribunal, the tribunal rejected the claim of disability discrimination on the basis that the provision of a taxi amounted to the provision of an auxiliary aid or service for the purposes of section 28G(3)(b) of the Disability Discrimination Act and was therefore within the exception to the duties set out in section 23G. The High Court quashed that decision, holding that a taxi was not necessarily an auxiliary aid or service and the finding on justification could not stand. On appeal the Court of Appeal held it was unable to determine whether or not the provision of a taxi was an auxiliary aid or service because, it said the necessary findings of fact had not been made and remitted the matter to a fresh tribunal to reconsider the case in its entirety. However, against the background that it was common ground that there was no breach of section 508B of the 1996 Act as the LA was transporting D to his home and back each day, Wall LJ (with whom Rix LJ agreed) noted that there must be situations in which a disabled child is 'placed at a substantial disadvantage in comparison with pupils who are not disabled' and in which it is reasonable for the LEA to take steps to ensure that this does not occur, for example children who are not disabled can attend after-school clubs and make their own way home afterwards. D cannot do so, which in principle appeared to place him at a substantial disadvantage.[191]

1.123 This case must now be read in light of the EqA 2010, which in principle removes the exemption for auxiliary aids or services.

Domestic challenges to school transport decisions based on Convention grounds

1.124 It is normally the case when it is alleged that a public authority has acted unlawfully that the court is concerned with the process by which the

---

[190] [2009] EWCA Civ 678.
[191] See para 17.

decision was reached. Accordingly it is trite law that, if, for example, the public authority has misdirected itself as to the relevant considerations its decision is unlawful and will be quashed by the court unless it decides to withhold relief in the exercise of its discretion. Challenges based on Convention grounds though fall within a different category. Here the court is concerned whether in fact the relevant Article has been breached not with whether the public authority directed itself correctly as to its terms. This important point was established in *R (on the application of Begum) v Headteacher and Governors of Denbigh High School*.[192] It is of general application to challenges under the Human Rights Act and is not confined to claims alleging breach of Article 9 or Article 2 of the First Protocol to the ECHR.

1.125 Challenges to decisions relating to school transport where the child attends a school as a result of a parental preference based on religion or belief have commonly been expressed as challenges based on discrimination arguments.

1.126 In *R (on the application of T) v Leeds City Council*[193] it was contended that the city council had breached Article 2 of the First Protocol and Article 14 in its transport policy by not providing free transport to some orthodox Jews to enable them to attend a school in Manchester. The policy did, however, confer a limited entitlement to free transport for those who were Church or England or Catholic, but no parallel entitlement to those who were Jewish. There were no orthodox Jewish schools in Leeds. Turner J held that there had been no breach of Article 4 of the Convention.[194]

1.127 In *R (R) v Leeds City Council/Education Leeds*[195] a challenge was brought to the decision of the LA not to fund a coach for nine children travelling from Leeds to attend Jewish schools in Manchester. The challenge was made on the grounds that the LEA's decision was *Wednesbury* unreasonable and contrary to Articles 8, 9 and 14 of the Convention and Article 2 of Protocol 1. Although the case was decided before amendments to the EA 1996, the points decided remain relevant. The court held that the decision not to fund the transport from Leeds to Manchester was reasonable taking into account the suitability of local schools and the LEA's limited resources as well as parental preference. It was further held that for the purposes of a claim of indirect discrimination there was no comparison between the children attending Christian schools within or just outside the LEA's boundaries, and the claimants for whom there was no Jewish school in or near the LEA's area and where the cost of providing transport to the preferred

---

[192] [2006] UKHL 15 at paras 26–31 per Lord Bingham, para 41 per Lord Nicholls, para 68 per Lord Hoffman, para 91 per Lord Scott and para 94 per Baroness Hale. This approach was subsequently confirmed in the House of Lords in *Miss Behavin' Ltd v Belfast City Council* [2007] UKHL 19 and *R (on the application of Nasseri) v Secretary of State for the Home Department* [2009] UKHL 23.

[193] [2002] ELR 91.

[194] Although decided before the statutory changes, the case remains relevant in terms of the discrimination arguments.

[195] [2006] ELR 25.

school would be so much greater. Importantly, it was held that Articles 8, 9 and Article 2 of the first protocol were not engaged as the LEA had not sought to prevent the claimants from attending a school of their choice. The claimants were in fact making the journey from Leeds to Manchester in order to do so; the only issue was as to who should fund the transport. Where, as will frequently be the case, there are significant budgetary implications in providing free transport which is additional to that presently required under domestic legislation, the reservation to Article 2 of the First Protocol is likely to be relied upon successfully. It is submitted that it is in any event doubtful, issues of discrimination apart, that the State is obliged to provide free school transport under the Convention. Just as the court held in the *Belgian Linguistic Case* that there was no obligation on the State to establish at its own expense or subsidise education of any particular type, it is likely to be held that an LA does not have to fund free school transport to any particular school absent any issue of discrimination.

LAW RELATING TO LOCAL AUTHORITIES IN WALES

1.128 The law in relation to Wales is to be found in the Learner Travel (Wales) Measure 2008, ('the 2008 Measure') the Safety on Learner Transport Measure 2011 ('the 2011 Measure') and statutory guidance in the form of the Learner Travel Operational Guidance.[196]

Duty to assess learner travel needs

1.129 Under section 2 of the 2008 Measure the LA must assess the learner travel needs[197] each academic year of certain specified persons. The section applies to learners[198] who have not attained the age of 19, learners who have attained the age of 19 who began a course of study before attaining that age continue on that course of study and such other learners as may be prescribed. Accordingly for those who have attained the age of 19 who change their course after attaining that age, there is no duty to assess their transport needs.

1.130 There is a non-exhaustive list of matters the LA must have regard to set out in section 2(4). They are: (a) the needs of learners who are disabled persons, (b) the needs of learners who are disabled persons, (c) the needs of children who are or were looked after by a LA, (d) the age of learners, and (e) the nature of the available routes. Curiously neither the needs of the parent nor the religion of either the child or his parents to be educated in accordance with their religious convictions are specifically mentioned either here or in section 4(5). There can be little doubt that both are at least permissible

---

[196] Issued under section 15 of the Measure (see http://wales.gov.uk/docs/det/publications/090401learnertraveguidanceen.pdf). The guidance came into force on 1 April 2009.

[197] The learner travel needs are defined by section 2(3) as the needs of learners who are ordinarily resident in the authority's area for suitable travel arrangements each day to and from relevant places where they receive education or training.

[198] See the 2008 Measure, s 2(1).

considerations.[199] It is submitted that they are both relevant considerations. Travel arrangements may not be suitable if they do not accommodate religious considerations or if they fail to take account of the fact that the child cannot get to school because it is too far to walk and neither parent can get him to school because of disability.

Duty to make transport arrangements

1.131 Section 3 of the Measure introduces a duty in specified circumstances for local authorities to 'make suitable transport arrangements to facilitate the attendance of the child each day at the relevant places where the child receives education or training' (section 3(2)). The phrase 'relevant places' is widely defined to include maintained schools, non-maintained special schools, independent schools named in a SEN statement, PRUs, other places where education is arranged under section 19(1) of the EA 1996, specified types of nursery education, further education institutions, specified places where education or training are provided or secured under the Learning and Skills Act 2000 and places where work experience is undertaken. Academies are not named but there can be little doubt that if the child has a statement naming an Academy, transport will fall to be provided to that Academy. It does not include access to higher education (see below). Transport arrangements include (but are not necessarily limited to) the provision of transport or the payment of the whole (but not part) of a child's transport expenses (section 3(4)). A distinction is made between transport arrangements (in section 3) and travel arrangements (in section 4).

1.132 The duty is to provide 'suitable' transport arrangements. Transport arrangements will not be suitable if they cause unreasonable levels of stress for the child, take an unreasonable amount of time or are unsafe[200] (section 3(5)). There is no statutory definition of a reasonable amount of time;[201] and the LA is not permitted to charge 'a child or a parent who is an individual' for the

---

[199] Paragraph 1.23 of the Guidance which states the contrary with regard to religious faith is of doubtful legality having regard to Article 2(1) of the First Protocol to the ECHR.

[200] Safety has been further dealt with by the Safety on Learner Transport (Wales) Measure 2011. Section 1 of that measure inserts a new section 14A into the 2008 Measure by virtue of which seat belts on all passenger seats are compulsory from 2014. There are further provisions for safety risk assessments, driver training and supervision of learners using learner transport.

[201] But see paras 1.46–147 of the Guidance: '1.46 Sections 3 and 4 of the Measure state that transport arrangements are not suitable if "they take an unreasonable amount of time". Although the Measure does not specify a time limit for all journeys, Welsh Ministers consider that normally journey times should be no more than 45 minutes for primary school travel and 60 minutes for secondary school travel. There may be some exceptional circumstances when those time limits cannot be adhered to such as delays due to heavier than normal traffic, roadworks, diversions and breakdowns. 1.47 It is also necessary to consider circumstances, perhaps in rural areas and especially in the secondary sector, where the nearest suitable school may be further away than such travel time limit would allow. In other circumstances children with special needs, additional learning needs or looked after children may need transport to establishments some distance away. There may also be circumstances where for those children that live part of the week with one parent and part of the week with another some distance away from their school the time limits cannot be met'.

transport arrangements (section 3(3)). This leaves open the possibility that the LA could charge another LA which is the parent of a looked after child; the power to do so is in section 18.

1.133 The notion of suitability is discussed in the guidance at paragraphs 1. 44–1.45 of the Guidance which state:

'1.44 The LA must make suitable transport arrangements to facilitate the attendance of the child each day at the relevant place where the child receives education or training. Transport arrangements are not suitable if they cause unreasonable levels of stress for the child; they take an unreasonable amount of time; or they are unsafe.

1.45 If a journey causes such stress that a child is unable to benefit from the education provided at the school then it is considered that would be unreasonable. A journey may cause unreasonable stress if for example a bus takes such a circuitous route that it takes over an hour and a half to arrive at the school whereas a direct route might take only 15 minutes, or if a child attending a primary school is required to change bus unaccompanied during the journey'.

1.134 Thus while a definition of suitability is canvassed in the legislation and the guidance, it is still possible to envisage situations where previous case-law would be useful.

1.135 The duty applies in the following circumstances (section 3(2), (7) and (8)):

(a) where a child is a registered pupil receiving primary education at a maintained school, pupil referral unit, named independent school or non-maintained special school, the conditions are that:

    (i) the child is ordinarily resident at a place two miles or more from the school or unit, measured by the shortest available route (ie a route that is safe for a child without a disability or learning difficulty to walk alone or (if too young to expect to walk alone) with an escort);

    (ii) no arrangements have been made by the LA for enabling the child to become a registered pupil at a nearer suitable maintained school, pupil referral unit, named independent school or non-maintained special school; and

    (iii) no arrangements have been made by the LA for suitable boarding accommodation at or near the school or unit;

(b) where a child is a registered pupil receiving secondary education at a maintained school, pupil referral unit, named independent school or non-maintained special school the same conditions apply as above, with the exception that the distance in condition (i) is three miles (instead of two miles);

(c)   where a child is enrolled full time and receiving education or training at a further education institution, the conditions are that:

   (i)   the child is ordinarily resident at a place three miles or more from the institution (measured in the same way as above); and
   (ii) no arrangements have been made by the LA for the child to enrol at a nearer suitable institution;

(d)   where a child is a registered pupil at a maintained school but is receiving secondary education at another relevant place (arranged by the LA or by or on behalf of the maintained school's governing body), the only condition is that they are ordinarily resident at a place three miles or more from the relevant place (measured in the same way as above); and

(e)   where a looked after child is a registered pupil receiving education at a maintained school, pupil referral unit, named independent school or non-maintained special school, the only condition is that they are ordinarily resident two miles (in the case of primary education)/three miles (in the case of secondary education) from the school (measured in the same way as above).

1.136   In considering whether there is a nearer school, unit or institution which is suitable, section 3(6) provides that it is suitable for a child 'if the education or training provided there is suitable, having regard to the age, ability and aptitudes of the child and any learning difficulties he or she may have'. Note that paragraph 1.23 of the Guidance provides that 'Neither the child's or parent's language preference or mother tongue, nor religious faith or conviction of the child or his or her parent have any bearing on whether a school is suitable'. That Guidance is of doubtful legality having regard to Articles 14 and 2 of the First Protocol to the ECHR. While in any given case an LA may be able to say it has no duty to provide free transport to enable the parent or child's religious preference to be accommodated in the choice of school, to provide that religion is not relevant in any case surely goes too far. The 2008 Measure cannot take precedence over Convention rights as it is subordinate legislation and the ECHR is given primacy by virtue of the Human Rights Act 1998.

Duty to make 'travel arrangements'

1.137   In addition to the duty in section 3 to make transport arrangements, there is a duty in section 4 to make other suitable travel arrangements to facilitate the attendance of an eligible child each day at the relevant place where the child receives education or training. Travel arrangements are wider than transport arrangements and include (but are not limited to) the provision of transport, escorts, the payment of the whole of the child's travelling expenses or the payment of allowances for particular modes of travel (sections 1(2) and

4(4)). Travel arrangements (like transport arrangements) are not suitable if they cause unreasonable levels of stress for the child, take an unreasonable amount of time or are unsafe (section 4(6)).

1.138 Section 4(5) provides that an LA must have regard to the following factors in considering whether travel arrangements are suitable or not:

(a)   the LA's statutory assessment of learner travel needs in the area;

(b)   the transport arrangements which must be provided to the child under section 3;

(c)   the age of the child;

(d)   any disability or learning difficulty; and

(e)   the nature of the routes which the child could reasonably be expected to take.

1.139 The duty applies in the following circumstances (section 4(1), (7), (8) and (9)):

(a)   the child is of compulsory school age, receives education or training at a relevant place and is ordinarily resident in the LA's area; and

(b)   the LA considers that travel arrangements are necessary to facilitate the attendance of the child at that relevant place;

(c)   in all cases, in considering the necessity of travel arrangements the LA must have regard to the factors set out in the preceding paragraph above;

(d)   if the child is not a looked after child and if arrangements have been made by the LA to enable the child to attend a nearer suitable relevant place, the LA may also have regard in particular to whether or not the child is attending the nearest suitable relevant place to their ordinary place of residence. As above, a relevant place is suitable for a child 'if the education or training provided there is suitable, having regard to the age, ability and aptitudes of the child and any learning difficulties he or she may have'.

Power to make travel arrangements

1.140   In addition to the duties in sections 3 and 4, the LA has a power under section 6 to make learner travel arrangements. The power is available where the learner is either ordinarily resident in the LA's area, or receives education (not including higher education) or training in the LA's area.

1.141   The definition of travel arrangements is wider than that in section 4, in that the LA has the option of only paying part of a pupil's reasonable travel expenses (section 1(2)). The travel arrangements must be made for the purpose of facilitating the attendance of the learner at a place where they receive education or training. The limits in section 5 do not apply and therefore the power can be used to make arrangements for travel between different sites of the same institution.

Behaviour

1.142 The Welsh Ministers have also issued a travel behaviour code as required by section 12 of the Measure. This applies to learners 'while they are travelling to and from the relevant places' where they receive education or training (whether or not the local authorities makes the travel arrangements).

1.143 Where there is an alleged breach of the code, the matter must be investigated. If the transport is provided or funded by the LA, it will lead the investigation. Otherwise, the school will investigate: paragraphs 1.13–1.15 and 3.5 of the statutory guidance. The guidance sets out a procedure in paragraph 4 which must be followed if the arrangements are made under the duties in section 3 or section 4, and should still be followed if the arrangements are made under the discretion in section 6.

Powers in relation to sixth form and further education transport

1.144 Section 7 contains a power to make regulations introducing a power and/or a duty for Welsh local authorities to transport learners to and from post-16 education and training. Part 3 of the Learning and Skills (Wales) Measure 2009 sets out the power under which Welsh Ministers may direct the governing bodies of schools and FE Colleges to provide 'learner support services' for young persons aged from 11 to 26.

POWERS OF THE SECRETARY OF STATE

1.145 Breach of the transport duty is capable of being remedied by the Secretary of State under his general powers under sections 496 and 497 of the EA 1996. Under section 496, if the Secretary of State is satisfied that any relevant authority (or governing body) has acted or is proposing to act unreasonably with respect to any of its powers under the Act, he may issue directions as to the exercise or performance of the relevant duty. Further, he has a power under section 497 to direct the LA to provide transport in accordance with their duties under the EA 1996. The latter power is not as circumscribed and appears to permit the Secretary of State to direct free school transport whenever he considers it appropriate for the purpose of facilitating the attendance of persons receiving education at schools or other relevant institutions.

1.146 These powers are potentially an adequate alternative remedy to which resort should be had prior to launching an application for judicial review. The attitude of the court to alternative remedies was helpfully considered by the courts in connection with the appeal to the Secretary of State that used to exist in connection with special educational needs and it is believed a similar approach is appropriate in the present context. In *R v London Borough of Newham ex parte R*,[202] Schiemann J (as he then was) set out the following principles:

'Judicial review is a discretionary remedy and relevant factors in deciding whether to exercise the discretion to grant leave to move for judicial review or to grant particular relief include a consideration of:

(1) whether a refusal to quash will be to leave the applicant without remedy; and, in particular;

(2) whether there is available an alternative forum in front of which the applicant can argue his substantive and legal points and which can dispose of them;

(3) whether the court's judgment will dispose of the outstanding issues;

(4) the chance of a point of law sought to be raised in the judicial review proceedings surfacing again in any alternative forum;

(5) the time implications of allowing the judicial review procedure to start or continue.

Where the material justifies the making of a general declaration, then the appropriate way of proceeding, if the declaration would be of value to the applicant, would be to go by way of judicial review. That is because this court is the only one having power to make such a declaration. In so far as the complaint is that a particular child has been the subject of a mistaken value judgement by the local education authority, then the appropriate way of proceeding is by way of appeal to the Secretary of State. Even if the complaint is that the mistaken value judgement by the local education authority was arrived at in part by reasons of mistakes of law, it is in general appropriate to proceed by way of appeal rather than by way of judicial review unless the alleged mistakes of law are likely to be repeated by the Secretary of State.'

1.147 While this concerned an alternative remedy by way of appeal, like principles are applicable here having regard to the wide direction-making power. In *R v Essex ex parte EB*[203] the court refused leave to move for judicial review on the basis of what are now sections 496 and 497 of the EA 1996. The main issue in that case was whether the nearest route was safe. The court held that the issue was best dealt with by the Secretary of State who, unlike the court, could look at the route himself. The court rejected a suggestion that it could give a quicker decision than the Secretary of State. The court also refused to grant leave simply because a number of children were interested in the point.

---

[202] [1995] ELR 168. For other cases in this context where review has been refused on the grounds that an appeal to the Secretary of State under the EA 1981, s 8 was an adequate alternative remedy, see *R v London Borough of Hackney ex parte GC* [1995] ELR 144 at 154G–155C, affirmed an appeal [1996] ELR 142, and *R v Mid Glamorgan County Council ex parte B* [1995] ELR 168 at 196G–197E.

[203] [1997] ELR 327.

The decision is obviously sensible. Safety issues are primarily issues of judgement that the court is ill equipped to deal with on an application for judicial review.

Chapter 2

CHALLENGING SCHOOL REORGANISATION DECISIONS IN THE COURTS

INTRODUCTION

2.1   School reorganisation, and in particular the closure of existing schools and the establishment of Academies, is in many cases a controversial and emotive subject and, as such, it generates significant litigation. As with judicial review in other areas, the courts are not concerned with the political merits of the decision but with its legality. Therefore, the scope of review in practice in this area is narrow. This Chapter deals first with the statutory framework[1] before discussing the persons who can mount a legal challenge and the timing of any application for judicial review. It then outlines the principles upon which the courts have acted when reviewing decisions relating to school closures, the establishment of new schools, amalgamations and significant changes in character.

THE STATUTORY FRAMEWORK

2.2   Generally, the starting point for any consideration of a school reorganisation is the statutory framework and in particular the general duties imposed on local authorities by Part I of the Education Act 1996 (EA 1996). Pursuant to that Part, local authorities have a duty to ensure that efficient primary and secondary education is available to meet the needs of the population of their area (EA 1996, s 13(1)).

2.3   The local authorities which have powers and duties relating to the provision of education used to be called 'local education authorities' but the current statutory term is simply 'LA'.[2] Local authorities must ensure that they exercise their functions in relation to the provision of education with a view to promoting high standards, ensuring fair access to educational opportunity and promoting the fulfilment by every child of his educational potential (EA 1996, s 13A(1)). They must also ensure that sufficient schools for providing primary

---

[1]   We have endeavoured to summarise the statutory framework rather than prepare a detailed commentary on the relevant legislation. The precise text of the relevant enactments should be considered in relation to any issue of statutory construction which may arise in any given case.

[2]   Local Authorities and Children's Services Authority (Integration of Functions) Order 2010, SI 2010/1158.

and secondary education are available for their area and, in doing so, they must secure diversity in the provision of schools and increasing opportunities for parental choice (EA 1996, s 14(1) and (3A)).

2.4   In exercising their functions to secure that sufficient schools are available for their area, local authorities must in particular have regard to the need to securing that primary and secondary education are provided in separate schools, the need to secure that special educational provision is made for pupils who have special educational needs, and the expediency of securing the provision of boarding accommodation (EA 1996, s 14(6)).

2.5   There are many ways in which, and by whom, mainstream schools can be established. There are also differences in procedure depending on the type of school concerned. Accordingly, the various categories of schools will be dealt with first, before dealing with the express powers of establishment, alteration and discontinuance.

SCHOOL CLASSIFICATION

2.6   Section 20(1) of the School Standards and Framework Act 1998 (SSFA 1998) sets out the various categories of maintained schools. These are:

(a)   Community schools.

(b)   Foundation schools.

(c)   Voluntary aided schools.

(d)   Voluntary controlled schools.

(e)   Community special schools.

(f)   Foundation special schools.

2.7   Those categories are acquired either:[3]

(a)   automatically by virtue of pre-existing status on the appointed day under the provisions of Schedule 2 (which allocates schools existing under the previous classification to the new classification);

(b)   by establishment under sections 28 or 31 of the SSFA 1998 or Part 2 of the Education and Inspections Act 2006 (EIA 2006);

---

[3]   Under the SSFA 1998, s 20(2).

(c) by virtue of Schedule 8 of the SSFA or sections 18–24 of the EIA 2006 (which enables changes to categories of school in accordance with the procedures therein set out).

2.8 Academies are not maintained by local authorities and, accordingly, they are independent schools for the purposes of the education legislation (EA 1996, s 463).

SCHOOL REORGANISATION

2.9 School reorganisations in England are now principally governed by Part 2 of the EIA 2006 and by Part II of the SSFA 1998 in Wales. The EIA 2006 introduced several important changes to the way in which maintained schools are established and re-organised. Section 29 of the EIA abolished the body formerly known as the School Organisation Committee (SOC). Each LA had one for its area – a body drawn from a wider membership than the authority, which had to make decisions on school closure following a statutory proposal for closure or re-organisation. SOCs never came into existence in Wales.

2.10 In England, the following Regulations apply in relation to different aspects of school reorganisation:

(a) The School Organisation (Establishment and Discontinuance of Schools) (England) Regulations 2007, ('the Establishment and Discontinuance Regulations');[4]

(b) The School Organisation (Prescribed Alterations to Maintained Schools) (England) Regulations 2007 ('the Alterations Regulations');[5]

(c) The School Organisation (Requirements as to Foundations) (England) Regulations 2007 ('the Foundation Regulations').[6]

2.11 In Wales, the key Regulations are:

(a) The Education (School Organisation Proposals) (Wales) Regulations 1999;[7]

(b) The Education (Maintained Special Schools) (Wales) Regulations 1999;[8]

---

[4] SI 2007/1288.
[5] SI 2007/1289.
[6] SI 2007/1287.
[7] SI 1999/1671.
[8] SI 1999/1780.

(c) The Change of Category of Maintained Schools (Wales) Regulations 2001.[9]

2.12 At the time of writing, the Welsh Ministers have introduced a new School Standards and Organisation (Wales) Bill. Part 3 of the Bill concerns school organisation and brings together the law in relation to school organisation for Wales. In addition, it requires the publication of a new Code on School Organisation and creates a new framework for the determination of proposals which receive objections. The procedures for school reorganisation remain essentially the same.

ESTABLISHING A NEW SCHOOL

In England

2.13 The power to establish and maintain primary and secondary schools is conferred on local authorities[10] by section 16 of the Education Act 1996. The processes for establishing new schools are laid down by Part 2 of the Education and Inspections Act 2006 and the School Organisation (Establishment and Discontinuance of Schools) (England) Regulations 2007.[11] The newly introduced section 6A of the EIA 2006 requires the LA to seek proposals to establish an Academy in the first instance where they identify a need for a new school. As independent schools, Academies are not subject to the normal regime for the establishment of new schools under Part 2 of the EIA 2006. Section 8 of the EIA 2006 which had allowed local authorities to propose the establishment of community school as part of a competitive process has been repealed. For a detailed account of how Academy schools are established, see Chapter 9 at paras **9.58–9.92**.

2.14 Despite the Academy presumption, in certain circumstances it is still possible to invite proposals for a new maintained school. In essence, the legislation envisages two different processes for establishing a new maintained school: on the one hand a competitive process initiated by the LA and, on the other hand, a non-competitive process which must be sanctioned by the Secretary of State.

2.15 The competitive process involves an LA publishing a notice inviting proposals for the establishment of a new school. Under section 7 of the EIA, the LA may, with the consent of the Secretary of State, invite proposals for a foundation, voluntary or foundation special school as well as an Academy. Before doing so, the LA must consult appropriate persons.

2.16 The information to be contained in proposals made in response to a competition notice is prescribed by regulation 6 of, and Schedule 2 to

---

[9]　SI 2001/2678.
[10]　Other persons can establish voluntary aided schools: see para **2.19** below.
[11]　SI 2007/1288.

SI 2007/1288. Once proposals have been submitted, the LA must publish them and, at the same time, it may publish its own proposals for the establishment of a foundation school or, if certain criteria are met, its own proposals for the establishment of a community school. The manner in which such proposals are to be published is laid down by regulation 8 of, and Schedule 5 to, the Regulations. There is, in addition, a duty on an LA to promote public awareness of any proposals published pursuant to a competitive process (EIA 2006, s. 9(2); Establishment and Discontinuance Regulations, regulation 10)

2.17 Schedule 2 of the EIA 2006 has been amended such that when a proposal is made for a new Academy, the Secretary of State must then decide whether to enter into Academy arrangements. Where there are both Academy proposals and non-Academy proposals, the Academy proposals must be determined first. If the Secretary of State decides not to enter into Academy arrangements, the non-Academy arrangements must be considered by the LA. If the Secretary of State does decide to enter into Academy arrangements, then it is for the Secretary of State to decide whether or not to direct that the non-Academy arrangements are to be considered.

2.18 Alternatively, with the consent of the Secretary of State, an LA may embark on a non-competitive process to propose the establishment of a new community, community special, foundation or foundation special school.[12]

2.19 The non-competitive process enables either an LA or any other person ('a proposer') to publish, with the consent of the Secretary of State, proposals to establish (in the case of an LA) a new community or foundation school or (in the case of a proposer) a new foundation or voluntary controlled school (EIA 2006, s 10(1) and (2)). Such proposals must contain the information prescribed in Schedule 3 to the Establishment and Discontinuance Regulations, regulations 11 and 12) and they must be published in accordance with regulation 13. Again, before publishing any such proposals, the local education authority or the proposer (as the case may be) must consult such persons as appear to them to be appropriate (EIA 2006, s 10(4)). If no proposals are made or none of the proposals result in Academy arrangements being made in response to a section 7 notice, the LA may then publish proposals of their own to establish a new community, community special, foundation or foundation special school (EIA 2006, s 11).

In Wales

2.20 Requirements on consultation, publication, consideration, approval and implementation of new school proposals are governed by section 28 and Schedules 6 and 7 of the SSFA 1998. The establishment of special schools by an LA in Wales is dealt with by section 31 of the SSFA 1998. The procedure is very similar to the establishment of a new school which is not also a special school.

---

12   EIA 2006, ss 10 and 11.

2.21   If an LA in Wales wishes to establish a new community or maintained nursery school, it must publish formal proposals to that effect by virtue of section 28(1)(a) and (aa) of the SSFA 1998. An LA may no longer publish proposals for the establishment of a new foundation school in Wales.[13] Section 28(3) provides that such proposals shall contain such information and be published in such a manner as may be prescribed. The relevant regulations are the Education (School Organisation Proposals) (Wales) Regulations 1999 (the 1999 Regulations).[14] Those Regulations contain detailed provisions relating to the manner of publication of formal proposals and the information those proposals should contain. What follows is a summary of some of the principal provisions.

2.22   By virtue of regulation 5(2)(a), the proposals must be posted in at least one conspicuous place in the area proposed to be served by the school. In addition, the proposals have to be published in at least one newspaper circulating in that area.[15] There are detailed provisions for the proposals to contain certain information under regulation 4(2) of, and Schedule 3 to, the 1999 Regulations. The proposals should state the name of the persons or body publishing the proposals, the date on which the proposals are planned to be implemented, and should include a statement explaining the right to make objections under paragraph 7 of Schedule 6 to the SSFA 1998, the date by which such representations should be made and where they should be sent, the location of the site of the proposed school, the numbers, age and gender of the pupils and whether the admission arrangements for the new school will make provision for selection by ability (banding), together with the arrangements for transport and various other matters.[16]

2.23   Before publication, the LA must consult such bodies as seem to it appropriate[17] and in discharging that duty must have regard to any guidance from the Welsh Assembly.[18]

2.24   By virtue of paragraph 7 of Schedule 6, any person may make objections to, or comments on, any proposals published under section 28 of the SSFA 1998. Those objections and/or comments should be sent to the LA, which in turn should send them with its comments to the Assembly.[19] Under regulation 7 of the 1999 Regulations objectors have, in general, a one month period to make representations and the LA has two weeks after that to make comments on those representations and submit them to the Assembly.

2.25   Some proposals require approval, some do not. A proposal from the LA requires approval if objections were made and not withdrawn, or the case is

---

13   SSFA 1998, s 28(2A).
14   SI 1999/1671.
15   Regulation 5(2)(b).
16   SI 1999/1671, Sch 3.
17   SSFA 1998, s 28(5).
18   Including Circulars 9/99 and 21/2009.
19   SSFA 1998, para 7(3) of Sch 6.

covered by paragraph 8(1) of Schedule 6. Where proposals require approval they are to be considered in the first instance by the Welsh Ministers. The Assembly has power to reject the proposals, approve them without modification, approve them with modifications or approve them subject to certain conditions being met.[20] The Assembly cannot approve with modifications unless it both thinks the modifications are desirable and it consults such bodies as may be prescribed.[21] Regulation 8 of the 1999 Regulations provides that the Assembly must consult the LA which it is proposed will maintain the new school before making any modification to the proposals.

2.26 Any approval can be expressed to take effect only if a specified event takes place by a specified date and regulations can prescribe what events may be specified.[22]

2.27 The LA is allowed to determine its own proposals where they do not 'require approval' by the Welsh Assembly Government.[23] This will be the case if the Welsh Assembly Government does not issue a notice within two months of receiving a copy of the proposals stating that they require approval and no objections have been received or all objections have been withdrawn in writing.

2.28 Implementation of proposals by the LA is dealt with in paragraphs 9 and 10 of Schedule 6 to the SSFA 1998. Paragraph 9(1) deals with the case where no objections were made in accordance with paragraph 7 of Schedule 6, or if made, they were withdrawn in writing within the objection period. If the case is governed by paragraph 9(1), then the LA must determine within four months of publication of the proposals whether to implement them and must notify the Assembly of its decision.[24]

2.29 It is the duty of the LA to implement proposals which have been approved by the Assembly under paragraph 8 of Schedule 6, or which it has itself determined to implement under paragraph 10 and Part III of Schedule 6. In general terms, the proposals must be implemented in the form in which they were approved, but there are a few exceptions. The Assembly can modify the proposals at the request of any prescribed body of persons after consulting prescribed persons and, in the case of approvals expressed to take effect only if a specified event takes place by a particular date, can modify the date by specifying a later date.[25] It does not have to be satisfied of any particular matter before modifying the proposals. The Assembly can also determine that there is no duty on the proposers to implement the proposals under paragraph 10(1) of Schedule 6 to the SSFA 1998. However, for it to so direct it must be satisfied either that implementation of the proposals would be unreasonably difficult or

---

20 SSFA 1998, para 8(2) and (3) of Sch 6.
21 SSFA 1998, para 8(2)(c) of Sch 6.
22 SSFA 1998, para 8(3) of Sch 6.
23 SSFA 1998, para 8 of Sch 6.
24 SSFA 1998, para 9(2) and (3).
25 SSFA 1998, para 10(2).

that circumstances have changed so much since approval was given that implementation would be inappropriate.[26] In addition, the promoters must have published proposals to the effect that they should not be obliged to implement the original proposals: paragraph 10(4) of Schedule 6.

CEASING TO MAINTAIN A SCHOOL

In England

2.30 In England, the discontinuance of schools is governed by Part 2, and Schedule 2, to the Education and Inspections Act 2006 (EIA 2006) and the Establishment and Discontinuance Regulations 2007.[27] In this context, the school is discontinued where the relevant LA ceases to maintain it: see section 15(8).

2.31 The statutory scheme is that, where an LA proposes to discontinue a school, it must publish proposals under section 15 of the EIA 2006. Discontinuance notices must contain the information specified in Schedule 4 of SI 2007/1288[28] including a contact address, the name of the school, the date that the planned proposals will be implemented and evidence of consultation before the proposals were published.

2.32 Section 16(2) requires that, before publishing any proposals to discontinue a community school other than a special school or a rural primary school, the LA must consult specified persons and such persons as appear to it to be appropriate and in doing so must have regard to any guidance given by the Secretary of State; see section 16(3).

2.33 Once the proposals have been published, the LA must allow representations to be made[29] before considering whether to approve the proposals.[30]

In Wales

2.34 If an LA in Wales wishes to cease to maintain a community, foundation or voluntary school or a maintained nursery school it must publish a formal proposal to that effect under section 29 of the SSFA 1998 for a mainstream school and section 31 of the SSFA 1998 for a special school. The details in the 1998 Act in relation to consultation, publication, representations, approval and implementation are at section 29 and Schedule 6 and are similar to those described above.

---

[26] SSFA 1998, para 10(3) of Sch 6.
[27] SI 2007/1288.
[28] Regulation 14 of SI 2007/1288.
[29] Regulation 16 of SI 2007/1288.
[30] EIA 2006, para 8 of Sch 2.

2.35 If objections are received, Welsh Ministers are the decision-makers on any such proposals, irrespective of which body has made them. Paragraph 9 of Schedule 6 applies to closures, allowing the relevant body to determine closure proposals where the Assembly does not have to determine the proposals, that is if the proposal has not been called in and there have been no objections or all objections were withdrawn in writing.

2.36 The Welsh Assembly can direct the LA to close a school without formal proposals by use of its power under section 19 of the SSFA 1998. That section covers the special case where the school is causing concern and is subject to a warning notice from the LA under section 15 of the SSFA 1998. Before the Assembly gives its direction, it must consult various interested parties, including the LA and the governing body.[31]

2.37 The Assembly also has power to direct the LA to discontinue a school if it considers it expedient to do so in the interests of the health, safety or welfare of a community or foundation special school.[32] Before it gives such a direction, it must consult the LA that maintains the school, any other LA which in his opinion would be affected by the discontinuance, the person who appointed the foundation governors (if applicable) and any other persons he considers appropriate.[33] If the Assembly gives such a direction, it must give notice of it in writing to the governing body and headteacher of the school.[34]

2.38 The National Assembly for Wales can also direct an LA in Wales to make proposals to close a school if it is of the opinion that the provision for primary or secondary education in maintained schools is excessive: see section 34 of, and Schedule 7 to, the SSFA 1998. If the LA does not comply with the direction, the Secretary of State can make proposals for the reduction of the surplus under paragraph 5 of Schedule 7 to the SSFA 1998.

2.39 Special schools in Wales can also be closed by the LA in a like manner to non-special schools. The relevant provisions are section 31 of, and Schedule 6 to, the SSFA 1998.

2.40 Section 30 of the SSFA 1998 governs closure by a governing body of a voluntary school. Discontinuance of a voluntary or foundation school by the governing body under section 30 of the SSFA 1998 applies to both England and Wales. The governors of a voluntary school cannot discontinue such a school except after serving at least two years' notice on the LA maintaining the school and the Secretary of State of their intention to do so.[35] Two years' notice means two clear years between service of the notice and the date of closure; see *Re Hector Whaling Ltd.*[36] No such notice can be served without the

---

[31] EIA 2006, s 19(2).
[32] EIA 2006, s 32(1).
[33] EIA 2006, s 32(3).
[34] EIA 2006, s 32(4).
[35] SSFA 1998, s 30(1).
[36] [1936] Ch 208.

consent of the Secretary of State if expenditure has been incurred otherwise than in connection with repairs by the Secretary of State, the Funding Agency for Schools, any LA or any body which was an LEA.[37]

2.41   It was held in *Inner London Education Authority v Secretary of State for Education and Science*[38] in relation to a predecessor of s 30[39] that the discretion given to the Secretary of State was not limited to financial considerations and he was entitled to take into account the future educational use of the premises, which in that case was to be as a City Technology College.[40] As there are no words limiting the matters that the Secretary of State is to have regard to when deciding to give his consent under section 30(2) of the SSFA 1998, it is very unlikely that a different result would be reached on the present section.

2.42   Before the notice is served, the governors must consult the Secretary of State (if the school is in England) or the Welsh Ministers (if the school is in Wales) if discontinuance of the school would affect the facilities for full-time education suitable to the requirements of persons over compulsory school age but below 19.[41] Once a notice has been given by the governors, they cannot withdraw it save with the consent of the LA: see section 30(7) of the SSFA 1998. If the governing body is unwilling or unable to carry on the school which is the subject of a notice under section 30 before that notice expires, the LA is empowered by section 30(4) of the SSFA 1998 to conduct the school as if it were a community school and may use the premises free of charge, but it must keep the premises under repair.[42] The governors remain entitled to use the premises when not required for the school by virtue of section 30(6) of the SSFA 1998.

PRESCRIBED ALTERATIONS

In England

2.43   Under sections 18 and 19 of the EIA 2006 alterations to schools in England, including a change of school category, must be dealt with in accordance with a prescribed procedure. Prescribed alterations to a maintained school in England are governed by the School Organisation (Prescribed Alterations to Maintained Schools) (England) Regulations 2007[43] and include:

---

[37]   SSFA 1998, s 30(2).
[38]   [1990] COD 412.
[39]   Education Act 1944, s 14.
[40]   City Technology Colleges were a statutory predecessor to Academies and were in many respects similar to them.
[41]   SSFA 1998, s 30(3).
[42]   SSFA 1998, s 30(5).
[43]   SI 2007/1289.

(a)   an enlargement, other than a temporary enlargement, of the premises of the school which would increase the capacity of the school by more than 30 pupils and 25 per cent of the previous capacity of the school or 200 pupils (whichever is the lesser);[44]

(b)   alteration of upper or lower age limit;[45]

(c)   change or removal of provisions reserved for pupils with special educational needs;[46]

(d)   admissions arrangements of a grammar school;[47]

(e)   changes from single sex to mixed provision or vice versa;[48]

(f)   introducing or ending boarding provision;[49]

(g)   transferring to a new site or discontinuing of use of a site;[50]

(h)   change of category.[51]

2.44   The procedure is again similar to that in relation to establishment of new schools and is not further detailed here. The Government has also published statutory and non-statutory guidance entitled 'Making Changes to a Maintained Mainstream School' for local authorities and governing bodies.

In Wales

2.45   Prescribed alterations in Wales also require formal proposals under section 28 of the SSFA 1998. Prescribed alterations in Wales are detailed in the Education (School Organisation Proposals) (Wales) Regulations 1999, SI 1999/1671.

2.46   What are prescribed alterations in Wales are set out in Schedule 2 of the 1999 Regulations. They are in many respects similar to the provisions in England and include:

---

[44]   The School Organisation (Prescribed Alterations to Maintained Schools) (England) Regulations 2007, SI 2007/1289, Sch 2, para 1(1).
[45]   2007 Regulations, Sch 2, paras 3 and 4.
[46]   2007 Regulations, Sch 2, para 5.
[47]   2007 Regulations, Sch 2, para 6.
[48]   2007 Regulations, Sch 2, para 7.
[49]   2007 Regulations, Sch 2, para 8.
[50]   2007 Regulations, Sch 2, para 10.
[51]   2007 Regulations, Sch 2, para 11.

(a) an enlargement, other than a temporary enlargement, of the premises of the school which would increase the capacity of the school by more than 30 pupils and 25 per cent of the previous capacity of the school or 200 pupils (whichever is the lesser);[52]

(b) the making permanent of a temporary enlargement of the school;[53]

(c) alterations in the age range of the school involving an extension or reduction of the age range by a full year or more;[54]

(d) the establishment or discontinuance of provision which is recognised as reserved for children with special educational needs;[55]

(e) the introduction of admission arrangements to which section 101(1) of the SSFA 1998 applies.[56] That section enables a maintained school to make provision for selection by ability if it is designed to secure that the pupils admitted to the school in any relevant age group are representative of all levels of ability among applicants for admission to the school in that age group and that no level of ability is substantially over, or under, represented;

(f) changes from single sex to mixed provision or vice versa unless incidental;[57]

(g) the establishment or removal of a significant number of boarding places;[58]

(h) the transfer of a school to a new site or discontinuance of a site where the school occupies more than one site.[59]

2.47 The above alterations are prescribed as alterations for which proposals must be published under section 28(2)(b) of the SSFA 1998 by the governing body of a community school. The information to be contained in the statutory notice is detailed in Schedule 3 of SI 2001/1671.

STANDING AND TIMING

2.48 For a general discussion on standing and timing, see Chapter 1 at paras **1.1–1.28**. What follows is a discussion of this issue in relation to a school reorganisation challenge.

---

[52] 1999 Regulations, Sch 2, para 1(1).
[53] 1999 Regulations, para 1(2).
[54] 1999 Regulations, para 2.
[55] 1999 Regulations, para 3.
[56] 1999 Regulations, para 4.
[57] 1999 Regulations, para 5.
[58] 1999 Regulations, para 7.
[59] 1999 Regulations, para 8, as amended by SI 2010/1142.

2.49 Anyone with sufficient interest can launch an application for judicial review to challenge a school reorganisation decision.[60] The courts now generally apply liberal rules of standing.[61] In the context of school reorganisation decisions, applications are usually brought by parents affected by the decision. It seems clear that the promoters of any proposed reorganisation would have standing to challenge the LA's, the Welsh Assembly's or the Secretary of State's decision on the proposals. Further, the objectors to the proposals or simply persons making representations on them would also have standing. Equally, it seems clear that depending on the nature of the challenge, the children affected would have standing.[62] As discussed in later Chapters, challenges to school admissions and the First-tier Tribunal should, generally, be brought by the parents and not the child but there the relevant statutory rights are vested in the parents. This is not the case with school closures. The point is of significance because of the availability of public funding. Children are likely to qualify for public funding where their parents do not simply because of differences in their income.

Proceedings brought in the name of the child

2.50 To date, most challenges to school reorganisations have been brought by parents (or by other interested parties). Is it an abuse to bring proceedings in the name of the child simply in order to obtain public funding for the litigation? This is a matter on which differing views have been expressed in the Court of Appeal. In the school admissions field it has been held, both in the High Court and in the Court of Appeal, that it would, however, ordinarily be an abuse of process simply to bring the challenge in the name of the child in order to qualify for public funding.[63] In *R (on the application of Boulton and Another) v Leeds School Organisation Committee*, which was a challenge to a school reorganisation decision, another division of the Court of Appeal held, when granting permission to move for judicial review, that it was not necessarily an abuse to bring proceedings in the name of the child.[64] When that case was heard substantively in the High Court, Scott Baker J held:[65]

---

[60]   Supreme Court Act 1981, s 31(3).

[61]   See *R v Secretary of State for Foreign and Commonwealth Affairs ex parte World Development Movement* [1995] 1 WLR 386 and *R v Somerset County Council ex parte Dixon* [1997] NPC 61. For general discussion of the topic see De Smith, Woolf and Jowell, *Judicial Review* (Sweet and Maxwell, 6th edn, 2006) at para 2.040–2.041.

[62]   In *R v Secretary of State for Education ex parte Bandtock* [2001] ELR 333 Collins J held, at para 12, that where the complaint was about a lack of consultation it was wrong to bring the proceedings in the name of the chid because a child of primary school age was not going to have any real input in relation to a consultation exercise. Pupils may come within 'any other interested party' in a given case but there is clearly no general rule that they should be consulted.

[63]   *R v Hackney LBC ex parte T* [1991] COD 454; *R v Richmond LBC ex parte JC* [2001] ELR 21 at paras 31 and 68.

[64]   *R (on the application of Boulton and Another) v Leeds School Organisation Committee* [2002] EWCA Civ 884 at para 7.

[65]   [2002] EWHC 1927, (Admin), [2003] ELR 67 at para 34.

(a)   that the observations of Kennedy and Ward LJJ in *R v Richmond LBC ex parte JC*,[66] suggesting it was an abuse to bring proceedings in the name of the child to get public funding, were limited to school admission disputes;

(b)   nevertheless,[67] that as far as school reorganisation disputes were concerned, it was ordinarily the parents who had the real and primary interest in bringing the case and it might be an abuse of process to proceed in the name of the child rather than a parent where this was done for the purpose of obtaining public funding and protection against a possible costs order;[68]

(c)   that clear evidence of such abuse would be needed and that it was not present in the case before him.

2.51   In *Boulton* the evidence of abuse was not present because the applicants were selected at random from a larger group and, had it been intended to choose claimants to get public funding, there were plenty of parents who were available as they were on state benefits.[69] The court emphasised that both the parent and the child had standing and the only issue was whether there had been an abuse of process.[70]

2.52   Accordingly, in this context, it is submitted that the courts will look carefully at the pre-existing practice and, if proceedings are commenced in the name of the child rather than the parent, require an explanation as to why that process has been adopted. As is suggested in Chapter 1,[71] a respondent should take the point in the acknowledgement of service if it appears that proceedings have been commenced in the name of the child simply to obtain public funding and, at the same time, should write to the claimants seeking an explanation. If an explanation does appear when the court considers whether to grant permission, it is possible that permission will be refused on that basis alone. If permission has been granted, attempts should be made to contact the Legal Services Commission to see if they are willing to continue to fund the case where there has been a prima facie abuse. If they do continue to fund, the court, while it could still refuse relief if satisfied there had been an abuse, may be reluctant to adopt this course.

2.53   Whether the applicant will have standing will also depend on the nature of the challenge brought. It is perfectly possible for the same person to have standing to raise some grounds of challenge but to lack standing in relation to

---

[66]   [2001] ELR 21 at paras 31 and 68.

[67]   At para 37.

[68]   To the same effect is *R v Secretary of State for Education ex parte Bandtock* [2001] ELR 333, per Collins J at para 12. In that case the point was not live because legal aid was, on the point being taken, also granted to the parent and the court held that the proceedings had been brought in the name of the child because it was believed (wrongly, the court held) that the child was the appropriate applicant.

[69]   [2002] EWCA Civ 884, para 36.

[70]   [2002] EWCA Civ 884, para 35.

[71]   See at para 1.2.

other grounds of challenge. In *R (Chandler v Secretary of State for Children Schools and another*,[72] the Secretary of State's decision to approve UCL as the sponsor for the new Academy was challenged on the basis that there had been a failure to comply with the public procurement requirements.[73] There was also by way of separate proceedings heard with this challenge a further challenge on a variety of other grounds ranging from consultation to improper purpose.[74] Forbes J rejected both challenges on the merits. He went on to hold[75] in relation to the procurement challenge that the claimant, a parent of school-age children living in the LA's area, did not have sufficient standing to bring a challenge under the procurement regime because, in particular, she was not an economic operator and there was no evidence that she or her children had been adversely affected by the approval of UCL as a sponsor. The Court of Appeal dismissed an appeal on the merits and affirmed the conclusions of Forbes J on the issue of standing.[76] Although they had not heard a detailed oral argument on the point and the issue was academic in the light of their conclusion on the merits, they held essentially that the parent lacked standing to raise the public procurement points because she was not interested in any way in those points as such but was merely opposed to Academy status. As she was therefore seeking to use the public procurement regime for a purpose for which it was not created she lacked standing.[77]

The need for promptness[78] in applying for judicial review

2.54   Under the provisions of CPR, r 54.5, any application for judicial review must be made promptly and, in any event, within three months after the grounds to make the claim first arose. It is well-known that in the education field generally, and in the context of school reorganisation decisions in particular, claimants must act swiftly so as not to have their challenges excluded on grounds of delay. In the school reorganisation context, the requirement that a challenge be brought promptly (see CPR, r 54.5(1)) may well require that it be brought well before the expiry of the three month 'back stop' time limit.

2.55   In *R (on the application of M (a child)) v School Organisation Committee*[79] M and nine other pupils applied for an extension of time within which to commence proceedings for the judicial review of a decision of the LA to reorganise the education system so as to remove middle schools in Oxford. The claimants were ten children. The court took a firm line with delay in cases which sought to challenge school reorganisation and held that the case was not of such public importance as to constitute an exception to the need for

---

[72]   [2009] EWHC 219, [2009] LGR 417. An appeal to the Court of Appeal was dismissed: [2009] EWCA Civ 1011, [2010] LGR 1.
[73]   See the second judicial review proceedings dealt with at para 114 of the High Court Judgment.
[74]   See at para 49 of the High Court judgment.
[75]   At paras 126, 136 and 137.
[76]   See at paras 69 and 70.
[77]   See at para 78 of the judgment of the court delivered by Arden LJ.
[78]   There is some debate about whether promptness in a case that raises community law points. This issue is discussed in Chapter 1 at paras **1.3–1.17**.
[79]   [2001] EWHC Admin 245; [2001] ACD 77.

promptness and lack of delay. The court refused to extend time by one day to bring the claimants within the three-month time limit and in any event, expressed the view that even if proceedings had been brought one day earlier, that the claimants would still have been substantially in breach of the obligation to proceed promptly.

2.56 A timing issue was also raised in *R (on the application of Brynmawr Foundation School Governors) v Welsh Ministers*.[80] The court found the claimant's lack of promptness in raising the point (over two months after the end of the consultation period) meant that it would not be appropriate to set aside the consultations and subsequent decisions.

The need to wait for the consideration of the decision-maker

2.57 Problems of timing in school reorganisation disputes are not limited to the concept of promptness. There is the additional problem of when the grounds for making the claim will be taken to have first arisen within the meaning of CPR, r 54.5. As indicated above, most school closures, or other reorganisations, require a whole series of steps, such as consultation, proposals and consideration by one or more persons of those proposals. It is possible that there may have been an error at an early stage of the process but impeccable consideration of the matter thereafter.

2.58 There is some controversy as to the appropriate time to bring an application for judicial review. A debate continues as to whether the target of a challenge in a discontinuance case, particularly where the challenge is to the adequacy of the consultation exercise, should be to the decision to publish the proposals to discontinue or whether it should be to the ultimate decision to approve the discontinuance. This debate was referred to but not resolved by the decisions of the High Court and Court of Appeal in the *Elphinstone* case.[81]

2.59 In the first edition of this book it was submitted[82] that the better view was that where the grounds of challenge were such that the proposals were fatally flawed and the decision-maker could not cure the defect, an application should be made before the decision-maker considered the matter. Where, by contrast, the defect was such that the decision-maker's consideration of the matter was capable either of curing it, or of being a powerful factor for the refusal of relief in the exercise of the court's discretion, then it was submitted that it would be appropriate to await the consideration of the decision-maker, providing the point of challenge was drawn to the attention of the proposer and the decision-maker at the earliest possible moment. It was further

---

[80]   [2011] EWHC 519 (Admin).

[81]   *R (on the application of Elphinstone) v Westminster City Council* [2008] EWHC 1287 (Admin); *R (Elphinstone) v Westminster City Council* [2008] EWCA Civ 1069. The decision of the High Court was to refuse permission, however the Court of Appeal was a substantive decision and referred with approval to the High Court decision. In the circumstances it is appropriate to refer to the High Court decision.

[82]   At para 1.32.

submitted[83] that defects which fell into the first category would be those where the statutory consultation had not, on its face, complied with the statutory requirements, or where either no proposals complying with the statute, or the wrong proposals, were used. A defect falling within the second category, it was submitted, would have been a *Wednesbury* challenge where the decision-maker's consideration of the merits of the proposal might have been fuller than the consideration of the LEA when it published the proposals.

2.60 It was further submitted[84] that the law did not then fully support that analysis. By contrast, in a number of cases the courts had permitted challenges to be brought to the Secretary of State's approval of proposals even though the grounds of challenge were apparent at the date formal proposals were published.[85] The furthest the courts had gone was to suggest that if the point was available at the date of publication of the proposals then the Secretary of State should have been notified at the earliest possible opportunity: see *ex parte Threapleton*.[86] *Nichol v Gateshead*[87] had indicated a more robust approach, but there the Court of Appeal had held that the challenge was in time. However, because of the extended delay in that case, it refused relief in the exercise of its discretion. Even in cases subsequent to *Nichol v Gateshead* the courts had entertained challenges brought after the Secretary of State's approval of proposals despite the fact that the grounds of challenge were available when the proposals were published and remained the same.[88]

2.61 In *R v Secretary of State for Education ex parte Bandtock*[89] Collins J considered this issue further. In that case, the claimant alleged that proposals published by the LA were unlawful because the LEA had failed to comply with its statutory duty to consult and that the notice of the proposals itself was flawed because of ambiguities therein contained. Collins J rejected the claims that there was a defect in the consultation process[90] or that the notice was invalid,[91] but he went on to deal with the question of timing where there was a two-tiered decision-making process. His consideration of this issue, therefore, is strictly obiter. He cited[92] with approval the analysis in paras **1.32–1.34** of the first edition of this book. He then considered the Divisional Court's decision in

---

[83]   At para 1.33.

[84]   At para 1.34.

[85]   *R v Secretary of State for Education ex parte Tebbutt* (unreported, CO/322/86, Div Ct, 26 June 1986, Woolf LJ and Hirst J, Transcript at 3F–4A) albeit the application in that case was made before the Secretary of State had made his decision; see 20E; *R v Secretary of State for Education and Science ex parte Threapleton* (1988) *The Times*, 2 June, CO/302/88, Div Ct, 12 May 1988, Woolf LJ and Hutchinson J, Transcript at 26D–27D; *R v Secretary of State for Wales ex parte Williams* [1997] ELR 100.

[86]   (1988) *The Times*, 2 June. Transcript CO/302/88 at 27D–27F.

[87]   (1988) 87 LGR 435 at 459–460.

[88]   *R v Cornwall ex parte Nicholls* (1989) *The Independent*, March 30; *R v Secretary of State for Wales ex parte Williams* [1997] ELR 100.

[89]   [2001] ELR 333.

[90]   At para 37.

[91]   At para 38.

[92]   At paras 47–50.

ex parte Threapleton[93] and, in particular, the remarks of Woolf LJ that it was normally appropriate to await the decision of the second decision-maker (then the Secretary of State) before making any application for judicial review, and stated he was singularly unpersuaded by it. He concluded by expressing the view that where it was contended that the proposals were unlawful, there ought to be a challenge to the proposals at that point and it was not appropriate to await the decision of the Secretary of State. He further observed that if a claimant waited for the Secretary of State's decision, and even if the challenge was technically in time, the court would not exercise its discretion to grant relief where the point taken arose from a flaw at an earlier stage of the decision-making process. In doing so he expressly followed the approach of the Court of Appeal in *Nichol v Gateshead Metropolitan Council.*[94]

2.62   It is submitted that the approach of Collins J in *Bandtock* has much to commend it. While it is obiter and cannot displace the authority of the Divisional Court in *Threapleton*, it is consistent with the Court of Appeal's approach in *Nichol v Gateshead* in so far as it suggests that a claimant, who waits for a second-tier decision-maker to take his decision when he has a case based on an illegality preceding the decision by the first-tier decision-maker, may find that relief is refused by the court in the exercise of its discretion. It is also consistent with the decision of the Court of Appeal in *R v Gloucestershire County Council ex parte Findlater.*[95] In that case, the claimants sought to allege that a decision of the LEA to publish proposals on 7 January 1999 was flawed by inadequate consultation. The Secretary of State had approved the proposals on 17 June 1999 and the application for judicial review was launched on 16 September 1999. During the course of the objection procedure the claimants had complained to the Secretary of State about the inadequacy of the consultation preceding the LEA decision of 7 January 1999. The Court of Appeal held that the consultation was not inadequate. It went on to say,[96] obiter, that even if there had been inadequate consultation, the challenge to the LEA decision was late and was not excused by a failed attempt to persuade the Secretary of State as to the inadequacy of the consultation. Although there is no trace of *Threapleton* being cited or discussed it is submitted that this decision does represent the modern trend of requiring these applications to be made promptly. The Court of Appeal expressly endorsed the remarks of Schiemann LJ in *R v Leeds City Council ex parte N*[97] as to the importance of giving early warning of challenges in this area so that the education system of the relevant LEA was not kept in suspense while legal proceedings dragged on. Accordingly, despite the suggestion to the contrary in *Threapleton*, claimants would be well advised not to wait for the decisions of second-tier decision-makers when they have a case of illegality by the first-tier decision-maker.

---

[93]   (1988) *The Times*, 2 June.
[94]   (1988) 87 LGR 435 at p 459.
[95]   (Unreported) 14 July 2000, Simon Brown and Waller LJ.
[96]   As above, at para 13 per Simon Brown LJ.
[97]   [1999] ELR 324 at 334.

2.63 At first blush, the decision of the House of Lords in *R (Burkett) v London Borough of Hammersmith and Fulham*[98] might be thought to support, from a claimant's point of view, a more relaxed approach to the question of delay than that suggested above. In *Burkett*, the issue was whether where there was a challenge to the grant of planning permission, grounds for the challenge first arose (within the meaning of what was then RSC Ord 53, r 4(1)) when an LA resolved to grant planning permission subject to certain conditions being fulfilled or whether time ran from the actual grant of planning permission. The House of Lords held that time ran from the date of grant of planning permission. However, in doing so, the Law Lords relied on the fact that the resolution had no legal effect until the grant of planning permission and might fall because the conditions were not fulfilled.[99] It cannot be said in the present context, however, that decisions of the first-tier decision-makers are in any sense provisional or of no legal effect. Although the LEA cannot close the school simply on publication of the proposals, those proposals do trigger a statutory right to make objections under para 2 of Sch 6 to the SSFA 1998 and cannot be withdrawn by the LEA if they have been determined by the SOC under para 3 of Sch 6.

2.64 Further, and importantly, Lord Steyn in *Burkett*, at paragraph 18 of his speech, expressly endorsed the manifest good sense of disputes about the allocation of places being brought speedily and before the school term starts. Although the context of this approval was the discretion of the court to refuse relief under section 31(6) of the Supreme Court Act 1981[100] where, even though the challenge was brought within three months there would be immense practical difficulties if relief were granted and not a refusal to entertain a case at all, it does illustrate the importance of speed in this area if effective relief is to be obtained.

2.65 In *R (on the application of Boulton) v Leeds School Reorganisation Committee*,[101] the Court of Appeal relied on *Burkett* in granting permission to move for judicial review where the claimant, although within three months, was arguably not prompt. The court remarked[102] that promptness was a tool to be used with great care, but went on to say that this was not a case where substantive relief should be granted if the challenge was otherwise well-founded because of the disruption that would follow from quashing a school reorganisation that was at that date almost complete. The court made clear that relief, in the event the case was successful, was to be limited to declaratory relief.

---

[98] [2002] UKHL 23, [2002] 1 WLR 1593.
[99] [2002] UKHL 23, [2002] 1 WLR 1593 at para 39 per Lord Steyn.
[100] Now the Senior Courts Act 1981P: see the Constitutional Reform Act 2005, s 59(5) and para 1 of Sch 11.
[101] [2002] EWCA Civ 884.
[102] [2002] EWCA Civ 884, at para 8.

2.66 In *R (on the application of Louden) v Bury Schools Organisation Committee*[103] Lightman J was faced with a challenge to a decision of the SOC based on an alleged invalidity of the LEA's decision to trigger the mechanism for closure under section 29 of the SSFA 1998. It was contended by the claimants, without having obtained permission to raise the point before the substantive hearing of the application for judicial review, that that decision had been taken by the Executive Committee of the LEA and that the Executive Committee did not have power to act on behalf of the full council because this was a matter involving expenditure not provided for in the council's approved budget and, therefore, under the council's constitution, not delegated to the Executive Committee of the council. The SOC submitted that this was a matter to be decided in proceedings against the LEA (which had not been commenced) and not in the proceedings against itself.

2.67 Lightman J offered the claimant an adjournment to enable an application to be made for the purpose of applying for permission to seek a declaration of invalidity against the LEA and joining the LEA as a defendant in the proceedings against the SOC before him. The claimant declined that opportunity and submitted that he was entitled to seek a determination as against the SOC alone, that the decision of the Executive Committee was invalid and that, in consequence, the subsequent decision of the SOC was invalid. Lightman J refused permission to raise this point on three grounds:

(a)   in the interests of fairness to the LEA and the SOC, the LEA should be made a party to raise the point;

(b)   without the LEA's involvement the court could not be confident it had the full facts on the alleged invalidity of the decision-making process before the LEA;

(c)   as it was conceded that the LEA decision was immune from challenge as against the LEA on grounds of delay, so was the SOC decision in so far as it was sought to rely on the alleged invalidity of the LEA decision as against the SOC.

2.68 It is respectfully submitted that the decision in *Louden* is to be welcomed. Although it does not refer to *Bandtock* or *Burkett*, it is submitted that it is consistent with the former and not inconsistent with the latter.

2.69 In the *Elphinstone* case in the High Court,[104] Kenneth Parker QC, siting as a deputy High Court Judge, inclined towards the view that in the present statutory context *Bandtock* was distinguishable, in that the LA was the decision-maker throughout and that it would potentially be able to correct any flaws in the process leading up to the publication of the statutory notices. His comments though were *obiter*. He also expressed the view that if he had to

---

[103]   (Unreported) Case No CO/4716/2002.
[104]   [2008] EWHC 1287 (Admin).

decide the issue, he was most influenced by the third of the policy reasons relied upon by Lord Steyn in *Burkett*, namely the desirability of curtailing premature challenges and of encouraging negotiation rather than litigation. Therefore, Kenneth Parker QC would not have ruled the application out of time. However, the Court of Appeal,[105] also *obiter*, expressed the view that there was much to be said for the respondents' submissions that any challenge should have been brought promptly after the decision to publish the statutory notices. The matter therefore still awaits definitive resolution by the courts.

CHALLENGING SCHOOL CLOSURES ON THE GROUNDS OF IRRATIONALITY

2.70 Conventional *Wednesbury* challenges[106] are difficult to maintain in this area. The high watermark of judicial restraint is to be found in the decision of the Court of Appeal in *R v Secretary of State for Education ex parte Avon (No 2)*.[107] In that case the Secretary of State had refused to approve proposals put before him by Avon for the reorganisation of secondary education in Bath. Because of falling school rolls there were insufficient sixth-form pupils in Bath for any individual school to provide a full range of courses for all pupils. It was in evidence that sixth formers were having to move from one part of Bath to another in order to attend their A-level classes. The council decided that the best way of remedying the problem was to remove the sixth forms from all the schools and to have a sixth form college in the centre of the town. This involved closing Beechen Cliff School and proposing to change it into a sixth form college. Both proposals required the approval of the Secretary of State for Education. However, Beechen Cliff also decided that it wished to acquire grant maintained status. That also required the approval of the Secretary of State. The consequence of the school acquiring grant maintained status was that the LEA would not be able to close it. The Secretary of State approved the proposal by Beechen Cliff to acquire grant maintained status and rejected the LEA proposals. The court commented in strong terms on its inability to review the political merits of the decision.[108] As Nicholls LJ put it:[109]

'The statutory provisions provide simply that the Secretary of State may reject proposals, or may approve them either without modification or, after consultation, with such modifications as he thinks desirable. By appointing the Secretary of State the decision-maker in this way, Parliament has given to him the responsibility of weighing the conflicting considerations, in the sense that the degree of importance (or "weight") to be attached to these considerations has been made a matter for his judgement. It is not for the court, in the exercise of its jurisdiction, to substitute its own evaluation of these considerations for that of the Minister.'

---

[105] [2008] EWCA Civ 1069.
[106] *Associated Provincial Picture House v Wednesbury Corporation* [1948] 1 KB 223.
[107] (1990) 88 LGR 737.
[108] See per Ralph Gibson LJ at 738, Nicholls LJ at 742 and Mustill LJ at 743.
[109] At 742.

2.71 While the court does not appear to have gone as far as suggesting that there is a higher threshold for *Wednesbury* challenges in this area than in others, it is clear that, in practice, it is very difficult to make good an irrationality challenge in relation to a school closure. Moreover, the courts regard it as inappropriate to have detailed evidence from an education expert in support of an irrationality challenge: see *R v Secretary of State for Education and Science ex parte Banham*[110] where the court also stressed[111] that the courts' role was purely supervisory and not in the nature of an appellate jurisdiction. This is an area where policy predominates and the courts are reluctant to weigh competing policy considerations.

2.72 Although the *Avon* case concerned a different statutory framework, the considerations are of a general nature and matters of weight are for the appropriate decision-maker. It is accordingly submitted that the approach of the court in *Avon* would be followed under the current statutory framework.

2.73 One example of an irrationality challenge which failed (albeit the challenge succeeded on other grounds) is *R v Secretary of State for Education ex parte Skitt*.[112] There, Sedley J rejected a claim that the Secretary of State's decision to approve proposals for the closure of Beacon School was irrational, despite the reliance by the Secretary of State on a stale inspector's report criticising the school, and the paucity of the proposals before the Secretary of State for the educational future of the children at the school. The court commented that irrationality or perversity was always a steep hill for an applicant to climb, but added the rider that it might be less steep if the same point was framed in terms of a want of logic. If this was intended to be the genesis of a different, and less strict, test for the intervention of the court on merits challenges, it is yet to claim general acceptance from the courts. It has not reappeared in subsequent case-law.

2.74 Another example of an irrationality challenge which failed was in relation to the closure of Hackney Downs School.[113] There, the Court of Appeal refused to hold that a closure of a school in the middle of an academic year was irrational. Although the Secretary of State's then policy, Circular 3/87, indicated it was desirable that closures should take place at the end of a school year, where the school was failing and the Educational Association reported to the Secretary of State that closure should take place as soon as possible, with special arrangements being made for pupils in Year 11, then it was not irrational for him to approve proposals to cease to maintain before the end of the school year.

2.75 A further irrationality challenge that failed was *R (on the application of B and another) v Schools' Organisation Committee of Lambeth London Borough*

---

[110] (1992) *The Times*, 9 March. Transcript, 4 March 1992, CO/2016/91, Macpherson J at 4D–4E.
[111] Transcript, 4B.
[112] [1995] ELR 388 at 398B–399D.
[113] *R v Secretary of State for Education ex parte Morris* [1996] ELR 162 at 210E–211E, CA.

Council.[114] In that case it was contended the closure decision was irrational because, in consequence, the severely physically disabled would be educated with children with 'challenging behaviour' and thereby placed at grave risk as to their safety and welfare. No fewer than four experts were called in support of the claimant's case. Although their evidence had not been available to the SOC, the substance of their concerns had been. However, the court found on the evidence that the experts and the objectors and the experts they had instructed had misunderstood the position and that children with emotional and behavioural difficulties were not to be educated with the severely physically disabled. Although the judge expressed sympathy with the claimants, he concluded, perhaps not surprisingly, that the decision was not irrational.

2.76 In *R (on the application of Roberts) v Welsh Ministers*[115] the claimant argued that the Welsh Ministers had acted irrationally in deciding that a particular school was not 'popular' within the meaning in the relevant guidance (Circular 21/2009). He declined to express a definitive view on whether the statutory obligation of an LA to have regard to policy guidance issued by the Welsh Assembly extended to section 2 of Circular 21/2009.[116]

2.77 Wyn Williams J held, applying *R (Raissi) v Secretary of State for the Home Department* [2008] QB 836, that the court was not limited to determining whether the Minister's interpretation had been a rational one, but had to determine for itself the meaning of the guidance contained in the Circular. Wyn Williams J considered that 'popular' was to be understood by the reasonable and literate man to mean a very well-attended school where surplus places were 10 per cent or less and this had to be measured over a period of time, years if possible. The reliance by the Welsh Ministers on the number of surplus places at a particular point in time to reach the conclusion that the school was 'unpopular' was irrational and unreasonable. The court held that the Ministers ought to have known that the number taken at a particular point in time was unlikely to be representative of the popularity of the school. The Welsh Ministers had also relied on one set of figures to assess the percentage of children from within the school's catchment area who attended the school as a measure of popularity. Wyn Williams J held that this strand of the defendant's conclusion was not irrational as there was nothing to suggest that the figure was markedly low compared with other years.

2.78 Despite finding that the Minister's conclusion was irrational on the basis of the number of surplus places, Wyn Williams J decided not to quash the decision because he was satisfied that even had the Welsh Minister applied the proper test, he would have reached the same conclusion.[117] Therefore, there was no point in remitting the matter for re-consideration.

---

[114] [2001] EWHC 515 (Admin), Harrison J.
[115] [2011] EWHC 3416 (Admin), Wyn Williams J.
[116] Paragraph 20.
[117] See at paras 153–158.

Relevant and irrelevant considerations

2.79 Successful challenges on these other two heads of *Wednesbury* are also rare.

2.80 The statutory scheme prescribes some conditions that the decision-maker must take into account and those he must ignore. For example, where an LA or governing body propose to discontinue a rural primary school, it must have regards to the matters in section 15(4) of the EIA 2006 including the likely effect of the discontinuance of the school on the local community, the availability and likely cost to the LA of transport to other schools, any increase in the use of motor vehicles which is likely to result from the discontinuance to the school and any alternatives to the discontinuance to the school.

2.81 'Having regard' to certain factors is a familiar concept in the education field and has been considered judicially on a number of occasions. In the context of section 76 of the Education Act 1944,[118] it was held that 'have regard' meant 'take account of'.[119]

2.82 The Secretary of State (or Welsh Assembly as appropriate) is also entitled to issue guidance which must be taken into account by the decision-maker. Section 29(4) of the SSFA 1998 imposes an obligation upon local authorities to have regard to any guidance issued by the Secretary of State when preparing proposals for publication under section 29.

2.83 By virtue of section 28(5) of the SSFA 1998 and section 9 of the EIA 2006, the LA is obliged, before publishing proposals, to consult and take account of any guidance issued by the Welsh Assembly or Secretary of State. Proposals under section 28 must include information prescribed by regulations[120] under section 29(3). There is little doubt that both the proposals themselves and objections and comments made within the prescribed period (ie those made within two months of first publication of the proposals)[121] are relevant considerations. While the decision-maker is probably not obliged to take into account non-statutory objections, there is no doubt that it is permissible for him to consider them, and, in fact, it was common for the Secretary of State when he was the only decision-maker to take them into account.

2.84 Guidance issued by the Secretary of State or Welsh Assembly Government, as appropriate, frequently changes and differs for those making proposals and also for those who have to make decisions on them. Not

---

[118] Repealed. See now the EA 1996, s 9.
[119] *Watt v Kesteven* [1955] QB 408 at 428–429; *Cummings v Birkenhead* [1972] Ch 12 at 25H–26C. Cf *Secretary of State for Education and Science v Tameside MBC* [1977] AC 1014 at 1063C per Lord Diplock.
[120] SI 1999/1671.
[121] Regulation 7 of SI 1999/1671.

surprisingly, it also differs depending on the type of proposals being made for those making the proposals and those who have to make relevant decisions on the proposals.

2.85 In *R v Secretary of State for Education and Science ex parte Threapleton*,[122] the Divisional Court considered whether the Secretary of State (the decision-maker under the then legislative scheme) had applied his policy:

> 'The Secretary of State's contention was that he had not disregarded his policy but applied his policy and if this be so, the parents cannot have any complaint. On the other hand, if the Secretary of State had not applied his policy when he thought he was doing so, this would mean that the Secretary of State had failed to take into account in coming to his decision a material consideration, namely that he was departing from his policy and, as Miss Baxendale [Counsel for the Secretary of State] accepted, in these circumstances his decision could be quashed by this court on conventional *Wednesbury* grounds.'

2.86 The court then construed the relevant policy and held on the facts that the Secretary of State had applied it correctly.

2.87 In September 1999, the National Assembly for Wales/the Welsh Assembly Government published Circular 9/1999 entitled 'Organisation of School Places'. It contains considerations to be taken into account in the determination of proposals to change the pattern of school provision. In September 2009, the Welsh Assembly Government published further guidance in the form of Circular 21/2009 entitled 'School Organisation Proposals'.

2.88 In *Roberts v Welsh Ministers* the court held that in making a decision about whether a school could properly be described as popular under the Circular, the Minister was entitled to consider all the characteristics of the school which reasonably and rationally bore on that issue. Wyn Williams J declined to identify or predict what circumstances and/or factors may exist in relation to a school which taken together could justify the conclusion that a school was popular. However, in the context of that case, the number of pupils attending the school could be a relevant measure of the school's popularity as could the percentage of eligible children who attended the school from its catchment area.

2.89 In addition, to the express requirements of the statute and the Secretary of State's policy, it is clear that the decision-maker is obliged to consider, even apart from the requirements to do so under the statutory guidance, the implications of the Equality Act 2010 (EqA 2010) when approving proposals. The need to consider the Sex Discrimination Act 1975 (SDA 1975) when approving proposals was conceded by the Secretary of State in *R v Secretary of*

---

[122] (1988) *The Times*, 2 June. Transcript, 12 May 1988, Woolf LJ and Hirst J at 21G–22A.

State for Education and Science ex parte Keating[123] and has not been questioned since. The problems of discrimination in this area are discussed in Chapter 3.[124]

2.90 There can also be little doubt that the effect of the European Convention on Human Rights is now a relevant consideration for the LA, Secretary of State and Welsh Assembly by virtue of section 6(1) of the Human Rights Act 1998.

2.91 Little guidance is given by the courts on what would be an irrelevant consideration to take into account. Clearly, just as the impact of discrimination legislation is a relevant consideration, a desire to remove opportunities on a gender or racially discriminatory basis would be an irrelevant consideration. A desire to remove denominational schools would probably not have been unlawful prior to the enactment of the Human Rights Act 1998, but may well now fall foul of Article 14 read with Article 2 of the First Protocol of the ECHR, especially if a decision is made to close only one type of denominational school (eg for Catholics).[125]

ILLEGALITY CHALLENGES

2.92 Illegality challenges by applicants have been more successful than *Wednesbury* challenges. Most successful challenges have involved a failure to comply with a mandatory procedural requirement laid down by the Education Acts. The areas which have most frequently created difficulty in the past are:

(a) the requirement for a council to consider a report from an Education Committee prior to taking decisions involving the exercise of any education functions (paragraph 6 of Part II to Schedule 1 to the Education Act 1944). This provision was frequently a trap for administrators: see *R v Kirklees ex parte Molloy*[126]) but has now been repealed;

(b) the duties upon the LA not to discriminate in the performance of their functions. This duty, which is alluded to above, is discussed in Chapter 3;[127]

(c) the need to publish formal proposals;

(d) the need to consult prior to publication of proposals. This is now statutory in most cases.

---

[123] 84 LGR 469 at 473.
[124] See at paras **3.31–3.45**.
[125] See at paras **2.116–2.143** below.
[126] (1988) 86 LGR 115.
[127] See at paras **3.31–3.45**.

CONSEQUENCES OF FAILURE TO COMPLY WITH STATUTORY REQUIREMENTS

2.93 As we can see from the summary of the statutory framework at para **2.13** et seq above, the law relating to school reorganisations is now very detailed and the possibility of there being an error at some stage in this complex process cannot be ignored. It is proposed to discuss problems at various stages of the process:

(a) Establishing a new school.

(b) Discontinuing a school.

(c) Complying with obligations as to consultation.

(d) Complying with statutory guidance.

(e) Consequences of a flaw by the LA on decisions by either the Secretary of State or Welsh Assembly. This question is related to the questions set out above and will be considered in that context.

Establishing a new school

2.94 The powers of local authorities to establish 'all-age' schools, which provide education for children of both primary and secondary ages, were considered in: *R (S) v Office of the Schools Adjudicator*[128] and *R (National Union of Teachers) v London Borough of Lewisham*.[129]

2.95 In the *Lewisham* case, the NUT sought to challenge a decision of the LA to establish a foundation school for children aged 3 to 16 and, concomitantly, to discontinue an existing maintained primary school. There were two main grounds of challenge. First, it was said that the Education Acts did not confer a power to establish an all-age school. Secondly, it was said that, in deciding to establish an all-age school, the LA had failed properly to have regard to the need for securing that primary and secondary education are provided in separate schools, as required by section 14(6) of the EA 1996. Blake J rejected both grounds of challenge.

2.96 In relation to the first ground of challenge, he held that an all-age school was a middle school for the purposes of the Education Acts and it was, therefore, lawful to establish such a school. In reaching this conclusion, Blake J placed particular reliance on the fact that section 4 of the EA 1996 provides that a school is an educational institution which provides 'one or more of' primary or secondary education and section 5(3) provides for a minimum, but not a maximum, age range for middle schools. Blake J did not purport to

---

[128] [2008] EWHC 3303 (Admin).
[129] [2009] EWHC 359 (Admin).

decide whether an all-age school which catered for children aged 2 to 18 would be lawful, however the DCSF contended that it would be, and it is likely that Blake J's reasoning applies equally to such schools.

2.97 In relation to the second ground of challenge, Blake J held that section 14 of the EA 1996 envisages that an LA would 'survey the scene' to assess whether it is providing sufficient schools for providing primary and secondary education (pursuant to section 14(1)), taking into account the elaboration of that duty in section 14(2) and the requirement to act with a view to securing diversity in the provision of schools and increasing opportunities for parental choice (pursuant to section 14(3A)). It was at this stage that the LA had to have particular regard to the need for securing that primary and secondary education were provided in separate schools in accordance with section 14(6)(a). However, once the LA had decided that a middle school appropriate, there was no ongoing need for it to have regard to that need, because section 14(7) provided that the section 14(6)(a) duty 'does not apply in relation to middle schools'.

2.98 As for what was actually meant by section 14(6)(a) of the EA 1996, which required an LA to have particular regard to the need for securing that primary and secondary education were provided in separate schools, Blake J held that it required an LA to take into account the actual educational benefit to children of being educated in separate schools or the loss of that benefit in being educated in a single school. As Blake J put it, 'in colloquial terms, the loss of such a benefit can be described as the disadvantages or negative aspects of proceeding with an all-age school'.

2.99 In the earlier *S* case, Plender J considered a challenge to a decision of the School's Adjudicator to approve the London Borough of Harrow's proposals to close a middle school and, concomitantly, to expand a first school. The challenge was based on an argument that the Adjudicator had failed properly to apply section 14(6)(a) of the EA 1996. Plender J concluded that there was no statutory impediment to the establishment of schools that bridged the traditional ages for primary and secondary education and that section 14(7) disapplied the section 14(6)(a) duty.

2.100 In *Chandler v London Borough of Camden*,[130] the LA decided that a new secondary school was required in its area. It decided not to adopt the competitive process for establishing a new school, but instead co-operated with University College London (UCL) to promote a new Academy sponsored by UCL. The claimant sought to challenge this decision and also to challenge the decision of the Secretary of State to approve UCL as the sponsor for the new Academy.

2.101 The claimant argued that the policy underlying the EIA 2006 was to ensure openness and transparency in the establishment of new schools,

---

[130] [2009] EWHC 219 (Admin).

particularly where there was local controversy, and that an LA could not exercise its discretion not to hold a competition in order to avoid the possibility of it losing control of either the decision-making process or the eventual outcome. This argument was rejected by Forbes J. It was held that the legislation plainly envisaged two different routes for the establishment of Academies and that Parliament had not placed any relevant restrictions on, or indicated any preference for, which route an LA might adopt.[131]

2.102 The claimant argued that the LA had circumvented the process of open competition by promoting an Academy to be sponsored by UCL. The claimant argued that the decision not to hold a competition ran contrary to the purpose of the Act and was improper. These arguments were rejected.[132]

2.103 In *R (on the application of Roberts) v Welsh Ministers*[133] the LA had a stated policy of providing 'local schools for local children'. The claimant submitted that the policy was unlawful as it conflicted with the relevant statutory provisions relating to parental choice. Section 9 of the Education Act 1996 imposes a duty on the LA to have regard to the general principle that pupils are to be educated in accordance with the wishes of their parents. Section 86(1) of the SSFA 1998 also obligated an LA to make arrangements for enabling a parent to express a preference as to the school at which they wished their child's education to be provided.

2.104 Wyn Williams J found that the LA's policy of providing 'local schools for local children' was not in conflict with the statutory provisions concerning parental choice. The relevant statutory provisions did not preclude the adoption of a policy which sought to match school places with the likely demand from children within the catchment area of a school and to have a policy which encouraged children to attend the school in whose catchment area they resided.

2.105 In *R v Buckinghamshire County Council ex parte Milton Keynes Borough Council*,[134] a challenge was brought to a decision of the county council to publish proposals for the establishment of a new grammar school when it knew that it would not be able to complete the process of establishment before its responsibility for education was transferred to the new unitary authority of Milton Keynes. It was argued that, in those circumstances, the county council did not have power to publish proposals because it did not intend to establish a new school. The court rejected this contention and held that there was power to publish proposals even when they would not be completed prior to reorganisation. Although the decision was in the context of establishment and not ceasing to maintain, it seems that it would apply equally to the latter context as the statutory framework is not materially different.

---

[131] See at paras 11–16.
[132] See at paras 73–83.
[133] [2011] EWHC 3416 (Admin).
[134] [1997] Admin LR 158.

2.106 One well-publicised case where a challenge succeeded against the Secretary of State is *R v Secretary of State for Education and Science ex parte Islam*.[135] In that case the promoters wished to establish a voluntary-aided school. When they published their proposals under section 13 of the Education Act 1980,[136] the LA area in which the school which was to become voluntary-aided was situated was short of school places. The consideration of the proposals by the Secretary of State was prolonged but when he came to determine the matter, the LA was no longer short of school places. That information was acquired by the Secretary of State from the LA without the proposers' knowledge. Had they known, they would have made representations on the figures and made the point that, because of the special nature of the school (it was a Moslem school), it drew children from beyond the boundaries of the LA. In quashing the decision the court held that the Secretary of State had to act fairly and that his action in rejecting the proposal on the ground that there was surplus capacity in the LA without putting this to the promoters was manifestly unfair.

2.107 It is now clear that the decision to establish or to refuse to establish an Academy is amenable to judicial review. For a detailed account of Academies, see Chapter 9.

Discontinuing a school

2.108 Most school closures require, as discussed at para **2.30** et seq above, the publication of formal proposals.

2.109 In *R (on the application of P) v Hertfordshire CC* as part of the procedure for the closure of a primary school, the LA sent a statutory notice as required under Schedule 4 of the 2007 Regulations. At the time the notice was sent approximately 50 per cent of the school's pupils had special educational needs, but the school was not a special school and did not have a special or reserved unit for such pupils. The claimant argued that the statutory notice was defective as it failed to state how the LA believed that its proposal would lead to improvements in the standard, quality and/or range of provision for children with special educational needs as then required by Schedule 4, paragraph 20.

2.110 The court found that the LA should have answered the question in its statutory notice. The failure to do so meant that a decision had been made by the LA without that relevant information and the decision of the LA was quashed. The court emphasised that the statutory notice did not bind the decision-maker but simply ensured that the decision-maker had the full information. The notice was deficient. The challenge was not to the validity of the notice but only to the validity of the decision. The effect was that a decision was made without an important piece of information. Since the decision the regulations have been amended and now only apply to accommodation which

---

[135] [1994] ELR 111.
[136] Now the SSFA 1998, s 28(2).

is recognised by the LA as being reserved for special educational provision.[137] Accordingly, the case before Burton J would now be decided differently on its particular facts. The principle though, that failure to have regard to relevant information as specified in regulations may flaw a decision, remains extant.

Obligations as to consultation

2.111 Before publishing proposals the LA is obliged to consult such persons as seem to them appropriate and to have regard to any guidance given by the Secretary of State.[138] Those requirements are phrased in mandatory language. The requirements of consultation are discussed below but, in summary,[139] there are four elements:

(a) the consultation must be when the proposals are still at a formative stage;

(b) sufficient reasons must be given for any proposal to permit of intelligent consideration;

(c) adequate time must be given for consideration and response; and

(d) the product of consultation must be taken into account in finalising the proposals.

2.112 It is submitted that the courts would regard failure to comply with the statutory duty to consult as leading to the illegality of the proposals by the LA and a ground for quashing the formal proposals or the any approval of them, subject to the refusal of relief in the exercise of the court's discretion.[140] This is discussed in more detail in para **2.140** et seq below.

Statutory guidance

2.113 What are the consequences if the LA or decision-maker has failed to have regard to, or misconstrued, the statutory guidance before it published the proposals?

2.114 It is well settled that the grant or refusal of a remedy sought by way of judicial review is ultimately discretionary although that discretion must be exercised judicially. In most cases in which a decision has been found to be flawed it would not be a proper exercise of discretion to refuse to quash the

---

[137] See SI 2009/1556.

[138] See, for example, s 29(5) of the SSFA 1998. Prior to there being a statutory duty to consult, the courts had held parents had a legitimate expectation of consultation; see e g *R v Brent London Borough ex parte Gunning* (1986) 84 LGR 168.

[139] *R v Brent LBC ex parte Gunning* (1986) 84 LGR 168.

[140] See *R v Secretary of State for the Environment ex parte Walters* (1988) 30 HLR 328,(1997) *The Times*, 2 September, CA. Albeit in a different context, it is an example of relief being refused in the exercise of the court's discretion where there had been a breach of a statutory duty to consult. The Court of Appeal refused to interfere with the judge's exercise of discretion to refuse relief.

decision. However, the key consideration for deciding whether or not a quashing order will be granted is the nature of the flaw in the decision in question.

2.115 In *R (on the application of Roberts) v Welsh Ministers*[141] Wyn Williams J concluded that the Welsh Ministers had erred in their interpretation of the word 'popular' in Circular 21/2009. However, it did not follow that the defendant's decision to approve the published proposals should be quashed. The judge found that although the defendant's approach was flawed, it was clear that even if the defendant were to reconsider the issue of popularity his conclusion would very likely to be that the school was not a popular school within the meaning in the Circular. Therefore, although the defendant's reasoning was flawed, the conclusion was undoubtedly correct. As the nature of the flaw in the decision-making was one of reasoning, it was not appropriate to grant a quashing order where the conclusion would be the same upon applying the correct approach.

2.116 In *R (on the application of Parents for Legal Action Ltd) v Northumberland CC*[142] whilst there had been a finding of procedural unfairness it did not entitle the claimant to a declaration that the LA's decision was unlawful and nor did it entitle them to a quashing order. Munby J concluded that the claimant was entitled to appropriate declaratory relief which did not require the entire consultation exercise to be reopened but only that part of the consultation which was flawed.

2.117 In *R (on the application of P) v Hertfordshire CC*[143] the LA's failure to provide information in the statutory notice about a high level of special educational needs meant that a decision was made without an important piece of information. Burton J noted that in many cases, the absence of that information would have been of no materiality but in that in the case before him where between 40 and 60 per cent of the children at the school were receiving special needs support, the information was material. The LA's decision was therefore quashed. However, in granting relief, the judge ordered that the existing consultation and literature should remain unchanged and the only additional factor that needed to be taken into account was that the information as to special needs should be answered properly. In addition, the judge took into account the consequences that might flow from granting a quashing order. He noted that if quashing the decision would have led to dramatically different and expensive and inconvenient steps for the defendant that he might have taken a different course. However, the absence of the information did not vitiate the entire consultation process. It was only necessary to ensure that the decision-maker had the full information to reconsider the decision.

---

[141] [2011] EWHC 3416 (Admin).
[142] [2006] EWHC 101 (Admin).
[143] [2008] EWHC 3379 (Admin). See the discussion of this case at para **2.109** above

2.118 Therefore, the consequences of a failure to publish information as required is likely to differ depending on what is not supplied. A failure to follow the regulations does not necessarily lead to a quashing of the subsequent decision. The claimant will be entitled to declaratory relief but the precise relief that will be appropriate will depend on the nature and extent of the failure to comply with a statutory requirement. In most cases, a failure to provide information in the published proposals or failure to comply with the manner of published proposals will not, in general, be fatal to the decision.

HUMAN RIGHTS CHALLENGES[144]

2.119 Most human rights challenges to school reorganisation decisions are likely to be centred around Article 14 of the ECHR read with Article 2 of the First Protocol. Article 2 of the First Protocol provides:

> 'No person shall be denied the right to education. In the exercise of any functions which it assumes in relation to education and teaching, the state shall respect the right of parents to ensure that such education and teaching in conformity with their own religious and philosophical convictions.'

2.120 The UK has entered a reservation in respect of the second sentence of Article 2 as follows:

> '... in view of certain provisions of the Education Acts in force in the United Kingdom, the principle affirmed in the second sentence of Art 2 is accepted by the United Kingdom only so far as it is compatible with the provision of efficient instruction and training and the avoidance of unreasonable public expenditure.'

2.121 Article 14 of the ECHR provides:

> 'The enjoyment of the rights and freedoms set forth in this Convention shall be secured without discrimination on any ground such as sex, race, colour, language, religion, political or other opinion, national or social origin, association with a national minority, property birth or other status.'

2.122 By virtue of section 6(1) of the Human Rights Act 1998 (HRA 1998), it is unlawful for a public authority to act in a way which is incompatible with a Convention right. Not all those concerned with school organisation decisions will be public authorities. While there can be little doubt that the LA, governing bodies of maintained schools, the Secretary of State and the Welsh Assembly are public bodies within the meaning of the HRA 1998, reorganisation proposals can be published by purely private persons and the establishment of an Academy under section 482 of the EA 1996 as amended by the EA 2002 does not even require the publication of formal proposals. A private person can

---

[144] For a general outline of the Strasbourg jurisprudence, see Chapter 10.

also establish an independent school. However, the point is likely to be of little practical importance in this particular context because at some stage a public authority will be involved.[145]

2.123 In *R (McDougal) v Liverpool City Council*[146] a challenge was brought in relation to the closure of a school which was the only mixed non-faith school in a deprived area. The court found that the council had not failed to have regard to the Convention rights of M under Article 14 and Article 2 of the First Protocol to the convention. There had been no discrimination against M because there was an objective and reasonable justification for any difference in treatment. The council had a legitimate aim in ensuring a reduction in the large number of surplus places at school in the areas of Liverpool and in ensuring that education was provided at the more successful and sought after schools. The school had by far the worst academic results and the highest predicted number of vacancies of the schools under consideration in the area. In any event, the complaint did not fall within the ambit of Article 2 of the first protocol because education was available to the claimant's children at a non-faith co-educational school to which free bus transport was provided by the council and which in any event was within three miles of the claimant's home. The claimant's children did not have the right to be educated at any particular school.

2.124 In *R (Roberts) v Welsh Ministers*[147] a challenge was brought under Article 2 of the First Protocol. The judge expressed the non-definitive view that if the policy of 'local schools for local children' was unlawful, it would also be in breach of Article 2 of the First Protocol. However, given the lawfulness of the policy, the judge concluded that Article 2 did not arise in this context.

2.125 Article 2 of the First Protocol is unlikely to be of much use on its own in challenging a school reorganisation decision. A disappointed promoter of a school is unlikely to get much help from Article 2 because of the decision in *Belgian Linguistics*[148] that the right it contains is to avail a person of the means of instruction existing at the time and does not oblige the State to establish new schools at its own expense.[149] Although Article 2 of the First Protocol includes a right to establish private schools,[150] the power of the Secretary of State to regulate such schools is likely to make successful challenges rare.

---

[145] Reorganisation decisions in relation to State schools will require at some stage a decision by the LA, the Secretary of State or the Welsh Assembly.

[146] [2009] EWHC 1861 (Admin).

[147] *R (on the application of Roberts) v Welsh Ministers* [2011] EWHC 3416 (Admin).

[148] This case is discussed in Chapter 10 at paras **10.4** and **10.5**.

[149] In *R v Secretary of State for Education and Employment ex parte Begbie* [2000] 1 WLR 1115 at 1128F–1129B the Court of Appeal rejected a challenge to the abolition of the assisted place scheme, based, inter alia, on Art 2 of the First Protocol on the ground that the Convention did not oblige a Member State to establish or subsidise at public expense education of a particular type.

[150] *Kjeldson* (1979–80) 1 EHRR 711. Although the court observed at para 50 that the text finally adopted, unlike some earlier versions, did not expressly enounce that freedom, it implied that such a guarantee was implicit in Art 2.

2.126 The Commission has expressly taken the view that Article 2 of the First Protocol guarantees the right to start and run a private school. In *Jordebo v Sweden*, the Commission considered that it followed from the court's judgment in *Kjeldsen* that such a right was guaranteed by Article 2, although it also expressly recognised that such a right could not be without conditions, but must be subject to regulation by the State in order to ensure a proper educational system as a whole.[151] Therefore, while upholding the right to start and run a private school, the Commission found nothing incompatible with Article 2 in the Education Authority's refusal to allow such a school to provide the higher stages of compulsory education on the ground that the education offered by the school at that level did not meet the necessary condition as to quality.

2.127 Accordingly, independent schools which are unhappy about the decision to refuse to register them, or to deregister them, under Part 10 of the EA 2002 are not likely to find much help in the Convention where the ground of decision relates to their suitability or lack of it. A policy decision by the Secretary of State not to register any more independent schools because he thought they were in principle unwelcome would be unlawful under the Convention and ultra vires sections 161(3), 165 and 169 of the EA 2002 which restrict refusal of approval or deregistration to matters relating to educational standards, risk of serious harm to welfare of pupils, and suitability of personnel.

2.128 That Article 2 of the First Protocol guarantees the right to start and run a private school was again confirmed by the Commission in *Verein Gemeinsam Lernen v Austria*,[152] although the substantive requirements of that provision were satisfied by the fact that the private school had been able to set up and had been widely recognised by the State. The provision did not go further and require the State to subsidise any particular form of education.

2.129 Unequal provision of State support to religious schools of particular denominations is likely to raise an issue of breach of Article 14 read with Article 2 of the First Protocol. A closure decision which had the effect that there were more State school places for those who wanted a Christian rather than a Moslem education is, prima facie, a breach of Article 14, but may not be unlawful. Potential defences include the reservation, justification and no discrimination. If, for example there was less demand for Moslem places than Christian places then, like the position in relation to sex discrimination, there would probably be no discrimination at all.[153] Further, a mere differential treatment would not be unlawful if it was justified because, as we have seen under the Convention, justification is a defence to even a complaint, adopting the terminology in the race and sex fields of direct discrimination. This means

---

[151] *Jordebo v Sweden*, No 11533/85, Decision 6.3.87, 51 DR 125 at 128.
[152] *Verein Gemeinsam Lernen v Austria*, No 23419/94, Decision 6.9.95, 82 DR 41, (1995) 20 EHRR CD78.
[153] See *R v Secretary of State for Education ex parte Avon (No 2)* (unreported) 24 May 1990 at 64G.

that it will never be to an applicant's advantage to allege a breach of the Convention when he has a complaint of sex or race discrimination because the rights are less advantageous than the existing domestic legislation. The Convention is useful when dealing with discrimination on grounds other than sex or race.

2.130 Justification is likely to cover a wide field, particularly having regard to the concept of margin of appreciation. An LA may conclude that it has to close a denominational school and thereby leave unequal provision for different denominations relative to demand because the school has poor educational standards or is too expensive to keep open.[154] Further, unlike the provision in relation to sex or race discrimination, administrative reasons (such as the time taken to consult and make formal proposals) which made it difficult or impossible immediately to equalise the provision for different religious minorities would probably mean that interim 'discrimination' while remedial action was being undertaken was not unlawful.

2.131 There is quite a bit of Convention jurisprudence on Article 14, particularly in the context of State subsidies to non-State schools. There is no obligation on the State to subsidise any particular form of education, but where the State chooses to do so, it must ensure that it does so in a non-discriminatory manner. That case-law has adopted a broad approach to questions of justification and therefore challenges on the basis of discrimination contrary to Article 14 will not be easy to maintain. In *X v UK*, for example, a parent from Northern Ireland committed to non-denominational (ie integrated) schooling, complained that whereas State schools received a 100 per cent subsidy from the State, private educational institutions received only an 85 per cent subsidy, so that private bodies wishing to set up non-denominational schools had to bear 15 per cent of the capital costs themselves.[155] This failure of the State to provide a 100 per cent grant for a private non-denominational school, it was argued, was contrary to Article 2 of the First Protocol. The Commission decided of its own motion to consider whether the difference in subsidy available to State schools on the one hand and voluntary schools on the other was a breach of Article 14, which required the authorities not to discriminate in the provision of available financial subsidies.

2.132 The Commission considered it legitimate for the State to exercise substantial control in the ownership and management of schools for which it provides a full 100 per cent subsidy, and reasonable for the State, in relation to bodies that seek ownership and decisive control over management policy in voluntary schools, to require some degree of financial contribution. It did not consider 15 per cent to be an unreasonable or disproportionate requirement, and therefore found that there had been no discrimination within the meaning of Article 14.

---

[154] These matters would also engage the UK's reservation.
[155] *X v UK*, No 7782/77, Decision 2.5.78, 14 DR 179.

2.133 In *Verein Gemeinsam Lernen v Austria*, a challenge was brought to the State's unequal subsidisation of private schools.[156] The applicant association, which set up and ran a non-religious private school, complained that State subsidies were allocated to church schools (which were also private) on a more favourable basis, contrary to Article 2 of the First Protocol taken together with Article 14. Subsidies were granted to church schools as a matter of course, whereas non-church schools such as the applicant association's had to fulfil the condition of corresponding to a 'need'.

2.134 The Commission agreed that Article 14 required that any subsidies that are made should not be made in a discriminatory fashion, but found that treating church schools differently from the applicant association's school could be justified in terms of Article 14 because the church schools were so widespread that if the educational services they provided fell to be met by the State, there would be a considerable burden on it as it would have to make up the shortfall in schools.[157]

2.135 In Scotland there has been some consideration of these issues. In *Dove and Another v Decision of Scottish Ministers*[158] a Convention challenge was made to the decision of the Ministers pursuant to section 17 of the Standards in Scotland's Schools Act 2000 to return a school to LA management following the abolition of self-governing status.[159] The challenge was based on Article 14 of the ECHR read with Article 2 of the First Protocol. It was sought to compare the school the Ministers put under management of the Education Authority (St Mary's) with Jordan Hill College, which had never had self-governing status but was financed by the Secretary of State as an independent school. The court had little difficulty in concluding, inter alia, that:

(a)   the measures complained of did not fall within the ambit of Article 2 of the First Protocol so the claim based on Article 14 failed in limine;

(b)   the two schools were not comparable and there was no differential treatment;

---

[156]   *Verein Gemeinsam Lernen v Austria*, No 23419/94, Decision 6.9.95, 82 DR 41.

[157]   See also *W and KL v Sweden* No 10476/83, Decision 11.12.85, 45 DR 143, in which the Commission declared inadmissible a complaint that a difference in treatment between pupils at one private school, who received an education allowance, and those at another, who did not, was in breach of Art 14 in conjunction with Art 2 of the First Protocol. The Commission found the difference in treatment to be based on the traditional independence of Swedish local authorities in matters within their jurisdiction, which was not without objective and reasonable justification.

[158]   [2001] Scotts CS 291.

[159]   The Self Governing Schools etc (Scotland) Act 1989. Part 1 of the 1989 Act was repealed by the Standards in Scotland's Schools etc Act 2000 and the Ministers were given power by order to specify that the self-governing school should cease to be such and accordingly the Education Authority in whose area the school was situated should manage the school. The self-governing status seems to be similar to grant-maintained status in England and Wales.

(c)   any differential treatment would have been justified as a matter of
      political judgement in the light of the legislative policy enacted in the 2000
      Act.

2.136   While the interpretation of Article 2 was a narrow one, it is submitted
that the interpretation of Article 14 would be followed in England.

2.137   There is unlikely to be much mileage on human rights challenges to
school organisation decisions based on other Articles of the Convention. It is
very unlikely that a school organisation decision will involve the determination
of civil rights and obligations within the meaning of Article 6 of the ECHR[160]
or that challenges based on Article 8 or Article 9 will, in practice, add much to
Article 2 of the First Protocol.[161]

2.138   It is possible to envisage challenges based on Article 8 of the
Convention in a school reorganisation decision. If the consequence of a closure
of a school catering for children with special educational needs was that the
children who went to that school as day pupils would have to board at another
school contrary to their wishes or their parents' wishes, then prima facie there
would be an interference with family life within the meaning of Article 8(1) of
the Convention. That was the view Sullivan J, in a different context, was
prepared to accept where he held that if, which it was not, an order of the
Special Educational Needs Tribunal (SENT) was to the effect that a child
should attend a boarding school, then it was prima facie an interference with
his Article 8 rights.[162] A well thought out education reorganisation should,
however, be capable of justification under Article 8(2) as being for the
protection of the rights and freedoms of others, viz their right to education
under Article 2 of the First Protocol.

2.139   Particular care must be taken when establishing or discontinuing single
sex schools in order to ensure that no breach of the EqA 2010 arises. These
problems are discussed at paras **3.31–3.45** of Chapter 3.

CONSULTATION

2.140   What is required by way of consultation has occupied the courts many
times. Until recently it could, with some confidence, have been said that it was a
four-part test summed up in the phrase 'the Sedley formulation', named after
Mr Stephen Sedley QC, as he then was. That formulation provides:

---

[160]   *Simpson v UK* Application No 14688/89 (1989) 64 DR 188.
[161]   Article 8, guaranteeing the right to respect for private and family life, was the subject of a
        complaint in both the *Belgian Linguistic* case (1979) 1 EHRR 252 and *Kjeldsen* (1979–80)
        1 EHRR 711. Art 9, guaranteeing freedom of thought, conscience and religion, was relied on
        in *Kjeldsen* and *Valsamis v Greece* (1997) 24 EHRR 294. Those Articles overlap with the rights
        and interests protected by Art 2 of the First Protocol.
[162]   *CB v London Borough of Merton and Special Educational Needs Tribunal* [2002] ELR 441 at
        para 20.

'First, that consultation must be at a time when proposals are still at a formative stage. Second, that the proposer must give sufficient reasons for any proposal to permit of intelligent consideration and response. Third ... that adequate time must be given for consideration and response and finally, fourth, that the product of consultation must be conscientiously taken into account in finalising any statutory proposals.'

2.141 That formulation was advanced by Stephen Sedley QC in *R v Brent ex parte Gunning*[163] and applied by Hodgson J in that case. It has been accepted by the courts on many occasions.[164]

2.142 In the *Hackney Downs* case the Court of Appeal emphasised[165] that the Sedley formulation is not an inflexible test:

'Consultation too is not in this context an absolute and inflexible concept. Lord Diplock in *CCSU*[166] spoke only of communicating to the person enjoying the benefit "some rational grounds for withdrawing it on which he has been given an opportunity to comment". A mechanistic approach to the requirements of consultation should be avoided. The nature, the scale, the period may all vary.'

2.143 What is required by way of consultation will depend on all the circumstances including the statutory context. As Simon Brown LJ put it in *Hackney Downs*:[167]

'Prominent amongst the considerations relevant to determining the precise demands of consultation in a given case will be:

(a) Whether the obligation is statutory and absolute or implied in common fairness. If the former, then plainly the process must satisfy in full measure all four of the requirements identified and approved in *ex parte Baker*[168] at 91. If, however, the obligation is merely implied, its scope may well be reduced. It may well have to be tailored to the practicalities of the situation.

(b) The urgency with which it is necessary to reach a decision. This may impose constraints lest the very process of consultation itself causes delay such as to pre-empt a particular proposal or other possibly appropriate decisions.

(c) The extent to which during earlier discussions or consultative processes opportunities have been afforded (and, indeed, taken) for views to be expressed by interested, and in particular opposing, parties and the likelihood, therefore, of material and informed additional views or information emerging upon further consultation. This consideration, of

---

[163] (1986) 84 LGR 168.
[164] *R v Coventry ex parte Newborn* (unreported) 26 September 1985, Mann J,; *R v London Borough of Sutton ex parte Hamlet* (unreported) 26 March 1986, Webster J; *R v Northamptonshire ex parte Tebbutt* (unreported) 26 June 1986, Woolf LJ and Hirst J; *R v Kent County Council ex parte Parker* (unreported) 26 June 1986, McCowan J; *R v Devon County Council ex parte Baker* [1995] 1 All ER 73 at 91; *R v Lambeth ex parte N* [1996] ELR 299.
[165] *R v Secretary of State for Education ex parte Morris* [1996] ELR 162 at 207C.
[166] *Council of Civil Service Unions v Minister for the Civil Service* [1985] AC 374.
[167] At 207D–207G.
[168] [1995] 1 All ER 73.

course, is only relevant provided that the views and information earlier elicited are available to the eventual decision-maker.'

2.144 Where there is a statutory duty to consult, then, as the Court of Appeal held in the passage quoted above, the Sedley formulation must be complied with in full. Where, however, as was the case in *Hackney Downs* itself, there is no statutory duty and there are circumstances of urgency which would make detailed consultation inappropriate, much less detailed consultation would be required. This is in accordance with general principles of public law.[169]

2.145 One of the main targets of challenges to decisions to discontinue a maintained school in order to replace it with an Academy has been the consultation exercise carried out prior to the publication of the statutory closure notices. Because each Academy is a creature of its own particular funding agreement and such funding agreements are rarely concluded until after proposals to discontinue the existing school have been approved, it is often said that the consultation on the proposals to discontinue are flawed by reason of a failure on the part of the LA to provide consultees with sufficient information about the Academy that is to replace the existing school.

2.146 In *P v Schools Adjudicator*[170] Wilkie J held that the fact that the legislation envisaged that a decision to discontinue a school could be made conditional upon the conclusion of a funding agreement for an Academy demonstrated that there was no power for, in that case, the Schools Adjudicator to insist upon the final funding agreement being in a specific form. In that case, however, the Adjudicator had been provided with a draft funding agreement and assurances and undertakings given by the sponsor of the Academy as to the eventual form of the Academy. Wilkie J held that the Adjudicator was obliged to consider whether and to what extent he could rely upon those matters.

2.147 The claimant in *R (Elphinstone) v City of Westminister*[171] attempted to take the argument a stage further. The challenge related to a decision by the LA to close Pimlico School in order for it to be replaced by an Academy. In that case, only an expression of interest document was available at the consultation stage. It was argued that consultees had to be provided with at least a draft funding agreement and similar assurances to those given in the *P* case before they would have sufficient information to enable them to give a properly informed response. The Court of Appeal rejected this argument, on the simple basis that there was nothing in the statutory scheme to suggest that such matters were 'conditions precedent' to a decision to approve proposals to discontinue a school and that the court should not be introducing further requirements to a comprehensive statutory scheme by way of implication.

---

[169] De Smith Woolf and Jowell *Judicial Review* (op cit) at para 7.016 where the view is expressed that this may negate a duty of consultation completely.

[170] [2006] EWHC 1934 (Admin).

[171] [2008] EWCA Civ 1069.

2.148 The Court of Appeal also held that neither an LA, nor consultees, required a 'mass of information' about the replacement Academy in order for the approval proposals to discontinue a school to make way for such an Academy to be lawful. Again, it held that there was nothing in the legislation to justify such a requirement. The basic principle was that an LA needed only to have before it sufficient details of the proposed replacement Academy to enable it to take a rational decision to approve the closure proposals. In this context, if an LA had sufficient information to take a rational decision, it was difficult to see how any consultation exercise which provided that same information to consultees could be flawed for want of information.

2.149 In *Chandler* the claimant argued that the consultation process undertaken by the LA was flawed because the consultation was not taken at a formative stage. However, in the circumstances, there was no obligation on the part of the LA to carry out any form of public consultation as it decided that the section 482 procedure was the appropriate route for the establishment of a new school in the area. This is no longer an option for local authorities as section 482 has now been repealed. In any event, the LA in the *Chandler* case did carry out several public consultations which were lawful in the circumstances.

2.150 In *R (on the application of Parents for Legal Action Ltd) v Northumberland County Council*[172] the claimant's application for judicial review was allowed in part because consultation has to be undertaken when proposals are at a formative stage only. This was a challenge under the first limb of the Sedley criteria. The authority conducted a relatively elaborate consultation about its proposals. The parents complained about its fairness, because at a relatively early stage, and without exploring the impact of a change of system on individual schools, the authority had decided to consult in detail on a two-tier system only. The judge found that there had been no consultations relating to specific school partnerships or specific schools at a formative stage.

2.151 In *R (on the application of Brynmawr Foundation School Governors) v Welsh Ministers*[173] the claimant brought a consultation challenge which was rejected. The court held that the Welsh ministers had been entitled to delegate their powers to consult and make proposals about the provision of sixth form education under section 113A of the Learning and Skills Act 2000 to an LA. The court held that individuals had not been denied any meaningful opportunity to express their views on the proposals.

2.152 In *R v Governors of Bacon's School ex parte ILEA,*[174] the Divisional Court had to consider whether there had been a failure to comply with the fourth requirement of the Sedley formulation, ie to give genuine consideration to the outcome of the consultation. It was argued that no genuine consideration was given because there was a 'guillotine motion'. The court gave

---

[172] [2006] EWHC 101 (Admin).
[173] [2011] EWHC 519.
[174] [1990] COD 414.

this argument short shrift holding that it was condescending to the point of insult. It also rejected an argument that it was appropriate to consider whether it was *Wednesbury* unreasonable to curtail debate as this had nothing to do with the principles of consultation.

2.153 In *R v Buckinghamshire County Council ex parte Milton Keynes Borough Council*[175] there was another challenge on the basis of an alleged failure to comply with the fourth requirement. It was contended that the imposition of a three-line whip amounted to a closing of minds against the results of a consultation which was therefore a sham. The court rejected this allegation on the facts, holding that there had been meaningful consideration of the results of the consultation despite the existence of the whip. In doing so, the court considered the earlier decision of the Court of Appeal in *R v Waltham Forest London Borough Council ex parte Baxter*[176] where it was held, in a non-consultation case, that it was not unlawful to vote in accordance with the party line providing that it was not done so blindly. As Russell LJ put it:[177]

> 'Party loyalty, party unanimity, party policy were all relevant considerations for the individual councillor. The vote becomes unlawful only when the councillor allows these considerations or any other outside influences so to dominate as to exclude other considerations which are required for a balanced judgement. If, by blindly toeing the party line, the councillor deprives himself of any real choice or the exercise of any real discretion, then his vote can be impugned and any resolution supported by his vote potentially flawed.'

2.154 In *R v Lambeth ex parte N*[178] Latham J quashed a decision by the LA to publish proposals to cease to maintain a special school. He held that there had been a failure to comply with the duty to consult.[179] It was not sufficient that parents were informed of the proposal to close the school, they also had to be invited to make representations, whether orally or in writing, not on simple generalities of policy, but on the specific proposal to close the school; including the proposed timetable and the effect on the parents and their children. Alternative arrangements for the children were a matter to be covered in the consultation process.

2.155 In general terms, in the absence of exceptional circumstances, it is likely that consultation of less than a month will be held to be unreasonably short. That was a conclusion arrived at by Donaldson J in *Lee v Department of Education and Science*[180] in a case under section 17(5) of the Education Act 1944, and this decision was applied in a school closure context in *R v Brent ex parte Gunning*.[181] In the challenge to the Hackney Downs closure decision[182] the Court of Appeal held that consultation had been adequate when the

---

[175]   [1997] Admin LR 158.
[176]   [1988] 1 QB 419.
[177]   At 428G–428H.
[178]   [1996] ELR 299.
[179]   Under what was then the Education Act 1993, s 184.
[180]   (1967) 66 LGR 211.
[181]   (1986) 84 LGR 168 at 192. Followed in *R v Secretary of State for Education and Employment*

Secretary of State had given ten days for interested parties to respond to a report of an Education Association recommending closure. However, there were special features in that case arising from the involvement of the Education Association, the urgent need to close the school before the close of the autumn term if the best interests of the children were to be promoted, and in any event there was a detailed history of recent consultation arising from an earlier decision by the LEA to publish proposals to cease to maintain. Against this extensive background of consultation it was perhaps not surprising that the Court of Appeal held ('emphatically') that the consultation of ten days by the Secretary of State was not unfair.

2.156 In *R v Kirklees Metropolitan Borough Council ex parte Beaumont*,[183] Newman J held that the failure of the LEA to produce a consultation document more than 24 hours before one-to-one surgeries with various parents did not flaw the consultation process. There were, however, a number of special features[184] about that case which render that conclusion less than surprising:

(a) the surgeries were only part of the consultation process which the council had elected to adopt and it was not inherent to the validity of the process that there should be one-to-one surgeries;

(b) when the difficulties were known, the school was notified and advice was sought as to whether the date for surgeries should be moved. The school considered it appropriate that they should continue because the school felt that it was in the interests of parents to continue with the dates set;

(c) some parents did attend and those who did not were given an open invitation to return to the school if they wished to engage in one-to-one surgeries. None of the parents took up that invitation.

2.157 The courts have had to consider whether it is appropriate to consult in languages other than English, for example when the local population contains substantial numbers of minorities who do not speak English. It is good practice for consultation in those circumstances to be in various of the minority languages, but the legal duty is only to consult in English.[185] Were the contrary to be the case, the LA could be placed in an impossible position.

BIAS

2.158 The problem of bias[186] has arisen in school reorganisation decisions.

---

ex parte McCarthy (1996) *The Times*, 24 July, where it was held that a consultation period of two weeks prior to withdrawal of approval from an independent special school was too short to be lawful.

[182] *R v Secretary of State for Education ex parte Morris* [1996] ELR 162 at 209H–210D.

[183] [2001] ELR 204.

[184] See paras 80–84.

[185] *R v Birmingham ex parte Kaur* (1991) 155 JPN 587.

[186] For bias generally, see *Porter v Magill* [2002] 2 AC 357 at paras 102–103 per Lord Hope: 'The

2.159 In *R v Kirklees Metropolitan Borough Council ex parte Beaumont*,[187] Newman J had to consider the problem of two councillors voting on school organisation proposals when they were also governors of one of the schools affected by those proposals. The council review of its provision focused on five schools in Dewsbury and one of the options was amalgamation of Birkdale and Westborough. Another option was closure of Birkdale. The governors of Westborough were opposed to amalgamation. A proposal was made to close Birkdale School at the meeting of the Education Committee on 9 July 1999. The votes were evenly split and the Chairman exercised his casting vote to vote in favour of the closure. Two of the governors of Westborough also voted in favour of closure of Birkdale. On 14 July the full council approved the decision of the Education Committee and on 22 July, statutory proposals were published stating that closure was to take place on 31 August 2003 and that there would be a significant enlargement of the premises at Westborough and expansion of its pupil numbers.

2.160 Newman J held that the councillors had a clear and substantial interest in the closure proposal by virtue of their membership of the governing body of a school directly affected by the proposals. He also held that they should not have voted and that those facts gave rise to a real danger of an appearance of bias and that the resolution of 14 July should be quashed.[188] He left open what the position would have been if they had disclosed their interest.

2.161 A bias point was also run in the case of *R (Brynmawr Foundation School Governors) v Welsh Ministers)*.[189] The claimant relied on the failure of Councillor Hillman to declare his personal and prejudicial direct interest at previous meetings at which he spoke in favour of the council's preferred option and against the position preferred by the school and its governors.

2.162 Councillor Hillman had a personal and prejudicial interest in the discussions about the school because his grandchild attended the school. He had written a letter expressly linking the treatment of his grandson to the proposed closure of the school's sixth form. The claimant argued that Councillor Hillman had a direct personal interest, contrary to the interests of the school, which triggered automatic disqualification under the principle in *R v Bow Street Magistrate ex parte Pinochet Ugarte (No. 2)*[190] and a fair minded and informed observer, when informed of the letter would conclude

---

question is whether the fair minded and informed observer, having considered the facts would conclude there was a real possibility that the tribunal was biased.'

[187] [2001] ELR 204.

[188] In doing so he expressly relied on *R v Local Commissioner for Administration in the North and North East of England ex parte Liverpool City Council* [2000] EWCA Civ 54, [2001] 1 All ER 462. In that case, seven councillors had voted in favour of a proposal by Liverpool FC without disclosing they were season ticket holders for the club. The Commissioner for Local Administration found this to be maladministration and the High Court and the Court of Appeal dismissed the challenge to her report.

[189] [2011] EWHC 519 (Admin).

[190] [2001] 1 AC 119.

that there was a real possibility of bias. Although noting that the letter was 'extraordinarily ill-advised', the judge did not decide the bias point because it had not been raised promptly.

2.163 Linked to the bias point was the argument that the outcome of the consultation was already predetermined. That was dismissed as the judge found that the consultees had not been denied any meaningful opportunity to comment on the proposals.

2.164 In *Chandler*[191] the claimant also argued that the LA was biased in its decision making. The court relied heavily on the case of *R (Lewis) v Redcar and Cleveland Borough Council*[192] where there was an allegation of bias or apparent bias on the part of the LA in making a planning decision. In that case, the Court of Appeal made clear that where the court is faced with the determination of a non-judicial body, such as the council, the 'test of apparent bias relating to predetermination is an extremely difficult test to satisfy.' Although the evidence showed that the councillors in the *Chandler* case had long been familiar with the issues relating to the proposed new school, there was no evidence that the councillors had closed their minds in relation to the decisions they took.

THE APPROVAL OF THE SECRETARY OF STATE OR THE WELSH ASSEMBLY

2.165 Under the previous law, the Secretary of State's approval of proposals did not take effect until formally communicated to the LA. In *R v Secretary of State for Education and Science ex parte Hardy*[193] the court had to consider the effect of a communication in confidence and in error. The Deputy Under Secretary had ticked the word 'approve' on proposals and that information had been communicated to the LEA by telephone in confidence and in error. The court held that the Secretary of State was not bound by this communication and was entitled to reject the proposals. It held that as long as a decision remained in the private office it was not irrevocable and it could not become a binding decision by being leaked innocently or maliciously. It is submitted that this approach would be applied in the present statutory context.

2.166 A related problem is the extent to which, once the final decision has been made and communicated, the Secretary of State or Welsh Assembly can reopen it. To some extent this is expressly dealt with by paragraph 8(3) of Schedule 6 to the SSFA 1998. Under those provisions the Welsh Assembly can give approval to take effect only if a specified event takes place by a certain date. It is expressly provided by paragraph 10(2)(b) of Schedule 6 to the SSFA

---

[191] [2009] EWHC 219 (Admin); [2009] LGR 158.
[192] (2008) 2 P&CR 436.
[193] (1988) *The Times*, 28 July.

1998 that the Assembly can, at the request of a prescribed body,[194] specify a later date by which the event in question can occur. Commenting on these provisions in *R v Gloucestershire County Council ex parte Findlater*,[195] Simon Brown LJ stated[196] that they strongly suggested that it was not appropriate to regard the decision-maker in those cases as *functus officio*. In that case the Court of Appeal was concerned with the previous law under sections 43 and 169 of the Education Act 1996 and did not explore the SSFA 1998 in depth. Under the old law, Simon Brown LJ expressed the view that if the Secretary of State (then the decision-maker) did have power to approve proposals subject to a condition subsequent and the condition thereafter failed, that he was not to be regarded as *functus officio* and could reconsider the matter afresh. If, however, he made an unqualified decision then he was to be regarded as *functus officio*.

2.167 It is very doubtful, however, that *Findlater* gives much support to the Secretary of State or Welsh Assembly having power to reopen decisions for reasons other than those expressly covered by the terms of paragraph 5(2) of Schedule 6. If, therefore, the Welsh Assembly has no request from a prescribed person to reopen the decision on the failure of a condition subsequent, it is very doubtful it has power to reopen the matter. To hold otherwise would be to defeat the express terms of the statute. *Findlater* is to be read on the new law merely as holding that the decision-maker is not *functus officio* only in relation to the matters expressly dealt with in the governing legislation (failure of conditions subsequent where there has been a request to reopen the matter from a prescribed person).

SCHOOL AMALGAMATIONS

2.168 The law relating to school amalgamations is essentially similar to that governing school closures. As appears above, consultation, formal proposals and in certain circumstances approval of the Welsh Assembly or Secretary of State are required here also. School amalgamations have, however, created some special problems. Two particular problems have arisen in this area which have not affected a mere school closure:

(a) what type of formal proposal the LA must publish when deciding upon a school amalgamation;

(b) whether the amalgamation will amount to a transfer of a business with attendant rights for employees and trade unions under the Acquired

---

[194] Regulation 9 of the Education (School Organisation Proposals) (Wales) Regulations 1999 (SI 1999/1671) prescribes the relevant bodies.

[195] (Unreported) 14 July 2000, CA.

[196] At para 20.

Rights Directive[197] or the Transfer of Undertaking (Protection of Employment) Regulations 2006,[198] as amended.

2.169 The first problem arises because the Education Acts do not specify a particular type of proposal which must be published for school amalgamations. By contrast, the Education Acts do require publication of proposals for the establishment of new schools, for ceasing to maintain schools, and for making prescribed alterations to existing schools. The solution to the problem was considered by Taylor J in *R v Secretary of State for Wales ex parte Russell*[199] and by Brooke J in *R v Secretary of State for Wales ex parte Williams.*[200] In both cases the LA proceeded by way of school closure followed by a proposal to create a new school. In both cases this method of approach was approved. Earlier authority[201] which suggested that it may be appropriate to proceed by way of a proposal for a significant change of character[202] does not preclude the route of closure followed by establishment of a new school.

2.170 As Taylor J put it in *R v Secretary of State for Wales ex parte Russell*, in the absence of bad faith, that is an attempt by the Education Authority to pull the wool over the eyes of those who would by statute have to see the notices, the court should not intervene.

Transfer of a business

2.171 This is a problem that has arisen as a result of the influence of European law. Where an amalgamation occurs there may be a transfer of a business. This point arose for decision in *Fidge v Governors of St Mary's Voluntary-aided School*[203] but the Industrial Tribunal and the Employment Appeal Tribunal (EAT) did not have to answer it because it was conceded by the applicants that the Transfer of Undertakings (Protection of Employment) Regulations 1981[204] (as they then stood) did not apply and the Industrial Tribunal and EAT held that the governing body were not an emanation of the State and, as a result, the Acquired Rights Directive could not be relied upon against them, even if it was otherwise capable of taking direct effect. Before the decision in that case, but not in force at the relevant date, the regulations were amended so that the exclusion in relation to undertakings not in the nature of a commercial venture was deleted. Moreover, the Court of Appeal reversed the

---

[197] Council Directive EEC/77/187 now replaced, from 12 March 2001, by 2001/23/EC.
[198] SI 2006/246.
[199] (Unreported) CO/175/83, 28 June 1983, Taylor J.
[200] [1997] ELR 100.
[201] *Bradbury v Enfield* [1967] 1 WLR 1311; *Wilford v West Riding of Yorkshire County Council* [1908] 1 KB 685.
[202] This concept no longer appears in the Education Acts. Instead there is a concept of prescribed alterations, see paras **2.44–2.48** above. None of these are amalgamations as such, although some of them (such as enlargement of the premises of the school) could clearly follow from an amalgamation.
[203] [1995] ICR 317.
[204] Now replaced by the 2006 Regulations, SI 2006/246.

decision of the EAT in *Fidge*[205] and held that the governing body was an emanation of the State and bound by the Directive.

2.172 The Court of Appeal considered whether a school amalgamation did involve the transfer of an undertaking in *Governing Body of Clifton Middle School v Askew.*[206] In that case, the applicant was a teacher employed by the LA at a middle school sharing a site with a first school. In 1993 the LEA ceased to maintain both schools and established a new primary school on the site. The applicant was dismissed by the LEA. He brought a claim for unfair dismissal against the LEA, the governing body of the old middle school and the governing body of the new school. He contended that there had been an amalgamation of his middle school and the first school which was a relevant transfer within the meaning of the 1981 Regulations and that, inter alia, his dismissal was a breach of regulation 8 as it was by reason of the transfer. Peter Gibson LJ held that:

(a) there was no amalgamation but a cessation of maintenance of two schools and the establishment of one new school;

(b) there was an undertaking capable of being transferred when Clifton First and Middle Schools ceased and Clifton Primary School commenced;

(c) under regulation 5 of the 1981 Regulations only those employed under a contract of employment by the transferor could transfer if there was a relevant transfer within the meaning of regulation 3;

(d) the council was not the transferor;

(e) Mr Askew was not employed by the old governing body.

2.173 Ward LJ held that:

(a) there was no transfer, merely a reorganisation of administrative functions between public administrative bodies;

(b) there had not been, and would not have been had the applicant been re-employed, any change of employer. The council would at all times have been the employer;

(c) the applicant had no rights under regulation 8 of the 1981 Regulations because he was not employed by the old governing body, therefore the council and not the old governing body was the transferor if anyone was;

(d) Mr Askew had no rights as against the old governing body capable of being transferred under Article 3 of Directive 77/187.

---

[205] [1997] ICR 334.
[206] [2000] ICR 286.

Chadwick LJ dissented on the transfer issue.

2.174 It will be observed that the reasoning of the Court of Appeal is not altogether consistent, but the majority view is that a teacher who loses his job as a result of a school amalgamation which proceeds by way of proposals for cessation of maintenance of two schools and establishment of a new school is unlikely to have rights under the 1981 Regulations[207] or Directive 2001/23/EC. The views of Ward LJ that there was no relevant transfer seem to have been reinforced by Art 1(c) of Directive 2001/23/EC, which provides:

> 'An administrative reorganisation of public administrative authorities, or the transfer of administrative functions between public administrative authorities, is not a transfer within the meaning of this Directive.'

DISCRETION

2.175 Discretion is a powerful argument against a court intervening in this area. The courts are sensitive to the disruption which would be caused by seeking to unscramble a school closure. Even where there has been a failure to comply with a mandatory procedural requirement, the court will withhold relief where no injustice has resulted and in substance, albeit not in form, all relevant matters have been taken into account.[208] Another ground is where there is delay and considerable detriment to good administration because virtually all the children have gone to other schools.[209]

2.176 In *R v Governors of Bacon's School ex parte ILEA*[210] the Divisional Court had to consider whether to refuse relief when the governors of a Church of England voluntary-aided secondary school voted to recreate the school as a City Technology College under section 105 of the Education Reform Act 1988.[211] The governors passed two resolutions, the first of which was conceded to be ultra vires because of the pecuniary interest of the governors. The court held that the second resolution, although it did not cure the

---

[207] See now the 2006 Regulations.
[208] See *R (on the application of Roberts) v Welsh Ministers* [2011] EWHC 3416 (Admin); *R (on the application of Parents for Legal Action Ltd) v Northumberland CC* [2006] EWHC 1081 (Admin); *R (on the application of P) v Hertfordshire CC* [2008] EWHC 3379.
[209] This was the situation which prevailed in *R v Northamptonshire ex parte K* [1994] ELR 397 at 404F–404G. In that case, all the children except the applicant had accepted places elsewhere. Although the challenge failed on the substantive merits, Rose LJ commented that that would have been a highly material matter had it come to the question of granting discretionary relief. He seems to have changed his mind, as in an earlier case, *R v Secretary of State for Education ex parte Malik* [1994] ELR 121, while he was still a puisne judge, he commented, obiter, that the remarks of Denning LJ in *Bradbury v Enfield* [1967] 1 WLR 1311 at 1324, to the effect that even if chaos should result the law must be obeyed, were still apt. It is submitted the modern approach is to take account of the detriment to good administration and that *Bradbury v Enfield* is no longer good law on this point.
[210] [1990] COD 414.
[211] Now repealed.

invalidity, was decisive because it plainly demonstrated the governors' true views of the school's best interests. As Simon Brown J put it:

> 'the fact remains that this court exercising its public law jurisdiction does have a discretion and must, in exercising that discretion, seek to strike a balance between the competing public interests that arise in a case like this. Clearly it would not be right routinely to refuse relief in cases involving breach of the regulations because of the probability that such a breach will not in fact have affected the decision in question. That would be to ignore the long term public interest in providing a sanction for these regulations and thereby protecting the integrity of the decisions of school governors generally. But it would equally be wrong to regard the regulations as sacrosanct and their strict enforcement as an absolute imperative in all situations. There is a continuing public interest in the children's future and in not frustrating the governors' wishes where, as here, these are clearly distinguishable.'

Stuart Smith LJ delivered a judgment to the same effect.

2.177 *Small Heath* was distinguished in *R v Kirklees MBC ex parte Beaumont*,[212] where the decision-making was flawed by reason of a private and personal interest of two of the councillors voting for the resolution. Newman J held[213] that the facts in that case were such that they gave rise to a real danger of the appearance of bias and, accordingly, justice required that the resolution should not stand.

INTERIM RELIEF

2.178 The courts had jurisdiction to stay a decision of the Secretary of State pending the full hearing of the substantive application for judicial review. The point arose in *R v Secretary of State for Education and Science ex parte Avon*,[214] but a stay was not granted as it was possible for the court to hear the matter quickly.

---

[212] [2001] ELR 204.
[213] [2001] ELR 204, at para 72.
[214] [1991] 1 QB 558.

Chapter 3

DISCRIMINATION

INTRODUCTION

3.1 There are three sources of anti-discrimination law in the field of education: the Equality Act 2010, provisions of European Union law, and Article 14 of the European Convention on Human Rights (ECHR). General principles of ECHR law so far as they relate to education are covered in Chapter 10, but this Chapter covers both discrimination under the ECHR and the Equality Act 2010. Matters of European Union law are touched on in this Chapter, but a detailed consideration of them is beyond the scope of this work.

3.2 The Equality Act 2010 (EqA 2010) received Royal Assent on 8 April 2010; most of its provisions came into force on 1 October 2010[1] and almost all of them now are at the date of this work. Its long title says that it is, amongst other things, an Act 'to reform and harmonise equality law and restate the greater part of the enactments relating to discrimination and harassment related to certain personal characteristics'. It repeals and replaces all of the various separate anti-discrimination legislation, including the Equal Pay Act 1970 (EPA 1970), the Sex Discrimination Act 1975 (SDA 1975), the Race Relations Act 1976 (RRA 1976) and the Disability Discrimination Act 1995 (DDA 1995).[2] It however does not purport to state the entirety of the applicable law even in the discrimination fields within its sphere of operation. It always has to be remembered that European Union Law has to be considered in the discrimination field. Some European Union law can be relied on directly by individuals either because it is a regulation and can be relied upon by a legal person in the same way as a provision of purely domestic law, or because it is a directly effective directive and can be relied upon by a person other than the State against the State or an emanation of the State.[3] Even directives which do not have direct effect may found an action against the State in damages.[4] Further legislation which is enacted to give effect to European Union Law has to be construed so far as possible to be consistent with it.[5] The EqA 2010 does

---

[1]   Paragraphs 2 and 5 of Sch 13 which oblige responsible bodies for schools to provide auxiliary aids where these would be a reasonable adjustment came into force on 1 September 2012: see SI 2012/2184. The prohibition on combined discrimination in s 14 was not in force as at 4 October 2012.

[2]   The full list of repeals and revocations is set out in Sch 27 to the Act. The Act specifically prohibits issues which have been finally decided in proceedings under the previous legislation from being re-opened: s 137.

[3]   *Van Gend en Loos v Nederlandse Administratie der Belastingen* [1963] ECR 1.

[4]   *Francovich v Italian Republic* [1991] ECR I- 5357.

[5]   *Marleasing SA v La Comercial Internacional de Alimentación SA* [1990] ECR I-4135 ECJ.

seek to deal with the EU dimension: by virtue of section 203 the Minster has power[6] to make orders harmonising the provision in the Equality Acts with EU law where there is an obligation to implement it under section 2 of the European Communities Act 1972, but it is important to remember that even prior to implementation of a harmonising measure directly applicable EU law will still have effect.

3.3   It is perhaps inevitable that the convenience of having several disparate pieces of legislation unified in a single Act comes at the cost of a very complex structure. The Act is based on the concepts of 'protected characteristics' and 'prohibited conduct', but, as will be seen, both of these vary from situation to situation. Further, there are various exceptions to the duties imposed which are found in a number of different places in the Act. At the broadest possible level, it is suggested that the three main questions to keep in mind when considering discrimination issues are: (1) what is the relevant duty under the Act? (2) has the prohibited conduct occurred? (3) does an exception apply?

3.4   Although it is Part 6 of the Act which is directly concerned with education, the full list of provisions which are relevant to the field of education law and are considered in this Chapter are as follows:

(a)   Section 29 (provision of services to the public and exercise of public functions), Schedule 2 (services and public functions: reasonable adjustments), Schedule 3 (services and public functions: exceptions).

(b)   Part 6, Chapter 1 (schools), Schedule 10 (accessibility for disabled pupils), Schedule 11 (schools: exceptions), Schedule 13 (education: reasonable adjustments).

(c)   Part 6, Chapter 2 (further and higher education), Schedule 12 (further and higher education exceptions), Schedule 13 (education: reasonable adjustments).

(d)   Part 6, Chapter 3 (general qualifications bodies), Schedule 13 (education: reasonable adjustments).

(e)   Section 149 (public sector equality duty), Schedule 18 (public sector equality duty: exceptions).

(f)   Part 9 (enforcement), Schedule 17 (disabled pupils: enforcement).

(g)   Schedule 14 (educational charities and endowments).

---

[6]   Note that in addition to the consultation and reporting obligations in s 203 there are further procedures set out in s 204. Apart from laying a draft statutory instrument before Parliament there has also to be placed before it an explanatory document containing the information specified in s 204(2).

3.5   There has been very little opportunity so far for courts or tribunals to rule on points of principle arising from the provisions that relate to education in the EqA 2010. Case-law in this field under the previous legislation may still be to some extent relevant. Case-law in other fields, such as employment, may also be relevant. Space does not permit this Chapter to examine the general body of case-law in other fields[7] which exists. Further caution is needed with cases decided other than under the EqA 2010, or under provisions in the EqA 2010 which are worded differently from those which apply to education. Moreover, case-law in some areas of discrimination law may provide little guidance for future cases because it is concerned with a highly fact-specific judgments such as in relation to reasonableness and proportionality. It does not follow that the decisions of the courts in this area never establish points of principle and are unworthy of detailed consideration.

3.6   The EqA 2010 was accompanied by lengthy and detailed Explanatory Notes which were subsequently revised and reissued in August 2010. That revised version of the notes is referred to in this Chapter where appropriate, although it must be remembered that they do not form part of the Act, have not been endorsed by Parliament and are not authoritative.[8]

OVERVIEW OF THE EQUALITY ACT 2010 AND BASIC PRINCIPLES

3.7   Only the provisions of the EqA 2010 that apply in the education field are directly relevant to this Chapter, but it is impossible to understand them without an overview of the Act as a whole. The key concepts in the Act are 'protected characteristics' (race, sex, disability etc – nine in total) and 'prohibited conduct' (discrimination, victimisation, harassment and failure to comply with the duty to make adjustments). The basic structure of the Act is to set out the duties not to discriminate by situation or context or relationship, the main ones being as follows:

(a)   Part 3: services to the public and public functions.

(b)   Part 4: premises.

(c)   Part 5: work.

(d)   Part 6: education.

(e)   Part 7: associations.

---

[7]   For example European Union law.

[8]   It is permissible to look at the explanatory notes to see the context in which legislation was enacted see: *R (Westminster City Council) v National Asylum Service* [2002] UKHL 38 at para 5 per Lord Steyn. Whether that principle applies to revisions to explanatory notes that postdate the relevant enactment is open to doubt.

(f)   Part 10: contracts.

(g)   Part 12: disabled persons: transport.

3.8   The Act also provides that a person (A) must not discriminate against or harass another (B) if the discrimination arises out of and is closely connected to a relationship which used to exist between them, and the conduct constituting the discrimination or harassment would, if it occurred during the relationship, contravene the Act.[9] A duty to make reasonable adjustments also applies to A in these circumstances if B is[10] placed at a substantial disadvantage.[11] Conduct which also amounts to victimisation of B by A, however, does not contravene this provision.[12]

3.9   The overview in this section looks at: (1) the protected characteristics, (2) the prohibited conduct, (3) general exceptions, and (4) some other general principles. Enforcement is deal with separately below.

Protected characteristics

3.10   The full list of protected characteristics,[13] together with the definitions in respect of each are as follows:

---

[9]   Section 108(1)–(2). For the purposes of enforcement a contravention of this section relates to the Part of this Act that would have been contravened if the relationship had not ended: s 108(6). The examples in the Explanatory Notes (see para 354) include that of a school which refuses to give a reference to an ex-pupil because of his or her religion or belief, which is said to be direct discrimination.

[10] The word 'is' was substituted for the original wording of 'in so far as B continues to be' by SI 2010/2279. The Explanatory Notes to that statutory instrument say this was to 'clarify an ambiguity'.

[11] As mentioned in s 20: s 108(4). For these purposes, ss 20–22 and the applicable Schedules are to be construed as if the relationship had not ended: s 108(5).

[12] Section 108(7).

[13] As set out in s 4.

Protected characteristic	References to a person who has a particular protected characteristic is a reference to:	References to persons who share a protected characteristic is a reference to:	Reference to discrimination on this ground is a reference to discrimination within the following sections:[14]	Applicable to education?
Age (s 5)	A persons of a particular age group[15]	Persons of the same age group[16]	13, 19	In part
Disability[17] (s 6)	A person who has, or has had, a particular disability[18]	Persons who have the same disability[19]	13, 15, 19, 21	Yes
Gender reassignment[20] (s 7)	A transsexual person[21]	Transsexual persons[22]	13, 16, 19	Yes
Marriage and civil partnership (s 8)	A person who is married or is a civil partner[23]	Persons who are married or are civil partners[24]	13, 19	No
Pregnancy and maternity (ss 17–18)	n/a[25]	n/a	17, 18	Yes

---

[14] See s 25.
[15] Section 5(1)(a). A reference to an age group is a reference to a group of persons defined by reference to age, whether by reference to a particular age or to a range of ages: s 5(2). The Explanatory Notes give the following examples (see para 37): '(1) An age group would include 'over fifties' or twenty-one year olds, (2) A person aged twenty-one does not share the same characteristic of age with 'people in their forties'. However, a person aged twenty-one and people in their forties can share the characteristic of being in the 'under fifty' age range.'
[16] Section 5(1)(b). For 'age group' see fn 2, above.
[17] The definition is considered in paras **3.11–3.16** below.
[18] Section 6(3)(a) and s 6(4). For persons who have had a disability, see below.
[19] Section 6(3)(b).
[20] A person has this protected characteristic if the person is proposing to undergo, is undergoing, or has undergone a process (or part of a process) for the purpose of reassigning the person's sex by changing physiological or other attributes of sex: s 7(1). A reference to a transsexual person is a reference to a person who has this protected characteristic: s 7(2).
[21] Section 7(3)(a).
[22] Section 7(3)(b).
[23] Section 8(2)(a).
[24] Section 8(2)(b).
[25] No definitions are given in this part of the Act, pregnancy and maternity discrimination being dealt with specifically and separately in each relevant context.

Protected characteristic	References to a person who has a particular protected characteristic is a reference to:	References to persons who share a protected characteristic is a reference to:	Reference to discrimination on this ground is a reference to discrimination within the following sections:[14]	Applicable to education?
Race[27] (s 9)	A person of a particular racial group[28]	Persons of the same racial group[29]	13, 19	Yes
Religion or belief (s 10)	A person of a particular religion or belief[30]	Persons who are of the same religion or belief[31]	13, 19	In part
Sex (s 11)	A man or a woman[32]	Persons of the same sex[33]	13, 19	Yes but with limited exceptions
Sexual orientation[34] (s 12)	A person who is of a particular sexual orientation[35]	Persons who are of the same sexual orientation[36]	13, 19	Yes

Disability

3.11　Where a claim of disability discrimination is made against a school and the child has a statement of special educational needs, it may well be that no

---

27　This includes colour, nationality and ethnic or national origins: s 9(1). A Minister of the Crown may amend this definition so as to provide for caste to be an aspect of race, as well as to amend the Act to provide for exceptions for its application to caste (see s 9(5)) indicating that unless and until this is done, caste is not to be considered an aspect of race.

28　Section 9(2)(a). A racial group is a group of persons defined by reference to race and a reference to a person's racial group is a reference to a racial group into which the person falls: s 9(3). The fact that a racial group comprises two or more distinct racial groups does not prevent it from constituting a particular racial group: s 9(4).

29　Section 9(2)(b).

30　Section 10(3)(a). 'Religion' means any religion and a reference to religion includes a reference to a lack of religion, and 'belief' means any religious or philosophical belief and a reference to belief includes a reference to a lack of belief: s 10(1)–(2). The Explanatory Notes give the following examples (see para 53): '(1) The Baha'I faith, Buddhism, Christianity, Hinduism, Islam, Jainism, Judaism, Rastafarianism, Sikhism and Zoroastrianism are all religions for the purposes of this provision. (2) Beliefs such as humanism and atheism would be beliefs for the purposes of this provision but adherence to a particular football team would not be.'

31　Section 10(3)(b).

32　Section 11(a).

33　Section 11(b).

34　This means a person's sexual orientation towards persons of the same sex, persons of the opposite sex or persons of either sex: s 12(1).

35　Section 12(2)(a).

36　Section 12(2)(b).

issue arises about whether the child is disabled. In *CP v M Technology School*[37] the Upper Tribunal held that the First-tier Tribunal had not been bound by the school's concession that the child was disabled, but also held that the tribunal had acted procedurally unfairly in deciding the point for itself at the hearing, after affording the unrepresented parents nothing more than a short adjournment and copies of relevant parts of the statutory guidance to consider in that time.[38]

3.12 However, where it is an issue, the definition of disability requires more detailed consideration. A person (P) has a disability if P has (or had) a physical or mental impairment and the impairment has a substantial[39] and long-term[40] adverse effect on P's ability to carry out normal day-to-day activities.[41] This basic definition is subject to further detailed provisions found in Schedule 1 to the Act[42] and regulations made pursuant to Schedule 1[43] which may be summarised as follows:

(a) The following are deemed to be disabled: (a) persons with cancer, HIV infection and multiple sclerosis,[44] and (b) persons who are certified by a consultant ophthalmologist as blind, severely sight impaired, sight impaired or partially sighted.[45]

(b) An impairment which consists of a severe disfigurement (except for tattoos and piercings)[46] is to be treated as having the relevant adverse effect,[47] as is an impairment for which measures[48] are being taken to treat or correct and were such measures not being taken would be likely to have that effect.[49] A person with a progressive condition which results in an

---

37 [2010] ELR 757 (UT).
38 See to similar effect *DR v LB Croydon* [2010] UKUT 387 (AAC), [2011] ELR 37, in particular affirming that the tribunal has an inquisitorial function and is entitled to take the issue of whether the child is disabled as a preliminary point but equally appearing to disapprove of the fact that there was nothing in the case management directions to alert the parties to the need to bring evidence or call witnesses on this issue: see at [29].
39 Defined as more than minor or trivial: s 212(1).
40 The effect of an impairment is long-term if: (a) it has lasted for at least 12 months, (b) it is likely to last for at least 12 months, or (c) it is likely to last for the rest of the life of the person affected: Sch 1, para 2(1). Further, an impairment which ceases to have the relevant effect it is to be treated as continuing to have that effect if that effect is likely to recur: Sch 1, para 2(2).
41 Section 6(1). The definition of disability in the EqA 2010 applies even where the matters complained of occurred before it came into force: Sch 1, para 9.
42 Which has effect by virtue of s 6(6).
43 Currently the Equality Act 2010 (Disability) Regulations 2010, SI 2010/2128.
44 Schedule 1, para 6. 'HIV infection' is defined as infection by a virus capable of causing the Acquired Immune Deficiency Syndrome: ibid.
45 SI 2010/2128, para 7.
46 SI 2010/2128, para 5.
47 Schedule 1, para 3.
48 'Measures' include in particular medical treatment and the use of a prosthesis or other aid: Sch 1, para 5(2). This does not apply in relation to the impairment of a person's sight, to the extent that the impairment is, in the person's case, correctable by spectacles or contact lenses: Sch 1, para 5(3).
49 Schedule 1, para 5(1). The relevant date is that of the acts complained of, so the effect of an

impairment which has (or had) an effect on day-to-day activities albeit not a substantial adverse one, is to be taken to have an impairment which has the relevant effect if the condition is likely to result in him having such an impairment.[50]

(c)　　The following are to be treated as not amounting to an impairment: (a) addiction to alcohol, nicotine or any other substance is deemed not to be an impairment, unless the addiction was originally the result of administration of medically prescribed drugs or other medical treatment;[51] (b) a tendency to set fires, to steal, or to physical or sexual abuse of other persons;[52] (c) exhibitionism or voyeurism;[53] the condition known as seasonal allergic rhinitis (hayfever).[54]

(d)　　Where a child under six years of age has an impairment which does not have the relevant effect, the impairment is to be taken to have the relevant effect where it would normally have that effect on the ability of a person aged 6 years or over.[55]

3.13　　Further, the Act permits the government to issue guidance about matters to be taken into account in deciding whether a person has a disability and obliges adjudicating bodies to take such account of such guidance as it thinks is relevant. The current guidance document was issued by the Office for Disability Issues in August 2010 and came into force in May 2011.

3.14　　The exclusion noted above of an impairment consisting of a tendency to physical abuse of others may be relevant where a claim of disability discrimination follows disciplinary action by a school for a physical assault by a pupil, and was considered by the High Court in *Governors of X Endowed Primary School v SENDIST*.[56] In that case, the pupil in question had Attention Deficit Hyperactivity Disorder (ADHD), a condition with which commonly associated problems include (it was said) non-compliant behaviour, temper tantrums, mood swings, learning problems and aggression. The pupil was excluded from the school following an assault on a member of staff and subsequently the school obtained a report from an external specialist team. The tribunal had found that the school had breached its duty to make reasonable adjustments in that it failed to enlist advice and support from that team before

---

impairment is long-term if it has lasted at least 12 months by the date of the acts complained of, or if the effect is likely, at that date, to last at least 12 months: *McDougall v Richmond Adult Community School* [2008] EWCA Civ 4, [2008] ICR 431, [2008] IRLR 227.

[50]　Schedule 1, para 8.

[51]　SI 2010/2128, para 3.

[52]　SI 2010/2128, para 4(1)(a), (b) and (c).

[53]　SI 2010/2128, para 4(1)(d) and (e).

[54]　SI 2010/2128, para 4(2). However, this does not prevent that condition being taken into account where it aggravates the effect of any other condition: see para 4(3).

[55]　SI 2010/2128, para 6. The Explanatory Note to the regulations says that this makes provision for assessing the ability of a child under six years of age to carry out normal day-to-day activities.

[56]　[2010] ELR 1.

the incident which led to the exclusion. Lloyd-Jones J held that the protection of the legislation does not extend to excluded conditions, whether or not they are manifestations of an underlying impairment and it followed from this that the failure to take reasonable steps had to be (at least in part) in respect of a protected disability. Nonetheless the tribunal's decision was upheld because on the facts the measures proposed by the external team were not limited to means of controlling a tendency to physical abuse and included measures for the management of pupils with ADHD generally which may be directed at non-compliant and disruptive behaviour falling short of a tendency to physical abuse.

3.15 Finally, in relation to disability, it is important to note that (subject to two exceptions which are not relevant to education) the Act applies in relation to a person who has had a disability in the same way as it applies in relation to a person who has the disability.[57] As such, all references (however expressed) to a person who has a disability include reference to a person who has had the disability, and a reference to a person who does not have a disability includes a reference to a person who has not had the disability.[58] So, for example, government guidance suggests it would be unlawful to harass a person because of a mental condition (meeting the Act's definition of disability) that person had in the past.[59] On the other hand, with the exception of direct discrimination, the EqA 2010 does not protect persons who are not disabled but are perceived as such.[60]

3.16 There is no doubt that in some cases the issue of whether a person has a disability may be very complicated but it must be remembered that there can be no discrimination arising from disability[61] by a person who does not know and could not reasonably have been expected to know of the disability.[62]

Prohibited conduct

3.17 The conduct which is prohibited by the Act is set out below in the same order as it appears in the Act itself. When comparing cases for the purposes of direct, indirect or combined discrimination, there must be no material

---

[57] Section 6(3). The exceptions are Part 12 (transport) and s 190 (improvements to let dwelling houses).

[58] Section 6(4).

[59] Guidance issued by the Government Equalities Office ('Equality Act 2010: What do I need to know? Quick start guide', July 2010, available on the Home Office's website), p 3.

[60] For attempts to argue this which have not been permitted or not succeeded, see *LB of Redbridge v Baynes* UKEAT 0923/09 (claimant employee not disabled in spite of losing sight in one eye but manager altered her duties because of what he called her 'disability'), *J v DLA Piper UK LLP* [2010] IRLR 936, [2010] ICR 1052, and *Aitken v Commissioner of Police of the Metropolis* [2011] EWCA Civ 582, [2011] All ER (D) 165, [2012] ICR 78. The position is different in relation to direct discrimination because it does not matter whether the complainant has the protective characteristic or not.

[61] Ie as defined in s 15.

[62] Section 15(2).

difference between the circumstances relating to each case.[63] The circumstances relating to a case include a person's abilities where the protected characteristic is disability in a case of alleged direct discrimination, or where it is one of the protected characteristics in a case of alleged combined discrimination.[64]

3.18   The prohibited conduct is as follows:

(a)   Direct discrimination: This is where, because of[65] a protected characteristic, a person (A) treats another (B) less favourably[66] than A treats or would treat others[67]. It does not matter whether A has the protected characteristic in question[68], nor (with one exception[69]) whether B has it either.[70] This definition of direct discrimination applies to all protected characteristics except for pregnancy and maternity, where the definition of discrimination is wider (see below). Where the protected characteristic is age, there is no discrimination if A can show the treatment to be a proportionate means of achieving a legitimate aim[71] but in all other cases, there is no defence of justification (even where the treatment is said to be mandated by religion[72]) and motive is irrelevant.[73] Where the protected characteristic is disability and B is not disabled, there is no discrimination only because A treats or would treat disabled persons more favourably than B.[74]

---

[63]   Section 23(1).

[64]   Section 23(2).

[65]   The previous legislation contained various definitions using the words 'on grounds of' but the view of the Explanatory Notes is that '[t]his change in wording does not change the legal meaning of the definition, but rather is designed to make it more accessible to the ordinary user of the Act': Explanatory Notes, para 61.

[66]   Where the protected characteristic is race, this includes segregating B from others: s 13(5). Where the protected characteristic is sex, this includes less favourable treatment of B because she is breast-feeding (although this does not apply for the purposes of Part 5 (work)): s 13(6)(a), (7).

[67]   Section 13(1).

[68]   Section 24(1). The following example is given in the Explanatory Notes (see para 95): 'An employer cannot argue that because he is a gay man he is not liable for unlawful discrimination for rejecting a job application from another gay man because of the applicant's sexual orientation.'

[69]   The exception is where the protected characteristic is marriage and civil partnership and only applies to a contravention of Part 5 (work). In this case the treatment must be because it is B who is married or a civil partner: s 13(4).

[70]   This follows from the wording and is confirmed by the exception in s 13(4) referred to in fn 68 above. As such, the definition covers cases where the less favourable treatment is because of the victim's association with someone who has the protected characteristic or because the victim is wrongly thought to have the protected characteristic himself. See Explanatory Notes, para 59.

[71]   Section 13(2).

[72]   *R (E) v JFS Governing Body* [2010] 2 AC 728.

[73]   *R v Birmingham City Council ex p Equal Opportunities Commission (No1)* [1989] AC 1155, *James v Eastleigh BC* [1990] 2 AC 751, *R (E) v JFS Governing Body*, above. These cases were decided under earlier legislation but there can be little doubt that the approach would be the same under the EqA 2010.

[74]   Section 13(3). Where the protected characteristic is sex and B is a man, no account is to be taken of special treatment afforded to a woman in connection with pregnancy or childbirth: s 13(6)(b).

(b) Combined discrimination: This occurs if, because of a combination of two relevant protected characteristics,[75] A treats B less favourably than A treats or would treat a person who does not share either of those characteristics.[76] This does not apply in education cases to a combination of characteristics that includes disability where a claim of direct discrimination because of disability alone would have to be brought in the First-tier Tribunal.[77] Where it does apply, B need not show that A's treatment of B is direct discrimination because of each of the characteristics in the combination taken separately.[78] However, B cannot establish a contravention of the Act by virtue of this provision if A can show (whether by relying on a provision in this Act or any other enactment) that his treatment of B is not direct discrimination because of either or both of the characteristics in the combination.[79] It does not matter whether A has one or both of the protected characteristics in the combination.[80] As at 4 October 2012 this provision was not in force.

(c) Discrimination arising from disability: A person (A) discriminates against a disabled person (B) if: (a) A treats B unfavourably because of something arising in consequence of B's disability, and (b) A cannot show that the treatment is a proportionate means of achieving a legitimate aim.[81] However, there is no such discrimination if A shows that A did not know and could not reasonably have been expected to know, that B had the disability.[82] This type of discrimination is what used to be known as 'disability related' discrimination and the wording is intended to reverse the effect of the decision of the House of Lords in *Malcolm v Lewisham*.[83]

(d) Gender reassignment discrimination: The definition in section 16(1) only has effect for the purposes of the application of Part 5 (work) so falls outside the scope of this work.

(e) Pregnancy and maternity: A person (A) discriminates against a woman if A treats her unfavourably because of a pregnancy of hers[84] or if, in the period of 26 weeks beginning with the day on which she gives birth,[85] A treats her unfavourably because she has given birth.[86] Section 18 makes

---

[75] For these purposes this means age, disability, gender reassignment, race, religion or belief, sex and sexual orientation, with marriage and civil partnership and pregnancy and maternity being excluded: s 14(2).

[76] Section 14(1).

[77] Section 14(5).

[78] Section 14(3).

[79] Section 14(4).

[80] Section 24(2).

[81] Section 15(1).

[82] Section 15(2).

[83] [2008] UKHL 43. This is confirmed by the Explanatory Notes at para 70.

[84] Section 17(2). The example given in the Explanatory Notes relevant to education is (see para 74): 'A school must not prevent a pupil taking an exam because she is pregnant'.

[85] For these purposes the day on which a woman gives birth is the day on which she gives birth to a living child or (if more than 24 weeks of the pregnancy having passed) a dead child: s 17(5).

[86] Section 17(3). This includes treating her unfavourably because she is breast-feeding.

further provisions in this regard but only for the purposes of the application of Part 5 (work) which is outside the scope of this work.

(f) Indirect discrimination: This is where A applies to B a provision, criterion or practice which is discriminatory in relation to a relevant protected characteristic[87] of B's.[88] For these purposes a provision, criterion or practice is discriminatory if: (a) A applies, or would apply, it to persons with whom B does not share the characteristic, (b) it puts, or would put, persons with whom B shares the characteristic at a particular disadvantage when compared with persons with whom B does not share it, (c) it puts, or would put, B at that disadvantage, and (d) A cannot show it to be a proportionate means of achieving a legitimate aim.[89]

(g) Discrimination consisting of a failure to comply with the duty to make adjustments: Wherever a duty to make reasonable adjustments is imposed by the Act, this is a reference to one or more of the three requirements set out in section 20,[90] and a failure to comply with any requirement imposed amounts to discrimination.[91] The person on whom the duty is imposed is referred to as A, who cannot require the disabled person to whom the duty is owed to pay to any extent A's costs of complying with the duty.[92] The three requirements are: (1) where a provision, criterion or practice of A's puts a disabled person at a substantial disadvantage in relation to a relevant matter in comparison with persons who are not disabled, a requirement to take reasonable steps to avoid the disadvantage;[93] (2) Where a physical feature[94] puts a disabled person at a substantial disadvantage in relation to a relevant matter in comparison with persons who are not disabled, a requirement to take reasonable steps to avoid[95] the disadvantage;[96] (3) Where a disabled person would, but for the provision of an auxiliary aid or service, be put at a substantial disadvantage in relation to a relevant matter in comparison with persons who are not

---

[87] For these purposes this means age, disability, gender reassignment, marriage and civil partnership, race, religion or belief, sex and sexual orientation, with pregnancy and maternity being excluded: s 19(2).

[88] Section 19(1).

[89] Section 19(2).

[90] Section 20(1), which must be read with ss 21–22 and the relevant Schedule (which is Sch 13 in the case of education duties).

[91] Section 21(2). Where imposed, the duty to comply with the first, second or third requirement applies only for the purpose of establishing whether A has contravened this provision and accordingly is not otherwise actionable: s 21(3).

[92] Section 20(7).

[93] Section 20(3). Where this relates to the provision of information, the reasonable steps include steps for ensuring that the information is provided in a format which is, in the circumstances, accessible: s 20(6).

[94] This includes: (a) a feature arising from the design or construction of a building, (b) a feature of an approach to, exit from or access to a building, (c) a fixture or fitting, or furniture, furnishings, materials, equipment or other chattels, in or on premises, or (d) any other physical element or quality: s 20(10).

[95] This includes removing the physical feature in question, altering it or providing a reasonable means of avoiding it: s 20(9).

[96] Section 20(4).

disabled, to take such steps as it is reasonable to have to take to provide the auxiliary aid or service.[97] It is up to a claimant to identify the reasonable steps the defendant should have taken but failed to take.[98]

(h) Harassment: This is where A engages in unwanted conduct related to a relevant personal characteristic[99] or unwanted conduct of a sexual nature, and that conduct has the purpose or effect of violating B's dignity or creating an intimidating, hostile, degrading, humiliating or offensive environment for B.[100] In deciding whether conduct has this effect, each of the following must be taken into account: (a) the perception of B, (b) the other circumstances of the case, and (c) whether it is reasonable for the conduct to have that effect.[101] A also harasses B if A or another person engages in unwanted conduct of a sexual nature or that is related to gender reassignment or sex, which conduct has the purpose or effect referred to above, and because of B's rejection of or submission to the conduct, A treats B less favourably than A would treat B if B had not rejected or submitted to the conduct.[102]

(i) Victimisation: This is where A subjects B[103] to a detriment because B does a protected act or A believes that B has done or may do a protected act.[104] Each of the following is a 'protected act' for these purposes: (a) bringing proceedings under the Act, (b) giving evidence or information in connection with proceedings under the Act, (c) doing any other thing for the purposes of or in connection with the Act, (d) making an allegation (whether or not express) that A or another person has contravened[105] this Act.[106] Giving false evidence or information, or making a false allegation, is not a protected act if the evidence or information given, or the allegation is made, in bad faith.[107] In the education field 'B' is extended to include a parent or sibling[108] of the child[109] in question.[110] In other words,

---

[97] Section 20(5), (11). Where this relates to the provision of information, see fn 92 above.

[98] *Dee Thomas-Ashley v Drum Housing Association Ltd* [2010] EWCA Civ 265, [2010] L & TR 17, (2010) 107(13) LSG 17, [2010] NPC 36, [2010] 2 P & CR 17. Going one step further, and in an education context, it will be difficult to show an error of law in a tribunal decision which focusses only the reasonable adjustments put forward by the parents in circumstances where no concrete suggestions are made as to other adjustments that could have been made: see *DP v Radley College* [2011] UKUT 66 (AAC), [2011] ELR 155.

[99] For these purposes this means age, disability, gender reassignment, race, religion or belief, sex and sexual orientation, with marriage and civil partnership and pregnancy and maternity being excluded: s 26(5). In the education field, the personal characteristics of gender reassignment, religion or belief and sexual orientation are also excluded: see s 85(10).

[100] Section 26(1)–(2).

[101] Section 26(4).

[102] Section 26(3).

[103] This section only applies where B is an individual: s 27(4).

[104] Section 27(1).

[105] The reference to contravening the Act includes a reference to committing a breach of an equality clause or rule: s 27(5).

[106] Section 27(2). References to the EqA 2010 include references to previous equality legislation (e g the SDA 1975): SI 2010/2317, art 8 (the full list of previous legislation is in art 1(3)).

[107] Section 27(3).

[108] Meaning a brother or sister, a half-brother or half-sister, or a stepbrother or stepsister: s 86(5).

subjecting a child to a detriment because his parent or sibling has done a protected act is also victimisation. It is the good or bad faith of the child, and not his parent or sibling that matters.[111] The Explanatory Notes say that the aim of this extension is to prevent parents being discouraged from raising an issue of discrimination with a school because of worry that their child may suffer retaliation as a result.[112]

General exceptions

3.19 As will be seen below, Parts 3 (services and public functions) and 6 (education) which are relevant to the education field, contain within them a number of exceptions, but the Act also contains a number of more general exceptions to its provisions. Those which are, or may be, relevant to the education field are as follows.

(a)   Sports: There is no contravention of the Act, so far as relating to sex, only by doing something in relation to the participation of another as a competitor in a gender-affected activity.[113] This is defined as 'a sport, game or other activity of a competitive nature in circumstances in which the physical strength, stamina or physique of average persons of one sex would put them at a disadvantage compared to average persons of the other sex as competitors in events involving the activity'.[114] When considering whether a sport, game or other activity is 'gender-affected' in relation to children, it is appropriate to take account of the age and stage of development of children who are likely to be competitors.[115] As such, whilst the Explanatory Notes suggest that it would be lawful to have men and women compete in separate 100 metre races they say that this would not necessarily be so with younger boys and girls.[116] Nonetheless, this provision is likely to ensure that reasonable different treatment of male and female pupils in sporting activities will not be unlawful.

---

[109]   Meaning a person who has not attained the age of 18: s 86(5).

[110]   Section 86(2).

[111]   Section 86(3)–(4). Thus the Explanatory Notes say (para 297) that where a parent or sibling maliciously makes or supports an untrue complaint the child is still protected from victimisation so long as the child has acted in good faith, but a child who has acted in bad faith is not protected, even where the parent or sibling makes or supports an untrue complaint in good faith.

[112]   Explanatory Notes, para 296. The examples which follow are: '(1) The parent of a pupil complains to the school that her daughter is suffering sex discrimination by not being allowed to participate in a metalwork class. The daughter is protected from being treated less favourably by the school in any way because of this complaint. (2) A pupil brings a case against his school claiming that he has suffered discrimination by a member of staff because of his sexual orientation. The pupil's younger brother, at the same school, is protected against any less favourable treatment by the school because of this case, even if is later found that the older brother was not acting in good faith.' It should be noted that in the latter case, the older brother would *not* be protected if it were later found that he (the older brother) was not acting in good faith.

[113]   Section 195(1).

[114]   Section 195(3).

[115]   Section 195(4).

[116]   Explanatory Notes, para 616.

(b) Positive discrimination: The Act does not prohibit what it calls 'positive action' where a person (P) reasonably thinks that persons who share a protected characteristic suffer a disadvantage connected to the characteristic, or that persons who share a protected characteristic have needs that are different from the needs of persons who do not share it, or participation in an activity is disproportionately low. In such circumstances, P is not prohibited[117] from taking proportionate action to address the disadvantage or needs or low participation.[118] The Explanatory Notes contain the following example relevant to the education field: 'Having identified that its white male pupils are underperforming at maths, a school could run supplementary maths classes exclusively for them'.[119]

(c) Employment in religious institutions: Although employment issues are outside the scope of this work, various exceptions from Part 5 (work) are worth noting. There is a general exception from the Act for schools of a religious character who do certain things permitted by various provisions in the School Standards and Framework Act 1998 (SSFA 1998).[120] These include dismissing teachers appointed to give religious education if they fail to give it efficiently, taking account of religious considerations in relation to certain appointments, preferring certain teachers at independent schools of a religious character and taking account of religious considerations in relation to certain teachers at Academies with religious character.[121] Further, there is no contravention of Part 5 in relation to certain posts in schools or institutions of further or higher education where their governing instrument requires the headteacher or principal to be of a particular religious order, or that a particular academic position must be held by a woman,[122] or where the legislation or instrument which establishes a professorship requires the holder to be an ordained priest.[123]

(d) Ordinary residence and nationality: The application of a provision, criterion or practice which relates to: (a) a person's place of ordinary residence, or (b) the length of time a person has been present or resident in or outside the United Kingdom or an area within it, which

---

[117] That is, by the EqA 2010 itself. Section 158(6) makes clear that these provisions do not permit P to do anything that is prohibited by or under any other enactment.

[118] Section 158.

[119] Explanatory Notes, para 517.

[120] The relevant provisions are ss 58(6)–(7), 60(4)–(5) and 124A.

[121] See Sch 22, para 4.The Explanatory Notes give (at para 985) the following examples: '(1) Voluntary controlled and foundation schools with a religious ethos may appoint a headteacher on the basis of his ability and fitness to preserve and develop the religious character of the school. (2) Voluntary aided schools with a religious ethos can restrict employment of teachers to applicants who share the same faith. For example, most Catholic schools may require that applicants to teaching positions be of the Catholic faith.'

[122] This exception only applies to instruments taking effect before 16 January 1990: Sch 22, para 3(4).

[123] See Sch 22, para 3.

discriminates against another does not amount to a contravention of Parts 3–6 providing this is done in accordance with a statutory provision or ministerial approval or a ministerial requirement.[124] Subject to the same proviso, anything which discriminates on the ground of nationality is also excluded.[125] An example of the effect of this given by the Explanatory Notes is that overseas students at universities in England and Wales can be required to pay higher tuition fees than local students.[126]

(e) Statutory authority: The exception for things done with statutory authority is worth noting because of its sheer breadth. There are exceptions from several Parts of the Act (including Parts 3 and 6 which are relevant to education) in relation to the protected characteristics of age, disability, religion or belief, sex and sexual orientation, for things required to be done by other enactments (whether pre- or post-dating the EqA 2010).[127] There is a particular exception for things done to comply with laws protecting women who are pregnant or who have recently given birth or guarding against risks specific to women.[128]

(f) Charities: Although only possibly of relevance to certain independent schools in some respects, the Act provides that a person does not contravene its provisions by restricting the provision of benefits to persons who share a protected characteristic if the person acts in pursuance of a charitable instrument and the provision of benefits is either a proportionate means of achieving a legitimate aim or for the purpose of preventing or compensating for a disadvantage linked to the protected characteristic.[129]

(g) There is no contravention of the Act so far as relating to sex discrimination or gender reassignment discrimination only because of anything done in relation to the admission of person to communal accommodation[130] or the provision of a benefit, facility or service liked to the provision of such accommodation.[131] However, there is a contravention of the Act in relation to admission of persons to communal

---

[124] Schedule 23, para 1(3). The proviso in full is that the thing must be done: (a) in pursuance of an enactment, (b) in pursuance of an instrument made by a member of the executive under an enactment, (c) to comply with a requirement imposed (whether before or after the passing of this Act) by a member of the executive by virtue of an enactment, (d) in pursuance of arrangements made (whether before or after the passing of this Act) by or with the approval of, or for the time being approved by, a Minister of the Crown, (e) to comply with a condition imposed (whether before or after the passing of this Act) by a Minister of the Crown: Sch 23, para 1(1).

[125] Schedule 23, para 1(2).

[126] Explanatory Notes, para 989.

[127] See Sch 22, para 1.

[128] See Sch 22, para 2.

[129] See ss 193–194 which contain detailed definitions, provisions and exceptions.

[130] Communal accommodation is defined as residential accommodation which includes dormitories or other shared sleeping accommodation which for reasons of privacy should be used only by persons of the same sex: see para 3(5) of Sch 23.

[131] Paragraph 3(1) of Sch 23.

accommodation if the accommodation is not managed in a way that is as fair as possible to both men and women.[132] In relation to admission of persons to communal accommodation and sex discrimination account has to be taken of whether and how far it is reasonable to expect the accommodation to be altered or extended or that further accommodation should be provided and the frequency of the demand or need for the use of the accommodation by persons of one sex as compared with those of the other.[133] In relation to admission of persons to communal accommodation and gender reassignment discrimination account has to be taken of whether and how far the conduct in question is a proportionate means of achieving a legitimate aim.[134]

Some other general principles

3.20 The Act makes general provision in relation to contract law, rendering unenforceable a term of a contract insofar as it constitutes, promotes or provides for treatment of any person that is of a description prohibited by the Act.[135] A term of a contract which purports to exclude or limit a provision of, or made under, the Act is unenforceable by the person in whose favour it would operate.[136] This does not apply to a contract which settles a claim in the county court.[137]

3.21 The Act contains prohibitions on instructing, causing or inducing contraventions of its provisions and on knowingly helping others to contravene the Act.[138]

3.22 The Act makes employers liable for things done by their employees in the course of their employment (as it does principals for things done by their agents with their authority).[139] Where proceedings are brought against employers on such a basis, it is a defence for the employer to show that it took all reasonable steps to prevent the employee from doing what is complained of or anything of that description.[140] Employees and agents are also liable,[141]

---

[132] Paragraph 3(2) of Sch 23.

[133] Paragraph 3(3) of Sch 23.

[134] Paragraph 3(4) of Sch 23. It is not clear whether this is in addition to the matters in para 3(3) or in substitution for them. The words 'must also' in para 3(4) suggest it is an additional matter but the wording of para 3(3)(b) suggests that the whole of the remit of para 3(3) is sex discrimination alone. The prudent course would be to regard both the para 3(3) and 3(4) matters as relevant matters in the case of gender re-assignment discrimination.

[135] Section 142(1). The Act also renders unenforceable 'non contractual terms' but these have no relevance to education, as they relate to the provision of employment services or insurance.

[136] Section 144(1).

[137] Section 144(3). The actual exemption is for claims 'within section 114', and since s 114(3) provides that this section does not apply to claims of disability discrimination in the First-tier Tribunal, such claims do not appear to come within this exemption. This is also the view taken by the Explanatory Notes (see para 464).

[138] Sections 111–112.

[139] Section 109(1)–(2). It does not matter whether that thing is done with the employer's or principals' knowledge or approval: s 109(3).

[140] Section 109(4).

unless they reasonably rely on a statement by their employer or principal that the thing complained of is not a contravention of the Act.[142] However, this does not apply in respect of complaints of disability discrimination in schools[143], with the result that such claims in the First-tier Tribunal can only be brought against the Responsible Body.[144]

3.23 Enforcement is covered separately below.

GENERAL DUTY NOT TO DISCRIMINATE IN PROVISION OF SERVICES AND EXERCISE OF PUBLIC FUNCTIONS: SECTION 29 OF THE EQA 2010

3.24 Part 3 of the EqA 2010 (sections 28–31) is concerned with the provision of services and exercise of public functions. Not all protected characteristics are covered by this Part: age, so far as relating to under-18s, and marriage and civil partnership are excluded entirely,[145] and religion and belief and sexual orientation are excluded from the prohibitions on harassment.[146] The obligations in this Part are imposed on two categories of persons:

(a) persons concerned with the provision of a service[147] to the public or a section of the public, whether for payment or not (referred to as 'service-providers') and

(b) persons exercising a public function[148] that is not the provision of a service to the public or a section of the public.

3.25 So far as (a) is concerned, four duties are imposed on service-providers:

(1) not to discriminate against or victimise a person requiring the service[149] by not providing[150] the person with the service;[151]

---

[141] Section 110(1). It does not matter whether in any proceedings the employer is found liable under section 109: s 110(2).

[142] Section 110(3). A person who knowingly or recklessly makes such a statement which is false or misleading in a material respect commits and offence and is liable on summary conviction to a fine not exceeding level 5 on the standard scale: s 110(4)–(5).

[143] Section 110(7).

[144] This is confirmed by the Explanatory Notes at para 361.

[145] Section 28(1).

[146] Section 29(8). This does not prevent conduct relating to those characteristics from amounting to a detriment for the purposes of discrimination within s 13 (direct discrimination) because of that characteristic: s 212(5).

[147] This includes the provision of goods or facilities, and also includes the provision of a service in the exercise of a public function: s 31(2)–(3). It also includes facilitating access to the service: s 212(4).

[148] This means a function of a public nature for the purposes of the Human Rights Act 1998: s 31(4).

[149] This includes a person who is seeking to obtain or use the service: s 31(6).

[150] This includes not providing the person with a service of the usual quality and not providing the service in the usual manner or on the usual terms: s 31(7).

(2) in providing the service, not to discriminate against or victimise a person (B) as to the terms on which A provides the service to B, by terminating the provision of the service to B, or by subjecting B to any other detriment;[152]

(3) not to harass[153] a person requiring the service or a person to whom the service-provider provides the service;[154]

(4) to make reasonable adjustments, ie to comply with the first, second and third requirements in section 20.[155]

3.26 So far as (b) is concerned persons exercising public functions are under two duties:

(1) not to do anything that constitutes discrimination, harassment[156] or victimisation;[157] and

(2) to make reasonable adjustments, ie to comply with the first, second and third requirements in section 20.[158]

3.27 In both cases, the Act makes further provision in respect of the obligation to comply with the three requirements of the reasonable adjustments duty. The reference in each of the three requirements[159] to 'a disabled person' is to be read as a reference to 'disabled persons generally',[160] which the Explanatory Notes say means the duty is an anticipatory one so that service providers and people exercising public functions must anticipate the needs of disabled people and make appropriate reasonable adjustments.[161] Additional modifications are made to the wording of section 20 to adapt it for the purposes of section 29.[162] The Act makes clear, however, that A is not required

---

[151] Section 29(1), (4).
[152] Section 29(2), (5).
[153] Religion or belief and sexual orientation are not relevant protected characteristics for the purposes of the duty not to harass: s 29(8).
[154] Section 29(3).
[155] Section 29(7) and Sch 2.
[156] Religion or belief and sexual orientation are not relevant protected characteristics for the purposes of the duty not to harass: s 29(8).
[157] Section 29(6).
[158] Section 29(7) and Sch 2.
[159] Ie in s 20(3), (4) or (5).
[160] Schedule 2, para 2(2).
[161] Explanatory Notes, para 676.
[162] These are set out in Sch 2, para 2(3)–(6) and are as follows: (1) In relation to each requirement the relevant matter is the provision of the service, or the exercise of the function, by A. (2) Being placed at a substantial disadvantage in relation to the exercise of a function means: (a) if a benefit is or may be conferred in the exercise of the function, being placed at a substantial disadvantage in relation to the conferment of the benefit, or (b) if a person is or may be subjected to a detriment in the exercise of the function, suffering an unreasonably adverse experience when being subjected to the detriment. (3) In relation to the second requirement (physical features), the duty is to take reasonable steps to avoid the identified disadvantage or to adopt a reasonable alternative method of providing the service or exercising the function.

to take any step which would fundamentally alter the nature of the service or the nature of A's trade or profession; similarly if exercising a public function there is no requirement to take a step which A has no power to take.[163]

3.28   However, these provisions do not apply to discrimination, harassment or victimisation that is prohibited by Part 4 (premises), Part 5 (work) or Part 6 (education), or which would be so prohibited but for an express exception.[164] As a result there can be no overlap with the duties in Part 6 (considered below), and so this section is unlikely to have any relevance for schools or other educational institutions in the field of education law, but it is important and relevant to local authorities in relation to their education functions not covered by Part 6.

3.29   There is no doubt that these functions are public functions (as defined) but it is less clear whether any of them (and if so which of them) would be held to constitute the provision of a service to a section of the public. However, little would seem to depend upon this given that such functions come within section 29 either way and the duty is effectively the same in either case.

3.30   Schedule 2 and Part 2 of Schedule 3[165] contains six important exceptions to the application of section 29 to the exercise by local authorities of their education functions:

(1)   The obligation to comply with the third requirement of the duty to make adjustments (provision of auxiliary aids) has not yet been brought into force in relation to local authorities exercising functions under the EA.[166]

(2)   Section 29 does not apply to the exercise of functions under sections 13 and 14 of the EA 1996[167] so far as relating to age discrimination or religious or belief-related discrimination.[168] The intended effect of this exception is to prevent local authorities from being bound to provide schools for pupils of different faiths, or no faith, or for particular age groups, in every catchment area.[169]

Further, 'physical feature' includes not just a physical feature in or on premises that A occupies but also a physical feature brought by or on behalf of A, in the course of providing the service or exercising the function, on to premises other than those that A occupies.

[163]   Schedule 2, para 2(7)–(8).

[164]   Section 28(2).

[165]   This Part of Sch 3 is to be construed in accordance with Ch 1 of Pt 6: Sch 3, Pt 2, para 12.

[166]   See SI 2010/2317, art 2(3)(b)(i). This mirrors the position in respect of s 85(6) and Sch 13.

[167]   Section 13 obliges local authorities to contribute towards the spiritual, moral, mental and physical development of the community by securing that efficient primary education, secondary education and (in England only) further education, are available to meet the needs of the population of their area. Section 14 obliges local authorities to ensure that sufficient schools for providing primary and secondary education are available for their area.

[168]   Schedule 3, Pt 2, para 1.

[169]   See the Explanatory Notes, para 686. Two examples are given: '(1) Catholic parents will not be able to claim that their LA is discriminating unlawfully if there is no Catholic school in their catchment area, or if there are fewer places in Catholic schools than in Church of England schools. (2) Parents of secondary age children will not be able to claim that it is age

(3) Section 29, so far as relating to sex discrimination, does not apply to the exercise of a local authority's functions in relation to the establishment of a school.[170] However, this does not disapply section 29 in relation to the exercise of the authority's functions under section 14 of the EA 1996[171] and this is considered in more detail below.

(4) Section 29, so far as relating to age discrimination, does not apply in relation to anything done in connection with: (a) the curriculum of a school, (b) admission to a school, (c) transport to or from a school, or (d) the establishment, alteration or closure of schools.[172]

(5) Section 29, so far as relating to disability discrimination, does not require a local authority (LA) exercising functions under the Education Acts[173] to remove or alter a physical feature.[174]

(6) Section 29, so far as relating to religious or belief-related discrimination, does not apply in relation to anything done in connection with: (a) the curriculum of a school, (b) admission to a school which has a religious ethos, (c) acts of worship or other religious observance organised by or on behalf of a school (whether or not forming part of the curriculum), (d) the responsible body of a school which has a religious ethos, (e) transport to or from a school, or (f) the establishment, alteration or closure of schools.[175]

3.31 The exception provided for at paragraph 8(2) of Schedule 3 referred to at para **3.30(3)** above requires further consideration. The Explanatory Notes state that this exception is designed to replicate the effect of provisions in the SDA 1975.[176] At paragraph 688 the Explanatory Notes state that the effect of these provisions is that an LA will not be prevented from establishing single sex schools but must provide similar numbers of places for boys and girls. It is

---

discrimination if their children have to travel further than younger ones to reach their school.' The author of the Explanatory Notes appears to have overlooked the fact that, by virtue of s 28(1), s 29 does not apply in any event to the protected characteristic of age, so far as relating to under-18s is concerned, and so this exception in the Sch is only of relevance to over-18s.

[170] Schedule 3, Pt 2, para 8(1).

[171] Schedule 3, Pt 2, para 8(2).

[172] Schedule 3, Pt 2, para 9. The Explanatory Notes give two examples (see para 691): '(1) School admissions policies can continue to be based on the ages of prospective pupils. (2) School transport can be provided for children of a particular age only.' See the comment above about this only being of any relevance for those over the age of 18.

[173] As defined in s 578 of the EA 1996: s 212(1).

[174] Schedule 3, Pt 2, para 10(1). The Explanatory Notes say at para 693 that this is excluded because 'such things will fall within the requirements on [local authorities] to produce accessibility strategies as set out in Sch 12'. The cross-reference is erroneous as accessibility strategies are dealt with in Sch 10.

[175] Schedule 3, Pt 2, para 11. The Explanatory Notes given two examples (see para 695): '(1) A public body will not be open to claims of religious discrimination as a result of its decision to establish, alter or close a faith school. (2) An LA can select a person of a particular religion or belief to be a governor of a school with a religious ethos.'

[176] Explanatory Notes, para 689.

unfortunate that the Explanatory Notes do not provide an entirely accurate description of what the law was under the SDA which they contend that the EqA 2010 was intended to replicate.

3.32   Clearly, just as under the previous legislative scheme, the intention is that it should be lawful to establish single sex schools. Of course once a single sex school is established machinery has to be present in the legislative scheme to ensure that the discrimination inherent in the existence of a single sex school is not unlawful. Under the SDA 1975 some, but by no means complete, provision was made to deal with the consequences of ensuring single sex schools were lawful. Accordingly, for example, section 26 of the SDA 1975 made it lawful for a single sex school not to admit children of the opposite sex and[177] section 27 enabled co-educational schools to become single sex schools and for discriminatory admissions during the transitional phase to be legitimised by application to the Secretary of State for what was known as a transitional exemption order.[178] Further, in relation to the duties of local authorities with regard to overall provision of schools and sex discrimination, the Act sought to restrict the enforcement of those duties to the Secretary of State.[179] Sections 26 and 27 of the SDA 1975 have equivalents[180] in the present statutory scheme, section 25 does not. Accordingly, while a single sex school is in itself lawful, that does not enable an LA to discriminate in relation to its overall provision of single sex schools and breach of such a duty can be the subject of legal proceedings in the Courts.

3.33   Under the previous legislative scheme the nature of the duty placed on the LA was considered a number of times by the courts. In *R v Birmingham City Council ex parte Equal Opportunities Commission*[181] the House of Lords held that the council was in breach of its duties under the SDA 1975 in knowingly maintaining a system of education in its area where the opportunities for selective education were considerably less for girls than for boys. The disparity arose from the fact that there were more voluntary aided single sex selective school places for boys than for girls and the LA, although it maintained these schools, was not responsible for admissions to them. The council could not simply cease to maintain the schools because that would have required the consent of the Secretary of State and it had no power to compel him to give such consent. Further, it could not change the schools to co-educational or comprehensive, as such an initiative had to come from the governors and also required the Secretary of State's consent. Nor could it in practice establish a new single sex selective school for girls because there was already over provision in the area and the Secretary of State's consent was not likely to be forthcoming in those circumstances. Despite these very real

---

[177]   See now to the same effect Sch 11, para 1 to the EqA 2010.
[178]   See now to the same effect Sch 11, para 3 to the EqA 2010.
[179]   See s 25(4) of the SDA 1975.
[180]   Schedule 11, paras 1 and 3 to the EqA 2010.
[181]   [1989] AC 1155.

practical difficulties, which the House of Lords recognized,[182] the council was held to be in breach of its duties under the SDA 1975.

3.34 In analysing the relevant duties under the SDA 1975, the House of Lords held that:

(a) it was not necessary for the applicants to show that selective education was better than non selective education; it was sufficient to show that it was an option reasonably regarded as of value;[183]

(b) intention or motive was irrelevant;[184]

(c) it was not necessary for the applicants to show that there was a breach by the council of its duties under section 8 of the EA 1944.[185] All that had to be shown was that the council, in the performance of its functions, did an act or deliberately omitted to do an act which constituted sex discrimination.[186] Moreover, 'constituted' was not to be construed in any restrictive sense as Woolf LJ had done in the Court of Appeal;

(d) the council had knowingly continued its acts of maintaining the various boys' and girls' schools which inevitably resulted in discrimination against girls because of the great disparity of places available for boys and girls in single sex education.[187]

3.35 It was unclear from this decision what the precise act of sex discrimination by the council was or, indeed, if there needed to be any precise act of discrimination. It appeared that the House of Lords held the LA to be responsible for the discrimination the girls suffered by the knowing maintenance of the relevant schools when that meant unequal opportunities for girls and boys. Accordingly, it was argued in *R v Birmingham ex parte EOC (No 2)*[188] that where the LA was not maintaining the relevant schools, because they were grant maintained,[189] it was not in breach of its section 23 duty. The Court of Appeal rejected this submission and held that the duty under section 8 of the EA 1944 was to secure that there were sufficient schools and that the council had to perform that 'securing function' having regard to all of the educational opportunities in its area.[190]

---

[182] [1989] AC 1155, at 1191H–1192A.

[183] [1989] AC 1155, at 1193H–1194A

[184] [1989] AC 1155, 1194A–1194D

[185] Now s 14 of the EA 1996

[186] [1989] AC 1155 at 1196D–1196F.

[187] [1989] AC 1155, at 1196H–1197B.

[188] [1994] ELR 282.

[189] Grant maintained status no longer exists. The acquisition of grant maintained status required a decision of the Secretary of State who, just like the present position with Academies, would also fund them. The local authorities had no control over grant maintained schools. For discussion of grant maintained schools see Ch 7 of the First Edition of this book.

[190] [1994] ELR 282 at 296D–297C.

3.36   The nature of the duty on what is now the LA was also considered by Ralph Gibson LJ in *R v Secretary of State for Education ex parte Avon (No 2)*.[191] He held:

(a)   The LA was both entitled and required to take into account the provision of all schools (including independent schools for the purpose of performing its duty under section 8 of the EA 1944.[192]

(b)   If 500 places were provided in a single sex school for boys, then there was an obligation to provide as many places in a single sex girls' school up to the number 500 as there were girls who wished to go to an LA single sex school;[193]

(c)   There was 'much force' in the submission (subsequently accepted in *Birmingham (No 2)*), that the LA had to mirror the provision made by a grant maintained school for boys by having equivalent provision for girls.[194]

(d)   There was no de minimis exception. If it was proved that there had been discrimination against one person, it was no answer to say it was only one.[195]

(e)   A mere difference in the number of places available was not an act of sex discrimination. An education authority did not discriminate against girls because there were more unfilled places in the boys only schools than there were in the girls only schools.[196]

3.37   These duties are almost impossible to perform. The problems set out below arise. Some of these arose under the previous statutory scheme and, it is submitted, continue to arise under the present scheme. Further fresh problems have been created by the new statutory scheme. Just some of the problems that arise are:

(a)   Single sex schools were, and continue to be, lawful. However, the LA is under a duty to ensure that a girl has the same chance of getting a single sex place as she would have done if she was a boy in any given year. It cannot perform this duty by having equal numbers of single sex places for girls and boys because, as is often the case in practice, there may be more

---

[191]   Unreported on this point. Transcript 24 May 1990. Mustill and Nicholls LJJ expressly reserved their position on the implications of the SDA 1975. They held that the Secretary of State did not have to reach a view on the then undecided point of the school acquiring grant maintained status.

[192]   (Unreported) 24 May 1990, at 61H to 62B. Section 8 of the EA 1944 was the predecessor to s 14 of the EA 1996.

[193]   (Unreported) 24 May 1990, at 62C–62F.

[194]   (Unreported) 24 May 1990, at 63D–64C.

[195]   (Unreported) 24 May 1990, at 64D–64F.

[196]   (Unreported) 24 May 1990, at 64G.

demand for single sex places, for girls rather than boys and vice versa.[197] Because the demand for single sex places is variable, but the capacity of single sex schools is not, the LA is at risk that in any given year its provision will be in breach of the Act, but it will, in practice have very limited power to do anything about it.[198] Whether this is an act of discrimination for which the LA is responsible has yet to be decided by the courts. In circumstances where an LA has done everything it reasonably can to ensure that its provision does meet the likely demand, it should not be held to be a breach of the EqA 2010 when in one year girls get places they would not have got had they been boys or vice versa, providing that there is no consistent pattern of one or other sex being treated less favourably. It is possible to argue that, in circumstances where the LA has not consistently maintained schools which inevitably discriminate against one sex, it does not commit the act of discrimination identified by the House of Lords in the first *Birmingham* case. Accordingly, so the argument would run, while there is discrimination against the individual girl or boy as the case may be, it is not discrimination for which the LA is responsible because it is not knowingly maintaining a system that inevitably discriminates against one sex. The difficulty with this argument is that in the second *Birmingham* case the Court of Appeal identified the act of discrimination as being a failure to secure equal educational opportunities in the LA area. Accordingly, reconsideration by the House of Lords is likely to be needed to resolve the point.

(b) Where there is an imbalance in the provision of single sex education places, the ability of the LA to take remedial action has been made more difficult by the EA 2011. Section 37 and paragraphs 1 and 2 of Schedule 3 to that Act inserted a new section 6A[199] into the Education and

---

[197] This was the conclusion reached by Hutton J in the High Court of Justice in Northern Ireland in the case of *In the Matter of an Application by the Equal Opportunities Commission for Northern Ireland, Kathleen Hackett, Leo Vincent Sharkey, Michael Woods and Patrick Lundy for Judicial Review* (unreported) 1 July 1988. The Judge held that the quota system for grammar school places was unlawful. The Department of Education and the Education and Library Boards had decided that 27 per cent of boys and 27 per cent of girls in the total transfer group in Northern Ireland for the year 1987/88 would be awarded the right to non-fee paying places in grammar schools on the basis of performance in the Eleven Plus Examination. The girls did better than the boys in the exam with the consequence that some boys got places they would not have done had they been girls. It was held that this was unlawful discrimination although relief was only granted to the Equal Opportunities Commission and not to the girls because they could not prove they would have got places had the unlawful discrimination not occurred. Although this is a decision of High Court of Justice of Northern Ireland on legislation only applying in Northern Ireland, there can be little doubt that the same result would follow under what is now the Equality Act 2010.

[198] It may be that its only power would be to purchase a single sex place in a fee paying school for the girl or boy who would otherwise be the victim of unlawful sex discrimination. However, the parents may have a perfectly reasonable objection to their child being educated at an independent school. In those circumstances it is difficult to see the LA would have any action it could take to remedy the possible breach. This problem has been known about for decades and it is a great pity that no action was taken to remedy it when the EqA 2010 was passed.

[199] In force from 1 February 2012 with transitional provisions for, broadly, proposals submitted before that date: see arts 3 and 4 of SI 2012/84.

Inspections Act 2006. If an LA in England think a new school has to be established (for example to address inequality of single sex provision for boys and girls) they have to seek proposals for an Academy. No provision is made for the LA to be immune from proceedings for sex discrimination while they are undertaking this procedure.

(c)   Where the single sex places are also selective and are now wholly situated in Academies, the severe problems that existed under the previous legislation are now even more acute. The LA has to take account of the fact[200] that there are selective places available in its area. If there is an imbalance the LA is powerless to remedy that like for like because, it cannot close vary or create Academy places[201] and is now prohibited from creating new grammar schools.[202] The EqA 2010 does not provide any clue as to how the LA can perform its equality duty in those circumstances. Of course it remains open to the LA to buy selective independent school places, but this may not satisfy the parents who object to independent schools and is not in any event the same as what the apparent victim of sex discrimination has lost.

(d)   There is equivalent demand for single sex education from boys and girls in the LA area and the LA has appropriate provision to meet that demand. However, one of the boys' schools is on the boundary of the LA and there is a large demand for places at that school from outside the LA area. Because the LA cannot treat those from outside the area less favourably than those within the area the consequence is that the boys from outside the area take up many of the available places at the boys' school with the consequence that boys in the LA area in which the school is situated have a less good chance than girls in getting a single sex place. This would seem to be a breach of the EqA 2010.

(e)   The LA is not in breach of its duty under the EqA 2010 because it has appropriate equivalent provision for single sex places for boys and girls. A single sex Academy is then established in the LA. The LA is immediately in breach of the EqA 2010 because it has to take account of the places in the Academy but cannot take steps immediately to remedy that breach.

3.38 The problems outlined above in relation to single-sex schools are problems of direct rather than indirect discrimination. In other words, it is no defence to the LA that it has not willingly breached the Act and that its action is justifiable having regard to administrative constraints upon it. In *R v Secretary of State for Education ex parte Malik*,[203] Rose J, obiter, suggested that

---

[200]   See paras **3.35** and **3.36** above.

[201]   The duty under s 6A of the Education and Inspections Act 2006 merely obliges the LA to seek proposals for Academies. It does not enable the LA to create Academies itself and if no proposals for Academies are forthcoming there is nothing the LA can do to remedy that.

[202]   Only schools which had selective admission arrangements in 1997/1998 can be designated by the Secretary of State as grammar schools under the SSFA 1998 as amended.

[203]   [1994] ELR 121 at 129H–130A.

it might be possible to view a school closure decision leading to potential breach of what were then ss 23 and 25 of the SDA 1975 as indirect rather than direct discrimination and hence justifiable. The point was not elaborated upon and it is difficult to reconcile this view of the law with the decision of the House of Lords in *R v Birmingham ex parte EOC*.[204] It is submitted that, despite the attractiveness of the suggestion that justification is in place in this area, there is at present no such defence. However, the absence of a defence of justification to a claim in direct discrimination was regarded as a defect in the law by the President of the Supreme Court in *R(E) v Governing Body of JFS and another*.[205] While there is much force in that remark, it is probably not open to the courts to create such a defence.[206] That makes it all the more unfortunate that Parliament failed to address these issues when passing the EqA 2010.[207]

The relevant pool – the LA area

3.39 Does the LA have to ensure that it has equal opportunities for boys and girls in each part of its area or in its area as a whole? This problem has been considered three times by the courts. In *R v Avon ex parte Keating*[208] Taylor J held that there was a breach of the act if boys had to travel further than girls to get a single-sex place. In *R v Kingston ex parte Emsden*[209] Schiemann J held that the LA's duties under section 8 of the EA 1944 were not breached when the opportunities for pupils in the area were not equal depending on where they lived. Although that case did not consider sex discrimination, it stressed that the section 8 duty is determined by the area as a whole. Further, *in R v Secretary of State for Education ex parte Connon and Davies*[210] Turner J held that the duty of the LEA under section 8 of the EA 1944 read with section 23 of the SDA 1975 was determined by the area as a whole and that the LEA was not obliged to ensure that there was equal provision in different parts of its area providing there were equal opportunities in the area as a whole. It is submitted that this is the better view. If the relevant pool is not the LA area then no guide is given in what is now the EqA 2010 as to what the pool is and it is wholly impracticable to ensure that no boy will have to travel more than a girl to get a single-sex place.

---

[204] [1989] AC 1155.

[205] [2009] UKSC 15, [2010] 2 AC 728 per Lord Philips at para 9. Lord Clarke, at para 152, regarded the absence of a justification defence as representing a deliberate policy choice by Parliament. Lord Hope noted at para 184 that the Act did not distinguish between discrimination which was invidious and that which was benign and described this as a problem before making reference to the absence of a test of justification for direct discrimination. Lord Walker noted at para 237 that the sharp distinction between the impossibility of justifying direct discrimination in any circumstances and the possibility of justifying indirect discrimination seemed 'sometimes' a little arbitrary.

[206] As Baroness Hale recognised at para 70.

[207] At the time of *JFS*, the Equalities Bill was going through Parliament. Baroness Hale noted this in terms at para 70 of her speech and in the light of that it is a great shame the opportunity she referred to as being available to deal with introducing a defence of justification was not taken.

[208] 84 LGR 469 at 477–479.

[209] 91 LGR 96 at 99–102.

[210] [1996] COD 454.

Duties in relation to different designation of schools

3.40 As we have seen at para **3.35** above, the Court of Appeal held in *Birmingham (No 2)* that the council had to take account of grant maintained schools when performing its duties. They suggested that the council also had to take account of independent schools provided under the assisted places scheme.[211] It follows from *Birmingham (No 2)* that a mere difference in legal status not relating to the character of the school falls to be ignored when determining whether an LA is in breach of its duty under the EqA 2010. It also follows from *Birmingham (No 2)*, albeit the point was given no consideration by the Court of Appeal in that case, that a difference between the funding arrangements between LA-maintained schools and other schools does not prevent them being equated.

3.41 How do Academies established under s 482 of the EA 1996 fit into the LA duties under the EqA 2010? These schools are independent schools established and funded by the Secretary of State and not the LA. Following the reasoning in *Birmingham (No 2)*, the LA would have to take them into account but it has no power to mirror their provision. If the Secretary of State agrees to establish a single-sex boys' Academy, how does the LEA take account of this when deciding what provision it needs to make for girls to avoid sex discrimination? While it could still seek to perform its duties under the EqA 2010 by having a maintained school that, as a matter of fact, provided education that was of the same standard it is difficult to see that that would be enough. In the first *Birmingham* case it was no defence to the city council that its comprehensive schools were as good as its selective schools because the issue was, had a parent been denied an option which was reasonably regarded as of value? A parent could reasonably say that the option of going to an Academy was reasonably regarded as of value and it was not sufficient that LA-maintained schools covered the same curriculum. Moreover, as we have see from paragraph **3.37(b)** above, the LA cannot merely establish a maintained school; the effect of section 6A of the Education and inspections Act 2006 is that if it needs a new school it has to seek proposals for the establishment of an Academy first.

3.42 In *R v Secretary of State for Education ex parte Connon and Davies*,[212] Turner J had to consider whether a school which had designated technology status (as distinct from being a City Technology College established under section 105 of Education Reform Act 1988)[213] had to be equally available for boys and girls. Schools with designated technology status did not enjoy a different status in law from other schools which are maintained by the LA,

---

[211] The duty of the Secretary of State to operate the assisted places scheme was abolished by the Education (Schools) Act 1997, the material provisions of which came into force on 1 September 1997. However, those currently with assisted places at secondary schools may keep their places until they complete their education at their current school, so the potential discrimination problem in relation to the assisted places scheme will continue for a few years.

[212] [1996] COD 454.

[213] See now s 482 of the EA 1996 as substituted by s 65 of the EA 2002. City Technology Colleges have, under that section, now been replaced by Academies.

although they did get better funding. It was held that the Secretary of State for Education had not behaved unlawfully in rejecting proposals for a technology school, Central Technology College, to go fully co-educational by admitting pre-sixth form girls, even though there was no other technology school available for girls in Gloucester, the nearest one being in Cirencester. One ground for the decision was that it was appropriate to take account of the school in Cirencester, but the judge appears also to have accepted the submission that it was appropriate for the Secretary of State to take account of the technology provision available for girls at Barnwood Park, which was eligible for technology status but had not yet acquired it.

3.43 If a school is not of a different legal status or character, then it is not discrimination to deprive one sex of the opportunity to go to that school. It is important to appreciate when formulating the test of deprivation (an option reasonably regarded as of value in *Birmingham (No 1)*) that the context was of an option which was undoubtedly of a different character (selective education). It is submitted that that test has no application where what is denied to one sex is neither of a different character or legal status. In that context, the court is simply concerned with whether one sex is treated less favourably than another. If the Secretary of State had considered in *Connon and Davies* that the opportunities at Barnwood Park were significantly less good than those at Central Technology College, no doubt she would rightly have held that rejection of the proposals would infringe the SDA 1975.

3.44 How the LA performs its duties under the EqA 2010 is a matter for it alone. Under the previous law the LA could lawfully publish proposals even where, if they were approved by the Secretary of State, at the moment of approval the duty on the LEA under the SDA 1975 was left unperformed, providing the LA was conscious of its duties under that Act.[214] It is probable that this is the position under the present law.

3.45 Most of the problems set out above are not new. Although these problems have not gone away, there have been no recent reported cases resolving these issues. This may be considered surprising but the increasing popularity of Academies means that it may not be long before these issues arise once more. If and when they do, it will not necessarily be in (or solely in) the context of sex discrimination: as has been seen, the provisions in the EqA 2010 now go much wider with only age and religious or belief related discrimination being excluded from the protected characteristics which are within the scope of section 29 of the EqA 2010 and also section 14 of the 1996 Act.

---

[214] *R v Northamptonshire ex parte K* [1994] ELR 397 at 402E.

DUTIES IN RESPECT OF SCHOOLS: PART 6, CHAPTER 1 OF THE EQA 2010

3.46 Part 6, Chapter 1 of the EqA 2010 (sections 81–89) is concerned with schools and applies to all schools (including Academies), whether maintained or independent.[215] Section 85 imposes a number of duties on the responsible body for a school not to discriminate against pupils and potential pupils.[216] In relation to independent educational institutions, alternative provision Academies that are not independent educational institutions and special schools not maintained by an LA, the responsible body is the proprietor.[217]

3.47 The responsible body in relation to maintained schools is either the LA[218] or the governing body,[219] the answer as to which it is in any situation appearing to depend upon which of the two is responsible for the matters alleged to constitute discrimination.[220] This identification may be important but even where there is no doubt, an understanding and appreciation of the division of responsibilities between a maintained school and an LA (and for that matter a parent) may be required. In *K v SENDIST*[221] a claim of disability discrimination against a school for refusing to clean and change an incontinent pupil failed on the basis that it was not safe for the school to do so, and it was for the LA, having been approached by the school for assistance and an amendment to his statement of special educational needs, to provide the additional facilities needed to clean and change him safely. There does not appear to have been any criticism of the LA on the facts of this case (either by the parent or the court) but the Court of Appeal found unattractive Mrs K's resistance to the school's attempts to have the statement amended, saying that 'if a parent obstructs the only realistic avenue open to a school to meet a disabled child's particular needs, that parent cannot at the same time accuse the

---

[215] The full list is as follows: (1) schools maintained by an LA, (2) independent educational institutions (other than a special school), (3) an alternative provision Academy that is not an independent educational institution, and (4) a special school (not maintained by an LA): s 85(7). Further definitions are provided as follows: (1) 'school' has the meaning given in s 4 of the EA 1996 (s 89(5)); (2) a reference to a school includes a reference to an independent educational institution in England, (3) a reference to an independent educational institution is a reference to an independent educational institution in England or an independent school in Wales (s 89(7)), (4) references to an independent educational institution in England is to be construed in accordance with Ch 1 of Pt 4 of the Education and Skills Act 2008 (s 89(6)), (5) in relation to Wales, independent school has the meaning given in s 463 of the EA 1996 (s 89(8)(a)), (6) special school has the meaning given in s 337 of the EA 1996. 'Alternative provision Academy' is not defined in the EqA 2010, but is an Academy that meets the requirements of s 1C of the Academies Act 2010.

[216] 'Pupil' has the meaning given in s 3(1) of the EA 1996: s 89(3).

[217] Section 85(9)(b). 'Proprietor' has the meaning given in s 579(1) of the EA 1996: s 89(4)(a). For the definitions of these types of schools see fn 214 above.

[218] As defined in s 162 of the Education and Inspections Act 2006: s 89(10).

[219] Section 85(9)(a).

[220] The DDA 1995 said the same but added 'according to which has the function in question': see Sch 4A, para 1. The omission of these words from the EqA 2010 suggests these words were otiose since it is difficult to discern a change of substance or at least what change was intended.

[221] [2007] EWCA Civ 165, [2007] ELR 234.

school of discriminating against the child if the school, as a consequence, is unable to provide the services which the child needs'.[222]

3.48 There are two important exceptions to all of the duties in this Chapter:

(1) The protected characteristics of age and marriage and civil partnership are entirely excluded from this Chapter, so discrimination on either of these grounds is not unlawful.[223]

(2) Nothing in this Chapter applies to anything done in connection with the content of the curriculum.[224] According to the Explanatory Notes,[225] this exception 'ensures that the Act does not inhibit the ability of schools to include a full range of issues, ideas and materials in their syllabus and to expose pupils to thoughts and ideas of all kinds'. The examples given are of a school curriculum which includes 'The Taming of the Shrew' on the syllabus and the teaching of evolution in science lessons, the first of which is said not to be discrimination against a girl, and the second of which is said not to be religious discrimination against a pupil whose religious beliefs include creationism. The Explanatory Notes do, however, make clear that the *way* in which the curriculum is taught *is* covered by the Act so as to ensure issues are taught in a way which does not subject pupils to discrimination.

Duties in section 85

3.49 The duties in section 85 fall into the following categories which are considered in turn: (a) admissions ('admissions duties'), (b) provision of education and access to benefits, facilities and services ('provision of education duties') and (c) the duty to make adjustments.

Admissions duties

3.50 The admissions duties consist of the following three duties imposed on a responsible body of a school:

(1) Not to discriminate against a person: (a) in the arrangements it makes for deciding who is offered admission as a pupil, (b) as to the terms on which it offers to admit the person as a pupil, or (c) by not admitting the person as a pupil.[226]

---

[222] [2007] EWCA Civ 165, [2007] ELR 234 at [53].

[223] Section 84. The Explanatory Notes give two examples to illustrate this (see para 291): '(1) It is not unlawful discrimination for a school to organise a trip for pupils in one year group, but not for pupils in other years. (2) It is not unlawful discrimination for a school to allow older pupils to have privileges for which younger pupils are not eligible, such as more choice of uniform or the right to leave school during the lunch period.'

[224] Section 89(2).

[225] See paras 302–303.

[226] Section 85(1). The Explanatory Notes give the following example (see para 295): 'A selective

(2)   Not to victimise a person in any of these ways in (1)(a)–(c).[227] As noted at
       para **3.18(i)** above, the definition of victimisation is extended in the
       context of schools to protect children from being victimised by protected
       acts done by a parent or sibling.
           (3) Not to harass a person who has applied for admission as a pupil.[228]

3.51   The admissions duties are subject to the following exceptions:

(a)   The duty not to discriminate, so far as relating to sex, does not apply in
       relation to a single-sex school or certain boarding schools.[229] A single-sex
       school is a school which admits pupils of one sex only or is deemed to do
       so by the Act for these purposes.[230] A school is deemed to be single-sex if
       it has pupils of the opposite sex but their admission to the school is either
       exceptional or their numbers are comparatively small and their admission
       is confined to particular courses or classes.[231] The boarding schools which
       are excluded are those schools (other than single-sex schools) which have
       some pupils as boarders and others as non-boarders and either: (a) admit
       as boarders pupils of one sex only, or (b) have boarders of the opposite
       sex but their numbers are small compared to the numbers of other pupils
       admitted as boarders.[232] A single-sex school which decides to become
       co-educational, or a boarding school which decides to change its
       admissions arrangements so that it will no longer benefit from the above
       exemptions, may require a transitional exemption order to avoid
       contravening the Act whilst that process is completed. The Act makes
       detailed provision is made about such orders,[233] but what is important to
       note is that they only relate to admissions.[234]

---

school imposes a higher standard for admission to applicants from an ethnic minority
background, or to girls. This would be direct discrimination.'

[227]   Section 85(4).
[228]   Section 85(3)(b).
[229]   Schedule 11, paras 1–2. The Explanatory Notes give the following five examples to illustrate
        the rules about single-sex schools (see para 862): '(1) A school which admits only boys is not
        discriminating unlawfully against girls. (2) If the daughters or certain members of staff at a
        boys' school are allowed to attend, it is still regarded as a single-sex school. (3) A boys' school
        which admits some girls to the Sixth Form, or which lets girls attend for a particular GCSE
        course not offered at their own school, is still regarded as a single-sex school. (4) A boys'
        school which admits girls to A-level science classes is not discriminating unlawfully if it refuses
        to admit them to A-level media studies or maths classes. (5) A boys' school which admits girls
        to the Sixth Form but refuses to let them use the same cafeteria or go on the same visits as
        other Sixth Form pupils would be discriminating unlawfully against them.' The example given
        about boarding schools is as follows (see para 863): 'A mixed-sex school has facilities for female
        boarders and can lawfully state in its prospectus that males cannot be accepted as boarders.'
[230]   Schedule 11, para 1(2).
[231]   Schedule 11, para 1(3)–(4).
[232]   Schedule 11, para 2.
[233]   Schedule 11, paras 3–4.
[234]   The Explanatory Notes say the following about these orders (see para 865): 'Where a
        transitional exemption order is made in accordance with the arrangements in para 4: (1) A
        boys' school which decides to become co-educational by starting to admit girls to Year 7 while
        keeping upper classes as they are, will not be discriminating unlawfully by refusing to admit
        girls to other years, until co-educational classes have been phased in throughout the school. (2)

(b) The duty not to discriminate in admissions, so far as relating to religion or belief, does not apply to foundation or voluntary schools with religious character,[235] or to independent schools who are registered as having a religious ethos.[236] However, deciding whether the discrimination relates to religion or belief may be difficult and controversial. In *R (E) v JFS Governing Body*,[237] it was held by six of a nine-judge Supreme Court that one of a Jewish school's admission requirements, namely matrilineal descent from a Jewish woman, was a test of ethnic origin and so constituted direct racial discrimination.

(c) There is no breach of the duty not to discriminate in admissions, so far as relating to disability, only as a result of the application of a permitted form of selection.[238] The forms permitted vary according to the type of school. In the case of a maintained school[239] which is designated as a grammar school, this means its selective admission arrangements.[240] In the case of a maintained school[241] which is not so designated, it means a form of selection which is permitted by law.[242] In the case of an independent educational institution, this means arrangements which provide for some or all of its pupils to be selected by reference to general or special ability or aptitude, with a view to admitting only pupils of high ability or aptitude.[243]

(d) In respect of the duty not to harass, none of the following is a relevant protected characteristic: gender reassignment, religion or belief and sexual orientation.[244] However, this does not prevent conduct relating to those

---

A girls' school which decides to become co-educational by initially admitting a certain number of boys to each year group will not be discriminating unlawfully by reserving a number of places in each year group for boys. (3) A school in the process of becoming co-educational must treat its male and female pupils equally once they have been admitted, since the transitional exemption order only relates to admissions.'

[235] That is, a school so designated under s 69(3) of the SSFA 1998.

[236] Schedule 11, para 5. The Explanatory Notes give the following example (see para 868): 'A Muslim school may give priority to Muslim pupils when choosing between applicants for admission (although the Admissions Code will not allow it to refuse to accept pupils of another or no religion unless it is oversubscribed). However, it may not discriminate between pupils because of any other of the protected characteristics, such as by refusing to admit a child of the school's own faith because she is black or a lesbian.'

[237] [2010] 2 AC 728.

[238] Schedule 11, para 8. The Explanatory Notes say (at para 874) that the effect of this exclusion is that: 'The parents of a disabled pupil cannot claim disability discrimination against a particular school if that pupil fails to meet any educational entry requirements set by the school.'

[239] 'Maintained school' has the meaning given in s 22 of the SSFA 1998: Sch 11, para 8(4).

[240] Within the meaning of s 104 of the SSFA 1998: Sch 11 para 8(2)(b).

[241] See fn 238 above.

[242] In other words, a form of selection mentioned in section 99(2) or (4) of the SSFA 1998.

[243] Schedule 11, para 8(2)(c).

[244] Section 85(10).

characteristics from amounting to a detriment for the purposes of discrimination within section 13 (direct discrimination) because of that characteristic.[245]

3.52   While a school cannot discriminate by refusing to admit a pupil who has a relevant protected characteristic, it is doubtful whether it can refuse to admit a pupil even when it knows that the reason the parents want the pupil to go the school is that they do not want the child to go to another school because of the presence there of other pupils with a relevant protected characteristic. This problem arose under the previous statutory scheme. By virtue of section 86 of the SSFA 1998,[246] a parent has a right to express a preference as to where his child should go to school. That preference must be acceded to unless one of the derogations referred to in section 86(2) of the SSFA 1998 are made out. In *R v Cleveland ex parte the Commission for Racial Equality*[247] the Court of Appeal held that an LA had to accept a preference made on racial grounds and that the court could not read into what is now section 86(3) of the SSFA 1998[248] a further exception enabling the LA to refuse to comply with such a preference. The Court of Appeal held that there had been no breach of the then applicable legislation, section 18 of the RRA 1976, but if there had been, it would have been rendered lawful by section 41(1)(a) of the RRA 1976[249] because the duty in what was then section 6 of the EA 1980[250] was mandatory.

3.53   The courts were driven to this conclusion because there was no machinery in the Act which enabled an LA to investigate the true reasons for the preference and it was accordingly accepted by counsel for the Commission for Racial Equality (CRE) that a council would have to act on the reasons expressed by the parent, even if it knew that those reasons were untrue. Therefore, had the court held that a choice based on racial grounds was unlawful, there was nothing to stop a parent expressing a preference and keeping quiet about race being the reason for the choice. In those circumstances it was conceded that the council would have to comply with the preference. Very little would have been gained, therefore, by holding that it was only the preference expressed on racial grounds which was unlawful.

3.54   Although this case was decided on the old law, it is submitted that it still applies under the EqA 2010. There has been no relevant amendment of the SSFA 1998 and the responsible body would still be forced to admit a child even when it knew that the choice had been made on racial grounds. Indeed the reasoning would be equally applicable where the choice had been made because of a relevant protected characteristic. It is to be regretted, however, that the law does apparently permit a choice of school to be made on such grounds.

---

[245]   Section 212(5).
[246]   Formerly s 6 of the EA 1980. For discussion see Ch 5 at paras **5.11–5.20** below.
[247]   [1994] ELR 44.
[248]   Formerly s 6(3) of the 1980 Act.
[249]   See now para 1 of Sch 22 discussed at para **3.19(e)** above.
[250]   Now s 86 of the SSFA 1998.

Provision of education duties

3.55 The provision of education duties consist of the following three duties imposed on the responsible body of a school:

(1) Not to discriminate against a pupil: (a) in the way it provides education for the pupil, (b) in the way it affords the pupil access to a benefit, facility or service, (c) by not providing education for the pupil, (d) by excluding the pupil from the school, or (e) by subjecting the pupil to any other detriment.[251] References to providing or affording access to a benefit, facility or service include a reference to facilitating access to the benefit, facility or service.[252]

(2) Not to victimise a pupil in the ways listed in (1)(a)–(e).[253] As noted at para **3.18(i)** above, the definition of victimisation is extended in the context of schools to protect children from being victimised by protected acts done by a parent or sibling.

(3) Not to harass a pupil.[254]

3.56 The provision of education duties are subject to the following exceptions:

(a) The duties in (1)(a)-(d), so far as relating to sex, do not apply in relation to boarding facilities at boarding schools which benefit from the exception in relation to admissions noted above (see para **3.51(a)**).[255] Neither do these duties prohibit 'deemed' single-sex schools (see the same para above) from confining pupils of the same sex to a particular course or classes.[256]

---

[251] Section 85(2). The Explanatory Notes give an example of this (see para 295): 'A school refuses to let a gay pupil become a prefect because of his sexual orientation. This would be direct discrimination.'

[252] Section 212(4).

[253] Section 85(5). The Explanatory Notes give the following examples (see paras 295 and 298): '(1) A pupil alleges, in good faith, that his school has discriminated against him because of his religion (for example claiming that he is given worse marks than other pupils because he is Jewish), so the school punishes him by making him do a detention. This would be victimisation. (2) The parent of a pupil complains to the school that her daughter is suffering sex discrimination by not being allowed to participate in a metalwork class. The daughter is protected from being treated less favourably by the school in any way because of this complaint. (3) A pupil brings a case against his school claiming that he has suffered discrimination by a member of staff because of his sexual orientation. The pupil's younger brother, at the same school, is protected against any less favourable treatment by the school because of this case, even if it is later found that the older brother was not acting in good faith.'

[254] Section 85(3)(a). The Explanatory Notes given the following example (see para 295): 'A teacher ridicules a particular pupil in class because of his disability, or makes comments which have the result of making the girls in the class feel embarrassed and humiliated. This would be harassment.'

[255] Schedule 11, para 2(2).

[256] Schedule 11, para 1(4).

(b)   The duties in (1)(a)–(d), so far as relating to religion or belief, do not
       apply to foundation or voluntary schools with religious character,[257] or to
       independent schools[258] who are registered as having a religious ethos.[259]

(c)   The duties in (1)(a)–(d) above, so far as relating to religion or belief, do
       not apply in relation to anything done in connection with acts of worship
       or other religious observance organised by or on behalf of any school
       (whether or not forming part of the curriculum).[260]

(d)   In respect of the duty not to harass, none of the following is a relevant
       protected characteristic: gender reassignment, religion or belief and sexual
       orientation.[261] However, this does not prevent conduct relating to those
       characteristics from amounting to a detriment for the purposes of
       discrimination within section 13 (direct discrimination) because of that
       characteristic.[262]

3.57   As we have seen from para **3.18(e)** above, prohibited conduct includes
treating a woman unfavourably because of pregnancy. A school may have a rule
that the pupils should not engage in sexual relations with each other. Breach of
such a rule might involve disciplinary sanctions. Suppose that as a result of
breach of such a rule the girl becomes pregnant. Can the school take
disciplinary action against the girl not for becoming pregnant but because she
broke the rule prohibiting sexual relations? It is submitted that the school can
because this is not a case like *James v Eastleigh BC*[263] where breach of the rule
and becoming pregnant are two sides of the same coin. True, the girl would not
have become pregnant unless she had broken the rule, but it was not a
necessary consequence of breach of the rule that she became pregnant. If
disciplinary action would have been lawful, as it is submitted it would, for
breach of the rule had she not become pregnant, then it is submitted that it

---

[257]   That is, a school so designated under s 69(3) of the SSFA 1998.
[258]   Schedule 11, para 5(b).
[259]   Schedule 11, para 5. The Explanatory Notes give the following example (see para 868): 'A
         Muslim school may give priority to Muslim pupils when choosing between applicants for
         admission (although the Admissions Code will not allow it to refuse to accept pupils of
         another or no religion unless it is oversubscribed). However, it may not discriminate between
         pupils because of any other of the protected characteristics, such as by refusing to admit a
         child of the school's own faith because she is black or a lesbian.'
[260]   Schedule 11, para 6. The Explanatory Notes say the following about this provision (see
         para 870): '(1) Under education law, a school must allow Jewish or Hindu parents to withdraw
         their children from daily assemblies which include an element of worship of a mainly Christian
         character, but it will not be discriminating unlawfully against those children by not providing
         alternative assemblies including Jewish or Hindu worship. (2) Schools are free to organise or to
         participate in ceremonies celebrating any faith, such as Christmas, Diwali, Chanukah or Eid,
         without being subject to claims of religious discrimination against children of other religions
         or of none.'
[261]   Section 85(10).
[262]   Section 212(5).
[263]   [1990] 2 AC 751.

should not cease to be lawful because she became pregnant as well. It is only imposing further sanctions on the girl for the pregnancy itself that is the prohibited conduct.

3.58 It is only the girl who is protected from less favourable treatment because of her pregnancy. Does this mean that the boy who also breached the relevant rule prohibiting sexual relations can be disciplined not only for breach of the rule but also for making the girl pregnant? As far as a breach of a rule prohibiting sexual relations is concerned it is submitted that the boy is in the same position as the girl and can be disciplined for its breach whether or not the girl becomes pregnant. Whether he can be disciplined for making the girl pregnant is less clear. If he can then he is treated less favourably than the girl which is prima facie sex discrimination but legitimised by section 13(6)(b) of the EqA 2010. However, it is less favourable treatment arising from the special protected status of pregnancy which he does not have. It seems therefore he could be disciplined for making the girl pregnant. In practice this may not matter if both the boy and girl can be disciplined for breach of a rule prohibiting sexual relations.

Duty to make adjustments

3.59 The duty to make reasonable adjustments applies only to disabled pupils (and disabled potential pupils). Its imposition by section 85(6) triggers the duties in sections 20–22 (see para **3.18(g)** above), but it is Schedule 13 which provides for how those duties apply in the education field. Schedule 13 provides first of all that that the responsible body is only obliged to comply with the first and third of the three requirements in section 20. As such, whilst the first requirement does not make clear (as did the DDA 1995) that it cannot oblige the provision of an auxiliary aid, this appears to be the only sensible reading of the Act. It follows from this that the issue of whether an adjustment sought constitutes an auxiliary aid may still arise, and thus there will be cause to regret that the Court of Appeal did not take the opportunity that was presented to it in *D v Bedfordshire CC*[264] to provide guidance on this point.[265]

3.60 In relation to the first requirement, Schedule 13 provides for how the wording of that requirement in section 20(3) is to be read in this context. Reading the two together, the duty on the responsible body (A) is as follows:

'where a provision, criterion or practice applied by or on behalf of A puts disabled persons/pupils[266] generally at a substantial disadvantage in relation to: (a) deciding who is offered admission as a pupil, or (b) the provision of education or access to

---

[264] [2009] EWCA Civ 678, [2009] ELR 361.

[265] The decision of the tribunal was quashed and remitted for reconsideration but that was simply on the basis that findings of fact the court considered necessary had not been made: see [20] and [26]. On the issue of 'auxiliary aid' the court did no more than note the dictionary definition of 'auxiliary' but say the argument was for another day: see [23].

[266] The relevant word is 'persons' in respect of (a) and 'pupils' in respect of (b).

a benefit, facility or service, in comparison with persons who are not disabled, to take such steps as it is reasonable to have to take to avoid the disadvantage.'

3.61   In deciding whether it is reasonable for A to have to take a step for the purpose of complying with any of the three requirements, A must have regard to two particular matters: (1) relevant provisions of a code of practice issued under section 14 of the EA 2006,[267] and (2) the extent to which taking the step is consistent with any request that has been made to keep confidential the nature or existence of the disabled person's disability.[268]

Miscellaneous: accessibility plans and strategies

3.62   Schedule 10 to the EqA 2010[269] provides that local authorities and schools[270] must prepare, implement, keep under review and revise if necessary, a written accessibility strategy or plan[271] and further such strategies or plans at such times as may be prescribed.[272] An accessibility strategy is a strategy for, over a prescribed period: (a) increasing the extent to which disabled pupils can participate in the schools' curriculums, (b) improving the physical environment of the schools for the purpose of increasing the extent to which disabled pupils are able to take advantage of education and benefits, facilities or services

---

[267]   Schedule 13, para 7. The EHRC has issued a Statutory Code of Practice 'Services, public functions and associations' which became law on 6 April 2011. That Code covers inter alia Part 3 of the Act but not Part 6: see para 1.6 of the Code. It is therefore of some relevance to the matters covered in this Chapter although does not cover the whole field and in particular the responsibility of schools under Part 6. The Commission's wesbite states that it had intended to produce further statutory codes of practice on the Public Sector Equality Duty and codes for the Further and Higher Education sector and schools but that it had been unable to proceed with its plans because the Government was 'keen to reduce bureaucracy around the Equality Act 2010 ...'.

[268]   Schedule 13, para 8. In respect of schools, the request (called a 'confidentiality request') is only valid if made by the disabled person's parents or by the disabled person and A reasonably believes that the person has sufficient understanding of the nature and effect of the request: Sch 13, para 8(3)–(5). In respect of further and higher education institutions the request can only be made by the disabled person: Sch 13, para 8(6).

[269]   Given effect by s 88.

[270]   The duty is imposed upon an LA in respect of schools for which it is the responsible body, and upon the responsible body of a school: Sch 10, paras 1 and 3. Responsible body means: (a) in relation to a maintained school or a maintained nursery school, the LA or governing body, (b) in relation to a pupil referral unit, the LA, (c) in relation to an independent educational institution or an alternative provision Academy that is not an independent educational institution, the proprietor, and (d) in relation to a special school not maintained by an LA, the proprietor: Sch 10, para 6(5). 'Governing body', in relation to a maintained school, means the body corporate (constituted in accordance with regs under s 19 of the EA 2002) which the school has as a result of that section: Sch 10, para 6(6). 'Maintained school' has the meaning given in s 20 of the SSFA 1998 and 'maintained nursery school' has the meaning given in s 22 of that Act: Sch 10, para 6(7).

[271]   The document local authorities are obliged to produce is termed a 'strategy', and that by schools a 'plan'.

[272]   Schedule10, para 1(1), (4)–(6), paragraph 3(1), (4)–(6). As at 4 October 2012 no regulations had been made.

provided or offered by the schools, and (c) improving the delivery[273] to disabled pupils of information which is readily accessible to pupils who are not disabled.[274] References to 'disabled pupils' include a disabled person who may be admitted to the school.[275] An accessibility plan is identical save that it relates only to the particular school for which it has been produced.[276]

3.63 In preparing these documents, local authorities and schools must have regard to the need to allocate adequate resources for implementing them[277] and local authorities must additionally have regard to any statutory guidance.[278] Strategies and plans must be made available for inspection at such reasonable times as the LA or school may decide and copies must be provided to a Minister of the Crown (if in England) or the Welsh Ministers (if in Wales) upon request.[279] School inspections[280] may extend to the performance by the responsible body of its functions in relation to the preparation, publication, review, revision and implementation of its accessibility plan.[281]

3.64 Enforcement of the duties under this Schedule is dealt with below.

DUTIES OWED BY FURTHER AND HIGHER EDUCATION INSTITUTIONS: PART 6, CHAPTER 2 OF THE EQA 2010

3.65 The duties imposed by Chapter 2 of Part 6 (sections 90–94) closely parallel those imposed in respect of schools by Chapter 1. As with schools, nothing in this Chapter applies to anything done in connection with the content of the curriculum.[282] However, the only protected characteristic

---

[273] The delivery must be within a reasonable time and in ways which are determined after taking account of the pupils' disabilities and any preferences expressed by them or their parents: Sch 10, para 1(3).

[274] Schedule 10, para 1(2).

[275] Schedule 10, para 6(4).

[276] Schedule 10, para 3(2)–(3). The example given by the Explanatory Notes (at para 859) is as follows: 'A school discusses with its disabled pupils their needs and requirements in order to help it develop a written accessibility plan. The plan includes a strategy to improve the physical environment of the school by putting in ramps and more easily accessible rooms, putting in hearing loops and producing newsletters in Braille.'

[277] Schedule 10, para 2(1)(a), 4(1).

[278] Schedule 10, para 2(1)(b), (2). Guidance may be issued by a Minster of the Crown for England and by the Welsh Ministers for Wales: Sch 10, para 2(4). The guidance to which regard must be had is about the content of an accessibility strategy, the form in which it is to be produced, persons to be consulted in its preparation, and about reviewing and revising of the strategy: Sch 10, para 2(2)–(3). There does not appear to be any relevant guidance in force.

[279] Schedule 10, para 2(6)–(7), 4(3)–(4).

[280] That is, inspections under Part 1 of the EA 2005 or Chapter 1 of Part 4 of the Education and Skills Act 2008 (regulation and inspection of independent education provision in England): Sch 10, para 3(8).

[281] Schedule 10, para 3(7).

[282] The Explanatory Notes give the following two examples (see para 316): '(1) A college course includes a module on feminism. This would not be discrimination against a male student. (2) A university requires students to use a computer for projects or essays. This would not be indirect discrimination against a member of a sect which rejects the use of modern technology.'

excluded from this Chapter of the EqA 2010 is that of marriage and civil partnership, so unlike in schools age discrimination is prohibited.[283] The provisions in Chapter 2 deal with three main areas:

(1)　admission and treatment of students;

(2)　further and higher education courses; and

(3)　recreational or training facilities.

Admission and treatment of students

3.66　The duties in this regard are set out in section 91, which applies to the following institutions: (a) universities,[284] (b) any other institution within the higher education sector,[285] (c) institutions within the further education sector,[286] and (d) a 16 to 19 Academy.[287] The duties are imposed on the responsible body for these institutions, which in the case of (a)–(c) is the governing body and in the case of (d) is the proprietor,[288] and they are owed to students and potential students.[289]

3.67　The duties imposed by section 91 are the same as those imposed on schools set out at paras **3.46–3.61** above. They are not repeated here but as a reminder are (in summary) not to discriminate against, victimise or harass, students or potential students in relation to their admission or education and to make reasonable adjustments.[290] However, in addition to these the following additional duties are imposed:

(a)　The responsible body must not discriminate against on the grounds of disability[291] or victimise a disabled person in the arrangements it makes for deciding upon whom to confer a qualification, as to the terms on which it is prepared to confer a qualification on the person, by not

---

[283]　Section 90.

[284]　A reference to a university includes a reference to a university college and a college, school or hall of a university: s 94(4).

[285]　A reference to an institution within the further or higher education sector is to be construed in accordance with s 91 of the Further and Higher EA 1992: s 94(5). 'Higher education' means education provided by means of a course of a description mentioned in Sch 6 to the Education Reform Act 1988: s 94(7).

[286]　Section 91(10). See fn 284 for the definition of 'institution within the further education sector'. 'Further education' has the meaning given in s 2 of the EA 1996: s 94(6).

[287]　A '16 to 19 Academy' is not defined in the EqA 2010 but is an Academy which meets the requirements of s 1B of the Academies Act 2010.

[288]　Section 94(12).

[289]　A reference to a student, in relation to an institution, is a reference to a person for whom education is provided by the institution: s 94(3).

[290]　They are set out in full at s 91(1)–(2), (5)(a)–(b), (6)–(7) and (9). The wording of these provisions is identical to that in s 85(1)–(6) save that the word 'pupil' is replaced by 'student' and 'school' by 'institution'.

[291]　Ie contrary to ss 13, 15, 19 or 21: s 25(2).

conferring a qualification on the person, or by withdrawing a qualification from the person or varying the terms on which the person holds it.[292]

(b) The responsible body must not harass a disabled person who holds or has applied for a qualification conferred by the institution.[293]

(c) In relation to the duty to make reasonable adjustments, in addition to the duties imposed on responsible bodies of schools, there is also a duty to comply with the 'second requirement' (physical features) in section 20(4),[294] and unlike with schools the duty to comply with the third requirement has been brought into force.[295] Paragraphs 3 and 4 make detailed and complex provision for how section 20 is to be read in this context.[296] Most importantly, a provision criterion or practice is said not to include the application of a competence standard.[297]

3.68 The exceptions, some of which are the same as those for schools, are as follows:

(a) The duty not to discriminate in respect of admissions,[298] so far as relating to sex, does not apply in relation to a single-sex institution.[299] As with schools, this includes institutions that are deemed to be single sex either because the admission of students of the opposite sex is exceptional or because the numbers admitted are comparatively small and they are confined to particular courses or classes.[300] The duties not to discriminate in the provision of education or the affording of access to benefits, facilities or services[301] do not prohibit 'deemed' single-sex institutions from confining pupils of the same sex to particular course or classes.[302] A single-sex institution which decides to become co-educational may require a transitional exemption order to avoid contravening the Act whilst that process is completed. Such an order only relates to admissions, and detailed provision is made about such orders.[303]

---

[292] Section 91(3), (4), (8). A reference to conferring a qualification includes a reference (a) to renewing or extending the conferment of a qualification, (b) to authenticating a qualification conferred by another person: s 94(11A).

[293] Section 91(5)(c).

[294] Schedule 13, para 3(2).

[295] See SI 2010/2317.

[296] The Explanatory Notes give the following example (see para 898): 'A university has a revolving door which causes some problems for disabled pupils and under these duties it may be reasonable for them to replace the door with a sliding one.'

[297] Schedule13, para 4(2). A competence standard is an academic, medical or other standard applied for the purpose of determining whether or not a person has a particular level of competence or ability: Sch 13, para 4(3).

[298] Ie that in s 91(1).

[299] Schedule 11, para 1(1).

[300] Schedule 12, para 1(1)–(3).

[301] Ie in s 91(2)(a)–(d), but not those in s 91(2)(e)–(f) (exclusion and general detriment).

[302] Schedule 12, para 1(4).

[303] Schedule 12, paras 2–3.

(b)   The responsible body of an institution which is designated by Ministerial order[304] for this purpose does not contravene the duty not to discriminate in respect of admissions, so far as relating to religion or belief, if in the admission of students to a course at the institution: (a) it gives preference to persons of a particular religion or belief, (b) it does so to preserve the institution's religious ethos, and (c) the course is not a course of vocational training.[305]

(c)   A person does not contravene the duties in respect of access to benefits, facilities or services,[306] so far as relating to age, only by providing or making arrangements for or facilitating the provision of,[307] care[308] for children[309] of a particular age group.[310]

(d)   A person (P) does not contravene the duties in respect of admission,[311] or in respect of the provision of education[312] if P shows that P's treatment of another person relates only to training that would help fit that other person for work the offer of which the other person could be refused in reliance on Part 1 of Schedule 9 (genuine occupational requirement).[313]

(e)   A person does not contravene any part of section 91, so far as relating to sexual orientation, by providing married persons and civil partners (to the exclusion of all other persons) with access to a benefit, facility or service.[314]

---

[304]   See the Equality Act 2010 (Designation of Institutions with a Religious Ethos) (England and Wales) Order 2010, SI 2010/1915.

[305]   Schedule 12, para 5.

[306]   Ie in s 91(2)(b) or (d).

[307]   This includes: (a) paying for some or all of the cost of the provision, (b) helping a parent of the child to find a suitable person to provide care for the child, and (c) enabling a parent of the child to spend more time providing care for the child or otherwise assisting the parent with respect to the care that the parent provides for the child: Sch 12, para 7(2). For the definition of 'child' see fn 308 below.

[308]   This includes supervision: Sch 12, para 7(4).

[309]   Child means a person who has not attained the age of 17: Sch 12, para 7(3).

[310]   Schedule 12, para 7. The Explanatory Notes give the following example (para 888): 'If a college provides a crèche for the pre-school children of students, this will not be unlawful age association discrimination against a student who is the parent of an older child. The college will not have to demonstrate that the provision and age limits are objectively justified.'

[311]   Ie in s 91(1).

[312]   Ie in s 91(2).

[313]   Schedule 12, para 4. The Explanatory Notes give the following example (see para 882): 'A Catholic theological college can refuse to admit a woman to a training course which was designed only to prepare candidates for the Catholic priesthood. However, a Church of England college could not confine training for the priesthood to men since women may also become Anglican priests.'

[314]   Schedule 12, para 6.

Further and higher education courses

3.69 These are defined as: (a) a course[315] of further or higher education secured by an LA,[316] and (b) a course of education provided by the governing body of a maintained school[317] under section 80 of the SSFA 1998.[318] The responsible body upon whom the duties are imposed is the LA in (a) and the governing body in (b)[319] and is under the following duties:

(a) Not to discriminate against or victimise a person in the arrangements it makes for deciding who is enrolled on the course, as to the terms on which it offers to enrol the person on the course, or by not accepting the person's application for enrolment.[320]

(b) Not to discriminate against or victimise a person who is enrolled on the course in the services it provides or offers to provide.[321]

(c) Not to harass a person who seeks enrolment on the course, is enrolled on the course or is a user of services provided by the body in relation to the course.[322]

(d) To make reasonable adjustments.[323] The content of this duty is the same as that imposed on universities and further education institutions (see para **3.67(c)** above), although the detailed provisions for how section 20 is to be read in this context are different.[324] However, where the responsible body is the governing body of a maintained school, it is not under any duty to comply with the second requirement[325] and the third requirement has not been brought into force.[326]

Recreational or training facilities

3.70 The duties in this regard are set out in section 93 which does not apply to the protected characteristic of age, so far as relating to persons who have not attained the age of 18.[327] The facilities to which it applies are those secured by

---

[315] In relation to further education, 'course' includes each component parts of a course if there is no requirement imposed on persons registered for a component part of the course to register for another component part of the course: s 92(9).
[316] As defined in s 162 of the Education and Inspections Act 2006: s 94(10).
[317] As defined in s 20(7) of the SSFA 1998: s 92(9).
[318] Section 92(7).
[319] Section 91(12).
[320] Section 92(1), (4).
[321] Section 92(2), (5).
[322] Section 92(3).
[323] Section 92(6).
[324] Schedule 13, para 5(3)–(4).
[325] Schedule 13, para 5(2).
[326] See SI 2010/2317.
[327] Section 93(9).

an LA in England under section 507A, 507B or 508 of the EA 1996.[328] The responsible body is the LA and is under the following duties:

(a) Not to discriminate against or victimise a person in the arrangements it makes for deciding who is provided with the facilities, as to the terms on which it offers to provide the facilities to the person, and by not accepting the person's application for provision of the facilities.[329]

(b) Not to discriminate against or victimise a person who is provided with the facilities in the services it provides or offers to provide.[330]

(c) Not to harass a person who seeks to have the facilities provided, is provided with the facilities or is a user of services provided by the body in relation to the facilities.[331]

(d) To comply with the first, second and third requirements of the duty to make reasonable adjustments.[332]

DUTIES OWED BY QUALIFICATION BODIES: PART 6, CHAPTER 3 OF THE EQA 2010

3.71 As with the previous Chapter of the Act concerning further and higher education, the only protected characteristic excluded from Chapter 3 is that of marriage and civil partnership.[333] This Chapter (sections 95–97) imposes duties on 'qualifications bodies', which are defined as authorities or bodies which can confer[334] a relevant qualification.[335] An authority or body is not a qualifications body in so far as it is the responsible body of a school or institution to which section 85 or section 91 applies, or it exercises functions under the Education Acts,[336] or as may be prescribed.[337]

---

[328] Section 93(7). The Explanatory Notes give the example of a summer camp for children from local schools which is put on by an LA (see para 313).

[329] Section 93(1), (4).

[330] Section 93(2), (5).

[331] Section 93(3).

[332] As set out in s 20: s 93(6) and Sch 13, para 6, which also makes provision for how the wording of s 20 is to be read in this context.

[333] Section 95.

[334] A reference to conferring a relevant qualification includes a reference to renewing or extending the conferment of a relevant qualification, and to authenticating a relevant qualification conferred by another person: s 97(6).

[335] Section 97(2). A relevant qualification is an authorisation, qualification, approval or certification of such description as may be prescribed by a Minister the Crown (in relation to conferments in England) or the Welsh Ministers (in relation to conferments in Wales): s 97(3). The current list is found in the Schedule to the Equality Act 2010 (General Qualifications Bodies) (Appropriate Regulator and Relevant Qualifications) Regulations 2010 (SI 2010/2245).

[336] As defined in s 578 of the EA 1996: s 212(1).

[337] Section 97(4)–(5).

3.72 A qualification body is under the following duties:

(a) not to discriminate against or victimise a person (B) in the arrangements it makes for deciding upon whom to confer a relevant qualification, as to the terms on which it is prepared to confer a relevant qualification on B or by not conferring a relevant qualification on B;[338]

(b) not to discriminate against or victimise a person (B) upon whom it has conferred a relevant qualification by withdrawing the qualification from B, varying the terms on which B holds the qualification or by subjecting B to any other detriment;[339]

(c) in relation to conferment by it of a relevant qualification, not to harass a person who holds the qualification or a person who applies for it;[340]

(d) to comply with the first, second and third requirements of the duty to make reasonable adjustments.[341]

3.73 The duty in (d) above is effectively the same as that imposed on universities and further education institutions (see para **3.67(c)** above) but with one important difference. The DDA 1995 had provided that there was no requirement to make a reasonable adjustment to a competence standard whereas now the Act makes provision for a regulator[342] to specify provisions, criteria or practices in relation to which the body is not subject to a duty to make reasonable adjustments, or in respect of which certain adjustments should not be made.[343]

---

[338] Section 96(1), (4).
[339] Section 96(2), (5).
[340] Section 96(3).
[341] As set out in s 20: s 96(6) and Sch 13, para 9, which also makes provision for how the wording of s 20 is to be read in this context.
[342] To be prescribed by a Minister of the Crown in relation to a qualifications body that confers relevant qualifications in England, and by the Welsh Ministers in relation to a qualifications body that confers relevant qualifications in Wales: s 96(10), s 97(7). For these purposes a relevant qualification is conferred in a part of Great Britain if there are, or may reasonably be expected to be, persons seeking to obtain the relevant qualification who are or will be assessed for those purposes wholly or mainly in that part: s 96(11).
[343] Section 96(7). The appropriate regulator must take certain matters into account (set out in s 96(8)), must consult (s 96(9)(a)), and must publish the matters so specified in such manner as is prescribed (s 96(9)(b)). The Explanatory Notes give the following examples (para 321): '(1) The regulator publishes, after appropriate consultation, a requirement that qualifications bodies cannot make reasonable adjustments by granting an exemption from components of the qualification which exceed a specified percentage of the total marks. (2) The regulator publishes, after appropriate consultation, a requirement on qualifications bodies not to use a specific reasonable adjustment, such as a reader in the independent reading element of a GCSE English exam. This would not be unlawful discrimination against a disabled candidate who would otherwise have been entitled to this specific adjustment.'

3.74 In England the appropriate regulator is the Office of Qualifications and Examinations Regulation (Ofqual)[344] and in Wales it is the Welsh Ministers.[345] The former published its specifications in December 2011 and they are available at http://www.ofqual.gov.uk/files/2011-12-15-specifications-in-relation-to-the-reasonable-adjustment-of-general-qualifications.pdf.

3.75 In summary they are as follows:

(a) An exemption must not be used as a reasonable adjustment, except where no other reasonable adjustment is available to the candidate.

(b) An exemption must not be used as a reasonable adjustment where it would form more than 40 per cent of the available (weighted) marks of a qualification.

(c) An exemption to part of a component must not be used as a reasonable adjustment. Exemptions must only be provided for whole components where a candidate cannot access any part of that component.

(d) Awarding organisations must not make reasonable adjustments for disabled candidates in relation to grade boundaries and pass marks, also known as 'cut scores'.

(e) Human readers must not be used as a reasonable adjustment where a candidate's reading ability is being assessed.

(f) Human scribes and voice recognition systems must not be used as a reasonable adjustment to demonstrate written skills where those written skills form part of the qualification's assessment objectives.

(g) British Sign Language must not be used as a reasonable adjustment where candidates are required to demonstrate their ability to speak or listen in English or a Modern Foreign Language.

(h) Practical assistants must not be used as a reasonable adjustment to carry out physical tasks or demonstrate physical abilities where those physical tasks or abilities form part of the qualification's assessment objectives.

3.76 The specifications document states that in developing these specifications Ofqual has taken account of: (a) the need to minimise the extent to which disabled persons are disadvantaged in attaining the qualification because of their disabilities, (b) the need to secure that the qualification gives a reliable

---

[344] Equality Act 2010 (General Qualifications Bodies) (Appropriate Regulator and Relevant Qualifications) Regulations 2010, SI 2010/2245, reg 3.

[345] Equality Act 2010 (General Qualifications Bodies Regulator and Relevant Qualifications) (Wales) Regulations 2010, SI 2010/2217, reg 2.

indication of the knowledge, skills and understanding of a person upon whom it is conferred, and (c) the need to maintain public confidence in the qualification.

3.77 It should be noted, however, that these are simply the areas where Ofqual has said reasonable adjustments should not be made. In other respects not covered qualifications bodies remain under a duty to make reasonable adjustments.[346]

PUBLIC SECTOR EQUALITY DUTY

3.78 Section 149 of the EqA 2010 obliges a public authority in the exercise of its functions, or any other person who exercises public functions, to have regard to the need to: (a) eliminate discrimination, harassment, victimisation and any other conduct that is prohibited by or under this Act, (b) advance equality of opportunity between persons who share a relevant protected characteristic[347] and persons who do not share it,[348] and (c) foster good relations between persons who share a relevant protected characteristic and persons who do not share it.[349] Compliance with the duties in section 149 may involve treating some persons more favourably than others, but that is not to be taken as permitting conduct that would otherwise be prohibited by or under the Act.[350]

3.79 The public authorities subject to this duty are specified in Schedule 19 and include local authorities, the governing bodies of maintained schools and other educational establishments maintained by local authorities[351] and the governing bodies of institutions within the further and higher education sector.[352] However, insofar as the duty relates to age it does not apply to provision of education, benefits, facilities or services to pupils in schools.[353]

---

[346] For a recent case on this (albeit decided under the DDA 1995), see *Burke v College of Law* [2012] EWCA Civ 37, [2012] ELR 195.

[347] This is all of the protected characteristics in s 4 apart from marriage and civil partnership: s 149(7).

[348] This involves having due regard, in particular to the need to: (a) remove or minimise disadvantages suffered by persons who share a relevant protected characteristic that are connected to that characteristic, (b) take steps to meet the needs of persons who share a relevant protected characteristic that are different from the needs of persons who do not share it, and (c) encourage persons who share a relevant protected characteristic to participate in public life or in any other activity in which participation by such persons is disproportionately low: s 149(3). So far as (b) is concerned, the steps involved in meeting the needs of disabled persons that are different from the needs of persons who are not disabled include, in particular, steps to take account of disabled persons' disabilities: s 149(4).

[349] This involves having due regard, in particular to the need to tackle prejudice and promote understanding: s 149(5).

[350] Section 149(6).

[351] As defined in s 162 of the Education and Inspections Act 2006: Sch 19, Pt 1.

[352] As defined in s 91(3) and 91(5) of the Further and Higher Education Act 1992.

[353] Schedule 18, para 1(1)(a)–(b). 'Pupil' and 'school' have the same meaning as in Ch 1 of Pt 6: Sch 18, para 1(2). The Explanatory Notes give the following example (see para 924): 'A school will not be required to consider advancing equality of opportunity between pupils of different ages. Nor will it be required to consider how to foster good relations between pupils of

3.80 The Explanatory Notes give one example relating to education, saying that this duty 'could lead a school to review its anti-bullying strategy to ensure that it addresses the issue of homophobic bullying, with the aim of fostering good relations, and in particular tackling prejudice against gay and lesbian people'. However, it does not follow that a school that does not do this would be failing to comply with its duty.

3.81 This duty has been the subject of much litigation but rather than attempting to analyse all of that and the principles established, this Chapter confines itself to considering three cases in the education field.

3.82 First, the predecessor to this duty in section 49A of the DDA 1995 was relied upon by a university student in the case of *R (AM) v Birmingham CC*.[354] The claimant's disabilities included muscular dystrophy and he could not move his lower limbs by himself, had limited movement in his arms and was dependent on others for all aspects of his care. He was accepted on a university course and had his needs assessed by the LA. Although a package of support was put together the dispute concerned the LA's refusal to provide the claimant with a mobile hoist in order to access toilet facilities at the university, it assessing the likelihood of him needing to use them as low and the possibility of returning to his nearby home in the event of an emergency. The court rejected the argument that the council's decision was in breach of section 49A because it failed to have due regard to the need to promote equality of opportunity. Although the decision did not refer to this duty, Cranston J said that 'form takes a back seat to substance in these matters' and the issue was whether the council had 'in substance incorporated the thought processes required by section 49A'. The judge held that it had:

> 'The assessment took into account the importance of the claimant's choice to attend university. It accepted that the claimant had a critical need for services to assist him to attend university and it reassessed the extent of his needs for assistance to do that. As I have described, it increased the care services to be provided to him above what had been decided in the 9 September assessment. It will be recalled that the council concluded that it was necessary to meet the claimant's needs by providing him with five and a half hours escorted travel and 40 hours of personal care. The assessment took into account that the claimant was a disabled person who did not have the same opportunities or facility to attend university as persons without disabilities. In assessing the claimant's disability, it took into account the need to spend money to provide him with services which the council would not spend in relation to an able bodied person. It paid due regard to the fact that there was no toileting suitable for him at the university and explored the possibility that he might require special assistance in that regard. In assessing that risk, however, it concluded that it was low or very low and that relevant alternative measures were available.'

---

different ages. But it will still need to have due regard to the need to eliminate unlawful discrimination, advance equality of opportunity and foster good relations between pupils in respect of the other protected characteristics.'

[354] [2009] EWHC 688 (Admin).

3.83 The case of *R (on the application of Essex County Council) v Secretary Of State For Education*[355] also concerned the predecessors to section 149, in this case section 71(1) of the RRA 1976 as well as section 49A of the DDA 1995. The High Court upheld the contention of the claimant LA that the Secretary of State had failed to fulfil these equalities duties in considering the impact of his decision to reduce the amount of funding it would receive for, amongst other things, pre-school education. There was no express consideration of these duties in the decision-making process and although the Secretary of State submitted that the impact would be obvious, and that was accepted so far as disabled children were concerned, the High Court held that the extent of any impact on ethnic minorities was not. The High Court also rejected the argument that since the LA decided how to spend the money it was given it was better placed to discharge these duties, saying that the Secretary of State could have put himself in a position in which it was able to evaluate the impact of the measures on the relevant groups.

3.84 Finally, in *R (on the application of (1) Hurley (2) Moore) v Secretary Of State For Business Innovation & Skills*[356] the government's decision to increase to £9000 the maximum amount of tuition fees that universities may charge students was challenged on, amongst other grounds, an alleged failure to comply with the duties in section 149 and in particular that what the Secretary of State had done focussed insufficiently on the full range of the duties in section 149. Elias LJ said as follows:

> '95…There can in my view be no doubt that there will be a number of features of the equality duties that will simply not be engaged at all by the policies. For example, nothing in these particular policies raises any concerns about harassment of the disabled, nor does it relate to attitudes towards them. It cannot be the case that whenever any legislation is passed, attention necessarily has to focus on these matters. It will always be possible to tag onto any legislation a provision, for example, giving greater grants to disabled students. But possibilities of that kind do not have to be canvassed in order to satisfy the equality duty. There must be some reason to think that the exercise of the functions might in some way relate to a particular aspect of the duty under consideration. As Aikens LJ pointed out in Brown (para 89), a public body might decide not to have an equality impact assessment on (in that case) the effect of a policy on the disabled precisely because it is not thought that it will have any impact on them at all. I made a similar observation in *R (Elias) v Secretary of State for Defence* [2005] EWHC 1435 (Admin); [2005] IRLR 488, para 96:
>
>> "No doubt in some cases it will be plain even after a cursory consideration that section 71 is not engaged, or at least is not relevant. There is no need to enter into time consuming and potentially expensive consultation exercises or monitoring when discrimination issues are plainly not in point."
>
> For these reasons, in my judgment there has on any view been very substantial compliance with these equality duties.

---

[355] [2012] EWHC 1460 (Admin).
[356] [2012] EWHC 201 (Admin).

96. However, I accept that if there is any doubt about whether a particular statutory objective is engaged, the issue needs to be explored before any conclusion can be safely reached that it is not. In so far as the EIA purported to focus on the full package of reforms then under consideration and not merely the decision to increase fees, I cannot be sure that this has been done. I cannot discount the possibility that a more precise focus on the specific statutory duties might have led to the conclusion that some other requirements were potentially engaged and merited consideration. I recognise that it was envisaged that there would be a further assessment, but it was never explained, if it be the case, that certain matters were not thought relevant for the initial so-called interim assessment on the grounds that they would be addressed in a later one.

97. I therefore conclude that the Secretary of State did not carry out the rigorous attention to the PSEDs which he was obliged to do. Having said that, I am satisfied that he did give proper consideration to those particular aspects of the duty which related to the principle of levying fees and the amounts of those fees, and by seeking a quashing of the regulations, the claimants have focused on that aspect of the policy.'

3.85 However, taking into account the fact that there had been 'very substantial compliance', a subsequent Equality Impact Assessment, and the administrative chaos and economic implications that would otherwise follow, the court refused to quash the regulations.

ENFORCEMENT

3.86 The Act is prescriptive about enforcement, providing that proceedings relating to a contravention of its provisions must be brought in accordance with Part 9[357] although this does not prevent a claim for judicial review[358] and the Act also preserves the power of the Secretary of State to act in certain circumstances.

3.87 The Act makes two provisions about enforcement which are of general application.[359] First, a person (P) who thinks that that any contravention of the Act has occurred in relation to P may use prescribed forms to question a person P he thinks has committed the contravention and in certain circumstances a court or tribunal in subsequent proceedings can draw an inference from a failure to answer or an evasive or equivocal answer.[360]

---

[357] Section 113(1).
[358] Section 113(3)(a). Although not relevant to education, for completeness s 113(2) and 113(3)(b)–(c) also provide that s 113(1)(a) does not apply to proceedings under Part 1 of the EqA 2010, and (b) does not prevent proceedings under the Immigration Acts or the Special Immigration Appeals Commission Act 1997.
[359] Two other general provisions of no, or marginal relevance to education law, are found in s 137 (findings in proceedings under the previous equality legislation cannot be reopened) and s 140 (transfer between employment tribunal and county court where conduct gives rise to separate proceedings).
[360] Section 138.

3.88 Secondly, where proceedings relating to a contravention of the Act are brought then if there are facts from which the court or tribunal could decide, in the absence of any other explanation that a person (A) contravened the provision in question, the court/tribunal must hold that the contravention occurred unless A shows that there was no contravention.[361]

3.89 The provisions that are relevant to education fall to be considered under five separate headings: (1) claims in the county court, (2) claims of disability discrimination against a school or LA,[362] (3) direction by the Secretary of State in respect of duties under section 85, (4) direction by the Secretary of State or Welsh Ministers in respect of accessibility strategies and plans duties, and (5) alternative complaint procedures.

County court proceedings

3.90 Primary jurisdiction to determine a claim relating to a contravention of Part 3 (services and public functions) or Part 6 (education) is conferred on the county court.[363] Such claims must be brought within six months of the date of the act to which the claim relates unless the court considers it just and equitable to allow a longer period.[364] This time period is extended in three situations: (1) where the claim is against a university[365] and a complaint is referred under the student complaints scheme within the six month time period,[366] to nine months, (2) in respect of any other claim relating to a dispute which is referred for conciliation pursuant to arrangements under section 27 of the Equality Act 2006 (ie by the Equality and Human Rights Commission),[367] to nine months, (3) in cross-border disputes where a mediation starts before the time limit expires, to eight weeks after the mediation ends.[368]

3.91 In such proceedings assessors must be appointed by the court[369] unless there are good reasons for not doing so,[370] and although (if appointed) their assistance must be used by the judge, the ultimate decision remains that of the judge: see the detailed guidance given by the Court of Appeal in *Nadeem Ahmed v University of Oxford*.[371] Where the court finds that there has been a contravention of any provision in Parts 3–7, it has the power to grant any

---

[361] Section 136(1)–(3). This does not apply to criminal proceedings brought under the Act: s 136(5).

[362] Section 114(3).

[363] Section 114(1).

[364] Section 118(1).

[365] To be precise, a 'qualifying institution', as defined in the Higher Education Act 2004: s 114(8).

[366] Section 118(2)–(3).

[367] Section 118(2), (4). This does not apply in certain immigration cases but this is not relevant to education.

[368] Sections 118(1) and 140A. Cross-border disputes are those to which the Directive 2008/52/EC applies but in short are those where at least one of the parties is domiciled or habitually resident in a Member State (excluding Denmark) other than that of any other party on the date mediation is agreed or ordered.

[369] Under s 63(1) of the County Courts Act 1984.

[370] Section 114(7).

[371] [2003] 1 WLR 995.

remedy which could be granted by the High Court in proceedings in tort or on a claim for judicial review,[372] subject to two limitations: (1) where the court finds there has been indirect discrimination but is satisfied that there was no intention to discriminate, then it must not award damages unless it first considers whether to make any other disposal,[373] (2) it must not grant a remedy other than damages or a declaration unless satisfied that no criminal matter would be prejudiced by doing so.[374] Any award of damages may include compensation for injured feelings whether or not it includes compensation on any other basis.[375]

3.92 Such claims can be settled without any special requirements applying, as they do to claims in the employment tribunal.[376]

Tribunal proceedings: claims of disability discrimination against a school or LA

3.93 Claims by a parent[377] that a responsible body has contravened Chapter 1 of Part 6 of the Act (schools) cannot be brought in the county court.[378] Such claims must (with two exceptions) be made to the First-tier Tribunal (FTT) or the Special Educational Needs Tribunal for Wales (SENTW), depending upon where the school is.[379] The procedural rules governing such claims are the Tribunal Procedure (First-tier Tribunal)(Health, Education and Social Care Chamber) Rules 2008[380] and the Special Educational Needs Tribunal for Wales Regulations 2012[381] respectively.

3.94 The exceptions are where the claim is in respect of an admissions decision[382] or exclusion decision[383] and appeal arrangements have been made for such decisions[384] in which case the claim must be made under those arrangements.[385] These provisions have been the subject of case-law. In *AS v*

---

[372] Section 119(2).
[373] Section 119(5)–(6).
[374] Section 119(7).
[375] Section 119(4).
[376] Section 144(3).
[377] As defined in the EA 1996: s 212(1).
[378] Section 114(3), s 116 and Sch 17.
[379] Section 116(1) and Sch 17 Pts 1 and 2.
[380] SI 2008/2699, as amended.
[381] SI 2012/322.
[382] A decision of a kind mentioned in s 94(1) or (2) of the SSFA 1998 or a decision as to the admission of a person to an Academy taken by the responsible body or on its behalf: Sch 17, para 13(5).
[383] A decision of a kind mentioned in s 52(3) of the EA 2002 or a decision taken by the responsible body or on its behalf not to reinstate a pupil who has been permanently excluded from an Academy by its headteacher: Sch 17, para 14(5).
[384] Arrangements under s 94 of the SSFA 1998 (in respect of admissions), under s 52(3) of the EA 2002 (in respect of an exclusion), or under an agreement between the responsible body for an Academy and the Secretary of State under s 482 of the EA 1996 (in respect of either) enabling an appeal to be made by the person's parent against the decision: Sch 17, paras 13(4), 14(4).
[385] Section 116(2) and Sch 17, Pt 4.

Buckinghamshire County Council[386] the Upper Tribunal (UT) held that the FTT had had no jurisdiction to entertain a challenge to the testing arrangements the council had made for transfer to grammar schools. The claimant was dyslexic and contended that he should have had a reader or a different test to determine his suitability for grammar school education. The testing decisions took place before any allocation of school places was made, but anyone failing the test had no chance of admission to a grammar school. The UT held that section 94 of the SSFA 1998 was widely drawn and it conferred a right of appeal from the testing decision to an Independent Appeal Panel and hence not to the FTT.[387]

3.95 Where a tribunal has found disability discrimination in respect of a pupil's fixed-term exclusion and that pupil is later permanently excluded for subsequent incidents which are different but may be described as 'more of the same', an appeal panel which leaves out of account the previous fixed-term exclusions and the tribunal decision relating to them, does not commit any error of law.[388] Where separate claims are brought simultaneously against two different schools, it is better for them to be heard by entirely separate panels.[389]

3.96 Claims can only be brought against the responsible body and not against any individual.[390] They must be brought within six months of the date when the conduct complained of occurred,[391] but a claim which is out of time may nonetheless be considered.[392]

3.97 If the tribunal finds that the contravention alleged has occurred it may make such order as it thinks fit.[393] This power may be exercised with a view to obviating or reducing the adverse effect on the person of any matter to which the claim relates.[394] There is, however, no power to order the payment of compensation.[395] Where a tribunal has made such an order and the Secretary of State (or the Welsh Ministers as appropriate) is satisfied, whether or not on

---

[386] [2010] UKUT 407 (AAC).

[387] See at paras 26–36.

[388] *R(N) v LB of Barking and Dagenham Independent Appeal Panel* [2009] EWCA Civ 108, [2009] ELR 268. Rix LJ expressed the view that it would have been wiser for the appeal panel to have considered the tribunal decision so that it could confirm, by reference to it, that the events which led to the permanent exclusion were properly to be regarded as being insulated from any prior behaviour or errors, but its failure to do so was not an error of law: see [53].

[389] *DP v Governing Body of Radley College* [2011] UKUT 66 (AAC), [2011] ELR 155.

[390] Section 110(7). See also the Explanatory Notes to the Act at para 361.

[391] Schedule 17, para 4(1). For these purposes: (a) if the contravention is attributable to a term in a contract, the conduct is to be treated as extending throughout the duration of the contract, (b) conduct extending over a period is to be treated as occurring at the end of the period, and (c) a failure to do something is to be treated as occurring when the person in question decided on it: Sch 17, para 4(5). In the absence of evidence to the contrary, a person (P) is to be taken to decide on failure to do something (a) when P acts inconsistently with doing it, or (b) if P does not act inconsistently, on the expiry of the period in which P might reasonably have been expected to do it: Sch 17, para 4(6).

[392] Schedule 17, para 4(3). This does not apply if the tribunal has previously decided under that sub-para not to consider a claim: Sch 17, para 4(4).

[393] Schedule 17, para 5(2).

[394] Schedule 17, para 5(3)(a).

[395] Schedule 17, para 5(3)(b).

a complaint, that the responsible body concerned has acted or is proposing to act unreasonably in complying with the order, or has failed to comply with the order, then he may give the responsible body such directions as he thinks expedient as to compliance by the body with the order.[396] Such a direction may not be given to the responsible body of a school in England in respect of a matter which has been complained about to the local government ombudsman,[397] or which the Secretary of State thinks could have been so complained about.[398] However, where such a complaint has been made and the ombudsman has made a recommendation to the responsible body[399] which has not been complied with, then the power of the Secretary of State to give such a direction remains.[400] The Secretary of State and Welsh Ministers may vary or revoke such direction and can also apply to the High Court for them to be enforced by a mandatory order in accordance with section 31 of the Senior Courts Act 1981.[401]

3.98 A settlement of such a claim may fall foul of the prohibition on contractual terms which purport to exclude or limit a provision of, or made under, the EqA 2010.[402] Whilst this prohibition does not apply to county court claims,[403] or to employment tribunal claims settled in accordance with special requirements,[404] the Act does not make any provision in respect of these claims to the FTT or SENTW. It is unclear whether this is oversight, although the different nature of such claims (including the fact that compensation cannot be ordered and the greater involvement by the tribunal) means the point may matter little in practice.

Direction by Secretary of State in respect of duties under section 85

3.99 The powers of the Secretary of State under sections 496 and 497 of the EA 1996 apply to the performance of a duty under section 85[405] by the responsible body of a maintained school or a special school not maintained by an LA.[406]

---

[396] Schedule 10, para 5(4)–(5).
[397] In accordance with Ch 2 of Pt 10 of the Apprenticeships, Skills, Children and Learning Act 2009 (parental complaints against governing bodies etc.): Sch 10, para 5(7)(a).
[398] Schedule 10, para 5(7).
[399] Under s 211(4) of the Apprenticeships, Skills, Children and Learning Act 2009 (statement following investigation): Sch 10, para 5(8).
[400] Schedule 10, para 5(8).
[401] Schedule 10, para 5(9).
[402] Section 144(1).
[403] Section 144(3).
[404] See ss 144(4) and 147.
[405] The duties under s 85 are considered at paras **3.49**–**3.61** above.
[406] Section 87.

Accessibility strategies and plans

3.100 The duties on local authorities and schools in respect of accessibility strategies and plans have been considered at paras **3.62** and **3.63** above. Where the Secretary of State (or Welsh Ministers as appropriate) is satisfied, whether or not on a complaint, that a responsible body has acted or is proposing to act unreasonably in the discharge of those duties, or has failed to discharge any of those duties, then he may give a responsible body such directions as he thinks expedient as to the discharge by the body of the duty.[407] There are other more specific direction-making powers in relation to non-maintained special schools and Academies.[408] The fact that the performance of the duty in question may be contingent on the opinion of the responsible body does not prevent such a direction being given.[409]

3.101 As with the enforcement of tribunal orders, there is no power to give directions to the responsible body of a school in England in respect of a matter which has been complained about to the local government ombudsman[410] (or which the Secretary of State thinks could have been so complained about)[411] but where such a complaint has been made and the ombudsman has made a recommendation to the responsible body[412] which has not been complied with, then the power remains.[413] Also, as with the enforcement of tribunal orders, the Secretary of State and Welsh Ministers may vary or revoke their directions and can also apply to the High Court for them to be enforced by a mandatory order in accordance with section 31 of the Senior Courts Act 1981.[414]

Alternative complaint procedures

3.102 The decision of the Court of Appeal in *R (Shelley Maxwell) v Office of the Independent Adjudicator for Higher Education*[415] may well affect the way allegations of disability discrimination in such complaints are considered in future. In that case the Office of the Independent Adjudicator (OIA) had received a complaint from a student against her university which included a complaint of disability discrimination. The OIA found that the complaint was justified and made various recommendations favourable to her, but refused to make any findings about her complaint of disability discrimination even though it had formed a view about it. The student brought a claim for judicial review contending that it was obliged to disclose its view about the complaint of disability discrimination. The Court of Appeal held that the issue before the

---

407 Schedule 10, para 5(1), (5).
408 Schedule 10, paras 5(2) and (3).
409 Schedule 10, para 5(6).
410 In accordance with Ch 2 of Pt 10 of the Apprenticeships, Skills, Children and Learning Act 2009 (parental complaints against governing bodies etc): Sch 10, para 5(7)(a).
411 Schedule 10, para 5(7).
412 Under s 211(4) of the Apprenticeships, Skills, Children and Learning Act 2009 (statement following investigation): Sch 10, para 5(8).
413 Schedule 10, para 5(8).
414 Schedule 10, para 5(9).
415 [2011] EWCA Civ 1236.

OIA was whether the complaint was justified, which it had determined, and it could not be judicially reviewed for declining to give a decision on the different issue of whether there had been unlawful discrimination. In his judgment Mummery LJ (with whom Hooper and MacFarlane LJJ agreed) emphasised the importance of issues of disability discrimination being determined through the formal procedures of the courts and tribunals rather than those operated by complaints bodies such as the OIA:

'29. I start from a position on which I think that most people would be in agreement: that a complaint of disability discrimination by a student against an institution that exists to provide courses in Higher Education is a serious matter. It is serious both from the point of view of the student claiming to be a victim and from the point of view of the institution as the alleged perpetrator. The outcome of the complaint and the proper procedure for achieving it are significant and sensitive for both sides.

...

32... [T]he practice and procedures for the review and resolution of a wide range of student complaints under the independent scheme operated free of charge and largely as an inquisitorial on a confidential basis by the OIA under the 2004 Act, is quite different from civil proceedings. Its informal inquisitorial methods, which are normally conducted on paper without cross examination and possibly leading to the making of recommendations in its Final Decision, mean that the outcome is not the product of a rigorous adversarial judicial process dealing with the proof of contested facts, with the application of the legislation to proven facts, with establishing legal rights and obligations and with awarding legal remedies, such as damages and declarations. The issue for the OIA in this matter was not to decide whether Ms Maxwell was in fact the victim of disability discrimination or whether the University is liable to her for such discrimination. The OIA's task was to review Ms Maxwell's complaint, which included a complaint of discrimination, to see whether the University's decision was reasonable in all the circumstances and was justified and, if so, to what extent, and what recommendations should be made to the University.

33. In my judgment, the courts are not entitled to impose on the informal complaints review procedure of the OIA a requirement that it should have to adjudicate on issues, such as whether or not there has been disability discrimination. Adjudication of that issue usually involves making decisions on contested questions of fact and law, which require the more stringent and structured procedures of civil litigation for their proper determination.'

3.103 Of course, it does not follow from this case that if the OIA *had* made findings of disability discrimination it would have been acting unlawfully but the points made by Mummery LJ may well discourage findings being made by it and similar bodies in the future.

EDUCATIONAL CHARITIES AND ENDOWMENTS

3.104 Schedule 14 to the EqA 2010,[416] replicating provisions in section 78 of the SDA 1975, provides for trust deeds or other instruments concerning educational charities which restrict benefits to a single sex to be modified by a Minister of the Crown. This cannot be done within 25 years of the trust being created without the consent of the donor or the personal representatives of the donor or testator. Applicants need to publish particulars of the proposal and invite representations for the Minister to consider before making the order. The Explanatory Notes give as an example a boys' grammar school which now allows girls into its sixth form and wishes to modify a trust deed which offers scholarships and help with tuition for boys of the school wanting to go to university so that it can also offer help to girls.[417]

DISCRIMINATION UNDER THE ECHR[418]

3.105 Article 14 of the Convention provides:

'The enjoyment of the rights and freedoms set forth in this Convention shall be secured without discrimination on any ground such as sex, race, colour, language, religion, political or other opinion, national or social origin, association with a national minority, property, birth or other status.'

3.106 The French speaking parents in the *Belgian Linguistic Case*[419] alleged that various of the provisions of the Belgian language law constituted discrimination contrary to Article 14 taken with Article 2 of the First Protocol. The court held:

(a) while the guarantee laid down in Article 14 had no independent existence, 'a measure which in itself is in conformity with the requirements of the Article enshrining the right or freedom in question may however infringe this Article when read in conjunction with Article 14 for the reason that it is of a discriminatory nature';

(b) it did not forbid every difference in treatment in the exercise of the rights and freedoms recognised, only those based on a distinction which has no objective and reasonable justification;

(c) in assessing whether such justification existed:

    (i)   the difference of treatment must pursue a legitimate aim;

    (ii) there must be a reasonable relationship of proportionality between the means employed and the aim sought to be achieved.

---

[416] Given effect by s 99.

[417] Explanatory Notes, para 900.

[418] For detailed consideration see '*The Law of Human Rights*' by Clayton and Tomlinson, 2nd Edn, OUP, paras 17.149–17.197.

[419] (1979–80) 1 EHRR 252. For discussion of this case see Ch 10 at para 4 et seq.

3.107 In the case itself, the court held that Article 14, read in conjunction with Article 2 of the First Protocol, could not be interpreted as guaranteeing to every child and their parent a right to education in the language of their choice. Its effect was said to be much more limited. Only one small aspect of the challenge was therefore upheld on the basis of Article 14.

3.108 In the education context, Article 14 has been relied on in a number of different contexts including State subsidies to non-State schools, in cases where there are different educational arrangements for children on the basis of their ethnic origins and in a school organisation dispute. In relation to State subsidies, there is no obligation on the State to subsidise any particular form of education, but where it does so it must ensure it does so in a non discriminatory manner. In *X v UK*[420] a parent from Northern Ireland committed to non-denominational schooling, complained that whereas State schools received a 100 per cent subsidy from the State, private education institutions received only an 85 per cent subsidy, so that private educational institutions wishing to set up a non-denominational school had to bear 15 per cent of the capital costs themselves. The claim failed; it was held that it was legitimate for the State to exercise substantial control in the ownership and management of schools for which it provided 100 per cent subsidy and to require some degree of financial contribution for other schools for which it was not responsible. The amount of financial contribution was held to be reasonable.

3.109 In *DH v Czech Republic*,[421] the Grand Chamber held that Roma children had been discriminated against on the grounds of their ethnic origin contrary to Article 14 read with Article 2 of the First Protocol when they were placed in special schools at which they were denied access to the normal educational curriculum and the opportunity to integrate with other children. A similar conclusion was reached by the Grand Chamber in *Orsus v Croatia*,[422] the applicants complained that their teaching in Roma only classes and the subsequent length of time it had taken to litigate their rights in the domestic courts in Croatia violated their rights under Articles 6 and Article 2 of the First Protocol of the Convention read with Article 14. The Grand Chamber held, unanimously that there had been a breach of Article 6 and, by a majority, of Article 2 of the First Protocol read with Article 14. They did not reach a conclusion on Article 2 of the First Protocol read alone. The measures taken were disproportionate because, inter alia, the children were placed in Roma classes on the basis of inadequate grasp of the Croatian language without any proper testing of their language ability, the curriculum followed in the Roma only classes was not as extensive as that for pupils attending the general classes, and no other group that had difficulty with the Croatian language was treated in a like manner.

---

[420] (1978) 14 DR 179. See to similar effect *Verein Gemeinsam Lernen v Austria* (1995) 82 DR 41 and *W and KL v Sweden* (1985) P 45 DR 143.
[421] (2007) 47 EHRR 3
[422] (2010) 28 BHRC 558.

3.110 An unsuccessful attempt was made to challenge a school reorganisation on the basis of breach of Article 14 read with Article 2 of the First Protocol in *R(McDougal) v Liverpool City Council*.[423] In that case the council was faced with a vast surplus of secondary school places in central Liverpool. It decided to reduce the number of schools in the area from four to three and after extensive consultation chose the worst performing school, Croxteth Community Comprehensive School, a co-educational non-faith school. The council further agreed to provide free transport for the displaced pupils and their siblings to a comparable school, Fazakerly High School. The claimant was concerned at the loss of the only mixed non-faith school in the Croxteth and Norris Green areas of Liverpool and claimed her rights under Article 14 and Article 2 of the First Protocol had been infringed. Silber J held[424] that there had been no discrimination because there was an objective and reasonable justification for the alleged difference in treatment. The council had a legitimate aim in ensuring a reduction in its surplus places and ensuring that education was provided in the best schools. In any event education was available to the claimant's children at a non-faith co-educational school at Fazakerley High School to which free bus transport was provided by the council and which in any event was within three miles of M's home.

DISCRIMINATION UNDER THE EU CHARTER

3.111 Since 1 December 2009, the EU Charter has had the same legal status among Member States of the EU as the EU treaties themselves.

3.112 Article 14 of that Charter provides:

'1. Everyone has the right to education and to have access to vocational and continuing training.
2. This right includes the possibility to receive free compulsory education.
3. The freedom to found educational establishments with due respect for democratic principles and the right of parents to ensure the teaching of their children in conformity with their religious, philosophical and pedagogical convictions shall be respected, in accordance with the national laws governing the exercise of such freedom and right.'

It is very doubtful whether this Charter will add anything of substance in education disputes because:

(a) It purports to be declaratory of existing rights under the EU treaties.[425]

(b) Article 1 of the protocol provides that it does not extend the ability of the ECJ or any court or tribunal of the United Kingdom to find that the laws

---

[423] [2009] EWHC 1821 (Admin); [2009] ELR 510.
[424] See at paras 61–72.
[425] See the preamble thereto.

of the UK are inconsistent with the fundamental rights, freedoms and principles that the Charter re-affirms.

(c)   The Charter only applies where the case concerns the application of EU law.[426]

UNIFORM DISPUTES AND DISCRIMINATION[427]

3.113   School uniform disputes have engaged the courts a number of times. Most of the challenges have been based on the ECHR, but some have turned on purely domestic provisions of discrimination law. The leading case on the Convention involving school uniform is the decision of the House of Lords in *R (Begum) v Head Teacher and Governing Body of Denbigh High School.*[428] In that well publicised case, Ms Begum contended that her rights under Article 9 of the Convention had been infringed when she was not permitted to wear strict Islamic dress, a jilbab at Denbigh High School. No case was advanced prior to the hearing in the House of Lords that this action was also a breach of Article 14 of the Convention.[429] The House of Lords held by a majority that there had been no interference with Ms Begum's Article 9 rights because she had freely consented to the school uniform and could have gone to another school where she would have been able to wear the jilbab.[430] They were unanimous that in any event the conduct of the school was justified having regard to the guidance of the European Court of Human Rights in *Sahin v Turkey.*[431] On the facts the school policy was justified, inter alia, on the basis that its uniform policy promoted the school policy of inclusiveness and that if the jilbab was permitted in school some vulnerable children would be pressurised to wear it against their will.[432] Although the House of Lords did not specifically address the argument based on Article 14 of the Convention, it is submitted that the same considerations as justified the actions of the school under Article 9 would have justified their actions under Article 14. Indeed it is inconceivable the House of Lords would not have addressed Article 14 expressly had they though the result would have been any different under that Article.

3.114   There is, however, some tension between the guidance derived from *Sahin v Turkey* and applied in *Begum* and the earlier decision of the House of Lords in *Mandla v Lee.*[433] In the earlier case a school had sought to justify a uniform policy in a very diverse school, inter alia, on the basis of a desire to

---

[426]   See Art 51(1) of the Charter.
[427]   See 'School Uniform and the European Convention on Human Rights', by Richard McManus QC [2006] *Education Law Journal* 87.
[428]   [2006] UKHL 15, [2007] 1 AC 100.
[429]   See [2007] 1 AC 100 at 107C.
[430]   See at paras 25, 50–54 and 87.
[431]   Application No 44774/98 at paras 104–111. That guidance stressed the importance of religious harmony and tolerance between opposing groups.
[432]   See paras 54, 65, 97 and 98.
[433]   [1983] 2 AC 548.

minimise external differences. That was held to be insufficient justification.[434] The House of Lords in *Begum* did not seek to resolve the tension between *Sahin v Turkey* and *Mandla v Lee* in this regard. It would be unfortunate if matters that were relevant to justification under the Convention were irrelevant under the EqA 2010, but the point can only be resolved by the Supreme Court.

3.115 In *Begum* the school had submitted that there had been no interference with Ms Begum's rights for two separate reasons, first she had freely agreed to the restrictions in question and secondly the existence of adequate alternatives to manifest their religion.[435] There was some debate post *Begum* as to whether a person's Article 9 rights could be interfered with if only one of these reasons was present but it was held in *R(X) v Head Teacher of Y school*,[436] it is submitted correctly, that there would be no interference if either reason was present. In that case the applicant had wished to wear the niqab, just as her sisters had done at the same school when they were older. The policy prohibiting the niqab was not sufficiently settled as for the school to be able to show that the applicant had agreed to it. There was, however, an alternative school the applicant could go to and on that basis Silber J held there had been no interference with the applicant's Article 9 rights. He nevertheless considered whether the policy was justified and having noted the importance of cohesion[437] held that it was.[438] Two other arguments not raising convention issues were also dismissed. They were that the applicant had a legitimate expectation she would be allowed to wear the niqab because her sisters had been and also, based on the same fact, that she was entitled to similar treatment. It is of note that in the context of the legitimate expectation argument the court relied on the same material as justifying a departure from any legitimate expectation as it had in relation to the Article 9(2) question and in particular relied on arguments of cohesion.[439]

3.116 A further attempt to invoke Articles 9 and 14 of the ECHR in relation to a school uniform dispute failed in *R(Playfloot) v Governing Body of Millais School*.[440] The pupil wished to wear a purity ring as a symbol of her commitment to chastity before marriage. The court held that the wearing of the ring was not a manifestation of her belief within the meaning of Article 9[441] but, if it was, her Article 9 rights had not been interfered with because she voluntarily accepted the policy and could manifest any belief within the meaning of Article 9 in other ways without undue difficulty.[442] For good measure the court held the policy was justified, inter alia, on the basis that it

---

[434] See at 566C–per Lord Fraser.
[435] See [2007] 1 AC 100 at 103H.
[436] [2007] EWHC 298 (Admin) at paras 27–39.
[437] See para 52.
[438] See paras 64–100.
[439] See paras 125–126.
[440] [2007] EWHC 1698 (Admin).
[441] See paras 23 and 24.
[442] See paras 30–32. In particular she would have been permitted to wear the ring on her bag and there was no evidence she could not have gone to another school.

promoted social cohesion.[443] The claim on Article 14 was based on the facts that the school had permitted various items of what it believed to be religious dress in other cases, such as headscarves and the Kara. The applicant contended that this showed that she as Christian was discriminated against. The court rejected this argument holding that the school had made exceptions to its policy on the basis of what it believed to be requirements of faith and pointing out in particular that the headscarf had been permitted to a Christian from a minority sect.[444] Understandably the court made detailed reference to *Begum* in reaching its conclusions and it is to be noted in particular both that the case did allege discrimination, albeit only under Article 14, and that cohesion was relied on as a legitimate matter capable of forming justification, albeit only expressly in the context of the Article 9 claim.

3.117 In *R (Watkins-Singh) v Governing Body of Aberdare Girls' High School*[445] Silber J upheld a claim of race discrimination by a girl who had not been permitted to wear the Kara[446] at school. He held that there had been both indirect discrimination contrary to what was then section 1(1A) of the RRA 1976 and the Equality Act 2006 and also a breach by the governing body of its duty under what was then section 71 of the RRA 1976.[447] It is the first finding which is relevant here. The court held that the appropriate pool for comparison for the purposes of indirect discrimination was all those whose religious or racial beliefs were compromised by the uniform code on the issue of the Kara or other similar item of jewellery.[448] He then went on to hold that the applicant had suffered a particular disadvantage[449] and that the failure to make an exception to the school uniform policy in the applicant's case was not justifiable.[450]

3.118 It is respectfully submitted that much of the reasoning on both the question of particular disadvantage and justification is questionable:

(a) The learned judge seems to have equated the questions whether the applicant was put under a disadvantage with whether persons in the relevant poll who shared her characteristics were placed under a particular disadvantage.[451] These were separate questions under the then legislative scheme and remained so under the EqA 2010. In effect the court simply looked at the detriment the applicant suffered and failed to see whether the group of similarly placed individuals who shared her characteristics suffered a disparate impact (particular disadvantage) when compared with

---

[443] See paras 36–38.

[444] See para 41.

[445] [2008] EWHC 1865 (Admin).

[446] The nature of the Kara is set out at para 1 of the judgment. It is a plain steel bangle commonly worn by Sikhs and regarded by them as of great significance.

[447] This was replaced by s 149 of the EqA 2010. The nature of this duty is discussed at paras **3.78–3.85** above.

[448] See para 46.

[449] See paras 52–71.

[450] See paras 72–92.

[451] See para 49.

those who did not share that characteristic. Particular disadvantage looked at disparate impact which the court did not analyse.

(b) His purported distinguishing of the earlier school uniform cases when dealing with the question of justification on the basis that the earlier cases were concerned with ostentatious religious symbols[452] is very unsatisfactory. Nowhere in the earlier cases had the highly visible nature of the symbol been regarded as in the least relevant. It is respectfully submitted that the learned judge was right to regard the desire to promote cohesion[453] as a potential justification of a school uniform policy but wrong to hold that this did not apply where the dress in question was not ostentatious. A Kara is a visible sign and if it is worn the school community can be readily divided into racial and religious groups.

3.119 Although, it is respectfully submitted, much of the reasoning in *Aberdare* is questionable, the decision may be right on its facts. Unlike the case of *Begum* there was no evidence that the wearing of the Kara would in fact lead to an undermining of cohesiveness in the school, or create any particular problems. In those circumstances to refuse to admit an exception to the school uniform policy was unreasonable.

3.120 Finally in *G v St Gregory's Catholic Science College Governors*[454] Collins J had to consider the validity of a ban on 'corn row' hairstyles in a school policy. He held:

(a) the prohibition on corn rows amounted to indirect discrimination;[455]

(b) it was not justified;[456] and

(c) it was not sex discrimination.[457]

3.121 Although the case concerned the previous legislative scheme, it was accepted by both parties and held by the court that so far as the case concerned indirect race discrimination the result would have been the same under the EqA 2010.[458] On the issue of particular disadvantage, Collins J said that more than choice was needed to show this but suggested that Silber J had put it too high in *Aberdare* when saying that the disadvantage must be exceptional.[459] He held that whatever the threshold the claimant had suffered it because he was not prepared to have his hair cut and being turned away from the school was

---

[452] See paras 77 and 78
[453] See para 78(c).
[454] [2011] EWHC 1452 (Admin).
[455] See paras 25–41.
[456] See paras 42–51.
[457] See paras 52–60.
[458] See para 11.
[459] See para 37.

traumatic for him.[460] His findings on justification were fact specific. The school had contended that the policy was needed to keep out gang and pop culture influences[461] but cornrows were not indicative of any gang membership or pop culture.[462] Further, the school had accepted that religious reasons could justify exceptions to the policy and the judge held there was no difference between that and the claimant's case.[463] That it is respectfully submitted is questionable because a person who has a religious objection to a school uniform policy is in a much stronger position than a person who does not as the earlier cases such as *Playfoot* had shown. On more solid ground was the point the judge made that the uniform policy was not applied to sixth formers. The judge expected exceptions to be made for the policy only if there was a genuine cultural and family practice of not cutting males' hair and wearing corn rows.[464]

---

[460] See para 38. This analysis it is submitted is deficient in the same way as that of Silber J in *Aberdare* in focussing on detriment to the claimant rather than disparate impact in the relevant groups.

[461] Accepted as a legitimate aim at para 46.

[462] See paras 46–47.

[463] See paras 49–50.

[464] See para 48.

Chapter 4

SPECIAL EDUCATIONAL NEEDS

INTRODUCTION

4.1   The courts are frequently concerned with disputes relating to children with special educational needs (SEN). This Chapter examines the role of the courts in relation to such disputes.[1] There are two principal areas of litigation: challenges to decisions of local authorities and challenges to decisions of the First-tier Tribunal (FTT).[2]

THE STATUTORY FRAMEWORK – AN OUTLINE

4.2   The relevant legislation is now to be found in the Education Act 1996 (EA 1996) as amended. This re-enacted Part III of the Education Act 1993. Some of the relevant case-law dates back to the Education Act 1981 which was in similar, but not identical, form.

4.3   By virtue of section 312(1) of the EA 1996, a child has special educational needs if he has a learning difficulty which calls for special educational provision to be made for him.

4.4   By virtue of section 312(2), subject to certain exceptions, a child has a 'learning difficulty' if he has a significantly greater difficulty in learning than the majority of children of his age,[3] he has a disability which prevents or hinders him from making use of educational facilities of a kind generally

---

[1]   For accounts of the general law relating to special educational needs, see John Ford, Mary Hughes and David Ruebain, *Education Law and Practice* (Jordans, 2009); Simon Oliver and Paula Clements, *Special Educational Needs and the Law* (Jordans, 2007); Oliver Hyams, *Law of Education* (Jordans, 2004) and Simon Whitbourn, *Special Educational Needs and Disability in Education – A Legal Guide* (Butterworths, 2002).

[2]   The Tribunal was formally known as the Special Educational Needs and Disability Tribunal (SENDT), and prior to that, as the Special Educational Needs Tribunal (SENT). The FTT was created by s 3(1) of the Tribunals, Courts and Enforcement Act 2007. With effect from 3 November 2008, the Transfer of Tribunal Functions Order 2008 (SI 2008/2833) transferred the functions of SENDT to the FTT and abolished the SENDT, regs 3, 4 and Sch 1. The 2008 Order applies only in England. In Wales, appeals continue to be heard by the Special Educational Needs Tribunal for Wales, EA 1996, s 333.

[3]   It does not follow that a child with high intelligence may not have special educational needs; see, for example, *R v Secretary of State for Education ex parte C* [1996] ELR 93 at 96E–96F.

provided for children of his age in schools within the area of the LA or he is under compulsory school age and would be likely to have such difficulties when over that age.[4]

4.5 'Special educational provision' is defined by section 312(4) of the EA 1996. In relation to a child who has attained the age of two it means educational provision which is additional to, or otherwise different from, the educational provision made for children of his age in schools maintained by the local authority (LA) (not counting special schools). In relation to children who have not attained that age it means educational provision of any kind.

4.6 By virtue of section 316(2) of the EA 1996,[5] children with special educational needs but without a statement of such needs maintained under section 324 have to be educated in a mainstream school. Children with statements of SEN must be educated in mainstream schools subject to two exceptions.[6] There is no duty so to educate them if it is incompatible with the wishes of the parent or the provision of efficient education for other children.

4.7 The definition of mainstream school in section 316 is an extended one. It excludes a special school, however, and it excludes independent schools save for where the independent school is a city technology college, city college for the technology of the arts or an Academy.[7] The extent of the duty in section 316 to educate a child in a mainstream school is elaborated upon in section 316A. There is no prohibition against a pupil being educated in an independent school which is not a mainstream school or in a school approved under section 342,[8] provided that the LA is not paying the cost.[9]

4.8 Section 316A(3) makes clear that the duties in section 316 do not cut down the operation of section 348 (special educational provision at a non-maintained school which is named in a statement or, if not so named, is required at that particular school, because the interests of the child render it necessary) or of paragraph 3 of Schedule 27, which deals with the ability of parents to express a preference for their child when he requires a statement of SEN.

---

[4]   As to the distinction between educational and non-educational provision, see paras **4.198–4.206** below.

[5]   As substituted by s 1 of the Special Educational Needs and Disability Act 2001 and amended by para 6(3) of Sch 7 to the Education Act 2002.

[6]   EA 1996, s 316(3).

[7]   EA 1996, s 316(4).

[8]   As amended by s 142 of the Education and Skills Act 2008. This section confers power on the 'appropriate national authority' to approve schools which are specially organised to make special educational provision for SEN and which are not community or foundation special schools. S 337A of the EA 1996 (inserted by s 142 of the Education and Skills Act 2008) defines the 'appropriate national authority' as being the Secretary of State, in relation to a school in England, and the Welsh Ministers, in relation to a school in Wales.

[9]   EA 1996, s 316(A).

4.9   Section 316A(4) provides that if the LA decide to make a statement but not to name the school for which the parent has expressed a preference, pursuant to paragraph 3 of Schedule 27, then the LA is bound by section 316(3). The paragraph 3 process must be completed first, and if effect is not given to parental preference pursuant to that process, the obligations under sections 316 and 316A remain.[10]

4.10   In *Bury Metropolitan Council v SU*[11] Upper Tribunal Judge Ward held that section 316(3) does not require a parent to choose mainstream education: if a parent expressed no view an LA would have to name a mainstream school unless that would be incompatible with the provision of efficient education for other children.

4.11   Section 316A(5) and (6) is designed to limit the effect of section 316(3)(b). The LA and the authority responsible for a particular mainstream school will not be able to say that a child cannot be educated in a mainstream school because it is incompatible with the provision of efficient education[12] for other children, unless there are no reasonable steps which the LA or another authority responsible for the school could take to prevent the incompatibility.[13] It is submitted that this imposes a high threshold and requires something more than mere prejudice to the provision of efficient education for other children.[14] Rather, the FTT must consider whether any adverse impact on the provision of efficient education for other children would be so great as to be incompatible with the provision of such education.[15]

4.12   The question of what is reasonable is to be dealt with by guidance to which the authority must have regard[16] and is dealt with in paras 45 and 46 of the statutory guidance. The guidance does not purport to be exhaustive and lists a large number of relevant factors which include:

---

[10]   See *R (H) v SENDT* [2004] EWCA Civ 770; [2004] LGR 844 at para 71; *CCC v London Borough of Tower Hamlets* [2011] UKUT 393 (AAC) per Upper Tribunal Judge Lane at para 28 and *R (LR) v FTT* [2012] UKUT 213 (AAC) per Upper Tribunal Judge Ward at para 36.

[11]   [2010] UKUT 406 (AAC); [2011] ELR 14 at para 19.

[12]   The EA 1996 does not define 'efficient education'. Judge Mesher in *NA v London Borough of Barnet* [2010] UKUT 180 (AAC), [2010] ELR 617 stated that an efficient education did not connote the very highest desirable standard or the very basic minimum, but something in between, and that incompatibility with the provision of efficient education did not entail no meaningful education being provided (at paras 33–34).

[13]   The burden of demonstrating incompatibility with efficient education and that no reasonable steps could cure the incompatibility was said by Upper Tribunal Judge Lane in *CCC v London Borough of Tower Hamlets* [2011] UKUT 393 (AAC) to fall on the LA (at para 28).

[14]   See, by analogy, *Essex County Council v SENDT* [2006] EWHC 1105 (Admin), [2006] ELR 452 at paras 27–29 per Gibbs J where he considered the similar wording in para 3(3)(b) of Sch 27 to the EA 1996.

[15]   See *Hampshire County Council v. R* [2009] EWHC 626 (Admin); [2009] ELR 371 at para 96 per Stadlen J.

[16]   EA 1996, ss 316A(8) and (9). The Statutory Guidance is *Inclusive Schooling – Children with Special Educational Needs*, DfES Guidance 0774/2001.

(a) whether taking the step would be effective in overcoming the incompatibility;

(b) the extent to which it is practical for the maintained school or LA to take the step;

(c) the extent to which steps have already been taken to facilitate the child's inclusion and their effectiveness;

(d) the financial and other resource implications of taking the step; and

(e) the extent of any disruption which taking the step would cause.

4.13 In *Bury Metropolitan Council v SU*[17] Upper Tribunal Judge Ward held that neither resources, nor compatibility of a mainstream school with a child's SEN were relevant factors to take into account under section 316(3) of the EA 1996.[18] He accepted, however, that the question of resources was relevant in determining whether reasonable steps could be taken to prevent the incompatibility under sections 316A(5) and (6) of the EA 1996. Further, Judge Ward accepted that it might not be reasonable to take steps to remove the incompatibility with the education of others if the effect of doing so would be a material adverse effect on the pupil with SEN to receive the provision that he requires.[19]

4.14 Section 316A(2) sets out exceptional circumstances where a pupil without a statement can be educated in a special school. These are where the pupil:

(a) is admitted to a special school for the purposes of an assessment under section 323;

(b) remains admitted to the special school in prescribed circumstances following an assessment under section 323;

(c) is admitted to a special school with the agreement of specified persons following a change in circumstances;

(d) is admitted to a community or foundation special school which is established in a hospital.

4.15 For the first exception to be available, the admission to the special school must be with the agreement of the LA, the headteacher of the school (or its governing body if it is in Wales), the parent and any person whose advice is to be sought under paragraph 2 of Schedule 26.[20] The second category of case

---

17 [2010] UKUT 406 (AAC); [2011] ELR 14.
18 [2010] UKUT 406 (AAC); [2011] ELR 14 at paras 22–23.
19 [2010] UKUT 406 (AAC); [2011] ELR 14 at para 23.
20 A wide range of professionals ranging from the medical to the educational must give advice in

(admission following assessment) is detailed in regulation 13 of the Education (Special Educational Needs) (England) Regulations 2001.[21] It is very limited in scope. The child can stay for ten school days after the LA serve a notice under section 325 informing the child's parent that it does not propose to make a statement or until a statement is made. The third category requires a change of circumstances, the agreement of the LA, the headteacher of the school,[22] and the parent. The Explanatory Notes[23] suggest that the change of circumstances must be sudden, but there is nothing in the section expressly to that effect. Nor is there any guidance as to what change of circumstances suffices for the purpose of section 316A(2)(c). Clearly, if any change of circumstances was sufficient, this would have the effect of undermining the general rule in section 316(2) that a child without a statement must be educated in a mainstream school. While the requirement of consent by the LA, the school, and the parent would provide some control on open-ended admissions to special schools, if any change of circumstance was sufficient to take a child's case outside the general prohibition in section 316(2) there would, in practice, be a limitation on the ability of those bodies to refuse their consent. The public bodies would have to act rationally and further the purposes of the Act and, in refusing consent which would thwart, on this hypothesis, a purpose of the Act, would be amenable to challenge by judicial review on *Padfield*[24] grounds.

4.16 It is submitted that, in its statutory context, any change of circumstance is insufficient for there to be power to place a child without a statement in a special school. What the section is concerned with is change of circumstances for the worse which suggest that the child's needs can no longer be met in a mainstream school and that a statement might be necessary.

4.17 It is also submitted that section 316A(2)(c) is concerned with, as the Explanatory Notes suggest,[25] essentially sudden changes of circumstance. Both section 316A(2)(a) and 316A(2)(b) are concerned with essentially interim arrangements as an adjunct to the statementing process and it is submitted that they lend colour to the type of change of circumstances that is relevant to section 316A(2)(c). Section 316A(2)(d), admission to hospital, is not necessarily temporary; but when it is not temporary, it is a sufficiently exceptional case not to displace the general character of section 316A(2) being concerned with interim arrangements.

---

connection with a formal assessment by virtue of regs 7–10 of the Educational (Special Educational Needs) (England) Regulations 2001 (SI 2001/3455) and regs 7–10 of the Educational (Special Educational Needs) (Wales) Regulations 2002 (SI 2002/152), made under para 2 of Sch 26 to the EA 1996.

21 SI 2001/3455. The parallel provision for Wales is reg 13 of the Educational (Special Educational Needs) (Wales) Regulations 2002 (SI 2002/152).

22 Or governing body of the school if the school is in Wales.

23 To s 1 of the Special Educational Needs and Disability Act 2001 which inserted this section into the EA 1996.

24 *Padfield v MAFF* [1968] AC 997.

25 It is legitimate to look at explanatory notes in order to see what Parliament's purpose was in passing legislation: see *R (Westminster City Council) v National Asylum Support Service* [2002] UKHL 38, [2002] 1 WLR 2956 at para 5 per Lord Steyn.

4.18 Section 317A[26] of the EA 1996 is concerned with the duty of a headteacher, or the governing body of a school, to inform a parent when a child is receiving special educational provision. This section applies if the child is a registered pupil at a community, foundation or voluntary school, a maintained nursery school or a pupil referral unit. In addition, the following conditions must be satisfied:

(a) the child must not have a statement maintained under section 324;

(b) the child must be in receipt of special educational provision because it is considered he has SEN;

(c) the parent must not have been previously informed that the child was in receipt of special educational provision at the school.

4.19 Who is required to inform the parent pursuant to the duty under section 317A(1) depends on the institution the child is attending. If this is a pupil referral unit, it is the headteacher who must inform the parent, but the statutory duty to secure that the headteacher so informs the parent is placed on the LA, not the headteacher himself. If the pupil is at a school, then the duty to inform the parent is on the governing body.

4.20 By virtue of section 321 of the EA 1996,[27] the LA is under a duty to identify children who have SEN where it is necessary for the LA to determine the special educational provision required for any learning difficulty identified. That duty is confined to children who are in the LA's area and registered as pupils at a maintained school or a maintained nursery school, or who are educated at a school which is not a maintained school or nursery school at the expense of the LA. Those who are not registered pupils at school are still the responsibility of the LA providing they are not under the age of two or over compulsory school age and have been brought to the attention of the LA as probably having special educational needs.[28]

4.21 If the LA considers that a child has, or probably has, SEN and that it is necessary for it to determine the child's special educational provision, section 323 of the EA 1996[29] provides for the LA to assess the child's needs.[30]

---

[26] As inserted by s 7(1) of the SSFA 2001, and as amended by the Education Act 2002, s 215, Sch 21, para 42.

[27] As amended by the SSFA 1998, Sch 30, paras 57 and 76, and by the Education Act 2002, s 215, Sch 21, para 42.

[28] EA 1996, s 321(3) as amended by the SSFA 1998, Sch 30, paras 57 and 76. This section was considered in its previous form in *R v Dorset and Further Education Funding Council ex parte Goddard* [1995] ELR 109, Auld J; *Rv Oxfordshire ex parte B* [1997] ELR 90, CA; *S v Essex County Council and SENT* [2000] ELR 718; and *Wakefield MDC v E* [2001] EWHC (Admin) 508, [2002] ELR 203. The question of the nature of the duty of the LA to children over 16 who are not registered at schools is discussed at paras **4.207–4.215** below.

[29] As amended by the Special Educational Needs and Disability Act 2001, para 11(1) of Sch 8.

[30] In *NM v London Borough of Lambeth* [2011] UKUT 499 (AAC) (at para 16) Upper Tribunal Judge Mark concluded that para 7.34 of the Code of Practice (see para **4.27** below), that

There is a notice procedure to the parents and the LA then must decide, having considered any representations and evidence submitted to it, whether to carry out the assessment. Where an LA decides to make an assessment, it must give notice to the child's parent of the decision and their reasons for making it.[31] Conversely, if after serving notice on the child's parents, an LA decides not to assess the educational needs of the child, they shall give notice in writing to the child's parent of that decision.[32] If an assessment is carried out, Schedule 26 to the EA 1996 and the Education (Special Educational Needs) (England) (Consolidation) Regulations 2001[33] detail the range of evidence and manner in which the assessment is to be conducted.

4.22 Section 324 of the EA 1996 provides that if, following an assessment under section 323, it is necessary for the LA to determine the special educational provision which any learning difficulty he may have calls for, the authority shall make and maintain a statement of his special educational needs. In *NC & DH v Hertfordshire*[34] the Upper Tribunal Judge held that an LA must ask two questions when determining whether to issue a statement of special educational needs: (i) whether the special educational provision identified as necessary for the child in the assessment carried out under section 323 is in fact available within the resources normally available to a mainstream school, and (ii) if so, can the school reasonably be expected to make such provision from within its resources. Further, the Upper Tribunal accepted that the resources 'normally available' will differ from case to case and from LA to LA but that it was proper for an LA to take account of the money and personnel provided to a school by a delegated budget.[35]

4.23 Detailed procedures set out in section 324 of, and Schedule 27 to, the EA 1996 provide how a statement is to be made and maintained. The statement must give details of the authority's assessment of the child's special educational needs, and these are set out in Part 2 of the statement.[36] The statement must specify the special educational provision to be made for the purpose of meeting those needs: these are set out in Part 3 of the statement.[37] Finally, the statement must specify the type of school or other institution which the LA considers would be appropriate for the child: this is done in Part 4 of the statement.[38]

---

suggested that an assessment would be necessary where there was 'convincing evidence' that a child's special educational needs have not been remedied sufficiently by steps taken by the school, was incorrect. He held that it was impossible to reconcile with the language of s 323 which requires only that a child 'probably': (i) has special educational needs, and (ii) that is necessary for the LA to determine the special educational provision which any learning difficulty he may have calls for.

[31]   EA 1996, s 323(4).
[32]   EA 1996, s 323(6).
[33]   SI 2001/3455, regs 6–13. There are similar regulations for Wales: see SI 2002/152.
[34]   [2012] UKUT 85 (AAC) at para 32.
[35]   [2012] UKUT 85 (AAC) at paras 35–38.
[36]   EA 1996, s 324(3)(a).
[37]   EA 1996, s 324(3)(b).
[38]   EA 1996, s 324(3)(c).

Parts 2 and 3 have been likened to a medical diagnosis and prescription.[39] The LA (and where appropriate the FTT) must identify or diagnose the need before going on to prescribe the educational provision to which that need gives rise, and only once the necessary educational provision has been identified can the LA specify the institution or type of institution which is appropriate to provide it.[40]

4.24 Sullivan J in *S v City of Swansea and Confrey* stated that the mischief to be avoided is 'putting the cart before the horse'[41] but accepted that once Parts 2 and 3 had been settled, the 'prescription in the remainder of Part 3 may be "informed" by what is actually available at a particular school'.[42]

4.25 There is a right of appeal to the FTT against a decision not to make a statement following an assessment under section 325.[43]

4.26 There are duties to review the child's needs under section 328 and to assess the child's needs under section 329 if the parents so request. There is a similar duty under section 329A[44] to assess at the request of the responsible body of a relevant school. Relevant schools are defined by section 329A(12) and include both maintained and independent schools. The responsible body is defined by section 329A(13) and is, in general, the proprietor or headteacher of the school in question.

4.27 The Secretary of State is empowered by section 313 of the EA 1996 to issue and revise a Code of Practice, to which LAs and others exercising relevant functions must have regard. The Code[45] makes detailed provision as to the practice in relation to SEN. It must be consulted about in draft and must be approved by a resolution of each House of Parliament: see section 314.

4.28 Local authorities are under a general duty under section 315 to keep under review the arrangements made by them for special educational provision. In performance of that duty they are obliged, to the extent that seems to them necessary or desirable for the purpose of co-ordinating provision for children with SEN, to consult with governing bodies of community, foundation and voluntary, and community and foundation special schools in their area.

---

[39] *R v Secretary of State for Education and Science, ex parte E* [1993] 2 FCR 753; [1992] 1 FLR 377, 388–389.

[40] *Learning Trust v MP and SENDIST* [2007] EWHC 1634 (Admin) at para 42 per Andrew Nicol QC sitting as a Deputy Judge of the High Court.

[41] [2000] ELR 315 at 322H.

[42] [2000] ELR 315 at 323A. See also *GC & JC v Tameside Metropolitan Borough Council* [2011] UKUT 292 (AAC) at paras 34–38 per Upper Tribunal Judge Wikeley.

[43] As amended by Sch 8, para 6 and Sch 9 to the Special Educational Needs and Disability Act 2001.

[44] As inserted by s 8 of the Special Educational Needs and Disability Act 2001, and amended by Childcare Act 2006, s 103, Sch 2 para 22 and the Education Act 2002, s 215, Sch 21, para 44 and Sch 22, Pt 3.

[45] The present Codes of Practice came into force on 1 January 2002 for England and 1 April 2002 for Wales; see SI 2001/3943 and SI 2002/157.

Governing bodies of community, foundation or voluntary schools, and maintained nursery schools, are under a duty under section 317 of the EA 1996 to use their best endeavours to ensure that children at their school who have SEN get the appropriate special educational provision. There are also duties under that section to secure that teachers know that a child has SEN and the importance of identifying and providing for those needs. Where those duties are on the governing bodies, the LA is empowered by section 318 to provide goods and services to the governing bodies to assist them in the performance of those duties.

4.29 Section 312A of the EA 1996 provides that the provisions of Part IV do not apply to a child who is subject to a detention order and detained in relevant youth accommodation.[46] A statement maintained for a child immediately before the beginning of the detention by an LA is to be treated as being maintained by that authority from the child's release.[47]

CHALLENGING DECISIONS OF THE LOCAL AUTHORITY IN THE COURTS

The First-tier Tribunal

4.30 The FTT was established by section 3 of the Tribunals, Courts and Enforcement Act 2007.[48] Section 7(1) of the 2007 Act empowers the Lord Chancellor, with the concurrence of the Senior President of the Tribunals, by order to make provision for the organisation of the FTT into a number of chambers. The Health, Education and Social Care Chamber has jurisdiction to hear appeals concerning special educational needs.[49] It is the body which

---

[46] Inserted by the Apprenticeships, Skills, Children and Learning Act 2009, s 52. EA 1996, s 562(1A) defines a 'detention order' and 'relevant youth accommodation'.

[47] EA 1996, s 312A(3).

[48] The FTT was created by s 3(1) of the Tribunals, Courts and Enforcement Act 2007. With effect from 3 November 2008, the Transfer of Tribunal Functions Order 2008 (SI 2008/2833) transferred the functions of SENDT to the FTT and abolished the SENDT, regs 3, 4 and Sch 1. The 2008 Order applies only in England. In Wales, appeals continue to be heard by the Special Educational Needs Tribunal for Wales, EA 1996, s 333 applying the Special Educational Needs and Disability Tribunal (General Provisions and Disability Claims Procedure) Regulations 2002 (SI 2002/1985). Pursuant to s 313(5) of the EA 1996, references to 'the Tribunal' in Pt IV of the EA 1996 are references to the FTT, where the LA concerned is in England, or references to the Special Educational Needs Tribunal for Wales, where the LA concerned is in Wales.

[49] See the First-tier Tribunal and Upper Tribunal (Chambers) Order 2010 (SI 2010/2655), reg 2 (which states that the chambers of the First-tier Tribunal shall include the Health, Education and Social Care Chamber. Reg 4 sets out the functions of the Health, Education and Social Care Chamber of the FTT. These include an appeal against a decision related to children with special educational needs. The FTT is for this purpose constituted as a three person panel, a judge and two other members where each member has substantial experience of education, childcare, health or social care matters, see the Practice Statement 'Composition of Tribunals in relation to matters that fall to be decided by the Health, Education and Social Care Chamber on or after 3 November 2008' (15 December 2008).

decides the merits of disputes between the LA and parents in relation to children with special educational needs.

4.31 The required composition of the FTT varies. A decision that disposes of proceedings before the FTT, made at or after a hearing, must be made by one judge and two other members where each member has substantial experience of education, childcare, health, or social care matters. Interlocutory decisions, including decisions on an application to strike out a claim, are determined by a judge sitting alone.[50]

4.32 The right of appeal to the FTT is vested in the parent.[51] A parent includes a person who is not a parent of the child but who has parental responsibility for him, or who has care of the child.[52] A parent includes a foster parent.[53]

4.33 A parent has a right of appeal to the tribunal under:

(a) Section 325(1) and (2) of the EA 1996 where the council refuses to make a statement following an assessment under section 323.

(b) Section 326 of the EA 1996 against the contents of a statement.

(c) Section 328(3)(b) of the EA 1996 in relation to a refusal to assess (in relation to a child for whom a statement is maintained).

(d) Section 328A(3) of the EA 1996 where the LA refuses to amend a statement following an annual review.

(e) Section 329(2)(b) of the EA 1996 also in relation to assessments (in relation to a child for whom a statement is not maintained).

(f) Section 329A(8) of the EA 1996 when the LA decides not to assess a child following a request from the responsible body under that section.

---

[50] See the Practice Statement on the 'Composition of Tribunals in Relation to Matters that Fall to be Decided by the Health, Education and Social Care Chamber on or after 18 January 2010' (16 December 2009), made pursuant to reg 1 of the First-tier Tribunal and Upper Tribunal (Composition of Tribunal) Order 2008 (SI 2008/2835).

[51] In Wales, amendments to the EA 1996 Act made by the Education (Wales) Measure 2009, ss 1–3, confer a right of appeal to the tribunal on the child for all appeals under Part IV of the EA 1996. This appeal is to be exercised concurrently with that of the parent. The provisions have yet to be brought into force.

[52] Education Act 1996, s 576(1). The phrase 'parental responsibility' has the same meaning as in the Children Act 1989. Pursuant to s 576(4), when determining whether an individual has the care of a child, any absence of the child at a hospital or boarding school and any other temporary absence shall be disregarded.

[53] See *F v Humberside* [1997] ELR 12. It was argued by the county council that a foster parent did not have a right of appeal. Laws J rejected this argument. He commented that the position would have been different in relation to a nanny or a babysitter. The Judge commented that it would be unsatisfactory if the only parent for the foster child was the LA as it would then be wearing two conflicting hats.

(g) Paragraph 8(3)(b) of Schedule 27 where a parent of a child, for whom a statement is maintained which specifies the name of a school or institution, has a request for a change of school turned down.

(h) Paragraph 11(2)(b) of Schedule 27 in relation to a decision to cease to maintain a statement.

4.34 There has been some debate in the courts about the scope of the above rights of appeal. It will be observed that the right of appeal under section 325(1) and (2) against a decision not to make a statement requires there to have been a prior assessment under section 323. In *O v Harrow LBC*[54] the Court of Appeal held that one prior assessment under section 323 was sufficient to ground more than one appeal. The facts in that case were a little unusual. There had been an assessment and the LA concluded that a statement was not necessary. Instead, it issued a note in lieu and the parents appealed. On appeal, the SENDT remitted the matter to the LA for reconsideration. There was no fresh assessment prior to the reconsideration and the LA decided not to issue a statement but to amend its note in lieu. On a fresh appeal, the SENDT acceded to an application to strike out for want of jurisdiction. The High Court held on appeal that the SENDT did, indeed, lack jurisdiction to hear the fresh appeal, but the appeal was subsequently allowed by the Court of Appeal.

4.35 The court concluded[55] that multiple appeals could be controlled by the SENDT exercising (in an appropriate case) the power it then had to strike out appeals that were scandalous or vexatious. The court was influenced by the desirability of matters in this field being considered by the tribunal rather than the courts on an application for judicial review.[56] It is respectfully submitted that this was a sound policy consideration. Unfortunately, the consequence of the decision is that the assessment, which was plainly intended to inform the process as to whether there should be a statement, becomes a purely arbitrary trigger to a right of appeal and, in practice, there will be little restraint on multiple appeals. It will nearly always be possible to have some extra expert evidence, falling short of the full requirements of a statutory assessment, which suggests that the LA decision should be reconsidered.[57]

4.36 The process for appealing to the FTT is dealt with in detail in the Tribunal Procedure (First-tier Tribunal) (Health, Education and Social Care Chamber) Rules 2008 (the FTT Rules).[58] By virtue of rule 20 the parent must

---

[54] [2001] EWCA Civ 2046, [2002] 1 WLR 928.

[55] [2001] EWCA Civ 2046, [2002] 1 WLR 928 at paras 22 and 30.

[56] At paras 25, 28 and 30.

[57] By contrast, in *East Sussex County Council v Hughes (President of SENDT)* [2004] EWHC 1834 (Admin) Jack J held that there was no right of appeal to the Tribunal against a statement of SEN issued pursuant to a Tribunal order under para 11(3)(b) of Sch 27 to the EA 1996 (at paras 34–35).

[58] SI 2008/2699. See also the Practice Direction for the FTT, Health, Education and Social Care Chamber, *Special Educational Needs or Disability Discrimination in Schools Cases* (30 October 2008). The procedural rules for the Special Educational Needs Tribunal for Wales are the Special Educational Needs Tribunal Regulations 2001 (SI 2001/600).

send or deliver an application notice to the Tribunal within two months[59] after written notice of the decision being challenged was sent to the parent.[60] Pursuant to rule 21, upon receipt of an application notice the LA must send or deliver the Tribunal a response, so that it is received within 30 days.[61] The Tribunal has the power to extend time, upon a request being made, for both the application notice and for the response.[62]

4.37 The FTT has wide case management powers. Rule 2(1) contains the 'overriding objective' which is 'to enable the Tribunal to deal with cases fairly and justly'. Rule 2(3) requires the FTT to seek to give effect to the overriding objective when it exercises any power under the FTT Rules or interprets any rule or practice direction. Rule 2(4) requires the parties to 'help the Tribunal to further the overriding objective' and to 'cooperate with the Tribunal generally'. Pursuant to rule 2(2), dealing with cases fairly and justly includes:

(a)   dealing with the case in ways which are proportionate to the importance of the case, the complexity of the issues, the anticipated costs and the resources of the parties;

(b)   avoiding unnecessary formality and seeking flexibility in the proceedings;

(c)   ensuring, so far as possible, that parties are able to participate fully in the proceedings;

(d)   using any special expertise of the FTT effectively;

(e)   avoiding delay, so far as compatible with the proper consideration of the issues.[63]

4.38 Rule 5(1) of the FTT Rules provides that the FTT may regulate its own procedure. Rule 5(3) sets out, without restricting the general powers in rule 5(1), the powers of the FTT in relation to case management.[64] A problem

---

[59]   Rule 12 of the FTT Rules contains special provision for the calculation of time. Most notably August and the period between 25 December and 1 January are entirely discounted. Rule 10(4) of the FTT Rules provides that the FTT can direct that the rules on time do not apply.

[60]   The contents of the application notice are prescribed by r 20 and the Practice Direction for the FTT, Health, Education and Social Care Chamber, *Special Educational Needs or Disability Discrimination in Schools Cases* (30 October 2008) (at paras 3–5). In Wales, reg 7(5) of the Special Educational Needs Tribunal Regulations 2001 requires a parent to deliver the notice of appeal to the secretary of the tribunal so that it is received no later than the first working day after the expiry of two months from the date that the authority gave him notice under Part IV of the EA 1996 that he had a right of appeal, reg 7(3) of the 2001 Regulations.

[61]   FTT Rules, r 21(1). The contents of the response are prescribed by r 21 and the Practice Direction for the FTT, Health, Education and Social Care Chamber, *Special Educational Needs or Disability Discrimination in Schools Cases* (30 October 2008) (at paras 9–10).

[62]   See reg 20(4) (application notice) and reg 21(4) (response) of the FTT Rules. In Wales, the President has the power to extend time, with or without an application, in exceptional circumstances, reg 51 of the Special Educational Needs Tribunal Regulations 2001.

[63]   These principles derive from the Tribunals, Courts and Enforcement Act 2007, s 22(4).

[64]   Those include, for example, the power to extend or shorten time for complying with any rule or

that occurred with frequency prior to 3 November 2008 was parents refusing to permit their children to be the subject of an assessment by an LA expert witness prior to a tribunal hearing. That eventuality is now addressed in rule 15(4) of the FTT Rules which in SEN cases empowers the FTT to require the parent of a child, or any other person with care of the child or parental responsibility for him, to make the child available for examination or assessment by a suitably qualified professional person. Rule 15(5) of the FTT Rules permits the FTT to consider a failure by a party to comply with a requirement made under paragraph (4), in the absence of any good reason for such failure, as a failure to cooperate with the FTT which 'could lead to a result which is adverse to that party's case'.

4.39 The FTT must hold a hearing before making a decision which disposes of proceedings unless each party has consented to the matter being decided without a hearing and the FTT considers that it is able to decide the matter without a hearing.[65] The child is entitled to attend the hearing and the FTT may permit the child to give evidence and to address the FTT.[66] Hearings in SEN cases are to be held in private unless the FTT considers that it is in the interests of justice for the case to be held in public.[67] If a party fails to attend a hearing, the FTT may proceed with the hearing if the FTT is satisfied that the party has been notified of the hearing or that reasonable steps have been taken to notify the party of the hearing and the FTT considers that it is in the interests of justice to proceed with the hearing.[68]

4.40 The FTT must provide to each party as soon as reasonably practicable after making a decision which finally disposes of all issues in the proceedings a decision notice stating the FTT's decision, written reasons for the decision, and notification of any rights of review or appeal against the decision and the time within which, and the manner in which, such rights of review or appeal may be exercised.[69]

---

practice direction, permit or require a party to amend a document, permit or require a party to provide documents, information or submissions to the FTT, and adjourn or postpone a hearing. Rule 6 sets out the procedure for applying for and giving directions. Rule 7 provides various sanctions for a failure by a party to comply with a requirement of the FTT Rules, a Practice Direction or a direction. Rule 8 gives the FTT the power to strike out a party's case. Rule 9 empowers the FTT to substitute or add parties. Rules 13–16 make provision for evidence and documents. In *HJ v London Borough of Brent* [2010] UKUT 15 (AAC) the Upper Tribunal gave guidance on the approach that the FTT should adopt to the late submission of evidence at paras 13–19.

[65] Rule 23(1) of the FTT Rules.

[66] Rule 24 of the FTT Rules. The FTT must give the parties reasonable notice of the time and the place of the hearing which should ordinarily be 14 days (unless the parties consent or in urgent or exceptional circumstances), see r 25 of the FTT Rules.

[67] Rule 26(2) of the FTT Rules.

[68] Rule 27 of the FTT Rules.

[69] Rule 30(2) of the FTT Rules. Rule 29 of the FTT Rules permits the FTT at the request of the parties, but only where it considers it appropriate, to make a consent order disposing of proceedings and making such other appropriate provision as the parties have agreed. There is no need for the FTT to hold a hearing before making a consent order, or for the FTT to provide reasons for the consent order.

4.41 A decision of the tribunal to extend time is only reviewable if the exercise of the tribunal's discretion was perverse or revealed an error of law.[70] It has further been held that it is not an error of law to refuse to extend time because of a mistake by advisers who held themselves out as competent so to act, whether or not they were legally qualified.[71]

4.42 The right of appeal to the FTT should be resorted to rather than an application made to the court for permission to move for judicial review. It is a general principle of judicial review that the courts will not entertain a challenge in the exercise of their discretion where there is an adequate alternative remedy. Those rights of appeal are an adequate alternative remedy.[72] They do not, however, cover the whole field; for example, as was pointed out in *White v Ealing and others*,[73] the tribunal has no jurisdiction to rule on the funding obligation of an LA.[74]

4.43 It is to be noted that it is only a parent who has a right of appeal to the tribunal.[75] It is submitted that this does not mean that the child can launch an application for judicial review, rather than appeal to the tribunal through his parents. This would be a clear abuse of process if it was done in order to obtain public funding.[76] It may not be an abuse of process if the child is over the age of 16 and the parent will not appeal to the tribunal.

4.44 In *R v Barnet ex parte Barnett*,[77] Hidden J refused an application for leave to move for judicial review of a decision of a LA where there was a dispute about whether the tribunal had jurisdiction to hear any appeal. The applicant had obtained advice from the tribunal to the effect that it lacked

---

[70] *R v SENT ex parte J* [1997] ELR 237 at 240D.

[71] *R v SENT ex parte J* at 239D–239G and *S and C v Special Educational Needs Tribunal* [1997] ELR 242.

[72] In *R v SENT ex parte F* [1996] ELR 213, Popplewell J set aside leave to move for judicial review when the right of appeal had not been exercised. He held, at 216G–217C, that if there was a statutory right of appeal it was to be exercised and that, save in exceptional circumstances, judicial review should not be granted.

[73] [1998] ELR 203: see para **1.97(a)** above. Followed by Ognall J in *G v SENT and Barnet*, CO/1335/1997 (unreported) 22 October 1997. As noted at para **1.97(a)** above, the Court of Appeal defeated the application of this principle in *Dudley v Shurvinton* [2012] EWCA Civ 346 by characterising a dispute about who should pay the transport to the parents' preferred school as one about educational provision.

[74] Other areas where judicial review is the only appropriate remedy are discussed at paras **4.110**, **4.111**, **4.112**, **4.113** and **4.114** below.

[75] *S v SENT* [1995] 1 WLR 1627 at 1629H–1631B, Latham J; affirmed on appeal [1996] 1 WLR 382.

[76] See *R v SENT ex parte South Cambridgeshire CC and Chapman* CO/1752/96, Ognall J, Current Law 1996 Reference 967210. There has been a debate, which is discussed at paras **1.1–1.2** above, about whether it is an abuse of process to bring proceedings for judicial review in the name of the child, rather than the parent, when there is no doubt that judicial review is the correct way to commence proceedings. It is submitted that this debate does not affect the position that it is an abuse of process to bring proceedings for judicial review, rather than by way of statutory appeal, simply to obtain public funding.

[77] (Unreported) 27 November 1995, Hidden J.

jurisdiction, but had not formally appealed. Hidden J refused leave and held that the applicant should institute an appeal to the tribunal and then appeal on a point of law.

Interim relief

4.45 An amendment to a statement of SEN takes effect forthwith despite any appeal; there is no statutory provision in the EA 1996 or elsewhere that suspends the effect of a decision of a LA to amend a statement of SEN, save in one regard. Paragraph 11(5) of Schedule 27 to the EA 1996 (inserted by section 6 of the Special Educational Needs and Disability Act 2001) provides that an LA may not cease to maintain a statement if the parent of a child has appealed against the authority's determination to cease to maintain the statement and the appeal has not been determined by the FTT or withdrawn.[78] Further, there is no provision for the FTT to grant interim relief pending a tribunal hearing, either in the EA 1996 or in the FTT Rules.

4.46 A court with a judicial review jurisdiction has power to order relief, including interim relief, pending the decision of the FTT.[79] A court will, however, be reluctant to exercise this power. Interim relief will in general be granted only where there are 'exceptional circumstances'.[80] That is for the following reasons. First, the statutory structure clearly envisages that amendments to statements of SEN take effect forthwith despite any appeal which is in contrast to decisions to cease to maintain a statement, which are suspended pending an appeal. Secondly, when the EA 1996 was amended by section 6 of the Special Educational Needs and Disability Act 2001, Parliament chose not to include provision for a stay in respect of an amendment to the statement of SEN. Thirdly, Parliament envisaged that this might well lead to a period of time elapsing between the lodging of the appeal and the hearing of the appeal.[81]

4.47 In the limited number of cases in which interim relief has been granted, the effect of that relief has been to maintain the status quo, in terms of both school placement and funding for that school placement. A stay of the decision to amend a statement of SEN was granted in *R (G) v London Borough of*

[78] A decision prior to the insertion of para 11(5) of Sch 27 to the EA 1996, *R v Oxfordshire County Council, ex p Roast* [1996] ELR 381, concerned a decision to cease to maintain a statement of SEN pending an appeal to the tribunal. Under the law then applicable an amendment took effect when made and subsisted to and beyond the appeal unless the tribunal decided otherwise on an appeal (at 387D–387E). Dyson J recognised that this construction could produce unfortunate results involving disruption to a child's education, as inevitably there will be a time gap between the decision of the LA and the decision of the tribunal.

[79] That is the High Court, and in the circumstances pertaining in s 15 of the Tribunals, Courts and Enforcement Act 2007, the UT.

[80] See *R (G) v London Borough of Barnet* [2005] EWHC 1946 (Admin); [2006] ELR 4 per Ouseley J (considering the decision of the Court of Appeal in *Re M (A Minor)* [1996] ELR 135) and *R (JW) v The Learning Trust* [2009] UKUT 1997 (AAC); [2010] ELR 115 at para 29.

[81] See, for example, *R (JW) v The Learning Trust* [2009] UKUT 1997 (AAC); [2010] ELR 115 at paras 27–29.

Barnet[82] and in *R (S) v Norfolk County Council*[83] where the result of the amendment would have been to terminate a place at a residential school previously funded by the LA.

4.48 By way of contrast, in *R v Worcestershire County Council, ex p S*,[84] the parent sought an injunction to compel the LA to fund the provision of the Lovaas programme to their son pending the issue of an assessment and statement some six weeks or so after the judicial review hearing. The parents had been paying for the programme, but were unable to continue to fund it. Popplewell J refused to grant the relief, noting that that maintaining the status quo 'with a totally different paymaster' did not, in fact, constitute maintaining the status quo.

4.49 In *R (JW) v The Learning Trust* the Upper Tribunal considered the following factors to be relevant in its decision to decline relief: the time period until the hearing was relatively short, there was no evidence that any provision being considered for JW at the parent's school in respect of which he would lose an opportunity if he could not start it immediately, indeed there was evidence that the programme at the parent's school was individualised and so capable of being delivered from a later start date, the parent had allowed an entire school term to elapse after lodging an appeal before seeking judicial review and further, the parent had failed to apply for her appeal to the tribunal to be expedited.[85]

4.50 As we have seen,[86] there is, in general, a two-month time-limit for appealing to the tribunal but there is a discretion to extend time in exceptional circumstances. What is the status of the statement, where the LA has issued a notice to cease to maintain a statement, but an appeal to the tribunal is lodged out of time? It is submitted that the LA is not bound to desist from its decision to cease to maintain a statement once the time period for appealing has expired simply because of the possibility that there might be an appeal out of time, coupled with an application for an extension of time. The contrary result would have the undesirable result of requiring the LA to maintain a statement for a possibly indefinite period of time based on a theoretical possibility of an out-of-time future appeal.

4.51 It does not follow that the LA should in all circumstances cease to maintain a statement as soon as the primary period for appealing has expired. For example, if the LA knows that an appeal is to be lodged, but that wholly exceptionally the parent has been prevented from doing so by reason of illness, it would not be reasonable to cease to maintain the statement in the interim. It would also be an improper purpose, and subject to attack on *Padfield* grounds, if the LA motivation for doing so was to defeat the manifest intention of

---

[82]   [2005] EWHC 1946 (Admin); [2006] ELR 4.
[83]   [2004] EWHC 404 (Admin); [2004] ELR 259.
[84]   [1999] ELR 46.
[85]   [2009] UKUT 1997 (AAC); [2010] ELR 115, at paras 31–37.
[86]   See para **4.36** above.

paragraph 11(5) of Schedule 27, which is that in a case involving a cessation of a statement, the status quo should be maintained pending an appeal.

4.52 The courts have also had to consider the problem that arises when an LA names in a statement a school with which the parents are so unhappy that they refuse to send the child to any school at all pending their appeal to the tribunal. Can section 19 of the EA 1996 be used, in effect, to oblige the LA to provide home tuition for the child for the period that it takes for the appeal to be determined?

4.53 Section 19 obliges the LA to make arrangements for the provision of suitable education[87] at school or otherwise for children who, by reason of illness exclusion or otherwise, may not receive suitable education unless such arrangements are made for them. In *R (G) v Westminster City Council* Lord Philips MR, giving the judgment of the court, held that if there was no suitable education available that is reasonably practicable for the child to attend, the LA will be in breach of section 19. If suitable education has been made available which is reasonably practicable, but for one reason or another the child is not taking advantage of if, the LA will not be in breach of section 19.[88] Lord Philips stated that the fact that parents have objections to their child attending a particular school does not make the situation one in which it is not reasonably practicable for the child to receive education so as to give rise to an obligation on the part of the authority to provide alternative arrangements.[89] Lord Philips added however, that it was possible to conceive of exceptional situations in which the LA school provides suitable education and there was no physical impediment in the child attending the school, yet it was nonetheless not reasonable to expect the child to attend the school. The example given was that of a situation in which three other children in the school were facing criminal charges, which they denied, of sexually assaulting that child. The LA would then come under a duty under section 19 to make alternative arrangements.[90]

4.54 The test of 'reasonable practicability' was described by Blake J in *R (R) v Kent County Council* as being 'strict ... verging upon but not quite the same as impossibility'.[91]

4.55 There has been some discussion in the case-law as to who is to decide whether a school is 'suitable' and whether it is 'reasonably practicable' for a child to attend the LA school. Without any reasoning on the point, the Court of Appeal in *R (G) v Westminster City Council* determined for itself whether or not it was reasonably practicable for G to attend the LA school.[92] In *C v*

---

[87] EA 1996, s 19(6) defines 'suitable education' as being 'efficient education suitable to his age, ability and aptitude and to any special educational needs he may have'.
[88] [2004] EWCA Civ 45; [2004] 1 WLR 1113 at paras 42–48.
[89] [2004] EWCA Civ 45; [2004] 1 WLR 1113, at para 47.
[90] [2004] EWCA Civ 45; [2004] 1 WLR 1113, at para 48.
[91] [2006] EWHC 2135; [2007] ELR 648 at para 25.
[92] [2004] EWCA Civ 45; [2004] 1 WLR 1113 at paras 42–48.

London Borough of Brent the Court of Appeal held that in the exercise of its statutory duty under section 19, it is for the LA to exercise a professional judgment as to what is 'suitable', a judgment which is open to challenge only where the LA has erred in law.[93] Subsequent decisions have held that questions of suitability, and what is 'reasonably practical', are for the LA in the first instance subject to the supervision of the courts on traditional public law grounds (for example, rationality).[94]

CHALLENGING DECISIONS OF THE FIRST-TIER TRIBUNAL

General

4.56 Since 3 November 2008, both the FTT and the Upper Tribunal (the UT) have, in certain circumstances, jurisdiction to amend or set aside a decision of the FTT. The UT was created by section 3 of the Tribunals, Courts and Enforcement Act 2007. It is a superior court of record.

4.57 Prior to 3 November 2008, section 11 of the Tribunals and Inquiries Act 1992 created a right of appeal from the SENDT on a point of law to the High Court.[95] Many of the older cases, therefore, are decisions of the Administrative Court.

Jurisdiction of FTT to amend or set aside its own decisions

4.58 The FTT has jurisdiction to amend, or set aside, its decisions in certain circumstances. The first circumstance pertains where there has been a clerical mistake or other accidental slip or omission in a decision, direction or any other document produced by the FTT. In those circumstances, the FTT may at any time correct the error by sending notification of the amended decision or direction, or a copy of the amended document, to all parties.[96]

---

[93] [2006] EWCA Civ 728; [2006] ELR 435 at paras 45 (per Smith LJ), 52 (per Laws LJ). It followed, said Smith LJ, that the focus of inquiry was not on the reasonableness or otherwise of the conduct of the parents in withdrawing the child from the school, see para 39.

[94] See *R (R) v Kent County Council* [2006] EWHC 2135; [2007] ELR 648 at paras 21–22 per Blake J; *R (B) v London Borough of Barnet* [2009] EWHC 2842 (Admin) in which HHJ McKenna sitting as a deputy Judge of the High Court held that it was not reasonably practicable for a child to attend a school which the headteacher had described as not being a suitable placement, see para 39; *R (HR) v Medway Council* [2010] EWHC 731 (Admin) at paras 44–45, per Geraldine Andrews QC sitting as a deputy judge of the High Court; and *R (KS) v Croydon London Borough Council* [2010] EWHC 339 (Admin); [2011] ELR 109 in which Lindblom J held that a language college was not suitable for a looked after child, see paras 35–38).

[95] There was a further right of appeal to the Court of Appeal from the High Court, but only with permission, s 11(5) of the Tribunals and Inquiries Act 1992.

[96] Regulation 44 of the FTT Rules.

4.59 The second circumstance applies where there has been a prescribed form of procedural impropriety.[97] The tribunal may set aside a decision which disposes of proceedings, or part of a decision, and re-make the decision or the relevant part of it if the tribunal considers that it is in the interests of justice to do so.[98]

4.60 Thirdly, the FTT has the power to review its own decisions. The extent of the power to review is limited by section 9 of the Tribunals, Courts and Enforcement Act 2007 and by regulations 47–49 of the Tribunal Procedure (First-tier Tribunal) (Health, Education and Social Care Chamber) Rules 2008 (the FTT Rules). Pursuant to regulation 49(1) of the FTT Rules, the FTT has the power to review its own decision in two circumstances: first, where circumstances have changed,[99] and second, on an application to the FTT for permission to appeal to the Upper Tribunal. Before considering whether or not to grant permission to appeal, the FTT must consider whether or not to review the decision.[100]

4.61 The power of the FTT to review a decision is exercisable of its own initiative or on application by a person who has a right of appeal in respect of a decision.[101]

4.62 The powers of the FTT on a review are contained in section 9(4) of the Tribunals, Courts and Enforcement Act 2007. Where the FTT has reviewed a decision it may, in the light of the review, correct accidental errors in the decision or in a record of the decision, amend the reasons given for a decision, and set a decision aside. Where, as a result of a review, the FTT sets a decision aside, it must either re-decide the matter or refer it to the Upper Tribunal.[102] In re-deciding the matter, the FTT may make such findings of fact as it considers appropriate.[103] A decision of the FTT may only be reviewed once (and if a decision is reviewed, set-aside and re-decided, it cannot be reviewed again).[104]

---

[97] Namely a document relating to the proceedings was not sent to or was not received at an appropriate time by a party or a party's representative, a document relating to proceedings was not sent to the tribunal at an appropriate time, a party or a party's representative was not present at a hearing related to the proceedings, or there has been some other procedural irregularity in relation to the proceedings, reg 45(2) of the FTT Rules.

[98] Regulation 45(1) of the FTT Rules. Such an application must be made no later than 28 days after the date on which the tribunal sent the decision notice to the party. The tribunal does, however, have power to extend time.

[99] Rules 48 and 49 of the FTT Rules. This power is unique to SEN cases. An application for a review must be made in writing within 28 days of the day on which the decision notice was sent to the party making the application. The tribunal has a power to extend time for the application.

[100] See para **4.67** below.

[101] Rule 9(2) of the FTT Rules. A person who has a right of appeal in respect of the decision is defined in s 11(2) as being 'any party to a case'.

[102] Tribunals, Courts and Enforcement Act 2007, s 9(5).

[103] Tribunals, Courts and Enforcement Act 2007, s 9(8).

[104] Tribunals, Courts and Enforcement Act 2007, s 9(10) and (11).

The tribunal must notify the parties in writing of the outcome of any review, and of any right of appeal in relation to the outcome.[105]

Appeal to the Upper Tribunal

4.63 The UT was established by section 3 of the Tribunals, Courts and Enforcement Act 2007.[106] The UT has its own rules of procedure, the Tribunal Procedure (Upper Tribunal) Rules 2008 (the UT Rules).[107]

4.64 Section 11(2) provides that any party to a case has a right to appeal. That is defined in subsection (1) as being 'a right of appeal to the Upper Tribunal on any point of law arising from a decision made by the First-tier Tribunal'. The FTT is not a party to an appeal to the UT.

4.65 The UT does not have jurisdiction to consider an appeal from an 'excluded decision'.[108] A party dissatisfied with a decision of the FTT that is an excluded decision must issue an application for judicial review.[109]

4.66 The meaning of the word 'decision' in sections 11(1) and 13(1) of the Tribunals, Courts and Enforcement Act 2007 was considered by the UT in *LS v London Borough of Lambeth*.[110] A FTT Judge of the Social Entitlement Chamber had ruled that he had no jurisdiction to hear the claimant's appeal against a housing benefit decision as the appeal had been lodged outside of the time period prescribed by statute. The claimant sought permission to apply for judicial review of that decision and also sought permission to appeal. The former application was made as the case-law prior to the Tribunals, Courts and Enforcement Act 2007 had indicated that a tribunal's refusal to admit an appeal for want of jurisdiction did not constitute a 'decision'. The three-judge

---

[105] Rule 49(2) of the FTT Rules. The FTT Rules contemplate that the FTT may make a decision on an application for a review ex parte. Where the FTT does so, however, the notice to the parties must state that any party that did not have an opportunity to make representations may apply for such action to be set aside and for the decision to be reviewed again, r 49(3).

[106] Tribunals, Courts and Enforcement Act 2007, s 7 gave power to the Lord Chancellor to make, with the concurrence of the Senior President of Tribunals, orders for the UT to be organised into a number of chambers. Reg 9 of the First-tier Tribunal and Upper Tribunal (Chambers) Order 2010 (SI 2010/2655) provides for there to be an Administrative Appeals Chamber. Reg 10(a) provides that it is a function of the Administrative Appeals Chamber to hear an appeal from the FTT and from the Special Educational Needs Tribunal for Wales.

[107] SI 2008/2698.

[108] Tribunals, Courts and Enforcement Act 2007, s 11(1). An excluded decision includes, relevantly, a decision of the FTT to review or not review one of its own decisions, see s 11(5). In *LM v London Borough of Lewisham* [2009] UKUT 204 (AAC) the UT held that there was a right of appeal against a refusal to review a case management direction, stating that 'the purpose of the exclusion in s 11(5)(d) is to prevent an appeal being brought against a review decision when it should be brought against the decision which it has been sought to have reviewed'.

[109] See paras **4.112** and **4.119** below.

[110] [2010] UKUT 461 (AAC). The UT had previously taken a similar view without hearing full argument on the point. See, for example, *AW v Essex County Council* [2010] UKUT 74 (AAC) per Upper Tribunal Judge Jacobs at paras 7–11; and *KC v London Borough of Newham* [2010] UKUT 96 (AAC) at per Upper Tribunal Judge Jacobs at para 2.

panel concluded that the word had to be read broadly, and that there was a right of appeal against an interlocutory decision unless it fell within the category of 'excluded decisions'.[111] In *LS* the UT concluded that an appeal lay against the FTT Judge's ruling. Moreover, the UT dismissed the claimant's application for judicial review on the grounds that she had an adequate alternative remedy by way of an appeal under section 11 of the 2007 Act.[112]

4.67 An appeal to the UT requires permission; this may be given by the FTT or the UT on an application by a party.[113] Permission must first be sought from the FTT,[114] for which the FTT Rules make provision.[115] Before considering whether to grant permission to appeal, the FTT must consider whether to review the decision on the basis that it discloses an error of law.[116] If the FTT decides not to review the decision, or reviews the decision and decides to take no action in relation to the decision or part of it, the FTT must consider whether to give permission to appeal to the UT (of the decision or part of it).[117] It is obvious, therefore, that the FTT and the UT have an overlapping jurisdiction to deal with errors of law in a decision of the FTT. In *R (RB) v First-tier Tribunal*[118] the UT considered when the FTT should review its own decision, and when it should grant permission to appeal to the UT. The UT stated:

'22. The power to review decisions is an important and valuable one. It is common ground that the power of review on a point of law is intended, among other things, to provide an alternative remedy to an appeal. In a case where the appeal would be bound to succeed, a review will enable appropriate corrective action to be taken without delay ...

... 24. It cannot have been intended that the power of review should enable the First-tier Tribunal to usurp the Upper Tribunal's function of determining appeals on contentious points of law. Nor can it have been intended to enable a later First-tier Tribunal judge or panel, or the original First-tier Tribunal judge or panel on a later occasion, to take a different view of the law from that previously reached, when both views are tenable. Both these considerations demonstrate that if a power of review is to be exercised to set aside the original decision because of perceived error of law, this should only be done in clear cases.'

[111] [2010] UKUT 461 (AAC) at para 90.
[112] [2010] UKUT 461 (AAC) at para 97.
[113] Tribunals, Courts and Enforcement Act 2007, s 4.
[114] Rule 46 of the FTT Rules.
[115] Rule 46 of the FTT Rules. An application must identify the decision of the tribunal to which it relates, identify the alleged error or errors of law in the decision, and state the result the party making the application is seeking, r 46(5) of the FTT Rules.
[116] Rule 47(1) of the FTT Rules.
[117] Rule 47(2) of the FTT Rules.
[118] [2010] UKUT 160 (AAC). The decision in *RB* was confirmed to apply to cases involving special educational needs by the UT in *B v Worcestershire County Council* [2010] UKUT 292 (AAC) at para 8.

4.68 If the FTT refuses permission to appeal, it must send a record of its decision to the parties as soon as practicable.[119] In those circumstances, it must send with the record of its decision a statement of the reasons for such refusal, notification of the right to make an application to the UT for permission to appeal together with the time limits for and methodology of the application.[120]

4.69 A party may renew its application for permission to appeal in the UT.[121] Such an application must be made in writing, within one month of the date on which the FTT sent notice of its refusal of permission to appeal or refusal to admit the application to the appellant,[122] and must contain certain prescribed matters.[123]

4.70 Does the UT has jurisdiction to determine whether to grant permission to appeal where the FTT has not reached a determination on review or permission to appeal? There is conflicting authority in the UT. In *CSDLA/574/2008*[124] Upper Tribunal Judge Gamble stated that the UT did not have jurisdiction in such circumstances, and further it did not have the power to waive the requirement for consideration by the FTT under rule 7(2) of the UT Rules. By contrast, in *CAF/2752/2008*[125] Upper Tribunal Judge Bano considered that rule 7(2) of the UT Rules did give the UT the power to waive the requirement for the application for permission to appeal to have been considered by the FTT. It is submitted that the latter interpretation is correct for the reasons given by the Judge, namely:[126]

> '... there is no power to waive the requirement that permission to appeal must have been granted either by the First-tier Tribunal or by the Upper Tribunal before an appeal can be determined by the Upper Tribunal. The requirement is one which is imposed by primary legislation and therefore cannot be overridden by the Upper Tribunal's power under rule 7(2) of the Rules of Procedure (Upper Tribunal) Rules 2008 to waive a requirement "...if a party has failed to comply with any

---

[119] Rule 47(3) of the FTT Rules.

[120] Rule 47(4) of the FTT Rules. The FTT may give permission on limited grounds, but must comply with r 47(4) in relation to any grounds on which it has refused permission. It will be noted that the FTT Rules envisage the procedure of an application for permission to appeal to be an ex parte application.

[121] Rule 21(2) of the UT Rules provides that a person may apply to the UT for permission to appeal to the UT against the decision of another tribunal only if they have made an application for permission to appeal to the tribunal which made the decision challenged and that application has been refused or has not been admitted.

[122] Rule 21(3) of the UT Rules. The UT has the power to extend time for the application for permission, see r 21(6). If the appellant makes an application to the UT for permission to appeal against the decision of the FTT, and that other tribunal refused to admit the appellant's application for permission to appeal because the application for permission was not made in time, the application to the UT for permission to appeal must include the reason why the application for permission to the FTT was not made in time, and the UT must only admit the application if the UT considers that it is in the interests of justice to do so, see r 21(7).

[123] Rules 21(4) and (5) of the UT Rules.

[124] [2009] UKUT 40 (AAC) at para 7(d).

[125] [2009] UKUT 57 (AAC) at para 9.

[126] [2009] UKUT 57 (AAC) at para 9. The Judge declined to waive the requirement as there had been an inordinate delay (some two years) which was largely unexplained, see para 11.

requirement in these Rules". But it seems to me that the requirement in rule 21(2) that a person may apply to the Upper Tribunal for permission to appeal only if an application has been made to the First-tier tribunal and the application has been refused or not admitted *is* a requirement of the rules of procedure, which does not arise under any primary legislation (unlike the requirement to apply for permission from the Upper Tribunal in order to apply for leave to appeal to the Court of Appeal … see section 13(4) of the Tribunals, Courts and Enforcement Act 2007). I therefore see no jurisdictional bar on the Upper Tribunal waiving the requirement imposed by rule 21(2) and itself considering whether to grant permission to appeal, even though for some reason the First-tier Tribunal has neither refused nor not admitted such an application.'

4.71 If the UT refuses permission to appeal, it must send written notice of the refusal and of the reasons for the refusal to the appellant.[127] If permission was refused without an oral hearing, or granted permission on limited grounds only, the appellant may (within 14 days of the UT sending written notice of the refusal) apply for the decision to be reconsidered at an oral hearing of the UT.[128]

4.72 It will be noted that consideration of the application for permission to appeal by the FTT and by the UT are envisaged to take place ex parte. There is no requirement in the FTT Rules or in the UT Rules for the appellant or the tribunal (either the FTT or the UT) to notify the respondent that an application for permission has been made until permission is granted.[129] After permission is granted, the UT Rules make provision for the respondent to provide a response to the appeal.[130]

4.73 Like the FTT Rules, the UT Rules contain an 'over-riding objective' to deal with cases 'fairly and justly'.[131] Rule 5(1) of the UT Rules provides that the UT may regulate its own procedure. Rule 5(3) sets out, without restricting the general powers in rule 5(1), the powers of the FTT in relation to case management.[132]

---

[127] Rule 21(1) of the UT Rules.

[128] Rules 22(3) and (4) of the UT Rules.

[129] Where the FTT granted permission, r 23 of the UT Rules provides that an appellant must serve a notice of appeal on the UT so that it is received within one month of the date on which the FTT gave permission. The UT must then serve the notice of appeal on the respondent. If the UT grants permission, it must sent written notice of the permission to each party, r 22. The application for permission to appeal stands as the notice of appeal, subject to any direction of the UT, r 22(2)(b).

[130] Rule 24 of the UT Rules provides that a response must be in writing and be received by the UT no later than one month after the date on which the UT sent a notice of appeal to the respondent, but the UT has the power to extend time for the response. The response must contain various prescribed matters, see r 24(3).

[131] Rule 2 of the UT Rules. Dealing with cases 'fairly and justly' is defined in r 2(2) in identical terms to r 2(2) of the FTT Rules; the principles laid out therein are derived from the Tribunals, Courts and Enforcement Act 2007, s 22(4). Rule 2(3) of the UT Rules requires the UT to seek to give effect to the overriding objective when it exercises any power under the UT Rules or interprets any rule or practice direction. Further, parties must help the UT to further the overriding objective and co-operate with the UT generally.

[132] Further case management powers are contained in rr 6–9, and 14–16 of the UT Rules.

4.74 The UT Rules provide a great deal of flexibility in the manner in which appeals can be determined. Appeals can be determined at the permission stage,[133] or without a hearing.[134] An appeal may be disposed of by consent.[135]

4.75 If the UT concludes that the decision of the FTT involved the making of an error on a point of law, the UT may (but need not) set aside the decision of the FTT. If the UT does set aside the decision of the FTT, the UT must either remit the case to the FTT with directions for its reconsideration or re-make the decision.[136] If the UT decides to remit the case to the FTT it may also direct that the members of the FTT who are chosen to reconsider the case are not to be the same as those who made the decision that has been set aside and the UT may give procedural directions in connection with the reconsideration of the case by the First-tier Tribunal.[137] If the UT decides to re-make the decision itself, it may make any decision which the FTT could make it if were re-making the decision, and the UT may make such findings of fact as it considers appropriate.[138]

Suspension of the decision of the FTT or the UT

4.76 The FTT has the power to suspend the effect of its own decision pending the determination by the FTT or the UT of an application for permission to appeal against, and any appeal or review of, that decision.[139] The UT has a similar power, on an appeal or an application for permission to appeal, against the decision of the FTT to suspend the effect of the FTT's decision pending the determination of permission to appeal, and any appeal.[140] An application for a stay should be made in the application for permission to appeal to the FTT and/or the UT, as appropriate.

4.77 The power of the UT to order a stay was considered by the UT in *Carmarthenshire County Council v M & JW*.[141] Upper Tribunal Judge Jacobs held, applying the decision of Sullivan LJ in *Department for the Environment,*

---

[133] Rule 22 of the UT Rules.

[134] Rule 34 of the UT Rules, although the UT must have regard to any view expressed by a party when determining whether to hold a hearing into any matter. Rule 38 of the UT Rules permits the UT to proceed without a hearing if either party fails to attend a hearing where it is satisfied that a party has been notified of the hearing or that reasonable steps have been taken to notify the party of a hearing, and that it is in the interests of justice to proceed with the hearing.

[135] Rule 39 of the UT Rules.

[136] Tribunals, Courts and Enforcement Act 2007, s 12(2).

[137] Tribunals, Courts and Enforcement Act 2007, s 12(3).

[138] Tribunals, Courts and Enforcement Act 2007, s 12(4).

[139] Rule 5(3)(l) of the FTT Rules. The Special Educational Needs Tribunal for Wales has no such power, see *Carmarthenshire County Council v. M & JW* [2010] UKUT 348 (AAC) per Upper Tribunal Judge Jacobs at para 4. In *Carmarthenshire* the parties applied directly to the UT, and the UT waived the requirement in r 21(2)(b) of the UT Rules that would have required the tribunal below to have refused or not admitted an application for permission to appeal to the UT, see r 7(1) and 7(2)(a) of the UT Rules.

[140] Rule 5(3)(m) of the UT Rules.

[141] [2010] UKUT 348 (AAC).

Food and Rural Affairs v Downs,[142] that two questions had to be asked in determining whether to grant a stay. The first was: have solid grounds been put forward by the applicant for the effect of the FTT's decision to be suspended? If it has, the second question is: on balance should the effect of the decision be suspended?[143] He accepted that the authorities treated these as separate stages, although he doubted whether the distinction could be easily maintained or whether it had practical value.[144]

4.78 In relation to the first question, Upper Tribunal Judge Jacobs held that the strength of the applicant's appeal is not a threshold criterion. He accepted that there was some similarity between interim relief and suspension, but stated that the power to suspend must be interpreted and applied in its context. It may have to be exercised before the grounds of appeal are known. Further, the power may also be exercised before the UT is in a position to make a judgment on the strength of the appeal. He noted that this occurred in *The Mayor and Burgesses of the London Borough of Camden v Hodin and White*[145] and in *R (Kent County Council) v H*[146] but the judge in both cases was able to undertake a balancing exercise.[147] The chances of the appeal succeeding were not, however, irrelevant and could be taken into account as the background or context of the balancing exercise or in the exercise of the tribunal's discretion.[148] Insofar as there was a need to find a 'solid ground', it existed in the need to act at all times in the interests of the child.[149] It follows that 'solid ground' is a lower threshold than that the test applied for interim relief of a serious question to be tried.

4.79 The Judge held that authorities are unlikely to be helpful in cases involving a judgment of balance. He referred to the decision of Collins J in *The Mayor and Burgesses of the London Borough of Camden v Hodin and White*[150] but stated that in applying the balancing exercise, Collins J did not lay down a principle of law. Rather the case merely illustrated the application of the balancing exercise that has to be undertaken. Each balancing exercise must be undertaken afresh for each case; comparison was not appropriate.

4.80 The Judge accepted that the public interest was relevant.[151] He also accepted that delay might be a relevant factor, particularly if it had any effect on the interests of the child.[152] In carrying out the balancing exercise, and ordering a suspension of the FTT's decision, Upper Tribunal Judge Jacobs

---

142 [2009] EWCA Civ 257; [2009] 3 CMLR 1544.
143 [2010] UKUT 348 (AAC) at para 17.
144 [2010] UKUT 348 (AAC) at para 24.
145 [1996] ELR 430 at 432.
146 [2006] EWHC 3591 (Admin) at paras 7 and 10.
147 [2010] UKUT 348 (AAC) at para 20.
148 [2010] UKUT 348 (AAC) at para 21.
149 [2010] UKUT 348 (AAC) at para 26.
150 [1996] ELR 430 at 433E.
151 [2010] UKUT 348 (AAC) at paras 27–28.
152 [2010] UKUT 348 (AAC) at paras 29–31.

placed particular emphasis on the fact that the LA applicant for the stay had made appropriate short-term provision to protect the child's placement until his ultimate placement was known.[153]

4.81 *Carmarthenshire* was a case involving the UT's powers to suspend. Given that the relevant rule in the FTT Rules is in identical terms to that in the UT Rules, it is submitted that the FTT should follow the same approach in determining an application to suspend the effect of its own decision under rule 5(3)(l) of the FTT Rules.

Scope of appeals to the Upper Tribunal

4.82 The appeal to the UT is on a point of law only. As stated by Richards J in *Bradley v The Jockey Club*, the function of the UT is not to take the primary decision but to ensure that the decision-maker has operated within lawful limits.[154] What is a point of law was the subject of detailed comment by Carnwath J (as he then was) in *South Glamorgan County Council v L and M*.[155] He applied the well-known formulations in *Edwards v Bairstow*[156] and *IRC v Scottish and Newcastle Breweries*.[157] A point of law includes the case where there is no evidence to support a primary finding of fact and where the conclusion of the tribunal is inconsistent with the primary facts as found by them so that it can be said the decision is perverse: see also *R v Kingston upon Thames and Hunter*.[158]

4.83 An appeal to the UT cannot be used to rehear the primary facts.[159] In the context of the employment tribunal, Mummery LJ in *Yeboah v Crofton*[160] set out the constraints that apply where there is an appeal on a point of law only:[161]

> 'Only the employment tribunal hears all the evidence first hand. The evidence available to the Employment Appeal Tribunal and to the Court of Appeal on an appeal on a question of law is always seriously and incurably incomplete. Much as one, or sometimes both, of the parties would like it to be so, an appeal from the employment tribunal is not a re-trial of the case. The scope of the appeal is limited to questions of law, which it is claimed arise on the conduct of the proceedings and the decision of the employment tribunal. The legal points must, of course, be considered in the context of the entirety of the proceedings and the whole of the decision, but with an awareness of the limitations on the court's competence to question the evidential basis for findings of fact by the employment tribunal. It is

---

[153] [2010] UKUT 348 (AAC) at para 41.
[154] [2004] EWHC 2164 (QB). The comments were approved on appeal by Lord Philips MR in that case when giving the judgment of the court, [2005] EWCA Civ 1056 at para 17.
[155] [1996] ELR 400 at 410B–413A.
[156] [1956] AC 14.
[157] [1982] 1 WLR 322.
[158] [1997] ELR 223 at 230H–231B.
[159] See *Green v Minister of Housing* [1967] 2 QB 606 at 615B–615F, 616A, 616G–617A. Followed in *G v SENT and Barnet* CO/1335/1997, Ognall J, 22 October 1997, (unreported).
[160] [2002] IRLR 634.
[161] [2002[IRLR 634 at para 12.

a rare event for the appellate body to have all of the documents put in evidence in the employment tribunal. No official transcript of the oral evidence exists. If an order is made for the production of the chairman's notes, it is usually on a selective basis, related to the particular grounds of appeal, which should always be particularised on a perversity challenge. Most important of all, none of the witnesses give evidence on an oral appeal.'

4.84 This statement of principle was approved as applying to a SEN appeal such that FTT and UT could be substituted for employment tribunal and employment appeal tribunal by Upper Tribunal Judge Wikeley in *DC v London Borough of Ealing*.[162] The Judge confirmed that there was a limited scope for challenging the FTT's findings of fact on an appeal to the UT on a point of law, and stated that findings of fact could be challenged only in the limited circumstances identified by the Court of Appeal in *R (Iran) v Secretary of State for the Home Department*.[163] Those circumstances occur where the FTT has: (i) made perverse or irrational material findings of fact, (ii) failed to take into account and/or resolve conflicts of fact or opinion on material matters, (iii) given weight to immaterial factors, or (iv) made a mistake as to a material fact, which could be established by objective and uncontentious evidence, and which results in unfairness.[164]

4.85 The weight to be attached to any particular evidence is essentially a matter for the Tribunal, unless the approach can be shown to be so illogical or as to be irrational or perverse.[165]

4.86 There had been a line of authority which suggested that a 'margin of appreciation' should be given to the decisions of the FTT by the UT.[166] It relied upon the dicta of Lady Hale in *AH (Sudan) v Secretary of State for the Home*

---

[162] [2010] UKUT 10 (AAC) at para 30.

[163] [2005] EWCA Civ 982; (2005) *The Times*, 19 August. *DC v London Borough of Ealing* [2010] UKUT 10 (AAC) at para 31.

[164] In relation to the latter point, see *A v Kirklees MBC* [2001] ELR 657. The child was physically and mentally disabled and had suffered three accidents, including a serious accident when his wheelchair overbalanced, at Fairfields school. The parents sought a change of school. They were unhappy about the LA proposal of Highfields school and wished him to go to Hollybank instead. The tribunal upheld the LA choice. It later emerged that the LA, through nobody's fault, had failed to inform the parents, or the tribunal, of an accident similar to the child's last accident at Fairfields, which had taken place at Highfields in 1993. The Court of Appeal held that the parents' case could be put either on the basis that a material factor had not been taken into account by the tribunal or that the family was denied a fair hearing. It dismissed the appeal before the court on the basis that the omitted information could not have made any difference to the tribunal.

[165] See *WS (by his litigation friend, Mr S) v Governors of Whitefield Schools and Centre* [2008] EWHC 1196 (Admin), per Dobbs J at para 27.

[166] See *DC v London Borough of Ealing* [2010] UKUT 10 (AAC) at para 36 per Upper Tribunal Judge Wikeley; *FC v Suffolk County Council* [2010] UKUT 368 (AAC) per Upper Tribunal Judge Pearl at para 32 and *West Sussex County Council* [2010] UKUT 349 (AAC) per Upper Tribunal Judge Pearl at para 27. But cf *MW v Halton Borough Council* [2010] UKUT 34 (AAC) in which Upper Tribunal Judge Ward stated that he was 'not convinced that these observations are apt to impose an additional need for restraint on the Upper Tribunal ... going beyond what is integral in its jurisdiction in relation to appeals being confined to appeals on a point of law in any event', at para 43.

Education and the Courts

Department (United Nations High Commissioner for Refugees Intervening[167] where she stated (in comments made in relation to what was then the Asylum and Immigration Tribunal):

> 'This is an expert tribunal charged with administering a complex area of law in challenging circumstances. To paraphrase a view I have expressed about such expert tribunals in another context, the ordinary courts should approach appeals from them with an appropriate degree of caution; it is probable that in understanding and applying the law in their specialised field the tribunal will have got it right ... They and they alone are judges of the facts. It is not enough that their decision on those facts may seem harsh to people who have not heard and read the evidence and arguments which they have heard and read. Their decisions should be respected unless it is quite clear that they have misdirected themselves in law. Appellate courts should not rush to find misdirections simply because they might have reached a different conclusion on the facts or expressed themselves differently.'

4.87 From these early decisions of the UT, it appeared accepted that a cautious approach was required by the UT as it did not sit (in the SEN jurisdiction) with expert members itself.

4.88 However, Upper Tribunal Judge Ward in *MW v Halton BC*[168] stated that Lady Hale's comments should not be seen as imposing 'an additional need for restraint on the Upper Tribunal'. In other words, appellate courts and tribunals should adopt an appropriate degree of caution when scrutinising the decisions of fact-finding tribunals, but no more.

4.89 Upper Tribunal Judge Ward's approach was endorsed by the Court of Appeal in *AP (Trinidad and Tobago) v Secretary of State*.[169] Carnwath LJ stated that Lady Hale's comments could not be applied to the appellate role of the UT as to do so would be to negate the purpose for which the UT was established, namely to provide specialist guidance of issues of law arising in the FTT. He noted that the chambers structure in the UT is designed to ensure that the equivalent specialist expertise is available for each category of its work.[170] Carnwath LJ added that this conclusion should not be confused with the more general principles which apply to any appellate court or tribunal.[171]

4.90 Subsequent cases have therefore adopted the approach that the *AH (Sudan)* case does not mean that anything other than an ordinary degree of caution is apt.[172] This does not change the basic premise that an Upper Tribunal judge cannot substitute his own view of the facts for that taken by the tribunal.

---

[167] [2007] UKHL 49; [2008] 1 AC 678 at para 30.
[168] [2010] UKUT 34 (AAC) at para 43.
[169] [2011] EWCA Civ 551, and see also *Chapple v Suffolk County Council* [2011] EWCA Civ 870 at para 46 per Carnwath LJ.
[170] [2011] EWCA Civ 551, at para 46.
[171] [2011] EWCA Civ 551, at para 47.
[172] *GC & JC v Tameside Metropolitan Borough Council (SEN)* [2011] UKUT 292 (AAC).

4.91 Is it a point of law when it cannot be said that there was no evidence for the conclusion of the tribunal, nor that its decision is perverse, but it can be said that there is 'insufficient' evidence for the conclusion? In principle, 'insufficiency' of evidence on its own would appear simply to engage the factual merits of an appeal, not to be a point of law. Nevertheless, there is some case-law suggesting that insufficiency of evidence for the tribunal decision will amount to a point of law. In *T v LB of Islington*,[173] Wilson J (as he then was) held that the SENDT had insufficient evidence to justify its conclusions on Part IV of the statement[174] and therefore the appeal should be allowed on that basis. In reaching his decision he relied[175] on a dictum of Sullivan J in *S v City and Council of Swansea and Confrey*:[176]

> 'Provided it is appropriate to meet the needs specified in part 2 and the objectives specified in part 3, the prescription in the remainder of part 3 may be "informed" by what is actually available at a particular school. It is, however, a corollary of this approach, that if a particular school is to be relied upon to meet a particular need, the tribunal must have accurately defined the need in part 2 and must have been able to satisfy itself that the school will be able to provide the special educational provision specified in the statement.'

4.92 That statement of principle is wholly conventional. It does not, however, say that it is a point of law if the tribunal is satisfied on insufficient evidence that the school which the tribunal considers should be specified in the statement will be able to provide the special educational provision specified in the statement. *T v LB of Islington*, in so far as it suggests that insufficiency of evidence is a point of law, is based on authority which did not support that approach.

4.93 *Confrey* was also relied on by Sullivan J (as he then was) in *R (on the application of W) v Bedfordshire County Council*.[177] In that case, the SENDT accepted evidence that British sign language was inappropriate for the child,[178] but then made amendments to the statement which failed to give effect to that point.[179] Not surprisingly, Sullivan J concluded[180] that the SENDT had not satisfied itself that the school could meet the needs of the child. The decision in that case was plainly perverse and it was not a case of the High Court concluding that it could intervene simply if the tribunal decision was based on insufficient evidence.

4.94 It is accordingly submitted, both on principle and on authority, that mere insufficiency of evidence is not a point of law entitling the UT to intervene on an appeal against the decision of the FTT. Only *T v LB of*

---

173 [2001] EWHC 1029 (Admin),[2002] ELR 426.
174 [2001] EWHC 1029 (Admin),[2002] ELR 426, at paras 43–46.
175 [2001] EWHC 1029 (Admin), [2002] ELR 426 at para 44.
176 [2000] ELR 315 at 323A–323B.
177 [2001] ELR 645.
178 [2001] ELR 645, at para 21.
179 [2001] ELR 645, at para 22.
180 [2001] ELR 645, at paras 26 and 27.

Islington actually proceeds on this ground. The case is not supported by the authority to which it refers, it contains no detailed analysis of whether insufficiency of evidence is a point of law and it is submitted that the case should not be followed.

4.95 A point of law will cover a pure point of statutory construction.

4.96 Allegations of breach of the duty of fairness also amount to a point of law. In *London Borough of Islington v LAO (by his mother and litigation friend, O)*[181] Judge Waksman QC, sitting as a deputy judge of the High Court, held that a decision of SENDT to direct that the LA produce a statement of SEN, given without providing the LA with an opportunity to give evidence, or make submissions, was unlawful.

4.97 In *R (L) v London Borough of Waltham Forest*[182] Beatson J (as he then was) stated that 'where the specialist tribunal uses its expertise to decide an issue, it should give the parties an opportunity to comment on its thinking and to challenge it'.

4.98 In *H v Gloucestershire County Council and Bowden (Chair of the SENDIST)*, however, Elias J (as he then was) stated that tribunals have to conduct their own affairs, and as such it was 'only in the case of a very clear unfairness that the court should intervene in a case of this kind, where it is alleged that the Tribunal did not properly conduct the proceedings.'[183]

4.99 It could at one time confidently have been stated that breach of the duty to give reasons was not a point of law for the purposes of the right of appeal on a point of law.[184] However, there is now an established practice of the courts allowing appeals where the reasoning of the tribunal is thought to be inadequate.[185]

Appeal to the Upper Tribunal – time-limits

4.100 The relevant time limits involved in an appeal to the UT are as follows. First, an appellant must apply to the FTT for permission to appeal so that it is received by the FTT no later than 28 days after the FTT sends the reasons for

---

[181] [2008] EWHC 2297 (Admin) at para 82.

[182] [2003] EWHC 2907 (Admin); [2004] ELR 161.

[183] [2000] ELR 357 at para 48.

[184] *S v SENT* [1995] 1 WLR 1627 at 1637D applying *Mountview Court Properties Ltd v Devlin* (1970) 21 P & CR 689. The Court of Appeal in *S v SENT* did not hear oral argument on this point but commented that it considered on the basis of the written arguments that the judge was right on this and the other conclusions he reached for the reasons he gave: see [1996] 1 WLR 382 at 386A. See also *R v Northamptonshire County Council ex parte Marshall* [1998] Ed CR 262.

[185] *L v Clarke and Somerset* [1998] ELR 129; *H v Kent County Council* [2000] ELR 660; *JL v Devon County Council* [2001] EWHC 958 (Admin); *R (on the application of B) v Vale of Glamorgan CBC* [2001] ELR 529; and *Crean v Somerset County Council* [2002] ELR 152. On reasons challenges see paras **4.242–4.254** below.

the decision.[186] Secondly, if the FTT refuses permission to appeal, the appellant may renew its application for permission to appeal to the UT. This application must be made in writing, within one month of the date on which the FTT sent notice of its refusal to appeal or refusal to admit the application to the appellant.[187] In the case of both applications, if the appellant sends or delivers the application so that it is received after the prescribed time, the application for permission to appeal must include a request for an extension of time and the reason why the application was not provided in time. Unless the tribunal extends the time for the application the tribunal must not admit the application.[188] Both the FTT and the UT have the power to extend the time for complying with a rule.[189]

4.101 Where, however, an appellant makes an application for permission to appeal to the UT against the decision of the FTT, and the FTT refuses to admit the appellant's application for permission to appeal as it was not made in time, the appellant's application for permission to appeal to the UT must include the reasons why the application for permission for appeal to the FTT was not made in time, and the UT must only admit the application if the UT considers that it was in the interests of justice to do so.[190]

4.102 Finally, where the UT refuses permission without an oral hearing or granted permission on limited grounds only, the appellant may within 14 days of the UT sending written notice of the refusal apply for the decision to be reconsidered at an oral hearing of the UT.[191]

4.103 The respondent's response must be received by the UT no later than one month after the date on which the UT sent a notice of appeal to the respondent. If the respondent provides the response to the UT later than the prescribed time, the response must include a request for the extension of time and the reason why the response was not provided in time.[192]

4.104 Both the FTT Rules and the UT Rules contain specific provisions about the calculation of time.[193]

4.105 The UT has declined to lay down general principles for the exercise of the power to extend time, following the comments of Black J in *Howes v Child Support Commissioner*[194] in which she noted that the Court of Appeal in *Audergon v La Baguette*[195] had 'deplored the creation of judge-made checklists which it considered an approach which carried the inherent danger that a body

---

[186] Rule 46 of the FTT Rules.
[187] Rule 21 of the UT Rules.
[188] Rule 46(4) of the FTT Rules; r 21(6) of the UT Rules.
[189] Rule 5(3)(a) of the FTT Rules, and r 5(3)(a) of the UT Rules.
[190] Rule 21(7) of the UT Rules.
[191] Rules 22(3) and (4) of the UT Rules.
[192] Rule 24 of the UT Rules.
[193] Rule 12 of the FTT Rules and r 12 of the UT Rules.
[194] [2007] EWHC 559 (Admin) per Black J at para 39.
[195] [2002] EWCA Civ 10, (2002), *The Times*, 31 January.

of satellite authority may be built up ... leading in effect to the rewriting of the relevant rule through the medium of judicial decision'.[196] The UT has emphasised that the power to extend time in the FTT Rules and in the UT Rules is unfettered. The UT has accepted, however, that the test in deciding whether or not to extend time was the overriding objective of dealing with cases fairly and justly. Further, the considerations listed in rule 2(2) of the FTT Rules and the UT Rules will be material in reaching that determination.[197]

4.106 In *CD v First-tier Tribunal*[198] the FTT (Social Entitlement Chamber) had declined to extend time so as to admit a late appeal in a criminal injuries case. The provision governing extensions of time in the Tribunal Procedure (First-tier Tribunal) (Social Entitlement Chamber) Rules 2008 is in material respects identical to that in the FTT Rules. Upper Tribunal Judge Turnbull declined to hold that the correct approach for a judge of the FTT who is considering whether to extend time for appealing is to have regard to the matters listed in CPR Rule 3.9. In reliance on *Howes v Child Support Commissioner*[199] Upper Tribunal Judge Turnbull stated that there was no provision in the relevant rules in the terms of CPR Rule 3.9 and that it was not right to import it by way of analogy. He stated that the power to extend time in the relevant rules was unfettered and the circumstances which would be relevant in exercising it would vary from case to case.[200]

4.107 In *Ofsted v AF*[201] the appellant sought to challenge a decision by a judge in the First-tier Tribunal (Health, Education and Social Care Chamber) to admit a late appeal by a childminder against the cancellation of her registration. Upper Tribunal Judge Levenson declined to follow the decision of the Court of Appeal in *Jurkowska v Hlamd Ltd*[202] on extensions of time in the employment tribunal. The Judge stated that the structure of proceedings was different, and that employment tribunal proceedings were more adversarial.[203] He concluded that 'these were questions of judgment on the facts and circumstances of each particular case'.[204]

4.108 In *Information Commissioner v PS*[205] Upper Tribunal Judge Wikeley expressed agreement with the decisions in *CD v First-tier Tribunal* and in *Osted v AF*. He declined to find as a general principle that once a time limit has expired time should not be extended unless an applicant has acted with reasonable expedition. The Judge stated that each case was fact sensitive.[206]

---

[196] See, for example, *Information Commissioner v PS* [2011] UKUT 94 (AAC) at para 63.
[197] See *Information Commissioner v PS* [2011] UKUT 94 (AAC) at para 64.
[198] [2010] UKUT 181 (AAC).
[199] [2007] EWHC 559 (Admin) per Black J at para 39.
[200] [2010] UKUT 181 (AAC) at paras 26 and 27.
[201] [2011] UKUT 72 (AAC).
[202] [2008] EWCA Civ 231; [2008] ICR 841.
[203] [2011] UKUT 72 (AAC) at para 38.
[204] [2011] UKUT 72 (AAC) at para 41.
[205] [2011] UKUT 94 (AAC).
[206] [2011] UKUT 94 (AAC) at para 49.

4.109 The approach of the UT, in declining to lay down any general principles as to when time ought to be extended, leads to inevitable inconsistency in approach. It has the further, undesirable, consequence that parties applying for an extension of time are unable to judge the prospects of success of an application.

Judicial review

4.110 It is a general principle of judicial review that the courts will not entertain a challenge in the exercise of their discretion where there is an adequate alternative remedy. It is clear that, just as the right of appeal from the LA to the FTT is regarded as an adequate alternative remedy, so too is the subsequent right of appeal to the UT.[207]

4.111 Although, in the light of the statutory right of appeal to the FTT and then the UT, judicial review has a much diminished role in this area, it has not been extinguished because rights of appeal do not cover the whole field of possible disputes. Where, for example, the LA is not arranging the educational provision specified in a statement of SEN, the appropriate course is not to appeal to the tribunal but to seek judicial review ordering the LA to perform its duty under s 324(5)(a) of the EA 1996.[208] Similarly, if there has been a failure of the LA to comply with an order of the FTT, the only appropriate action is judicial review.[209]

4.112 Further, and as noted above,[210] the UT does not have jurisdiction to consider an appeal from an 'excluded decision'. A party that is dissatisfied with a decision of the FTT that is an excluded decision must issue an application for judicial review. The proper defendant to such an application will be the FTT. The other party to the FTT proceedings should be joined as an interested party.

4.113 Prior to 3 November 2008, when appeals from the SENDT lay to the High Court pursuant to section 11 of the Tribunals and Inquiries Act 1992, the SENDT (through the Chairman of the relevant panel) was the proper respondent to an appeal. The usual practice of the SENDT was to appear only where there were issues of general principle as to jurisdiction and procedure

---

[207] See *R v Special Educational Needs Tribunal, ex parte South Glamorgan* [1996] ELR 326, CA; *LS v London Borough of Lambeth* [2010] UKUT 461 (AAC) at para 97.

[208] See, for example, *R (N) v North Tyneside Borough Council* [2010] EWCA Civ 135; [2010] ELR 312.

[209] Regulation 25 of the Education Special Educational Needs (England) (Consolidation) Regulations 2001 (SI 2001/3455) lays down certain time-limits for compliance with orders of the FTT, but does not provide a sanction for failure to comply. While in *O v Harrow* [2001] EWCA Civ 2046, [2002] 1 WLR 928, at para 25, one of the considerations that weighed with the Court of Appeal was the desirability of the SENDT remitting a case and reviewing the decision on remission, the case is not authority for the proposition that the tribunal has general power to police and enforce the orders it makes.

[210] See para **4.65** above.

raised or allegations of bias against the SENDT.[211] It appears likely that the FTT will adopt a similar approach in relation to applications for judicial review of excluded decisions.[212]

4.114 The Tribunals, Courts and Enforcement Act 2007 confers jurisdiction on the UT to hear certain claims for judicial review.[213] This power has been exercised in SEN cases.[214]

CHALLENGES TO THE DECISION OF THE UPPER TRIBUNAL

4.115 The UT has the same power as the FTT to correct clerical mistakes and accidental slips or omissions,[215] and to set aside a decision which disposes of proceedings where there has been a procedural irregularity.[216]

4.116 Section 10 of the Tribunals, Courts and Enforcement Act 2007 gives the UT the same right to review its own decisions as the FTT.[217] Provision is made for this in the UT Rules.[218]

4.117 Section 13 of the Tribunals, Courts and Enforcement Act 2007 provides for a further right of appeal on a point of law to the Court of Appeal. There is no right of appeal in respect of an 'excluded decision'.[219] Permission to appeal

---

[211] See, by way of example, *S v SENT* [1995] 1 WLR 1627 (the first appeal under Ord 55 which raised a number of points) and *Joyce v Dorset (bias)* [1997] ELR 26.

[212] See, for example, *R (LR) v FTT* in which the FTT did not appear, and the LA, an interested party, defended the FTT's decision.

[213] The rules on when the Upper Tribunal has jurisdiction in judicial review claims are complex. The Tribunals, Courts and Enforcement Act 2007, s 15 empowers the UT to grant a mandatory order, a prohibiting order, a quashing order, a declaration or an injunction where the conditions in s 18 are met or where the case is transferred to it by the High Court. The UT Rules, s 16 and r 28 preserves the ordinary requirements for permission and promptness (with a three month longstop time limit). By s 18, if four specified conditions are met in respect of an application for judicial review made to the UT then it has the function of deciding the application, otherwise it must transfer the application to the High Court. Section 19 amends the Supreme Court Act 1981 by inserting a new s 31A. This provides that if four specified conditions are met, the High Court must transfer the application to the UT. If all conditions except condition 3 are satisfied, then the High Court may transfer the application if it considers it just and convenient to do so.

[214] See, for example, *R (JW) v The Learning Trust* [2009] UKUT 1997 (AAC); [2010] ELR 115.

[215] Rule 42 of the UT Rules.

[216] Rule 43 of the UT Rules.

[217] See paras **4.60–4.62** above.

[218] Rules 43, 45–46 of the UT Rules.

[219] This is defined in s 13(8) as, inter alia, a decision of the UT on an application under s 11(4)(b) (application for permission or leave to appeal), or a decision of the UT under s 10 to review or not to review an earlier decision of the UT (or to take no action in the light of a review, or to set aside an earlier decision of the UT).

is required,[220] and may be given either by the UT or by the Court of Appeal.[221] On receiving an application for permission to appeal, the UT may review the decision, but may only do so if:

(a)   when making the decision, the UT overlooked a legislative provision or binding authority which could have had a material effect on the decision; or

(b)   since the UT's decision a court has made a decision which is binding on the UT and which, had it been made before the UT's decision, could have had a material effect on the decision.[222]

4.118   An application for permission to appeal may be made to the Court of Appeal only if permission has been refused by the UT.[223] Permission to appeal to the Court of Appeal shall not be granted unless the UT, or where the UT refuses permission, the Court of Appeal, considers that the proposed appeal would raise some important point of principle of practice or there is some other compelling reason for the relevant appellate court to hear the appeal.[224]

4.119   The decision of the UT to refuse permission to appeal from the FTT, an 'excluded decision' pursuant to section 13(8) of the Tribunals, Courts and Enforcement Act 2007, is susceptible to judicial review, but only where the proposed appeal raised some important point of principle or practice, or where there was some other compelling reason.[225]

4.120   Section 14 of the Tribunals, Courts and Enforcement Act 2007 sets out the powers of the Court of Appeal where it determines the making of the decision by the UT involved the making of an error on a point of law. The Court of Appeal may (but need not) set aside the decision of the UT. If it does, it must either remit the case to the UT or to the FTT with directions for its reconsideration, or re-make the decision. If the Court of Appeal remits the case, it may direct that persons who are chosen to reconsider the case are not the same as those who have previously made the decision, and it may give procedural directions for the reconsideration of the case by the UT or the FTT. If the Court of Appeal re-makes the decision, it may make any decision that the UT could have made if it were re-making the decision, and may make such findings of fact as it considers appropriate.[226]

---

[220]   Tribunals, Courts and Enforcement Act 2007, s 13(3).
[221]   Tribunals, Courts and Enforcement Act 2007, s 13(4).
[222]   Rule 45(1) of the UT Rules.
[223]   Tribunals, Courts and Enforcement Act 2007, s 13(5). The procedure for making an application for permission to appeal is set out in rule 44 of the UT Rules.
[224]   Appeals from the Upper Tribunal to the Court of Appeal Order 2008 (SI 2008/2834), reg 2.
[225]   *R (Cart) v Upper Tribunal* [2011] UKSC 28 at paras 27, 94, 96, 101, 105 and 134.
[226]   Tribunals, Courts and Enforcement Act 2007, s 14.

PROCEDURAL POINTS

Adjournments

4.121   The FTT has a broad discretion to adjourn or postpone a hearing.[227] The authorities disclose two broad approaches by appellate courts reviewing decisions to grant or refuse an adjournment.

4.122   The first, and more limited, approach was adopted by the Court of Appeal in *Carter v Credit Change Ltd*.[228] That case concerned the discretion to adjourn vested in the ET by the predecessor to reg 10(2)(m) of the Employment Tribunals (Constitution and Rules of Procedure) Regulations 2004.[229] The Court of Appeal held, under the then version of the rule, that the exercise by a tribunal[230] of this discretion will not easily be overturned on appeal. The Court of Appeal approved a passage in *Bastick v James Lane (Turf Accountants) Ltd*,[231] stating the limited grounds on which the EAT would interfere with such a decision:[232]

> 'Either we must find ... that the tribunal, or its chairman, has taken some matter which it was improper to take into account or has failed to take into account some matter which it was necessary to take into account in order that discretion might be properly exercised; or alternatively, if we do not find that, that the decision which was made by the tribunal, or its chairman, in the exercise of its discretion was so far beyond what any reasonable tribunal or chairman could have decided that we are entitled to reject it as perverse.'

4.123   That test was approved by the Court of Appeal in *Teinaz v Wandsworth London Borough Council*[233] and in *Andreou v Lord Chancellor's Department*.[234]

4.124   In the SEN field, in *West Glamorgan County Council v Confrey*,[235] Popplewell J held that the court was concerned with whether the discretion to refuse an adjournment was exercised properly and not with whether it would have come to the same conclusion.

4.125   The alternative approach is that, in reviewing the refusal of an adjournment, the court should apply the natural justice test (ie whether the refusal of an adjournment led to the denial of a fair hearing): see *R v Thames Magistrates Court ex parte Polemis*[236] and *R v Cheshire County Council, ex*

---

[227]   Rule 5(3)(h) of the FTT Rules.
[228]   [1980] 1 All ER 252.
[229]   SI 2004/1861. For r 10(2)(m) see para 16 and Sch 1 to the Regulations.
[230]   Under the then rules the discretion was vested in the tribunal. The discretion is now vested in the Employment Judge.
[231]   [1979] ICR 778 at 782.
[232]   [1980] 1 ALL ER 252 at 257b–257e.
[233]   [2002] EWCA Civ 1040, [2002] ICR 1471 at para 20.
[234]   [2002] EWCA Civ 1192; [2002] IRLR 728.
[235]   CO/3042/95 (unreported) 22 April 1996 at 5E–7A.
[236]   [1974] 1 WLR 1371.

parte C.[237] In *ex parte C* Sedley J observed 'it follows that in the ordinary case, where a power of adjournment is at large, there is no true margin for the Tribunal; the court itself will decide on the relevant material whether fairness required an adjournment'. However, in neither *Polemis* nor *ex parte C* was there reference to the *Carter v Credit Change* line of authority. *Ex parte C* was followed by Dyson J in *L v Royal Borough of Kensington and Chelsea*,[238] again, without reference to *Carter v Credit Change*. He held, on the facts of that case,[239] that it was wrong in law to refuse an adjournment when the hearing had been brought forward at short notice and expert evidence going to a central issue in the case could not be given in person.[240]

4.126 The two lines of authority may not be irreconcilable. A refusal to grant an adjournment may not lead to an unfair hearing, but may still be perverse.[241] Accordingly, any refusal to adjourn may have to satisfy both the *Wednesbury* and fairness tests. Indeed, in *R (R) v SENDT and Bournemouth Borough Council* [2008] EWHC 473 (Admin) Mitting J described the difference between Sedley J in *ex parte C* and Popplewell J in *Confrey* as being 'at the highest theoretical level'.[242] Whichever test is applied, the balance of authority now appears to be that if the refusal of an adjournment would lead to an unfair hearing, the courts will intervene on appeal. In general terms therefore, it is submitted that if the refusal of an adjournment would lead to an unfair hearing, the court will intervene save in exceptional circumstances.[243]

4.127 In *London Borough of Hammersmith and Fulham v First-tier Tribunal (Health, Education and Social Care Chamber)*[244] Cranston J stated that it was

---

[237] (1997) 95 LGR 299; [1998] ELR 66, Sedley J.

[238] [1997] ELR 155 at 159D.

[239] [1997] ELR 155 at 159D, at 160B–160C.

[240] To similar effect in the planning context is *West Lancashire District Council v Secretary of State for the Environment* (unreported) CO/1910/97, where an adjournment was refused despite the unavailability of the main witness on the day for the hearing. This was held to be both unfair and to fail a *Wednesbury* test.

[241] In *R v Cheshire ex parte C* Sedley J referred to the unreported decision of the Court of Appeal in *R v Immigration Appeal Tribunal ex parte Adrees* (18 April 1996), where Staughton LJ seemed to have contemplated that both the *Wednesbury* and fairness tests had to be satisfied and Sedley J in fact applied both tests, albeit on the hypothesis he was wrong that the test was not one of fairness. He held the refusal unfair because the need for the adjournment had been created by the last minute unavailability of a solicitor for personal reasons over which the parent had no control.

[242] [2008] EWHC 473 (Admin) at para 21.

[243] For an example of the court doing this see *S (A Child) v Hounslow LBC* [2000] Ed CR 680. In that case the appellant was unable to arrange child care on the date fixed for the hearing and she contacted a social worker at the council to inform her. In due course the social worker, having spoken to the tribunal, informed her that an adjournment had been arranged. The tribunal was unaware of this assurance and refused an adjournment (the appellant not attending but a charity worker making the application) on the date of the hearing. The court allowed the appeal on the ground that the refusal to adjourn was without the SENT being aware of the assurance the parent had received that the matter had been adjourned and remitted the case to a fresh tribunal. The court referred to the conflict in the authorities as to whether a *Wednesbury* or fairness test applied but found it unnecessary to resolve that issue.

[244] [2009] EWHC 1694 (Admin); [2009] ELR 486 at paras 18–19.

best practice for the FTT to inform the other party of an application to adjourn made *ex parte*, but that the FTT had not erred in law in failing to do so.

Taking points on appeal not run below

4.128 In the EAT, where appeals also lie on a points of law, it has become the established practice not, save in exceptional circumstances, to allow new points to be raised on appeal which were not raised before the ET especially where that would require fresh evidence.[245] In *B v Harrow*,[246] the Court of Appeal referred to this line of authority and allowed a point to be taken on appeal because the interests of justice required it. Weight was placed[247] on the fact that the tribunal was meant to be an informal tribunal and that representation was discouraged there. This, it is respectfully submitted, is an insubstantial ground on which to distinguish the line of authority concerning the EAT. The ET is also intended to be an informal tribunal where unrepresented litigants are commonplace. Of more weight was the point relied on[248] that the case was of general importance which might set a precedent.

4.129 The issue was reconsidered in *L v Hereford and Worcester County Council and Hughes*,[249] *S v London Borough of Hackney*[250] and *T v SENT & Wiltshire CC*.[251] In all three of those cases it was sought to raise on appeal points on the ECHR which had not been ventilated before the tribunal. In the last of those authorities, Richards J reviewed[252] the earlier case-law and held that although *B v Harrow* did not appear to have been cited in either the *Hereford and Worcester* case or the *Hackney* case, it was right to follow the approach in those cases and refuse permission to raise a fresh point on the ECHR. He held that in circumstances where the appellant was represented before the tribunal by a highly competent solicitor, and that the point sought to be raised was not one of pure statutory construction, nor one of general importance, it was appropriate to distinguish *B v Harrow*.[253]

4.130 Until the matter is reconsidered in the Court of Appeal the principles set forth in *B v Harrow* will continue to govern the approach of the courts to entertaining fresh points on appeal from the FTT. Greater indulgence will be shown when the parent or LA were unrepresented before the FTT than if they

---

[245] *Kumchyk v Derby City Council* [1978] ICR 1116; *Hellyer Brothers v McCleod* [1987] ICR 526; *Jones v Governing Body of Burdett Coutts School* [1998] IRLR 521, CA; *Mensah v East Hertfordshire NHS Trust* [1998] IRLR 531, CA; *Glennie v Independent Magazines UK Ltd* [1999] IRLR 719, CA; *Gloystarne & Co Ltd v Martin* [2001] IRLR 15, EAT.

[246] [1998] ELR 351.

[247] [1998] ELR 351 at 356A–356C.

[248] [1998] ELR 351, at 356C.

[249] [2000] ELR 375.

[250] [2001] EWHC 572 (Admin), [2002] ELR 45.

[251] [2002] EWHC 1474 (Admin), [2002] ELR 704.

[252] [2002] EWHC 1474 (Admin), [2002] ELR 704, at para 39(i).

[253] See also, to the same effect, the comments of Elias J in *R (Aladay) v London Borough of Richmond* [2004] EWHC 1290 (Admin) at paras 48–55.

were represented; regard will be had also to whether the point is of general importance. Although in *T v SENT and Wiltshire*, Richards J also made reference to that fact that the point sought to be raised before him was not one of pure construction, it does not follow that if a point is one of pure statutory construction it would not require fresh evidence. Indeed, in *B v Harrow*, the point would have required fresh evidence[254] had the House of Lords not reversed the Court of Appeal on the issue of construction.[255]

4.131 It is difficult to see why the courts should take a more indulgent approach to the raising of a fresh point on appeal from the FTT than from the EAT. It is submitted that there is no principled reason why the approach should be different and the matter is ripe for reconsideration by the courts.

Notes of evidence or transcript of the hearing

4.132 There is no obligation upon either party to procure a signed copy of the note of the FTT judge for the use of the UT on an appeal.[256]

4.133 In *South Glamorgan County Council v L and M*[257] Carnwath J held that it was only in exceptional circumstances that it would be necessary to seek a note of evidence from the Chairman because the point of law should be apparent from the statement of reasons or the general documents in the case.

4.134 In *Staffordshire County Council v J and J*[258] Collins J, without having had detailed argument on the issue, considered, obiter, the grounds upon which production of the notes of evidence should be ordered:

'It will only be necessary to have them if there is an issue which depends upon having those notes. So far as I can see, there would only be likely to be such an issue if the point taken on appeal was that the conclusion reached by the tribunal or any finding of fact by the tribunal was itself perverse in that it was either based on no evidence or was contrary to the evidence put before the tribunal.'

4.135 In *Joyce v Dorset County Council*[259] a transcript was voluntarily produced by the SENT because serious allegations of bias were made: in particular, it was said that various of the applicant's witnesses had been prevented from giving their evidence fully. This allegation, made on affidavit, was abandoned when the transcript showed it to be groundless.[260] Now, this would be a case where it would be incumbent upon the appellant to obtain notes of the evidence because it would plainly be relevant to a ground of appeal that the tribunal had behaved unfairly.

---

[254] As was submitted to the Court of Appeal at 355E.
[255] [2000] 1 WLR 223.
[256] Contrary to the position under CPR Part 52, which pertained prior to 3 November 2008.
[257] [1996] ELR 400 at 411E.
[258] [1996] ELR 418.
[259] [1997] ELR 26.
[260] See 30D–30E.

4.136 These decisions, and the decision of the EAT in *Webb v Anglian Water Authority*[261] were considered by McCullough J in *Sythes v London Borough of Camden and Special Educational Needs Tribunal*.[262] He held[263] the principles in *Webb v Anglian Water* applied equally in the education field. Accordingly, in order for the Chairman's notes to be ordered:

(a) the notice of appeal had to raise a permissible ground of attack. Permissible grounds were that:

  (i) there was no evidence to support a particular finding of fact;
  (ii) the SENT misunderstood the evidence;
  (iii) the finding of fact was perverse;

(b) the party seeking the notes had to specify the exact finding which was attacked or the finding which he contended should have been made.

4.137 It is submitted that what are described here as permissible grounds of attack in the notice of appeal would now be relevant grounds of appeal for the purposes of obtaining any official transcript. It is also submitted that the notice of appeal would have to specify with particularity exactly which findings of fact by the tribunal are attacked and what finding it is submitted should have been made.

4.138 In *Fisher v Hughes*[264] there were allegations that the hearing before the tribunal was unfair, inter alia, because of the profound deafness of the applicant's representative. Keene J ordered production of the tape of the hearing and the Chairman's signed note. On the test to be applied, he said that:

(a) it was common ground that the question to be asked was was it necessary for the notes and/or transcript to be produced in order to dispose properly of an issue raised in the appeal;[265]

(b) earlier decisions suggesting that an order for production of notes would only be made in exceptional circumstances were not laying down a rule of law to that effect but merely stating that as a matter of expectation occasions of necessity would rarely arise.[266]

4.139 If the notes of evidence have been produced and, on appeal, the appellant then seeks to make use of them to elevate questions of fact into ones of law, he is likely to get little sympathy from the court. In *Joyce v Dorset County Council*[267] the court deprecated that conduct and commented:[268]

---

[261] [1981] ICR 811 at 814B–814D.
[262] (Unreported) CO/3991/95, 21 June 1996.
[263] Transcript 3C–5C and 6H–7B.
[264] [1998] ELR 475.
[265] [1998] ELR 475, at 476F.
[266] [1998] ELR 475, at 477G.
[267] [1997] ELR 26.

'Because of the original allegation in relation to the behaviour of the tribunal, a transcript was produced of the hearing. The appellant has sought to make use of that transcript to elevate decisions of fact to issues of law. None were justified. It will only be in very rare cases that a transcript will be necessary. And in those cases, the court would be unlikely to be impressed by any arguments based upon the transcript which had not been raised before.'

Keene J expressly endorsed those comments in *Fisher v Hughes*.[269]

4.140 In *R (London Borough of Hammersmith and Fulham) v Pivcevic and Goh and the Special Educational Needs and Disability Tribunal* Stanley Burnton J stated:[270]

'In my judgment, the court would not exercise its power to order a tribunal to produce signed notes of evidence merely because they would be "useful" or "beneficial" for the parties to see them. It must be shown that the notes of evidence are required fairly to determine grounds of appeal or of review which (subject to seeing those notes) appear to have a reasonable prospect of success. Where there is an apparently substantial allegation that there was no evidence to support a significant finding made by the tribunal, the notes should be produced, and in such circumstances the court will normally if necessary make an order for their disclosure. If the notes are produced voluntarily, and no application is made by the appellant for an order for their production, in a disputed case, unless it is clear from the tribunal's decision that it's finding was not based on the oral evidence, the court may have no means of knowing whether the finding in question was reasonably based on that evidence; and so the court may be unable to determine whether this ground of appeal is well-founded. There may also be cases where procedural impropriety or unfairness is alleged, which the court cannot properly determine without the chairman's notes of evidence.'

4.141 In *Carmarthenshire County Council v MW & JW* Upper Tribunal Judge Jacobs appeared to take a more generous approach under the UT Rules.[271] He determined that a typed transcript of the hearing before the Special Educational Needs Tribunal for Wales obtained by the LA was admissible before the UT. He applied the following principles:

'15. First, the Upper Tribunal is entitled to all of the evidence that was before the tribunal. That includes the oral evidence. There is no difference between providing copies of the documents that were before the hearing and providing a transcript of the oral evidence and argument at the hearing. A transcript is not evidence of what was said at the hearing, it is the record of the proceedings. No satellite issues can arise as are possible when the evidence is provided by witness statements.

16. Second, the issues raised in a particular case may be such that the Upper Tribunal is able to decide the case without seeing all the evidence.

---

[268] [1997] ELR 26, at 34B.
[269] [1998] ELR 475 at 477G.
[270] [2006] ELR 594 at para 49.
[271] [2010] UKUT 348 (AAC) at paras 15–20.

17.   Third, there is no formal procedure that has to be followed. There is no need
      for an application that a party be allowed to produce or rely on a transcript
      …

18.   Fourth, the transcript may only be used in support of an argument that the
      tribunal made an error of law.

19.   Fifth, the other party must not be taken by surprise. Natural justice and the
      Convention right to a fair hearing require that all the parties have a
      reasonable time to prepare their cases.

20.   Sixth, the production of a transcript may be relevant in an application for
      costs.'

4.142 In *NC & DH v Leicestershire County Council* the Upper Tribunal held
that in the absence of a transcript the hand written note of the Chairman is the
only authoritative guide to the evidence that was given before the FTT.[272]
Upper Tribunal Judge Pearl added that an appellant would only be able to raise
an arguable error of law, in the sense of perversity in the decision making of the
tribunal of first instance, if the handwritten note is entirely unambiguous, and
if the treatment of that evidence by the decision maker crosses the threshold of
perversity.[273]

Witness statements

4.143 In *Oxfordshire County Council v GB and others*[274] the Court of Appeal
commented on the practice of parties filing witness statements in an appeal to
the High Court from the SENDT in the following terms:

'If reference needs to be made to the evidence for the purposes of the statutory
appeal, the ordinary resort is to as much of the documentation and notes of
evidence as will help to determine what material basis there was for the impugned
part of the decision: see *Webb v Anglian Water Authority* [1981] ICR 811, *South
Glamorgan CC v L and M* [1996] ELR 400; McManus, *Education and the Courts,*
paras 3.40 to 3.44. Fresh evidence, even on judicial review, has a restricted ambit
(see *R v Secretary of State for the Environment, ex parte Powis* [1981] 1 WLR 584;
R v Westminster City Council, ex parte Ermakov [1996] 2 All ER 302) which can be
no larger on a statutory appeal. Decisions such as that of Latham J in *S v SENT*
[1995] 1 WLR 1627, 1635, admitting evidence on the question whether there had
been any admissible basis for the SENT's decision, may fall within this restricted
field, especially since SENT reasons are permitted by the SENT Regulations 1994,
reg 30(2) to be in summary form; but the practice described (without doubt
accurately) in McManus, *op cit*, para 3.45 of parties submitting evidence at will to
the court hearing an appeal against a SENT decision is in our present view
unacceptable. The one class of fresh information which the special nature of such
appeals may call for is up-to-date evidence about the child's schooling and needs,
but purely – as the present case will illustrate – in order to enable relief to take a
suitable form.

---

[272] [2012] UKUT 85 (AAC) at para 18.
[273] [2012] UKUT 85 (AAC) at para 19.
[274] [2001] EWCA Civ 1358, [2002] ELR 8.

10. For these reasons we would pay no attention to the evidence that was submitted to the Administrative Court by all three parties. That of the LEA sought to recanvass the facts; that of the tribunal chair sought to advance ex post facto reasons for the written decision; and that submitted by the parents sought to make out a better case for the decision than the tribunal itself had done. Since we have not heard oral submissions on this aspect of the case, what we have said above is based upon the written materials helpfully submitted by both counsel at the court's request at the conclusion of argument. It should not be taken to be a comprehensive consideration of the problem.'

4.144 While those comments are expressly not a comprehensive consideration of the problem, and without the benefit of oral argument, it is submitted they do signal a general reluctance to accept further evidence other than that which is relevant to relief.[275] It is submitted that this general reluctance is in principle sound and was so on the facts of that case. It is one thing to make sure that the court has the material before the tribunal to enable it to make a judgment about whether the tribunal decision was perverse. It is quite another to seek to justify or undermine the decision of the tribunal on the basis of witness statement evidence that was not before the tribunal and is not confined to describing what happened before that body.

4.145 There are, however, circumstances in which evidence which was not before the FTT is properly admissible. Recourse may be had to a witness statement where there is a material dispute about the oral evidence of a witness.[276] To the extent that the evidence goes beyond an account of what was said to the FTT, it is inadmissible.[277]

Costs

4.146 The FTT has a limited jurisdiction to make an order in respect of costs. Pursuant to r 10(1) of the FTT Rules it may do so in two circumstances. The first is an order under section 29(4) of the Tribunals, Courts and Enforcement Act 2007 for wasted costs. Section 29(4) permits the FTT to disallow or order the legal or other representative to meet the whole or part of any wasted costs.[278]

---

[275] The approach advocated in *Oxfordshire* was followed in *Renshaw v Sheffield City Council* [2002] EWHC 528 (Admin), in *B v Worcestershire County Council* [2010] UKUT 292 (AAC) at para 12 and in *NC & DH v Leicestershire County Council* [2012] UKUT 85 (AAC) at para 23.

[276] *The Learning Trust v MP* [2007] EWHC 1634 (Admin) per Andrew Nicol QC sitting as a deputy Judge of the High Court at paras 29–30.

[277] *R (TS) v Bowen (Chair of SENDIST)* [2009] EWHC 5 (Admin); [2009] ELR 148 per Lord Carlisle of Berriew QC sitting as a deputy Judge of the High Court at para 32.

[278] 'Wasted costs' are defined in s 29(5) of the Tribunals, Courts and Enforcement Act 2007 as being any costs incurred by a party as a result of any improper, unreasonable or negligent act or omission on the part of any legal or other representative or any employee of such a representative or which in the light of any such act or omission occurring after they were incurred, the FTT considers it is unreasonable to expect that party to pay. A 'legal or other representative' is defined in subsection (6) to mean any person exercising a right of audience or right to conduct the proceedings on behalf of a party to proceedings.

4.147   The FTT has power, second, to make an order where it considers that a party or its representative has acted unreasonably in bringing, defending or conducting the proceedings. The meaning of 'unreasonable' was discussed by the Court of Appeal in *Ridehalgh v Horsefield*:[279]

> '"Unreasonable" also means what it has been understood to mean in this context for at least half a century. The expression aptly describes conduct which is vexatious, designed to harass the other side rather than advance the resolution of the case, and it makes no difference that the conduct is the product of excessive zeal and not improper motive. But conduct cannot be described as unreasonable simply because it leads in the event to an unsuccessful result or because other more cautious legal representatives would have acted differently. The acid test is whether the conduct permits of a reasonable explanation. If so, the course adopted may be regarded as optimistic and as reflecting on a practitioner's judgment, but it is not unreasonable.'

4.148   The power to award costs where a party or its representative has acted unreasonably was considered in *HJ v London Borough of Brent*,[280] a case in which the LA conceded the father's appeal at the door of the tribunal. Upper Tribunal Judge Jacobs applied the comments made in the context of employment tribunal proceedings by Mummery LJ in *McPherson v BNP Paribas (London Branch)*.[281] First, the proper issue was the conduct of proceedings and not the decision to withdraw. Secondly, the costs that may be awarded are not limited to those that are attributable to the unreasonable conduct: the receiving party does not have to prove that specific unreasonable conduct by the paying party caused particular costs to be incurred. Thirdly, costs must not be punitive. Fourthly, the unreasonable conduct is relevant at three stages: it is a precondition to an order for costs, and it is also a relevant factor to take into account in deciding whether to make an award for costs and the form of the order.[282]

4.149   Upper Tribunal Judge Jacobs stated that two principles deriving from another decision of the Court of Appeal concerning employment law, *Kovacs v Queen Mary and Westfield College*[283] were relevant, namely that a party's ability to pay is not a relevant factor, and that an award should cover as a minimum the costs attributable to the unreasonable behaviour.[284] It is submitted that the former factor is not relevant in SEN appeals in the FTT: it conflicts with the requirement in rule 10(6) of the FTT Rules that the FTT may not make an order for costs against an individual without considering that person's financial means.

4.150   Upper Tribunal Judge Jacobs declined to make an award of costs in favour of the father. He stated that he could not make an award of costs simply

---

[279]   [1994] Ch 205, at 232.
[280]   [2011] UKUT 191 (AAC).
[281]   [2004] ICR 1398 at paras 30, 40 and 41.
[282]   [2011] UKUT 191 (AAC) at paras 8–12.
[283]   [2002] ICR 919.
[284]   [2011] UKUT 191 (AAC) at para 13.

because the father won his case.[285] Further, it was not proper to second guess a party's decisions in the course of litigation. He stated that 'merely because particular evidence in the end secured a particular outcome, it does not follow that it was unreasonable to defend the case or that it was unreasonably conducted'.[286]

4.151 The FTT may make an order in respect of costs on an application or on its own initiative.[287] A person making an application for an order under this rule must send or deliver a written application a schedule of the costs claimed with the application.[288] An application for a costs order may be made at any time during the proceedings but it may not be made later than 14 days after the date on which the FTT sends the decision notice recording the decision which finally disposes of all issues in the proceedings.[289]

4.152 The FTT may not make a costs order against a person ('the paying person') without first giving that person an opportunity to make representations; and if the paying person is an individual, considering that person's financial means.[290] The amount of costs to be paid may be determined by summary assessment by the FTT, by agreement between the parties or by assessment of the whole or a specified part of the costs incurred by the receiving party, if not agreed.[291]

4.153 The UT may make an award of costs only in the circumstances that the FTT had the power to make an order in respect of costs.[292] The UT may make an order for costs on an application or on its own initiative.[293] The UT may, however, make an award of costs in judicial review proceedings.[294]

SUBSTANTIVE POINTS OF LAW

4.154 It is not proposed to detail here the whole of the substantive law of special educational needs. What is dealt with are the points most commonly arising in practice which either raise accepted points of law, or are contended to do so.

---

[285] [2011] UKUT 191 (AAC) at para 16.
[286] [2011] UKUT 191 (AAC) at para 17.
[287] FTT Rules, r 10(3).
[288] FTT Rules, r 10(4).
[289] FTT Rules, r 10(5).
[290] FTT Rules, r 10(6).
[291] FTT Rules, r 10(7). If there is an order for an assessment under r 10(7)(c), the paying person or the receiving person may apply to the County Court for a detailed assessment of the costs in accordance with the Civil Procedure Rules 1998 on the standard basis, or if specified in the order, on the indemnity basis, see FTT Rules, r 10(8).
[292] UT Rules, r 10(1).
[293] UT Rules, r 10(4). The procedure by which an application is to be made, and the powers of the UT upon such an application mirror the FTT Rules, r 10(4)–(8), see UT Rules r 10(5)–(9).
[294] UT Rules, r 10(3).

Challenges to the form of the statement

4.155 It is well established that a statement of SEN has to identify each and every special educational need and the provision for meeting those needs: see *R v Secretary of State for Education and Science ex parte E.*[295] At first, the courts adopted a practical approach to challenges based on the form of the statement. They did not take too technical an approach to whether the needs and the provision to meet those needs was detailed enough, nor were they prepared to grant relief in the exercise of their discretion unless some useful purpose was served by doing so. The latter point appears from the decision of the Court of Appeal in *Re L*,[296] where the court commented:[297]

> 'Before proceeding to consider the detail of Mr Friel's [counsel for the appellant] argument it is right to remark that the case of *ex parte E* (above) must be applied in a context such as the present with caution. In explaining that the purpose of Part III is to match the needs identified in Part II, the court was not inviting a line by line examination of the parts in order to gauge the degree of correspondence between them. Inelegant or even imperfect matching, whether or not the product of poor draftsmanship, would not be enough. Only if there was a clear failure to make provision for a significant need would the court be likely to conclude that there was such a dereliction of duty by a local education authority as called for the intervention of an appeal committee or, in default, of the Secretary of State or, indeed, the High Court. In short, the case does not justify a detailed comparison between the parts of a statement in support of a challenge to its sufficiency.'

4.156 It was contended by the appellant that the approach of the authority was contrary to the approach recommended by the Court of Appeal in *Ex parte E.*[298] The court held that this submission was entirely misconceived and that the question was not one of approach but content.

4.157 This practical approach also appeared in the decision of Latham J in *Joyce v Dorset County Council.*[299] In that case, the applicant argued that although numeracy was mentioned in the statement as a particular area of special educational needs, it was not specifically addressed when dealing with the child's needs. The court refused to intervene holding that the SENT must have concluded that the provision met the child's needs as a whole and that the statement though apparently deficient was not in truth so.

4.158 It should be noted that the tribunal has a discretion to correct any deficiency in the statement before hearing an appeal if the parties consent: see s 326(5) of the EA 1996. It also has power to amend the statement without the parties' consent by virtue of s 326(3)(b). In *Joyce v Dorset CC*[300] the court held that there was no error of law when a tribunal which could have ordered an

---

[295] [1992] 1 FLR 377.
[296] [1994] ELR 16, CA.
[297] [1994] ELR 16, CA, at 22E–22F.
[298] [1992] 1 FLR 377.
[299] [1997] ELR 26.
[300] [1997] ELR 26 at 33D.

amendment of an unclear statement chose not to. Further, the court, in hearing an appeal from the tribunal, is not bound to allow the appeal even if there has been a misdirection. An example of this is *Knight v Dorset CC*,[301] where it was held that the tribunal had misdirected itself by failing to consider properly whether the child had a significantly greater learning difficulty than the majority of children of the same age, but the appeal was dismissed on the basis that it was likely the tribunal would have reached the same conclusion had it adopted the correct approach and thus there had been no miscarriage of justice.

4.159 Accordingly, the approach the courts adopted in the past was such that purely formal challenges to the statement were unlikely to succeed unless it could be shown that the child had been thereby prejudiced. A particular aspect of this problem is whether a statement, when detailing provision of a particular nature, such as speech therapy, should specify the number of hours. Here, dating from the decision of Laws J in *L v Clarke and Somerset County Council*,[302] the courts for some time adopted a stricter approach. He held:[303]

'In my judgment, a requirement that the help to be given should be specified in a statement in terms of hours per week is not an absolute or universal precondition of the legality of the statement ... There will be some cases where flexibility should be retained. However, it is plain that the statute requires a very high degree of specificity ... in very many cases it will not be possible to fulfil the requirement to specify the special educational provision considered appropriate to meet the child's needs, including specification of staffing arrangements and curriculum, unless hours per week are set out.

The real question, as it seems to me, in relation to any particular statement is whether it is so specific and so clear as to leave no room for doubt as to what has been decided is necessary in the individual case. Very often a specification of hours per week will be necessary and there will be a need for that to be done.'

4.160 In that case the statement provided that the child's progress in various subjects should be 'monitored' and that his individual action plan should include regular, preferably daily, individual or small group work and the amount and timing of his support should be negotiated with him. Laws J held that this was not sufficiently specific.

4.161 The judgment of Laws J in *L v Clarke* marked the beginning of a more interventionist approach by the courts at first instance to challenges to the form of a statement, at least where the challenge related to the failure of the

---

301 [1997] COD 256.
302 [1998] ELR 129. He relied on some observations of Schiemann J in *R v Cumbria ex parte P* [1995] ELR 337 to the effect that if all the statement had said was £6,000 was allocated to pay for all the child's needs that would not have been lawful. However, Schiemann J in that case upheld as lawful, although not without criticism, a statement which did not specify a given number of speech therapy sessions and merely stated that speech therapy should be provided 'as appropriate'.
303 [1998] ELR 129, at 136G.

statement to quantify the number of hours required for a particular form of support, and spawned a considerable amount of litigation.[304]

4.162 The issue was then considered by the Court of Appeal in *E v Newham LBC*[305] and *R (on the application of IPSEA Ltd) v Secretary of State for Education and Schools.*[306] The first of these was a substantive appeal and the second an application for permission to appeal, but they were heard by the same court and two separate judgments of that court were delivered on the same day.

4.163 In the *Newham* case the statement did not quantify the therapy to be provided in terms of hours, or otherwise, and provided, in effect, that the individual education plan should be developed and determined by others. At first instance, Stanley Burnton J[307] dismissed the appeal from the tribunal decision and in turn the Court of Appeal dismissed the appeal from his decision. It held that:[308]

(a)   the tribunal could not delegate its statutory duty to some other person, however well qualified;

(b)   the statutory duty was not discharged if the description of the special educational provision was so vague and uncertain that it was not possible to discern what the tribunal had decided;

(c)   the degree of flexibility which was appropriate was for the tribunal to decide, taking into account all relevant factors;

(d)   in some cases, a high degree of flexibility might be required; in others not;

(e)   in the case before the court it was appropriate to leave the education plan to be determined by the designated school in conjunction with therapists because:

  (i)   the parents had reconciled themselves to a special school for the time being;
  (ii) the reason for the debate on provision in the past was a contest between mainstream and special schooling;
  (iii) for mainstream schooling, greater specificity might be required because staff had to be brought in, whereas for a special school such staff were available;

---

[304]   The principal authorities were helpfully reviewed by Stanley Burnton J in *E v Newham and SENT* [2002] EWHC 915 (Admin), [2002] ELR 453 at paras 24–31. The case went to the Court of Appeal which upheld the High Court [2003] EWCA Civ 09, [2003] ELR 286 but the review at first instance remains a useful collection of the earlier authorities.

[305]   [2003] EWCA Civ 09, [2003] ELR 286.

[306]   [2003] EWCA Civ 7, [2003] ELR 393.

[307]   [2002] ELR 453.

[308]   At paras 63–66.

(iv) it was important to get the child back to school and the professional advice was out of date through no fault of the LA;

(v) there was much to be said for flexibility and assessing both needs and provision in the school context;

(vi) there were no conflicting reports by experts;

(vii) the previous decision of the Court of Appeal in *Bromley v Special Educational Needs Tribunal and others*[309] had upheld as lawful a statement which did not specify the number of hours required for speech therapy.

4.164 In the *IPSEA* case, IPSEA sought permission to appeal against the refusal of its application for permission to move for judicial review of the 'SEN Toolkit', non-statutory guidance which was issued by the Secretary of State. It was submitted that the Toolkit was inconsistent with the statutory guidance in the Code of Practice issued under section 313 of the EA 1996. The Court of Appeal refused the application for permission to appeal.

4.165 The Code of Practice provides[310] at para 8.37:

'Provision should normally be quantified (e g in terms of hours of provision, staffing arrangements) although there will be cases where some flexibility should be retained in order to meet the changing special educational needs of the child concerned. It will always be necessary for LEAs to monitor, with the school or other setting, the child's progress towards identified outcomes, however provision is described. LEAs must not, in any circumstances, have blanket policies not to quantify provision.'

4.166 Objection was taken to three paragraphs in the SEN Toolkit:

(a) paragraph 30 which, it was alleged, suggested that flexibility was appropriate not only to meet the changing needs of the child, but also to reflect particular class, or school, arrangements;

(b) paragraph 38 which, it was alleged, suggested that flexibility was appropriate for reasons other than the changing needs of the school, and, it was alleged, drew an impermissible distinction between special schools and mainstream;

(c) paragraph 39 which, it was suggested, created impermissible extensions of the exceptions to a presumption of quantification.

4.167 The Court of Appeal held that:[311]

(a) specification did not mean quantification;

---

[309] [1999] 3 All ER 587.

[310] DfES/581/2001 issued in November 2001. Para 8.37 of this Code is materially identical to the Code of Practice issued in 1993.

[311] [2003] EWCA Civ 7 at paras 14–17.

(b)   the statement had to clearly spell out the provision appropriate to meet the particular needs of, and objectives identified for, the particular child. It had to be addressed to the needs of the child rather than the needs of the system;

(c)   the statement of Laws J in *L v Clarke and Somerset County Council* to the effect that in very many cases the number of hours of particular provision which should be set out in the statement was correct;

(d)   the needs of the child could not be judged in a vacuum, and might differ depending on the peer group or teachers he was with, and it was in that sense the Toolkit was to be understood;

(e)   the general rule in the Code that precision was required, but flexibility was appropriate where this best met the needs of the child, remained the law.

4.168   Accordingly, following the judgments of the Court of Appeal, the law on specificity now appears to be as follows.

(a)   The Code of Practice at paragraph 8.37 correctly states the law and accordingly special educational provision should normally be quantified in terms of hours.[312]

(b)   While the tribunal cannot delegate its duty, it can, in an appropriate case, leave the detail of the provision required for the child to be determined by others.[313]

(c)   The degree of flexibility in any case is a matter for the tribunal, taking account of all relevant factors.[314]

(d)   Quantification will not be required if flexibility is in the best interests of the child.[315]

(e)   Flexibility is appropriate to meet the changing needs of the child which can include how the child progresses with a particular peer group or teachers.[316]

(f)   Greater specificity may be required if the child is to be educated in a mainstream school rather than a special school.[317]

(g)   Specificity will not be required where there is no material, such as conflicting experts' reports, from which the tribunal can come to any

---

[312] *IPSEA*, para 17.
[313] *Newham*, para 64.
[314] *Newham*, para 64.
[315] *IPSEA*, para 17.
[316] *IPSEA*, para 15.
[317] *Newham*, para 65.

precise quantification.[318] However, if the tribunal lacks the necessary information to specify in any great detail, by reason of the absence of appropriate evidence, it should consider an adjournment to enable such evidence to be obtained, although a court is unlikely to accede to an appeal based on a failure of the FTT to adjourn where no application was made for it to do so.[319]

(h) Specifying minimum hours with provision for amendment as a result of monitoring would be lawful.[320]

4.169 The *Newham* and *IPSEA* cases marked a change in practice by the courts. The reference to the flexibility that is appropriate being a matter for the judgment of the tribunal signalled a diminution in successful challenges in the courts,[321] although, of course, it left open the argument, in any given case, that the LA has misdirected itself, failed to take account of relevant considerations, or reached a perverse result. It is of note in this regard that none of the earlier case-law was overruled and that the decision of Laws J in *L v Clarke and Somerset* was expressly approved in *IPSEA*.

4.170 The decision in *Newham* represents a pragmatic approach to the problem of specificity. It is difficult to see, as a matter of principle, how it is permissible to delegate any of the specification of detail of the provision to meet a child's needs, but it is unworkable to have a system whereby each matter of detail has to be in the statement with the consequence that the statement would have to be formally amended as the child's needs changed from week to week.

Relevance of resources

4.171 Resources are a relevant factor within closely circumscribed limits in relation to special educational needs. Accordingly, there is no duty to accede to the parent's choice of maintained school if that would prejudice the efficient

---

[318] *Newham*, para 65 and *S v City and Council of Swansea and Confrey* [2000] ELR 315 at 327G–328E.

[319] *Newham* at first instance [2002] ELR 453 at para 38. The Court of Appeal took the view, at para 61, that if the statement was compliant, no sensible legal attack could be launched on the failure of the SENDT to adjourn of its own motion. In the light of this, while it may be sensible for the SENDT to consider an adjournment of its own motion, its failure to do so is unlikely to provide grounds for appeal.

[320] *Newham*, para 64; *S v City of Council of Swansea and Confrey* [2000] ELR 315 at 327G–328E.

[321] See, for example, *A v Birmingham City Council* [2004] EWHC 156 (Admin), *T v Devon County Council* [2006] EWHC 395 (Admin), *T v Hertfordshire County* Council [2004] EWCA Civ 927, Y *v London Borough of Lambeth* [2009] EWHC 690 (Admin).

use of resources[322] and there is no duty to accede to the parent's choice of an independent school if that would involve unreasonable public expenditure.[323]

4.172   The courts/tribunals have had to consider the extent to which the LA is obliged to meet the cost of special educational provision in a statement where there is a scheme of delegation and the school is in receipt of a delegated budget. In *R v Oxfordshire ex parte P*[324] it was argued that the LA was obliged to pay for the cost of statemented provision out of centrally retained funds. The court rejected this argument, holding that there was no delegation by the LA of its duties under what was then section 7(2) of the Education Act 1981[325] so long as the school agreed to meet the costs out of its delegated budget.[326] In a subsequent case, *R v Hillingdon ex parte Governing Body of Queensmead School*,[327] the court held that the needs of the child always had to be met, and that where the LA proposed a reduction in funding, it was obliged to notify the school first so that it could make appropriate representations. The court emphasised that budgetary considerations had no part to play in the assessment of the special educational needs, although it could be relevant in deciding how the needs were to be met. This is in accordance with well-established authority in this field. In *R v Surrey County Council Education Committee ex parte H*,[328] the Court of Appeal emphasised that LAs were not obliged to provide the best possible education for the child but merely to meet the needs of the child.[329] That decision was held to be applicable to what is now section 324 of the EA 1996 in *R v Cheshire ex parte C*,[330] where Sedley J, after referring to *ex parte H*, commented:

> '[It] is ... fair to read that case, which involved the local education authority's choice of mainstream as opposed to a special needs school, as endorsing the limitation of the authority's duty under s 168 [now s 324 of the EA 1996] to the selection of *an* appropriate school. Although the statutory regard to cost is relevant only as a constraint on parental choice, which is strictly not in issue at this point, there is nothing in the statutory scheme which calls upon the local

---

[322]   See paras 3(3)(b) and 8(2)(b) of Sch 27 to the EA 1996. For attendance to be incompatible with the efficient use of resources it must result in significant additional expenditure: see *Surrey County Council v P* [1997] ELR 516. See also *R (on the application of Hampshire County Council) v R* [2009] EWHC 626 (Admin) for the high threshold imposed by the notion of 'incompatibility'.

[323]   See s 9 of the EA 1996.

[324]   [1996] ELR 153.

[325]   See now s 324(5)(a) of the EA 1996.

[326]   See also *Coventry v Browne* [2007] EWHC 2278 (Admin), [2008] ELR 1: any monies spent on a child attending a school (whether from the LA's central funds or from the school's delegated budget need to be included when calculating cost for the purposes of para 3(3)(b) of Sch 27 of the EA 1996 and s 9 of the EA 1996.

[327]   [1997] ELR 331, Collins J.

[328]   (1984) 83 LGR 219.

[329]   Latham J relied on this under the Education Act 1993: see *S v SENT* [1995] 1 WLR 1627 at 1638B–C.

[330]   (1997) 95 LGR 299 at 313.

education authority to specify the optimum available provision and much in its general duty of financial husbandry to entitle it to choose the least expensive of the appropriate options.'[331]

4.173 Under paragraph 3(3) of Schedule 27 to the EA 1996, the LA does not have to accede to the parent's choice of maintained school if, inter alia, the child's attendance at that school would be incompatible with the efficient use of resources. This is frequently an area of debate in the tribunal and the questions have arisen as to whose, and what, resources are taken into account. In *B v London Borough of Harrow*,[332] the House of Lords, reversing the Court of Appeal and upholding the trial judge, held that the reference to resources in paragraph 3(3) of Schedule 27 meant the resources of the LA making the statement of SEN[333] and not those of some other authority which did not have to pay for the provision.[334]

4.174 Resources are also relevant under section 9 of the EA 1996. Under that provision, the Secretary of State and LAs are to have regard to the general principle that pupils are to be educated in accordance with the wishes of their parents so far as that is compatible with, inter alia, the avoidance of unreasonable public expenditure. In that context, the issue has arisen regarding what resources are taken into account; is this just costs which fall to be paid for out of the LA educational budget or does it include social services provision as well? There is a conflict of authority on this point, but the balance of authority is that all costs to the public purse are to be taken into account.

4.175 In *O v Lewisham*[335] Andrew Nicol QC (sitting as a deputy high court judge) ruled that all public expenditure could be taken into account. The facts of the case were that the appellant was a child who was the subject of a statement of educational needs. His parents wanted him to attend a residential maintained school, but the LA had identified a maintained day school as being appropriate. The appellant's mother appealed to the special educational needs and disability tribunal. The LA calculated that it would cost approximately £20,000 more to place the appellant at his parents' choice of school. However, the appellant's mother argued that if he was placed at a residential school, respite care provided by the authority's social services department would not be

---

[331] See also *R (A) v Hertfordshire County Council* [2006] EWHC 3428 (Admin), [2007] ELR 95 at [25] per Judge Gilbart QC, 'need' in this context means 'what is reasonably required'.

[332] [2000] 1 WLR 223.

[333] Note: in *B v London Borough of Harrow (No 2)* Latham J held that the costs of transporting a child to and from school, as well as the costs of occupational therapy, were properly taken into account under para 3 of Sch 27 of the EA 1996. He was faced in that case with an argument that transport costs should not have been taken into account because the parents had offered to pay them, but he held that the tribunal were entitled to find as a fact that the parent would be unable to meet that commitment and the LA had accordingly properly taken it into account as a cost it would bear. As a matter of current practice in tribunals, it is accepted that transport costs should not be taken into account where a parent has agreed to pay transport costs as long as appropriate wording is included in Part IV of the statement (see Chapter 1 – School Transport).

[334] Ibid, at 228H–229C per Lord Slynn. The rest of the House agreed with his speech.

[335] [2007] EWHC 2092 (Admin), [2007] ELR 633.

necessary, and, taking that into account, the additional cost of her preferred school was only about £3,500. The tribunal rejected that submission, and, by reference to paragraph 3(3) of Schedule 27 to the EA 1996, refused to amend the statement to reflect the parental preference. The appellant applied for judicial review.

4.176 The issue arose as to whether cost savings to a local social services department could be taken into account as 'public expenditure' for the purposes of section 9 of the EA 1996, or whether such was limited to the cost to the LA by reference to the interpretation placed on 'resources' in paragraph 3(3) of Schedule 27 to the Act.

4.177 The LA also argued that since, having regard to previous authorities, the test in paragraph 3(3) of Schedule 27 to the Act 'superseded' or was 'substituted for' section 9, section 9 did not apply to the instant case. As to the proper construction of 'public expenditure', it relied, inter alia, on the fact that the tribunal would not be able to discover the costs of services provided by other agencies, on the distinction that Parliament had maintained between the functions of a local education authority and a local social services authority, and on the fact that the cost of providing such other services would fluctuate with changes in circumstances.

4.178 The Judge ruled: (i) that section 9 was still in play when the parent was expressing a preference for a maintained school and that paragraph 3(3) of Schedule 27 of the EA 1996 did not supersede section 9, and (ii) that all expense to the public purse should be taken into account when considering section 9.[336]

4.179 It is submitted that the basis for both these conclusions is flawed. The first conclusion is flawed given the decision of the House of Lords in *B v London Borough of Harrow*. The second conclusion is flawed for the following reasons:

(a)   The learned judge was departing from two earlier authorities, namely, *C v Special Educational Needs Tribunal*[337] and *S v Somerset County Council*.[338]

(b)   He placed no weight on the practical difficulties that such an interpretation would create. The responsible LA will simply not know what prejudice to public expenditure there is if it covers public expenditure that it is not responsible for.

(c)   There is no necessary reason to construe unreasonable public expenditure differently from paragraph 3(3) of Schedule 27. To the contrary neither

---

[336] For a decision to contrary effect, see *S v Somerset County Council* [2002] EWHC 1808 (Admin), [2003] ELR 78.
[337] [1997] ELR 390.
[338] [2002] EWHC 1808 (Admin), [2003] ELR 78.

expression expressly indicates what expenditure is included and there is no natural and ordinary meaning that points one way or the other. The statutory context though of decisions being taken at a LA level points plainly to the relevant expenditure being that of the responsible LA.

(d) While it might now be the case that because local authorities have replaced local education authorities[339] regard has to be had to all the home LA expenditure, that change does not support a submission that the responsible LA has to take into account the expenditure of all other authorities providing they are 'public authorities'. Despite these apparent flaws, the first conclusion reached by Andrew Nichol QC has been approved by the UT in the case of *CM v London Borough of Bexley*[340] and the second conclusion, the 'public purse' aspect of the *O v Lewisham* case, has been expressly approved by the UT in *K v Hillingdon*.[341]

4.180 In *CM v London Borough of Bexley*[342] the UT followed *O v Lewisham* on the meaning of resources in section 9 of the EA 1996, but held that section 9 was a 'weak provision'. Accordingly, although a reasoned parental preference could in an appropriate case outweigh the prejudice to the responsible authority's resources, the remarks of Lord Slynn in *B v London Borough of Harrow* that section 9 of the EA 1996 was subject, inter alia, to the prejudice to the responsible authority's resources, though technically obiter, were to be given respect. He held further that an unreasoned parental preference was unlikely to have much weight.[343]

4.181 The current position is therefore that:

(a) even when considering two maintained schools, section 9 has to be taken into account;

(b) section 9 is a weak provision and only imposes a duty to 'have regard to' parental preference;

(c) when considering the notion of unreasonable public expenditure under section 9, all expenses incurred to the public purse should be taken into account. This includes the expense to the 'home' authority.

4.182 In *Oxfordshire County Council v GB and others*[344] the Court of Appeal analysed how section 9 and the avoidance of unreasonable public expenditure was to be judged. It held that:

---

[339] See ST 2010/1158 which inserted the word 'LA' for 'local education authority' in s 9 of the EA 1996 with effect from 10 May 2010.

[340] [2011] UKUT 215.

[341] [2011] UKUT 91.

[342] [2011] UKUT 215.

[343] Judge Ward remitted the matter to the FTT to determine in that case whether parental preference outweighed the prejudice to the responsible body's resources. On remission the FTT held that it did not.

[344] [2001] EWCA Civ 1358, [2002] ELR 8 at paras 16 and 17.

(a)   it was for the LA, or on appeal, the tribunal, to judge whether expenditure
      on the parent's preferred independent school was unreasonable;

(b)   that meant striking a balance between the educational advantages of the
      placement preferred by the parent and the extra cost to the LA as against
      what it would cost the LA to place the child in a maintained school;

(c)   where the child's needs could not be met by the state system, the LA had
      no choice and had to pay the cost;

(d)   where the choice was between two independent schools, the cost to be
      taken into account was simply the respective annual fees of the two
      schools;

(e)   where the choice was between two maintained schools, then para 3 of
      Sch 27 substituted a test of suitability for the particular child, efficiency in
      education and efficient use of resources. That last criterion included
      comparative on-costs such as transport and personal support, but in most
      cases did not require apportioning of the LA accounts or balance sheet;

(f)   where the choice was between an appropriate independent school and an
      appropriate maintained school, the comparison that fell to be made was
      between the annual fee to the LA of placement at the independent school
      as compared with the additional cost to the LA on its annual budget of
      placing the child at the maintained school. The existing costs of staffing
      the school, or having a particular unit at the school, did not fall to be
      taken into account.

4.183   The *Oxfordshire* case remains the leading authority on how costs should
be calculated for both paragraph 3(3) of Schedule 27 of the EA 1996 (where
parents are seeking a maintained school) and section 9 of the EA 1996 (where
parents are seeking an independent school). There has, however, been an
on-going debate about how costs should be calculated.

4.184   Since the decision of the Court of Appeal in *Oxfordshire County
Council v GB and others* the approach to the cost of placement in Part 4 of a
statement of special educational needs (SSEN) was that only the marginal or
additional cost to the local education authority should be taken into account.

4.185   Hence, where an LA has prefunded a set number of places in a special
school and there are still places available at the time that costs are under
consideration there will be a nil additional cost to the child attending the
special school. Similarly, a finding that specialist teaching had to be provided
under Part 3 would incur a nil additional cost if a specialist teacher was
employed at the proposed placement and had capacity to provide the teaching
required by Part 3.

4.186 In *Coventry City Council v SENDIST and AB and MB*[345] Underhill J held that additional expenditure incurred by a school using delegated funding should also be included under section 9 of the EA 1996. This decision did not, however, challenge the orthodox position set out in *Oxfordshire*.

4.187 In *Slough Borough Council v SENDIST and others*[346] Sedley LJ appeared to backtrack on the position he and the other members of the Court of Appeal adopted in *Oxfordshire*. But the orthodoxy was reasserted by the Court of Appeal in *EH v Kent County Council*.[347]

4.188 In *EH*, Sullivan LJ's judgment sought to reconcile the apparently conflicting approaches to the identification of the costs to the public purse taken by Sedley LJ in the *Oxfordshire* and *Slough* cases as responses to extreme positions adopted in submissions. The Court of Appeal endorsed the orthodox *Oxfordshire* approach, holding that the LA's budgetary arrangements for an individual school would usually be a sensible starting point for the FTT (rather than the school's accounts as was contended by the appellant). If the LA arrangements made provision for the payment of an age-weighted pupil unit (AWPU) to the school there was no reason ordinarily and in this case why the FTT should not accept that the AWPU, together with any additional costs specifically incurred in respect of the child in question (such as transport and therapy), were a fair reflection of the cost to the public purse of educating the child at that school. Ultimately, Sullivan LJ held that whether a placement involved unreasonable public expenditure was a question of fact to be answered by the FTT in a common-sense way.

4.189 However, the Court of Appeal held that it is for the FTT to decide what evidence it considers most helpful and it is entitled to have regard to other information, such as a school's accounts, if it is not satisfied that the figures based on the LA's budgetary arrangements are a fair reflection of the cost to the public purse of educating the child at the school in question. Although they would not necessarily provide the definitive answer, the LA's budgetary arrangements for an individual school would usually be a sensible starting point. It should only be in those cases where there was no AWPU payment by the LA, or where the FTT was satisfied that, for some cogent reason, the AWPU plus any additional costs did not fairly reflect the cost to the public purse of placing the child in a particular school, that the FTT would consider it necessary to adopt some other method of calculating the public expenditure under section 9 of the EA 1996.

4.190 By this decision, the Court of Appeal largely restored the well-understood *Oxfordshire* approach. However, it does leave the door open for parents to invite the FTT to depart from this approach where they can show a 'cogent reason' for doing so on the facts. It reinforces the need for LAs to adduce proper evidence on the issue of costs before the FTT and not rely on

---

[345] [2007] EWHC 2278 (Admin).
[346] [2010] EWCA Civ 688.
[347] [2011] EWCA Civ 709.

'nil cost' and no evidence. Further, whilst this could be said to be the last word on the section 9 issue when a maintained mainstream school is being judged against an independent school, there is scope for a different approach when a maintained special school (which is funded differently from a maintained mainstream school) is being considered.

4.191   The task of the tribunal, when assessing whether the school the parent wishes the child to attend would be incompatible with the efficient use of resources, does not involve looking at the costs of the child attending a school that is neither named by the LA nor the parent's preferred option. In *H v Leicestershire County Council*[348] the parent contended the tribunal should have taken into account the cost to the LA of the child attending a school that neither the LA nor the parent named. Dyson J rejected the argument[349] on the basis that the tribunal was not obliged to consider the hypothetical cost of each LA school that was suitable for the child and then to compare it with the costs of the parent's preferred school.

4.192   The impact of section 9 has been considered by the courts where the tribunal has rejected the school named by the LA as appropriate and is faced with an expensive school desired by the parents. In *Hereford and Worcester County Council v Lane*,[350] the Court of Appeal held that the tribunal erred in law in ordering the LA to name a school which provided more than the child needed by way of special educational provision. The tribunal had held that the school named by the LA did not meet the child's needs and therefore concluded that it should order the naming of the school preferred by the parents even though this school, on the court's own findings of fact, provided a 24-hour curriculum that the child did not need. The Court of Appeal held[351] that section 9 of the EA 1996 should have been considered and that the tribunal should have considered using its powers under section 326(3)(b) of the Act to order an amendment of the statement as to the type of school or provision before ordering the LA to name a school which provided a curriculum which the child did not need.

4.193   It does not follow from *Lane* that in all cases where the tribunal considers that the school named by the LA in Part IV of the statement is inappropriate, it is obliged to let the LA have the chance of naming less expensive independent schools than those desired by the parents. In *Rhondda Cyon Taff County Council v Special Educational Needs Tribunal and V*,[352] *Lane* was distinguished by Newman J on the basis that the latter case decided that over provision in a school was capable of being regarded as inappropriate provision and that in the case before him the LA should have argued at the tribunal that the parent's preferred school over-provided for the child and was

---

[348]   [2000] ELR 471.
[349]   [2000] ELR 471, at 483G–484A.
[350]   [1998] ELR 319.
[351]   [1998] ELR 319, at 334H–335C and 337E–338C.
[352]   [2001] EWHC 823 (Admin), [2002] ELR 290 at para 10.

inappropriate. He went on to hold[353] that because the LA had not done this, and had accepted that the school the parents wanted was appropriate, and not argued that unreasonable expenditure arose from the need of the child to board at the parents' choice of school, it did not come within the principles set out in *Lane*. He held[354] that *Lane* was not authority for the proposition that, at the conclusion of every case where the tribunal considered that the school named by the LA in Part IV of the statement was inappropriate, it was obliged to let the LA have the chance of naming less expensive independent schools than those desired by the parents. He also held that such a principle would be contrary to the priority given to expedition in the resolution of SEN disputes; would give undue prominence to resource considerations, which, though an important factor, were not the only one, because the interests of the child were also important; and would relieve the LA of its duty to put forward its full case at the outset.

4.194 Where there is no extra cost to the LA in the child attending a school outside the United Kingdom because a private benefactor is prepared to meet the cost, the LA should decide purely on educational grounds what school should be named in the statement.[355]

4.195 If a non-maintained school is named in a statement then, by virtue of section 348 of the EA 1996, the LA has to meet the cost of the child attending that school. Where the LA cannot meet the child's needs outside the named non-maintained school, it has a duty under section 348[356] to pay for the provision which it cannot exclude: see *R v Kent ex parte W*.[357]

4.196 In *Finn*[358] the court had to consider whether there was a duty on an LA to pay school fees under section 324(5)(a)(i) prior to sections 348 or 517(6) of the EA 1996 being brought into force. In that case, the parents had raised funds privately to enable the child to go to an independent school prior to the tribunal naming the school in the statement. Dyson J held that the duty to arrange under section 324(5)(a) meant to organise, or ensure that the special educational provision was available, and that this did not necessarily include paying. However, in a non-maintained school, as the learned judge held, it would usually be the case that provision would not be available unless it was paid for and that, accordingly, the duty on the LA was to ensure the special educational provision was paid for either by itself or by someone else. Accordingly, while as a matter of construction of section 324, the duty to arrange did not impliedly carry with it the duty to pay, as matter of fact, the LA might have to pay if it is to arrange the special educational provision.

---

[353] [2001] EWHC 823 (Admin), [2002] ELR 290, at para 11.
[354] [2001] EWHC 823 (Admin), [2002] ELR 290, at para 14.
[355] *R v Cheshire County Council ex parte C* [1998] ELR 66.
[356] In force from 1 September 1997: see SI 1997/1623.
[357] [1995] ELR 362 at 369B and 370H.
[358] Dyson J, [1997] EWHC 651 (Admin), [1998] ELR 203. This case was heard with *White v Ealing*, which went to appeal: see [1998] ELR 319.

4.197 The duty on the LA under section 324 applies only if the parents have not made suitable arrangements. Whether suitable arrangements have been made is not a question of fact for the court but for the LA, subject to the usual *Wednesbury* attacks.[359] However, suitable arrangements must include arrangements for funding for a reasonable period of time.[360]

Educational/non-educational provision

4.198 Under section 324(5)(a)(i) of the EA 1996, the LA is obliged to arrange that the special educational provision specified in the statement is made available to the child unless the parent has made suitable alternative arrangements. The Court of Appeal recently emphasised the mandatory nature of that duty, stating that there was no 'best endeavours' defence in the legislation.[361] Under section 324(5)(a)(ii), the LA has, by contrast, a discretion whether or not to arrange for non-educational provision. It is, accordingly, usually a matter of importance whether any particular provision is properly to be regarded as educational or non-educational. This issue has arisen in the courts in the context of speech and language and other therapies.

4.199 The leading authority remains the decision of the Court of Appeal in *London Borough of Bromley v SENT*.[362] There, the Court of Appeal held[363] that there was no hard and fast line to be drawn between educational and non-educational provision and there was a large intermediate area which was capable of being either. Which applied in any given case was, the Court of Appeal held, to be judged on a case-by-case basis by the LA and the tribunal. The effect of *Bromley* is that the courts are less likely than they might have been in the past to accede to a challenge that the tribunal has got the classification wrong. They are more likely to defer to the tribunal decision and review it only on *Wednesbury* lines.[364] In the *Bromley* case itself, the tribunal conclusion, that physiotherapy, occupational therapy and speech therapy were all in that case educational, was upheld[365] as one that could properly be reached.

4.200 Nevertheless, earlier case-law does remain of some relevance, at least as a guide to the possible correct classification, in any future case. While the tribunal will not be obliged to adopt the courts' earlier classification before the decision in *Bromley* in every future case, there are limits to the 'large

---

[359] *White v Ealing and others* [1997] EWHC 651 (Admin), Dyson J; [1998] ELR 203.

[360] As above, following Auld J in *R v Hackney ex parte GC* [1995] ELR 144 at 153B and Turner J in *R v Kent County Council ex parte W* [1995] ELR 362 at 370F.

[361] R (N) v North Tyneside Borough Council [2010] EWCA Civ 135

[362] [1999] ELR 260.

[363] [1999] ELR 260, at 295F–296C.

[364] The *Bromley* approach has been adopted in a number of subsequent cases. See *K v Governing Body of a Grammar School* [2006] EWHC 622 (Admin), [2006] ELR 488; *A v Hertfordshire County Council* [2006] EWHC 3428 (Admin), [2007] ELR 95 and *R (on the application of TS) v Bowen* [2009] EWHC 5 (Admin), [2009] ELR 148.

[365] Ibid, at 296F.

intermediate area' where the therapy in question can be properly classified as either educational or non-educational. Accordingly the previous case-law is set out below.

4.201 In the past, speech therapy has been classified as ordinarily an educational need. This was established by the Court of Appeal in *R v Lancashire ex parte M*.[366] The test adopted for whether it was educational or non-educational was as propounded by the Divisional Court:

> 'At the one end of the scale, it seems to me that speech therapy may well be akin to teaching; at the other, it may be a purely medical procedure, such as surgery or requiring drug treatment.'

The Court of Appeal went on to say:[367]

> 'To teach an adult who has lost his larynx because of cancer might well be considered as treatment rather than education. But to teach a child who has never been able to communicate by language, whether because of some chromosomal disorder as in the *Oxfordshire* case, or because of some social cause (eg because his parents are themselves unable to speak, and thus he cannot learn by example as normally happens) seems to us just as much educational provision as to teach a child to communicate by writing.'

4.202 Although the Court of Appeal adopted a test which stated that speech therapy was not necessarily educational, that test means that, for all practical purposes, it will be educational, because speech therapists do not ordinarily get involved in surgery and the like. That speech therapy is, in practice, usually to be regarded as educational is an approach which is supported by the current Code of Practice on Special Educational Needs which provides at para 8.49:

> 'Since communication is so fundamental in learning and progression, addressing speech and language impairment should normally be recorded as educational provision unless there are *exceptional* reasons for not doing so.'

4.203 That approach, and the decisions on which it is based, creates real practical difficulties for LAs because they do not employ speech therapists. The classification of provision as educational or non-educational has the important consequence that the LA is either under a duty to provide it (if it is educational) or simply has a discretion to so do.[368] Nevertheless, it has been confirmed by the courts that the duty is non-delegable and it is no defence for the LA to blame the health authority for failing to perform its duty.[369] If the health authority has failed to appoint a speech therapist, it is the obligation of the LA to acquire a speech therapist elsewhere, such as in the private sector.

---

[366] [1989] 2 FLR 279. Cf *R v Oxfordshire County Council ex parte W* [1987] 2 FLR 193.

[367] Ibid, at 301G.

[368] See *City of Bradford Metropolitan Council v A* CO/3788/95, Brooke J, Transcript at 6C–6G not following *R v Hereford and Worcester County Council ex parte P* [1992] 2 FLR 207 at 215.

[369] *R v Harrow LBC ex parte M* [1997] ELR 62, Turner J. See also *R (N) v North Tyneside Borough Council* [2010] EWCA Civ 135.

Moreover, the health authority has a wide discretion how it allocates resources and just one of its priorities is the assistance of the LA. This means it is, in practice, difficult to review the decision of the health authority not to assist in relation to the provision of speech therapists: see *R v Brent and Harrow Area Health Authority ex parte London Borough of Harrow.*[370]

Case-law prior to *Bromley* tended not to classify occupational therapy or physiotherapy as special educational provision. This point was touched on in *Re L,*[371] where Part V of the statement provided:

'V Additional non-educational provision

Advice from occupational therapists particularly on handwriting skills. Speech therapy overview.'

4.204 It was contended by the applicant that both the speech therapy and the occupational therapy should have been specified in the statement as educational provision rather than non-educational provision and hence should have appeared in Part III of the statement. The court refused to intervene but it is not clear from the judgment whether this was because it did not accept the argument as correct or because it was refusing relief in the exercise of its discretion.

4.205 Further consideration was given to the question of occupational therapy in *B v Isle of Wight*[372] where it was held, applying the speech therapy test, that in this case occupational therapy was non-educational rather than educational because the therapies in question would not teach the child any school subject. In some other cases prior to *Bromley* the assumption seems to have been made that occupational therapy was educational provision.[373]

4.206 Provision of nursing care is not capable of being special educational provision as a matter of law: see *Bradford MBC v A.*[374] Neither is the provision of lift for a disabled child: see *R v Lambeth London Borough Council ex parte M.*[375] Provision of an interpreter or interpreting support is not normally to be regarded as educational provision but it can be properly so regarded in a particular case.[376]

---

[370] [1997] ELR 187.
[371] [1994] ELR 16, CA.
[372] [1997] ELR 279.
[373] *R v London Borough of Harrow ex parte M* [1997] ELR 62 where it was assumed that occupational therapy and physiotherapy were properly educational provision without any apparent debate on the point. The case is therefore of little weight on the point. See also *C v SENT* [1997] ELR 390.
[374] [1997] ELR 417, Brooke J.
[375] (1995) 94 LGR 122.
[376] *Vu v London Borough of Lewisham and Another* (unreported) CO/1590/99, Richards J, 31 July 2000 at para 9.

Duration of the LA's responsibility

4.207 As discussed above,[377] the LA's duty is confined by section 321 of the EA 1996 to those who are registered pupils at school or, if not so registered, are not under the age of two or over compulsory school age. By virtue of section 8 of the EA 1996, a person ceases, in broad terms, to be of compulsory school age when they are 16. Since the Further and Higher Education Act 1992 the LA has not had responsibility for further and higher education. This has meant that children wishing to go to a college of further education, rather than a school, apparently cease to be the responsibility of the LA.

4.208 In *R v Dorset ex parte Goddard*,[378] Auld J had held that once the child had been the subject of a statement the LA had to continue to maintain the statement after the child had reached 16 and could not rely on it automatically lapsing when the child left school. This decision gave no effect to what was then paragraph 7 of Schedule 1 to the Education Act 1981 and was disapproved by the Court of Appeal in *R v Oxfordshire ex parte B*.[379] That is the current law because paragraph 9(2) of Schedule 27 to the EA 1996 is materially identical to what was paragraph 7 of Schedule 1 to the Education Act 1981.

4.209 However, an LA cannot seek to evade its responsibilities by seeking to prevent a child over 16 being registered at a school if it is apparent that the school is the only suitable provision for the child. In *Oxfordshire* the Court of Appeal approved the decision of Auld J on the facts because the LA decision had been a sham.[380] The case of *Oxfordshire* was, however, different on the facts from *Goddard* because it was a long-standing policy in Oxfordshire that children should be educated in colleges of further education and there was no question of a sham.

4.210 In *S v Essex County Council and SENT*,[381] Turner J was concerned with a case where the LA had given notice to cease to maintain a statement after the child had left a school which only catered for children up to compulsory school age. As a result, from that moment the child ceased to be registered at any school. The tribunal accordingly declined jurisdiction to hear the appeal. Turner J held that it was wrong to do so on the basis that Parliament cannot have intended such a result and the definition in section 312(5) of 'child' in the Act was inclusive.

4.211 It is respectfully submitted that the decision in *Essex*, while understandable on its facts,[382] is flawed because:

---

[377] At para **4.20** above.
[378] [1995] ELR 109.
[379] [1997] ELR 90 at 96G–97A and 98E–99A.
[380] [1997] ELR 90, at 96E–G per Butler Sloss LJ and at 98E per Swinton Thomas LJ.
[381] [2000] ELR 718.
[382] It was regarded, obiter, as correctly decided by Collins J in *Wakefield MDC v E* [2001] EWHC 508 (Admin), [2002] ELR 203 at paras 34–37, but that was in the context of distinguishing it as

(a)   none of the earlier case-law is referred to in the judgment and it is not apparent whether it was cited;

(b)   while the definition of 'child' in section 312(5) was inclusive, and that in section 579 was 'unless the context otherwise requires', the responsibility of the LA in that case, by virtue of section 321, turned not on the definition of child in those sections, but on whether the child was registered at a school;

(c)   holding that 'child' in the circumstances of that case meant a child who was the subject of a statement of SEN at the time the LA decided to give notice to determine to cease to maintain the statement and therefore that the decision should be quashed is a difficult argument to follow. That test would mean that the requirement for a child to be registered at a school if over the age of 16 in order for the LA to be responsible under section 321(3)(d) would be rendered nugatory. This was not a case where the LA had given notice to the child of a decision to cease to maintain the statement before the child had reached compulsory school age[383] or in order to defeat any right of appeal.

4.212   The Code of Practice seeks to deal with this problem in para 8.124:

> 'Where the young person's present school does not cater for children aged 16 plus, the LEA should consider whether to amend the statement to name another school or cease the statement if an appropriate further education course is identified. The LEA should formally propose to amend the statement to name the alternative school or formally propose to cease the statement. In both cases the LEA must also notify the parents of their right to appeal to the tribunal and the time limits for lodging the appeal.'

4.213   The need for a child over the age of 16 to be registered at a school rather than a college of further education in order to enjoy the protection of a statement of SEN is illustrated by the decision of Collins J in *Wakefield MDC v E.*[384] In that case, the tribunal refused to name a particular further education college for the child because, had it done so, the child would not have remained the responsibility of the LA since he was over 16 and would no longer have been registered at a school and entitled to a statement of SEN. Collins J held that it was correct to do so.

4.214   Since the decision of the Court of Appeal in *Oxfordshire* there has been considerable case-law on the question of when the responsibility of an LA ceases in relation to those who have attained the age of 16 but are no longer

---

not applicable in the case then before the court. More importantly similar reasoning seems to have been adopted by the Court of Appeal in *Hill v Bedfordshire County Council* [2008] EWCA Civ 661; [2008] ELR 660 see para **4.214** below.

[383]   [2000] ELR 718 at para 33.

[384]   [2001] EWHC 508 (Admin), [2002] ELR 203.

registered at a school.[385] The trend of the case-law has to be to extend the duration of the LA's responsibility, no doubt for understandable reasons, beyond that which is the ordinary and natural meaning of the relevant legislative provisions. In *Hill*[386] the Court of Appeal held that the LA was responsible for a person who was over the age of 16 but no longer registered at a school because the school which he had been attending had gone insolvent. They accepted that this was not the literal meaning of section 321(3) but, seemingly[387] that this result followed because the person qualified as child under section 312(5) because he was under 19 and could have been registered at another school. That analysis is impossible to reconcile either with the clear words of section 312(5) which require that the child be both under 19 and registered at a school. It also defeats what the Court of Appeal accepted was the literal interpretation of section 321(3) which was that the responsibility of the LA should cease once the person ceased to be registered at a school.

4.215 That expansive approach does though have limits. In *Essex County Council v Williams*[388] the Court of Appeal confined the decision in *Hill* to its special facts and held that it did not have the consequence that the LA continued to be responsible for a person who had reached the age of 19 however much she might need a statement of special educational needs.

Parental preference

4.216 There used to be no right of preference for children with SEN equivalent to what is now section 86 of the School Standards and Framework Act 1998.[389] The right of preference under that section still does not apply to children in special schools or with statements of SEN maintained under section 324.[390] However, rights of preference are, to some extent, conferred elsewhere under the SEN scheme.

4.217 There is a right of preference under paragraph 3 of Schedule 27 to the EA 1996 similar to that in section 86 of the SSFA 1998. There is also a similar right under paragraph 8 of Schedule 27. Those rights are, however, confined to maintained schools and are expressly qualified if compliance with the preference would be incompatible with efficient education, or the efficient use of resources, or the school would be unsuitable to the child's age, ability, aptitude or special educational needs.

4.218 Section 9 of the EA 1996 also applies to children with special educational needs, but its effect is much more limited than paragraph 3 of

---

[385] *Wolverhampton City Council v SENDIST* [2007] EWHC 1117 (Admin), *Hill v Bedfordshire County Council* [2008] EWCA Civ 661, *B v Islington* [2010] EWHC 2539 and *Essex County Council v W* [2011] EWCA Civ 1315.

[386] [2008] EWCA Civ 661.

[387] See *Essex County Council v Williams* [2011] EWCA Civ 1315 at para 34.

[388] [2011] EWCA Civ 1315.

[389] As amended by para 3 of Sch 4 to the EA 2002.

[390] SSFA 1998, s 98(6) and (7).

Schedule 27. Under the former provision the LA only has to 'have regard' to the general principle that children are to be educated in accordance with the wishes of the subject to, inter alia, the avoidance of unreasonable public expenditure,[391] whereas under paragraph 3 of Schedule 27, the LA is obliged to give effect to that preference subject to similar exceptions.[392] Accordingly, where there are two adequate schools, but one is markedly more suitable than the other for the child's needs, the tribunal is not obliged by section 9 to give effect to the parent's choice for the least suitable of the two schools.[393]

4.219   Despite the restricted role of section 9 of the EA 1996 in relation to children with special educational needs, it has figured a number of times in litigation. In the past, parents' reliance upon it was not very successful.[394] In *W-R v Solihull MBC*[395] Latham J held[396] that once a tribunal had compared the two schools contended for and concluded that the material before it showed one was preferable for the meeting of the child's needs, section 9 could, thereafter, have little significance. As a matter of everyday practice however before the FTT, section 9 is often determinative of parental appeals in favour of the parents. It has been increasingly applied by the tribunal as meaning that if both schools are suitable, parental preference should prevail unless the LA can show a significant difference in cost between the two provisions. It has been elevated beyond a duty to 'have regard to' into a duty to comply with parental preference unless the LA is able to make out a substantial costs differential. As noted above, however, this expansive approach has been limited by the decision in *CM v Bexley Borough Council*, where Judge Ward reiterated the weak nature of section 9.[397]

4.220   In *T v Special Educational Needs Tribunal and Wiltshire County Council*[398] the parents wished the child to be educated at home. The tribunal found that the LA placement at a school was appropriate and therefore section 319 of the EA 1996, which empowered the LA to arrange special educational provision for a child otherwise in a school when satisfied that provision in a school would be inappropriate, was not in play. It was sought to be argued that section 9 required the tribunal to follow the parental preference where two proposals were equally appropriate and cost-neutral. Richards J rejected this argument. Section 9 was merely a general principle to be taken into account and where, as in that case, the dispute was between school and

---

[391]   *Watt v Kesteven* [1955] 1 QB 508 and *Cummings v Birkenhead* [1972] Ch 12.
[392]   *Catchpole v Buckinghamshire County Council* [1999] BLGR 321 at 328e–328g.
[393]   Catchpole at 331a–331f.
[394]   See for example *S v London Borough of Hackney and SENT* [2001] EWHC 572 (Admin), [2002] ELR 45, Collins J. For a rare example where s 9 has been relied on successfully see *Southampton County Council v TG Hewson and Stanton* [2002] EWHC 1516 (Admin), [2002] ELR 698. That, however, was an obvious error where the tribunal in making its calculations had failed to take account of one year of expenditure that would have been incurred where the difference was, on the figures accepted by the tribunal, significant.
[395]   [1999] ELR 528.
[396]   [1999] ELR 528, at 533H–534E.
[397]   [2011] UKUT 215. See para **4.180** above.
[398]   [2002] EWHC 1474 (Admin), [2002] ELR 704.

non-school provision, it could not override section 319 of the Act, which only empowered the LA to make non-school provision if a school was not appropriate.[399]

4.221 It is now doubtful whether the decision in *T v Special Educational Needs Tribunal and Wiltshire County Council* can have much operation in the future. In *TM v London Borough of Hounslow*[400] the Court of Appeal held that it was not sufficient to simply ask whether the child could be educated in school. Rather, the LA had to take account of section 319 of the Education Act 1996 in the assessment process and determine whether, having regard to parental wishes for education at home, it was inappropriate for the child to be educated at school.[401] That process involved consideration of all the circumstances of the case including the child's background and medical history, the child's particular educational needs, the facilities that could be provided in and out of school, the comparative costs of the various alternative provisions, the child's reactions and the parents' wishes. While the decision in *T v Special Educational Needs Tribunal and Wiltshire CC* was not overruled, it was said to be not on point and of no particular help.[402]

Fairness

4.222 Allegations of bias made against the tribunal are rare. The first reported case was in *Joyce v Dorset*.[403] Allegations were made of both actual and apparent bias but, the allegation of actual bias, on the basis that the tribunal had prevented witnesses giving their evidence properly, was abandoned at the outset of the hearing.[404] The allegation of apparent bias was, however, pursued and the court had to rule on it. What happened was that after the hearing one of the tribunal members started to chat to the LA representative and the parent formed an impression of bias.[405] The court held that there was no real danger of bias and that it was a pity that the allegation had been made and persisted in after receipt of the affidavit evidence from the tribunal.[406] The court did, however, caution against informal contact with one party or its witnesses during the course of the hearing. The test now for bias is to be found in the House of Lords decision in *Porter v Magill*:[407]

> 'The question is whether the fair-minded and informed observer, having considered the facts, would conclude that there was a real possibility that the tribunal was biased.'

---

[399] [2002] EWHC 1474 (Admin), [2002] ELR 704, at para 38(ii) and (iii).
[400] [2009] EWCA Civ 859.
[401] [2009] EWCA Civ 859 at paras 25–28.
[402] [2009] EWCA Civ 859 at para 29.
[403] [1997] ELR 26.
[404] [1997] ELR 26 at 30D–E.
[405] [1997] ELR 26, at 30F–31C.
[406] [1997] ELR 26, at 31D–32E.
[407] [2001] UKHL 67, [2002] 2 AC 357; see per Lord Hope at para 103.

4.223 While the above test is different in formulation from that applied by Latham J in *Joyce*, it is submitted that the result in that case would still be the same. That was the conclusion of Lightman J in a slightly different context in *R (on the application of Opoku v Principal of Southwark College.*[408] The facts in *Opoku* were that the principal of the college had decided to exclude Mr Opoku and he had then exercised his right of appeal before the governors. They were due to hear the appeal in the principal's office and she had collected some papers from her office just before they were due to begin, and again subsequently, but had adduced evidence to the effect that the time she was in the office was brief, and she had not discussed the appeal with them. Lightman J had no difficulty in concluding that this conduct would not lead any fair-minded and informed observer to conclude that there was any real possibility of bias.

4.224 It is not proposed to discuss here all the cases which might arise of apparent bias. It is useful, however, to consider some of the problems that might be said in this context to give rise to a case of apparent bias by the tribunal. The following cases are considered:

(a)   the tribunal chairman is part-time but sits regularly. He also appears as an advocate before the tribunal and when doing so addresses tribunal members with whom he has sat;

(b)   the tribunal chairman repeatedly interrupts the parties and cross examines their experts;

(c)   the tribunal chairman has written extensively on the subject and expressed views as to the law on doubtful points.

4.225 The first problem was considered, in the context of employment tribunals, in *Lawal v Northern Spirit Ltd*[409] where the Court of Appeal had held, by a majority, that it did not give rise to apparent bias.[410] This decision was reversed by the House of Lords,[411] which held that the practice should cease and that there should be a restriction on part-time judges appearing as counsel before a panel of the EAT consisting of one or two lay members with whom they had previously sat. The House relied in this connection on a similar restriction imposed, in relation to employment tribunals, by the 'Terms and Conditions of Service and Terms of Appointment of Part-Time Chairman of Employment Tribunals'.[412] There is no reason to think that the courts would now adopt a different approach in relation to the FTT. Accordingly, there would be apparent bias if a part-time chairman appeared as counsel in the FTT with one or two lay members with whom he had sat judicially.

---

[408]   [2002] EWHC 2092 (Admin) at para 18, (2002) 94 (44) LSG 33.
[409]   [2002] EWCA Civ 1218, [2002] ICR 1507.
[410]   Pill LJ dissented and Lord Phillips MR suggested that if the advocate sits frequently as a part-time chairman the result might be different: see at para 52.
[411]   [2003] UKHL 35, [2003] ICR 856.
[412]   Issued October 2000 at para 16.

4.226 The problem of frequent interruption and cross examination by the court has arisen a number of times. Excessive and undesirable interruption and cross examination by a judge may be a breach of Article 6 of the ECHR, but whether or not it is so, will depend on the facts.[413] While the right to education is not a civil right within the meaning of Article 6 of the ECHR, a similar principle will govern whether a tribunal has shown apparent bias by excessive interruptions or cross examination of witnesses.[414]

4.227 In *H v Gloucestershire*[415] it was sought to be argued that an unfair hearing had taken place, not because of interruptions by the tribunal, but because of interruptions of an expert called by the parents by the LA representative. There was a conflict of evidence about the nature, and extent, of the interruptions, and the parents sought an order for cross examination, which was refused by the trial judge. In the Court of Appeal, on an application for permission to appeal, the parents sought to contend that they had a right to cross examine where there was a conflict of evidence going to procedural fairness. The Court of Appeal rejected this submission and held that the exercise of the judge's discretion not to order cross examination was not to be interfered with.[416]

4.228 Bias, on the basis of predetermination, can arise from the tribunal members having published, in an academic capacity, views on the law which indicate to a fair-minded observer that they are not impartial. This was a problem that arose in the joined cases considered in *Locabail (UK) Ltd v Bayfield Properties.*[417] There, the Court of Appeal set out the governing principles as follows:[418]

'It is not inappropriate for a judge to write in publications of the class to which the recorder contributed. The publications are of value to the profession and for a lawyer of the recorder's experience to contribute to those publications can further rather than hinder the administration of justice. There is a long established tradition that the writing of books and articles or the editing of legal textbooks is not incompatible with holding judicial office and the discharge of judicial functions. There is nothing improper in the recorder being engaged in his writing activities ... Anyone writing in an area in which he sits judicially has to exercise considerable care not to express himself in terms which indicate that he has preconceived views which are so firmly held that it may not be possible for him to try a case with an open mind ... The specialist judge must therefore be circumspect in the language he uses and the tone in which he expresses himself. It is always

---

[413] *CG v United Kingdom* (2002) 34 EHRR 31. It was held that there was no breach in that case.
[414] *R v Gakhar (Laj pat)* CA 24 February 1995 and *Montanaro (formerly Price) v The Home Office* [2002] EWCA Civ 462 are example of appeals being allowed because of the judge's excessive interruptions and cross examination of witnesses. *Cairnstores Ltd v Aktiebolaget Hassle* [2002] EWCA Civ 1504, (2002) 25(12) IPD 25081 is an example where the interruptions and cross examination of experts by the judge did not exhibit apparent bias.
[415] (Unreported) CA, 19 June 2000.
[416] (Unreported) CA, 19 June 2000, at paras 49 and 50.
[417] [2000] QB 451.
[418] [2000] QB 451, at para 85.

inappropriate for a judge to use intemperate language about subjects on which he has adjudicated or will have to adjudicate.'

In that case it was held that the tone of the article written by the recorder extra-judicially was such that apparent bias was made out.[419]

4.229 Problems of predetermination have also arisen when the tribunal, having determined an issue without giving one of the parties an opportunity to make proper representations on the issue, then seeks to remedy its earlier error by carrying out a review. In *E v Oxfordshire*,[420] Elias J (as he then was) held that it was not inherently unfair for the same tribunal to hear the review as made the original error and that the regulations contemplated this course.

4.230 The question has arisen as to what principles govern how members of the tribunal can act upon their own knowledge and experience in disputes before them. In *White v Ealing Borough Council*[421] the Court of Appeal held that the members could act on the basis of their own experience and it was preferable, if that led them to consider that a particular course was appropriate, to canvas that with the parties, but that a failure to do so did not render the decision procedurally unfair.

4.231 In the context of employment tribunals, it has been held that it is not necessarily procedurally unfair for such a tribunal to decide a case on the basis of authorities with which the parties have not had an opportunity of dealing, although it is preferable for the tribunal to invite comment on such authorities before reaching its decision.[422] A similar approach, it is submitted, would be followed in relation to the FTT.

Religion

4.232 Cultural or religious factors are not special educational needs in themselves: see *R v ILEA ex parte Futerfas*.[423] However, if a child has other needs which are special educational needs and they cannot be met at a non-denominational school, there is a duty to educate the child at a

---

[419] [2000] QB 451, at para 89.
[420] [2001] EWHC 816 (Admin), [2002] ELR 256 at para 26.
[421] [1998] ELR 319 at 331G–332C, 338C–338E, 342H–343B and 343H–344B.
[422] *Stanley Cole (Wainfleet) v Sheridan* [2003] IRLR 52, EAT.
[423] (Unreported) 10 June 1988 at 11F to 12A. In *G v SENT and Barnet* [1997] EWHC 912 (Admin), Ognall J held, at para 8, that this was still the law under the EA 1996 despite para 4.50 of the then Code of Practice on SEN made under s 313 of the EA 1996, which provided that denominational considerations were a relevant factor in determining the appropriateness of the provision for a child. Para 8.65 of the current Code of Practice provides that the LA should consider very carefully a preference by the parents for a denominational mainstream maintained school and representations made by parents for a denominational non-maintained special school, or independent school, but that denominational considerations cannot override the requirements of s 316 of the EA 1996.

denominational school: see *R v Secretary of State for Education ex parte E.*[424] The impact of the Human Rights Act 1998 on religious or cultural factors is considered below.[425]

The duty to name a school

4.233 The courts have had to consider whether there is a duty to name a school under section 324 of the EA 1996. In *White v Ealing and others*[426] the Court of Appeal held that there was no absolute duty on the LA or the tribunal to name a school as part of the special educational provision where it was of the view that such provision should be made in a special school. While special educational provision could include the naming of a particular school under section 324(4)(b), that did not mean that there was a duty in all cases to name the school as part of that provision. The Court considered, it is submitted rightly, that neither the decision of Auld J nor the Court of Appeal in *R v London Borough of Hackney ex parte GC*[427] compelled a contrary result. If the special educational needs of the child were so unusual that they could only be met by specifying a particular school, the LA might have to name that school. The question whether to name a school was one for the judgment of the tribunal, challengeable on the usual public law grounds.

4.234 The conclusion of the Court of Appeal was confirmed in relation to a non-special school in the case of *R (on the application of M) v Sutton London Borough Council.*[428]

4.235 By virtue of a legislative amendment made by section 9 of the Special Educational Needs and Disability Act 2001, there is no duty to name a school under section 324(4)(b) of the EA 1996 if the child's parents have made suitable arrangements for the special educational provision specified in the statement to be made for the child.[429]

4.236 It should be noted that even where there is a duty to name a school, the tribunal is concerned with the present, and future, needs of the child, and an order by it that a particular school should be named does not have retrospective effect, with the consequence, in relation to a fee-paying school, that the LA is not liable for fees incurred by the parents since the child was placed at the school, but before the order of the tribunal that that school should be named in Part IV of the statement.[430]

---

[424] [1996] ELR 312 at 321E–322A.
[425] See at paras **4.262–4.278** below.
[426] [1998] ELR 319, CA.
[427] [1995] ELR 144, [1996] ELR 142.
[428] [2007] EWCA Civ 1205 at paras 16–19.
[429] EA 1996, s 324(4A).
[430] *R v London Borough of Barnet ex parte B* [1998] ELR 281, CA; *R v Secretary of State for Education and Science ex parte Davis* [1989] 2 FLR 190.

Residential school

4.237   One of the issues frequently raised in FTT appeals is whether the child has a need for a residential school or, as it is often referred to, a 'waking day' or 24 hour curriculum.

4.238   In the *Learning Trust v SENDIST and MP*[431] Andrew Nicol QC, sitting as a deputy judge of the High Court, stated that when considering whether residential provision is required, the focus must be on whether or not the child requires educational programmes continuing after the end of the school day. The fact that a child has a need for a consistency of approach in his dealings with adults outside of school as well as inside school does not mean necessarily that this is an *educational* need that needs to be met with *educational* provision beyond the school day.[432]

4.239   In *Hampshire County Council v JP* the UT held that the test for whether a child needed a residential school named in Part 4 of the statement of special educational needs was 'whether his need for a consistent programme was such that his education could not reasonably be provided unless he was accommodated on the site where he was educated'.[433]

4.240   In *H v East Sussex County Council*[434] the tribunal had concluded that the education proposed by the LA, supported as it was by social service provision and therapy support outside of the ordinary school day, was appropriate for the child. The child's parent appealed on the basis that the additional therapy and the social services support were part of the child's educational provision. The tribunal had, accordingly, failed to specify or quantify in the child's statement what educational provision was required.

4.241   The Court of Appeal held in a case where after care after school is important, support from other agencies will be a relevant consideration in considering the position overall. The court concluded, however, that the provision of carers was not the provision of education and neither did the tribunal consider them to be so.[435]

REASONS CHALLENGES

4.242   Rule 30 of the FTT Rules provides that the FTT must provide to each party as soon as reasonably practicable after making a decision which finally disposes of all issues in the proceedings a decision notice stating the tribunal's decision and 'written reasons for the decision'.

---

[431]   [2007] EWHC 1634 (Admin); [2007] ELR 658.
[432]   See also *T v Hertfordshire County Council* [2004] EWCA Civ 927, [2005] LGR 262.
[433]   [2009] UT 239 (AAC) at para 29.
[434]   [2009] EWCA Civ 249; [2009] ELR 161.
[435]   [2009] EWCA Civ 249; [2009] ELR 161 at para 48. See also *Bedfordshire County Council v Haslam* [2008] EWHC 1070 (Admin).

4.243 Previously, regulation 36 of the Special Educational Needs Tribunal Regulations 2001 had required 'a statement of reasons (in summary form) for the tribunal's decision'. The phrase 'in summary form' is not repeated in rule 30 of the FTT Rules. A number of cases considered the nature of the duty imposed by SENDT by regulation 36.

4.244 In *W v Leeds City Council and SENDIST*[436] Ward LJ considered four judgements of the Administrative Court that dealt with the duty on the SENDT to give reasons.[437] He stated (at paragraphs 53–54):[438]

'53. I do not think it necessary for this court to add to the already substantial jurisprudence on this topic. Speaking for myself, I have always regarded the judgment of Sir Thomas Bingham MR (as he then was) in this court in *Meek v Birmingham City Council* [1987] IRLR 250 (even though it substantially antedates the incorporation into English Law of ECHR) as the definitive exposition of the attitude superior courts should adopt to the reasons given by Tribunals. Whilst, of course, some aspects of the reasoning processes of different specialist tribunals are unique to the particular speciality which is engaged, I see no reason, in this context, to distinguish between Employment Tribunals and what are now SENDISTs. Sir Thomas said:

"It has on a number of occasions been made plain that the decision of an Industrial Tribunal is not required to be an elaborate formalistic product of refined legal draftsmanship, but it must contain an outline of the story which has given rise to the complaint and a summary of the Tribunal's basic factual conclusions and a statement of the reasons which have led them to reach the conclusion which they do on those basic facts. The parties are entitled to be told why they have won or lost. There should be sufficient account of the facts and of the reasoning to enable the EAT or, on further appeal, this court to see whether any question of law arises ..."

53. The Master of the Rolls added:

"Nothing that I have said is, as I believe, in any way inconsistent with previous authority on this subject. In *UCATT v Brain* [1981] IRLR 225, Donaldson LJ (as he then was) said at p 227: 'Industrial tribunals' reasons are not intended to include a comprehensive and detailed analysis of the case, either in terms of fact or in law ... their purpose remains what it has always been, which is to tell the parties in broad terms why they lose or, as the case may be, win. I think it would be a thousand pities if these reasons

---

[436] [2005] EWCA Civ 988; [2005] ELR 617.

[437] Being *S v Special Educational Needs Tribunal and the City of Westminster* [1996] ELR 102; *H v Kent County Council and the Special Educational Needs Tribunal* [2000] ELR 660; *R (on the application of M) v Brighton and Hove City Council and Special Educational Needs Tribunal* [2003] ELR 752, and *R (on the application of L) v London Borough of Waltham Forest and another* [2004] ELR 161.

[438] The approach of Ward LJ is consistent with the approach of the courts to reasons in other contexts, see, for example, the decision of the House of Lords concerning the provision of reasons in planning cases, *South Bucks District Council v Porter (No 2)* [2004] 1 WLR 1953, per Lord Brown at 1964D–G.

began to be subjected to a detailed analysis and appeals were to be brought based upon any such analysis. This, to my mind, is to misuse the purpose for which the reasons are given.'''

4.245 The duty on SENDT to give reasons was revisited by the Court of Appeal in *H v East Sussex County Council*.[439] The appellant had asserted a conflict between the authorities at first instance as to the obligation of a tribunal when giving reasons dealing with expert evidence. The appellant suggested that Grigson J had been correct when he stated in *H v Kent County Council and SENDIST*[440] that a 'specialist tribunal such as SENDIST can use its expertise in deciding issues but if it rejects expert evidence it should say so specifically. In certain circumstances it may be required to say why it rejects it'. That statement was contrasted by the appellant with the words of Wilkie J in *KW and VW v London Borough of Lewisham*[441] in that 'where there are contending points of view being expressed by various professionals on either side of the argument, the tribunal has given sufficient reasons by identifying which side of the argument has succeeded'.

4.246 Waller LJ (with whom Scott Baker and Toulson LJJ agreed) criticised this approach as seeking to elevate statements of Grigson J and Wilkie J into propositions of law in all cases. That was, in his view, an entirely wrong approach.[442] Waller LJ stated that the requirement to give reasons was concerned with fairness. He reaffirmed the guidance given by Ward LJ in *W v Leeds City Council and SENDIST*.[443]

4.247 Finally, Waller LJ stated that the duty contained in regulation 36 was one to give reasons in 'summary form'. He stated that summary reasons should not contain a full comprehensive analysis or spell out every step in the reasoning or deal with every conceivable point: their purpose was to tell the parties in broad terms why they lost or won.[444]

4.248 The duty imposed on the FTT to give reasons by the FTT Rules has been the subject of consideration by the Upper Tribunal. In *DC v London Borough of Ealing* the Upper Tribunal considered the duty of the FTT to provide reasons for its decisions pursuant to the FTT Rules.[445] Judge Wikeley noted that the requirement that reasons be in 'summary form' has been omitted from the FTT Rules. He nevertheless proceeded on the basis that the decisions in *W v Leeds City Council and SENDIST* and in *H v East Sussex County Council* applied with equal force to rule 30 of the FTT Rules.[446]

---

[439] [2009] EWCA Civ 249; [2009] ELR 161.
[440] [2000] ELR 660.
[441] [2006] EWHC 1853 (Admin), [2007] ELR 11.
[442] [2009] EWCA Civ 249; [2009] ELR 161, at paras 9–10, 14–15.
[443] [2009] EWCA Civ 249; [2009] ELR 161, at paras 14–19.
[444] [2009] EWCA Civ 249; [2009] ELR 161, at para 19.
[445] [2010] UKUT 10 (AAC).
[446] See also *GC & JC v Tameside Metropolitan Borough Council* [2011] UKUT 292 (AAC) at paras 19–22.

4.249   The decision of the UT in *Hampshire County Council v JP*[447] concerned a tribunal's decision on an appeal relating to a statement of special educational needs. A challenge by the LA to the tribunal's reasoning was one of the grounds of appeal. The three-judge panel stated:[448]

> 'The fact that an expert has stated an opinion is not in itself an adequate reason for a tribunal to adopt that opinion unless the opinion is unchallenged. In the event of a conflict of opinions, it is necessary for a tribunal to give an opinion for preferring one opinion rather than the other. Where an opinion is fully reasoned, a tribunal accepting the opinion may be taken to have adopted the reasoning and in those cases merely referring to the opinion may be sufficient provided that the expert has given adequate reasons for disagreeing with any opposing view.'

4.250   The UT concluded: 'where there is a crucial disagreement between experts and the dispute involves something in the nature of an intellectual exchange, with reasons and analysis advanced on either side, the judge must enter into the issues canvassed before him and explain why he prefers one case over the other' (relying on *Flannery v Halifax Estate Agencies Limited* [2001] 1 WLR 377 (CA)).[449]

4.251   Attempts by the FTT to supplement the reasons given for a decision when refusing to review the decision or when refusing to grant permission to appeal have been met with disapproval by the UT.[450]

4.252   In *B v Worcestershire County Council*[451] Upper Tribunal Judge Williams stated that the FTT's decision refusing to review its original decision, where additional reasons were provided, was not relevant to his decision on the appeal.[452] He relied upon *Oxfordshire County Council v GB*[453] in which the Court of Appeal stated '... we do not consider it generally appropriate that a statutory tribunal which is required to give reasoned decisions should respond to an appeal by purporting to amplify its reasons'.

4.253   In *MM & DM v London Borough of Harrow*[454] Upper Tribunal Judge Jacobs stated that the UT was not concerned with the reasons given by the FTT when refusing permission. This decision is consistent with the decision of the Court of Appeal in *Albion Water Ltd v Dŵr Cymru Cyf*[455] in which it stated that the reasons given by a lower court for refusing permission cannot be used to show that a point of law arises.

---

[447]   [2009] UKUT 239 (AAC).
[448]   [2009] UKUT 239 (AAC) at para 37.
[449]   [2009] UKUT 239 (AAC) at para 39.
[450]   This can be contrasted with the position under the old Order 52 regime in which the courts had admitted evidence to explain the reasons already given for a decision or (in exceptional circumstances) to add to the reasons given provided that these were the true reasons at the time, see *S v SENT* [1995] 1 WLR 1627 at 1637A, 1636G–1637C.
[451]   [2010] UKUT 292 (AAC).
[452]   [2010] UKUT 292 (AAC), at para 10.
[453]   [2001] EWCA Civ 1358 at para 9.
[454]   [2010] UKUT 395 (AAC) at para 4.
[455]   [2009] 2 All ER 279 at para 67.

4.254   The UT has considered the duty on the FTT to provide reasons for its interlocutory decisions. In *KP v Hertfordshire County Council*[456] the parents sought to appeal to the UT against an interlocutory decision of the FTT made pursuant to rule 15(4) of the FTT Rules to order that the parents make their child available for assessment by a speech and language therapist. One of the grounds of appeal before the UT was that the reasons given by the FTT for giving the direction were insufficient. The UT rejected the appeal. Judge Wikely noted that rule 6(4) of the FTT Rules, which requires written notice of any direction given to be sent to every party and to any other person affected by the direction, did not contain a requirement to provide reasons. He stated that the FTT had a discretion to provide reasons in each case, depending on whether it was appropriate or not. He rejected the submission that the principle in *H v East Sussex County Council*, that a party should know in broad terms whether it has won or lost, applied to an interlocutory decision. He observed that the application did not involve anyone 'winning' or 'losing', but was rather one of the many steps along the way to a resolution of the substantive issues in dispute.[457]

STRIKING OUT A PARTY'S CASE

4.255   The FTT has various powers[458] to strike out the whole or a part of a party's case.[459] The proceedings, or the appropriate part of them, will automatically be struck out if the applicant has failed to comply with a direction that stated that failure by the applicant to comply with the direction would lead to the striking out of proceedings or that part of them.[460] The FTT must strike out the whole or a part of the proceedings if the FTT does not have jurisdiction in relation to the proceedings or that part of them; and does not exercise the power in rule 5(3)(k)(i) (transfer to another court or tribunal) in relation to the proceedings or that part of them.[461] The FTT may strike out the whole or the part of the proceedings if:

(a)   the applicant has failed to comply with a direction which stated that failure by the applicant to comply with the direction could lead to the striking out of proceedings or part of them;

---

[456]   [2010] UKUT 233 (AAC).

[457]   [2010] UKUT 233 (AAC) at paras 26–28.

[458]   The FTT has powers short of strike out to deal with a failure to comply with the rules or a direction. Rule 7(2) empowers the FTT to take such action as it considers just, which may include waiving the requirement, requiring the failure to be remedied, referring the case to the UT to ask it to exercise its powers in relation to witnesses, or to restrict a party's participation in the proceedings.

[459]   It should be noted that, in contrast to the Special Educational Needs Tribunal Regulations 2001, the FTT Rules do not contain a power to strike out an appeal which is, or has become, scandalous, vexatious or frivolous. On the application of the latter power, see *White v Aldridge* [1999] ELR 150; *G v South Gloucestershire Council* [2000] ELR 136; *R (on the application of A) v London Borough of Lambeth* [2001] EWHC 379 (Admin), [2002] ELR 231 and *East Sussex County Council v Hughes* [2004] EWHC 1834 (Admin).

[460]   FTT Rules, r 8(2).

[461]   FTT Rules, r 8(3).

(b)   the applicant has failed to co-operate with the FTT to such an extent that the FTT cannot deal with the proceedings fairly or justly;

(c)   the FTT considers there is no reasonable prospect of the applicant's case or part of it, succeeding.[462]

4.256   The FTT may not exercise its discretion to strike out proceedings under rules 8(3) or 8(4)(b) or (c) of the FTT Rules without first giving the applicant an opportunity to make representations in relation to the proposed striking out.[463] If the proceedings, or part of them, have been struck out under rule 8(2) or (4)(a) of the FTT Rules, the applicant may apply for the proceedings, or part of them, to be reinstated.[464]

4.257   Rule 8 of the FTT Rules applies to a respondent as it applies to an applicant except that a reference to the striking out of proceedings is to be read as a reference to the barring of the respondent taking further part in the proceedings; and a reference to an application for the reinstatement of proceedings which have been struck out is to be read as a reference to an application for the lifting of the bar on the respondent from taking further part in the proceedings.[465] If a respondent has been barred from taking further part in the proceedings, the FTT need not consider any response or other submission made by the respondent and may summarily determine any or all issues against that respondent.[466]

4.258   Considering rules 8(3) and (4) of the FTT Rules in *AW v Essex County Council*,[467] Upper Tribunal Judge Jacobs applied the definition of jurisdiction given by Diplock LJ in *Garthwaite v Garthwaite*:[468]

> 'In its narrow and strict sense, the "jurisdiction" of a validly constituted court connotes the limits which are imposed on its power to hear and determine issues between persons seeking to avail themselves of its process by reference (i) to subject-matter of the issue, or (ii) to the persons between whom the issue is joined, or (iii) to the kind of relief sought, or any combination of these factors.'

The Judge stated that the test under rule 8(3) of the FTT Rules was whether the FTT had authority to decide an issue; the test under rule 8(4) was what decision the FTT is entitled to give on an issue.[469]

---

[462]   FTT Rules, r 8(4).
[463]   FTT Rules, r 8(5).
[464]   FTT Rules, r 8(6). Such an application must be made in writing and received by the Tribunal within 28 days after the date on which the FTT sent notification of the striking out to that party, FTT Rules, r 8(7).
[465]   FTT Rules, r 8(8).
[466]   FTT Rules, r 8(9).
[467]   [2010] UKUT 74 (AAC) at para 14.
[468]   [1964] P 356 at 387.
[469]   [2010] UKUT 74 (AAC) at para 15.

4.259   In *London Borough of Camden v FG*[470] the respondent failed to comply with the case management directions made by the FTT. The directions stated that a failure to comply might result in the exercise of the FTT's powers under rule 8 to strike out all or part of a party's case. The FTT, applying rule 8(4)(a), made an order that the respondent be barred from taking any further part in the proceedings. The FTT dismissed the respondent's subsequent application to be reinstated. A representative from the respondent attended the hearing before the FTT, but was not permitted to remain whilst the appeal was heard.

4.260   On appeal, the UT rejected the respondent's argument that the decision to bar the respondent from the proceedings was disproportionate, had not taken proper account of the overriding objective and would be appropriate only if there had been wilful and repeated disobedience.[471] The UT held that the respondent ought to have sought permission to appeal from the FTT's decision not to reinstate it, rather than waiting until after the final hearing to appeal.[472]

4.261   Rules 7 and 8 of the UT Rules are in materially identical terms to rules 7 and 8 of the FTT Rules. In *FC v Suffolk County Council*[473] Upper Tribunal Judge Pearl considered rule 7(2)(d) (the power to restrict a party's participation in proceedings where it has failed to comply with a requirement of the UT Rules or a direction). The respondent had failed, in breach of a case management direction, to file a defence and lodge a skeleton argument no later than five days prior to the hearing. The Judge refused to restrict the respondent's participation in the proceedings, and stated that rule 7(2)(d) was 'a draconian provision' which should be used 'only in the most blatant cases of disregard on the part of a party to the proceedings'.[474]

HUMAN RIGHTS CHALLENGES

4.262   In other areas of public law, challenges based on Article 6 of the ECHR have loomed large.[475] This has not been reproduced in cases involving special educational needs. There are two principal reasons for this. The first is that the existence of the FTT, and previously, SENDT, has meant, in practice, that most disputes involving special educational needs are, in fact, heard by that tribunal and nobody has suggested that it is, in general, not an independent and impartial tribunal.[476] The second is that at an early stage the European Commission decided, when declaring an application inadmissible, that the right

---

[470]   [2010] UKUT 249 (AAC).

[471]   [2010] UKUT 249 (AAC) at para 51.

[472]   [2010] UKUT 249 (AAC) at para 54.

[473]   [2010] UKUT 368 (AAC).

[474]   [2010] UKUT 368 (AAC) at para 13, although it should be noted that the appellant was legally represented and the skeleton was sent prior to the hearing so that counsel for the appellant had an opportunity to read it.

[475]   See, for example, the discussion in the House of Lords in *Runa Begum v Tower Hamlets* [2003] UKHL 5, [2003] 2 WLR 388.

[476]   If it was somehow lacking in independence or impartiality and Art 6 was engaged there would

to education in Article 2 of the First Protocol was not a civil right within the meaning of Article 6 of the ECHR.[477] Despite this, there has been some reference to Article 6 of the ECHR in cases involving the tribunal. In *A v Kirklees*,[478] where the tribunal was unaware that an accident had taken place at the school that was named as appropriate for the child some six years previously, the appellant sought to rely on Article 6 of the ECHR. Sedley LJ[479] found it unnecessary to comment on whether Article 6 was in play because he did not regard it as adding to domestic law principles on the facts of that case.

4.263 There have been a number of attempts to use Article 2 of the First Protocol to the ECHR in this field. On the whole, these have not been successful. There are two relevant rights in Article 2: the right to education and the right to respect for the parents' religious and philosophical convictions. The general nature of these rights is discussed in Chapter 10.[480] The impact of those general principles on children with special educational needs is discussed here.

4.264 In *Simpson v UK*,[481] the parents of a dyslexic child contended that their child's right to education in accordance with the first sentence of Article 2 was denied when the LA insisted that the child should be educated in a maintained school rather than an independent school. The Commission held that the application was inadmissible, inter alia, because a place was available at a maintained school with appropriate teaching facilities for children with special educational needs.

4.265 In *Ford v UK*,[482] it was contended that the right to education had been denied by an LA placing a child in a special school. Once again, the Commission declared the application inadmissible, relying on the State's margin of appreciation, which it considered was reasonably based on expert evidence as to what education best met the needs of the child.

4.266 In *McIntyre v United Kingdom*[483] the Commission dismissed an application alleging that the right to education was breached by failing to provide a lift for a disabled child so that she could freely use the school facilities.

---

then be an argument about whether the appeal to the UT on a point of law was sufficient to mean that, overall, Art 6 had been complied with.

[477] *Simpson v UK* Application No 14688/89 (1989), 64 DR 188. The merits of this decision are discussed in Chs 5 and 6 relating to admissions and exclusions where the point has been the subject of debate.

[478] [2001] EWCA Civ 582, [2001] ELR 657.

[479] [2001] EWCA Civ 582, [2001] ELR 657, at para 19. The other two members of the Court did not refer expressly to Art 6 and applied domestic law principles.

[480] Article 2 of Protocol 1 to the European Convention on Human Rights has now been considered compressively by the House of Lords in *Ali v Headteachers and Governors of Lord Grey School* [2005] UKHL 14; [2006] 2 AC 363 and by the Supreme Court in *A v Essex CC* [2010] UKSC 33; [2011] AC 280.

[481] (1989) 64 DR 188.

[482] [1996] EHRLR 534.

[483] Application 29046/95, 21 October 1998, E Comm HR.

4.267 In *H v Gloucestershire County Council*[484] it was sought to be argued that a decision of the tribunal which was not irrational nevertheless breached the right to an 'effective education ... pursuant to a combination of Art 8 and Art 2'. The court rejected this argument,[485] inter alia, on the ground that it added nothing to ordinary principles and it was for the tribunal to carry out a balancing act on the evidence before it.

4.268 In *H v Kent CC*[486] it was argued that the refusal of the LA, upheld on appeal by the tribunal, to carry out a statutory assessment of a child, was a breach of the right to education. That argument was rejected[487] because the child was not being deprived of her education, merely the machinery by which her needs were to be assessed. The same argument was also rejected by Elias J (as he then was) in *S v Special Educational Needs Tribunal*.[488]

4.269 The second sentence of Article 2 is concerned with respecting the parents' 'religious and philosophical convictions'. That is not simply the same as respecting their wishes. A number of cases before the Commission have raised the question of the extent to which the obligation to respect parents' philosophical convictions in the second sentence of Article 2 requires the State to act in accordance with the wishes of parents of children with special educational needs. In each case the Commission expressly left open the question whether the parents' disagreement with the education authorities about the appropriate school for their child could be said to be based on 'deep-founded philosophical convictions', rather than a mere difference of view as to the best way of providing their child with an education.[489]

4.270 In three cases, the parents of children with disabilities who each wanted their child to be educated in a mainstream school complained that the education authorities' decision that they be educated in a special school constituted a violation of Article 2 of the First Protocol.[490] The parents contended that they held deep philosophical convictions about the need for integrated, rather than segregated, education for disabled children generally, and for their child in particular, and that by placing each child in a special school, the education authorities were failing to respect the parents' right to have their child educated in accordance with those philosophical convictions.[491]

---

[484] (Unreported) 19 June 2000, CA.

[485] (Unreported) 19 June 2000, CA, at paras 80 and 81.

[486] [2000] ELR 660.

[487] [2000] ELR 660, at para 59.

[488] [2005] EWHC 196 (Admin); [2005] ELR 443.

[489] However, in *Family H v UK*, No 10233/83, Decision 6.3.84, (1984) 37 DR 105, the Commission accepted that the beliefs of the parents of four dyslexic children, who educated them all at home because they found the state school system 'repugnant', were of a 'philosophical' nature for the purposes of Art 2 of the First Protocol.

[490] *PD and LD v UK* No 14135/88, Decision 2.10.89, 62 DR 292; *Graeme v UK*, No 13887/88, Decision 5.2.90, 64 DR 158; *Klerks v Netherlands*, No 25212/94, Decision 4.7.95, 82 DR 41.

[491] In *PD and LD v UK*, the applicant parents also put the argument in terms of a lack of

4.271 The Commission held that, even assuming that such convictions were in issue, the child's right to education in Article 2 of the First Protocol was predominant.[492] The Commission observed that 'there is an increasing body of opinion which holds that, whenever possible, disabled children should be brought up with normal children of their own age', but it also recognised that this policy could not apply to all disabled children, and that 'there must be a wide measure of discretion left to the appropriate authorities as to how to make the best use possible of the resources available to them in the interests of disabled children generally'. While it was incumbent on those authorities to place weight on parental convictions, it could not be said that the second sentence of Article 2 required the placing of a disabled child such as the applicants' child in a mainstream school, with the expense of the additional teaching staff which would be needed or to the detriment of the other pupils, rather than in an available place in a special school.

4.272 The Commission noted that the requirement to respect, as far as possible, parents' philosophical convictions did not require the State to provide special facilities to accommodate particular convictions.[493] In the two cases against the UK, the Commission also referred to the UK's reservation to the second sentence of Article 2 and noted the similarity between the terms of that reservation and the provision in the relevant domestic legislation[494] providing that a child with special educational needs should be educated in an ordinary school if that is compatible with the special education the child requires, the provision of efficient education for other children at the school and the efficient use of resources.

4.273 The Commission concluded that the education authorities had respected the parents' convictions, as well as the child's right to have as effective an education as possible, and the applications were therefore declared inadmissible.

4.274 In a case not involving special educational needs, *Campbell and Cosans v United Kingdom*,[495] the court gave guidance on what was a philosophical conviction for the purpose of the second sentence of Article 2 of the First Protocol:

'In its ordinary meaning the word "convictions" taken on its own, is not synonymous with the words "opinions" and "ideas" such as are utilised in Art 10 of the Convention, which guarantees freedom of expression; it is more akin to the term "beliefs" (in the French text: "convictions") appearing in Art 9 – which guarantees freedom of thought, conscience and religion – and denotes views that attain a certain level of cogency, seriousness, cohesion and importance.

adequate choice of state schools for parents of disabled children, contrary to what they contended was Art 2's guarantee of the provision of a reasonable range of practical choices within the state school system.

[492] *Kjeldsen* at para 52.
[493] Citing *X v UK*, No 7782/77, Decision 2.5.78, 14 DR 179.
[494] Education Act 1981, s 2; see now ss 316, 316A and especially para 3 of Sch 27 to the EA 1996.
[495] (1982) 4 EHRR 293 at para 36.

As regards the adjective "philosophical" it is not capable of exhaustive definition ... the word philosophy ... is used to allude to a full-fledged system of thought or, rather loosely, to views on more or less trivial matters ... neither of these extremes can be adopted ... philosophical convictions ... denotes ... such convictions as are worthy of respect in a democratic society and such as are not incompatible with human dignity; in addition, they must not conflict with the fundamental right of the child to education, the whole of Art 2 being dominated by its first sentence.'

4.275 In *R (on the application of Williamson) v Secretary of State for Education and Employment*,[496] Elias J (as he then was) held that a belief that one measure is more effective than another is not a philosophical conviction, even if the reason for holding that belief was based on a religious text.[497]

4.276 In *T v SENT and Wiltshire CC*,[498] the parents argued that their views as to the appropriate form of educational provision for their child constituted a philosophical conviction for the purposes of Article 2 of the First Protocol of the ECHR. Richards J held that the point was not open to them because it had not been raised below.[499] He went on to consider[500] the merits of the argument and held that, although the criteria in *Campbell and Cosans* were far from clear cut, and the matter was not susceptible of precise analysis, the correct characterisation of the parents' preference for the particular programme they wished the child to undertake, the Lovaas programme, was not that they had any philosophical conviction in its favour, but simply that they entertained a judgement that it was the best education for their child.[501] Even if it was properly to be regarded as a conviction, for the purposes of Article 2 of the First Protocol, the learned judge held that the tribunal had given due weight to the parent's preference to the extent permitted by section 319 of the EA 1996 and that section was not incompatible with the ECHR.

4.277 In *Re S*[502] Buxton LJ was prepared to give a wide construction to 'convictions' under Article 2 and to hold that the views of the parents as to whether the child should be educated in a learning centre or in mainstream education fell within its scope. The basis for this decision does not appear from the report and there is no material recited showing that the parents had

---

[496] [2001] EWHC 960 (Admin), [2002] ELR 214, Elias J.
[497] In the Court of Appeal, [2002] EWCA Civ 1926, (2002) *The Times*, 18 December, Buxton LJ expressly approved that conclusion of Elias J but Rix LJ and Arden LJ held that the parents in that case did have a religious belief or a philosophical conviction: see at paras 176 and 305.
[498] [2002] ELR 704.
[499] [2002] ELR 704, at para 39(i).
[500] [2002] ELR 704, at para 39(iii) and (iv).
[501] He placed reliance upon the reasoning of Elias J in *R (on the application of Williamson) v Secretary of State for Education and Employment* [2001] EWHC (Admin) 960, [2002] ELR 214. That case was affirmed on appeal (see [2002] EWCA Civ 1926) but the majority disagreed with the judge there was no philosophical conviction in play in that case: see at paras 152, 175 and 305. It is submitted this does not undermine the reasoning in *T* because in *Williamson* the court was concerned as, it held, with religious and philosophical convictions, and not simply a question of what action was efficacious.
[502] [2002] EWCA Civ 191. Thorpe LJ did not deal with this point. The matter came before the court on an application for permission to appeal (see para 17) and was dealt with by a two-judge court.

anything other than a preference for a particular institution to educate their child. However, because the parents did not agree as to which institution that should be, the Court of Appeal held that the ECHR did not assist the court.

4.278 The Commission has allowed the State's assessment of the child's right to education to override the parents' conviction that the child should be educated at home. Accordingly, where parents of a dyslexic child failed to comply with a school attendance order and were convicted, the Commission held[503] that it was not its task to decide whether the parents or the State were correct as to what form of education was better for the child, because the State had a responsibility to verify and enforce educational standards and the parents were obliged to co-operate in the performance of that duty.

4.279 In *CB v London Borough of Merton*,[504] it was sought to be argued that a decision of the tribunal that a boarding school should be named in the statement was an interference with the child's and parent's right to family life where neither parent nor child wanted boarding education. Sullivan J had no difficulty in concluding[505] that there had been no interference within the meaning of Article 8(1) and that, if there had, it was justified under Article 8(2). As the judge held, an order of the tribunal that a particular school should be named does not oblige the parent to send the child to that school, but does oblige the LA to name the school in the statement. If the child does not attend any school, the LA can take matters further, but until it does there can be no interference with the right to family life. In any event, as the judge held, where, as in that case, there was no suitable school for the child other than the one named by the tribunal, any interference under Article 8(1) would be plainly justified under Article 8(2) as necessary to protect the child's right to education.

4.280 Similarly, in *R (O) v Hammersmith and Fulham London Borough Council* the claimant asserted that a refusal to place a child at a special residential school constituted an unlawful interference with his rights under Article 8. The Court of Appeal held 'where the LA simply chooses one way of meeting a child's needs rather than another, it cannot be said to have interfered with the exercise by the child or their parents of their right to respect to their private or family life'.[506] The Court of Appeal concluded that there had been no breach of Article 8.

4.281 Finally, issues of deprivation of liberty under Article 5 have been raised in relation to special schools. In *C v A Local Authority and others*[507] the Article 5 rights of a pupil attending a residential special school were found to have been violated by his regular confinement in a room designed for his seclusion (a fact conceded by the LA). C was an 18 year with severe autism who was placed at a residential special school for pupils with severe learning

---

[503] *Family H v United Kingdom* (1984) 37 DR 105.
[504] [2002] EWHC 877, [2002] ELR 441.
[505] [2002] EWHC 877, [2002] ELR 441, at paras 19–22.
[506] [2011] EWCA Civ 925, [2011] 3 FCR 17 at para 43.
[507] [2011] EWHC 1539.

difficulties and complex needs. The school, amongst other things, frequently placed C in the 'blue room', a 10 feet square room designed by an autism adviser in 2007. This action had the approval of C's mother, and was said to have a calming influence on him. The blue room had padded walls and a secure door and window, although it could not be locked. The school's records showed that restraint techniques were being used on C on average more than twice a day. In June 2010 the blue room door was held closed so as to confine C on 192 occasions (6.4 times per day).

4.282 C brought a claim for judicial review seeking a number of matters, including damages for breach of Articles 3, 5 and 8. Subsequent proceedings issued in the Court of Protection by the LA were consolidated and determined together.

4.283 Ryder J held that neither the LA nor the school had any power to deprive C of his liberty, he was deprived of his liberty, and this was unlawful and contrary to Article 5. The Judge held that whether the facts surrounding the deprivation of liberty were such as to also violate the child's rights under Articles 3 and 8 would require a more detailed examination of the facts at a further hearing.[508] Once an incapacitated child in residential provision reaches the age of 16, consideration needs to be given to applying to the Court of Protection under the Mental Capacity Act 2005 for authorisation for any deprivation of liberty.[509] In the absence of any corresponding guidance that is applicable to a severely learning disabled child who is resident in a special school and whose condition *prima facie* falls within the definition of a mental disorder, the guidance in the Mental Health Act 1983 Code of Practice applies, with the consequence that regard must be had to it and the reasons for any departures from it explained and recorded.[510] Further, where a child's learning disability does not fall within the definition of a mental disorder, the Code should be applied in any event as good practice (para 71).[511]

4.284 In considering whether a school's practice amounts to a deprivation of a child's liberty, the LA and the school will need also to have regard to recent decisions of the Court of Appeal in the context of the deprivation of liberty in residential[512] case homes.

---

[508] [2011] EWHC 1539 at para 113.
[509] [2011] EWHC 1539 at para 64.
[510] [2011] EWHC 1539 at paras 69–70.
[511] [2011] EWHC 1539 at para 71.
[512] See *P & Q (aka MIG and MEG) v Surrey CC* [2011] EWCA Civ 190, [2011] 1 FCR 559 and *Cheshire West and Chester Council v P* [2011] EWCA Civ 1257.

APPEALS BY CONSENT AND ALTERNATIVE DISPUTE RESOLUTION

4.285   Express provision[513] is made for an LA to concede appeals made to the FTT. Such appeals are treated as having been determined in favour of the appellant but the tribunal is not required to make any order. Instead, the LA is to required to make a statement of SEN or (essentially) take such other action as the appeal relates to within a prescribed period.[514]

4.286   Under section 332B(1) of the EA 1996,[515] an LA in England must make arrangements with a view to avoiding or resolving disputes between parents and authorities about the exercise by authorities of their functions in relation to SEN. Under section 332B(2), the LA must also make arrangements with a view to avoiding, or resolving, disagreements between the parents of a relevant child and the proprietor of the school about the special educational provision made for the child. 'A relevant child' is a child with special educational needs who is a registered pupil at a maintained school, or a maintained nursery school, a pupil referral unit, a city technology college, city college for the technology of the arts, or a city Academy, an independent school or a school approved under s 342.[516]

4.287   The arrangements the LA makes must provide for the appointment of an independent person with the function of facilitating the avoidance or resolution of such disagreements.[517] It is also obliged to have regard to any guidance from the Secretary of State[518] in making its arrangements[519] and must take such steps as it considers appropriate to make the arrangements known to parents, headteachers and proprietors, and such other persons as seem appropriate in its area.[520]

4.288   Those arrangements do not affect the entitlement of any parent to appeal to the tribunal.[521] Indeed rule 3(1) of the FTT Rules provides that the FTT should seek, where appropriate, to bring to the attention of the parties the availability of any appropriate alternative procedure for the resolution of the dispute and, if the parties wish (and provided that it is compatible with the overriding objective) to facilitate the use of the procedure.

---

[513]   EA 1996, s 326(a) as inserted by s 5 of the Special Educational Needs and Disability Act 2001.

[514]   EA 1996, s 326A(4). The period prescribed ranges from 2 to 5 weeks and depends on the nature of the appeal: see reg 26 of the Education (Special Educational Needs) (England) (Consolidation) Regulations 2001, SI 2001/3455.

[515]   As inserted by s 3 of the Special Educational Needs and Disability Act 2001. Note that s 332BA of the EA 1996 applies to the resolution of disputes in Wales. Further, s 332BB of the EA 1996 imposes a duty on LAs in Wales to make arrangements for the provision of independent advocacy services in their area.

[516]   EA 1996, s 332B(7) and (8).

[517]   EA 1996, s 332B(3).

[518]   See the SEN Toolkit 0558/2001 at s 3.

[519]   EA 1996, s 332B(4). In Wales the guidance from the National Assembly for Wales must be taken into consideration.

[520]   EA 1996, s 332B(5).

[521]   EA 1996, s 332B(6).

Chapter 5

SCHOOL ADMISSIONS

THE STATUTORY FRAMEWORK

School Admissions Code

5.1   Under section 84(1) of the School Standards and Framework Act 1998 (SSFA 1998) the Secretary of State is obliged to issue a code for school admissions (the Admissions Code) containing such provision as he thinks appropriate in respect of the discharge by various specified bodies of their functions under Chapter 1 of Part III of the SSFA 1998. The bodies specified by section 84(1) are local authorities (LAs), the governing bodies of maintained schools, admission forums, appeal panels and Adjudicators. The Code may impose requirements and include guidelines setting out the aims, objectives and other matters in relation to the discharge of their functions under Chapter 1 of Part III of the SSFA 1998 by LAs and governing bodies.[1]

5.2   There is a difference between section 84(1) and (2). Section 84(1) applies to the five specified bodies,[2] section 84(2) applies only to two[3] of those five bodies. Accordingly, the guidance under section 84(2) does not apply to either admission forums, appeal panels or Adjudicators. The reason for this is that the guidance that is to be provided under section 84(1) is different from that to be provided under section 84(2). Under section 84(1) the guidance is cast very broadly to include such 'provision' as the Secretary of State thinks appropriate. In section 84(2) the guidance can impose requirements and may include guidelines setting out 'aims, objectives and other matters'.

5.3   The current School Admissions Code came into force with immediate effect on 1 February 2012. There is a separate Code of Practice for England dealing with School Admission Appeals which came into force on the same day. The School Admissions Code provides that its purpose is to ensure that all school places for maintained schools (excluding maintained special schools) and Academies are allocated and offered in an open and fair way.[4] Admission

---

[1]   SSFA 1998, s 84(2). Although Academies – being independent schools – are not listed in s 84(1), the funding arrangement between an Academy company and the Secretary of State requires the Academies to comply with the Code and admissions law although the Secretary of State has power to vary this requirement where there is demonstrable need: see para 4 of the Admissions Code.

[2]   LAs, governing bodies of maintained schools, admission forums, appeals panels and Adjudicators.

[3]   LAs and governing bodies of maintained schools.

[4]   See para 12.

authorities must ensure that the practices and criteria used to decide the allocation of school places are fair, clear and objective.[5] The Code makes clear that parents should be able to look at a set of arrangements and understand easily how places for a particular school will be allocated.[6]

5.4   In drawing up admissions arrangements the School Admissions Code provides that admission authorities must act in accordance with the School Admissions Code, the School Admission Appeals Code and other laws relating to admissions and relevant human rights and equalities legislation.[7] Admissions authorities are obliged to set a planned admission number[8] and oversubscription criteria. Although the School Admissions Code does not purport to give a definitive list of acceptable over subscription criteria,[9] detailed principles and guidance in relation to such criteria are set out in it.[10]

5.5   There is a statutory duty upon the five bodies specified in section 84(1) to act in accordance with the Code when exercising their functions under Chapter 1 of Part III of the SSFA 1998.[11] There is a similar statutory duty on any other person when exercising any function of the purposes of the discharge by the LA or the governing body of their functions under Chapter 1 of Part III of the SSFA 1998.[12]

Admissions forum

5.6   Section 85A of the SSFA 1998[13] obliges an LA in Wales[14] to establish an admissions forum to advise it on such matters connected with the exercise of the authority's functions under Chapter 1 of Part III of the SSFA 1998 as may be prescribed and to advise the admissions authorities for maintained schools in the area for which the forum is established on such matters connected with the determination of the admission arrangements and such other matters connected with the admission of pupils as may be prescribed.

---

[5]   See para 14
[6]   See para 14
[7]   See para 1.1
[8]   See para 1.2
[9]   See para 1.10
[10]   See para 1.6 and following.
[11]   SSFA 1998, s 84(3)(a) as amended by the Education and Inspections Act 2006. Prior to the amendment by the Education and Inspections Act 2006, the duty in s 86(3)(a) was merely to 'have regard' to the Code. Previous case-law, such as *R (on the application of Metropolitan Borough Council of Wirral) v Chief Schools Adjudicator* [2001] ELR 574, Ouseley J, needs to be understood in that light.
[12]   SSFA 1998, s 84(3)(b).
[13]   As inserted by s 46 of the EA 2002.
[14]   SSFA, s 85A(1) was amended by the Education Act 2011, s 34(1), (2)(a)(i) to limit its application to Wales. The amendment took effect on 1 February 2012: see Art 3 of the Education Act 2011 (Commencement No 2 and Transitional and Savings Provisions) Order 2012, SI 2012/84.

5.7 The role of an admissions forum is set out in regulation 3 of the Education Admissions (Admission Forums) (Wales) Regulations 2003[15] and is a broad one. Its role is to:

(a) consider how well existing and proposed admission arrangements serve the interests of children and parents within the area of the authority;

(b) promote agreement on admission issues;

(c) consider the comprehensiveness and accessibility of the admissions literature and information for parents, produced by each admission authority within the area of the forum;

(d) consider the effectiveness of any proposed co-ordinated admission arrangements;

(e) consider the means by which admissions processes might be improved and how actual admissions relate to the admissions numbers published;

(f) monitor the admission of children who arrive in the authority's area outside a normal admission round with a view to promoting arrangements for the fair distribution of such children among local schools, taking account of any preference expressed in accordance with arrangements made under section 86(1) of the Act;

(g) promote effective admission arrangements for children with special educational needs, looked after children and children who have been excluded from school;

(h) insofar as not included within subparagraphs (a)–(g) consider any admissions issues arising.

5.8 Membership of the admissions forum is dealt with in regulation 5 of the 2003 Regulations. The forum is to comprise core members appointed by the authority and, if the core members consider it desirable, other interested parties who appear to the core members to represent any section of the local community and are not members of the LA. The Core members are to be appointed by the LA and must comprise:

(a) at least one and not more than five who are members or officers of the LA;

(b) at least one and not more than three who are nominated by the appropriate diocesan authority of the Church of Wales;

---

[15] SI 2003/2962.

(c) at least one and not more than three who are nominated by the appropriate diocesan authority of the Roman Catholic diocese in the area;

(d) at least one and not more than three from each school group;

(e) at least one and not more than three who are parent governor representatives;

(f) not more than three who are not members of the authority who appear to the authority to represent the interests of any section of the local community.

5.9 The LA, the admissions authorities for maintained schools in the area for which the forum is established, and the governing bodies of the Academies in the area have to have regard,[16] in carrying out their functions, to the advice of the admissions forum.[17]

Rights of preference

5.10 Rights for parents to express a preference as to where they wish their children to be educated were introduced by section 6 of the Education Act 1980.[18] That Act supplemented the more general right of preference under section 76 of the Education Act 1944. The relevant rights are now to be found in section 9 of the EA 1996 and sections 86 and 87 of the School Standards and Framework Act 1998 (SSFA 1998). Section 86 of the SSFA 1998 is dealt with first as it is more important.

5.11 By virtue of section 86(1), an LA has a mandatory duty to make arrangements enabling the parent of a child to express a preference as to the school at which he wishes education to be provided in the exercise of the authority's functions and to give reasons for his preference. An LA must also provide advice and assistance to parents in connection with such preferences.[19]

5.12 The LA and the governing bodies of maintained schools are under a duty to comply with that preference unless:

(a) compliance with the preference would prejudice the provision of efficient education or the efficient use of resources;[20] or

---

[16] As to what 'have regard' means, see fn 11 to para **5.5** above and the discussion at paras **5.30–5.32** below in connection with what is now s 9 of the EA 1996.

[17] SSFA 1998, s 85A(4) and 85(B)2. Section 85A(4) will only apply to LAs in Wales from a date to be appointed by virtue of the Education Act 2011. Section 85B(2), which applies to Academies, will be repealed from a date to be appointed. As at 29 February 2012, no date had been appointed.

[18] There are similar rights of preference for children with statements of special educational needs under para 3(3) of Sch 27 to the EA 1996.

[19] SSFA 1998, s 86(1A) as inserted by the Education and Inspections Act 2006, s 42; see also para 1.6 and App 5 of the Code.

[20] Section 86(3)(a).

(b) in the case of a school where the arrangements for admission are based wholly on selection, by reference to ability or aptitude and are so based with a view to admitting only pupils with high ability or aptitude, if compliance with the preference would be incompatible with selection under those arrangements;[21]

(c) the child has been permanently excluded from two or more schools for a period of less than two years since the last of those expulsions;[22]

(d) where there is a scheme for co-ordinated admission arrangements and a parent has expressed preference for more than one school.[23]

5.13 A failure to give effect to the parental preference can only be justified on the specified exceptions.[24] The duty in section 86(1) does not apply in relation to sixth form education or any other education to be provided to a child who is, or will be before his course starts, above compulsory school age.[25]

5.14 Children who are below compulsory school age, do not, in general, enjoy rights of preference under section 86(2).[26] There is an exception where the arrangements for the admission of pupils to a maintained school provide for the admission of children who will be under compulsory school age at the time of their proposed admission. Such children do have rights of preference in relation to their admission to the school otherwise than for nursery education.[27] Children who are admitted to school for nursery education and are then subsequently transferred to a reception class at the school are to be regarded as admitted to school (otherwise than for nursery education) on being so transferred.[28]

5.15 There are no rights of preference under section 86 for children who have statements of SEN or are at special schools.[29] Such children have similar rights of preference under paragraphs 3 and 8 of Schedule 27 to the EA 1996.

5.16 The duty under section 86(2) applies to the admission of children who are not in the area of the LA maintaining the school in question: see

---

[21] SSFA 1998, s 86(2) and (3)(c). For the purposes of education above compulsory school age, arrangements are to be taken to be wholly by reference to ability or aptitude even where there are additional criteria applied, provided that the number of children in a relevant age group who are assessed as having the relevant ability or aptitude is greater than the number of pupils which it is intended to admit to the school: see SSFA 1998, s 86(9).

[22] SSFA 1998, ss 86(2) and 87.

[23] SSFA 1998, ss 86(2A) and 89(b).

[24] *R v Cleveland County Council, ex p Commission for Racial Equality* [1994] ELR 44.

[25] SSFA 1998, s 86(1ZA).

[26] SSFA 1998, s 98(3).

[27] SSFA 1998, s 98(4).

[28] SSFA 1998, s 98(1).

[29] SSFA 1998, s 98(6) and (7); *R v Essex ex parte C* [1994] ELR 54 at 62B, Jowitt J, [1994] ELR 273 at 277F–277G, CA; *R v Governors of Hasmonean High School ex parte B* [1994] ELR 343 at 347H–348B, CA.

section 86(8)(a). It also applies to parents who are seeking the naming of a particular school in a school attendance order.[30]

5.17 What can and cannot amount to prejudice to the provision of efficient education or the efficient use of resources is further elaborated upon at section 86(4), (5), (5A) and (5B). Prejudice may arise by reason of measures required to be taken in order to ensure compliance with the duty under section 1(6) to adhere to limits on infant class sizes.[31]

5.18 Conversely, the general rule is that prejudice cannot arise if the number of pupils in a relevant age group admitted to the school does not exceed the number determined under section 89 as the number of pupils in that age group that it was intended to admit to the school in that year. There is an exception to this general rule if the conditions set out in section 86(5A) are met in relation to the school and the school year.[32] Those conditions are that the school is one at which boarding accommodation is provided for pupils and that the determination under section 88C (or section 89 which applies to Wales) by the admission authority of the admission arrangements which are to apply for that year include the determinations mentioned in paragraphs (a) and (b) of sections 88D(2) or 89A(2) (which applies to Wales).

5.19 Where the conditions set out in section 86(5A) are met in relation to a maintained school and a school year, no prejudice is to be taken to arise from either the admission of boarders to the school in that year of a number of pupils in a relevant age group which does not exceed the number determined under section 89 as the number of pupils in that age group it intended to admit in that year as boarders. This also applies to the admission of non-boarders.

5.20 The LA has a discretion to make arrangements for the parent of a child to express preferences for more than one school.[33] Where such arrangements are made and a scheme is adopted or made by virtue of section 89B, the admissions authority for a particular maintained school for which a preference is expressed is not obliged to offer admission to the child if the child is offered admission to a different school for which the parent has also expressed a preference.

Co-ordinated admission arrangements

5.21 Sections 88M and 88N (and 89B and 89C[34] in respect of Wales) empower the Secretary of State to make regulations[35] in relation to co-ordinated admission arrangements for both primary and secondary school

---

30 SSFA 1998, s 86(8)(b).
31 SSFA 1998, s 86(4).
32 SSFA 1998, s 86(5).
33 SSFA 1998, s 86(2A) as inserted by the EA 2002, s 51, Sch 4, para 3(1) and (3).
34 As inserted by the EA 2002, s 48.
35 See the School Admissions (Co-ordination of Admission Arrangements) (England) Regulations 2008, SI 2008/3090. These regulations were revoked and replaced by the School

admissions. The Code deals with this at Chapter 3 and Appendix 2. As is provided in paragraph 1.37 of the Code, the duty to comply with parental preference is not affected by co-ordinated admission arrangements except where more than one place could be offered. In those circumstances, the duty to comply applies to the single offer that should be made in accordance with the co-ordinated arrangements and not the other possible offers; the authority in which the parents resides must ensure so far as is reasonably practicable that the parent is offered a place at whichever of the schools is their highest preference.[36] Co-ordinated schemes do not affect the rights and duties of the governing bodies of voluntary-aided and foundation schools to set and apply their own admission arrangements and over-subscription criteria, nor for Academies to agree their own arrangements with the Secretary of State.[37]

5.22 The School Admissions (Co-ordination of Admission Arrangements) (England) Regulations 2012[38] detail how the LA is to go about its task. It must prepare a qualifying scheme relating to every primary and secondary school in its area no later than 1 January in the relevant 'determination year'.[39] The determination year is the academic year beginning two years before the admission year.[40] A qualifying scheme has to comply with the requirements specified in Schedule 2 to the 2012 Regulations.[41] Those requirements are split into five sections: general requirements, requirements of a qualifying scheme relating to applications made in the course of a normal admission round, requirements of a qualifying scheme relating to applications for in-area schools, additional duties on an authority relating to applications for out-of area schools, and duties of governing bodies under a qualifying scheme. The general requirements are that a qualifying scheme must:[42]

(a) ensure, so far as is reasonably practicable, that each parent in the area of an authority who has made an application on the common application form in respect of the admission of a child to a school receives a single offer of a school place under the scheme;

Admissions (Co-ordination of Admission Arrangements) (England) Regulations 2012 with savings for admissions up to the 2013–14 academic year. They are accordingly not dealt with in this text.

36 Paragraph 3.15(d) of the Code.
37 Paragraph 3.8 of the Code.
38 SI 2012/8.
39 The School Admissions (Co-ordination of Admission Arrangements) (England) Regulations 2012, at regs 26 and, 27 and Sch 2.
40 The School Admissions (Co-ordination of Admission Arrangements) (England) Regulations 2012 at reg 3(1).
41 The School Admissions (Co-ordination of Admission Arrangements) (England) Regulations 2012, at reg 4(2).
42 The School Admissions (Co-ordination of Admission Arrangements) (England) Regulations 2012, at Sch 1, para 1.

(b) ensure, so far as is reasonably practicable, in any case where a child is eligible to be granted admission to more than one school, that the child is granted admission to whichever of those schools is ranked highest on the common application form;

(c) require a common application form to be completed, enabling a parent in an authority's area:

  (i)   to provide their name and address, and the name, address and date of birth of the child;
  (ii)   to apply for not less than three schools, whether or not any school for which such application is made is within the authority's area;
  (iii) to give reasons for their application; and
  (iv)   to rank each application in relation to any other application,

(d) identify for each school to which the scheme applies whether it is the authority or the governing body who are the admission authority;

(e) where the governing body is the admission authority for such a school and has made arrangements for another body to determine the order of priority under paragraph 5(b), identify that body; and

(f) specify that any notification of acceptance of a school place must be received by the authority within two weeks after the date of the offer.

5.23 The requirements of a qualifying scheme relating to applications made in the course of a normal admission round are that the qualifying scheme must:[43]

(a) require the common application form to be submitted to the authority by 31 October in the offer year, in relation to applications for secondary schools, and 15 January in the offer year, in relation to applications for primary schools;

(b) specify how applications submitted after the 31 October and 15 January will be processed;

(c) require an authority to send any determination granting or refusing admission to a school to a parent on the offer date (such determination being sent on behalf of the school's governing body in any case where the authority are not the admission authority for the school); and

(d) specify the dates by which each of the steps required to be taken in accordance with the Schedule is to be performed, including where the date is specified in the Schedule.

---

[43] The School Admissions (Co-ordination of Admission Arrangements) (England) Regulations 2012, at Sch 2, para 2

5.24 A qualifying scheme relating to applications for in-area schools must require the local authority:[44]

(a) to forward the common application together with any supporting information provided by the parent to the governors where it is the admissions authority;

(b) where it is the admissions authority for each school, to determine the order of priority in which the application for the school is ranked;

(c) where the child is eligible for admission to more than one school or none, to determine whether the child is to be granted or refused admission to any school in its area;

(d) to notify the governing body of its determination where it is not the admissions authority;

(e) to communicate any determination granting or refusing admission to the parent;

(f) where the parent lives in a different LA, to notify that LA of its determination.

5.25 Where the parent in the home authority applies for a school in a different authority, the home authority must notify that authority of the application and forward to them details of it, together with any supporting information provided by the parent.[45] A qualifying scheme must:[46]

(a) specify whether the child is to be granted or refused admission to any school in the home authority's area for which an application has also been made, that authority will have regard to any information provided by the other authority as to whether the child is to be granted admission to a school within that authority's area; and

(b) require the home authority to send any determination granting or refusing admission to the school in the other authority's area to the parent (such determination being sent on behalf of the school's governing body in any case where they are the admission authority for the school).

---

[44] The School Admissions (Co-ordination of Admission Arrangements) (England) Regulations 2012, at Sch 2, para 3.
[45] The School Admissions (Co-ordination of Admission Arrangements) (England) Regulations 2012, at Sch 2, para 4(1) and (2).
[46] The School Admissions (Co-ordination of Admission Arrangements) (England) Regulations 2012, at Sch 2, para 4(3).

5.26 A qualifying scheme must require a governing body who are the admission authority for a school:[47]

(a)   to forward to the LA any application made directly to the school together with any supporting information provided by the parent;

(b)   to determine (or make arrangements for another body to) by reference to the school's admissions criteria the order of priority for each application to the school;

(c)   to notify the LA of that determination. Where another body not being the LA will make the determination the governing body are to arrange for that body to notify the LA.

5.27 The procedural requirements for the adoption of qualifying schemes are set out in regulation 27. Where the qualifying scheme is substantially different to the qualifying scheme adopted for the preceding academic year, or the authority have not consulted on a qualifying scheme adopted in the preceding seven academic years, the authority is then obliged to consult[48] each governing body who are the admission authority for a school in the authority's area and any other LA as the authority may determine.[49] The consultation with LAs in other areas must be undertaken with a view, in particular, to securing that the arrangements for the admission of pupils to schools in the areas of different LAs are, so far as reasonably practicable, compatible with each other.[50] Once the consultation is complete, the LA must determine the qualifying scheme and take all reasonable steps to secure its adoption by themselves and each governing body they consulted in relation to it.[51] The Secretary of State is to be informed by 15 April in the determination year whether the LA has secured adoption of a qualifying scheme.[52]. He has default powers to impose a scheme himself when not so informed.[53]

5.28 For the normal admissions round, the date on which decisions are made is to be a single date.[54] In respect of secondary schools, the single date on which

---

[47]   The School Admissions (Co-ordination of Admission Arrangements) (England) Regulations 2012, at Sch 2, para 5.

[48]   The School Admissions (Co-ordination of Admission Arrangements) (England) Regulations 2012 at reg 27(3).

[49]   The School Admissions (Co-ordination of Admission Arrangements) (England) Regulations 2012, at reg 27(4).

[50]   The School Admissions (Co-ordination of Admission Arrangements) (England) Regulations 2012 at reg 27(5).

[51]   The School Admissions (Co-ordination of Admission Arrangements) (England) Regulations 2012, at reg 27(6).

[52]   The School Admissions (Co-ordination of Admission Arrangements) (England) Regulations 2012 at reg 28.

[53]   The School Admissions (Co-ordination of Admission Arrangements) (England) Regulations 2012, at reg 29.

[54]   The School Admissions (Co-ordination of Admission Arrangements) (England) Regulations 2012 at reg 30.

decisions have to be communicated to the parent is prescribed as 1 March.[55] For primary schools the date is 16 April unless this is a non-working day in which case it is the next working day.[56]

5.29 The Secretary of State's general default powers under sections 496 and 497 of the Education Act 1996 apply to the LA and governing bodies in relation to the obligations imposed under a qualifying scheme or an imposed scheme.[57]

RIGHTS OF PREFERENCE

General

5.30 Section 86 of the SSFA 1998 is a more extensive right than section 9 of the EA 1996. Section 9 provides that in exercising all their respective powers and duties under the Education Acts, the Secretary of State, LAs and the funding authorities are obliged to have regard to the general principle that pupils are to be educated in accordance with the wishes of their parents, so far as that is compatible with the provision of efficient instruction and training and the avoidance of unreasonable public expenditure. This replaced section 76 of the Education Act 1944, which was similar.

5.31 The 1944 Act was considered by the Court of Appeal in *Watt v Kesteven*.[58] The Court of Appeal held:[59]

> 'It only lays down a general principle to which the county council must have regard. This leaves it open to the county council to have regard to other things as well, and also to make exceptions to the general principle if it thinks fit to do so.'

The point was reconsidered in *Cummings v Birkenhead*:[60]

> 'There are many other things to which the education authority may have regard and which may outweigh the wishes of the parents. They must have regard, for instance, not only to the wishes of the parents of one particular child, but also to the wishes of the parents of other children and of other groups of children.'

5.32 Accordingly, while section 9 of the EA 1996 is not confined to admissions, unlike section 86 of the SSFA 1998, and is in that sense broader than section 86, it is, in practice, of much less utility to disappointed parents

---

55   The School Admissions (Co-ordination of Admission Arrangements) (England) Regulations 2012, at reg 30(3)(b). It is the next working day if 1 March is not a working day.
56   The School Admissions (Co-ordination of Admission Arrangements) (England) Regulations 2012 at reg 30(3)(a).
57   The School Admissions (Co-ordination of Admission Arrangements) (England) Regulations 2012, at reg 32.
58   [1955] 1 QB 408.
59   At 424 per Denning LJ. Parker LJ at 429 was to similar effect.
60   [1972] Ch 12 at 36. See also the authority referred to in fn 11 at para **5.5** above.

challenging an admissions decision, because their wishes can more easily be defeated under section 9 of the EA 1996 than under section 86 of the SSFA 1998.

5.33   In exercising its duties under section 86(1)(a) of the SSFA 1998, the LA must make arrangements enabling parents to express a preference before allocating places. Accordingly, where an LA had a policy that school places would be allocated to those who were in a designated catchment area unless they expressed a preference to go to a different school without the beneficiaries having to take any action, it was held that the LA had not made arrangements enabling the parents to express a preference.[61] Expression of a preference denoted a positive act.

5.34   The LA must also make arrangements[62] for enabling the parents to express reasons for their preference. Just as the duty, under section 86(1)(a) of the SSFA 1998, to make arrangements to enable parents to express a preference has created difficulties, so has this duty to make arrangements to enable parents to express reasons for their preference. In *R (on the application of K) v London Borough of Newham*[63] one of the priority criteria for admission to a school was whether the parents stated they preferred mixed or single-sex education. The admissions form stated that this was to be found out by looking at the type of school the parent had applied for as their first preference. There was no specific place for the parent to state their reasons for choosing a single-sex school. Although there was a space for additional information, the form stated there that all allocations would still be made in accordance with the admissions criteria. Accordingly, a parent was not encouraged to explain why he had expressed the preference he had. Collins J held that the parents had not been enabled to give reasons for their preference; their silence, in accordance with the format and guidance on the admissions form as to why they preferred a single-sex school could not be inferred to amount to a statement that the school was preferred because it was single-sex.[64] He further held that due weight had to be given to the religious conviction of the parents as a result of Article 2 of the First Protocol to the ECHR.[65]

5.35   Is the LA obliged to take account of the reasons the parents express in support of their preference? This may seem a surprising question. In principle, it would seem obvious that the reasons the parents give for expressing a preference were a relevant matter to be taken into account and it is difficult to see why Parliament should have imposed the duty on the LA to make arrangements to enable the parents to give reasons for the expressed preference if those reasons could simply be ignored. However, in *R v Rotherham MBC ex parte Clarke* Buxton LJ recorded his understanding[66] that both counsel in that

---

[61]   *R v Rotherham MBC ex parte Clarke* [1998] ELR 152, CA.
[62]   Under the SSFA 1998, s 86(1)(b).
[63]   [2002] EWHC 405 (Admin), [2002] ELR 390.
[64]   [2002] EWHC 405 (Admin), [2002] ELR 390, at paras 30–34 and 41.
[65]   [2002] EWHC 405 (Admin), [2002] ELR 390, at paras 29 and 38.
[66]   [1998] ELR 152 at 178B–178D.

case agreed that the LA was free to ignore whatever reasons the parents expressed. He was conscious that this construction made it difficult to see why the LA was obliged to make arrangements to enable reasons to be expressed. Morritt LJ[67] expressed the view that reasons might be of importance at a later stage of the process if it was not possible to give effect to all expressed preferences. Lord Bingham CJ stated[68] that he agreed with what Buxton LJ had said about reasons. Accordingly, a majority of the Court of Appeal in *Rotherham* appear to suggest that reasons can be ignored. That apparent holding, however, is obiter. In *Rotherham* there was no question of the LA ignoring the reasons parents had given for their preferences. The question did not arise because the LA did not make arrangements at all for the parents to give reasons for their preference. It is submitted therefore, that *Rotherham* does not bind future courts to hold that reasons once expressed can be ignored by the LA.

5.36 The point was revisited by Collins J in *R (on the application of K) v London Borough of Newham*.[69] Having considered the judgment of Buxton LJ[70] in *R v Rotherham ex parte Clarke*, he held that, while there might be some reasons which could not be overcome or be relevant to the relevant policy applied by the admissions authority, there were other reasons, such as religious convictions, which could be relevant.

5.37 It is submitted that the current position is that the LA should have regard to the reasons given by parents for expressing their preferences because:

(a) while it is true that section 86 of the SSFA 1998 does not state that the LA is obliged to take account of the reasons for the parental preference, Parliament cannot possibly have intended that the LA should ignore those reasons, since it is obliged to make arrangements to enable the parents to express them. The contrary construction makes the duty under section 86(1)(b) a meaningless one that serves no useful purpose;

(b) *Rotherham* is obiter, proceeded apparently on a concession, is not strictly binding, and is of limited persuasive authority.

Of course, it does not follow that a reason for a preference will always be of weight. If the reasons expressed by the parent are wholly unrelated to the admissions criteria, it is difficult to see that they will have any weight even if they have to be taken into account. If, however, they relate to the admissions criteria in question, they may be of weight, either at the initial allocation stage, or subsequently, on appeal. An LA may have a sibling link admission criterion and have to rank a number of children who meet that criterion. It is not difficult to envisage that some siblings may have stronger reasons for wishing to be educated in the same school than others and that a reason to the effect that

---

67 [1998] ELR 152, at 181E.
68 [1998] ELR 152 at 183C.
69 [2002] EWHC 405 (Admin) at paras 36–38.
70 [1998] ELR 152 at 178B–178D.

a particular child was very shy and close to his siblings may be of weight compared with the case where the siblings were independent-minded.

R v Greenwich

5.38 In *R v Greenwich London Borough Council ex parte Governors of John Ball Primary School*[71] the Court of Appeal held that neither the local authority nor the governing body could discriminate against an applicant for admission on the basis that he was outside the LA area. This decision has created very real practical problems for local authorities and has been a source of much further litigation. In *R v Royal Borough of Kingston upon Thames ex parte Kingwell*,[72] an in-borough parent argued that the LA, by changing its admissions policy to remove discrimination against out-borough applicants, was in breach of its more general duties under what are now sections 13 and 14 of the EA 1996, because he was now denied a chance of a place for his child at the school of his choice, a single-sex grammar school. The court held that the primary duty was not to discriminate against out-borough applicants and that they were bound to dismiss the application as a result of the decision of the Court of Appeal in *Greenwich*.

5.39 At the same time as delivering judgment in the *Kingwell* case the Divisional Court also gave judgment in *R v Bromley London Borough Council ex parte C*.[73] In that case, a challenge was brought by three out-borough applicants. Bromley had revised its policy post-*Greenwich* so that it provided that in the event of over-subscription preference would be given to siblings and then, inter alia, on the basis of proximity. The policy then contained a proviso:

> 'The council will only depart from the results which would be produced by applying the above criteria if and to the extent that such departure is necessary in order to comply with ss 7 and 8 of the Education Act 1944.'

5.40 Bromley maintained that the proviso was necessary because without it there would necessarily be denial of places at Bromley schools to the children of Bromley residents and a breach of their duties under what are now sections 13 and 14 of the EA 1996. The Divisional Court held, despite these practical difficulties, that the policy was unlawful. It stated, contrary to the position as it appeared to the Court of Appeal in *Greenwich*, that it saw much practical difficulty with what the Divisional Court termed 'troublesome legislation' and indicated that it was not surprised that representations had been made to the Secretary of State urging a change in the law.[74] The court,

---

[71] 88 LGR 589.

[72] [1992] 1 FLR 182.

[73] [1992] 1 FLR 174.

[74] According to para 4(iii) of Annex C to DfEE Circular 6/93 (no longer in force) the Secretary of State considered whether to amend the law and determined it was not necessary because there was no evidence of significant practical difficulties and because of the increasing numbers of grant-maintained schools. Although grant-maintained schools have gone, the present Admissions Code regards the *Greenwich* judgment as a sensible recognition of the pattern of cross-border choices of school.

however, refused to grant anything other than declaratory relief because of the detriment to good administration in setting aside the whole admissions procedure in Bromley for that year.

5.41 In *R v Kingston upon Thames RLBC ex parte Emsden*,[75] the court had to consider again the problems highlighted by *Greenwich*. In that case the LA, in order to comply with *Greenwich*, adopted an admissions criterion based, in the final resort, on distance from the school. The effect was that some pupils in the LA area were effectively denied a right of access to a popular selective school because out-borough applicants lived nearer to the school. It was held that the policy was lawful.

5.42 There was yet a further challenge to an admissions policy on the basis of *Greenwich* in *R v Wiltshire ex parte Razazan*.[76] In that case, the LA gave priority to those children who had no priority of a place at another school but the policy applied equally to those inside and outside the LA boundary.[77] It is, perhaps, not surprising in those circumstances that the court had no difficulty in dismissing the challenge based on *Greenwich*.

5.43 In *R v Rotherham MBC ex p LT*[78] it was contended that giving priority to those who were in a catchment area that coincided to any extent with the LA boundaries was unlawful. The Court of Appeal rejected this argument, holding that catchment areas had to be carefully considered so that they interlocked with each other and had regard to areas of population, bus routes, safe walking distances and matters of that sort.[79]

LAWFUL ADMISSIONS CRITERIA

5.44 The Court of Appeal in *Greenwich*[80] held that an LA was entitled to have any reasonable admissions policy it thought fit and that this did not have to be capable of promoting efficient education or the efficient use of resources. The Admissions Code, at paragraph 1.8, provides that oversubscription criteria should be:

> '... reasonable, clear, objective, procedurally fair, not complex and comply with all relevant legislation, including equalities legislation.'

Paragraph 1.9 of the Admissions Code contains a detailed list of prohibitions in relation to admissions arrangements. Paragraph 1.10 of the Admissions Code makes clear it is for admission authorities to decide which over subscription criteria are the most suitable for a school having regard to local

---

[75] 91 LGR 96.
[76] [1996] ELR 220, Popplewell J, affirmed by Court of Appeal for the same reasons [1997] ELR 370 at 376C.
[77] See at 225C–225E.
[78] [2000] ELR 76.
[79] [2000] ELR 76, at 82B–82C.
[80] 88 LGR 589 at 599.

circumstances. It provides that the Code does not give a definitive list of acceptable oversubscription criteria but then sets out at paragraphs 1.11–1.41 a detailed commentary on the criteria most commonly used. Some of the commentary on the commonly used criteria is set out in mandatory language and therefore must be followed. Where mandatory language is not used, admissions authorities will have power to depart from the guidance. However, where they choose to do so, they will have to justify their decision, in the event of an objection to the Adjudicator.

Sibling link

5.45 While the Admission Code no longer describes this in terms as an acceptable criterion, paragraphs 1.11–1.12 proceed on the assumption it is lawful. Sibling links were expressly approved as lawful in *Greenwich*[81] and there has been no subsequent case-law casting doubt on their legality.

5.46 The Admissions Code provides at paragraph 1.11 that Admissions authorities must state clearly in their arrangements what they mean by a sibling. The Code assumes that a sibling could include a step sibling, foster sibling, adopted sibling and other children living permanently at the same address as well as siblings of former pupils. Where former pupils are included a clear and simple definition must be given and regard must be had to the restrictions in paragraph 1.9 of the Admissions Code. The only one of those restrictions that is expressly concerned with a sibling oversubscription criterion is paragraph 1.9(j) which prohibits priority being given to siblings in designated grammar schools that rank children by pass mark. If there is evidence that a sibling criterion would involve discrimination or disadvantaging disabled children or those with special educational needs this would also be of doubtful legality.[82] An LA will have to consider with care whether adoption of a sibling criterion breaches the Equality Act 2010; however, save for the problem of indirect discrimination, there is no reason to suppose that such a criterion will not, in general, continue to be regarded as lawful by the courts.[83] The Admissions Code goes on at paragraph 1.12 to provide that if sibling priority is given in relation to pupils attending another state funded school, that must be

---

[81] 88 LGR 589 at 599.

[82] See para 1.9 (h) of the Admissions Code

[83] It is unlikely that a sibling criterion would in general fall foul of Art 14 of the ECHR. The right in Art 2 of the First Protocol does not confer a right to be educated in a particular school and, accordingly, criteria which discriminated between applicants to particular schools would not be a breach of Art 2. While Art 14 does not require that there should have been a breach of another Article of the Convention, in order for it to operate a parent would have to show that the criterion that operated to his disadvantage in relation to a particular school also operated in relation to the enjoyment of the right to education more generally and this may be difficult to establish on the facts. The nature of most over-subscription criteria, including sibling links, is to distinguish between applicants for a particular school and not to deny any education to those who do not meet the over-subscription criteria for a particular school. In any event any discrimination would probably not be unlawful because the desirability of educating siblings together would almost certainly be justifiable. In *R (on the application of K) v London Borough of Newham* [2002] ELR 390, at para 39, a sibling criterion was regarded by Collins J as very important and necessary in the light of Art 8 of the ECHR.

clearly stated in the arrangements. It is assumed that it is lawful to give such priority where the relevant schools have close links (by being on the same site or being a pair of single sex schools) but this is no more than an assumption.

Distance

5.47 It is clear from *R v Kingston upon Thames RLBC ex parte Emsden*[84] that the courts have in the past regarded this criterion as lawful.[85] Further, the Secretary of State's view[86] assumes that this is an acceptable criterion. At paragraph 1.13 of the Admissions Code, he states that the over-subscription criterion should make clear how distance from home to school will be measured. The Secretary of State goes on to deal with the case of a child living with different parents with shared responsibility for different parts of a week. In those circumstances, the over-subscription criterion needs to make clear how the home address will be decided. Unhelpfully the Secretary of State gives no guidance on how the LA should decide which of two competing home addresses should be adopted. Where the child spends more time with one parent that the other it is submitted it is reasonable for the LA to adopt the home address where the child spends the majority of his time. Where the child spend an equal amount of time with each parent then it is submitted that it is reasonable for the LA to choose either home address or to let the parents nominate either home address. Outside these two alternatives the position is less certain, but, as the issue would be tested on traditional *Wednesbury* grounds, it is submitted that in general an LA will act lawfully in choosing either of the home addresses of the parents providing it is made clear in advance in the oversubscription criteria that this will be done.

Catchment areas

5.48 The Admissions Code assumes catchment areas are an acceptable criterion.[87] Previous case-law was to the same effect, provided that the LA boundary was not used to define the catchment area; see *Greenwich*.[88] If the catchment area uses the LA boundary, that would negate what is now section 86(8)(a) of the SSFA 1998.[89] The Admissions Code makes clear at paragraph 1.14 that a catchment area does not prevent a parent who lives outside the area, from expressing a preference for the school.

---

[84] 91 LGR 96.

[85] For similar reasons to those canvassed above in relation to the sibling criterion, it is submitted that this criterion would not, in general, breach the HRA 1998. Even if there was discrimination it is submitted that a distance criterion is justifiable as it promotes local schools in a community and the minimisation of travelling time for pupils.

[86] At para 1.13 of the Admissions Code.

[87] Paragraph 1.14.

[88] 88 LGR 589 at 599 and 602–603. The mere fact of coincidence of part of the boundary of the catchment area with the LA boundary does not invalidate the catchment area: *R v Rotherham MBC ex parte LT* [2000] ELR 76, CA.

[89] Formerly s 6(5) of the Education Act 1980.

5.49 The courts have had to consider the legality of catchment areas drawn up after all the parental preferences have been expressed. The Secretary of State formerly[90] stressed the importance of the catchment area being defined in advance of the admissions cycle.[91] This was no doubt because of the statutory duty to publish particulars of the arrangements for admission under what is now section 92 of the SSFA 1998.[92] The courts have, however, on two occasions, upheld the defining of catchment areas after the event, despite the duty to publish this information. In *R v East Sussex ex parte D*[93] the relevant priority provided[94] 'children living within a total area defined each year to satisfy as many parents' first preferences as possible'.

5.50 The admissions booklet provided:[95]

> 'The area referred to under priority (ii) is based on the geographical distribution of addresses of children whose parents have given a first preference for the school. An area is drawn only if these first preferences exceed the places remaining after the needs of children coming within priority (i) have been met (and a small number of places have been held back to meet the needs of children in priority (ii) at the review stage). Where it is necessary to draw an area it may well change from year to year in response to parental preferences and reflecting the different home addresses of children.'

It is perhaps not surprising in the light of that information that it was submitted by the applicant[96] that it was impossible for a parent to know what chance there was of getting his preference in relation to any individual school. The court accepted[97] the submissions[98] that the mere fact the area was not defined beforehand did not make the policy irrational, nor was it arbitrary, because the line could be drawn in a variety of places. The court, while not expressly referring to the submission[99] that breach of an information obligation under what is now section 92 of the SSFA 1998, and regulations made thereunder, did not render the admissions policy unlawful, appears implicitly to have accepted this also.

5.51 In *R v Bradford MBC ex parte Sikander Ali*,[100] there was a similar process of drawing up catchment areas after the event was deployed[101] but with the added degree of certainty that those areas where there were stronger

---

[90] In para 4 of Annex C to circular 6/93.
[91] The present Admissions Code does not make any express comment on this.
[92] The regulations made thereunder are the School Information (England) Regulations 2008, SI 2008/3093 and the Education (School Information) (Wales) Regulations 2011, SI 2011/1944.
[93] Unreported on this point, Transcript, 15 March 1991, Rose J.
[94] (Unreported) 15 March 1991, at 8G.
[95] (Unreported) 15 March 1991, at 9E–9H.
[96] (Unreported) 15 March 1991, at 12B–12C.
[97] (Unreported) 15 March 1991, at 38F–39A.
[98] (Unreported) 15 March 1991, at 30E–31D.
[99] (Unreported) 15 March 1991, at 35D–35F.
[100] [1994] ELR 299.
[101] [1994] ELR 299, at 303D–303E.

community ties were favoured.[102] It was argued[103] that 'traditional links' were too nebulous to be lawful and[104] that a parent could not make an effective choice because, in breach of section 8(1) of the Education Act 1980,[105] the parent would not know which were the traditional areas. The court accepted[106] that a criterion so nebulous as to be unlikely to produce any result other than one which was quixotic, arbitrary or whimsical would be *Wednesbury* unreasonable but that, on the evidence, that was not the case before it. The court also held[107] on the evidence that the LA was not in breach of its duty to publish information because it did not have to spell out every nut and bolt of what was to be done, but that if it had been in breach of that duty, relief would have been refused in the exercise of the court's discretion.[108]

5.52 It is submitted that it is open to doubt whether catchment areas drawn up after the parents have expressed their preferences would be regarded as lawful under the current legislation but the present Admissions Code gives no guidance on the point. Paragraph 1.14 merely states that catchment areas must be designed so that they are reasonable and clearly defined. Although as a matter of language this would seem to admit of the possibility that definition could take place after a preference was expressed, it is submitted that catchment areas drawn up after the expression of a preference are unlikely now to be regarded as lawful because they hinder an effective expression of preference.

Feeder primary or nursery schools

5.53 The Admissions Code provides at paragraph 1.15 that naming of a feeder school as an oversubscription criterion must be transparent and made on reasonable grounds. Again, it simply assumes that feeder schools are a lawful criterion if reasonable grounds exist and does not give guidance on when such grounds will exist save that the naming of independent schools as feeder schools is prohibited.[109] Previous case-law suggests that the use of feeder schools is prima facie a lawful admissions criterion. While *Sikander Ali*[110] concerned the legitimacy of 'traditional links', rather than feeder schools, the reasoning necessarily would legitimise feeder schools. An earlier circular[111] sounded two notes of caution, both of which, it is submitted, continue to have force. The first is the need to justify on objective grounds the feeder school and to avoid breach of *Greenwich* indirectly, and the second is the need not to use

---

102 [1994] ELR 299, at 303E–303G.
103 [1994] ELR 299, at 308D–308E.
104 [1994] ELR 299, at 316C–316H.
105 Now the SSFA 1998, s 92 and the School Information (England) Regulations 2008, SI 2008/3093 and the Education (School Information) (Wales) Regulations 2011, SI 2011/1944.
106 [1994] ELR 299 at 308E.
107 [1994] ELR 299, at 318B–318C.
108 [1994] ELR 299 at 318D–318E.
109 See para 1.9 (l) of the School Admissions Code.
110 [1994] ELR 299.
111 Circular 6/93 at Annex C, para 5. The point is not discussed in the present Admissions Code.

independent schools as feeder schools.[112] The rational for this latter concern is the prohibition in section 450 of the EA 1996 on charging for admission to any maintained school. To give priority to those who can afford to go to an independent school is not directly charging for admission to a maintained school, but would indirectly undermine the force of this prohibition and hence be amenable to challenge on *Padfield*[113] grounds. It is not surprising therefore that the use of independent schools as feeder schools is expressly prohibited in paragraph 1.9(l) of the School Admissions Code.

Ability

5.54 The Admissions Code deals with oversubscription criteria in relation to ability at paragraphs 1.17–1.33. Only designated grammar schools are permitted to select their entire intake on the basis of high academic ability.[114] These schools are not obliged to fill up spare places if candidates have not reached the required standard.

5.55 Partial selection by ability is dealt with at paragraphs 1.21–1.23 of the Admissions Code. Partially selective schools must not exceed the lowest proportion of selection that has been used since the 1997/98 school year.[115] The entry requirements for selective places have to be published and if there are spare places after selection has taken place they must be filled regardless of whether the applicants have met the criteria for selection. Looked after children are to be given priority for the remainder of places after selection. They are also to be given priority for selective places where the selective admission arrangements are not based on the highest scores in the selection test providing they meet the pre-set standards of the test. They do not need to be given priority in relation to the selective intake where selection is based on the highest score in the selection test.

5.56 Selection by aptitude is dealt with at paragraphs 1.24–1.33 of the Admissions Code. Schools that have arrangements to select by aptitude must not allow for more than 10 per cent of the total admissions intake to be allocated on the basis of such aptitude even if the school has more than one specialism. The specialist subjects on which a school may select by aptitude are, broadly, sport, the performing and visual arts, modern languages and, with a temporal restriction, design and technology and information technology. All tests for selection, whether by ability or aptitude, must be clear, objective and give an accurate reflection of the child's ability, irrespective of sex race or disability.[116]

---

[112] This is the subject of an express prohibition in the current Admissions Code see para 1.9(h).

[113] *Padfield v Minister of Agriculture, Fisheries and Food* [1968] AC 997.

[114] Paragraph 1.18.

[115] SSFA 1998, s 100.

[116] Paragraphs 1.31–1.32 of the Admissions Code. A challenge to the selective tests in Buckinghamshire by a dyslexic child failed in *AS v Buckinghamshire County Council* [2010] UKUT 407 (AAC) on the basis the First Tier Tribunal did not have jurisdiction to hear it.

Other acceptable criteria

5.57　The Admissions Code indicates or assumes that the following additional criteria are acceptable:

(a)　social or medical need (paragraph 1.16);

(b)　whether the child is 'looked after' (paragraph 1.7). As is therein specified these children must be given the highest priority unless otherwise provided by the Code;

(c)　banding (paragraphs 1.25–130 of the Admissions Code and section 101 of the SSFA 1998).

(d)　random allocation providing this is not used as the principal oversubscription criteria for which the LA is the admissions authority (paragraphs 1.34–1.35).

In relation to medical or social needs an earlier Admissions Code provided that this criterion could be used to give children a higher priority, whether the need was that of the parents or the child.[117] The present Admissions Code is silent on the point and merely provides, at paragraph 1.16, that the need must be defined with clear details of what supporting evidence is required.[118] Decisions on the application of this criterion have to be consistent.

5.58　'Looked after' children in public care are further dealt with in paragraphs 1.19–1.20 and 1.28 of the Code.[119] Where admission arrangements are wholly based on selection by reference to ability, no priority needs to be given to looked after, or previously looked after, children. Where the admissions arrangements are not based solely on highest scores, such priority has to be given provided the children have met the pre-set standards of the ability test. It is further provided that schools designated by the Secretary of State as having a religious character must give priority to looked-after children of their faith over those children belonging to other faiths.[120] It is permissible to give priority to looked after or previously looked after children whether or

---

[117]　The example given in the 2010 Admissions Code was where one or both parents had a disability that made travel to a school further away more difficult: para 2.28 of the Code.

[118]　In *R v St Edward's College* [2009] EWHC 2050, [2010] ELR 159, the court held that the requirement in the (then) Code for 'professional documentary evidence (from either a registered health professional such as a doctor or social worker)' was not ambiguous, nor exclusive – the use of the word 'professional' focussed on the requirement of independence and expertise but did not exclude evidence from other sources, for example, a headteacher in a case of bullying

[119]　See also reg 7(1) of the School Admissions (Admission Arrangements and Co-Ordination of Admission Arrangements) (England) Regulations 2012, SI 20128/8, which states that looked after children must be given first priority, except where regs 8 to 11 apply. Those regulations relate to grammar schools, schools with a religious character (although there are exceptions here), schools with pre-existing arrangements and schools which select by pupil banding.

[120]　Paragraph 1.37 of the Admissions Code.

not of the faith[121] and if priority is given for any children who are not of the faith the first priority has to be for looked after or previously looked after children.[122]Where banding is used, looked after and previously looked after children have to be given priority in each band. It is submitted that these provisions do not infringe Article 14 of the ECHR. Even if they have the effect that looked-after children are treated generally more favourably in relation to the right to education than those who are not in public care, the treatment is probably justifiable. Children in public care are among the most vulnerable children in society and it is submitted that the policy is a proportionate response to that problem.

5.59   Earlier guidance[123] suggested that the following additional criteria were also acceptable:

(a)   travelling time;

(b)   ease of access by public transport;

(c)   educational reasons, contribution to the life of the school/pastoral benefit;

(d)   a desire for single-sex or co-educational education;

(e)   religious affiliation.

Save in relation to religious affiliation, the legality of these criteria has not been the subject of litigation in England. There can be little doubt that travelling time, ease of access by public transport and the desire for single-sex or co-educational education are lawful criteria. As for educational reasons and contribution to the life of the school, it is likely that these would not be lawful unless they fell within the permitted partial selective arrangements authorised under section 99(2) and (4) of the SSFA 1998.[124] The relevance of religious affiliation to admissions is dealt with further below.[125]

Random allocation

5.60   In earlier guidance[126] the Secretary of State expressed the view that admission by lot was unlawful. The courts have not, in the past, accepted this view. In *R v Bradford MBC ex parte Sikander Ali*[127] Jowitt J, in meeting a

---

[121]   Paragraph 1.37 of the Admissions Code.
[122]   Paragraph 1.37 of the Admissions Code.
[123]   Circular 6/93 at paras 8–12, and para 2.36 of the 2010 Admissions Code.
[124]   In Northern Ireland an admissions criterion which provided for admission on the basis of extra-curricular activities evidenced by a certificate was held not to constitute a test of the pupil's ability nor to unlawfully infringe Art 14 of the ECHR by discriminating against lower socio-economic groups; see *Re A (A child)(Application for Judicial Review)* [2001] NI 454. Such a criterion would now be unlawful by virtue of paragraph 1.9(i) of the Admissions Code.
[125]   See paras **5.66–5.74** below.
[126]   Paragraph 18 of Circular 6/93.
[127]   [1994] ELR 299 at 312B.

submission that everyone had to have an equal chance of admission to a preferred school, commented that no subscription criteria could give everyone an equal chance of success unless the outcome were decided by lottery. He did not state whether such a policy would be lawful because he rejected the submission that everyone had to have an equal chance.

5.61 The point was dealt with directly by Macpherson J in *R v Lancashire County Council ex parte West*.[128] He held that such a policy was neither unfair nor unlawful. The decision does, however, highlight the desirability of admissions criteria being justifiable on educational grounds.

5.62 The present Admissions Code states at paragraph 1.34 that local authorities must not use random allocation as the sole or principal oversubscription criterion for allocating places at all the schools in the area for which they are the admissions authority. The Code though goes on to assume that partial random allocation is lawful providing the operation of such a criterion is clear, transparent and looked after and previously looked after children are prioritised. Random allocations have to be supervised by a person independent of the school and must be used each time a person is offered a place from a waiting list.[129]

UNLAWFUL OVERSUBSCRIPTION CRITERIA

5.63 The Admissions Code states that the admissions authorities must not:[130]

(a) place any conditions on the consideration of any application other than those in the oversubscription criteria published in their admission arrangements;

(b) take into account any previous schools attended, unless it is a named feeder school;

(c) give extra priority to children whose parents rank preferred schools in a particular order, including 'first preference first' arrangements;

(d) introduce any new selection by ability;

(e) give priority to children on the basis of any practical or financial support parents may give to the school or any associated organisation, including any religious authority;

(f) give priority to children according to the occupational, martial, financial or educational status of parents applying(although children of staff may be prioritised in arrangements;

---

[128] Unreported; see Liell (ed) *The Law of Education* (Butterworths, 9th edn) at F712.
[129] Paragraph 1.35 of the Admissions Code.
[130] Paragraph 1.9 of the Code.

(g)   take account of reports from previous schools about children's past behaviour, attendance, attitude or achievement, or that of any other children in the family;

(h)   discriminate against or disadvantage disabled children or children with special educational needs;

(i)   prioritise children according to their, or their parents' current or previous hobbies or activities save that schools which have been designated as having a religious character may take account of religious activities as laid out by the body or person representing the religion or religious denomination;

(j)   in the case of designated grammar schools that rank all children according to a pre-determined pass mark and allocate places to those who score highest, give priority to siblings of current or former pupils;

(k)   in the case of schools with boarding places rank children on the basis of suitability for boarding;

(l)   name fee-paying independent schools as feeder schools;

(m)   interview children or parents.[131] In the case of sixth form applications, a meeting may be held to discuss options and academic entry requirements for particular courses, but this meeting cannot form part of the decision making process on whether to offer a place. Boarding schools may interview children to assess their suitability for boarding;[132]

(n)   request financial contributions (either in the form of voluntary contributions, donations or deposits (even if refundable)) as part of the admissions process – including for tests; or

(o)   request photographs of a child for any part of the admissions process, other than as proof of identity when sitting a selection test.

As admissions authorities now have to act in accordance with the Admissions Code and the language of paragraph 1.9 is mandatory, no issue arises as to the legality of these criteria.

OTHER POTENTIALLY UNLAWFUL CRITERIA

5.64   Thus far, consideration has been given to those criteria the current Admission Code described as unacceptable. An earlier circular[133] listed the following additional unacceptable criteria:

---

[131]   This reflects the prohibition in the SSFA 1998, s 88(A)1.
[132]   This reflects the SSFA 1998, s 88A(2).
[133]   DfEE Circular 6/93 at paras 13–21.

(a)   governors' reserved right;

(b)   lot;

(c)   distinguishing between applicants on religious grounds in non-denominational schools.

The legality of these additional criteria is considered here. Questions of admission by lot have already been dealt with at paras **5.60–5.62** above.

Governors' reserved right

5.65   It is submitted that the Secretary of State was right to conclude that it was unlawful for the governors to reserve to themselves the right to refuse admission to the school of any prospective pupil.

Religion

5.66   The Admissions Code provides[134] that schools designated by the Secretary of State as having a religious character[135] may give preference in their admissions arrangements to members of a particular faith or denomination (as may be required by their Trust Deed), providing this does not conflict with other legislation.[136] It would seem, accordingly, that a distinction is drawn between schools designated as having a particular religious character and those that are not so designated, with only the former being able to give priority on the basis of the faith of the applicant.[137] Particular care must be taken not to infringe equalities legislation.[138]

5.67   It is clear that religious considerations can be used for determining priorities in the case of over-subscription at a denominational school: see *R v Governors of the Bishop Challenor Roman Catholic Comprehensive Girls' School ex parte Choudhury.*[139]

5.68   Religious considerations could take a variety of forms. The most obvious is evidence that someone practised a particular faith; but what evidence was required to establish that someone was a practising member of a particular faith should be clearly specified in the admissions criteria.[140]

---

[134]   At paras 1.36–138.
[135]   Schools are so designated under the SSFA 1998, s 69(3).
[136]   See para 1.1 of the Admissions Code
[137]   The distinction reflects long-standing policy to the same effect: see paras 12 and 20–21 of Annex C to Circular 6/93.
[138]   In *R(E) v Governing Body of JFS* [2009] UKSC 15, [2010] 2 AC 728 an oversubscription condition that provided that priority would be given to children who were recognised as Jewish by the Office of the Chief Rabbi was held unlawful race discrimination because those who had converted to Judaism were not recognised as Jewish by the Office of the Chief Rabbi.
[139]   [1992] 2 AC 182 at 192–194. This is reflected in para 1.36 of the Admissions Code.
[140]   In *R v Governors of La Sainte Union Convent School* [1996] ELR 98, Sedley J granted leave to move for judicial review on the basis that a baptism certificate was evidence that at least one of

5.69 It appears that it may be lawful to give priority on the basis of parish boundaries, provided that they are not chosen in order to defeat the *Greenwich*[141] judgment. This is very similar to the position in relation to catchment areas which have been held to be lawful.

5.70 It is to be noted that the view of the Secretary of State in earlier guidance[142] was that the LA should take care not to define an area which, in practice, contravened the guidelines in *Greenwich*.[143]

Preserving the religious character of a school

5.71 It used to be lawful to have admissions criteria which were intended to preserve the character of the school under section 91 of the SSFA 1998. That section was repealed by the EA 2002[144] with effect from 1 October 2002.

Religion and non-denominational schools

5.72 As indicated above, the Code appears[145] to indicate that it is acceptable to give priority on the basis of religion for schools designated as religious schools by the Secretary of State, but not to afford preference on the basis of religious criteria to a non-designated school. Previous case-law,[146] has not, in terms of legality, invalidated admissions criteria based on religion for non-denominational schools. In *R v Lancashire CC ex parte M*,[147] Popplewell J had to consider the legality of an admissions criterion for county schools which gave preference to those who had not attended Roman Catholic primary schools. After having considered Circular 6/93, which was not in existence at the date of the appeal committee decision under challenge, he concluded that the appeal committee was not acting unreasonably if it took religion into account.

5.73 In *R v Lancashire County Council ex parte Foster*[148] the Divisional Court had to consider the legality of the same admissions criterion for county schools. It was held that such a policy was lawful. The court was, however, guarded about the extent to which religious considerations in general could determine priority for county schools and it seems that it was heavily

---

the parents was a practising Roman Catholic. The case never proceeded to a substantive hearing so there was no ruling on the legal issues. The Code at para 1.37 provides that parents must be easily be able to understand how the faith-based criteria will be satisfied. Faith based oversubscription criteria must have regard to any guidance from the body or person representing the religion or religious denomination: para 1.38 of the Admissions Code.

141 88 LGR 589.
142 Paragraph 4(vi) of Annex C to DfEE Circular 6/93.
143 88 LGR 589.
144 Section 49 and Sch 22, Pt 3.
145 At para 1.36.
146 Prior to there being the statutory Admissions Code but where there was guidance to similar effect in Circular 6/93 at paras 12 and 20–21 of Annex C.
147 [1994] ELR 478.
148 [1995] ELR 33.

influenced by the special facts in Lancashire which would have meant that, if the policy was not in place, those who were not Roman Catholics would not receive places:[149]

> 'Standing in isolation and without explanation a policy which allocates places to Roman Catholic children attending a Roman Catholic school only after other applications have been met sounds discriminatory and unsustainable, but when set out in the context, as it exists in this local education authority's area, it seems to be impossible for this court to say that it is so unreasonable that the court should interfere. Put very simply, the situation is that a large number of children have to be accommodated in a finite number of secondary schools which fall into two groups: the county high schools and the Roman Catholic schools. Because of arrangements made between the Roman Catholic diocesan authorities and the local education authority pursuant to the 1980 Act, very few non-Catholic children can be accommodated in Roman Catholic schools even if they wanted to go there.

> If too many Roman Catholic children from the Roman Catholic primary schools express a preference to go to county schools and those preferences are considered in the same way as all other preferences, the local education authority will be left with a number of children who cannot be given places, as they should be, in the areas in which they live, so the local education authority has formulated its policy and, after carefully considering the advice of the Department for Education, has decided to adhere to it. It may be that for those who have to formulate the policy the arguments are, as the Roman Catholic and diocesan authorities observed, finely balanced, but we are not entrusted with that task.'

5.74 It is submitted that this case-law is not dated by the Admissions Code. The Code does not provide that it is never appropriate to have admissions criteria on the basis of religion for schools not designated as religious by the Secretary of State. Nor does the Code seek to deal with the special facts that existed in *Lancashire*. As the case-law seems to have been very guarded, it seems, therefore, that in the absence of special facts like those which existed in *Lancashire*, the courts will not uphold admissions criteria based on religious considerations to schools not designated by the Secretary of State as having a religious character.

CHALLENGING ADMISSIONS CRITERIA

5.75 Admissions criteria may be sought to be challenged on procedural or substantive grounds. The question arises as to how and when such challenges should be mounted. The following possibilities arise:

(a) exercise of statutory rights of consultation, objection to and determination by an Adjudicator with possible judicial review thereafter of his decision;

---

[149] [1995] ELR 33, at 40H–41D.

(b) judicial review of the admissions authority decision;

(c) challenges in the course of the hearing of an admissions appeal with possible judicial review thereafter of that decision.

5.76 Of the potential courses of action listed above, it is submitted that the first is, in general, the course which should be followed. Case-law exists evidencing all three forms of challenge and this is discussed below.

Consultation and objection to an Adjudicator

5.77 There are duties of consultation under section 88C of the SSFA 1998 upon local authorities in England prior to the admissions arrangements being settled.[150] The content of the duty is set out in detail in the School Admissions (Admission Arrangements and Co-ordination of Admissions Arrangements) (England) Regulations 2012.[151] Consultation is not required on proposed admission arrangements where the admissions authority consulted on its proposed admission arrangements in accordance with section 88C(2) in any of the seven preceding determination years, and the proposed admission arrangements are the same as those determined following the last such consultation.[152] The manner of[153] and time for[154] consultation is also prescribed by regulations.

5.78 Once admission arrangements have been determined, they cannot be revised save in limited circumstances prescribed by regulations,[155] namely where the variation is necessary to give effect to the School Admissions Code, the mandatory requirements of Part 3 of SSFA 1998, any determination of the Adjudicator and a correction to a misprint in the admission arrangements.[156] If, as a result of a 'major change in circumstances' a variation is required, the LA must refer the proposed variation to the adjudicator and notify the prescribed bodies.[157] The phrase 'major change in circumstances' is not defined by the SSFA.

---

[150] Inserted by the Education and Skills Act 2008.

[151] SI 2012/8. See reg 12 for the full list of consultees. For guidance, see the Admissions Code at paras 1.42–1.50.

[152] Regulation 15(2) of the School Admissions (Admission Arrangement and Co-ordination of Admissions Arrangements) (England) Regulations 2012, SI 2012/8.

[153] Regulation 16 of the School Admissions (Admission Arrangement and Co-ordination of Admissions Arrangements) (England) Regulations 2012, SI 2012/8.

[154] Regulation 17 of the School Admissions (Admission Arrangement and Co-ordination of Admissions Arrangements) (England) Regulations 2012, SI 2012/8.

[155] SSFA 1998, s 88E(9)(b) pursuant to which the School Admissions (Admission Arrangement and Co-ordination of Admissions Arrangements) (England) Regulations 2012, SI 2012/8 were made.

[156] Regulation 21(3) of the School Admissions (Admission Arrangement and Co-ordination of Admissions Arrangements) (England) Regulations.

[157] Section 88E(2) of the SSFA 1998 and paras 3.6–3.7 of the Code.

5.79 There are then rights of objection to an Adjudicator under section 88H of the SSFA 1998.[158]

5.80 Parents were formally eligible to make an objection only if they fell within prescribed categories. Now under section 88H(2) of the SSFA any body or person can make an objection providing they give their name and address to the adjudicator.[159]

5.81 The Secretary of State also has a power to refer admission arrangements to the adjudicator if it appears to him that they do not, or may not, conform with the requirements.[160]

5.82 In broad terms the Adjudicators have responsibility for determining disputes between Academies, local admissions authorities and schools or parents over admissions arrangements.[161] The decision of the Adjudicator is binding.[162] The Adjudicator must publish a report of his decision which must include reasons.[163]

5.83 An Adjudicator is not required to determine an objection referred under section 88H(2) of the SSFA 1998 unless it is received by the Adjudicator on or before 30 June in the determination year.[164] Previously an objection which was received after the then due date of 31 July was to be regarded as properly referred if it was not reasonably practicable for the objection to have been received earlier than the time it was received.[165] There is no like provision in the current regulations. Accordingly the clear intention seems to have been to make the present time limit of 30 June an absolute one. However, the regulation merely states that the Adjudicator is 'not required' to consider a late application. That language in itself suggests that although the Adjudicator is not bound to consider a late application he may have a power to do so. It is submitted that that is not what Parliament intended because this regulation is under the heading 'objections that may not be referred to the Adjudicator' and the jurisdiction conferred under section 88H(2) of the SSFA excludes prescribed objections. Late objections are prescribed objections under regulation 23. The position may be harsh where it was not reasonably

---

[158] Inserted by the Education and Skills Act 2008. See also regs 21–24 of the School Admissions (Admission Arrangement and Co-ordination of Admissions Arrangements) (England) Regulations 2012, SI 2012/8 which set out what objections may or may not be referred to the Adjudicator and the procedure to be followed.

[159] See reg 24 of the School Admissions (Admission Arrangement and Co-ordination of Admissions Arrangements) (England) Regulations 2012.

[160] SSFA 1998, s 88I.

[161] SSFA 1998, s 88H(1), (1A) and regs 21 and 22 of the School Admissions (Admission Arrangements) (England) Regulations 2012, SI 2012/8. The full extent of the Adjudicator's powers and duties is contained in s 88H–88P.

[162] Section 88K(2).

[163] Section 88K(3).

[164] Regulation 23.

[165] Regulation 25(2) of the School Admissions (Admission Arrangements) (England) Regulations 2008, SI 2008/3089 (repealed).

practicable for an objector to present an application in time but the detriment to good administration in late application and possible amendment of admission arrangements is obvious.

5.84 If the matter falls within the Adjudicator's jurisdiction he must determine it on its merits. Case-law has considered the nature of the jurisdiction vested in the Adjudicator. In *R v the School Adjudicator ex parte Metropolitan Borough of Wirral*,[166] the council decided, supported by a considerable majority of primary schools and all its grammar schools, to adopt an 'elevated preference option', whereby a parent was enabled to express a first preference for a grammar school, but (if the child did not get a place there) to express a first preference for an all-ability school. The council rejected a 'rank order option', where parents simply expressed their preferences in order. One of the non-selective schools objected to the arrangement on the basis that it gave parents of able children two first choices and thereby put parents of other children at a disadvantage. The objection was forwarded to the Adjudicator who wrote to the council asking it to provide further information. The council explained that a consultation exercise had revealed that the elevated preference option had strong public support. The Adjudicator decided that the elevated preference option was unfair and, in effect, imposed the rank order option which had been rejected by the council. It was alleged, inter alia, that the Adjudicator was wrong to substitute his own judgement for that of that council. The court held that the Adjudicator was entitled to take that decision because he possessed an original jurisdiction to determine the matter.[167] While he had to take into account[168] the LA decision and that the LA was comprised of elected representatives, he was free to reach a decision at variance with that decision. Accordingly, the question for the court on the substantive merits[169] was whether the Adjudicator's decision was perverse. On the particular facts of the case, the court held that it was not. Where objections are made by parents, the Adjudicator is entitled to consider the substance of the objections and is not expected to treat them as if they were pleadings.[170]

Judicial review of an admissions authority

5.85 There can be little doubt that, where a right of objection exists to the Adjudicator, this should be used rather than an application for judicial

---

[166] [2000] ELR 620, Latham J.

[167] [2000] ELR 620, at para 19. This aspect of the case was followed by Ouseley J in *R (on the application of the Metropolitan Borough of Wirral) v The Chief Schools Adjudicator* [2001] ELR 574 at para 15 and in *Drayton Manor High School, R (on the application of) v The Schools Adjudicator & Anor* [2008] EWHC3119 (Admin), [2009] ELR 127, para 28.

[168] Other relevant considerations are the submissions of all interested parties and the Admissions Code. See further para **5.93** below.

[169] There was also a procedural fairness challenge which did not succeed.

[170] *R (on the application of Wandsworth London Borough Council) v Schools Adjudicator* [2003] EWHC 2969, where Goldring J commented that it was 'vitally important in these matters not to become over legalistic'.

review.[171] That is plainly an adequate alternative remedy in the light of his original jurisdiction. Moreover, the courts are likely to be very unsympathetic to applications for judicial review simply because the time-limit for objecting to the Adjudicator has passed. It would ordinarily be an abuse to seek to move for judicial review simply because the time for the exercise of statutory rights of challenge had expired.[172] It is submitted that the courts would not, in the exercise of their discretion, entertain judicial review of a decision of the LA that the Adjudicator would have had jurisdiction to consider, had the objection been made in time. The fact that speed is of the essence in this area[173] also strongly militates against the courts entertaining judicial review outside the objection period where a matter does fall within the Adjudicator's jurisdiction.[174]

Challenges during the course of an admissions appeal

5.86 It used to be controversial as to whether it was appropriate to seek to challenge the legality of admissions criteria during the course of an admissions appeal. The School Admissions Appeals Code 2012 now expressly provides at paragraph 3.2 that the Appeal Panel must consider whether the admission arrangements comply with the mandatory requirements of the School Admissions Code and Part 3 of the School Standards and Framework Act 1998. The reach of this provision is not entirely clear. Earlier case-law on previous provisions suggests a limited rather than extensive jurisdiction is vested in appeal panels to consider the legality of admissions arrangements.

5.87 In *R v Sheffield ex parte H*,[175] the Court of Appeal, by a majority, held that under an earlier statutory scheme, the appeal panel had jurisdiction to consider whether the admissions policy applied by the LA was lawful or not. Even Laws LJ, who dissented on this point, considered[176] that the appeal panel had jurisdiction to consider the question of legality under paragraph 12 of

---

[171] Before the creation of the Adjudicator the common way of challenging admissions criteria was by judicial review. This is now likely to be a residual jurisdiction.

[172] *R v SENT ex parte F* [1996] ELR 213 at 217A–217B.

[173] Latham J dismissed the procedural unfairness challenge in *R v School Adjudicator ex parte Metropolitan Borough of Wirral* [2000] ELR 620 at para 30 on the ground that requirement for speed militated against the Adjudicator being obliged in the interests of fairness to make preliminary decisions so as to enable the interested parties to make further representations: see at paras 27–31.

[174] It does not follow that where a matter does not fall within the Adjudicator's jurisdiction the courts should by analogy require an application for judicial review to be made within the timescale for the exercise of the statutory right of challenge: *R (on the application of Burkett) v Hammersmith and Fulham London Borough Council* [2002] UKHL 23, [2002] 1 WLR 1593 at para 53. However, unless the challenge is made in time for a dispute to be determined by the court before the beginning of the new school year, leave to move for judicial review may be refused under s 31(6) of the Supreme Court Act 1981 on the ground of detriment to good administration: *R v Rochdale MBC ex parte B, C and K* [2000] Ed CR 117, David Pannick QC (sitting as a Deputy High Court judge), approved in *Burkett* at para 18.

[175] [1999] ELR 511.

[176] [1999] ELR 511, at 520C–520F.

Schedule 24 to the SSFA 1998. The conclusion of the Court of Appeal on this point was technically obiter because it dismissed the appeal on other grounds.

5.88 The matter was reconsidered by the Court of Appeal in *R (on the application of Hounslow LBC) v Schools Admission Appeal Panel for Hounslow LBC.*[177] *Sheffield* was distinguished[178] on the grounds that:

(a) it concerned a different statutory framework;

(b) the unlawfulness of the admissions criteria had been judicially determined and admitted and did not require judicial review proceedings.

5.89 Nevertheless, in *Hounslow* the Court of Appeal went on to state[179] that the appeal panel could look at the legality of admissions arrangements but discouraged a focus on such issues, still less any adjournment of the appeal to enable judicial review proceedings to take place. While that statement was in the context of paragraph 12(a) of Schedule 24 to the SSFA 1998 (which limited the scope of an appeal to one of perversity where the admissions authority have refused admission in order to avoid class size prejudice) it was not, apparently, so confined. *Sheffield* was not such a case and it was expressly endorsed[180] in *Hounslow*.

5.90 In *R (Buckinghamshire County Council) School Admissions Independent Appeal Panel for Buckinghamshire,*[181] Blake J also adopted a conservative approach to role of the admissions panel in relation to the legality of admissions arrangements. While he held[182] that changes in the applicable scheme meant that the guidance in *Hounslow* no longer had to be given full effect by appeals panels, he went on to hold[183] that the words 'mandatory requirements' themselves limited what a panel could properly look at. He stated that a mandatory requirement was likely to be one that was precise and certain in its application to a given set of facts. That which required a panel to make a broad judgment preferring one of a number of potential means of addressing a problem was not normally something the panel should be concerned with.

5.91 Accordingly, the position seems to be that the appropriate place and time to challenge admissions criteria is before the Adjudicator, or, where there is no right of objection to the Adjudicator, by way of application for judicial review. However, a failure to bring a challenge then would not preclude a parent challenging the application of admissions criteria if the contention was that the admissions arrangements failed to comply with a mandatory requirement of the SSFA or the Admissions Code. Nevertheless a parent would be well advised

---

[177] [2002] EWCA Civ 900, [2002] ELR 602.
[178] [2002] EWCA Civ 900, [2002] ELR 602, at para 22.
[179] [2002] EWCA Civ 900, [2002] ELR 602, at paras 59–61.
[180] [2002] EWCA Civ 900, [2002] ELR 602, at para 59.
[181] [2009] EWHC 1679 (Admin).
[182] At paras 19 and 20.
[183] At para 47.

not to wait for an appeal to the appeal panel before challenging admissions criteria because the school the parents wish their child to attend may be full by the time of an appeal and admission of the child and others in a like position may seriously prejudice the provision of efficient education or efficient use of resources within the meaning of paragraph 3.6 of the School Admission Appeals Code. The appeal cannot, therefore, be an adequate alternative remedy in those circumstances.

JUDICIAL REVIEW OF THE ADJUDICATOR

5.92 In the light of the original jurisdiction of the Adjudicator to determine admissions criteria, the chances of successfully reviewing the Adjudicator on the substantive merits are slim. An irrationality challenge where matters of educational judgment predominate is going to be difficult to sustain. A challenge based on the fact that the Adjudicator has decided the matter at variance with the Admissions Code could be made as he is now obliged to act in accordance with it.[184] Challenges on the basis of illegality, if for example the Adjudicator determined that the admissions authority should apply criteria which were illegal, would have mileage, as would a challenge based on the failure to have regard to all material considerations.[185]

5.93 What is capable of being a relevant consideration has been discussed by the courts in two cases involving Wirral Metropolitan Borough Council.[186] In the first of these cases, Latham J held[187] the Adjudicator should take account all matters submitted to him by the interested parties, the LA decision, the fact that the LA had elected representatives who could be expected to know the area and the Code of Practice.[188] In the second case, Ouseley J stated:[189]

'The Adjudicator is a specialist, with his own experience, which it is expected he will bring to bear ... There will be certain material considerations which are expressly, or by obvious implication, identified by the Act as those to which regard must be had, whether or not they are raised by the affected parties. The Code of Practice is one such consideration. These will be considerations fundamental to his

---

[184] *R (on the application of Wirral MBC) v Chief Schools Adjudicator* [2001] ELR 574 at para 75; *R (on the application of M) v London Borough of Barking and Dagenham* [2002] EWHC 2483 (Admin) at para 55 were decided before the Education and Inspections Act 2006 amended the SSFA so as to oblige the Adjudicator to act in accordance with the Code.

[185] For an example of a challenge to an Adjudicator's decision succeeding on the basis of a failure to take account of all relevant considerations, see *R (on the application of Watford Grammar School for Girls and another) v Adjudicator for Schools* [2003] All ER (D) 135, Collins J.

[186] *R v The School Adjudicator ex parte Metropolitan Borough of Wirral* [2000] ELR 620, Latham J and *R (on the application of the Metropolitan Borough of Wirral) v the Chief Schools Adjudicator* [2001] ELR 574, Ouseley J.

[187] [2000] ELR 620 at paras 19 and 20.

[188] There is an express statutory duty to have regard to the Admissions Code by virtue of the SSFA 1998, s 84(1)(d) and (3).

[189] [2001] ELR 574 at paras 52–53. At para 68 he held that points not raised by the council before the Adjudicator did not meet this test of being relevant considerations and accordingly could not be relied upon before him as invalidating the decision of the Adjudicator.

decision. There will be other considerations which are relevant in the sense that if raised it would be lawful for him to take them into account, but they are ones he cannot be expected to know or discover for himself or to consider or attribute weight to unless they are raised for his consideration ... He has to consider those consequences which the reasonable decision-maker, fulfilling that particular statutory duty, would realise were necessary or fundamental considerations arising as part and parcel of his very determination. It is his determination itself which can create the fundamental materiality of such consequences. But unless particular consequences are drawn to his attention, he is only required to consider those which any reasonable Adjudicator would regard as obvious and significant in the sense of being fundamental to his decision or at least ones which, upon being considered, would lead to a real possibility of a different decision.'

Accordingly, it behoves any objector to put his full case before an Adjudicator. A failure to do so, while, not necessarily fatal, is likely to weaken his chances of successfully contending that the Adjudicator has failed to take account of all relevant considerations.

5.94 There is scope for procedural challenges against decisions of the Adjudicator. As far as the duty to act fairly is concerned, the decisions of Latham J and Ouseley J in the two cases involving Wirral establish that the Adjudicator is not obliged to make a provisional decision and then invite representations on it from interested parties because the requirements of a speedy decision-making process militate against this.[190] If, however, a new point arises, then the interest of fairness would require him to invite further representations from interested parties.[191]

5.95 The Adjudicator must publish his decision and the reasons for it.[192] Unlike the position with regard to the First-tier Tribunal,[193] the duty on the Adjudicator to give reasons is not a summary one, nor does a question arise in this context of whether a failure to give reasons is an error of law for the purposes of a statutory right of appeal. The reasons the Adjudicator is obliged to give must deal with the substantial issues raised.[194] A failure to comply with the duty to give reasons would be a ground for quashing the decision.[195]

---

[190] [2000] ELR 620 at paras 22–31 per Latham J; [2001] ELR 574 at paras 51 and 53 per Ouseley J. See also *R v Clark ex parte JD* (2000) *The Times,* 26 May, Maurice Kay J, 27 March 2000.

[191] [2000] ELR 620 at paras 22–31 per Latham J; [2001] ELR 574 at paras 51 and 53 per Ouseley J. See also *R v Clark ex parte JD* (2000) *The Times,* 26 May, Maurice Kay J, 27 March 2000.

[192] SSFA 1998, s 88K(3).

[193] See the discussion in Chapter 4 at paras **4.242–4.254**.

[194] *R v Downes ex parte Wandsworth LBC* [2000] ELR 425 at 442G.

[195] This was a ground on which the decision was quashed in *R v Downes ex parte Wandsworth LBC* [2000] ELR 425. It does not follow that any failure to give reasons will lead to a decision being quashed in the light of the court's discretion to refuse relief.

ADMISSIONS NUMBERS[196]

5.96 Admissions authorities are obliged under section 88D(1) of the SSFA 1998[197] to determine the number of pupils in each relevant age group that it is intended to admit to the school in that year. That duty is part of the duty to determine admission arrangements under section 88C of the SSFA and accordingly the duties of consultation there set out apply. Under section 88D(2) the determination may include, in the case of boarding schools, separate numbers for boarders and non-boarders in each relevant age group. The admissions number has to take into account the children with statements of special educational needs admitted during a normal admission round to a relevant age group.[198]

5.97 In fixing the number, the admissions authority must have regard to any prescribed method of calculation or other prescribed matter.[199] The relevant regulations were the School Admissions (Admission Arrangements) (England) Regulations 2008.[200] Regulation 4 provided that the admissions authority, in determining the admissions number, must have regard to the indicated admissions number for a relevant age group. The indicated admissions number was that number calculated in accordance with the DfES guidance 'Assessing Net Capacity in Schools'.[201] The admissions authority was not obliged to have an admissions number as high as the indicated admissions number, but if it was lower, then there were publication obligations under regulation 20 which were designed to assist parents to make any desired statutory objection to the Adjudicator.

5.98 Once the admission number has been set, pupils can be admitted to the school in a given year in excess of that number without that constituting an increase in the PAN.[202] In a normal year of entry, a child must not be refused admission on the grounds of prejudice to efficient education or the efficient use of resources, except where the number of applications for admission exceeds the admissions number.[203]

---

[196] See paras 1.2–1.5 of the Admissions Code 2012.
[197] As inserted by the EA 2002, s 47(2).
[198] SSFA 1998, s 98(9).
[199] SSFA 1998, s 88(D3).
[200] SI 2008/3089. These regulations were revoked by reg 3(1) of the School Admissions (Admissions Arrangements) (England) Regulations 2012 save that they continue to have effect in relation to arrangements under which pupils are admitted to schools in England for the academic years 2011–2012 and 2012–2013. Currently there are no regulations which deal with planned admissions limits for the academic years 2013–2014 and beyond.
[201] Published August 2002.
[202] See paras 1.4 and 1.5 of the Admissions Code 2012.
[203] SSFA 1998, s 86(5).

ADMISSIONS APPEALS

5.99 Parents have rights of appeal to an appeal panel from admissions decisions of LAs and governing bodies.[204] By virtue of section 94(1) of the SSFA 1998, the LA must make arrangements for enabling the parent to appeal where the decision was made by or on behalf of the LA as to the school at which education is to be provided or, in the case of a community or voluntary controlled school, the decision to refuse admission was made by or on behalf of the governing body.

5.100 The governing body of a foundation or voluntary school has a similar duty to make such arrangements under section 94(2) of the SSFA 1998. Joint arrangements can be made by governing bodies of two or more foundation or voluntary-aided schools maintained by the LA as a result of section 94(3) of the SSFA 1998.

5.101 There are no rights of appeal for parents where parental preference has been denied as a result of the child having had two permanent exclusions within the ambit of section 87(2) of the SSFA 1998: see section 95(1) of the SSFA 1998. There are, however, rights of appeal for the governing body of the relevant school where the LA is the admissions authority and it decides to admit a child to whom section 87(2) of the SSFA 1998 applies: see section 95(2). By virtue of section 95(4) of the SSFA 1998, the decision of the appeal panel is binding on the LA and the governing body. The School Admissions (Admissions Appeals Arrangements) (England) Regulations 2012[205] deal with the constitution of the appeal body in this category of case.[206] The procedure for these appeals is now dealt with in the School Admissions Appeals Code 2012.[207]

5.102 By virtue of section 94(5) of the SSFA 1998,[208] an appeal under that section is to an appeal panel constituted in accordance with regulations. By virtue of section 94(5A) of the SSFA 1998,[209] regulations may contain provisions as to the procedure on such appeals, the grounds on which an appeal panel can act in an infant class size appeal and for allowances to members of the appeal panels. The Education (Admissions Appeals Arrangements) (England) Regulations 2012[210] also deal with the constitution of appeal panels for this category of case.[211] The procedure for these appeals is now dealt with

---

[204] There is an exception in the case of an admission following a direction by the LA under the SSFA 1998, s 96 or 97A. The direction-making power of the LA under ss 96 or 97A is an exceptional one and is discussed at paras **5.164–5.168** below.
[205] SI 2012/9; see reg 5 and the Schedule to the regulations. See also s 1 of the School Admissions Appeal Code 2012.
[206] SSFA 1998, s 95(3) as amended by para 9 of Sch 4 to the EA 2002.
[207] See s 6 of the School Admission Appeals Code.
[208] As substituted by the EA 2002, s 50.
[209] As substituted by the EA 2002, s 50.
[210] SI 2012/9; see reg 5 and the Schedule.
[211] See also s 1 of the School Admission Appeals Code 2012.

by sections 2–4 of the Admissions Appeals Code 2012. By virtue of section 94(6),[212] the decision of the appeal panel is binding on the LA and the governing body.

5.103 The rights of appeal conferred by section 94 of the SSFA 1998 do not apply to Academies. However, the Secretary of State when he enters into Funding Agreements with Academies requires them to comply with the Code and the law relating to admissions although he will waive this where there is a demonstrable need.[213] Academies will in general therefore be responsible for arranging admissions appeals but they can ask local authorities to carry out some or all of the relevant functions on their behalf.[214] If the applicant for an Academy place has no right of appeal because the Secretary of State has waived the requirement for the particular Academy to have such appeals, it is submitted that judicial review would lie against a decision to refuse an Academy place because of the statutory underpinning for Academies,[215] and the case-law holding that judicial review of city technology colleges was available.[216]

ADMISSIONS APPEALS AND THE COURTS

5.104 Litigation involving admissions appeals has been concentrated on the following areas:

(a)   the process by which the decision is reached;

(b)   the extent to which the appeal panel can entertain questions going to the legality of the admission arrangements;

(c)   the impact of the ECHR;

(d)   the extent of any duty to give reasons.

The extent to which the appeal panel can question the legality of the admissions arrangements has been considered above.[217] The remaining questions are considered below.

---

[212]   As amended by the EA 2002, Sch 4.
[213]   See para 5 of the School Admission Appeals Code.
[214]   See para 6 of the School Admission Appeals Code.
[215]   EA 1996, s 482 as substituted by the EA 2002, s 65.
[216]   *R v Governors of Haberdashers Aske's Hatcham College Trust ex parte Tyrell* [1995] COD 399, Dyson J.
[217]   At paras **5.86–5.91** above.

Decision-making process of appeal panel

5.105 It was well established under the statutory scheme which prevailed prior to the SSFA 1998 that the appeal committee[218] should reach its decision by a two-stage process:

(a) first, to decide whether the LA has made out its case that there would be prejudice to efficient education to admit further children to the school;

(b) secondly, to decide whether, if there was prejudice whether it was outweighed in the particular case, by the parental preference. This is a balancing exercise.

This two-stage process was established in *R v South Glamorgan Appeals Committee ex parte Evans.*[219] It was accepted as correct in many subsequent authorities.[220]

5.106 Paragraph 3.1 of the Admission Appeals Code 2012 provides that the Panel must follow a different process, described somewhat inaccurately, as a two-stage process, in all appeals other than those relating to infant class size prejudice. What is described as the first stage is set out at paragraphs 3.2–3.7 of the School Admissions Appeals Code 2012. The panel must consider:

(a) whether the admission arrangements comply with the mandatory requirements of the School Admissions Code and Part 3 of the SSFA 1998;

(b) whether the admission arrangements were correctly and impartially applied in the case in question;[221]

If the appeal panel considers that the admissions arrangements did not comply with admissions law or had not been correctly and impartially applied a further

---

[218] Now an appeal panel constituted in accordance with The School Admissions (Appeal Arrangements)(England) Regulations 2012. Under the previous statutory scheme the appeal lay to an appeals committee constituted under the provisions of Sch 33 to the EA 1996. Both terms are used in the text below reflecting the different nomenclature at different times but all references to an appeal committee should, in the absence of contrary indication, be seen as equally applicable to an appeal panel.

[219] (Unreported) 10 May 1984, Forbes J.

[220] See *R v Commissioner for Local Administration ex parte Croydon London Borough Council* [1989] 1 All ER 1033. It was assumed to be correct without any endorsement to that effect in *R v Governors of Bishop Challenor Roman Catholic Comprehensive Girls' School ex parte Choudhury* [1992] 3 WLR 99 at 110C–110G. It was accepted as correct in *R v Lancashire ex parte M* [1995] ELR 136; *R v Appeal Committee of Brighouse School ex parte G* [1997] ELR 39; and *R v Education Appeal Committee of Leicestershire County Council ex parte Tarmohamed* [1997] ELR 48 where, at 52B, Sedley J, after commenting that the case had been inexplicably unreported, remarked that it had been commended, adopted and followed by other judges and by public authorities. See also to the same effect *R v South Gloucestershire Appeals Committee ex parte C* [2000] ELR 220.

[221] See para 3.2 of the School Admission Appeals Code 2012.

question then arises.[222] If the panel is satisfied that had the admission arrangements complied with admissions law or had they been correctly and impartially applied the child would have been offered a place, then it must uphold the appeal. That seemingly applies regardless of the prejudice to the efficient use of resources.[223] It is difficult to see how this provision is workable. If the admissions arrangements were incorrectly applied to one person who would have been given a place had they been correctly applied at the time, admitting such a child months later when the school is full regardless of the prejudice to the efficient use of resources is likely to cause detriment. That though is what the School Admission Appeals Code appears to provide for. If, by contrast, the admissions arrangements were incorrectly applied to more than one person who would have been given places had they been correctly applied at the time, then serious prejudice to the efficient use of resources is to be considered before the children are admitted. Accordingly the panel should then proceed to what is described as stage 2.

5.107 What is the approach the panel should adopt when deciding whether the child would have been offered a place had the admission arrangements been correctly and impartially applied? In *R (M) v Haringey Independent Appeal Panel* the Court of Appeal held obiter and without consideration of relevant previous authority,[224] in relation to the 2009 Admission Appeals Code, that the correct approach was one of reviewing the reasonableness of the LA decision where any issue of judgment arose.[225] Wilson LJ relied on three matters[226] none of which it is submitted has force. First he relied on the fact that the 2009 Admissions Appeals Code drew a distinction between the panel considering various matters and deciding others. Secondly, he relied on the fact that the consideration by the panel was retrospective. Thirdly, he held that consideration of whether a place would have been offered if the arrangements had been applied correctly would never arise if the appeal was a full merits one.

5.108 As far as the first matter is concerned, while reference to both the concepts of consideration and decision can be found in the 2012 Admission Appeals Code,[227] that is a distinction that does not help on what the nature of the decision has to be because, for example at paragraph 3.7 for all the questions at the first stage the Code uses the concept of 'finding'. A decision or

---

[222] See para 3.5(a) of the School Admission Appeals Code 2012. They must also refer the matter to the appropriate admissions authority: see para 3.4 of the School Admission Appeals Code 2012.

[223] Paragraph 3.3 suggests that prejudice to the efficient use of resources must be considered after the questions in para 3.2. However, para 3.5(a) provides that an appeal must be allowed in the circumstances therein described which do not include prejudice to the efficient use of resources. That is not a mere oversight as the prejudice to the efficient use of resources is included at para 3.5(b). It is submitted that the correct reading of para 3.3 is that sequentially prejudice to the efficient use of resources is to be considered after the para 3.2 questions but it is not relevant under para 3.5(a).

[224] See paras **5.119–5.120** below for a discussion of these other authorities.

[225] See [2010] EWCA Civ 1103 at paras 37–38.

[226] See at para 37.

[227] See for example at paras 3.2 and 3.3.

a finding can as easily be on the merits or applying a concept of reasonableness. As far as the second point Wilson LJ relied on is concerned, it is inevitable an appeal post dates the decision of the LA and will look back. That is the nature of an appeal. It does not follow that that the appeal is limited to review of reasonableness rather than by way of full merits. As far as the third matter is concerned, there is nothing in this point either. It is perfectly possible for the panel to hold that the admission arrangements were incorrectly applied but that the child would still not have been offered a place because he had a lower priority than children with a higher but lawful oversubscription criteria. Nevertheless, despite these reservations about the reasoning of Wilson LJ, it is probable a court would hold that the test to be applied by the panel on an appeal was one of review on rationality grounds because *Haringey* is referred to on a different point in a footnote to paragraph 3.3 of the 2012 Admission Appeals Code and there is no suggestion that the approach it suggests was wrong. Had the Secretary of State considered the approach was not the one that had been intended he could and would have taken the opportunity to make this clear in the 2012 Admission Appeals Code.

5.109 If, in the case of unlawful or incorrect application of admission arrangements, the panel is not satisfied that the child would have been offered a place, then it must consider whether the admission of additional children would prejudice the efficient use of resources.[228] If the panel concludes that no such prejudice arises then it must allow the appeal. However, here there is an exception in the case of multiple appeals. If a number of children have been denied places they would have got had there been no error in the legality or application of the admission arrangements, then if there is serious prejudice to the provision of efficient education or efficient use of resources the panel must go to the second stage.[229] This suggests that if there is prejudice to the provision of efficient education or efficient use of resources but that that prejudice is not serious, then the appeal must be allowed without going to the second stage.

5.110 The second stage involves balancing the prejudice to the school against the appellant's case for the child to be admitted to the school. The panel must take into account the appellant's reasons for expressing a preference for the school, including what the school can offer the child that the allocated or other schools cannot.[230] If the panel considers that the appellant's case outweighs the prejudice to the school, it must allow the appeal.

5.111 Detailed provision is made in the Admission Appeals Code as to the consideration of the issue of prejudice. For multiple appeals, the panel is directed not to compare the individual cases when deciding whether the appellant's case outweighs the prejudice to the school.[231] However, the Code goes on to provide that where the panel finds there are more cases which outweigh prejudice than the school can admit, it must compare the cases and

---

[228] See para 3.5(b) of the Admission Appeals Code 2012.
[229] See para 3.6 of the Admission Appeals Code 2012.
[230] See para 3.8 of the Admission Appeals Code 2012.
[231] See para 3.9 of the Admission Appeals Code 2012.

only admit the strongest ones up to the number the school can admit without causing prejudice. This is a curious use of language, because *ex hypothesi* by the time what is termed in the Admission Appeals Code the second stage, is reached, there will already have been established that the admission of one further child will cause prejudice. What paragraph 3.9 must be intended to mean is that the panel should admit up to the number where it considers the parental preference is sufficiently strong to outweigh a tolerable level of prejudice.[232] It is unfortunate that the Code is unclear on this point and does not specify what level of prejudice is sufficient to outweigh parental preference.

5.112 Paragraph 3.10 of the Admission Appeals Code provides that in considering prejudice the panel must be able to demonstrate prejudice over and above the fact that the published admissions limit has been reached but they must not reassess the capacity of the school. The panel are directed to consider the impact on the school of admitting additional children. Four factors are identified which the panel are permitted to have regard to.[233] These are:

(a) what effect an additional admission would have on the school in the then current and subsequent academic years as the year group moves through the school;

(b) whether any changes have been made to the school's physical accommodation or organisation since the admission number was set for the relevant year group;

(c) the impact of the locally agreed Fair Access Protocol;

(d) the impact on the organisation and size of classes, the availability of teaching staff, and the effect on children already at the school.

5.113 In *Haringey Independent Appeal Panel v R ex p M*[234] the Court of Appeal concluded that under paragraph 3.1(a) of the 2009 Admission Appeals Code the panel was required to address three matters:

(1) whether the admission arrangements complied with the mandatory requirements;

(2) whether they were correctly applied in the individual case; and

(3) whether prejudice would arise were the child to be admitted.

---

[232] Whatever that may mean.

[233] These are expressly permissible rather than mandatory considerations, but the prudent course would be for the panel to have regard to them anyway as absent good reason not to follow guidance the courts are more likely to hold a decision would be flawed: see for example the decisions on the previous version of the SSFA 1998, s 84(3), most notably *R (Metropolitan Borough of Wirral) v Chief Schools Adjudicator* [2001] ELR 574.

[234] [2010] EWCA Civ 1103, [2010] ELR 823 at para 16.

This cannot be an exhaustive summary of the current law. As we have seen under the 2012 Admission Appeals Code, before the panel considers prejudice under paragraph 3.5(a) it must consider whether the child would have been offered a place had the admission arrangements been lawful or correctly and impartially applied.[235]

5.114 As to the nature of the exercise *Haringey* is authority for the proposition under the 2009 Code that when the panel is considering the issue of prejudice *at the first stage* of the enquiry it applies an essentially objective test and does not, save to a very limited extent, consider the particular attributes of the child.[236]

5.115 For infant class size appeals, paragraph 4.6 of the Admission Appeals Code 2012 provides that the appeal panel can allow the appeal only if it finds: (a) that the admission of additional children would not breach the infant class size limit,[237] or (b) that the admission arrangements did not comply with admissions law or were not correctly and impartially applied and the child would have been offered a place if the arrangements had complied or had been correctly and impartially applied, or (c) that the decision was not one which a reasonable admissions authority would have made in the circumstances of the case. The School Admission Appeals Code deals with these appeals at paragraphs 4.1–4.2. Here the position is more complex and although the School Admission Appeals Code directs at paragraph 4.3 that a two-stage process should be undertaken in certain circumstances, the nature of what is involved in the first stage of the process is somewhat different from the non-class size appeal.

5.116 For class size appeals, the School Admission Appeals Code directs[238] the appeal panel to consider all of the following matters at the first stage:

(a)   whether the admission of an additional child/additional children would breach the infant class size limit;

---

[235] That was also the case under para 3.2(a) of the 2009 Admissions Appeal Code. In the light of the fact Wilson LJ, as he then was, set this out at para 18 of his judgment he cannot be taken to have held that in all cases there were three questions which fell to be considered at the first stage.

[236] See at para 28. Wilson LJ recorded in this paragraph the submissions of all Counsel that balancing at the second stage did involve consideration of the particular attributes of the child but did not comment on whether those submissions were well founded. It is difficult to see that a child's attributes are irrelevant when balancing under para 3.8 of the 2012 Admission Appeals Code. If, as this paragraph provides, the reasons for the preference and what the school can offer the child are taken into account, then, eg, not only should a stated desire for high quality musical education which the school can offer be relevant, but also it must be relevant that the child has musical ability.

[237] The limit is in general 30 pupils in an infant class: see reg 4 of the School Admissions (Infant Class Sizes) (England) Regulations 2012, SI 2012/10.

[238] At para 4.4.

(b) whether the admissions arrangements (including the area's co-ordinated admission arrangements) complied with the mandatory requirements of the School Admissions Code and Part 3 of the School Standards and Framework Act 1998;

(c) whether the admissions arrangements were correctly and impartially applied in the case(s) in question;

(d) whether the decision to refuse admission was one which a reasonable admission authority would have made in the circumstances of the case.

5.117 If any of these matters are established, the panel may uphold the appeal at the first stage.[239] Although the word used is 'may', it would seem odd that an appeal should be refused even if good grounds were established and it is difficult to envisage that it would be lawful to dismiss the appeal in those circumstances. There is no difficulty about the first ground; if the panel finds the admission of children would not breach the infant class size limit the ground is established and the appeal may be allowed. For unlawful or incorrectly applied admission arrangements, the appeal panel has to find in addition the child would have been admitted to the school had the arrangements been lawful or correctly applied before it allows the appeal. There is no requirement to find the child would have been admitted if the decision of the admissions authority is found to have been unreasonable. The only caveat is that in the case of multiple appeals the panel has to move to the second balancing stage if satisfied that to admit all the children who would have been offered places under paragraph 4.6 would seriously prejudice efficient education or resources. This caveat is curious because although it expressly applies to all paragraph 4.6 cases, as just noted the panel only needs to consider whether a place would have been offered in the paragraph 4.6(b) category. It appears to be intended that in the case of multiple appeals if the panel is of the view that allowing all the appeals would cause serious prejudice it must move to the balancing exercise.

5.118 The question whether the admissions arrangements had been properly applied by the admissions authority would seem, at first blush, to involve the panel deciding that issue as a matter of objective, primary fact, rather than simply applying a *Wednesbury* test, ie whether the admissions authority could reasonably have concluded that the child should not be admitted to the school in question on the application of the criteria. The contrast in this regard between the language of paragraph 4.6(b) and paragraph 4.6(c) of the School Admission Appeals Code 2012 is marked. Indeed, if it had been intended that paragraph 4.6 (b) should import simply a test of reasonableness, it is difficult to see that there would be many appeals under sub-paragraph (b) that would not also succeed under sub-paragraph (a) and/or (c).[240]

---

[239] See para 4.6 of the Admission Appeals Code.

[240] The only difference, on this hypothesis, is that sub-paragraph (c) directs attention to the decision the reasonable admissions authority would make and sub-paragraph (b) to the decision that would have been made had the arrangements been applied properly. Accordingly,

5.119 Nevertheless, in *R v South Gloucestershire Education Appeal Committee ex parte Bryant*,[241] under a materially identical earlier statutory scheme,[242] Buxton LJ appeared to suggest the contrary. He stated, at para 29, that 'the job for the committee is to decide whether such decisions have passed outside what can properly discerned to be the boundary of the policy'. Chadwick LJ delivered a concurring judgment but also expressly endorsed[243] the reasons of Buxton LJ. Aldous LJ simply agreed. Accordingly, there can be no doubt that the Court of Appeal was unanimous in apparently adopting a *Wednesbury* approach to the question of whether the admissions criteria been properly applied. However, as Buxton LJ makes clear,[244] that approach is only applicable if the criteria involve an exercise of judgement. If the admissions authority, for example, is simply wrong about a matter of fact (such as satisfaction of a sibling criterion), there is no warrant for the panel to look at the decision of the admissions authority only in *Wednesbury* terms.

5.120 Judgment was given in the *South Gloucestershire* case on 28 June 2000. Just over a month later a different division of the Court of Appeal gave judgment in *R v London Borough of Richmond ex parte JC*.[245] It does not appear that *South Gloucestershire* was cited in the latter case. However, in *ex parte JC*, the Court of Appeal was unanimous that the task of the panel under sub-paragraph (b) of what was then paragraph 11A of Schedule 33 to the EA 1996 was to see whether the admissions authority applied the admissions arrangements correctly as a matter of primary fact.[246] While *ex parte JC* did not consider expressly the question of criteria involving an exercise of judgement, the approach adopted to sub-paragraph (b) was general and not restricted to criteria which did not involve an exercise of judgement.

5.121 As noted in paras **5.107–5.109** above the CA in *R (M) v Haringey Independent Appeal Panel* adopted, obiter, a *Wednesbury* approach where the exercise was one of judgment. Neither of the earlier decisions of the Court of Appeal on the point were referred to. There are thus conflicting decisions of the Court of Appeal. It is respectfully submitted that it is open to doubt whether, even in cases involving the exercise of judgement by the admissions authority, it is appropriate for the panel to restrict itself to a *Wednesbury* approach. That approach, it is respectfully submitted, sits uneasily with the language of the

---

an irrational application of criteria at the original stage, leading to an incorrect application of admissions criteria, would lead to an appeal not succeeding under sub-paragraph (a) only if the circumstances of the case had changed so that it was now reasonable to refuse admission of the child to the school. This cannot be a common case.

[241] [2001] ELR 53.

[242] Paragraphs 12(a) and (b) of Sch 24 to the SSFA 1998.

[243] [2001] ELR 53 at para 42.

[244] [2001] ELR 53, at para 28 and the first sentence of para 29.

[245] [2001] ELR 21. See also *R (K and S) v Admissions Appeal Panel of Cardiff County Council* [2003] EWHC 436 (Admin).

[246] [2001] ELR 21, at paras 41, 45, 46, 48, 49, 75(2), 80 and 91.That is in accordance with the position taken by McCullough J in *R v Dame Alice Owens School Governors ex parte S* [1998] Ed CR 101 and also in Northern Ireland; see *Farrah's Application* (1990) 6 NIJB 72 CA and *Re Hughes* [2001] NIQB 38 at para 7, Weatherup J.

Admissions Appeal Code 2012 although, as noted above, *Haringey* is cited in the 2012 Code on a different point and not commented on with disapproval in relation to the present point. *R v Richmond ex parte JC*, it is submitted, is to be preferred, but future clarification by the Court of Appeal on the point is still necessary.

5.122 For an infant class size appeal it is not sufficient for the admissions authority to show that the admissions number has been reached. The Admission Appeals Code 2012 assumes, at paragraph 4.9, that the panel may allow an appeal on the ground that the admissions authority could take measures to avoid the infant class size limit being breached such as hiring another teacher. That is in accordance with the decision in *R (on the application of O) v St James Roman Catholic Primary School Appeal Panel.*[247] If the appeal panel finds that a reasonable admissions authority would admit the child, the appeal panel does not have to go further: it simply allows the appeal unless there are potentially more successful appellants than could be admitted before class size prejudice would arise. If there are such multiple appeals, and admission of all the children would cause serious prejudice, then the Admissions Appeals Code 2012 states[248] that the appeal panel should proceed to the second stage. The balancing exercise requires a comparison of the individual appeals and admission up to the number where the class size limit would not be breached if necessary by taking measures to avoid breach which would not be prejudicial to efficient education or the efficient use of resources.[249]

5.123 The 2012 Admission Appeals Code gives guidance as to consideration of reasonableness at paragraph 4.10. The guidance is conventional. It does not deal with the question whether the panel can look at evidence for this purpose that was not before the admission authority. It is submitted that evidence that did not exist at the time of the decision of the admission authority is not relevant to the issue of whether the admissions authority acted reasonably. Evidence that a reasonable admissions authority would have obtained at the time but failed to do so, is, it is submitted, admissible before the appeal panel.

5.124 If, at the first stage, the appeal panel concludes prejudice has not been made out, then the appeal succeeds: see *R v Local Commissioner ex parte Croydon LBC.*[250] In that case the Divisional Court held that while it was generally unhelpful to look at the questions in terms of onus of proof, that it was for the LA to establish prejudice, and thereafter the balancing exercise had to be carried out without any regard to onus of proof.[251]

5.125 The panel must actually consider whether there is prejudice to efficient education. It is not sufficient that it simply asks whether the school thinks there

---

[247] [2001] ELR 469 at para 11.
[248] At para 4.7.
[249] See para 4.9.
[250] [1989] 1 All ER 1033 at 1040j.
[251] [1989] 1 All ER 1033, at 1041b–104d.

would be prejudice. Accordingly, in *R v Appeal Committee of Brighouse School ex parte G*,[252] the court quashed decisions where the appeal committee simply asked itself whether the school had a case, rather than performing an independent evaluation of that case.

5.126 Does section 86(3)(a) of the SSFA 1998 direct attention to the prejudice to efficient education or to the efficient use of resources at schools other than that which the parent prefers? In *R v Education Appeal Committee of Blackpool Borough Council ex parte Taylor*[253] Kay J decided it was an arguable point that the appeal committee was entitled to consider the impact on efficient education and use of resources at other schools. He relied on the decision of the Court of Appeal in *B v London Borough of Harrow*.[254] That decision was reversed by the House of Lords,[255] but Lord Slynn expressed the view[256] that where a child was not applying to a special school for children with special educational needs, but wished to go to a school outside the LA area, the resources of the receiving authority and 'perhaps' also of the sending authority would fall to be considered under what was then section 411(3)(a) of the EA 1996.[257] That was, expressly, not a final view and strictly obiter because the case before him concerned a child with special educational needs.

5.127 In *R v Essex CC ex parte Jacobs*,[258] Collins J held that an admissions appeal committee had acted unlawfully in relation to the balancing exercise. The applicant wished his twins to attend the same school as their older sisters. He was divorced from their mother and both of them lived approximately one mile outside the school's designated catchment area. The children spent time at both addresses and the applicant chose the school for its convenience. The committee dismissed the appeal. It was held that they had done so unlawfully because they had effectively discounted that the elder siblings attending the school benefited from its convenient location to both parents' addresses and had taken an irrelevant matter into account by suggesting the elder sibling could move schools so that all the children could attend the same school.

5.128 The balancing exercise can involve looking at whether the child had a legitimate expectation that he would be allocated a place at the preferred school. In *R v Beatrix Potter School ex parte K*,[259] the headteacher had offered the child a place and the mother had bought a school uniform in reliance upon that offer. The offer was then withdrawn. The Secretary of State refused to intervene. The court held that the parent had a legitimate expectation that the child would be admitted to the school, but that was only one factor to be considered when considering the rationality of the decision to refuse

---

[252] [1997] ELR 39.
[253] [1999] ELR 237.
[254] [1998] ELR 351.
[255] [2000] 1 WLR 223.
[256] [2000] 1 WLR 223, at 227G. The rest of the House concurred in his speech.
[257] Now SSFA 1998, s 86(3)(a).
[258] [1997] ELR 190.
[259] [1997] ELR 468.

admission. However, the court held that the decision to refuse admission was neither irrational nor unfair. In *R v Birmingham City Council ex parte L*[260] the letter notifying the parent of the appeal committee decision mistakenly suggested that the parent had succeeded in obtaining a place at her first choice of school. Once the mistake was discovered, the LA offered a rehearing, but the parent refused that offer and brought proceedings for judicial review, contending that she had a legitimate expectation of a place at the preferred school. Latham J held that there was no clear and unambiguous promise on the facts and, accordingly, no legitimate expectation. He went on to indicate that even had he found a clear and unambiguous representation, it would not have been an abuse of process for the LA to refuse to give effect to it, having regard to the prejudice to the school in having additional children.[261] The School Admissions Code 2012 now provides[262] that once an admissions authority has made an offer of a place it may only be withdrawn if it was offered in error, the parent has not responded within a reasonable time, or it is established that the offer was obtained through a fraudulent or intentionally misleading application. The School Admissions Code states[263] that where a place is withdrawn on the basis of misleading information, the application must be considered afresh, and a right of appeal offered if a place is refused. The School Admissions Code also provides[264] that where the parent has not responded to an offer, the admissions authority must give the parent a further opportunity to respond and explain that the offer might be withdrawn if they do not do so.

5.129 It is quite common for an appeal committee to hear a number of appeals all at once before giving a decision on any of them. This can sometimes lead to problems. In *R v Camden Education Committee ex parte X*[265] one of the members of the appeal committee was able to hear the appeals on the first of two days set aside, but not the second. For the second day he was replaced by someone else who gave a decision on an appeal heard on the first day. The court quashed the decision, holding that it was unlawful for a different committee to decide an appeal from the one which heard the appeal.[266] That conclusion seems inevitable. The School Admission Appeals Code provides[267] that where there are multiple appeals by parents who all wish for their children to attend a

---

[260] [2000] ELR 543.
[261] [2000] ELR 543, at paragraphs 14 and 17–19. An additional point was raised in that case that the appeal committee was functus officio once the decision was made and the LA was bound by a decision even in the case of mistake. The court had no difficulty in rejecting that contention on the basis that there was no question of a fresh decision being made but, by contrast, a fresh and correct expression of the decision actually made originally: see paras 9 and 10.
[262] At paras 2.12–2.13.
[263] School Admissions Code 2012, at para 2.12.
[264] School Admissions Code 2012, at para 2.12.
[265] (1991) 89 LGR 513.
[266] The School Admission Appeals Code now provides to the same effect at para 1.9. If a member is ill or otherwise unable to continue after commencement of the hearing, then the hearing should be postponed until he recovers or is able to resume the appeal. If he is not able to resume the appeal, then the appeal should be reheard.
[267] At para 2.18.

particular school, that the admissions authority should take reasonable steps to ensure that the same panel hears the appeals. If, exceptionally, this is not possible, the Code provides[268] that each panel must take its decision independently; no doubt this is because decisions can only be taken by members who heard the appeals, and then only on the basis of the evidence put forward in the appeal hearing in the presence of both parties.

5.130 Some valuable guidance was given on multiple appeals in *R v Education Appeal Committee of Leicestershire County Council ex parte Tarmohamed.*[269] Where appeals are heard together and the appeal committee concludes that prejudice to efficient education will result if more than a given number are admitted, then it may be necessary to rank the appellants in order of merit.[270] This does not mean that each parent has a right to comment on the other appellants' cases, but if comments are made and the committee feels duty bound to take account of them, it should enable the affected parent to reply in the interests of fairness.[271]

5.131 The Code is mindful of the danger of the admissions authority case changing during the course of a series of individual appeals and provides that panels must not make decisions on individual cases until they have heard all the appeals (paragraph 2.18). It provides that the appeal panel must ensure that the presenting officer does not produce new evidence in later appeals but recognises that it is possible that challenge to his evidence by an appellant might lead to new material coming out.[272] If new evidence does come out the Code provides that the clerk must ensure that the panel considers what bearing that evidence may have on all appeals. This is singularly unhelpful because no guidance is given as to what the panel should do if the evidence is relevant. It is possible, for example, that during questioning by one parent the presenting officer may give credible evidence that potentially damages the case of other parents but which, if they had an opportunity to deal with it, they might have an answer. It is submitted that in these circumstances, the interests of fairness would require the panel to reconvene earlier appeals so the parents had an opportunity of dealing with this new material.

---

[268] At para 2.18.

[269] [1997] ELR 48.

[270] [1997] ELR 48, at 59C–59E. This approach is advocated in the Admissions Code at para 4.71. Compare *R v Hackney London Borough ex parte T* [1991] COD 454. In that case the court held that staggered hearing of appeals, while constituting a blemish which meant that later appellants had a less good chance of getting a place, did not render the process unlawful. It is unlikely that the courts would now take this approach in the light of para 4.69 of the Admissions Code, which provides, in the case of multiple appeals, that no decisions should be taken until all the appeals have been heard. There is an exception if a parent wishes his case to be heard significantly later than the others; in that event, the Code suggests at para 4.69 that it might not be reasonable to hold up decisions of the majority.

[271] At 59F–60H.

[272] See para 2.19.

HUMAN RIGHTS AND ADMISSIONS

5.132 Although human rights challenges have been brought, the courts have not shown much enthusiasm for intervening on such grounds. Case-law has focused around two questions:

(a) challenges based on Article 6 of the ECHR;

(b) challenges based on Article 8 of the ECHR.

The traditional view is that the right to education is not a civil right within the meaning of Article 6 of the ECHR.[273] Even if it is such a right, it has been held that the arrangements for admissions appeals[274] do comply with Article 6 of the ECHR.[275]

5.133 In *R (on the application of the Mayor and Burgesses of the London Borough of Hounslow) v the School Admission Appeals Panel for the London Borough of Hounslow*[276] it was sought to be argued that an admissions policy which gave priority to those children who lived in nearby areas rather than those with siblings already at the school contravened Articles 8 and 14 read with Article 2 of the First Protocol to the ECHR. At first instance Kay J dismissed the challenge summarily. He was upheld, on this point, by the Court of Appeal.[277]

---

[273] See *Simpson v United Kingdom* (1989) 64 DR 188; *R v Richmond ex parte JC* [2001] ELR 21 and the discussion in Chapter 1 at para **1.16** above.

[274] The constitution of Admissions Appeal Panels is dealt with by reg 3 of, and Sch 1 to, the Education (Admissions Appeals Arrangements) (England) Regulations 2002, SI 2002/2899.

[275] *R (on the application of B) v Head Teacher of Alperton Community School and others* [2001] EWHC 229 (Admin), [2001] ELR 359 at paras 70–72. This case was heard with two exclusion appeals. One of those exclusion appeals was in due course the subject of an appeal to the Court of Appeal and was heard with two further appeals from the decisions of Scott Baker J and Turner J. That Court of Appeal decision, *S, T and P v London Borough of Brent and others* [2002] EWCA Civ 693, [2002] ELR 556, accordingly did not have an admission case before it and Newman J's decision is the relevant authority on the point. The Court of Appeal recognised there were difficulties in applying Art 6 of the ECHR to education cases but were prepared to make the assumption that it applied to an exclusion case. It went on to hold that the appeals panels were compliant with Art 6. Accordingly nothing in the Court of Appeal's decision undermines the authority of Newman J's decision at first instance.

[276] [2002] EWHC 313, [2002] ELR 402 at paras 80 and 81. In *R (on the application of South Gloucestershire LEA) v the South Gloucestershire Schools Appeal Panel* [2001] EWHC 732 (Admin), [2002] ELR 309, Stanley Burnton J held that a policy that discriminated against siblings on the basis of residence was within the scope of Art 14 of the ECHR and required objective justification. However, he refused to decide whether it was lawful because, inter alia, he had not had placed before him full material relating to that issue. Cf *R on the application of K v London Borough of Newham* [2002] EWHC 405 (Admin) 405 at para 39, [2002] ELR 390 where Collins J relied on Art 8 in connection with a sibling criterion.

[277] *R (Hounslow LBC) v School Admissions Appeals Panel for the London Borough of* [2002] EWCA Civ 900, [2002] ELR 602. The Court of Appeal held, at para 62, that although there was discrimination, the limit on infant class sizes provided the necessary objective justification. The court considered both the decision of Kay at first instance and the decision of Stanley Burnton J in *South Gloucestershire*. See also *R (on the application of Khundakji) v Admissions Appeal of Cardiff County Council* [2003] EWHC 436 (Admin), [2003] ELR 495, Richards J,

5.134 In *R (on the application of O) v St James Roman Catholic Primary School Appeal Panel*,[278] Newman J was prepared to accept that Article 8 of the ECHR and Article 2 of the First Protocol were engaged by an admission decision to a religious school, but held that they conferred no absolute right to admission. The provision of efficient education or the efficient use of resources could outweigh the Article 8 rights and the UK reservation was relevant to the rights in Article 2 of the First Protocol.[279] He further held that a school would act compatibly with Article 8 by having in its admissions policy a sibling criterion.

5.135 An Article 8 challenge was also given short shrift by the Court of Appeal in *R v Richmond ex parte JC*.[280] In that case it was sought to be argued that the failure to accede to parental preference breached Article 8 because of the health of the child and the mother. That challenge failed because the relevant evidential base was not adduced before the LA and also because the rights of other children not to have an overcrowded class was sufficient justification under Article 8.2.[281]

THE EXTENT OF THE DUTY OF APPEAL PANELS TO GIVE REASONS

5.136 Paragraph 2.24 of the School Admissions Appeals Code provides that the panel must communicate the decision in each appeal, including the reasons for that decision, in writing to the appellant, the admission authority and the LA as soon as possible after the hearing but not later than five school days later unless there is good reason.

5.137 Under the previous statutory scheme[282] the relevant duty was to communicate the decision and the 'grounds upon which it was made' in writing. There was extensive case-law on this provision[283] as to the extent of the duty therein contained. Now that the relevant duty has been cast in terms of reasons

---

where it was held that an allegation that Art 2 of the First Protocol to the ECHR would be breached because the child would be late if required to go to a school other than the preferred school added nothing to domestic law. The court held that the issue of lateness had to be considered under domestic law and nothing in the ECHR dealt specifically with it.

[278] [2001] ELR 469.

[279] [2001] ELR 469, at para 36. This case predated the coming into force of the HRA 1998 but the judge accepted the invitation by both parties to be informed in his approach by the ECHR.

[280] [2001] ELR 21.

[281] [2001] ELR 21, at paras 57, 58 and 87.

[282] See para 1(8) of Sch 2 to the Education (Admissions Appeals Arrangements)(England) Regulations 2002, SI 2022/2899 which re-enacted materially identical provisions dating back to para 9 of Sch 2 to the Education Act 1980.

[283] See paras **5.131–5.146** of the Second Edition of this book. See also *London Borough of Lambeth, R (on the application of) v Lambeth Independent Appeals Panel & Anor* [2012] EWHC 943 (Admin), where the decision of the Appeal Panel was quashed, inter alia, for failing to give adequate reasons.

rather than grounds and there is express provision in the Code as to the nature of the reasons that should be supplied, caution should be adopted in looking at this earlier case-law.

5.138   The content of the duty to give reasons is dealt with in paragraph 2.25 of the School Admission Appeals Code 2012. That provides that the decision must be easily comprehensible so that the parties can understand the basis upon which the decision was made. The paragraph goes on to provide that the letter must contain a summary of relevant factors that were raised by the parties and considered by the panel. The paragraph concludes by providing that clear reasons are to be given by the panel for this decision which must explain how any issues of fact or law raised at the hearing were resolved by them.

5.139   Paragraph 2.25 of the School Admission Appeals Code 2012 clearly provides for a higher standard of reasoning than the early case-law on the previous statutory framework required. It must now be doubtful whether, in any case standard form, decision letters will be lawful. It must also be doubtful whether a panel could lawfully omit to refer to any argument raised before it, or whether it could lawfully fail to explain what its view was on each of the points raised.

5.140   Where there is a defect in reasons it will not necessarily in itself be sufficient for the court to intervene. In *R v Governors of the Buss Foundation Camden School for Girls ex parte Lukasiewicz*,[284] the court held that even though the reasons might have been expressed differently, the failure did not undermine the decision nor flaw the decision-making process, nor was it of such materiality that the decision should be set aside. To similar effect is the decision of Morrison J in *R (on the application of L) v Independent Appeal Panel of St Edward's College*, where it was held that the letter on balance did not meet the required standard.[285] Morrison J refused relief because the complaint was more form than substance. The reasons had been elaborated upon subsequently and, had there been a letter before action, which there was not, the judge was of the view that the problem could have been cured. He also relied on the fact that, at the time of the hearing,[286] the school year was in mid-course and there was nothing to stop a re-application the following year. In *R v Birmingham City Council Education Appeals Committee ex parte B*[287] the decision was quashed for inadequacy of reasons. In that case the balance was in favour of granting relief in the exercise of the court's discretion. The boy was out of school and the court heard the case in October. There was an urgent need for him to be back at school and a real risk that the appeal panel had approached the matter incorrectly. Similarly, in *McKeown v Cardinal Heenan*

---

[284]   [1991] COD 98.
[285]   [2001] EWHC 108 (Admin), [2001] ELR 542.
[286]   6 February.
[287]   [1999] ELR 305.

High School,[288] Carnwath J quashed a decision which failed to reveal, either in its text or in evidence before the court, why the parents had lost.[289]

STANDING AND TIMING

5.141 The rights of preference conferred by section 86 of the SSFA 1998 are vested in the parent, not the child. Further, the wishes that count under section 9 of the EA 1996 are those of the parents, not the child. Considerations of this nature, in relation to what is now section 86 of the SSFA 1998, led Hutchison J to comment that it was a matter of concern if proceedings were brought in the name of the child in order to obtain legal aid: see *R v Hackney LBC ex parte T.*[290] However, despite this, in a number of subsequent cases challenges were brought by the child without any point being taken on standing.[291] In the first edition of this book it was submitted[292] that *R v Hackney LBC ex parte T* was correct and that it was an abuse of legal aid to bring judicial review proceedings in the name of the child simply to get legal aid where, as here, the relevant rights were vested in the parents and not the child.

5.142 The point was revisited by the Court of Appeal in *R v London Borough of Richmond ex parte JC.*[293] Kennedy LJ accepted that the child might have sufficient interest to mount the challenge and that in some exceptional cases it might even be appropriate for him to bring the application for judicial review, but expressed the clear view that it would normally be an abuse for an application to be brought in the name of the child simply in order to obtain legal aid and to protect the parents from costs. He held that if that device was used in the future, it might well be appropriate for judicial review to be refused on that ground. Ward LJ gave judgment to the same effect. While there has been some discussion about whether *ex parte JC* has any broader application in the education field,[294] and what material is needed before an application for permission can be refused on the grounds of abuse, it is submitted that this approach is authoritative in the admissions field and application for permission to move for judicial review should not now, in the ordinary course of events, be brought in the name of the child.

---

[288] [1998] ELR 578.

[289] The exercise of discretion is perhaps a surprising one as it was mid-way though the school year and the school was already grossly over-subscribed. Nevertheless, Carnwath J held that there was a realistic possibility of the decision being altered in the child's favour on any reconsideration.

[290] [1991] COD 454.

[291] See for example *W (A Minor) v Education Appeal Committee for Lancashire County Council* [1994] ELR 530 and *R v Lancashire ex parte M* [1994] ELR 478.

[292] At para **5.83**.

[293] [2001] ELR 21 at paras 31 and 69 per Kennedy LJ and Ward LJ. Mantell LJ agreed with Kennedy LJ and, in so far as Ward LJ was to the same effect (which he was on this point), with him as well, therefore the Court of Appeal was unanimous on this point.

[294] See paras **1.1** and **1.2** above.

5.143 Time is of the essence in challenging admissions decisions. An applicant has the dilemma of whether to challenge a decision in the courts as soon as the LA has made one, or whether to wait until the appeal panel has given its decision. If the applicant goes for judicial review before the appeal panel hears an appeal, then it might be said he should have exhausted the appeal first on the ground that it is an adequate alternative remedy. If the applicant waits until the appeal panel gives its decision, it may be too late for the court to grant effective relief, even if the challenge is well founded, because of the detriment to good administration.

5.144 Accordingly, where the ground of challenge is a point of general application affecting the admissions policy of an LA, it is sensible to challenge the policy by way of objection to the Adjudicator, or by application for judicial review if no statutory right of objection is available, as soon as possible. As is discussed generally above,[295] the panel's jurisidiction to entertain legality challenges is not at large and the panel may be unable to grant any effective relief even where it is proper for it to entertain arguments as to legality. Moreover, the appeal panels have no power to order the council to reconsider cases not the subject of appeals and it may well be that unless such cases are reconsidered, the school to which the applicant wishes to go will be full.

5.145 Where the ground of challenge does not relate to a general policy but is particular to the decision-making process in the particular case, it is probably better to appeal and then seek to challenge the decision of the appeal panel if it reproduces the error or makes one of its own.[296] Such challenges should be made promptly and it is not sufficient to bring them just within the three-month period prescribed by CPR, r 54.5. This was stressed in relation to the equivalent rule in RSC by Sedley J in *R v Appeal Committee for Brighouse School ex parte G*[297] and in *R v Education Appeal Committee of Leicestershire CC ex parte Tarmohamed.*[298]

DISCRETION

5.146 As discussed above, the court will refuse relief in the exercise of its discretion on the grounds of delay. The detriment to good administration is

---

[295] See at paras **5.86–5.91** above.
[296] In *R (on the application of M) v London Borough of Barking and Dagenham* [2002] EWHC 2483, Jack Beatson QC held that there was no undue delay while the parent was seeking to appeal against a decision of an admissions authority, but that thereafter there was a particular need for promptness: see para 75. As the claimant did not move to challenge until just before expiry of the three months from the appeal decision, he held that, in that case, there was undue delay and refused relief on the ground of detriment to good administration.
[297] [1997] ELR 39 at 47B–47C.
[298] [1997] ELR 48 at 61B–61D. To similar effect, see *R v Education Appeal Committee of Blackpool Borough Council ex parte Taylor* [1999] ELR 237 at 240F–241B. While the judge in that case did not express a concluded view, he indicated that delay caused by inviting the intervention of the Secretary of State and the Local Government Ombudsman, neither of whom had power to set aside the decision under challenge, could not excuse the need to apply for judicial review promptly.

always a problem where the challenge affects large numbers of children and to grant certiorari would require the LA to go through the whole admissions process again. Where that is the case, the courts are unlikely to grant any more than declaratory relief: see *R v Bromley LBC ex parte C.*[299] Even where only one child has been the victim of illegality, to grant relief may be detrimental to good administration if the school in question has a long waiting list and a high demand for places.[300]

SCHOOL ATTENDANCE ORDERS

5.147 By virtue of section 437 of the EA 1996, if it appears to the LA that a child of compulsory school age in its area is not receiving suitable education, either by regular attendance at school, or otherwise, the LA is obliged to serve a notice on the parent requiring him, in not less than 15 days, to satisfy the LA that the child is receiving such appropriate education. If the LA is not so satisfied and considers it expedient that the child should attend school, it is obliged to serve a school attendance order on the parent. The parents are given a degree of choice as to the school named in the order by virtue of section 438 of the EA 1996 and can get the named school changed subsequently under section 440.

5.148 For a child with a statement of SEN, the school named in the school attendance order is to be the school in the statement if there is one, by virtue of section 441(2). If the statement does not name a school, it is to be amended and then that named school is to appear in the school attendance order: see section 441(3). The order is to be changed when the statement changes, by virtue of section 441(4).

5.149 The parent can apply for the school attendance order to be revoked on the ground that suitable arrangements have been made for the child to receive suitable education otherwise than at school.[301] If the LA is satisfied as to this, it must comply with the request.[302] If it is not satisfied, the parent can take the matter up with the Secretary of State, who can give such direction as he thinks fit.[303] If the child is the subject of a statement naming a school, the parent cannot apply for the school attendance order to be revoked on these grounds.[304] If the statement does not name a school, the Secretary of State's power of direction is limited to directing an amendment of the statement.[305]

---

[299] [1992] 1 FLR 174.

[300] *R v Gateway Primary School Governors ex parte X* [2001] ELR 321. In that case the child was unlawfully deleted from the admissions register. Moses J held that there was good reason for delay while an appeal was being lodged and decided but not thereafter. He held that there would be a detriment to good administration in allowing the child to jump the queue in the long waiting list or to be admitted, which would increase the class size above the limit of 30.

[301] EA 1996, s 442(2).

[302] EA 1996, s 442(2).

[303] EA 1996, s 442(3).

[304] EA 1996, s 442(5)(a).

[305] EA 1996, s 442(5)(b).

5.150 It is an offence to fail to comply with an attendance order unless the parent proves that he is causing the child to receive suitable education otherwise than at school: see section 443(1) of the EA 1996.[306] The burden is also on the parent to prove that the child is not of compulsory school age.[307] If the parent is acquitted, the court can order that the school attendance order should cease to have effect, but this does not absolve the LA of its duty to take further action under section 437 if it considers, having regard to any change of circumstances, that it is expedient to do so.[308] Only the LA can commence proceedings for this offence[309] (see section 446), but before doing so it should consider (under section 447) whether it is appropriate to apply for an education supervision order as an alternative or additional step. A direction to apply for a supervision order is also in the range of sanctions of the court (see section 447(2)), but the LA can decide not to apply for one, albeit it must inform the court and give its reasons under section 447(3).

5.151 It has been held that it is not appropriate to seek to enforce a school attendance order by making the child a ward of court: see *Re Baker.*[310]

5.152 It is open to debate whether the reverse onus of proof provisions in section 443(1) of the EA 1996 comply with Article 6(2) of the ECHR. Here, the offence is not one of strict liability but one where a burden of proof is expressly placed on the accused. A burden of proof on the accused is legitimate, provided that it is kept within reasonable limits which take into account the importance of what is at stake and that it maintains the rights of the defence.[311] As such, the courts would have to investigate whether the provision pursued a legitimate aim and was proportionate. The facts which the parent has to prove, ie, that the child is receiving suitable education, are particularly within the parent's knowledge and that is a relevant matter.[312] The aim is legitimate[313] and the means proportionate. That was the conclusion of the Irish Supreme Court in relation to a similar offence in Ireland in *Best v Attorney General*.[314] It is submitted that that decision would be followed in England.

---

[306] In *Oxfordshire County Council v JL* [2010] EWHC 798, the court held that this was neither unjust nor a violation of the ECHR.

[307] EA 1996, s 445.

[308] EA 1996, s 443(3).

[309] This also applies to the offence under s 444 which is considered below.

[310] [1961] 3 All ER 276, CA.

[311] *Salabiaku v France* (1988) 13 EHRR 379 at para 28. For discussion of this topic generally see, for example, Clayton and Tomlinson *The Law of Human Rights*, (Oxford University Press, 2009) at paras 11.259–11.261; *Sheldrake v DPP* [2005] 1 AC 264, *R v Keogh* [2007] 1 WLR 1500 CA, *DPP v Wright* [2009] EWHC 105 (Admin).

[312] *R v Davies* [2002] EWCA Crim 2949, [2003] ICR 586.

[313] *Barnfather v LB Islington* [2003] EWHC 418 (Admin), [2003] 1 WLR 2318. The court was split on whether the offence under s 444 was proportionate not on whether the aim it pursued was legitimate: see paras 30–32 and 50–52. Elias J specifically adverted to a reasonable and proportionate approach, which would have been to have a reverse burden of proof rather than strict liability. Permission to appeal to the HL was refused.

[314] [1999] IESC 90.

Challenging school attendance orders

5.153 As we have seen, breach of a school attendance order is a criminal offence. Should a parent seek to challenge the validity of a school attendance order by way of an application for judicial review or will he be able to take *vires* points by way of defence to the criminal proceedings? This raises the problem of collateral challenge in public law.[315] In *Phillips v Brown*,[316] the Divisional Court on appeal by way of case stated from a conviction for failure to comply with a school attendance order under what was then section 37 of the Education Act 1980, held that it was appropriate for the justices to inquire whether it could reasonably appear to the LA that the parent was in breach of the duty to cause the child to receive efficient full-time education suitable to his age, ability and aptitude. The court made clear that the justices would be concerned with the essentially public law issue of whether the LA had directed itself correctly on relevant matters and could reasonably have decided that it appeared the parents were in breach of duty; but that, in the absence of the parents providing information that the child was receiving education in response to a request for information prior to the institution of the school attendance procedure, it could very easily be concluded that the parents were in breach of duty and it was open to the LA to reach this conclusion. The court indicated that while this *vires* issue was open, parents would be well advised to concentrate on the defence on the merits, under what was then section 37(5), that the child was receiving efficient full-time education suitable to his age, ability and aptitude otherwise than at school.

5.154 The law on enforcement notice prosecutions in the planning field might seem to be at odds with this. In *R v Wicks*[317] it was held by the House of Lords that it was not open to a defendant to seek to challenge the decision to issue an enforcement notice which was valid on its face. Their Lordships held expressly that no generalisation was possible and that all depended on the true construction of the relevant Acts of Parliament.[318] By contrast, *Boddington v British Transport Police*[319] does seem to allow a general rule that, on a prosecution for a criminal charge, a defendant will be allowed to raise all grounds of invalidity available to him. In that well-known case, the defendant, who was prosecuted for smoking in breach of a byelaw, was allowed to contend[320] that the byelaw was invalid.[321]

---

[315] As to this generally see De Smith, Woolf and Jowell *Judicial Review of Administrative Action* (op cit) at 5-049–5-077; *Wade on Administrative Law* (Oxford University Press, 8th edn, 2000) at 287–294; Lewis *Judicial Remedies in Public Law* (Sweet & Maxwell, 2nd edn, 2000) at paras 3-042–3-5057.

[316] (Unreported) 20 June 1980. See Peter M Liell (ed) *The Law of Education* (Butterworths, 9th edn) at F 412.

[317] [1997] 2 WLR 876.

[318] [1998] 2 AC 92.

[319] [1999] 2 AC 143.

[320] Unsuccessfully, as it turned out.

[321] See also *R v Reading Crown Court ex parte Hutchinson* [1988] QB 384.

5.155 Although section 37 of the Education Act 1944 was different from section 437 of the EA 1996, the basic structure of various facts having to appear to the LA before it could proceed to serve an attendance order was the same.

5.156 It is unclear whether the courts would now follow the approach in *Phillips v Brown* in relation to the initial decision to commence a school attendance order process, as distinct from any other point going to the validity of the school attendance order. The decision to start proceedings for the service of a school attendance order is not unlike the decision to institute trespass proceedings in *Avon County Council v Buscott*,[322] where it was held that a challenge to the decision to issue proceedings was not a defence and had to be raised by way of application for judicial review. That decision is to be contrasted with that of the High Court in *Postermobile plc v Brent London Borough Council*,[323] where the court allowed an appeal by way of case stated in circumstances where it was unfair for the local authority to bring proceedings. It is submitted that the courts are now more likely to let all points relating to invalidity to be taken by way of defence on a prosecution, including those relating to the decision to prosecute.

Parent's offence for non-attendance of child at school where registered pupil

5.157 It is also an offence under section 444(1) of the EA 1996 if a child of compulsory school age does not attend regularly the school at which he is a registered pupil. This offence is not dependent on there being a school attendance order. The offence is committed by the parent. Section 444(3) provides that the child (if not a boarder) shall not be taken to have failed to attend regularly by reason of his absence if it was:

(a)   with leave;

(b)   [repealed]; or

(c)   on a day exclusively set aside for religious observance by the religious body to which his parent belonged.

5.158 Section 444(2A)–(6) has further defences (in relation to non-boarders). Under section 444(2A) the child is not to be taken to have failed to attend the school at which he is registered regularly by reason of his absence at any time if the parent proves[324] that at that time the child was prevented from attending by reason of sickness or unavoidable cause. Under section 444(3B) where the child's home is in England it is a defence if the parent proves that the LA is in breach of its transport duties under section 508B(1) or 508E(2)(c) of the EA

---

[322]   [1988] QB 656.
[323]   (1997) *The Times*, 8 December.
[324]   As to the validity of such burden of proof issues having regard to Art 6(2) of the ECHR see para **5.152** above.

1996. There is a similar defence for children whose home is in Wales under the equivalent Welsh measures.[325] Under section 444(3D) where the school is an independent school that is not a qualifying school the child shall not be taken to have failed to attend regularly at the school if the parent proves that the school is not within walking distance[326] of the child's home, that no suitable arrangements have been made by the LA for boarding accommodation for him at or near the school and that no suitable arrangements have been made for him to become a registered pupil at a school nearer to his home. Under section 444(6) if a child has no fixed abode, then the transport related defences in subsections (3B), (3D) and (4) do not apply. There is a defence for such a child if the parent proves that he is engaged in a trade or business of such a nature as to require him to travel from place to place, the child has attended at a school as regularly as the nature of that trade or business requires and the child has attained the age of six and has made at least 200 attendances during the period of 12 months ending with the date on which the proceedings were instituted.

5.159   For boarders, the only defence is sickness or unavoidable cause if the child is absent without leave: see sections 444(2) and (7). The offence under section 444(1) is punishable on summary conviction by a fine not exceeding level 3 on the standard scale: section 444(8).

5.160   A new and more serious offence was created by the Criminal Justice and Court Services Act 2000 in relation to offences committed after 1 March 2001. That Act inserted new subsections (1A), (8A) and (8B) into section 444. This new offence is punishable on summary conviction by a fine at level 4 or three months' imprisonment or both.[327] Further, if, on trial for the offence under section 444(1A), the defendant is found not guilty of that offence, the court can find him guilty of the offence under section 444(1). The new offence under section 444(1A) imports both mens rea and fault. The parent must know the child is failing to attend regularly and, in addition, must fail to cause him to do so.

5.161   A child fails to attend regularly if he fails to attend at the times prescribed by the LA.[328] Further, if the child does attend, but is in breach of the school's disciplinary code as to dress so that he is sent back home, the offence is still committed: see *Spiers v Warrington Corporation*.[329] The offence is absolute and there is no defence that the parent did not know of the child's

---

[325]   See s 444(3F) and (4).
[326]   Walking distance is defined by s 444(5) as two miles for a child under eight and three miles for a child who has attained the age of eight.
[327]   EA 1996, s 444(8A).
[328]   *Hinchley v Rankin* 59 LGR 190.
[329]   [1954] 1 QB 61. But this does not apply if the school uniform policy is unlawful: *Watkins-Singh, R (on the application of) v The Governing Body of Aberdare Girls' High School & Anor* [2008] EWHC 1865 (Admin).

absence.[330] It is equally no defence that the child had left home shortly before her sixteenth birthday and the parent did not know where she was.[331]

5.162 The courts held that the defence of unavoidable cause in what was section 444(3)(b), and is now section 444(2A), does not cover matters of conscience. Accordingly, where a parent refused to send her children to school because she objected to corporal punishment, the offence was committed.[332] Further it is very doubtful that it is a defence under section 444(1) that the parent acted under duress from the child.[333] The unavoidable cause must be that of the child and it is not sufficient to make out the defence that the parent has done all she reasonably can to secure the attendance of the child at school.[334]

5.163 In Scotland it has been held that the equivalent offence under section 35(1) read with section 42 of the Education (Scotland) Act 1980 contravened the ECHR and, in particular, Article 6(2) thereof by its failure to provide any defence 'arising out of [the parent's] practical innocence, whether based on force majeure, reasonable diligence or the like'.[335] In that case the court relied[336] on section 3 of the HRA 1998 to interpret the offence as permitting a wide defence of reasonable excuse contrary to earlier pre-HRA 1998 case-law[337] which would have been otherwise binding on the court. The approach in Scotland approach has not, ultimately, commanded acceptance in England. At first, in *Helmsley v West Sussex County Council*,[338] Judge Barrett QC and justices accepted section 444(1) was inconsistent with Article 6(2) of the ECHR and read into the offence a fault requirement, but in *Barnfather v London Borough of Islington*,[339] the Divisional Court held that Article 6(2) was simply not engaged. The court was divided on the question, which did not then arise, whether the strict liability offence it created was contained within reasonable limits and was proportionate. It is respectfully submitted that the Divisional Court was correct to conclude that Article 6(2) of the ECHR was not engaged for the reasons they gave. On the question of justification, it is respectfully submitted that, had the issue arisen, the judgment of Elias J is to be preferred to that of Maurice Kay J.

---

[330] *Crump v Gilmore* (1969) 68 LGR 56.
[331] *Bath and North East Somerset District Council v Jennifer Warman* [1999] ELR 81, DC.
[332] *Jarman v Mid Glamorgan Education Authority* (1985) *The Times*, 11 February.
[333] *Hampshire County Council v E* [2007] EWHC 2584 (Admin), [2008] ELR 260.
[334] *Jenkins v Howells* [1949] 2 KB 218, *R(R) v Leeds Magistrates' Court* [2005] EWHC 1479, *London Borough of Islington v D* [2011] EWHC 990(Admin).
[335] *John O'Hagan, Director of Administration, North Lanarkshire Council v Lorraine Rea* [2001] Scots SC1 at para 8.
[336] *John O'Hagan, Director of Administration, North Lanarkshire Council v Lorraine Rea* [2001] Scots SC1, at paras 13 and 14.
[337] *Kiley v Lunn* 1982 SCCR 436 and *McIntyre v Annan* 1991 SCCR 465. This is to the same effect as the English case-law: see *Jenkins v Howells* [1949] 2 KB 218; *Spiers v Warrington Corporation* [1954] 1 QB 61; *Crump v Gilmore* (1969) 68 LGR 56; *Bath and North East Somerset District Council v Jennifer Warman* [1999] ELR 81, DC; and *Barnfather v London Borough of Islington* [2003] EWHC 418 (Admin), [2003] 1 WLR 2318 at para 7.
[338] (Unreported) 12 September 2001.
[339] [2003] EWHC 418 (Admin), DC.

POWER OF LA TO DIRECT ADMISSION TO SCHOOL

5.164   Under section 96 of the SSFA 1998, the LA can direct the governing body of a school, which is the admissions authority for the school, to admit a child where the child in question has been refused admission to, or permanently excluded from, every suitable school within a reasonable distance of the child's home. Any direction given must specify a school which is a reasonable distance from the child's home and from which the child is not permanently excluded.[340] A direction, unless it is given on the determination of the Adjudicator appointed by the Secretary of State[341] under section 97(4) of the SSFA 1998, must specify a school in the LA area.[342] While this provision prevents one LA seeking to export problem children to another LA area, it has the consequence, in the absence of a direction from the Adjudicator appointed by the Secretary of State, that a school which is within a reasonable travelling distance of the child's home and which is both suitable for the child and with available capacity cannot be specified in an LA direction. No direction can be made specifying a school that selects by reference to ability unless the child satisfies the selection criteria: section 96(3A).

5.165   A direction cannot specify a school if admission to that school would prejudice efficient education or the efficient use of resources[343] by reason of measures required to be taken to ensure compliance with the limits on infant class sizes. If a direction is made, the governing body is obliged to admit the child to the school, although this does not affect its ability to exclude from the school a pupil who is already registered there.[344]

5.166   Section 97 of the SSFA 1998 deals with the procedure for making a direction under section 96. Before making the direction the LA is obliged to consult both the parent of the child and the governing body of the school it is proposed to specify in the direction.[345] The next stage is for the LA to make a decision as to whether to make the proposed direction. If it so decides, it must then give notice in writing of its decision to the governing body and the headteacher of the school. It cannot make the direction until at least the 15-day period for referral to the appropriate authority[346] has expired.[347] If the matter is not referred to the appropriate authority within that period, the LA can make the direction. If the matter has been referred to the appropriate authority, the LA cannot make a direction until the appropriate authority has made a decision.

---

[340]   SSFA 1998, s 96(2).
[341]   For Wales the decision maker is the Assembly.
[342]   SSFA 1998, s 96(3).
[343]   SSFA 1998, s 96(4) and s 86(3)(a) and (4).
[344]   SSFA 1998, s 96(5) and (6).
[345]   SSFA 1998, s 97(1).
[346]   Defined by s 49(6A) of the Education and Inspections Act 2006 as the Adjudicator in relation to LAs in England and the Assembly in relation to local authorities in Wales.
[347]   SSFA 1998, s 97(2)(b) and 97(3).

5.167 The statutory procedures do not provide for the appropriate authority to consult anyone prior to making his decision. While there is an argument that he is not under a duty to consult in the light of the express duty on the LA to consult in section 97(1), it is unlikely that the courts would accede to this argument. It is probable that the courts would hold that the interests of fairness do oblige the appropriate authority to elicit all relevant views (including those of the LA proposing to make the direction) before making a direction. Not only would there be obvious unfairness in the appropriate authority making a direction without consulting affected persons, but there is a real risk that he would not have all the relevant information if he did so. In this context, it is to be noted that the appropriate authority is not constrained to specify a school in the LA area.[348] He would not, therefore, have before him in the papers submitted by the governing body for the school which the LA was proposing to specify, all relevant information as to an out-of-area school that he then proposed to specify.

5.168 The appropriate authority has a similar constraint to the LA in relation to specifying a school where the effect would be to breach the requirements on infant class sizes.[349] Once the appropriate authority has made a decision, if the LA is the admissions authority for the school to which he has determined the child should go, the LA must admit the child to that school and give notice in writing of the appropriate authority's determination to the governing body and headteacher of that school.[350] If the LA is not the admissions authority for the school concerned, it must specify the school in question in its direction.[351] A direction under section 96 is to be given in writing and the LA is to give a copy of the notice to the headteacher of the school.[352] LAs in England can give a similar direction in respect of looked after children, under section 97A.

OTHER POWERS OF THE SECRETARY OF STATE IN RELATION TO ADMISSION

5.169 In addition to the powers of the Secretary of State under section 97 of the SSFA 1998, he enjoys his general powers under what used to be sections 68 and 99 of the Education Act 1944.[353] The ability to intervene under these powers is not confined to admissions decisions and applies generally in the education field. The discussion here is accordingly of general application. Section 496 entitles the Secretary of State to intervene if he is satisfied that an LA or governing body of a state school is acting or proposing to act unreasonably. The Secretary of State does not need to have a complaint to

---

[348] SSFA 1998, s 96(3) assumes the Secretary of State's powers under s 97(4) are not so constrained.
[349] SSFA 1998, s 97(5).
[350] SSFA 1998, s 97(4)(a).
[351] SSFA 1998, s 97(4)(b).
[352] SSFA 1998, s 97(6).
[353] See now the EA 1996, ss 496 and 497.

exercise his power. If the Secretary of State is satisfied that a body is acting unreasonably he can give such directions as appear to him expedient.

5.170 The scope of this power of intervention, when it was contained in section 68 of the Education Act 1944, was considered in the famous case of *Secretary of State for Education and Science v Tameside Metropolitan Borough Council.*[354] In that case, the Secretary of State had approved proposals that the LA schools should go comprehensive in September 1976. In May 1976 there was a change of control in the LA from Labour to the Conservatives and the Conservatives were opposed to turning the grammar schools into comprehensive schools. They so informed the Secretary of State on 7 June 1976. This led to the Secretary of State issuing a direction on 11 June 1976 under what was then section 68, directing the LA to implement the approved proposals by November 1977 and to implement the previous arrangements for non-selective allocation of school places. Her application for *mandamus* to enforce the direction failed. It was held that in order to intervene, the Secretary of State had to be satisfied that no reasonable authority could have taken the view it did after he had taken reasonable steps to acquaint himself with the relevant information.[355] It was not sufficient that the Secretary of State disagreed with the policy of the LA.

5.171 Section 497 of the Education Act 1996 enables the Secretary of State to intervene when he is satisfied that the public body to which the section applies is in default of any duty imposed on it by, or for the purposes of, the Act. The bodies are the same bodies as are covered by section 496. There has been litigation as to the extent to which the powers of intervention of the Secretary of State under what are now sections 496 and 497 exclude the right to apply for judicial review.

5.172 The Secretary of State has a discretion to issue a direction under section 497 of the EA 1996 when a body to which that section applies[356] is failing to discharge any duty imposed upon it. It has been confirmed by the courts that this is indeed a discretion and the Secretary of State is entitled to take account of the fact that a child has a place at another school when deciding whether or not to maintain a direction that the child be admitted to a school of choice.[357] While the Secretary of State has to take into account parental preference under section 9 of the EA 1996, he is also under a duty to take into account the best interests of the child and if the school of choice were refusing to teach the child that was a relevant matter for him to take into account.

---

[354]   [1977] AC 1014.

[355]   [1977] AC 1014, at 1064H–1065B per Lord Diplock.

[356]   The bodies to which the section applies are LAs and governing bodies of community, foundation or voluntary schools or governing bodies of community or foundation special schools: EA 1996, s 497(2).

[357]   *R v Secretary of State for Education and Employment ex parte W* [1998] ELR 413 at 421E–422E. The Secretary of State has express power to revoke directions he has previously given under s 570 of the EA 1996 and it was his revocation which was sought to be challenged, unsuccessfully, in that case.

5.173 The Secretary of State has further general direction-making powers to secure the proper performance of LA functions under sections 497A, 497AA and 497B of the EA 1996.

5.174 Section 497A[358] enables the Secretary of State to intervene if he is satisfied that the LA are failing to perform any function to which the section applies either at all or to an adequate standard.[359] It accordingly prescribes a lower threshold for intervention than sections 496 or 497 of the EA 1996. The section applies to all the education functions of the LA.[360] The Secretary of State has power to direct that the function in question be performed on behalf of the LA by a third party, and may require the LA to enter into a contract or other arrangement with that third party containing such terms as he may specify in the direction.[361] He can also direct that the function be performed by the Secretary of State or a person nominated by him[362] and that the LA shall comply with any instructions of the Secretary of State or his nominee in relation to the exercise of the function. He can give such other directions as he thinks expedient for the purpose of securing that the function in question is performed to an adequate standard. The powers are exercisable simply on the Secretary of State being satisfied as to inadequate performance. That can be by way of complaint, but does not need to be, although the Secretary of State would, by analogy with *Tameside*, have to take reasonable steps to inform himself of relevant matters. Where he is contemplating exercise of his functions he has to notify the LA who are then under a duty to give him such assistance as they are reasonably able to give.[363] The Secretary of State is also under a common law duty to behave fairly: see *R (Shoesmith) v OFSTED and others*.[364] In that case it was held by the Court of Appeal that the Secretary of State had adopted an intrinsically unfair procedure before exercising his power to, in effect, replace the Director of Children's Services.[365] In those circumstances fairness required that the existing incumbent had a fair opportunity to put her case as to why she should not be replaced. There is no reason to limit the duty of fairness which the Court of Appeal found breached in that case to situations analogous to dismissal. Judicial review of the exercise of these powers on substantive grounds is unlikely to be easy in view of their width.

5.175 Section 497B contains the necessary consequential provisions to ensure that directions under section 497A are effective. In addition, to various specific duties on the LA to assist any person the Secretary of State specifies in a

---

[358] As amended by s 60 of the EA 2002 and applies to England. Section 497A as inserted by s 8 of the SSFA 1998 continues to apply to Wales.

[359] Section 497A(2). He can also exercise his powers under s 497A(4), (4A) or (4B) where he has previously given the LA a direction under those subsections and he is satisfied that, if no further direction was given under those subsections, the LA would fail to perform the relevant function either at all or to the requisite standard: s 497A(2A).

[360] EA 1996, s 497A(1).

[361] EA 1996, at s 497A(4).

[362] EA 1996, at s 497A(4A).

[363] EA 1996, s 497AA.

[364] [2011] EWCA Civ 642.

[365] See at para 67.

direction, such as providing access and relevant documents, there is a general duty on the LA to give the specified person every such assistance with the performance of the specified function or functions as it is reasonably able to give.[366]

5.176 The old law on what are now sections 496 and 497 of the EA 1996 was that these sections, in certain cases, excluded the power to apply to the court: see *Watt v Kesteven*[367] and *Cummings v Birkenhead*.[368] It is unlikely now that the courts would analyse these sections, or sections 497A to 497B, in the same way when considering whether the right to apply for judicial review is limited or excluded.[369] Instead, they would look at whether these default powers are an adequate alternative remedy in the same way as they consider whether an appeal should be pursued rather than an application made for judicial review. Certainly, as we have already seen above, in the admissions context the courts have not failed to intervene to quash either an unlawful policy or an unlawful admissions decision on the ground that application should instead have been made to the Secretary of State.

THE DUTY TO GIVE INFORMATION

5.177 By virtue of section 92 of the SSFA 1998[370] regulations may:

(a) require the publication by the LA of such information relating to admissions as may be prescribed;

(b) require the publication by the governing body of a foundation or a voluntary-aided school of such information relating to admissions as may be prescribed;

(c) require or allow the publication by the governing body of any school maintained by an LA, or by the LA on behalf of the governing body, of such information relating to the school as may be prescribed;

(d) make provision as to the time by which, and the manner in which, information required to be published under these provisions is to be published.

---

[366] EA 1996, at s 497B(4).

[367] [1955] QB 408.

[368] [1972] Ch 12 at 38A–38D and 39B.

[369] It is not in dispute that in analysing whether breach of s 8 of the Education Act 1944, now s 14 of the EA 1996, gave rise to a private law right of action whether for breach of a duty of care or breach of statutory duty the courts have placed reliance on the ministers default powers under what are now ss 496 and 497 of the EA 1996: see *X v Bedfordshire* [1995] ELR 404 at 454G. Whether a private law right of action exists does not have any bearing on the question whether judicial review for breach of public law duties is available and it is submitted it is.

[370] As substituted by the Education and Skills Act 2008, s 169, Sch 1, Pt 2, paras 53 and 65.

The relevant regulations for England were the Education (School Information) (England) Regulations 2008.[371] For Wales they are the School Information (Wales) Regulations 2011.[372] They are detailed and only an outline of the relevant provisions are dealt with here. There are three relevant Schedules to both the English and Welsh regulations.

5.178 Regulation 5(1) and Schedule 2 of the English regulations[373] prescribed the general information that the LA must publish in a composite prospectus; the information covers a range of issues in addition to admissions (such as transport strategy).[374] The composite prospectus must be published no later than 12 September each year: (i) on the local authority's website, and (ii) by making copies available to parents on request.[375]

5.179 Regulation 5, read with Schedule 2 of the English regulations, concerns the publication of admissions related information. The relevant information is that specified in Part 1, paragraphs (2), (3) and (7), and Part 2, paragraphs 12–16 of Schedule 2.[376] Those paragraphs provide that the information to be provided is as to the admissions policy for the school; the number of places for pupils of the normal age of entry to the school which were available at the start of the year immediately following the reporting school year;[377] and any objections that have been made in respect of admission arrangements.

5.180 Under paragraph 2 of Part 1 of Schedule 2 of the English regulations the composite prospectus had to include an explanation of the stages in the process of applying for a school place including:

(a)   how to apply, including how to apply on-line, and by what date;

(b)   when offers of places will be communicated to parents;

---

[371]   SI 2008/3089. The regulations were primarily consolidating Regulations which revoked and re-enact, the Education (School Information) (England) Regulations 2002 and two sets of amending Regulations, with some changes. They were in turn largely revoked by SI 2012/8 but continued to have effect for the academic years 2011/2012 and 2012/2013. The School Information (England)(Amendment) Regulations 2012, SI 2012/1124 replaced the duty to publish an annual prospectus with a duty to publish relevant information on the school website.

[372]   SI 2011/1944.

[373]   The equivalent provisions in the Welsh regulations are reg 4 and also Sch 2.

[374]   For the information that has to be published on the School Website from 1 September 2012 see para 2(5) of the School Information (England) (Amendment) Regulations 2012, SI 2012/1124 which inserts a new Sch 4 to the revoked 2008 regulations.

[375]   Regulations 5(1) and 6(1) of the English Regulations. By virtue of reg 5(1) of the Welsh regulations the composite prospectus must be published before 1 October in the publication school years and not later than six weeks before the date up to which parents may express a preference for a school in respect of the admission school year.

[376]   The provisions of the Welsh Schedule 2 are similar, but not identical.

[377]   'Reporting school year' is defined in reg 3 as the school year immediately preceding the 'publication school year'. 'Publication school year' means the school year immediately preceding the 'admission school year'. 'Admission school year' means a school year at the beginning of which pupils are to be admitted to any school.

(c) when appeals will be heard; and

(d) how applications made otherwise than in the course of a normal admission round would be dealt with.

5.181 Regulation 8 and Schedule 3 of the English regulations[378] were concerned with publication of non-admissions related information, and in relation to that, changes decided upon but not yet implemented.

5.182 That information was to be published during the offer year, and no later than six weeks before the date up to which parents may express a preference for a school.[379] Regulation 9 set out the manner of publication.

5.183 Failure to publish the required information would attract either the Secretary of State's intervention under his general default powers in sections 496 and 497 of the EA 1996 or the sanction of judicial review. It is unlikely, however, that each information failure would flaw subsequent admissions decisions. The consequences must depend on the nature of the breach and the effect, if any, it had on the subsequent decision of the LA or the admissions appeal panel.

5.184 In *R v Stockton on Tees BC ex parte W*[380] it was sought to be argued that an admissions decision was flawed by the failure under the then extant regulations[381] to publish the school admissions arrangements for parents moving into the area and to supply a map of the school catchment area. The Court of Appeal held that there had been no illegality and did not go on to consider what the effect of such illegality would have been on the admissions decisions.

---

[378] Schedule 3 of the Welsh regulations is different.
[379] Regulation 8(2).
[380] [2000] ELR 93.
[381] Education (School Information) (England) Regulations 1994, SI 1994/1421.

Chapter 6

SCHOOL DISCIPLINE AND EXCLUSIONS

DISCIPLINE

6.1 It is the responsibility of the governing body of a relevant school[1] in England and Wales to ensure that, on the part of its pupils, policies designed to promote good behaviour and discipline are pursued at the school.[2] In particular, section 88(2) of the Education and Inspections Act 2006 (EIA 2006) requires the governing body to make, and from time to time review, a written statement of general principles to promote good behaviour and discipline.[3] The headteacher must have regard to this written statement in determining measures under section 89(1) of the EIA 2006 to be taken with a view to promoting among pupils self-discipline and proper regard for authority, encouraging good behaviour and respect for others on the part of pupils and in particular preventing all forms of bullying among pupils, securing that the standard of behaviour of pupils is acceptable, securing that pupils complete any tasks reasonably assigned to them in connection with their education and otherwise regulating the conduct of pupils. Those measures can include the making of rules and provision for disciplinary penalties as defined by section 90 of the EIA 2006. They may also, to such extent as is reasonable, include measures to be taken with a view to regulating the conduct of pupils at a time when they are not on the premises of the school and are not under the lawful control or charge of a member of the staff of the school under section 89(5) of the EIA 2006.

6.2 Where the governing body considers that it is desirable that any particular measures should be determined by the headteacher, or that he should have regard to any particular matters, the governors are to notify him of those measures or matters and may give him such guidance as they consider appropriate.[4] In exercising their functions under section 88(2) the governors are to have regard to any guidance given by the Secretary of State in relation to England and by the Welsh Assembly in relation to Wales.[5]

---

[1] Relevant school means a community, foundation or voluntary school, a community or foundation special school, a maintained nursery school, a pupil referral unit or a school approved by the Secretary of State under s 342 of the EA 1996: s 88(5) of the EIA 2006.

[2] EIA 2006, s 88(1).

[3] EIA 2006, s 88(2). This requirement was previously contained in s 61(2)(a) of the SSFA 1998, which was repealed by the EIA 2006.

[4] EIA 2006, s 88(2)(b).

[5] EIA 2006, s 88(4).

6.3   Before the governors make or revise the statement required by section 88(2)(a) of the EIA 2006, they are obliged to consult, in such manner as appears to them to be appropriate, the headteacher and parents of pupils registered at the school as well as such other persons who work at the school, whether or not for payment, as it appears to the governing body to be appropriate to consult.[6]

6.4   The headteacher of a relevant school, in determining what measures shall be taken for, inter alia, promoting self-discipline and proper regard for authority among pupils under section 89 of the EIA 2006, is to act in accordance with the current statement made by the governors under section 88(2)(a) and to have regard to any notification or guidance given to him under section 88(2)(b).[7] The standard of behaviour which is to be regarded as acceptable at the school is to be determined by the headteacher in so far as it is not determined by the governors.[8] The measures determined by the headteacher under section 89 are to be publicised by him in the form of a written document and are to be made generally known within the school and to parents of pupils registered at the school.[9] In addition, the headteacher is obliged at least once in every school year to take steps to bring the measures to the attention of all pupils and parents and all persons who work at the school (whether or not for payment).[10]

6.5   The disciplinary measures adopted by the headteacher of a school in England pursuant to section 89(1) must identify the items for which a search may be made.[11] In England, searches may be carried out in certain circumstances by the headteacher or any member of staff authorised by the headteacher.[12] There is a similar but less widely drawn power to search pupils in Wales.[13]

6.6   The local authority (LA) has a reserve power in certain circumstances to prevent a breakdown of discipline at a maintained school[14] under section 62 of the School Standards and Framework Act 1998 (SSFA 1998). It can take steps either to prevent the breakdown or to end continuing breakdown of discipline

---

6   EIA 2006, s 88(3).
7   EIA 2006, s 89(2)–(2A). In relation to a school in Wales, the headteacher must also require pupils to comply with the travel behaviour code made by the Welsh Ministers under s 12 of the Learner Travel (Wales) Measure 2008: EIA 2006, s 89(2A)(c).
8   EIA 2006, s 89(3)–(3A). In relation to a school in Wales, the standard of behaviour which is to be regarded as acceptable may also be determined by the Welsh Ministers: EIA 2006, s 89(3A)(c).
9   EIA 2006, s 89(6)(a).
10   EIA 2006, s 89(6)(b).
11   EIA 2006, s 89(4A) (inserted by the EA 2011 with effect from 1 April 2012).
12   EA 1996, ss 550ZA–550ZD (inserted by the Apprenticeships, Skills, Children and Learning Act 2009 with effect from 1 September 2010) (as amended by the EA 2011 from 1 April 2012: see SI 2012/924. The power to search pupils in England was previously found in the EA 1996, s 550AA.
13   EA 1996, s 550AA (inserted by the Violent Crime Reduction Act 2006 with effect in Wales from 31 October 2010).
14   Maintained school includes a maintained nursery school: SSFA 1998, s 62(5).

at the school, including the giving of any direction to the governing body or headteacher.[15] The LA can only take such steps in certain circumstances. The first[16] is that, in the opinion of the authority, the behaviour of registered pupils at the school or any action taken by such pupils or their parents is such that the education of any registered pupils at the school is (or is likely in the immediate future to become) severely prejudiced and that the governing body has been informed in writing of the authority's opinion.

6.7 The second category of case[17] is where the LA has given a warning notice,[18] referring to the safety of pupils or staff at the school being threatened by a breakdown of discipline at the school, the governing body have failed to comply, or secure compliance with the notice to the authority's satisfaction within the compliance period, and the LA has given reasonable notice that it proposes to exercise its powers under section 62(1), whether or not in conjunction with their other powers.[19]

6.8 In relation to maintained schools in Wales,[20] the Welsh Assembly has power under section 127 of the SSFA 1998 to issue Codes of Practice containing such practical guidance as it thinks appropriate with a view to securing effective relationships between LAs in Wales and the schools maintained by them in relation to the promoting of high standards of education in such schools and the discharge of such functions as the Assembly may determine are exercisable by such authorities in relation to such schools. The LA, governing body and headteacher must all have regard to this Code in discharging their functions in relation to any maintained school in Wales.[21]

---

[15] SSFA 1998, s 62(1), (4).

[16] SSFA 1998, s 62(2).

[17] SSFA 1998, s 62(3).

[18] Notice is to be given in accordance with the EIA 2006, s 60(2) in the case of a school in England and the SSFA 1998, s 15(2) in the case of a school in Wales. This enables the LA to give a warning notice where they are satisfied, inter alia, that the safety of pupils or staff is threatened by a breakdown of discipline, the LA has previously informed the governors or headteacher of the matters on which that conclusion is based and the matters have not been remedied to the LA's satisfaction within a reasonable period. This notice is a precursor to the LA exercising its powers of intervention under the SSFA 1998, ss 16 and 17, to appoint additional governors or suspend the school's delegated budget.

[19] These powers include the EIA 2006, ss 63–66 in the case of a school in England; and the SSFA 1998, ss 16, 16A and 17 in the case of a school in Wales.

[20] The application of the SSFA 1998, s 127 to England was removed by the EIA 2006, s 58.

[21] SSFA 1998, s 127(2).

DISCIPLINARY SANCTIONS

Corporal punishment

6.9   Section 548 of the EA 1996 provides that corporal punishment is unlawful in all relevant educational institutions[22] in England and Wales. Corporal punishment is defined[23] as anything which is done for the purpose of punishing the child and which would, apart from any justification, be battery. It does not include anything done for the purpose of averting an immediate danger of personal injury or the property of any person including the child.[24]

6.10 In *R (on the application of Williamson) v Secretary of State for Education*[25] it was sought to be argued that this provision contravened Article 9(1) and Article 2 of the First Protocol to the European Convention on Human Rights (ECHR). The claimants were teachers and parents at certain independent schools which had been established to provide Christian education based on biblical observance. They contended that they had a religious belief that corporal punishment should be carried out. The House of Lords held that this was a religious belief for the purpose of Article 9 of the ECHR and of Article 2 of the First Protocol, and that while section 548 interfered with those Articles,[26] this was justified because corporal punishment was prescribed by primary legislation in clear terms and the interference was necessary in a democratic society for the protection of rights and freedoms and pursued the legitimate aim of protecting children and promoting their wellbeing in a proportionate manner.

Reasonable force

6.11 Section 93 of the EIA 2006[27] provides that members of staff at a school in England and Wales may use, in relation to any pupil at the school, such force as is reasonable for the purpose of preventing the pupil from committing any offence, causing personal injury to, or damage to the property of, any person including the pupil himself and engaging in any behaviour prejudicial to the maintenance of good order and discipline at the school, or among its pupils, whether that behaviour occurs during a teaching session or otherwise. That power does not permit corporal punishment,[28] but does enable the member of

---

22   Relevant educational institution means a school or an independent educational institution (as defined by the Education and Skills Act 2008, s 92) in England other than a school: s 548(7A), (7B).

23   EA 1996, s 548(4).

24   EA 1996, s 548(5).

25   [2005] UKHL 15, [2005] 2 AC 246, [2005] ELR 291.

26   Because the alternative means available to the parents to manifest their religion were held not to be adequate.

27   This power was previously contained in the EA 1996, s 550A (as inserted by the Education Act 1997, s 4), which was repealed by the EIA 2006.

28   EIA 2006, s 93(4).

staff to take action while on the premises of the school or elsewhere when, as a member of staff, he has lawful control or charge of the pupil concerned.[29]

6.12 Non-statutory guidance on the use of reasonable force has been issued by the Department for Education.[30] The governing body of a school in England is required to ensure that a procedure is in place for recording each significant incident in which a member of the staff uses force on a pupil for whom education is being provided at the school and reporting certain incidents to the parent of the pupil[31] and, in some cases,[32] the LA.[33]

6.13 In one case it was argued that the fact of working at a special school for pupils with emotional, behavioural and social needs constitutes implied consent to being assaulted by the school's pupils. Unsurprisingly that contention was rejected.[34]

Detention

6.14 Section 92 of the EIA 2006[35] empowers a school to detain a pupil who has not attained the age of 18 after the end of the school session without the parent's consent providing certain conditions are satisfied. The headteacher must have previously determined, and made generally known within the school, and taken steps to bring to the attention of every person who is a parent of a pupil registered at the school that detention of pupils after the end of a school session is one of the measures that might be taken with a view to regulating the conduct of pupils.[36] In addition, the detention must be imposed by the headteacher or by another person at the school specifically or generally authorised by him or her for the purpose and it must be reasonable in all the circumstances.[37] In Wales, the pupil's parent must have been given at least 24 hours' notice in writing that the detention was due to take place.[38]

6.15 In judging whether detention is reasonable, proportionality is expressly referred to, together with any special circumstances relevant to its imposition including, in particular, the pupil's age, any special educational needs he may

---

[29] EIA 2006, s 93(3).
[30] 'Use of Reasonable Force: Guidance for headteachers, staff and governing bodies', May 2012.
[31] No such report must be made where it appears to the person on whom the reporting obligation would otherwise fall that significant harm would fall on the pupil if the incident was reported to the parent: s 93A(5)(a).
[32] Where there is no parent to whom the incident could be reported without, in the belief of the LA, significant harm being inflicted on the pupil.
[33] EIA 2006, s 93A (inserted by the Apprenticeships, Skills, Children and Learning Act 2009, s 246) as amended by SI 2010/1158 and with effect from 5 May 2010.
[34] *R (H) v Crown Prosecution Service* [2010] EWHC 1374 (Admin).
[35] This power was previously contained in the EA 1996, s 550B (as inserted by the Education Act 1997, s 5 and amended by the SSFA 1998 and the EA 2002), which was repealed by the EIA 2006.
[36] EIA 2006, s 92(3)(b).
[37] EIA 2006, s 92(2) and s 91(3) and (4).
[38] EIA 2006, s 92(3)(d). This requirement was removed in England by the EA 2011, s 5 with effect from 15 January 2012.

have, any disability he may have, any religious requirements affecting him and, where arrangements have to be made for him to travel from the school to his home, whether suitable alternative arrangements can reasonably be made by his parents.[39]

EXCLUSION

Meaning of exclusion

6.16 The statutory definition of the term 'exclude' states that it means 'exclude on disciplinary grounds', and the term 'exclusion' is to be construed accordingly.[40]

Non-disciplinary suspensions

6.17 Where the school imposes a rule which the pupil does not wish to comply with, the pupil's refusal to attend compliant with the rule does not constitute an 'exclusion'. It was for a time suggested that if a school imposes a requirement on attendance, which requirement was later found to have been unreasonable or otherwise unlawful, then the pupil would have been 'excluded' during the currency of the dispute over that rule.[41] That view is probably not correct. Exclusion is a term of art and does not cover all de facto absences even when triggered by some action on behalf of the school.[42] The Supreme Court clarified the position in *JR 17's Application for Judicial Review*.[43] The correct analysis is that this is not an exclusion in the statutory sense. There was never any attempt to impose a disciplinary sanction on the pupil. A school's decision which results in a pupil staying away from the school may be subsequently found to be unlawful, but it will be an unlawful decision or policy, rather than an unlawful exclusion of the pupil.

6.18 In *JR 17's Application for Judicial Review*[44] the school had purported to suspend the claimant on 'precautionary grounds', without any findings as to his guilt of the matters alleged. The suspension was held to have been unlawful as the pupil had not been afforded an opportunity to give his account.[45] However, the Supreme Court also held that there was no provision in the relevant legislative and policy scheme for a precautionary suspension, and schools had no such power at common law. Accordingly, pupils could not

---

[39] EIA 2006, ss 91(6) and 92(5).
[40] EA 2002, s 51A(10) for England (inserted by the EA 2011, s 4), and s 52(10) for Wales.
[41] *R (SB) v Governors of Denbigh High School* [2006] UKHL 15, [2007] 1 AC 100, para 39 per Lord Bingham; *R (Singh) v Aberdare Girls School* [2008] EWHC 1865 (Admin), [2008] ELR 561, paras 146–153 *per* Silber J.
[42] See *Ali v Head Teacher and Governors of Lord Grey School* [2006] UKHL 14 per Lord Hoffmann at paras 37–40.
[43] [2010] UKSC 27, [2010] ELR 764, Also note *Spiers v Warrington Corp* [1954] 1 QB 61, 66 per Lord Goddard CJ.
[44] [2010] UKSC 27, [2010] ELR 764.
[45] [2010] UKSC 27, [2010] ELR 764, para 50 per Dyson JSC.

lawfully be excluded on that basis.[46] The court held that if headteachers were to have the power to suspend or exclude pupils for reasons other than breaches of discipline, such as a suspension on precautionary grounds, then the legislative framework needed to be altered.[47] The absence of a power of precautionary exclusion is inconsistent with any de facto absence from school caused by the headteacher or governors amounting to an exclusion in law. For the absence of the child to amount to an exclusion, the school must have intended to exclude the child on disciplinary grounds.[48] Although *JR 17* concerned the particular scheme in Northern Ireland, the same result would probably be reached in England and Wales.

Legislative framework for exclusions

6.19   The passage of the Education Act 2011 (EA 2011) changed the regime of school exclusions in England. The most significant change was the repeal of the right to appeal against certain exclusions, which has been replaced with the right to have such exclusions reviewed. The changes were brought about the insertion of a new section 51A into the Education Act 2002 (EA 2002) with effect from 1 September 2012.[49] Section 52 of the EA 2002, which applied to exclusions in schools in England and Wales prior to 1 September 2012, only applies to exclusions in Wales from 1 September 2012. The changes introduced by the EA 2011 do not affect the exclusions process in Wales.

6.20   As well as being governed by the relevant sections of the EA 2002, exclusions in England and Wales are also subject to secondary legislation and statutory guidance. The EA 2002 provides that regulations shall make provision about a range of matters including the procedure to be followed on appeal[50] or on review.[51] The applicable legal frameworks may be summarised as follows:

(a)   In relation to exclusions in England from 1 September 2012:

---

[46]   [2010] UKSC 27, [2010] ELR 764, para 84 per Lord Phillips, para 86 per Lord Rodger, para 107 per Lord Brown.

[47]   [2010] UKSC 27, [2010] ELR 764, para 47 per Sir John Dyson SCJ, para 71 per Lord Philips P. Some have considered it desirable that such a power should exist as it would enable a pupil who is accused of a serious criminal offence in relation to another pupil to be removed from the school prior to determination of guilt or innocence and without any subsequent criminal trial being prejudiced or the alleged victim being put at risk by the alleged offender remaining at the school.

[48]   See *Ali v Head Teacher and Governors of Lord Grey School* [2006] UKHL 14 per Lord Hoffmann at para 40, *Re JR 17* [2010] ELR 764 at para 45 per Sir John Dyson SCJ, at para 86 per Lord Roger and at para 107 per Lord Brown.

[49]   EA 2011, s 4. Section 51A applies with modifications to Academies in England: reg 21 of SI 2012/1033.

[50]   Section 52(3)(f) in England prior to 1 September 2012 and in Wales.

[51]   Section 51A(3)(e) in England from 1 September 2012. The Court of Appeal has described this as synonymous with the processing of appeals. It dismissed a challenge to the lawfulness of a regulation about the standard of proof, which was said to have been a regulation about evidence rather than procedure: *R (V) v Independent Appeal Panel for Tom Hood School* [2010] EWCA Civ 142, [2010] ELR 291 at para 43.

(i)   section 51A of the EA 2002;

(ii)   the School Discipline (Pupil Exclusions and Reviews) (England) Regulations 2012, SI 2012/1033;[52]

(iii) 'Exclusions from maintained schools, Academies and pupil referral units in England' (the 2012 Guidance on Exclusions in England).

(b)   In relation to exclusions in England between 1 September 2008 and 31 August 2012:

(i)   section 52 of the EA 2002 (prior to the amendments introduced by the EA 2011);

(ii)   the Education (Pupil Exclusions and Appeals) (Maintained Schools) (England) Regulations 2002, SI 2002/3178;[53]

(iii) the Education (Pupil Exclusions and Appeals) (Pupil Referral Units) (England) Regulations 2008, SI 2008/532;[54]

(iv)   'Improving behaviour and attendance: guidance on exclusion from schools and pupil referral units' (the 2008 Guidance on Exclusions in England).[55]

(c)   In relation to exclusions in Wales from 1 September 2004 onwards:

(i)   section 52 of the EA 2002;

(ii)   the Education (Pupil Exclusions and Appeals) (Maintained Schools) (Wales) Regulations 2003, SI 2003/3227;[56]

(iii) Education (Pupil Exclusions and Appeals) (Pupil Referral Units) (Wales) Regulations 2003, SI 2003/3246;[57]

(iv)   'Exclusion from Schools and Pupil Referral Units' ('the 2004 Guidance on Exclusions in Wales).[58]

---

[52] See Pt 2 in relation to maintained schools, Pt 3 in relation to pupil referral units and Pt 4 in relation to Academies. The provisions relating to exclusions from pupil referral units in England from 1 September 2012 are very similar to those applying to maintained schools and Academies and are not set out in detail in this Chapter.

[53] SI 2002/3178 came into force on 20 January 2003. Annex D of the model funding agreement for Academies stipulates that the Academy Trust shall act and shall ensure that the Principal and the governing body act in accordance with the law on exclusions as if the Academy were a maintained school, subject to minor exceptions.

[54] SI 2008/532 came into force on 1 April 2008. The provisions relating to exclusions from pupil referral units in England prior to 1 September 2012 are very similar to those applying to maintained schools and are not set out in detail in this Chapter.

[55] The 2008 Guidance on Exclusions in England came into force on 1 September 2008. Annex D of the model funding agreement for Academies provides that the Academy Trust shall ensure that the Principal and the Governing Body of the Academy have regard to 2008 Guidance on Exclusions in England when excluding, or reviewing the exclusion of a pupil and in relation to any appeals or review process as if the Academy were a maintained school, subject to minor exceptions.

[56] SI 2003/3227 came into force on 9 January 2004.

[57] SI 2003/3246 came into force on 9 January 2004. The provisions relating to exclusions from pupil referral units in Wales are very similar to those applying to maintained schools and are not set out in detail in this Chapter.

[58] The 2004 Guidance on Exclusions in Wales first came into force on 9 January 2004. It was amended in September 2004 and further amendments were made on 15 May 2012.

6.21 The regulations provide that the statutory guidance[59] in force at the time must be taken into account by the following persons and bodies when exercising functions under the EA 2002:

(a) the headteacher of a maintained school[60] and the principal of an Academy;[61]

(b) the governing body of a maintained school;[62]

(c) the LA responsible for a maintained school;[63]

(d) the proprietor of an Academy;[64]

(e) the review panel and the SEN expert where there is a review of the exclusion;[65] and

(f) the appeal panel where there is an appeal against the exclusion.[66]

THE DECISION TO EXCLUDE

Who can exclude?

6.22 The power to exclude pupils for a fixed period or permanently is vested in the headteacher.[67] The power may also be exercised by an acting headteacher.[68]

---

[59] Statutory guidance on exclusions in England is issued by the Secretary of State; statutory guidance on exclusions in Wales is issued by the Welsh Assembly.

[60] Regulation 9(a) of SI 2012/1033 (for maintained schools) in England from 1 September 2012; reg 7(1)(a) of SI 2002/3178 in England prior to 1 September 2012; reg 8(1)(a) of SI 2003/3227 in Wales.

[61] Regulation 27(a) of SI 2012/1033 in England from 1 September 2012. For the remainder of this Chapter, for 'headteacher' substitute 'principal' with reference to Academies: see reg 21 of SI 2012/1033.

[62] Regulation 9(b) of SI 2012/1033 in England from 1 September 2012; reg 7(1)(a) of SI 2002/3178 in England prior to 1 September 2012; reg 8(1)(a) of SI 2003/3227 in Wales.

[63] Regulation 9(c) of SI 2012/1033 in England from 1 September 2012; reg 7(1)(b) of SI 2002/3178 in England prior to 1 September 2012; reg 8(1)(b) of SI 2003/3227 (as amended by SI 2010/1142) in Wales.

[64] Regulation 27(b) of SI 2012/1033 in England from 1 September 2012.

[65] Regulation 9(d)–(e) of SI 2012/1033 (for maintained schools) and reg 27(c)–(d) of SI 2012/1033 (for Academies) in England from 1 September 2012.

[66] Regulation 7(1)(c) of SI 2002/3178 in England prior to 1 September 2012; reg 8(1)(c) of SI 2003/3227 in Wales.

[67] EA 2002, s 51A(1) in England from 1 September 2012; EA 2002, s 52(1) in England prior to 1 September 2012 and in Wales.

[68] 'Headteacher' includes acting headteacher pursuant to the Education Act 1996, s 579(1); see also para 1 of the 2012 Guidance to Exclusions in England.

Powers and procedure to be followed by headteacher

6.23 The headteacher has only two options if he decides to exclude a pupil: either to exclude the pupil for one or more fixed periods (which may not exceed 45 days in any one school year), or to exclude the pupil permanently.[69]

6.24 Once the headteacher has decided to exclude a pupil he or she must, without delay, inform the relevant person[70] of the following matters relating to the exclusion:

(a) the period of exclusion, or that it is permanent if this is the case;

(b) the reasons for exclusion;

(c) the scope of the right to make representations; and

(d) the means by which such representations may be made.[71]

6.25 Where a pupil is excluded in England from 1 September 2012, the headteacher is required to notify the relevant person of the above matters (as well as where and to whom any representations should be sent) *in writing* without delay.[72]

6.26 There is also a duty to inform other bodies about school exclusions. The headteacher must, without delay, inform the LA and the governing body of a maintained school or the proprietor of an Academy of the period of exclusion

---

[69] Regulation 4 of SI 2012/1033 (in relation to maintained schools) and reg 22 of SI 2012/1033 (in relation to Academies) in England from 1 September 2012; reg 3 of SI 2002/3178 in England prior to 1 September 2012; reg 3 of SI 2003/3227 in Wales.

[70] In England the relevant person is the pupil's parent if the excluded pupil is under the age of 18 and the pupil himself or herself if he or she has attained the age of 18: reg 2 of SI 2012/1033 and reg 2 of SI 2002/3178. In Wales the relevant person is: (a) the parent of a pupil who was aged 10 or below on the day before the beginning of the school year in which that pupil is excluded, (b) the pupil and the pupil's parent if the pupil is of compulsory school age and was aged 11 or above on the day before the beginning of the school year in which that pupil was excluded, and the pupil himself or herself if he or she is above compulsory school age: reg 2 of SI 2003/3227.

[71] Regulation 5(1)–(3) of SI 2012/1033 (for maintained schools) and reg 23(1)–(3) of SI 2012/1033 (for Academies) in England from 1 September 2012; reg 4(1)–(2) of SI 2002/3178 in England prior to 1 September 2012; reg 4 of SI 2003/3227 in Wales. The applicable guidance includes further detail about matters that must and should be included in notification to the relevant person: paras 25–31 of the 2012 Guidance for Exclusions in England from 1 September 2012; paras 88–89 of the 2008 Guidance for Exclusions in England prior to 1 September 2012; paras 1.5–1.6 of the 2004 Guidance for Exclusions in Wales.

[72] Regulation 5(1)(b) of SI 2012/1033 (for maintained schools) and reg 23(1)(b) of SI 2012/1033 (for Academies). The written notice must also state that the person notified may attend and be accompanied by a friend or represented at a meeting of the governing body or the proprietor if this is held to consider the exclusion where a pupil is excluded permanently or excluded for a fixed term where the result of the exclusion is that the pupil will be excluded from the school for a total of more than five school days in any one term or lose the opportunity to take any public examination or National Curriculum test: reg 5(3)(b)(v) of SI 2012/1033 (for maintained schools) and reg 23(3)(b)(v) of SI 2012/1033 (for Academies).

(or that it is permanent if that is the case) and the reasons for it where a pupil is excluded permanently or excluded for a fixed term where the result of the exclusion is that the pupil will be excluded from the school for a total of more than five school days in any one term or lose the opportunity to take certain examinations.[73]

6.27 There is also a duty to inform the LA and the governing body of a maintained school or the proprietor of an Academy of all other fixed term exclusions, but this information must be passed on each term rather than after each exclusion.[74] The governing body of a school in Wales must provide particularly detailed information about exclusions to the relevant LA on a termly basis, including the excluded pupil's name, age, date of birth, gender and ethnic group as well as whether he or she has a statement of special educational needs or is looked after by an LA.[75]

THE ROLE OF THE GOVERNING BODY OR PROPRIETOR TO CONSIDER REINSTATEMENT

6.28 The governing body of a maintained school and the proprietor of an Academy must decide whether or not to reinstate a pupil in circumstances where the pupil been has excluded in any of the following circumstances:

(a) the pupil has been excluded permanently;[76]

(b) the pupil has been excluded for a fixed term and as a result of the exclusion the pupil will:

    (i) lose the opportunity to take certain examinations;[77]

    (ii) be excluded for more than five school days in any one term (and representations have been made to the governing body);[78] or

---

[73] Regulation 5(2) and 5(3)(a) of SI 2012/1033 (for maintained schools) and reg 23(2) and 23(3)(a) of SI 2012/1033 (for Academies) in England from 1 September 2012; reg 4(3)–(4) of SI 2002/3178 in England prior to 1 September 2012; reg 4(3)–(4) of SI 2003/3227 in Wales. This is any public examination or National Curriculum test under SI 2012/1033 and any public examination under SI 2002/3178 and SI 2003/3227.

[74] Regulation 5(5) of SI 2012/1033 (for maintained schools) and reg 23(5) of SI 2012/1033 (for Academies) in England from 1 September 2012; reg 4(5) of SI 2002/3178 (as amended by SI 2006/2189 and SI 2007/1870) in England prior to 1 September 2012; reg 4(5) of SI 2003/3227 in Wales.

[75] Regulation 5(1) of SI 2003/3227 (as amended by SI 2004/1805 and SI 2010/1142). An LA must provide information about exclusions to the National Assembly for Wales upon request: reg 5(2) of SI 2003/3227 (as amended by SI 2010/1142).

[76] Regulation 6(1)(a) and 6(2) of SI 2012/1033 (for maintained schools) and reg 24(1)(a) and 24(2) of SI 2012/1033 (for Academies) in England from 1 September 2012; reg 5(1)(a) and 5(2) of SI 2002/3178 in England prior to 1 September 2012; reg 6(1)(a) and 6(2) of SI 2003/3227 in Wales.

[77] This is any public examination or National Curriculum test under SI 2012/1033 and any public examination under SI 2002/3178 and SI 2003/3227.

[78] Such representations must be made under reg 5(3)(b) of SI 2012/1033 (for maintained schools)

(iii) be excluded for a total of more than 15 school days in any one term.[79]

6.29 The governing body or the proprietor has the power to direct the headteacher to reinstate a pupil.[80] The headteacher must comply with any direction to that effect.[81]

Procedure for the governing body or proprietors

6.30 The procedure to be followed by the governing body or proprietors in considering whether to reinstate an excluded pupil is governed by the regulations in force at the time.

6.31 There is no express provision in the relevant regulations for the governing body of a maintained school or the proprietor of an Academy to hear witnesses but unless they do so it will, in practice, be difficult for them to consider the circumstances of the case. The guidance accordingly assumes that the governing body may consider witness statements and hear witnesses.[82]

Procedure for the governing body or proprietor in England from 1 September 2012

6.32 From 1 September 2012, the governing body of a maintained school or the proprietor of an Academy in England must, in order to decide whether or not a pupil should be reinstated:

(a) consider the interests and circumstances of the excluded pupil, including the circumstances in which the pupil was excluded, and have regard to the interests of other pupils and persons working at the school or Academy (including persons working voluntarily);

---

and reg 24(3)(b) of SI 2012/1033 (for Academies) in England from 1 September 2012; reg 4(1)(c) of SI 2002/3178 in England prior to 1 September 2012; reg 4(1)(c) of SI 2003/3227 in Wales.

[79] Regulation 6(1)(b)–(c) and 6(2) of SI 2012/1033 (for maintained schools) and regulation 24(1)(b)–(c) and 24(2) of SI 2012/1033 (for Academies) in England from 1 September 2012; reg 5(1)(c)–(d) and 5(2) of SI 2002/3178 in England prior to 1 September 2012; reg 6(1)(c)–(d) and 6(2) of SI 2003/3227 in Wales.

[80] Regulation 6(4) of SI 2012/1033 (for maintained schools) and reg 24(4) of SI 2012/1033 (for Academies) in England from 1 September 2012; reg 5(4) of SI 2002/3178 in England prior to 1 September 2012; reg 6(4) of SI 2003/3227 in Wales.

[81] Regulation 6(5) of SI 2012/1033 (for maintained schools) and reg 24(5) of SI 2012/1033 (for Academies) in England from 1 September 2012; reg 5(5) of SI 2002/3178 in England prior to 1 September 2012; reg 6(5) of SI 2003/3227 in Wales.

[82] See para 58 of the 2012 Guidance for Exclusions in England from 1 September 2012; paras 106 and 149–154 of the 2008 Guidance for Exclusions in England prior to 1 September 2012; para.2.1 of the 2004 Guidance for Exclusions in Wales.

(b) consider any representations about the exclusion made to the governing body or proprietor by or on behalf of the relevant person,[83] the headteacher or the LA;

(c) take reasonable steps to arrange a meeting at which the exclusion is to be considered for a time and date when each of the following persons is able to attend:

  (i) the headteacher;
  (ii) the relevant person (and, where requested by the relevant person, a representative or friend of the relevant person); and
  (iii) a representative of the LA in the case of a maintained school and where this is requested by the relevant person in the case of an Academy.[84]

6.33 The headteacher and the relevant person (and, where requested by the relevant person, a representative or friend of the relevant person) must be allowed to attend the meeting and make representations about the exclusion.[85] Where a pupil has been excluded from a maintained school, the governing body must also allow a representative of the LA to attend and make representations.[86] Where a pupil has been excluded from an Academy, a representative of the LA may attend the meeting as an observer and may only make representations with the permission of the proprietor.[87]

Procedure for the governing body in England prior to 1 September 2012 and the governing body in Wales

6.34 Governing bodies in England considering exclusions that took place prior to 1 September 2012 were required, before deciding whether or not to reinstate a pupil, to give the relevant person[88] and the LA an opportunity to make oral representations at a meeting of the governing body.[89] The governors were obliged to consider the circumstances in which the pupil was excluded and all representations made to them.[90] These requirements continue to apply to governing bodies in Wales.[91]

---

[83] For the definition of 'relevant person' see fn 70 to para **6.24** above.
[84] From 1 September 2012, reg 6(3)(a)–(c) of SI 2012/1033 for maintained schools and reg 24(3)(a)(d) of SI 2012/1033 for Academies.
[85] From 1 September 2012, reg 6(3)(d) of SI 2012/1033 for maintained schools and reg 24(3) of SI 2012/1033 for Academies.
[86] From 1 September 2012, reg 6(3)(d) of SI 2012/1033.
[87] Regulation 24(3)(e) of SI 2012/1033 in England from 1 September 2012.
[88] For the definition of 'relevant person' see fn 70 to para **6.24** above.
[89] Regulation 5(2)(c) of SI 2002/3178.
[90] Regulation 5(2)(a)-(b) of SI 2002/3178.
[91] Regulation 6(2) of SI 2003/3227 (as amended by SI 2010/1142). Governing bodies in Wales must also consider any representations made by the excluded pupil where the pupil is not the relevant person and by the headteacher: reg 6(2)(b) of SI 2003/3227.

6.35   The governing body or proprietor will need to make sufficient findings of fact before making a decision to exclude a pupil. In one case the relevant body[92] decided to permanently exclude a pupil for dealing in a substance the pupil believed to be cannabis, but without that body reaching any findings as to the true nature of the substance. This was held to constitute an error of law. The true nature of the substance may have significantly altered the body's view of appropriate sanction, and so a factual finding had to be made.[93]

Reinstatement by the governing body or proprietor

6.36   If the governing body of a maintained school or the proprietor of an Academy decide to reinstate a pupil, they must consider whether the pupil should be reinstated immediately or by a particular date.[94] They must inform the relevant person and the LA and direct the headteacher accordingly.[95] From 1 September 2012, the governing body of a maintained school or the proprietor of an Academy in England must inform the relevant person and the LA of the decision and the reasons for the decision *in writing* without delay.[96]

6.37   Notification requirements also arise where a decision is taken not to reinstate a pupil who has been excluded on a fixed term basis. From 1 September 2012, the governing body of a maintained school or the proprietor of an Academy in England must inform the relevant person and the LA of the decision and the reasons for the decision in writing without delay.[97] In England prior to 1 September 2012 and in Wales, the relevant person, headteacher and the LA must be informed of the decision not to reinstate a pupil excluded for a fixed term but there is no requirement in the regulations that this notification be provided in writing.[98]

---

[92]   The case concerned a decision by an Independent Appeal Panel, however the principle would apply generally.

[93]   *R (A) v Independent Appeals Panel for Sutton* [2009] EWHC 1223 (Admin), [2009] ELR 321, paras 71–75 per Hickinbottom J.

[94]   Regulation 6(2) of SI 2012/1033 (for maintained schools) and reg 24(2) of SI 2012/1033 (for Academies) in England from 1 September 2012; reg 5(3) of SI 2002/3178 in England prior to 1 September 2012; reg 6(3) of SI 2003/3227 in Wales. The governing body in Wales must additionally consider whether it would not be practical for the headteacher to comply with a direction requiring the reinstatement of the pupil: reg 6(3) of SI 2003/3227.

[95]   Regulation 6(4) of SI 2012/1033 (for maintained schools) and reg 24(4) of SI 2012/1033 (for Academies) in England from 1 September 2012; reg 5(4) of SI 2002/3178 in England prior to 1 September 2012; reg 6(4) of SI 2003/3227 (as amended by SI 2004/1805) in Wales (unless the governing body consider that it would not be practical for the headteacher to comply with a direction requiring re-instatement). This notification must be given 'without delay' under SI 2012/1033 and SI 2003/3227 and 'forthwith' under SI 2002/3178.

[96]   Regulation 6(4)(d) of SI 2012/1033 (for maintained schools) and reg 24(4)(d) of SI 2012/1033 (for Academies) in England from 1 September 2012.

[97]   Regulation 6(6)(a) of SI 2012/1033 (for maintained schools) and reg 24(6)(a) of SI 2012/1033 (for Academies) in England from 1 September 2012.

[98]   Regulation 5(6)(a) of SI 2002/3178 in England prior to 1 September 2012; reg 6(6)(a) of SI 2003/3227 in Wales. This notification must be given 'forthwith' under SI 2002/3178 and 'without delay' under SI 2003/3227.

6.38 More onerous notification requirements apply where a pupil has been permanently excluded. From 1 September 2012, if the governing body of a maintained school or the proprietor of an Academy in England decides not to reinstate the pupil they must, without delay, give the relevant person notice in writing of the following matters:

(a) that the exclusion is permanent;

(b) that the relevant person may apply for the proprietor's decision to be reviewed by a review panel;

(c) where the relevant person applies for a review, that the relevant person may require the proprietor to appoint a SEN expert to advise the review panel;

(d) the role of the SEN expert in relation to a review;

(e) how an application for a review may be made and what the application must contain;

(f) where and to whom to send the application and the date by which the application must be received;

(g) that the relevant person may, at their own expense, appoint someone to make representations for the purpose of the review; and

(h) that the relevant person may issue a claim under the Equality Act 2010 where the relevant person believes that unlawful discrimination has occurred, and the time within which such a claim should be made.[99]

6.39 In England prior to 1 September 2012 and in Wales, the governing body is required to give the relevant person notice in writing of the reasons for their decision, the right of appeal, the person to whom an appeal should be made, and that any notice of appeal must contain the grounds of appeal and the last date on which the appeal may be made.[100]

CHALLENGING THE DECISION OF THE GOVERNING BODY OR PROPRIETOR

Entitlement to apply for review or appeal

6.40 Where pupil has been permanently excluded and the governing body or proprietor decides not to reinstate them, there is a statutory entitlement to

---

[99] Regulation 6(6)(b) of SI 2012/1033 (for maintained schools) and reg 24(6)(b) of SI 2012/1033 (for Academies) in England from 1 September 2012.

[100] Regulation 5(6)(b) of SI 2002/3178 in England prior to 1 September 2012; reg 6(6)(b) of SI 2003/3227 in Wales.

challenge the refusal to reinstate. In England from 1 September 2012, a decision not to reinstate may be reviewed by application to a review panel.[101] In England prior to 1 September 2012 and in Wales an appeal may be made to an independent appeal panel.[102] The relevant provisions governing review panels and independent appeal panels are set out below.

Applying for a review or an appeal

6.41   The entitlement to apply for a review or appeal arises where a pupil has been permanently excluded and the governing body or proprietor has decided not to reinstate the pupil. The process of applying for a review or an appeal is essential the same.[103] Only the relevant person has a right of review[104] or appeal.[105] No application can be made after 15 school days from the date that the relevant person has been given the requisite notice.[106]. It seems, therefore, that if the notice of permanent exclusion does not state all the requisite matters, time does not begin to run for an appeal. For the purpose of calculating the time period for applying for a review or an appeal, an application is taken to be made, if first class post is used, on the second working day after the date of posting or, where the notice is delivered, on the date of delivery.[107]

6.42   If the relevant person gives notice in writing that he or she does not intend to apply for a review[108] or an appeal,[109] he or she is bound by that decision.

---

[101]   EA 2002, s 51A and reg 7 of SI 2012/1033 (for maintained schools) and reg 25 of SI 2012/1033 (for Academies) in England from 1 September 2012.

[102]   EA 2002, s 52 and reg 7 of SI 2002/3178 in England prior to 1 September 2012.

[103]   An application for a review must be in writing setting out the grounds on which a review is sought: para 9(a) of Sch 1 to SI 2012/1033 (for maintained schools and Academies) in England from 1 September 2012.

[104]   Regulation 7(1) of SI 2012/1033 (for maintained schools) and reg 25(1) of SI 2012/1033 (for Academies) in England from 1 September 2012.

[105]   Regulation 6(1) of SI 2002/3178 in England prior to 1 September 2012; reg 7(1) of SI 2003/3227 in Wales.

[106]   In relation to the notice requirements, see reg 6(6)(b) of SI 2012/1033 (for maintained schools) and reg 25(6)(b) of SI 2012/1033 (for Academies) in England from 1 September 2012; reg 5(6)(b) of SI 2002/3178 in England prior to 1 September 2012; regn 6(6)(b) of SI 2003/3227 in Wales. In relation to the 15 day time limit see paras 2(1) and 9(b) of Sch 1 to SI 2012/1033 (for maintained schools and Academies) in England from 1 September 2012; para 1 of Sch 1 to SI 2002/3178 in England prior to 1 September 2012; para 1 of Sch 1 to SI 2003/3227 in Wales. In England from 1 September 2012 the time limit is extended where the relevant person makes a claim under the Equality Act 2010 alleging that the exclusion amounts to unlawful discrimination: see para 2(1) of Sch 1 to SI 2012/1033 (for maintained schools and Academies).

[107]   Paragraph 1(2) of Sch 1 to SI 2012/1033 (for maintained schools and Academies) in England from 1 September 2012; para 1(2) of Sch 1 to SI 2002/3178 in England prior to 1 September 2012; para 1(2) of Sch 1 to SI 2003/3227 in Wales.

[108]   Paragraph 2(4) of Sch 1 to SI 2012/1033 (for maintained schools and Academies) in England from 1 September 2012.

[109]   Paragraph 1(3) of Sch 1 to SI 2002/3178 in England prior to 1 September 2012; para 1(3) of Sch 1 to SI 2003/3227 in Wales. In Wales, where the relevant person is both a pupil of compulsory school age who was aged 11 or above on the day before the beginning of the

REVIEW PANELS

Arrangement of the review panel

6.43   In England from 1 September 2012, where a relevant person applies for a review, the LA or proprietor that is the 'arranging authority'[110] must, at their own expense:

(a)   make arrangements for the review of the governing body's decision not to reinstate a pupil who has been permanently excluded; and

(b)   if requested by the relevant person, appoint, for the purpose of that review, a SEN expert to provide impartial advice on how special educational needs may be relevant to the decision to exclude the pupil permanently.[111]

Constitution of the review panel

6.44   The review panel must consist of three or five members appointed by the arranging authority. Where the review panel has three members, it must include one person from each of the following categories:

(a)   persons who are eligible to be lay members;[112]

(b)   headteachers, or persons who have held that position during the last five years; and

(c)   persons who are or have been:

    (i)   a governor of a maintained school;
    (ii) a member of a pupil referral unit management committee;
    (iii) a director of the proprietor of an Academy,
    provided they have served in that capacity for at least 12 consecutive months within the last five years and have not been a teacher or a headteacher in any school during the last five years.[113]

---

school year in which that pupil is excluded and a parent of his or hers, a notice in writing given by a parent of an intention not to appeal will be treated as final whether or not the pupil has given such notice in writing.

[110]   Paragraph 1(1) of Sch 1 to SI 2012/1033 (for maintained schools and Academies) in England from 1 September 2012.

[111]   For maintained schools, reg 7(1) of SI 2012/1033, for Academies, reg 25(1) of SI 2012/1033. The role of the SEN expert is discussed at paras **6.48–6.53** below.

[112]   A person is eligible to be a lay member if the person has never worked in a school in a paid capacity (disregarding any service as a governor or as a paid volunteer): para 3(4) of the Sch to SI 2012/1033.

[113]   Paragraph 3(2)–(3) of the Sch to SI 2012/1033.

6.45 Where the review panel has five members it must have one person who is eligible to be a lay member[114] and two people from each of the other categories referred to above.[115]

6.46 The following persons are disqualified from membership of the review panel for the purpose of that review:

(a) any member (or director) of the arranging authority or, if different, the responsible body;

(b) the headteacher of the relevant school (or any person who has held that position within the last five years);

(c) any person employed by the responsible body or the arranging authority (if different), other than the headteacher of a school other than the relevant school;

(d) any person who has, or at any time has had, any connection with:

(i)   the responsible body, the arranging authority (if different), the relevant school or the relevant person; or
(ii) the excluded pupil or the incident leading to the exclusion,
of a kind which might reasonably be taken to raise doubts about that person's impartiality.
        The lay member must chair the review panel.[116]

6.47 Review panel members and, if appointed, the SEN expert, must declare any known potential conflict of interest to the arranging authority before the review begins.[117] A review panel member may not be substituted or replaced with a different panel member for any reason after a review panel has begun.[118] Where a review panel has begun a review and for any reason it ceases to be constituted in accordance with this paragraph, the review must cease and a new review panel must be constituted to conduct the review afresh.[119]

---

[114] A person is eligible to be a lay member if the person has never worked in a school in a paid capacity (disregarding any service as a governor or as a paid volunteer): para 3(4) of the Sch to SI 2012/1033.

[115] Paragraph 3(2)–(3) of the Sch to SI 2012/1033 (for maintained schools and Academies) in England from 1 September 2012.

[116] Paragraph 3(10) of the Sch to SI 2012/1033 (for maintained schools and Academies) in England from 1 September 2012.

[117] Paragraph 3(13) of Sch 1 to SI 2012/1033 (for maintained schools and Academies) in England from 1 September 2012.

[118] Paragraph 3(11) of the Sc to SI 2012/1033 (for maintained schools and Academies) in England from 1 September 2012.

[119] Paragraph 3(12) of the Sch to SI 2012/1033 (for maintained schools and Academies) in England from 1 September 2012.

Role of the SEN expert

6.48 In England from 1 September 2012, the relevant person is entitled to request the involvement of an expert in special educational needs[120] ('SEN expert') in the review process. The relevant person must make this request in writing at the time as the application for review.[121] The right to request the appointment of an SEN expert exists regardless of whether or not the school has recognised that the child has special educational needs.[122]

6.49 Where the relevant person makes such a request, the LA in the case of a maintained school or the proprietor in the case of an Academy must, at its own expense, appoint an SEN expert.[123] The 2012 Guidance on Exclusions in England states that the SEN expert should be a professional with first-hand experience of the assessment and support of SEN, as well as an understanding of the legal requirements on schools in relation to SEN and disability.[124] The Guidance gives the following examples of suitable individuals: educational psychologists; specialist SEN teachers; special educational needs coordinators (SENCOs); and behaviour support teachers.

6.50 A person may not be appointed as the SEN expert for the purpose of a review if they have had any connection with the responsible body, the arranging authority, the relevant school or the relevant person or the excluded person or the incident leading to the exclusion of a kind which might reasonably be taken to raise doubts about that person's impartiality.[125] However, this does not prevent a headteacher or any employee of the LA being appointed as an SEN expert.[126]

6.51 The role of the expert is to provide impartial advice on how special educational needs may be relevant to the decision to exclude the pupil permanently.[127] The SEN expert's functions in relation to the review are limited to advising the review panel, orally or in writing or both, impartially, of the relevance of special educational needs in the context and circumstances of the review.[128] The regulations provide that it is not the role of an SEN expert to

---

[120] Special educational needs has the same meaning as the EA 1996, s 312: reg 2(1) of SI 2012/1033 (for maintained schools and Academies) in England from 1 September 2012.

[121] Regulation 7(3) of SI 2012/1033 (for maintained schools) and reg 25(3) of SI 2012/1033 (for Academies) in England from 1 September 2012.

[122] Paragraph 119 of the 2012 Guidance on Exclusions in England.

[123] Regulation 7(1)(b) of SI 2012/1033 (for maintained schools) and reg 25(1)(b) of SI 2012/1033 (for Academies) in England from 1 September 2012.

[124] Paragraph 122 of the 2012 Guidance on Exclusions in England.

[125] Paragraph 3(7) of the Sch to SI 2012/1033 (for maintained schools and Academies) in England from 1 September 2012.

[126] Paragraph 3(8) of the Sch to SI 2012/1033 (for maintained schools and Academies) in England from 1 September 2012.

[127] Regulation 7(1)(b) of SI 2012/1033 (for maintained schools) and reg 25(1)(b) of SI 2012/1033 (for Academies) in England from 1 September 2012.

[128] Paragraph 18 of the Sch to SI 2012/1033 (for maintained schools and Academies) in England from 1 September 2012.

make an assessment as to whether the pupil has special educational needs.[129] It is submitted that in practice it will at times be necessary for SEN experts to make such an assessment in order to determine the possible effect of any special educational needs on the exclusion.

6.52   The 2012 Guidance on Exclusions in England provides that the focus of the SEN expert's advice should be on whether the school's policies which relate to SEN, or the application of these policies in relation to the excluded pupil, were legal, reasonable and procedurally fair[130] (in line with the tests to be applied by the review panel).[131] If the SEN expert believes that this was not the case he or she should, where possible, advise the panel on the possible contribution that this could have made to the circumstances of the pupil's exclusion.[132]

6.53   Where the school does not recognise that a pupil has SEN, the SEN expert should advise the panel on whether he or she believes the school acted in a legal, reasonable and procedurally fair way with respect to the identification of any special educational needs that the pupil may potentially have, and any contribution that this could have made to the circumstances of the pupil's exclusion.[133] The SEN expert should not criticise a school's policies or actions simply because he or she believes a different approach should have been followed or because another school might have taken a different approach.[134]

Procedure for the review panel

6.54   The procedure for the review panel is governed by the applicable regulations. Any other matters of procedure not provided for by the regulations are to be determined by the arranging authority[135] and further information about the procedure to be followed is contained in the 2012 Guidance on Exclusions in England.

6.55   The arranging authority must set a date for the review panel to meet and review the decision not to reinstate the pupil.[136] Reasonable steps must be taken to schedule the review at a time that will allow the attendance of any person who is entitled to make representations and wishes to attend as well as any SEN expert that has been appointed.[137]

---

[129]   Paragraph 18 of the Sch to SI 2012/1033 (for maintained schools and Academies) in England from 1 September 2012.
[130]   Paragraph 156 of the 2012 Guidance on Exclusions in England.
[131]   Paragraph 148 of the 2012 Guidance on Exclusions in England.
[132]   Paragraph 156 of the 2012 Guidance on Exclusions in England.
[133]   Paragraph 157 of the 2012 Guidance on Exclusions in England.
[134]   Paragraph 158 of the 2012 Guidance on Exclusions in England.
[135]   Paragraph 20 of Schedule 1 to SI 2012/1033 (for maintained schools and Academies) in England from 1 September 2012.
[136]   Paragraph 10(1) of Sch 1 to SI 2012/1033 (for maintained schools and Academies) in England from 1 September 2012. This date must not be later than the closing date for reviews.
[137]   Paragraph 11 of Sch 1 to SI 2012/1033 (for maintained schools and Academies) in England from 1 September 2012.

6.56 The following persons, and any representative they instruct, have the right to attend the review and to make representations:

(a) the relevant person (and, if requested by the relevant person, a friend of the relevant person);

(b) the headteacher of the relevant school; and

(c) the responsible body and, if different, the arranging authority.[138]

6.57 The review panel must consider any written or oral representations made to it by these persons when determining a review.[139] In addition, where the relevant school is an Academy, if requested by the relevant person, a representative of the LA in which that Academy is located (and, if applicable, the home LA) must be permitted to attend the review as an observer but may only make representations with the consent of the arranging authority.[140]

6.58 In deciding whether the governing body's decision was flawed, and therefore whether to quash the decision, the panel must only take account of the evidence that was available to the governing body at the time of making their decision.[141] This includes any evidence which the panel considers would, or should, have been available to the governing body if they had been acting reasonably.[142] If evidence is presented that the panel considers is unreasonable to have expected the governing body to have been aware of at the time of their decision, the panel can take account of the evidence when deciding whether to recommend that the governing body reconsider their decision.[143]

6.59 A review panel may from time to time adjourn a review but, before doing so, must consider the effect of any adjournment on each of the parties to the review, any victim of the incident leading to the exclusion and the pupil or any parent of the pupil where they are not the relevant person.[144] If the relevant person has requested the appointment of a SEN expert but the SEN expert is not in attendance, the relevant person may ask the review panel to adjourn the review to a later date or time so that the SEN expert, or an alternative SEN

---

[138] Paragraph 12(1) of Sch 1 to SI 2012/1033 (for maintained schools and Academies) in England from 1 September 2012.

[139] Paragraph 12(2) of Sch 1 to SI 2012/1033 (for maintained schools and Academies) in England from 1 September 2012.

[140] Paragraph 12(3) of Sch 1 to SI 2012/1033 (for maintained schools and Academies) in England from 1 September 2012.

[141] Paragraph 134 of the 2012 Guidance on Exclusions in England.

[142] Paragraph 134 of the 2012 Guidance on Exclusions in England.

[143] Paragraph 135 of the 2012 Guidance on Exclusions in England.

[144] Paragraph 13(1) of Sch 1 to SI 2012/1033 (for maintained schools and Academies) in England from 1 September 2012.

expert, may attend.[145] A request for an adjournment due to the non attendance of the SEN expert must be granted by the review panel.[146]

6.60 Reviews must be heard in private except where the arranging authority directs otherwise.[147] Two or more reviews may be combined and dealt with in the same proceedings where the review panel considers that it would be fair and expedient to do so because the issues raised by the reviews are the same or connected and the parties to each review agree.[148]

6.61 The court considered the issue of whether challenges to exclusions should be heard together, or heard by the same panel, in the case of *R (S and B) v Independent Appeals Panel of Birmingham City Council*.[149] Although the case was decided under the previous regime when there were appeals rather than reviews it is submitted it remains of relevance under the present statutory scheme. Four boys were involved in contributing money towards buying marijuana and arranging to smoke it. All were permanently excluded and all appealed. Some were reinstated and some were not. The unsuccessful boys brought judicial review proceedings contending that there should have been a combined hearing.

6.62 Beatson J upheld the challenge, holding that where there was joint participation in the same incident and there was no evidence of substantially different participation by individuals or of different mitigation available to them, it was incumbent on the appeals panel to consider whether to combine the appeals, or to organise them so that the same members heard all four appeals.

6.63 In *R (O) v Independent Appeals Panel for Tower Hamlets*,[150] it was held that there is no general duty on an appeals panel to draw to the appellant's attention or his representative every procedural rule that might be relevant to the hearing.

6.64 Where a SEN expert is present the review panel must seek and consider the SEN expert's view on how special educational needs may be relevant to the pupil's exclusion.[151]

---

[145] Paragraph 13(2) of Sch 1 to SI 2012/1033 (for maintained schools and Academies) in England from 1 September 2012.

[146] Paragraph 13(3) of Sch 1 to SI 2012/1033 (for maintained schools and Academies) in England from 1 September 2012.

[147] Paragraph 14 of Sch 1 to SI 2012/1033 (for maintained schools and Academies) in England from 1 September 2012.

[148] Paragraph 15 of Sch 1 to SI 2012/1033 (for maintained schools and Academies) in England from 1 September 2012.

[149] [2007] ELR 57.

[150] [2007] ELR 468.

[151] Paragraph 3(17) of the Sch to SI 2012/1033 (for maintained schools and Academies) in England from 1 September 2012.

6.65 In exercising its functions, the review panel must consider the interests and circumstances of the excluded pupil, including the circumstances in which the pupil was excluded, and have regard to the interests of other pupils and persons working at the school (including persons working at the school voluntarily).[152]

Powers of the review panel

6.66 When determining an application for a review, the review panel may:

(a) uphold the decision of the responsible body;[153]

(b) recommend that the responsible body reconsiders the matter;[154]

(c) if it considers that the decision of the responsible body was flawed when considered in the light of the principles applicable on an application for judicial review, quash the decision of the responsible body and direct the responsible body to reconsider the matter;[155]

(d) direct the governing body to place a note on the pupil's educational record;[156]

(e) order that the LA are to make an adjustment to the school's budget share for the funding period during which the exclusion occurs in the sum of £4,000 if, following a decision by the panel to quash the governing body's original decision, the governing body:

    (i) reconsider the exclusion and decide not to reinstate the pupil; or
    (ii) fail to reconsider the exclusion within the time limit specified in the regulations.[157]

6.67 Critically, unlike an independent appeal panel, a review panel does not possess the power to decide to direct the reinstatement of a pupil. The review panel's decision is binding on the relevant person, the governing body, the headteacher and the LA or proprietor.[158]

---

[152] Regulation 7(4) of SI 2012/1033 (for maintained schools) and reg 25(4) of SI 2012/1033 (for Academies) in England from 1 September 2012.

[153] EA 2002, s 51A(4)(a) (as amended by the EA 2011) in England from 1 September 2012.

[154] EA 2002, s 51A(4)(b) (as amended by the EA 2011) in England from 1 September 2012.

[155] EA 2002, s 51A(4)(c) (as amended by the EA 2011) in England from 1 September 2012.

[156] Regulation 7(5)(a) of SI 2012/1033 (for maintained schools) and reg 25(5)(a) of SI 2012/1033 (for Academies) in England from 1 September 2012.

[157] Regulation 7(5)(b) of SI 2012/1033 (for maintained schools) and reg 25(5)(b) of SI 2012/1033 (for Academies) in England from 1 September 2012.

[158] Regulation 7(6) of SI 2012/1033 (for maintained schools) and reg 25(6) of SI 2012/1033 (for Academies) in England from 1 September 2012.

Decision of the review panel

6.68 In the event of a disagreement between the members of a review panel, the review under consideration must be decided by a simple majority of the votes cast and, where the votes are tied, the chair of the review panel is to have a second or casting vote.[159]

6.69 Upon conclusion of a review the review panel must without delay give notice of its decision in writing to the relevant person, the responsible body, the LA and, if applicable, the home LA.[160]

6.70 The notice must include:

(a) the review panel's decision, indicating whether the review panel:

    (i) upholds the responsible body's decision;
    (ii) recommends that the responsible body reconsiders its decision; or
    (iii) quashes the responsible body's decision;

(b) the reasons for the review panel's decision;

(c) any order under the regulations;[161] and

(d) any information that must be recorded on the pupil's educational record.[162]

Reconsideration by the governing body or proprietor following a review

6.71 The governing body or proprietor must reconsider the exclusion where the review panel:

(a) recommends that the governing body reconsider a decision not to reinstate a pupil who has been permanently excluded; or

(b) quashes the governing body's decision and directs the governing body to reconsider the matter.[163]

---

[159] Paragraph 16 of Sch 1 to SI 2012/1033 (for maintained schools and Academies) in England from 1 September 2012.
[160] Paragraph 19(1) of Sch 1 to SI 2012/1033 (for maintained schools and Academies) in England from 1 September 2012.
[161] Regulation 7 of SI 1012/1033 (for maintained schools) and reg 25 of SI 1012/1033 (for Academies) in England from 1 September 2012.
[162] Paragraph 19(2) of Sch 1 to SI 2012/1033 (for maintained schools and Academies) in England from 1 September 2012.
[163] Regulation 8(1) of SI 2012/1033 (for maintained schools) and reg 26(1) of SI 2012/1033 (for Academies) in England from 1 September 2012.

6.72 The governing body or proprietor must reconsider the exclusion within ten school days after notification of the review panel's decision.[164] When the governing body or proprietor have reconsidered their decision they must, without delay, inform the relevant person, the headteacher and the LA (and, if applicable, the home LA) of their reconsidered decision and the reasons for it.[165]

APPEAL PANELS

Arrangement of appeal panels

6.73 In England prior to 1 September 2012 and in Wales, an LA is required to make arrangements for enabling the relevant person to appeal against any decision of the governing body not to reinstate a pupil who has been permanently excluded from a school maintained by the authority.[166]

Constitution of appeal panels

6.74 An appeal panel is required to be constituted in accordance with the applicable regulations.[167] It must consist of three or five members appointed by the authority from three categories:

(a) persons who are eligible to be lay members;

(b) persons who are, or have been within the previous five years, headteachers of maintained schools in England and persons who are currently working in education or education management in Wales; and

(c) persons who are, or have been, governors of maintained schools, provided that they have served as governors for at least 12 consecutive months within the previous six years and have not been teachers or headteachers during the last five years.[168]

6.75 If the appeal panel consists of three members there must be one member from each of these three categories.[169] If the panel consists of five members

---

[164] The notification is to have been provided pursuant to para 19 of Sch 1 to SI 2012/1033 (for maintained schools and Academies) in England from 1 September 2012. The regulations give guidance on determining when notification is taken to have been given: reg 8(3) of SI 2012/1033 (for maintained schools) and reg 26(3) of SI 2012/1033 (for Academies).

[165] Regulation 8(2) of SI 2012/1033 (for maintained schools) and reg 8(2) of SI 2012/1033 (for Academies) in England from 1 September 2012.

[166] Regulation 6(1) of SI 2002/3178 in England prior to 1 September 2012; reg 7(1) of SI 2003/3227 (as amended by SI 2010/1142) in Wales.

[167] Paragraph 2 of Sch 1 to SI 2002/3178 in England prior to 1 September 2012; para 2 of Sch 1 to SI 2003/3227 in Wales.

[168] Paragraph 2(2) of Sch 1 to SI 2002/3178 (as amended by SI 2004/402) in England prior to 1 September 2012; para 2(2) of Sch 1 to SI 2003/3227 in Wales.

[169] Paragraph 2(3)(a) of Sch 1 to SI 2002/3178 in England prior to 1 September 2012; para 2(3)(a) of Sch 1 to SI 2003/3227 in Wales.

then one must be from the first category and two each from the remaining two categories.[170] A person is eligible to be a lay member if he is a person with personal experience in the management of any school or the provision of education in any school, save that experience as a governor or in any other voluntary capacity is excluded.[171]

6.76 The following persons are disqualified from being members of an appeal panel:[172]

(a) any member of the LA or of the governing body of the school in question;

(b) the headteacher of the school in question or any person who has held that position within the previous five years;

(c) any person employed by the authority other than as a headteacher;

(d) any person who has, or at any time has had, any connection with the authority[173] or the school or with any person within paragraph (c)[174] or the pupil in question or the incident leading to his exclusion of a kind that might reasonably be taken to raise doubts about his ability to act impartially.

6.77 In addition, a person is disqualified from membership of an appeal panel in England prior to 1 September 2012 if they have not satisfied the training requirements imposed by the regulations.[175]

6.78 The fact that members of an appeal panel must include persons who have been headteachers has raised the question whether this might infringe the rule against bias. It might be said that headteachers are more likely to uphold the decisions of other headteachers. The regulations dealing with disqualification might be said not to save the provision as they would only permit the headteachers in question to be replaced by headteachers in relation to whom there was no reasonable apprehension of bias. It is submitted that there is no reasonable apprehension of bias simply because someone is a headteacher. A

---

[170] Paragraph 2(3)(b) of Sch 1 to SI 2002/3178 in England prior to 1 September 2012; para 2(2)(3)(b) of Sch 1 to SI 2003/3227 in Wales.

[171] Paragraph 2(4) of Sch 1 to SI 2002/3178 in England prior to 1 September 2012; para 2(4) of Sch 1 to SI 2003/3227 in Wales.

[172] Paragraph 2(7) of Sch 1 to SI 2002/3178 in England prior to 1 September 2012; para 2(7) of Sch 1 to SI 2003/3227 (as amended by SI 2010/1142) in Wales.

[173] This does not include persons who are employed as headteachers in England or persons who are employed as headteachers or teachers in Wales: see para 2(8) of the Sch to SI 2002/3178 in England prior to 1 September 2012; para 2(8) of Sch 1 to SI 2003/3227 in Wales.

[174] In the case of Wales any person who has, or at any time has had, any connection with any person listed in para (b) of a kind which might reasonably be taken to raise doubts about his or her ability to act impartially is also disqualified from being a member of an appeal panel: see para 2(7)(d)(i) of Sch 1 to SI 2003/3227.

[175] Paragraph 2(7)(e) of Sch 1 to SI 2002/3178 (as amended by SI 2006/2189) in England prior to 1 September 2012. There is no equivalent regulation in Wales.

headteacher will be familiar with how a school is run and well qualified from his experience to judge whether exclusion was appropriate in a particular case. He will be aware that exclusion is a remedy of last resort and will not have a predisposition in its favour.

6.79 An appeal panel, if it consists of five members, can continue to hear an appeal if no more than two members die or become too ill to continue, provided that the remaining members consist of one person from each of the relevant categories.[176]

6.80 Under a previous statutory scheme it was contended that the composition of the appeal panel was such as to infringe the right of a person under Article 6 of the ECHR to the determination of his civil rights and obligations by an independent tribunal. What was objected to was that the members were appointed, paid and trained by the LA, that the LA had the opportunity to make representations to the appeal panel and that the members had no security of tenure.[177] Newman J held that Article 6 did not apply but that, even if it did, it had not been infringed.[178] It will be observed that members of appeal panels are still appointed, paid for, and indemnified by the LA, there is still no security of tenure and the LA is still able to make representations at the appeal.[179] There is no reason to think that the decision in *Alperton* would not continue to apply. In *R (V) v Independent Appeal Panel for Tom Hood School*[180] the Court of Appeal affirmed that Article 6 does not apply to the exclusion of pupils as the right to education does not guarantee education at a particular institution.[181] The same result had previously been reached in relation to fixed term exclusions.[182]

---

[176] Paragraph 2(9) of Sch 1 to SI 2002/3178 in England prior to 1 September 2012; para 2(9) of Sch 1 to SI 2003/3227 in Wales.

[177] See para 71 of *R (on the application of B) v Head Teacher of Alperton Community School and others* [2001] EWHC 229 (Admin), [2001] ELR 359, Newman J. One of the three cases considered by Newman J (the case of *T*) was considered by the Court of Appeal in *S, T and P v Brent LB* [2002] EWCA Civ 693, [2002] ELR 556, but no point was taken as to the composition of the appeal panel in itself leading to a breach of Art 6 or otherwise leading to an infringement of the rule against bias. The Court of Appeal recognised, at para 30, that there were difficulties in holding that a school exclusion appeal panel determined any civil right or obligation within the meaning of Art 6 of the ECHR but was prepared to make an assumption, which it regarded as tenable, that 'domestic human rights law' and 'arguably' the ECHR would today regard the right not to be permanently excluded without good reason a civil right for Art 6 purposes.

[178] [2001] EWHC 229 (Admin), [2001] ELR 359 at paras 70–73.

[179] In the light of the Court of Appeal's decision in *S, T and P v Brent LB* [2002] EWCA Civ 693 [2002] ELR 556 at paras 22–24 that the LA representations should be objective and not urge any particular outcome in the instant case it is difficult to see how their right to make representations could inhibit the impartiality of the appeal panel.

[180] [2010] EWCA Civ 142, [2010] ELR 291.

[181] Applying *Ali v Lord Grey School Governors* [2006] UKHL 14, [2006] 2 AC 363.

[182] *R (B) v Headteacher of St Michael's Church of England School* [2008] ELR 116, per Beatson J.

Procedure for appeal panel

6.81 The detailed procedure for appeals is set out in the applicable regulations.[183] The appeal is to be by notice in writing and must set out the grounds on which it is made.[184] It is to be heard at such time as the LA determines,[185] but in fixing the date, the LA is to take reasonable steps to ascertain any times when the relevant person and any other person who would be entitled to appear and make oral representations would be unable to attend.[186] Once those dates have been ascertained, the LA is to take them into account with a view to ensuring, so far as is reasonably practicable, that those persons are able to appear and make representations at the hearing.[187]

6.82 The appeal panel is required to give the relevant person an opportunity of appearing and making oral representations. In addition the panel has to allow him to be represented or to be accompanied by a friend.[188] The panel has also to allow the headteacher, governors and LA to make written representations and to appear and make oral representations.[189]

6.83 In *S, T and P v Brent LB*,[190] the Court of Appeal commented that an appeal panel had to be careful when hearing submissions by the LA not to acquiesce in an endeavour by the LA or any one else to determine or influence its final decision. The court gave, as an example, a submission by the LA that the panel's decision should not be such as to undermine the headteacher's authority. While the Court of Appeal considered such a submission was unobjectionable in itself, it considered that it might be readily perceived as an attempt to uphold an exclusion on inadmissible grounds. The court went on to state that consideration should be given to the layout and seating arrangements at panel hearings so as to avoid any impression that the LA and the school were ranged against the pupil.

6.84 The content of representations by the LA was also the subject of comment by the Court of Appeal in *S, T and P v Brent LB*, where it was held[191] that the LA had to maintain a completely objective stance. It is not part of its

---

[183] Paragraphs 6–16 of Sch 1 to SI 2002/3178 in England prior to 1 September 2012; paras 6–16 of Sch 1 to SI 2003/3227 in Wales.

[184] Paragraph 7 of Sch 1 to SI 2002/3178 in England prior to 1 September 2012; para 7 of Sch 1 to SI 2003/3227 in Wales.

[185] Which has to be not later than the closing date for appeals: see para 8(2) of Sch 1 to SI 2002/3178 in England prior to 1 September 2012; para 8(2) of Sch 1 to SI 2003/3227 in Wales.

[186] Paragraph 9(1) of Sch 1 to SI 2002/3178 in England prior to 1 September 2012; para 9(1) of Sch 1 to SI 2003/3227 (as amended by SI 2010/1142) in Wales.

[187] Paragraph 9(2) of Sch 1 to SI 2002/3178 in England prior to 1 September 2012; para 9(2) of Sch 1 to SI 2003/3227 (as amended by SI 2010/1142) in Wales.

[188] Paragraph 10(1) of Sch 1 to SI 2002/3178 in England prior to 1 September 2012; para 10(1) of Sch 1 to SI 2003/3227 (as amended by SI 2010/1142) in Wales.

[189] Paragraph 10(2) of Sch 1 to SI 2002/3178 in England prior to 1 September 2012; para 10(2) of Sch 1 to SI 2003/3227 (as amended by SI 2010/1142) in Wales.

[190] [2002] EWCA Civ 693, [2002] ELR 556 at para 25.

[191] [2002] EWCA Civ 693, [2002] ELR 556 at paras 22–24.

role to press for a particular conclusion in relation to a particular pupil or to submit that the pupil ought, or ought not to be, permanently excluded. Instead, it should confine itself to providing relevant information regarding the situation in various schools in its area.

6.85   The appeal panel has power to adjourn the hearing from time to time.[192] Ordinarily, appeals are to be heard in private but the panel can direct that one member of the LA may attend as an observer[193] and, in Wales, a member of the Council on Tribunals may also appear without a panel direction.[194] Two or more appeals may be dealt with in the same proceedings if the panel considers that it is expedient to do so because the issues raised by the appeals are the same or connected.[195] The guidance provides that the panel should check that no-one objects before taking this approach.[196]

6.86   Subject to the provisions of the relevant regulations and the guidance, it is for the appeal panel to decide how to conduct proceedings.[197] Curiously, as in the case of the hearing before the governors, there is no express provision in the regulations for the appeal panel to hear evidence, whether written or oral, nor for cross-examination. The guidance, however, provides that evidence may be given at the hearing[198] and that there will be questioning of the parties by the other parties and the panel.[199] This leaves open the questioning of witnesses who are not parties, but there can be little doubt that the interests of fairness would require that.[200]

6.87   Where issues arise as to the identification of a pupil, the technical rules of evidence in a criminal trial do not apply, but the appeal panel must be alive to the possibility of identification evidence being tainted and the interests of fairness require careful consideration of the circumstances of the identification. The appeal panel must inquire how identification came to be made. A failure to

---

[192]   Paragraph 10(3) of Sch 1 to SI 2002/3178 in England prior to 1 September 2012; para 10(3) of Sch 1 to SI 2003/3227 in Wales.

[193]   Paragraph 11 of Sch 1 to SI 2002/3178 (as amended by SI 2008/2683) in England prior to 1 September 2012; para 11(a) of Sch 1 to SI 2003/3227 in Wales.

[194]   Paragraph 11(b) of Sch 1 to SI 2003/3227 in Wales.

[195]   Paragraph 12 of Sch 1 to SI 2002/3178 in England prior to 1 September 2012; para 12 of Sch 1 to SI 2003/3227 in Wales.

[196]   See para 121 of the 2008 Guidance for Exclusions in England prior to 1 September 2012; para 3.1 of the 2004 Guidance for Exclusions in Wales.

[197]   See para 144 of the 2008 Guidance for Exclusions in England prior to 1 September 2012; para 7.1 of the 2004 Guidance for Exclusions in Wales.

[198]   See paras 149–154 of the 2008 Guidance for Exclusions in England prior to 1 September 2012; paras 8.1–8.8 of the 2004 Guidance for Exclusions in Wales.

[199]   See para 146 of the 2008 Guidance for Exclusions in England prior to 1 September 2012; para 7.3 of the 2004 Guidance for Exclusions in Wales.

[200]   See para 153 of the 2008 Guidance for Exclusions in England prior to 1 September 2012 and para 8.7 of the 2004 Guidance for Exclusions in Wales which seem to assume that if a witness is called they can be cross-examined because it notes that those who simply provide written statements cannot be interrogated.

make sufficient inquiry into these matters led to the quashing of an appeal decision in *R v Cardinal Newman's School ex parte S.*[201]

6.88 Where an independent appeals panel is considering whether to decline to order a pupil's reinstatement, it should give the parties a specific opportunity to address that issue.[202]

Decision-making by appeal panel

6.89 The appeal panel is obliged to have regard to the guidance of the Secretary of State when making any decision on appeal.[203] The appeal panel is not to determine that a pupil should be reinstated merely because of a failure to comply with procedural requirements imposed by or under the regulations in relation to a decision of the governing body not to reinstate or the exclusion or decision by the headteacher.[204]

6.90 Prior to 1 September 2012, an appeal panel in England was expressly required by the relevant regulations to have regard to both the interests of the excluded pupil and the interests of other pupils at the school and persons working at the school, including persons working there voluntarily.[205] There is no equivalent regulation to this effect in Wales.

6.91 The appeal panel may uphold the exclusion, direct that the pupil is to be reinstated (either immediately or by a date specified in the direction) or decide that because of exceptional circumstances, or for other reasons, it is not practical to give a direction requiring his reinstatement, but that it would otherwise have been appropriate to give such a direction.[206] Decisions are by majority vote with the chairman having a second or casting vote.[207] The decision and the grounds on which it is made must be communicated in writing to the relevant person, the LA, the governing body and the headteacher within two working days after the conclusion of the appeal hearing.[208]

---

[201] [1998] ELR 304, Moses J.

[202] *R (D) v Independent Appeal Panel of Bromley London Borough* [2008] ELR 12. This of course will no longer have direct relevance in England in relation to exclusion from 1 September 2012 because review panels have no power to order reinstatement from that date.

[203] Regulation 7(1)(c) of SI 2002/3178 in England prior to 1 September 2012; reg 8(1)(c) of SI 2003/3227 in Wales.

[204] Regulation 6(4) of SI 2002/3178 in England prior to 1 September 2012; reg 7(3) of SI 2003/3227 in Wales.

[205] Paragraph 6(3) of Sch 1 to SI 2002/3178 in England prior to 1 September 2012.

[206] Regulation 6(6) of SI 2002/3178 for schools and reg 7(6) of SI 2002/3179 for PRUs.

[207] Paragraph 13 of Sch 1 to SI 2002/3178 in England prior to 1 September 2012; para 13 of Sch 1 to SI 2003/3227 in Wales.

[208] Paragraph 14 of Sch 1 to SI 2002/3178 in England prior to 1 September 2012; para 14 of Sch 1 to SI 2003/3227 (as amended by SI 2010/1142) in Wales.

Content of the duty to reinstate

6.92 As a matter of language it might be thought that the duty to reinstate if ordered by the appeal panel or the governors meant that the school was obliged to restore the status quo. By a bare majority the House of Lords[209] decided that reinstatement did not bear this meaning but meant simply that a pupil was no longer excluded. It is respectfully submitted that the decision of the minority is to be preferred. To define reinstatement as simply meaning no longer being excluded is a departure from the natural meaning of the concept and essentially circular. It does not help on the content of the duty; indeed, as Lord Hoffman pointed out, it empties that concept of practical content. It also means that a decision of an appeal panel, which is intended to be binding,[210] is deprived of much of its force. According to the majority,[211] a pupil was reinstated when he was provided with work and a teacher in a room isolated from the mainstream of the school, and he was not allowed to return to his class or to circulate with other pupils at any stage of the day. The House of Lords accepted[212] that if reinstatement was a sham or the school was not acting in good faith then there would be no reinstatement in law; however, it is difficult to see how these will ever be established on the facts of any case if reinstatement has such little practical content.

6.93 The House of Lords was heavily influenced by the fact the headteacher had acted under the threat of industrial action from the staff. It was accepted before the House of Lords that the threat was a relevant consideration.[213] Once that was accepted the school was in the position where it could lawfully refuse fully to integrate the child back into school even where, but for that threat, the child would have been so integrated. The effect of the decision is therefore that the decision of the appeal panel can be defeated simply by the teachers in question refusing to teach the child who has won the appeal.[214] The union would enjoy immunity from the tort of inducing breach of contract because the dispute would be a trade dispute.[215] That is a position much to be regretted because it much reduces the efficacy of an appeal which Parliament intended to benefit the pupil who had been excluded. While the absence of an effective power of reinstatement on appeal is of declining practical importance in England because review panels can no longer order reinstatement in relation to exclusions from 1 September 2012 it remains of importance in Wales. It means that although the statutory schemes in England and Wales are different under both statutory schemes a pupil who wins his appeal or review may find that he is not restored to the status quo that existed prior to his exclusion.

---

[209] *R (on the application of L) (A Minor) v Governors of J School* [2003] UKHL 9, [2003] 1 All ER 1012. Lords Bingham and Hoffmann dissented.

[210] Regulation 6(5) of SI 2002/3178 and reg 7(5) of SI 2002/3179.

[211] At para 42.

[212] At para 47.

[213] See at para 80. Cf *R v Coventry City Council ex parte Phoenix Aviation* [1995] 3 All ER 37.

[214] While some appeals will be won even though the child has not been cleared on the merits of the incident alleged that led to the exclusion, that will not be true in all cases.

[215] *P v NASUWT* [2003] UKHL 8, [2003] 1 CR 386.

THE DECISION TO EXCLUDE – RELEVANT CONSIDERATIONS

6.94 Some help is found in the regulations on relevant considerations when making the decision to exclude. As noted above, review panels (and previously independent appeal panels) in England are expressly required by the regulations to have regard to both the interests of the excluded pupil and the interests of other pupils at the school and persons working at the school, including persons working there voluntarily.[216] In addition, the statutory guidance issued by the Secretary of State or the Welsh Assembly must be taken into account by the following persons and bodies in exercising their functions in relation to exclusions:

(a)   the headteacher of a maintained school[217] and the principal of an Academy;[218]

(b)   the governing body of a maintained school;[219]

(c)   the LA responsible for a maintained school;[220]

(d)   the proprietor of an Academy;[221]

(e)   the review panel and the SEN expert where there is a review of the exclusion;[222] and

(f)   the appeal panel where there is an appeal against the exclusion.[223]

6.95 The guidance deals with all stages of the process of the decision to exclude. The 2012 Guidance on Exclusions in England, which came into force on 1 September 2012, is far less prescriptive than the 2008 Guidance on Exclusions in England and the 2004 Guidance on Exclusions in Wales.

---

[216]   Regulation 7(4) of SI 2012/1033 (for maintained schools) and reg 25(4) of SI 2012/1033 (for Academies) in England from 1 September 2012; para 6(3) of Sch 1 to SI 2002/3178 in England prior to 1 September 2012. There is no equivalent reg to this effect in Wales.

[217]   Regulation 9(a) of SI 2012/1033 (for maintained schools) in England from 1 September 2012; reg 7(1)(a) of SI 2002/3178 in England prior to 1 September 2012; reg 8(1)(a) of SI 2003/3227 in Wales.

[218]   Regulation 27(a) of SI 2012/1033 in England from 1 September 2012. For the remainder of this Chapter, for 'headteacher' substitute 'principal' with reference to Academies: see reg 21 of SI 2012/1033.

[219]   Regulation 9(b) of SI 2012/1033 in England from 1 September 2012; reg 7(1)(a) of SI 2002/3178 in England prior to 1 September 2012; reg 8(1)(a) of SI 2003/3227 in Wales.

[220]   Regulation 9(c) of SI 2012/1033 in England from 1 September 2012; reg 7(1)(b) of SI 2002/3178 in England prior to 1 September 2012; reg 8(1)(b) of SI 2003/3227 (as amended by SI 2010/1142) in Wales.

[221]   Regulation 27(b) of SI 2012/1033 in England from 1 September 2012.

[222]   Regulation 9(d)–(e) of SI 2012/1033 (for maintained schools) and reg 27(c)–(d) of SI 2012/1033 (for Academies) in England from 1 September 2012.

[223]   Regulation 7(1)(c) of SI 2002/3178 in England prior to 1 September 2012; reg 8(1)(c) of SI 2003/3227 in Wales.

However, unless there are grounds to believe that the detailed guidance given in earlier versions no longer applies, it is likely that it will continue to inform good practice when making the decision to exclude. The 2008 Guidance on Exclusions in England and the 2004 Guidance on Exclusions in Wales specifically directed the independent appeal panel to consider whether the headteacher and governing body had regard to the statutory guidance.[224]

6.96 In *S, T and P v Brent LB*,[225] under a previous statutory scheme, the Court of Appeal commented on the proper role of the Secretary of State in issuing guidance and the extent to which the appeal panels were bound to follow it. It held[226] that the guidance should not seek to influence individual decisions, but could list factors the panels should seek to have regard to without indicating any preferred outcome. The panel should keep in mind that guidance was no more than that; it was not a direction and not rules. If the panel treated the guidance as something to be strictly adhered to it would be failing to exercise its own independent judgement, it would be treating guidance as rules and it would be fettering its discretion.

6.97 The exclusions guidance makes plain that exclusion is a sanction to be used only in response to serious (or persistent)[227] breaches of the school's behaviour policy and if allowing the pupil to remain in school would seriously harm the education or welfare of the pupil or others in the school.[228] Permanent exclusion is a serious matter and will usually, although not always, be the final step in a process for dealing with disciplinary offences following a wide range of other strategies which have been tried without success.[229] Although permanent exclusion should normally be used as a last resort, in exceptional circumstances the headteacher might consider it appropriate to exclude a child for a first or one-off offence.[230] The guidance gives as possible examples, serious actual or threatened violence against another pupil or member of staff, sexual abuse or assault, supplying an illegal drug or carrying an offensive weapon.

6.98 At each stage of the exclusions process, when establishing the facts in relation to an exclusion the decision-maker must apply the civil standard of proof, namely whether on the 'balance of probabilities' it is more likely than

---

[224] Paragraph 156 of the 2008 Guidance on Exclusions in England; Pt 1, para 9.2 of the 2004 Guidance on Exclusions in Wales.

[225] [2002] EWCA Civ 693, [2002] ELR 556 at para 19. For comment see Richard Gold 'The Legal Effect of Statutory Guidance' [2003] ELJ 100.

[226] [2002] EWCA Civ 693 at para 15.

[227] Persistent breaches are only referred to in the 2012 Guidance on Exclusions in England: see para 15.

[228] Paragraph 12 of the 2012 Guidance on Exclusions in England; para 13 of the 2008 Guidance on Exclusions in England; Pt 1, para 1.1 of the Guidance on Exclusions in Wales.

[229] Paragraph 16 of the 2008 Guidance on Exclusions in England; Pt 1, para 1.3 of the Guidance on Exclusions in Wales. This is not specifically addressed in the 2012 Guidance on Exclusions in England.

[230] Paragraph 17 of the 2008 Guidance on Exclusions in England; Pt 1, para 1.4 of the Guidance on Exclusions in Wales.

not that a fact is true, rather than the criminal standard of proof, namely 'beyond reasonable doubt'. A degree of uncertainty about this question was generated by the decision in *R (S) v The Governing Body of YP School*.[231] In that case Laws LJ stated that the right approach had been conceded by the parties, namely that in dealing with a disciplinary matter where the accusation amounts to a crime under the general law, the headteacher must be sure that the child has done what he has been accused of doing, essentially equating the degree of probability required with the criminal standard of proof.

6.99 Following this decision, the regulations in force at the time were amended to explicitly provide that where any fact fell to be established, any question as to whether that fact was established had to be decided on the balance of probabilities by the headteacher, the governing body and the appeal panel.[232] This was reiterated in SI 2012/1033 which provides that the civil standard is to be applied by the headteacher, the governing body or proprietor and the review panel.[233]

6.100 In *R (V) v Independent Appeal Panel for Tom Hood School*[234] the Court of Appeal affirmed that the regulation made in 2004[235] was lawful and upheld the decision of an appeal panel that applied the civil standard of proof even though the allegation in question, if established, would have amounted to the commission of a criminal offence.[236]

6.101 Drug related offences are dealt with in the 2008 Guidance on Exclusions in England and the 2004 Guidance on Exclusions in Wales. They provide that in making a decision whether to exclude for a drug-related incident the headteacher should have regard to the school's published policy on drugs and should consult the school's drugs co-ordinator in England or an appropriately trained member of staff in Wales.[237]

6.102 The 2008 Guidance on Exclusions in England and the 2004 Guidance on Exclusions in Wales provided that the headteacher should not exclude in the

---

[231] [2003] EWCA 1306, [2004] ELR 37.
[232] Regulation 7A of SI 2002/3178 (inserted by SI 2004/402) in England prior to 1 September 2012; reg 8A of SI 2003/3227 (inserted by SI 2004/1805) in Wales.
[233] Regulation 10 of SI 2012/1033 (for maintained schools) and ref 28 of SI 2012/1033 (for Academies) in England from 1 September 2012.
[234] [2010] EWCA Civ 142, [2010] ELR 291.
[235] Regulation 7A of SI 2002/3178 (inserted by SI 2004/402) in England prior to 1 September 2012.
[236] The particular allegation that would have amounted to a criminal offence was possession of a knife. The Court of Appeal held that Art 6 was not engaged as V did not have a civil right to be educated at a particular school and the sanction of permanent exclusion was insufficiently severe to render the charge against him criminal.
[237] Paragraph 22 of the 2008 Guidance on Exclusions in England; Pt 1, para 2.1 of the Guidance on Exclusions in Wales. This is not specifically addressed in the 2012 Guidance on Exclusions in England.

heat of the moment and that before excluding, whether for a fixed period or permanently, the headteacher should:[238]

(a)   ensure that a thorough investigation has been carried out in the case of a school in England and an appropriate investigation has been carried out in the case of a school in Wales;

(b)   consider all the evidence available to support the allegations, taking account of all relevant school policies;

(c)   allow the pupil to give his version of events;

(d)   check whether the incident may have been provoked;

(e)   if necessary, consult others, but not anyone who may have a later role in reviewing the headteacher's decision.

6.103   The 2008 Guidance on Exclusions in England and the 2004 Guidance on Exclusions in Wales provided that headteachers should consider alternative solutions to exclusion.[239] Although the 2004 Guidance on Exclusions in Wales states that exclusion should not be used if alternative solutions are available, this mandatory rule is of doubtful legality and as such[240] it can probably take effect as meaning that the headteacher should not normally exclude in those circumstances.

6.104   The 2012 Guidance on Exclusions in England provides that the behaviour of pupils outside school can be considered as grounds for exclusion.[241] The 2008 Guidance on Exclusions in England and the 2004 Guidance on Exclusions in Wales provided that pupils' behaviour outside school but on school business, such as school trips, was subject to the school's behaviour policy and should be dealt with in the same way as if it had occurred on the school premises.[242] Bad behaviour outside school but not on school business can be grounds for exclusion provided that, in the judgement of the

---

[238]   Paragraph 23 of the 2008 Guidance on Exclusions in England; Pt 1, para 3.1 of the Guidance on Exclusions in Wales. This is not specifically addressed in the 2012 Guidance on Exclusions in England.

[239]   Paragraph 11 of the 2008 Guidance on Exclusions in England; Pt 1, para 5.1 of the Guidance on Exclusions in Wales.

[240]   See by analogy *R v Social Fund Inspector ex parte Stitt* [1990] COD 288. See also on the inability of guidance to be mandatory *R (on the application of P) v Oxfordshire County Council* [2002] EWCA Civ 693, [2002] ELR 556 at para 15.

[241]   Paragraph 3 of the 2012 Guidance on Exclusions in England citing s 89(5) of the Education and Inspections Act 2006. Non-statutory guidance on maintained schools' powers to discipline outside of the school are set out in *Behaviour and Discipline in Schools – A Guide for Head teachers and School Staff (2012)*.

[242]   Paragraph 61 of the 2008 Guidance on Exclusions in England; Pt 1, para 12.1 of the Guidance on Exclusions in Wales.

headteacher, there is a clear link between that behaviour and maintaining good behaviour and discipline among the pupil body as a whole.[243]

6.105 Additional safeguards apply to the exclusion of pupils with special educational needs. The 2012 Guidance on Exclusions in England provides that headteachers should, as far as possible, avoid excluding permanently any pupil with a statement of SEN or a looked after child.[244] It states that where a school has concerns about the behaviour, or risk of exclusion, of a child with additional needs, a pupil with a statement of SEN or a looked after child, it should, in partnership with others (including the LA as necessary), consider what additional support or alternative placement may be required.[245] This should involve assessing the suitability of provision for a pupil's SEN. Where a pupil has a statement of SEN, schools should consider requesting an early annual review or interim/emergency review. The 2008 Guidance on Exclusions in England and the 2004 Guidance on Exclusions in Wales directs schools and governing bodies to have regard to the SEN Code of Practice.[246] They state that pupils with SEN should only be permanently excluded in the most exceptional circumstances.[247] If their statement of SEN can be changed or extra support provided, these strategies should normally be pursued and any existing exclusion should be withdrawn.[248]

6.106 There is also a duty to avoid discrimination in making exclusion decisions. In particular, this includes a duty not to discriminate on the grounds of disability or race.[249]

6.107 When the matter falls to be considered by the governing body or proprietor, the 2012 Guidance on Exclusions in England provides that in deciding whether or not to reinstate a pupil the governing body should consider whether the decision to exclude the pupil was lawful, reasonable and procedurally fair, taking account of the headteacher's legal duties.[250] The 2008 Guidance on Exclusions in England and the 2004 Guidance on Exclusions in Wales provide that where reinstatement is practical, the governing body should consider any representations made by the parent, the pupil and the LA and whether the headteacher has complied with the law on exclusion and had

---

243 Paragraph 61 of the 2008 Guidance on Exclusions in England; Pt 1, para 12.1 of the Guidance on Exclusions in Wales.
244 Paragraph 22 of the 2012 Guidance on Exclusions in England.
245 Paragraph 24 of the 2012 Guidance on Exclusions in England.
246 Paragraph 63 of the 2008 Guidance on Exclusions in England; Pt 1, para 13.1 of the 2004 Guidance on Exclusions in Wales.
247 Paragraph 64 of the 2008 Guidance on Exclusions in England; Pt 1, para 13.2 of the 2004 Guidance on Exclusions in Wales.
248 Paragraph 65 of the 2008 Guidance on Exclusions in England; Pt 1, para 13.3 of the 2004 Guidance on Exclusions in Wales.
249 Paragraph 8 of the 2012 Guidance on Exclusions in England; paras 68–76 of the 2008 Guidance on Exclusions in England; Pt 1, paras 14.1–15.3 of the 2004 Guidance on Exclusions in Wales.
250 Paragraph 67 of the 2012 Guidance on Exclusions in England.

regard to the guidance.[251] In addition, both the 2008 and the 2012 versions of the Guidance on Exclusions in England and the 2008 Guidance on Exclusions in England provide that the governing body should consider whether on a balance of probabilities the pupil did what he or she is alleged to have done.[252] The 2004 Guidance on Exclusions in Wales states that the governing body should consider appropriate school policies, including the school's published behaviour policy, equal opportunities policy, anti-bullying policy, special educational needs policy and race equality policy.[253] Where reinstatement is not practical the guidance provides that the governors must consider whether the headteacher's decision was justified on the evidence.[254]

6.108 Where there is an application for review, the 2012 Guidance on Exclusions in England provides that the review panel may only quash the decision of the governing body where it considers that it was flawed when considered in the light of the principles applicable on an application for judicial review.[255] The 2012 Guidance on Exclusions in England states that the panel should apply the following tests in this respect:

(a) Illegality – did the headteacher and/or governing body act outside the scope of their legal powers in taking the decision to exclude?

(b) Irrationality – was the decision of the governing body not to reinstate the pupil so unreasonable that it was not one a sensible person could have made?

(c) Procedural impropriety – was the process of exclusion and the governing body's consideration so unfair or flawed that justice was clearly not done?

While the guidance on these matters is helpful, it plainly is not an exhaustive statement of the principles upon which a court would intervene by way of judicial review. It does not, for example, include the power of the court to review a decision where the decision-maker has failed to take account of relevant considerations. The guidance cannot cut down the statutory right to have a review on the full panoply of judicial review grounds and were a review panel to limit its consideration of a review to the matters specified in the guidance it would itself be amenable to successful challenge by way of judicial review. In addition if the review panel jurisdiction is cut down by the statutory guidance to something less than a court would do on a judicial review then a

---

[251] Paragraph 109 of the 2008 Guidance on Exclusions in England; Pt 3, para 3.3 of the 2004 Guidance on Exclusions in Wales.

[252] Paragraph 62 of the 2012 Guidance on Exclusions in England; para 109 of the 2008 Guidance on Exclusions in England.

[253] Part 3, para 3.3 of the 2004 Guidance on Exclusions in Wales.

[254] Paragraph 112 of the 2008 Guidance on Exclusions in England; Pt 3, para 3.7 of the 2004 Guidance on Exclusions in Wales.

[255] Paragraph 132 of the 2012 Guidance on Exclusions in England. Statutory guidance on this consideration is provided by paras 148–151 of the Guidance.

parent might be justified in launching judicial review proceedings of a decision to exclude before a review on the ground that the review was not an adequate alternative remedy.

6.109 The 2012 Guidance on Exclusions in England explains that procedural impropriety means something that has a significant impact on the quality of the decision-making process. It gives the examples of bias, failing to notify parents of their right to make representations, the governing body making a decision without having given parents an opportunity to make representations, failing to give reasons for a decision and the headteacher taking part in the decision not to reinstate.[256]

6.110 If the relevant person appeals against the exclusion, the 2008 Guidance on Exclusions in England and the 2004 Guidance on Exclusions in Wales provide that the independent appeal panel should consider:[257]

(a)   whether the pupil did what he or she is alleged to have done. It is said that the panel should decide this on the balance of probabilities;

(b)   the basis of the headteacher's decision and the procedures followed, having regard to:

    (i)   whether the headteacher and the governors complied with the law and the guidance. Serious procedural defects may be sufficient to allow an appeal;

    (ii)   the school's published behaviour policy, equal opportunities policy and, if appropriate, anti-bullying policy, SEN policy and race equality policy;

    (iii) the fairness of the exclusion in relation to the treatment of any other pupils involved in the same incident,

(c)   whether exclusion was a reasonable response and, if not, whether the particular appeal is an exceptional one where reinstatement is not a practical way forward;

(d)   the interests of the excluded pupil and the interests of all other members of the school community;

(e)   if a claim of race or disability discrimination is made, whether there has been such discrimination.

6.111 In *R v London Borough of Camden and the Governors of the Hampstead school ex parte H*,[258] the Court of Appeal treated earlier guidance[259] as a

---

[256] Paragraph 149 of the 2012 Guidance on Exclusions in England.
[257] Paragraphs 155–161 of the 2008 Guidance on Exclusions in England; Pt 2, paras 9.1–9.6 of the 2004 Guidance on Exclusions in Wales.
[258] [1996] ELR 360 at 360 and 372C.
[259] Circular 10/94.

relevant consideration, but without either any debate or holding that it was, in fact, a relevant consideration. In *R v Northamptonshire ex parte Weighill*[260] Laws J, without having heard full argument on the point, but basing himself on that decision of the Court of Appeal, held that the then current circular was a relevant consideration. The current Guidance on Exclusions is, of course, expressly a relevant consideration under the regulations.[261] It does not follow that those with functions in relation to exclusion are obliged slavishly to follow the guidance; their only duty is to have regard to it. If, however, a matter is dealt with in the guidance, then the decision-maker probably has to give reasons for not following it. Case-law has shed some further light on other relevant considerations in this area.

Proportionality and conduct off school premises

6.112 In *R v London Borough of Newham ex parte X*[262] Brooke J held it was arguable that the behaviour of pupils towards each other off school premises was a relevant consideration[263] and that the penalty had to be proportionate to the offence. While the appropriate penalty was essentially a matter for the school authorities, he thought it arguably disproportionate to exclude a boy permanently for removing a younger boy's trousers and possibly his underpants, socks and shoes and then humiliating him. Accordingly, the judge granted leave to move for judicial review. While this was only a leave application, it is submitted that the learned judge was right to come to the conclusions he did as to the relevance of conduct off school premises and the importance of proportionality. This decision, in relation to behaviour off school premises, has been strengthened by the statutory guidance on exclusions.[264] While proportionality is not, as yet, a general principle of public law, it has gained acceptance in the context of administrative penalties.[265]

---

[260] [1998] ELR 291.

[261] See para **6.94** above.

[262] [1995] ELR 303.

[263] [1995] ELR 303, at 306H to 307A.

[264] See the discussion at para **6.104** above.

[265] See *R v Barnsley MBC ex parte Hook* [1976] 1 WLR 1052 at 1057 and De Smith, Woolf, and Jowell *Judicial Review of Administrative Action* at (op cit) pp 601–602. However, in this context of school expulsions Turner J suggested in *R v Governors of St Gregory's Roman Catholic School Aided High School* [1995] ELR 290 at 301G that proportionality was not part of domestic law in this context. The point was not elaborated upon and, it is submitted, not in accordance with the balance of authority in this area and would not now be followed. In *R v Secretary of State for the Home Department ex parte Mbandaka* [1999] Ed CR 656 Collins J did consider whether the penalties imposed in that case were disproportionate but refused to intervene, inter alia, on the ground that there was no evidence of a likelihood of any reoccurrence. The same judge had also considered that proportionality was relevant in *R v Governors of Bacon's City Technology College ex parte W* [1998] ELR 488. See also Richards J in *R v Muntham House School ex parte R* [2000] ELR 287 at 297H, where he adopted an approach of proportionality but held that the matter was not reviewable because the school in question was not amenable to judicial review.

Conduct of parent

6.113   The conduct of a parent may be relevant consideration. In *Secretary of State for Education and Science v Tameside MBC*,[266] Lord Diplock referred to the parents as partners with the LA and the Secretary of State in the education of their children. Turner J in *R v Neale and another ex parte S*,[267] founding on this and common sense, held, without making a definitive ruling on the point, that where the parent's attitude to the headteacher and governors was defiant, it was not necessarily an irrelevant consideration in deciding whether to make an exclusion permanent.

6.114   There is a question as to whether this remains accurate in the light of the clear position taken in the statutory guidance that it would be unlawful to exclude a pupil due to the actions of a pupil's parents[268] or to punish a pupil's parents.[269]

6.115   A variety of other strategies are available for dealing with difficult parents, such as prosecution under section 547 of the EA 1996, which makes it an offence for a trespasser on school premises to cause or permit a nuisance or disturbance and allows for the removal and prosecution of any person believed to have committed the offence. While, in the case of a serious incident, this may keep the parent off school premises, it will do nothing to repair what, by that stage, may be a serious breakdown in the relationship between parent and school.

6.116   Although the Guidance on Exclusions must be taken into account, it is submitted that it cannot have the effect that in no case would it be appropriate to exclude a pupil because of the conduct of the parent. The guidance cannot have such an absolute effect because of its nature as guidance[270] and it is submitted that the tentative ruling in *Neale* is correct and still good law. While it would be wrong to base an exclusion decision entirely on the conduct of the parent, because the child is not responsible for his parents, nevertheless if there is a total breakdown in the relationship of parent and school, the partnership between them simply cannot operate. If a child already merits punishment because of serious misconduct, having regard to the conduct of a difficult parent which aggravates the offence (for example a parent seeking to harass pupils who were victims of bullying by his child) may be sufficient grounds for excluding a pupil for the offence he committed. It is submitted, however, that it would be wrong in principle to exclude a child who was in no way at fault because his parent was difficult. In those circumstances there would have been no breach of the school's behaviour policy, or indeed, any other offence by the pupil meriting exclusion.

---

[266]   [1977] AC 1014 at 1063.

[267]   [1995] ELR 198 at 211E.

[268]   Paragraph 12 of the 20012 Guidance on Exclusions in England.

[269]   Paragraph 26(f) of the 2008 Guidance on Exclusions in England; Pt 1, para 4.1(f) of the 2004 Guidance on Exclusions in Wales.

[270]   *R (on the application of S) v Brent LBC* [2002] EWCA Civ 693, [2002] ELR 556.

6.117 The issue was considered by Kay J in *R v Bryn Elian High School Board of Governors ex parte W*.[271] In that case, two sisters were permanently excluded from school after a series of disruptive incidents. Their behaviour had been influenced by their father, a former headteacher of the school who, since his departure, had been very critical of it and its management. Kay J held it was proper for the headteacher to look at the way the father had behaved and the way in which that would have an effect on the way the children would behave, if not excluded; but he also held that the children had been excluded for their own conduct and not that of their father, the latter's conduct only being relevant to the question whether there was a reasonable prospect that the children's behaviour would improve.[272] Although this case pre-dates the present Guidance, it is submitted that it illustrates an approach that is still permissible.

Effect of not excluding on the victim

6.118 Where the conduct that leads to consideration of expulsion involves a victim, it is appropriate to consider not only the effect of exclusion on those who will be excluded, but also the effect on the victim if the offenders are not excluded. The point arose in *R v London Borough of Camden and the Governors of the Hampstead School ex parte H*.[273] In that case, the Court of Appeal reversed the decision of the judge and held that the effect on the victim of an assault should be taken into account when considering setting aside a headteacher's decision to exclude. If it was a choice between the victim remaining at school or the offenders then the justice of the case might be to let the victim remain.[274] While the case concerned the decision of the LA and the governors, it would seem that the headteacher should also consider the effect of not excluding the offender if the victim is to remain at school. The regulations provide that the effect of reinstatement on other pupils[275] at the school is now expressly a relevant consideration for the governing body in England from 1 September 2012[276] as well as for the review panel[277] or appeal panel.[278]

Previous conduct

6.119 Previous conduct is plainly a relevant consideration.[279] The 2012 Guidance on Exclusions in England explicitly recognises for the first time that exclusion may be appropriate in response to persistent breaches, as well as a

---

271 [1999] ELR 380.

272 [1999] ELR 380, at 398F–399B and 401D–401E.

273 [1996] ELR 360.

274 [1996] ELR 360, at 378H–379A.

275 The provision is not confined to victims and covers all other pupils.

276 Regulation 6(3)(a) of SI 2012/1033 (for maintained schools) and reg 24(3)(a) of SI 2012/1033 (for Academies) in England from 1 September 2012.

277 Regulation 7(4) of SI 2012/1033 (for maintained schools) and reg 25(4) of SI 2012/1033 (for Academies) in England from 1 September 2012.

278 Regulation 6(3) of SI 2002/3178 in England prior to 1 September 2012. There is no equivalent regulation in Wales.

279 *R v London Borough of Camden and the Governors of the Hampstead School ex parte H* [1996] ELR 360 at 379C–379D.

single serious breach, of the school's behaviour policy.[280] The 2008 Guidance on Exclusions in England and the 2004 Guidance on Exclusions in Wales acknowledge that permanent exclusion will usually be the final step in a process for dealing with disciplinary offences, following a wide range of other strategies which have been tried without success.[281] In *A v Staffordshire County Council*,[282] a pupil was permanently excluded for deflating a teacher's tyres on April Fool's day. The court held that the exclusion was not unlawful, having regard to the pupil's poor disciplinary record and the fact that his continued presence at the school would make it more difficult to deliver satisfactory education to the rest of the children.

Degree of injury

6.120   Where exclusion is based on an assault, it is appropriate to examine the injury actually sustained rather than punish someone for the hurt that may have been caused to a typical victim: see *R v London Borough of Camden and Governors of Hampstead school ex parte H.*[283] This does not mean that a medical report must be obtained as to the precise extent of the victim's injuries.[284]

Educational factors

6.121   Educational factors is a rather intangible concept. In *R v The Board of Governors of Stoke Newington School*,[285] in a challenge which succeeded on procedural grounds, the court held[286] that a decision as to whether the child should be reinstated was essentially one for those concerned with the administration of the school and the education of the child. Those persons should take account of educational factors which the court said were outside its province. The learned judge made reference to the history of the child being obstructive in class and preventing the education of others and the fact that the child had benefited from home tuition. It would seem, therefore, that these are relevant factors, although the second of these factors is not likely to be in play when the headteacher makes his initial decision. It has also been held to be a relevant consideration that the particular school had strict disciplinary standards.[287]

---

[280]   Paragraph 15 of the 2012 Guidance on Exclusions in England.
[281]   Paragraph 1 of the 2008 Guidance on Exclusions in England; Pt 1, para 1.3 of the 2004 Guidance on Exclusions in Wales.
[282]   (1996) *The Times,* 18 October.
[283]   [1996] ELR 360 at 379B–379C.
[284]   *R (on the application of C) v Sefton Metropolitan Borough Council Independent Appeals Panel and the Governors of Hillside High School* [2001] ELR 393, Scott Baker J.
[285]   [1994] ELR 131.
[286]   [1994] ELR 131, at 138G.
[287]   *R v Governors of St Gregory's RC Aided High School and Appeals Committee ex parte M* [1995] ELR 290 at 301D.

FACTORS NOT JUSTIFYING EXCLUSION

6.122 The Guidance on Exclusions provides in mandatory terms[288] when exclusion should not be used. That again can only take effect as meaning that exclusion should not normally take place in those cases. The examples given of when exclusion should not be used are:

(a) minor incidents such as failure to do homework or bring dinner money;

(b) poor academic performance;

(c) lateness or truancy;

(d) pregnancy;

(e) breaches of school uniform rules or rules on appearance except where these are persistent and in open defiance of such rules;

(f) punishing pupils for the behaviour of their parents.

6.123 It is submitted that these matters are, with limited exceptions, legitimate matters of policy for the Secretary of State to adopt and require little further comment. Two matters in this list do, however, merit comment. The guidance in relation to a parent's conduct has already been considered and it is submitted that there cannot be an inflexible rule to the effect that this is always irrelevant.

6.124 The second matter worthy of comment is the suggestion that it might, in certain circumstances, be appropriate to exclude for breaches of rules relating to dress or appearance. This is dealt with in detail in Chapter 3[289] and at paras **6.132–6.134** below.

WEDNESBURY AND HUMAN RIGHTS CHALLENGES

6.125 The extent to which the court will entertain a challenge to the merits of a decision to exclude was explored in *R v Governors of St Gregory's RC Aided High School and Appeals Committee ex parte M*:[290]

'It is as well at this stage to reiterate the familiar principle which must govern the court's approach to the reasonableness of the decision in the well known *Wednesbury* sense. The court is not concerned with a function of review or appeal. But it is concerned with the question whether or not the decision was (*Associated Provincial Picture Houses v Wednesbury Corporation* [1948] 1 KB 223 at p 229):

---

[288] At para 5.1. Although it is in mandatory terms it cannot take effect as anything other than guidance and the decision-maker is not bound to follow it: see *R (on the application of P (A Child))* v *Oxfordshire County Council Exclusion Appeals Panel* [2002] EWCA Civ 693, [2002] ELR 556.
[289] See at paras **3.113–3.121**.
[290] [1995] ELR 290 at 301E–301G.

"so absurd that no sensible person could ever dream that it lay within the power of the authority (so to act)."

This test has not to be diluted. It is far easier to establish that it has been met when it can be shown that the authority in question has either failed to take into, or left out of, account some material factor. That cannot be shown here. So the question becomes one for the court to assess whether or not a reasonable headteacher could have arrived at the decision reached in the present case. In my judgement, the applicant has failed to establish that he would not, and by a significant margin. The decision would have been the same even if the principle of proportionality formed a part of the domestic law of our courts.'

6.126 As observed above it may well be that the suggestion that proportionality was not relevant in this context is too restrictive. However, the case does illustrate the reluctance of the courts to intervene on merits-based challenges.[291] Subsequent appellate authority has taken a similarly restrictive view on acceding to irrationality challenges to school expulsion decisions. In *R (on the application of DR) v Head Teacher of S School*[292] the Court of Appeal applied the test in employment law,[293] ie was the decision under challenge 'certainly wrong' or 'perverse' rather than being a 'permissible option'. In that case a pupil was raped and the appellant was one of a group of five boys who had shut her in a darkened room where the attack took place. Although he dissociated himself from the incident by leaving the room before the rape took place, he had by then taken part in an indecent assault and made no attempt to alert anyone to the continuing attack on the girl. In those circumstances, the court found it impossible to say that the decision of the appeal panel in not allowing his appeal was perverse.[294]

6.127 It might be thought, questions of penalty apart, that proportionality was necessarily engaged in any decision to exclude because of Article 2 of the First Protocol to the ECHR. This, however, is not the case. As was established in *A v The Head Teacher and Governors of the Lord Grey School*:[295]

(a) the right to education in Article 2 does not exclude all disciplinary penalties;

(b) it would not be contrary to Article 2 of the First Protocol to exclude provided the national regulations did not prevent the child from enrolling in another establishment;

(c) the duty in Article 2 was imposed on the State and not any particular domestic institution;

---

[291] To similar effect, in a challenge that succeeded on procedural grounds is *R v Board of Governors of Stoke Newington School ex parte M* [1994] ELR 131 at 138F–138G.

[292] [2002] EWCA Civ 1822, [2003] ELR 104.

[293] *Piggott Brothers v Jackson and others* [1992] ICR 85 at 92. Applied at para 48 in this context.

[294] [2002] EWCA Civ 1822, [2003] ELR 104 at paras 49–51.

[295] [2006] UKHL 14, [2006] AC 363. This case is considered in detail in Chapter 7.

(d) Article 2 of the First Protocol did not create any right to be educated in any particular institution;

(e) if the child had no access to any particular alternative educational institution, there might be a breach of Article 2 of the First Protocol and the school authority might be liable in damages unless the cause of the unavailability is that of the LA (in which case it is liable) or the parent's decision (in which case the LA is not liable for a breach of Article 2);

(f) just as compliance with domestic law would not justify a breach of Article 2 of the First Protocol, nor would a failure to comply with domestic law necessarily lead to an infringement of that right.

6.128 In the particular case, one exclusion was held to be unlawful because, inter alia, it was neither fixed term nor permanent,[296] but it was held that this did not render the school liable for breach of Article 2 of the First Protocol to the ECHR. In relation to another period of exclusion, the court held it was neither reasonable nor justified under domestic law, but the school was not liable because alternative education was available pursuant to the LA's responsibilities under section 19 of the EA 1996.[297]

6.129 This approach was repeated in the subsequent Supreme Court case of *Re JR 17's Application for Judicial Review.*[298] Also see, in the context of special educational needs, *R v Essex County Council*,[299] which is considered further in Chapter 7.[300]

6.130 The *Lord Grey School* case was pursued as a complaint to the European Court of Human Rights, under the title *Ali v United Kingdom.*[301] The court held that the exclusion was in pursuit of a legitimate aim, although it recognised that the pupil was not technically excluded for disciplinary reasons or to ensure compliance with the school's internal rules.[302] It readily accepted that over and above the need to ensure observance with a school's internal rules, a measure resulting in the suspension of a pupil for a temporary period for reasons relating to an imperative not immediately connected with school rules – such as a criminal investigation into an incident at the school – could be considered justified.[303] The exclusion was also found to be foreseeable, despite the multiple procedural irregularities in the exclusions process.[304]

---

[296] See the decision at first instance: [2003] EWHC 1533, [2003] ELR 517, at para 93.
[297] [2003] EWHC 1533, [2003] ELR 517, at paras 107–114.
[298] [2010] UKSC 27, [2010] ELR 764, para 63 per Dyson JSC, para 67 per Phillips JSC, para 96 per Rodger JSC and para 113 per Brown JSC. Hale JSC at paras 103–104 expressed the matter slightly differently.
[299] [2010] UKSC 33, [2011] 1 AC 280.
[300] At paras **7.189–7.203**.
[301] [2011] ELR 85, Application no. 40385/06.
[302] [2011] ELR 85, Application no. 40385/06, para 56.
[303] [2011] ELR 85, Application no. 40385/06, para 57.
[304] [2011] ELR 85, Application no. 40385/06, para 58.

6.131   The court held that in determining whether or not an exclusion has resulted in a denial of the right to education the court would consider whether a fair balance was struck between the exclusion and the justification given for that measure.[305] The court listed the following factors as relevant to this question: the procedural safeguards in place to challenge the exclusion and to avoid arbitrariness, the duration of the exclusion, the extent of co-operation shown by the pupil or his parents with efforts to reintegrate him, the efforts of the school authorities to minimise the effects of the exclusion and in particular the adequacy of alternative education provided by the school during the period of exclusion, and the extent to which the rights of any third parties are engaged.

6.132   There are a number of cases in which human rights challenges have been brought where the pupil is out of school due to a refusal to comply with the school's dress code. The cases concerning this issue as it arises in the context of Article 9 are dealt with in Chapter 3[306] on discrimination. It is worth here noting other Articles of the ECHR relating to this issue.

6.133   The right of freedom of expression to be found in Article 10 of the ECHR would, in general, seem not to cover how a person dresses unless the individual dresses in a particular way to express ideas or opinions.[307] Where the individual does so dress, it should be possible for the school to show there is a legitimate interest in a school having a uniform and that it was necessary to enforce a rule that it should be worn. Rules about school dress are, in principle, reasonable and promote discipline and a persistent and open defiance of such rules would undermine school discipline. Exclusion on those grounds would appear to be proportionate. The restriction is probably sufficient as prescribed by law because school rules have as their legal basis section 61(4) of the SSFA 1998. Accordingly, it is submitted that exclusion as a last resort for breach of uniform requirements should not be a breach of Article 10 of the ECHR.

6.134   In *R on the application of Roberts v Chair and Governing Body of Cwemfelinfach Primary School*[308] the parent objected to the school policy that earrings should not be worn at school. An application for permission to move for judicial review was brought in reliance upon, inter alia, Articles 8 and 13 of the ECHR and Article 2 of the First Protocol. The reason for the school policy was because of a concern about the health and safety of young children wearing earrings during activities where they might be pulled or struck, such as PE, swimming, dancing, lunchtime play and school trips. When the claimant

---

[305]   [2011] ELR 85, Application no. 40385/06.

[306]   At paras **3.113**–**3.121**.

[307]   *Stevens v United Kingdom* (1986) 46 DR 245 at para 2. See the discussion in Clayton and Tomlinson *The Law of Human Rights* (Oxford University Press, 2003) at para 15.271. The issue might have arisen in *R (on the application of Roberts) v Chair and Governing Body of Cwemfelinfach Primary School* [2001] EWHC 242 (Admin) (Richards J), where the parent objected to the school policy that earrings should not be worn at school but confined the challenge under the ECHR to Arts 8 and 13 and Art 2 of the First Protocol. The application was unsuccessful and permission to move for judicial review was refused.

[308]   [2001] EWHC 242 (Admin), Richards J.

refused to comply with the policy, the school prevented her participating in the relevant activities. Richards J refused permission to apply for judicial review. A challenge that the 'exclusion' policy breached the provisions relating to the national curriculum failed.[309] Richards J rejected the argument under Article 13 on the basis that judicial review provided an adequate remedy.[310] The Article 8 argument was not developed before him and he saw nothing in it.[311] On the question of breach of Article 2 of the First Protocol he held that:[312]

(a) the right of access to educational institutions was not absolute or unqualified;

(b) the policy which had been adopted was rational and had been adopted for health and safety reasons;

(c) such a policy was a legitimate means of regulating access; it was confined to particular activities; it was not punitive in nature and did not go further than was necessary in accordance with the health and safety aspects of the policy;

(d) the parent's objection to the ban was not a religious or philosophical conviction and therefore the second sentence of Article 2 had not been breached.

Procedural challenges

6.135 Not surprisingly, it has been held that the rules of natural justice apply to the decision to exclude a pupil[313] and we have seen that there are opportunities under the relevant statutory schemes for interested persons to make representations at various stages.

6.136 In *R v Governors of the London Oratory School ex parte Regis*[314] the headteacher recommended expulsion and told the parents of their right of appeal to the governors. At the same time he informed them that he would act as clerk to the governors and at no stage was he asked to stand down from this task. He took no part in the decision-making process and withdrew with the applicants prior to that stage. The court dismissed an application for judicial review, holding that the rules of fairness did not require the headteacher to withdraw. This was also a plain case of waiver. It is well established that once a person knows the facts which entitle him to object, he must take the point there and then and cannot seek to raise the point later: see *R v Nailsworth Licensing Justices ex parte Bird*.[315]

---

[309] [2001] EWHC 242 (Admin), at paras 22–31.
[310] [2001] EWHC 242 (Admin), at para 42.
[311] [2001] EWHC 242 (Admin), at para 48.
[312] [2001] EWHC 242 (Admin), at paras 45–47.
[313] *R v Governors of the London Oratory School ex parte Regis* [1989] Fam Law 67.
[314] [1989] Fam Law 67.
[315] [1953] 1 WLR 1046. See to same effect *Wade on Administrative Law* (op cit) at p 481.

6.137   The *Regis* case is to be contrasted with *R (on the application of AM) v Governing Body of K School and Independent Appeal Panel of London Borough of E.*[316] In that case, the headteacher was alleged to have remained in the room after the hearing by the governors and to have spoken to the committee members. Because it was contended that any unfairness was cured by the hearing before the appeal panel, no evidence was adduced contradicting that allegation and it was therefore assumed to be true. At first instance, Mitchell J held that that failing, together with the failure to give considerable documentation to the father more than a day before the hearing and the refusal to allow him to adduce three witness statements, gave rise to apparent unfairness. The Court of Appeal endorsed that view, although it held that the unfairness had been cured by the hearing before the appeal panel.

6.138   In *R v Board of Governors Stoke Newington School*[317] the court held that the rules of natural justice had been infringed when a teacher-governor was present at the governors' meeting and was a relevant witness. There is no invariable rule, however, that a teacher-governor who knows the pupil it is sought to exclude cannot sit on the discipline committee of the governors, although such a governor should err on the side of caution and not sit even when the parent fails to object if there is a reasonable doubt as to his ability to act impartially as a result of his knowledge of the pupil.[318] It has been held not to infringe the rule against bias for an appeal panel to be advised by a clerk employed by a LA when the clerk simply advised on points of law and took no part in the decision-making process.[319]

6.139   In *E & Anor v Merchant Taylors School*[320] the Court of Appeal upheld the decision of a review panel convened by an independent school not to reinstate a pupil excluded by the headteacher, C. The pupil's parents argued that the hearing before the review panel was tainted by apparent bias because C knew one of the members of the review panel, J, who was another independent headteacher and attended the same church as C. There was evidence that C had once previously sought J's professional advice about an unrelated matter and that C and J's wives and children knew each other, but did not regularly spend time together. The Court of Appeal held that the relationship between J and C could not lead a fair minded observer to think that there was any real possibility of bias. In reaching this conclusion they took into account the fact that the number of independent school headteachers was small and therefore it was not surprising that C and J knew each other on a professional basis.[321]

---

[316]   [2002] EWCA Civ 1822(2002) *The Times*, 19 December at paras 18 and 45.
[317]   [1994] ELR 131.
[318]   *R (on the application of T) v Head Teacher of Elliot School* [2002] EWCA Civ 1349, [2003] ELR 160 at paras 16 and 47.
[319]   *R (on the application of S (a child)) v C High School Head Teacher* [2001] EWHC (Admin) 513, [2002] ELR 73.
[320]   [2009] EWCA Civ 1050.
[321]   [2009] EWCA Civ 1050, at paras 16–17.

Although they attended the same church there was no evidence that they socialised on even the most occasional basis. Accordingly the test for apparent bias was not met.

6.140 The courts have been prepared to intervene on the grounds of fairness even in relation to the initial decision to exclude by the headteacher. In *R v London Borough of Newham ex parte X*[322] the headteacher took the decision to exclude without giving the parents any opportunity to make representations. Despite rights of appeal, the court held, in the exceptional circumstances of that case, that it was appropriate to grant leave to move for judicial review. The child was in his GCSE year and every day was critical and so interim relief was granted to ensure that the child was back at school pending further order. The correctness of this decision was accepted by the Court of Appeal in *R (on the application of DR) v Head Teacher of S School*,[323] although it observed that it would expect judicial review of decisions below that of the appeal panel to be very few and far between.[324] It was suggested that judicial review would be confined to the cases where the decision-maker had acted quite improperly, where the court's guidance was required on some point of principle or, as in the case of *Newham*, where interim relief was necessary to enable the pupil to return to school to pursue work leading to external qualifications. Although the position that now exists in England for review of exclusions after 1 September 2012 is less favourable from a pupil's point of view than it was because he does not get a full merits appeal, it is probably still the case that the courts will only entertain an application for judicial review prior to an independent review hearing in exceptional cases.

6.141 How an appeal committee should examine evidence was considered in *R v Governors of St Gregory's RC Aided High School and Appeals Committee ex parte M*.[325] In that case a challenge was mounted that it was wrong for the appeal committee to:

(a) receive hearsay evidence of the incident itself;

(b) hear from the child directly without the parents being present.

6.142 The court rejected both challenges.[326] It was sought to be argued again in *R v Staffordshire ex parte Ashworth*[327] that the reception of hearsay evidence by an appeal committee flawed its decision, but again, the court refused to accede to that challenge.

6.143 The Secretary of State's previous Guidance on Exclusions provided expressly for the receipt of hearsay evidence. At paragraph 9.4 it provided that,

---

[322] [1995] ELR 303.
[323] [2002] EWCA Civ 1822, [2003] ELR 104.
[324] [2002] EWCA Civ 1822, [2003] ELR 104, at para 45.
[325] [1995] ELR 290.
[326] [1995] ELR 290, at 297G–297H.
[327] (1997) 9 Admin LR 373.

in the case of witnesses who are pupils of the school, it will normally be more appropriate for the panel to rely on witness statements. At paragraph 9.5 the guidance provided that all written statements must be attributed and signed unless the school has good reason to wish to protect the anonymity of pupils. The paragraph then went on to exhort the panel to bear in mind that a written statement might not encompass all the relevant issues, nor could the author be interrogated. While it is probably still the position that hearsay evidence can be considered, the warnings in the previous guidance about its limitations remain sensible.

6.144 The extent to which it is proper for the appeal panel to consider anonymous evidence has been the subject of a number of cases. In *R v Head Teachers and Independent Appeal Committee of Dunraven School ex parte B*[328] the appellant had been excluded on the basis of a witness statement which he had not seen and oral testimony which he had not heard. The Court of Appeal held that was a breach of the requirements of natural justice because the appellant had not had a fair opportunity of answering the case against him.[329] The court was sensitive about the need to protect confidentiality where there was a fear of reprisals against the informer. It applied[330] the guidance of the EAT in *Linford Cash and Carry Ltd v Thompson*:[331]

> 'Every case must depend upon its own facts ...
>
> 1.   The information given by the informant should be reduced into writing in one or more statements ...
> 2.   In taking the statements the following seem important:
>   ...
>   (D) whether the informant has suffered at the hands of the accused or has any other reason to fabricate, whether from personal grudge or any other reasons or principle.
> 5.   If the informant is prepared to attend a disciplinary hearing no problem will arise, but if, as in the present case, the employer is satisfied that the fear is genuine then a decision will need to be made whether or not to continue with the disciplinary process.
> 7.   The written statement of the informant – if necessary with omissions to avoid identification – should be made available to the employee and his representatives.
> 8.   If the employee or his representatives raises any particular and relevant issue which should be put to the informant, then it may be desirable to adjourn for the chairman to make further enquiries of that informant.'

6.145 It is to be noted that the Court of Appeal in *Dunraven* did not say that in no circumstances would it be appropriate for the appeal panel to act on the basis of anonymous evidence. Indeed, it expressly contemplated that it would

---

[328] [2000] ELR 156.
[329] To similar effect see *R v Governors of Bacon City Technology College ex parte W* [1998] ELR 488, Collins J, where it was held unfair to rely on witness statements the appellant had not seen.
[330] [2000] ELR 156 at 191F–192G.
[331] [1989] IRLR 235.

be proper to act on such evidence if it was necessary to protect the informant. What the court did say, however, is that if the informant's identity cannot be concealed, and that is necessary for his protection, then the appeal panel cannot act on the basis of his evidence and keep it from the appellant.

6.146 The Court of Appeal returned to the problem of anonymised witness statements in *S, T and P v Brent LB and others*.[332] After observing that *Dunraven* did not directly answer the problem of witness statements which were disclosed, but were shorn of evidence of authorship, they held that there might be very good reasons for anonymising such statements, but that the injustice of not using them might be even greater than the injustice of using them, and that appeal panels and governing bodies should be prepared to disregard such statements if they were damaging to the pupil in ways with which the pupil could not be expected to deal without knowing who had made the statement.

6.147 In *R (on the application of T) v Head Teacher of Elliot School*,[333] the appellant contended that *Dunraven* decided that statements which were not signed were inadmissible. The Court of Appeal rejected this contention[334] and then dealt more generally with unsigned statements. It was held[335] that the concept of admissibility was not a useful one in a school exclusion context. The panel had to look at the statements and decide whether to give them weight, bearing in mind that it might be unfair to do so in the absence of identification but that decisions in this area were fact-sensitive. In the particular case, it was held that it was not unfair for the panel to give weight to unsigned statements, but the court observed[336] that if the statements had been damaging in specific respects with which, in the judgement of the panel the pupil could not be expected to deal with without knowing the identity of the author, it would be wrong to give weight to them.

6.148 In *R (on the application of A) v Head Teacher of North Westminster Community School*,[337] Newman J reviewed the above case-law and stated the governing principles in the following terms:

'As the Court of Appeal identify ... the principle at play is fairness. The panel's task is to find the least unfair course. The results of applying the principle of fairness will vary according to the facts of the case in question. To this extent, the consequences or arguable consequences in a case such as this are, in my judgment, essentially driven by the facts of the case. In passages which I have cited, the Court of Appeal were giving instances of how unfairness can arise from the use of an anonymous statement. It was not stipulating a procedure to be followed in every case. For example, unfairness can arise where the statements are damaging to the pupil in ways the pupil cannot be expected to deal with, without knowing who has

---

[332] [2002] EWCA Civ 693, [2002] ELR 556 at para 29.
[333] [2002] EWCA Civ 1349, [2003] ELR 160.
[334] [2002] EWCA Civ 1349, [2003] ELR 160, at para 39.
[335] [2002] EWCA Civ 1349, [2003] ELR 160, at para 37.
[336] [2002] EWCA Civ 1349, [2003] ELR 160, at para 51 referring back to their own decision in *S, T and P v Brent* [2002] EWCA Civ 693, [2002] ELR 556 at para 29.
[337] [2002] EWHC 2351 (Admin), [2003] ELR 378 at paras 6–9.

made the statement. The same point was made in the case of *T*. The instances given were that there may be reasons for believing the witness, whose statement is available in an anonymised form, is unreliable and is well known to be unreliable, or is either a liar or an exaggerator, or there may be other circumstances where there is a possibility of bias. Equally, there are other things which the Court of Appeal have identified which should be borne in mind when they are used. The absence of cross-examination and the character of the maker, and in general, any information which might be available and cast doubt on the quality and reliability of the statement, can arise not simply from the character of the maker of the statement, but can also arise from the circumstances in which it was taken, the time in which it was taken and all the other matters with which the tribunal and courts are familiar when considering questions of reliability.'

6.149   In the case before him, Newman J held it was not unfair to rely on anonymised statements, some of which merely identified the appellant as having been in possession of fireworks. That conclusion was scarcely surprising as fireworks had been found in the appellant's bag. More fundamentally, one of the statements identified the appellant as being responsible for throwing a firework and this was the incident for which he was excluded. It was held not to be unfair to rely on this statement when there was no reason to doubt its accuracy and that line had not been explored by the appellant before the appeal panel.

6.150   It is fair for an appeals panel not to hear evidence from witnesses who have no first-hand knowledge of the incident which led to the exclusion when the claimant wished them to be called simply for the purpose of cross-examination. This may seem obvious but a contention to the contrary was advanced in *R (on the application of J) v A school.*[338] Davis J dismissed the application, holding that the desire of the claimant to cross-examine witnesses to whom he had given an account of the incident, but who had not seen it themselves, was a fishing expedition and there was no unfairness in the appeal panel hearing simply from the headteacher.

6.151   Further consideration was given to the way an appeal committee should approach its task in *R v London Borough of Camden and the Governors of the Hampstead School ex parte H.*[339] In that case, the governors failed to conduct a balanced investigation into the factual issues they had to determine, one of which was whether a shooting was deliberate or not. The offenders had suggested the shooting was accidental and the governors had not heard from the victim on this issue. The court held[340] that, while the governors and the LA were not obliged on every occasion to carry out searching inquiries involving the calling of bodies of oral evidence, if there were factual issues to be resolved reasonable inquiries had to be made and those inquiries had to be balanced. Further, where it was being contemplated not to exclude, it was important to obtain information on the effect this would have on the victim.[341]

---

[338]   [2003] All ER (D) 158.
[339]   [1996] ELR 360.
[340]   [1996] ELR 360 at 377E–377G.
[341]   [1996] ELR 360, at 378F–378G.

6.152 The courts will look at the whole procedure before both the headteacher and any appeal panel, before deciding whether there has been any breach of the duty to act fairly. Accordingly, a fair hearing at appellate level may lead to the conclusion that an earlier breach of the duty of fairness by the headteacher did not mean that the decision to exclude was unfair when the procedure was considered as a whole.[342] That was the approach taken by the Court of Appeal in *R (on the application of DR) v Head Teacher of S School.*[343] It accepted[344] that if the prior procedural fairness tainted the subsequent appeals, then the appeal decision would be in itself assailable, but commented that was not the case before the court and that, save for such a failing, it would find it difficult to think of any case where a decision reached upon a full merits hearing should be impugnable by reference to unfairness at an earlier stage. The court also commented that although there were three stages in an exclusion decision: decisions successively by the headteacher, governing body and appeal panel, the first two stages could sensibly be regarded as one because any case of permanent exclusion was automatically referred to the governing body.[345] This approach has been applied in numerous subsequent cases.[346] Now that the independent review process in England is less than a full merits appeal there will be more scope for arguing that a breach of the duty of fairness at earlier stages was not cured at the review stage. However, in those circumstances the point is likely to be academic because the review panel decision in those circumstances should have allowed the review on procedural grounds.

6.153 It is submitted that a similar approach to that governing procedural fairness would be adopted to the taking account of relevant considerations; if a headteacher failed to take account of a relevant factor but an appeal committee did take account of that factor, it is submitted that the court would not quash the decision of the appeal committee on the basis of the failure of the headteacher to take account of that factor.[347]

6.154 In relation to challenges to the procedure followed by headteachers and governing bodies when making exclusion decisions, it is generally inappropriate to seek to apply the special evidentiary requirements governing criminal proceedings.[348] The correct approach is to consider all the evidence and determine the weight to be accorded to each item of evidence, rather than to

---

[342] *R v Governors of St Gregory's RC Aided High School and Appeals Committee ex parte M* [1995] ELR 290 at 294C–295E.
[343] [2002] EWCA Civ 1822, [2003] ELR 104.
[344] [2002] EWCA Civ 1822, [2003] ELR 104, at para 43.
[345] [2002] EWCA Civ 1822, [2003] ELR 104, at para 37.
[346] Eg *R (A) v Independent Appeals Panel for Sutton* [2009] EWHC 1223 (Admin), [2009] ELR 321, para 44 *per* Hickinbottom J
[347] See also by analogy *R v Secretary of State for Education and North East London Education Association ex parte Morris* [1996] ELR 162 at 203E–205H.
[348] *R (M) v Independent Appeal Panel, Governing Body and Head Teacher of CH School* [2004] EWHC 1831 (Admin), [2005] ELR 48, para 12 per Newman J; *R (A) v Independent Appeals Panel for Sutton* [2009] EWHC 1223 (Admin), [2009] ELR 321, para 40 per Hickinbottom J.

seek to apply rules found in other areas of law, particularly the criminal law, relating to the admissibility of particular forms of evidence.[349]

EXCLUSIONS FOR CRIMINAL OFFENCES

6.155   Problems arise where a pupil is alleged to have committed a criminal offence which has led to the decision to exclude. How should the decision-maker deal with such allegations? What is the standard of proof and what action, if any, should be taken before a decision of the criminal courts as to guilt, or otherwise, of the alleged offender?

6.156   The Secretary of State's 2012 Guidance on Exclusions dealt with these issues. It is the Secretary of State's view that the decisions on exclusion are to be made on the simple balance of probabilities.[350] The Guidance then goes on to describe separately the approach to be adopted by the headteacher, governing body, LA and independent review panel.

6.157   In relation to the headteacher the Guidance provides[351] that he need not postpone his decision to exclude solely because of a police investigation and the possibility that criminal proceedings might be brought in respect of the same incident. It urged him to make a judgement on the basis of the evidence available to him at the time. It did not say in terms whether that judgment should be as to the guilt or otherwise of the pupil in relation to the incident alleged against him. In the light of the fact that precautionary exclusions have now been held not to exist in law[352] it seems likely that the headteacher will have to decide on the guilt or innocence of the pupil on the basis of incomplete materials. That is scarcely satisfactory as is the lack of Guidance on this question. The Guidance merely states lamely that where the evidence is limited by a police investigation or criminal proceedings a headteacher should give particular consideration to ensuring the decision to exclude is fair while being silent as to the factors the headteacher has to take account of in giving that particular consideration.

6.158   The Guidance goes to state at paragraph 172 that where the governing body have to consider an exclusion in these circumstances they cannot postpone their meeting and must decide whether or not to reinstate the pupil on the evidence available. In relation to the independent review panel, the Guidance stated at paragraph 173 that the fact that parallel criminal proceedings were in progress should not 'directly' determine whether the proceedings should be adjourned. It then specified four factors which it said should be considered on a non-exclusive basis. These were:

---

[349]   Eg *R (W) v Independent Appeals Panel of Bexley London Borough Council* [2008] EWHC 758 (Admin), per Burton J.

[350]   Guidance, para 7.

[351]   Guidance, para 170.

[352]   *JR 17's Application for Judicial Review* [2010] UKSC 27, [2010] ELR 764. See para **6.18** above.

(a)   whether any and if so what charge had been brought against the pupil;

(b)   whether relevant witnesses and documents are available;

(c)   the likelihood of delay if the hearing were adjourned and the effect it may have on the excluded pupil, the parents or any victim or the school itself;

(d)   whether an adjournment, or as the case may be, declining to adjourn might result in injustice.

6.159   The Guidance went on to state[353] that if the panel did decide to adjourn, the clerk or LA or Academy Trust should monitor the progress of any police investigation and/or criminal proceedings and should reconvene the panel at the earliest opportunity when the hearing can proceed to a final determination.

6.160   Paragraphs 140 and 174 of the Guidance provided that the panel could adjourn more than once. Earlier Guidance to the effect that where the panel reconvened following the disposal of any criminal proceedings, it should have regard to any information about those proceedings relevant to the issues it must determine has not been reproduced but, it is submitted, must still represent the position. Similarly, earlier Guidance which provided that where there had been an acquittal, the appeal panel should 'bear in mind' that this did not necessarily mean that the pupil had not committed the act alleged has not been reproduced. Again it is submitted the review panel would be entitled to draw a similar inference.

6.161   Is the guidance correct to suggest that the standard of proof is the ordinary civil one on the balance of probabilities? For some time there was a debate about this but the point is now settled the standard of proof is the ordinary civil one. Not only, as we have seen do the relevant regulations so provide but also that is the current effect of the case-law. In *Re B (Children) (Sexual Abuse: Standard of Proof)*[354] the House of Lords clarified the issue of standard of proof and *Re H*, explaining that there was only one civil standard of proof, and that this balance of probabilities test always means more likely than not.[355] This approach has been applied in the context of school exclusion decisions.[356]

---

[353]   Paragraph 174 of Part 5 of the Guidance.
[354]   [2008] UKHL 35, [2009] AC 11.
[355]   [2008] UKHL 35, [2009] AC 11, at para 13 *per* Lord Hoffmann and paras 69–73 per Baroness Hale. Also see *R (D) v Life Sentences Review Commission* [2008] UKHL 33, [2008] 1 WLR 1499, para 28 *per* Lord Carswell.
[356]   *R (V) v Independent Appeal Panel for Tom Hood School* [2010] EWCA Civ 142, [2010] ELR 291; *R (A) v Independent Appeal Panel for Sutton* [2009] EWHC 1223 (Admin), [2009] ELR 321, paras 46–55 *per* Hickinbottom J.

DUTY OF THE APPEAL PANEL TO STATE THE 'GROUNDS' OF ITS DECISION

6.162 Under the previous statutory scheme the appeal panel had to communicate 'grounds' for the decision. What 'grounds' meant in that context was the subject of much case-law and eventually the position was reached that was not very different from a statutory duty to provide reasons.[357] Now paragraph 143 of the 2012 statutory Guidance provides in express terms that the panel must issue a written notification of the decision to all parties without delay and that that notification must include the reasons for the decision.

6.163 There is no obligation upon an appeal panel to state more than reasons why it has reached its decision. In *R v Education Committee of Blackpool Borough Council ex parte Taylor*[358] it was sought to be argued, on an application for permission to move for judicial review, that the appeal committee should in its reasons deal with contentions that had been raised before it and explain, if the contentions were irrelevant, that it has not been influenced by them. Kay J rejected this argument in the following terms:

> 'That is an unsustainable argument. The need to give reasons is a requirement to give reasons which enable parents to understand the basis upon which the decision had been made ... To suggest that every consideration that has been raised which has not influenced them should be recited and then specifically disavowed is one that I find quite unarguable.'

6.164 The requirement to state the reasons for an exclusion decision requires the decision-maker to resolve any important issues of disputed fact.[359]

STANDING AND TIMING

6.165 It seems plain that the child who has been excluded has standing to bring an application for judicial review. He is plainly directly affected, even though he may not be the relevant person as defined by the legislative framework[360] because he has not attained the age of 18. Equally clearly, the parent, where he or she is the relevant person as defined by the legislative framework, would have standing to challenge a decision. Further, as we have seen, it has not been suggested that a victim has no standing to challenge a decision not to exclude.[361] The LA, headteacher and governors are all affected by decisions to exclude, or to reinstate, that are made by the others and would have standing to challenge those decisions where their rights are affected.

---

[357] See paras **6.99–6.104** of the second edition to this book. In view of the limited future relevance of this case-law it is not reproduced here.

[358] [1999] ELR 237.

[359] Eg *R (A) v Independent Appeal Panel for Sutton* [2009] EWHC 1223 (Admin), [2009] ELR 321, paras 71–75 *per* Hickinbottom J.

[360] See reg 2 of SI 2002/3178 and reg 2 of SI 2002/3179.

[361] *R v London Borough of Camden and the Governors of the Hampstead School ex parte H* [1996] ELR 360.

6.166 Subject to appealing or applying for an independent review in an appropriate case, any application for judicial review should be made promptly and well before the three-month time-limit.[362] A failure to move promptly may have the consequence that it is too late for the court to grant practical relief because by then the child has gone to another school or is otherwise no longer concerned in any practical sense with the expulsion. In those circumstances the court might refuse to grant any relief. This problem arose in *R v Neale ex parte S*.[363] The applicant had left the LA area and been accepted at another school and the court was unpersuaded that any useful purpose would be served by the court intervening or making any order. The court accepted as accurate a passage from Supperstone and Goudie *Judicial Review*[364] as to how the court should exercise its discretion in such cases:

'The court does not beat the air in vain. It may have become otiose or pointless to grant a remedy because the relevant detriment to the applicant has been removed or because nothing in practice will change if the remedy is granted.'

6.167 Although the court went on in that case to consider and dismiss the application on the merits, it was made clear[365] that relief would have been refused in the exercise of the court's discretion had the challenge been otherwise well founded, on the ground that no useful purpose would have been served by affording relief. To the same effect is the decision of the same judge in *R v Governors of St Gregory's RC Aided High School and Appeals Committee ex parte M*.[366]

6.168 It is now open to doubt whether the simple fact that the child has left the school in question and does not wish to go back is sufficient to render academic any challenge to an appeal decision. It is submitted that the courts would now regard as serving a useful purpose, an application simply designed to clear a pupil's name. In *R v Independent Appeal Panel of Sheffield County Council ex parte N*,[367] a girl pupil had accused a boy of a sexual assault. The matter had been reported to the police and a prosecution was pending. The appeal panel applied a presumption of innocence and ordered reinstatement of the boy. The boy was due to leave the school in any event in a matter of weeks. The girl sought permission to apply for judicial review and this was granted by Moses J, inter alia, on the basis that she had rights that ought to be vindicated.

---

[362] In *R (on the application of A) v Head Teacher of North Westminster Community School* [2002] EWHC 2351 (Admin), [2003] ELR 378 at para 3 Newman J emphasised that in expulsion cases it was appropriate to move at the beginning of the three-month period rather than the end. In the case of short fixed-term exclusions the obligation to move promptly may mean within a week or two from the relevant decision: see *R v Secretary of State for the Home Department ex parte Mbandaka* [1999] Ed CR 656. As to the law generally on the obligation of promptness in this context, see Chapter 1.

[363] [1995] ELR 198 at 210C–210F.

[364] Published by Butterworths (1992) at p 349.

[365] [1995] ELR 198 at 212G.

[366] [1995] ELR 290 at 301H–302A.

[367] [2000] ELR 700.

She was out of school at the time and, by clearing the boy on the grounds it had given, the panel had inevitably reflected on her integrity and reputation.

6.169　A pupil who has been accused of a serious breach of discipline has just as much interest in his name being cleared as a pupil who, as in the *Sheffield* case, has made allegations which have not been accepted by the appeal panel. Indeed, in *R (on the application of A) v Head Teacher of North Westminster Community School*,[368] Newman J did not regard it as a bar that the application before him was only to clear the pupil's name because the pupil had obtained a place at another school, although he dismissed the application on its merits.

Appeal or review

6.170　As we have seen, the statutory framework contemplates that decisions on reinstatement and appeal take place within a short timescale. Not all of these time scales are mandatory.[369] Where these statutory rights exist it is likely the court will, in the vast majority of cases, require them to be exhausted before any application for judicial review, as they are an adequate alternative remedy. That was the conclusion of the Court of Appeal in *R (on the application of DR) v Head Teacher of S School*.[370] Simon Brown LJ stated the governing principles in these terms:

> 'I recognise that, had they not appealed and instead sought judicial review of the (assumed to be) flawed decisions by the governing body, the more difficult question would then have arisen as to whether the court should properly exercise its supervisory jurisdiction or should rather leave the applicants to their right of appeal under the statute. For my part, whilst conscious of the risk that, were the courts never to permit such challenges, governing bodies might come to be regarded (and to regard themselves) as for all practical purposes immune from the judicial review jurisdiction ... I would expect cases where review is thought appropriate to be very few and far between. Save in a case where the governing body is plausibly said to have acted quite improperly, or where the court's guidance on some real point of principle is required or, as in *R v London Borough of Newham and another ex parte X* [1995] ELR 303, where not merely was permission to move for judicial review granted but also interim relief to enable the pupil to return to school to pursue GCSE course work, the court's proper response will almost always be to leave the applicant to his statutory remedy.'

6.171　Another example of a case, predating this decision of the Court of Appeal in *DR*, where the court thought it was appropriate to move for judicial review rather than appeal, was *R v Rectory School Governors ex parte WK*,[371] where a parent had not been given the opportunity of making oral representations about a fixed-period exclusion. The consequence of the

---

[368] [2002] EWHC 2351 (Admin), [2003] ELR 378 at para 2.

[369] In *R v Board of Governors of Stoke Newington School ex parte M* [1994] ELR 131 at 138D–138E Potts J held that the requirement for a reinstatement decision to be taken in 15 days was not mandatory.

[370] [2002] EWCA Civ 1822, [2003] ELR 104 at para 45.

[371] [1997] ELR 484.

fixed-period exclusion was that when there was a further incident, the only option open to the headteacher by way of exclusion was a permanent exclusion and this was the course he adopted. The court granted leave to move for judicial review because it held that the statutory right of appeal was not the appropriate mode of dealing with the issues of procedural fairness raised in the proceedings. Reliance was placed by Forbes J[372] upon the decision of Brooke J in *R v London Borough of Newham ex parte X*, although the issue in that case was very different.

INTERIM RELIEF

6.172   As we have just seen, in an exceptional case the court will grant interim relief ordering reinstatement of a child: see *R v London Borough of Newham ex parte X*.[373]

INDEPENDENT SCHOOLS

6.173   The rights and duties outlined above apply in relation to the State sector. There is no ability to challenge by way of judicial review the decision of an independent school to expel a pupil; *R v Fernhill Manor School ex parte A*.[374] That decision was applied in *R v Muntham House School ex parte R*[375] to a non-maintained residential school and in *R v Incorporated Froebel Educational Institute ex parte L*[376] in relation to an independent co-educational day school.

6.174   The court went on to hold in the latter case that the only remedy that was available to the parents was to seek a declaration as to their contractual rights. Specific performance of the contract was regarded as undesirable where, as there, the contract involved daily personal contact and some of the teachers had lost confidence and trust in the child who had been excluded for theft. While that may be regarded as unexceptional, what was of interest was that the child had been in school as a result of an interim injunction and the evidence was that that had been a success. It was held, however, that was insufficient for the court to continue the injunction that had been granted on an interim basis.

---

[372]   [1997] ELR 484, at 488D–488F.
[373]   [1995] ELR 303. Affirmed in *R (on the application of DR) v Head Teacher of S School* [2002] EWCA Civ 1822, [2003] ELR 104 at para 45.
[374]   [1994] ELR 67.
[375]   [2000] ELR 287, Richards J.
[376]   [1999] ELR 488.

Chapter 7

PRIVATE LAW ACTIONS IN DAMAGES

INTRODUCTION

7.1 This Chapter primarily deals with the circumstances in which children or their parents may have a private law action in damages against the school and/or the LA.[1] Most of the Chapter is concerned with an analysis of the circumstances in which a cause of action might arise in relation to the child's educational well-being and physical well-being. The Chapter then considers:

(a) time-limits;

(b) joint tortfeasors and contributory negligence; and

(c) quantum.

BREACH OF PUBLIC LAW DUTIES – EDUCATIONAL WELL-BEING

7.2 In relation to the educational well-being of the pupil the following potential causes of action are considered:

(a) liability in negligence of teachers and other professionals;

(b) liability of the LA for negligence arising out of performance of statutory functions;

(c) liability of the LA for breach of statutory duty under the Education Acts;

(d) liability of public authorities under the Human Rights Act 1998 (HRA 1998).

7.3 The first question that arises in relation to any possibility of liability for negligence is whether the public authority in question owes a duty of care.

---

[1] Throughout this Chapter reference is made to 'Local Authorities' (LAs) and not to 'Local Education Authorities'(LEAs). Before the Secretary of State made the *LAs and Children's Services Authority (Integration of Functions) Order* 2010, SI 2010/1158, the Education Acts and regulations made under them referred to 'local education authorities' but that terminology is no longer used. The change is not retrospective but for the sake of consistency, the term 'LA' is used throughout this Chapter save where it is material to distinguish between a local education authority and a LA for the purposes of the analysis.

There will first be examined the principles set out by the courts as governing whether a duty of care is owed in relation to the exercise by a public authority of education functions. There will then be examined the circumstances in which the courts have held that a duty of care is owed. Consideration will be then be given to the impact of the jurisprudence on Article 6 of the European Convention on Human Rights (ECHR) and whether, in consequence, it is possible to state in any given case that a duty of care is not owed in a particular case without there being a trial on the evidence first. There will then be discussed, in the light of these principles, the potential liability of a public authority for negligence in relation to education decisions where the errors alleged are not in the SEN field.

Principles upon which courts act when deciding whether a duty of care is owed

7.4   It remains convenient, when setting out the modern law on the question of whether a duty of care is owed, to start with the House of Lords decision in *X v Bedfordshire County Council*.[2] In each of five appeals that were before their Lordships in *X*, defendant LAs had applied to strike out claims against them on the ground that they disclosed no reasonable cause of action. Two of the appeals (the *Bedfordshire* and *Newham* cases) concerned allegations that the authorities had failed to carry out, or had negligently carried out, statutory duties imposed on them in order to protect children from child abuse; the other three appeals (the *Dorset*, *Hampshire* and *Bromley* cases) concerned similar allegations in relation to duties imposed upon them as education authorities by the Education Acts 1944 to 1981 in relation to children with SEN.

7.5   In the *Dorset* case, the plaintiff, who had SEN, initially attended a local primary school maintained by the county council. He claimed that the council were in breach of statutory duty[3] and negligent. The case was put in a number of ways:

(a)   that the LA negligently failed to make a proper statement or make proper provision for his special educational needs as required by the Education Act 1981;

(b)   that the LA provided a psychology service which negligently advised the plaintiff's parents who relied on that advice; and

(c)   that the psychologist and other officers employed by the authority owed a personal duty of care to use professional skill and care in their assessments and advice, for breach of which the LA was vicariously liable.

---

2   [1995] 2 AC 633.
3   The claim for breach of statutory duty was dismissed by the Court of Appeal and not appealed to the House of Lords: see at 760G.

7.6   In the *Hampshire* case, the plaintiff had attended a school run by the defendant LA from 1978 to 1984, and had manifested behavioural problems and learning difficulties consistent with dyslexia. In June 1984, the headteacher finally referred him to the Mid-Hampshire Teachers' Centre, an advisory service run by the defendant. They reported that the plaintiff had 'no serious handicaps' and that it was 'mainly a question of a good deal of regular practice'. It was alleged that:

(a)   the headteacher was in breach of a duty of care owed by him to the plaintiff, in failing to refer him either for formal assessment of his special educational needs, or to an educational psychologist; and

(b)   the advisory service was negligent, inter alia, in failing to ascertain that the plaintiff suffered from a specific learning disability, and in failing to diagnose that he was, in fact, dyslexic.

It was not disputed that the LA would be vicariously liable for a breach of any such direct duty of care owed by its employees.

7.7   In the *Bromley* case, the plaintiff had spent periods of time in a mainstream school, periods of time in no school and periods of time in a special school. He claimed damages for breach of statutory duty and negligence against the LA for failing to:

(a)   secure the availability of efficient primary or secondary education;

(b)   avoid placing the plaintiff in special schools when he did not have any serious disability and could and should have been placed in mainstream schools;

(c)   make arrangements for the provision of his special educational needs in particular by failing to make or maintain a statement of SEN;

(d)   provide a place for the plaintiff at any school in certain periods;

(e)   pay proper regard or heed to his mother's requests during the time he did not have a school place that he be provided with one and, that for certain periods that be at an ordinary school;

(f)   provide the plaintiff with any reasonable education.

7.8   Lord Browne-Wilkinson set out the following questions to be answered in deciding whether there was a duty of care.

(a)   Do the relevant functions under the Education Acts simply impose duties or do they impose duties which leave to the LA a discretion as to the extent to which, and the methods by which, those duties are to be performed? If the latter is the case, then the LA cannot be liable in negligence unless the manner of exercise of the discretion is irrational.[4]

(b) Does the decision include matters of policy? If it does, the courts cannot reach a conclusion that a decision was outside the ambit of the statutory discretion.[5] Policy matters include the allocation of finite resources[6] but it is important to ascertain what factors were taken into account by the authority in exercising its discretion. Care must be taken in reaching the conclusion that a decision involves policy issues and is therefore non-justiciable.

(c) Does the claim allege carelessness, not simply in the taking of a discretionary decision to do some act, but in the practical manner in which that act has been performed? If it does, the governing principles are as follows:

  (i)   Was the damage to the claimants reasonably foreseeable?
  (ii)   Was the relationship between the claimants and the defendants sufficiently proximate?
  (iii) Is it just and reasonable to impose a duty of care?[7]
  (iv)   Would imposition of a common law duty of care be inconsistent with or have the tendency to discourage the due performance by the public authority of its statutory duties?[8]

7.9 In *X v Bedfordshire* it was conceded[9] by the LA that it could foresee damage to the plaintiffs if it carried out its duties negligently and that the relationship between them was sufficiently proximate.

Conclusions of House of Lords in *X v Bedfordshire* on negligence

7.10 Applying those principles, Lord Browne-Wilkinson held that:

(a) the LA did not owe a direct duty of care to perform carefully the statutory duties imposed on it by the Education Act 1981 because: (i) that would replicate remedies of appeal the plaintiffs had under the statute,[10] (ii) the cases in which it could be successfully alleged that the LA had behaved irrationally would be small but the possibility of vexatious claims not so,[11] and (iii) in almost every case which could give rise to a claim for the negligent exercise of statutory discretions it was probable that there would

---

4   *X v Bedfordshire CC* [1995] 2 AC 633 at 736B.
5   *X v Bedfordshire CC* at 738G–738H.
6   *X v Bedfordshire CC* at 737F.
7   *X v Bedfordshire CC* at 739A–739B.
8   *X v Bedfordshire CC* at 739D.
9   *X v Bedfordshire CC* at 749E.
10   *X v Bedfordshire CC* at 761G.
11   *X v Bedfordshire CC* at 761H–762A.

be an alternative claim against the LA on the grounds of its vicarious liability for the negligent advice on the basis of which it exercised its discretion;[12]

(b) the LA did owe a direct duty of care once the decision was taken to provide a psychology service to the public, but if the psychology service was merely part and parcel of the system established by the LA for the discharge of its statutory duties under the Education Act 1981, the existence of any direct duty of care might have to be excluded or limited so as to not impede the due performance by the authority of its statutory duties;[13]

(c) educational psychologists and other members of the staff of the LA owed a duty to use reasonable professional skill and care in the assessment and determination of the pupil's special educational needs and the LA was liable vicariously for breach of such duties.[14] Again, if at trial it emerged that there was a conflict between the professional duty owed to the child by the psychologist and the discharge by the LA of its statutory duties, then it might be necessary to limit or exclude the duty of care to the child;

(d) in each case, the test to be applied was not that of the reasonable parent, but that applied to professional persons, the so-called '*Bolam*' test;[15] those persons were bound to exercise the ordinary skill of a competent psychologist, headteacher and advisory teacher as the case may be, and if they acted in accordance with the accepted views of a responsible body of such professionals, albeit that others might disagree, they would have discharged that duty.

7.11 In the child abuse cases, the House of Lords held that there was no duty of care. The reasons given were that the social workers and psychiatrists were retained by the LA to advise it and not the parents;[16] that the parents would not regulate their conduct on the basis of the advice given;[17] and considerations of witness immunity.[18] However, the first reason, at least, would be equally true in the education cases.[19]

---

[12]   *X v Bedfordshire CC* at 762B.
[13]   *X v Bedfordshire CC* at 762H–763D.
[14]   *X v Bedfordshire CC* at 763E–764C, 766B–766E and 771B–771D.
[15]   *Bolam v Friern Hospital Management Committee* [1957] 1 WLR 582.
[16]   *X v Bedfordshire CC* at 752G.
[17]   *X v Bedfordshire CC*, at 753C.
[18]   *X v Bedfordshire CC*, at 754.
[19]   Cf Lord Nolan 771H–772A.

Impact of *Phelps* in the House of Lords on questions of duty of care

7.12 In *Phelps and others v London Borough of Hillingdon and others*,[20] the House of Lords adopted a broader approach than in *X v Bedfordshire*. It heard four conjoined appeals.

7.13 The plaintiff in the first appeal, *Phelps v The Mayor and Burgesses of the London Borough of Hillingdon*, suffered from a specific learning difficulty or dyslexia, and brought a claim in negligence against the defendant LA based on its vicarious liability for the negligence both of its educational psychologist and of the school the plaintiff had attended.

7.14 Garland J, relying on *X v Bedfordshire*, found that the educational psychologist owed a duty of care directly to the plaintiff, on the basis that her findings, recommendations and advice would be communicated to and acted upon by the plaintiff, through her parents.[21] Although the defendant and the school would also rely on her advice, the judge found that it did not 'accord with reality or commonsense to regard her as owing a duty only to the defendants'. It was obvious that there would be discussions with the plaintiff's parents and it was expected that information derived from the educational psychologist would be passed on to them. They would have a number of choices open to them and could be expected to rely on that information in exercising those choices. The judge relied on the finding of the House of Lords in *X v Bedfordshire*, that in principle, an educational psychologist might owe a duty of care directly to a pupil, without addressing the matters expressly referred to by their Lordships, namely whether this would give rise to any potential conflicts of duty. The judge found on the facts that the educational psychologist was in breach of the duty of care. Her failure to diagnose the plaintiff as suffering from a specific learning difficulty or to carry out further tests, despite some clear indications (e g reading age far below chronological age and predicted reading age on basis of IQ; inability to write her own address aged 11 years 9 months) 'was more than an error of judgment: it was a failure to exercise the degree of care and skill to be expected of an ordinarily competent member of her profession'.[22] Further, she should have thought again when the plaintiff made so little progress despite special needs teaching. The Court of Appeal reversed Garland J.[23]

7.15 The second case heard by the House of Lords with *Phelps* was *Anderton v Clywd County Council*. That case had not gone to trial. The plaintiff had been privately diagnosed as dyslexic and contended that the LA had not investigated her problems adequately or at all and, as a result, had failed to make suitable educational provision for her, causing her to suffer from psychological problems. Her solicitors issued a summons under the then relevant rule of

---

[20] [2001] 2 AC 619.
[21] [1998] ELR 38 at 55F.
[22] [1998] ELR 38 at 57A–57B.
[23] [1999] 1 WLR 500.

court seeking pre-action discovery pursuant to section 33(2) of the Supreme Court Act 1981. That raised the question whether her claim was likely to be one for personal injuries. The master and judge ordered pre-action discovery but they were reversed by the Court of Appeal.

7.16 In the third appeal, *G v Bromley London Borough Council*, the plaintiff had a statement of SEN which emphasised the need for him to have access to a computer and to be trained in its use. He contended that the LA had negligently and in breach of duty failed to provide a proper education for him, in particular in computer technology and suitable training to enable him to communicate, and that as a result he had suffered damage in the form of lack of educational progress, social deprivation and psychiatric injury. His case had been struck out by the judge but the Court of Appeal had allowed his appeal.

7.17 In the fourth appeal, *Jarvis v Hampshire*, the plaintiff had been assessed under the Education Act 1981. The educational psychologist did not report that the plaintiff had dyslexia. The plaintiff's mother considered that he had dyslexia and should be placed in a unit specialising in that condition, but he was placed elsewhere. Proceedings were brought against the psychologist and the LA, contending that they had been negligent and had acted in breach of duty. It was alleged that the LA was vicariously liable for the negligence of the psychologist and directly for failing to provide competent advice through its psychology service. The judge refused to strike out the claim in negligence, but was reversed by the Court of Appeal.

7.18 When the four appeals reached the House of Lords, the following principles were set out:

(a) the LA could be vicariously liable for negligence by an educational psychologist employed by it in connection with its duties in relation to children with SEN. While there could be cases where to recognise such a vicarious responsibility would so interfere with the performance of the LA's duties that it would be wrong to recognise such liability, it was for the LA to establish that; it could not be presumed and the circumstances in which it was anticipated that it would be established would be exceptional.[24] This is, in practice, a significant qualification of *X v Bedfordshire*;

(b) the educational psychologist, psychiatrist, teacher and education officer concerned with children who had special educational needs might owe a duty of care to people whom it could be foreseen might suffer damage if injury or damage was caused by their failure to exercise reasonable care and skill.[25] In order for the psychologist to owe a duty of care it had to be shown that the psychologist was acting for the particular child in the sense

---

[24] [2001] 2 AC 619 at 652H–653F, 654H–655B, 665C, 665D, 665E, 676G, and 677G.
[25] [2001] 2 AC 619 at 653G–653H, 665C, 665D, 665E, 676G, and 677G.

that he was called in to advise in relation to the assessment and future provision of the child.[26] Nothing further by way of assumption of responsibility had to be shown;

(c) psychological damage caused by the failure of the educational psychologist to take reasonable care was damage for the purpose of the common law. In addition, where there was a failure to diagnose a congenital condition and take appropriate action as a result of which a child's level of achievement was reduced, loss of employment and wages was recoverable damage;[27]

(d) following the approach in *X v Bedfordshire*, the standard of care for the relevant professional was the ordinary skill and care of an ordinary and competent man exercising that art. It was not negligent if the relevant professional acted in accordance with a practice accepted as proper by a responsible body of men skilled in that particular art.[28] The decision in *Bolam v Friern Hospital Management Committee*[29] was expressly approved.

7.19 Applying those principles to the cases before them, the House of Lords held in *Phelps* that the plaintiff's case succeeded on the basis of vicarious liability of the LA but not on the basis it was in breach of a direct duty of care.[30] It was held that it did not matter that the educational psychologist was part of a multi-disciplinary team[31] and that the judge had been entitled to find on the evidence the educational psychologist had been negligent.[32]

7.20 In the *G* case, the action had not been struck out by the Court of Appeal and the House of Lords dismissed the appeal.[33] In the *Jarvis* case, the action had been struck out by the Court of Appeal and, accordingly, the House of Lords allowed the appeal. The vicarious liability case was allowed for the same reasons as in *Phelps* and the direct liability case was also allowed to stand because it was so closely linked with it and on the basis that it would be wrong to strike it out at that stage.[34]

7.21 In the *Anderton* case, the order for pre-action discovery was restored on the basis that the plaintiff was likely to be a party to proceedings for personal injury.[35] A broad definition of injury was adopted and it was held that a failure

---

[26] [2001] 2 AC 619 at 654C–654E, 665C, 665D, 665E, 676G, and 677G.
[27] [2001] 2 AC 619 at 654F–654G, 665C, 665D, 665E, 676G, and 677G.
[28] [2001] 2 AC 619 at 655B–655C.
[29] [1957] 1 WLR 582 at 586–587 per McNair J.
[30] [2001] 2 AC 619 at 657F.
[31] [2001] 2 AC 619 at 656A–656B. That is a significant limitation of the approach in *X v Bedfordshire*.
[32] [2001] 2 AC 619 at 656B–657D.
[33] [2001] 2 AC 619 at 658F–660A.
[34] [2001] 2 AC 619 at 662D.
[35] [2001] 2 AC 619 at 664F–665A.

to mitigate the adverse consequences of a congenital defect was capable of constituting personal injuries to a person.

7.22 In *X v Bedfordshire*[36] the House of Lords had answered in the negative, the question whether the LA owed a direct duty of care in relation to the exercise of education discretion in the SEN field.[37] In *Phelps* the House of Lords was not prepared to rule out that such a duty of care could be owed, but the matter was left in an uncertain state. Lord Slynn seemed to accept there could be a direct liability on behalf of the LA.[38] Lord Nicholls left the question open.[39] Lord Clyde also left the question open.[40] Lord Jauncey agreed with Lords Slynn, Nicholls and Clyde.[41] Lord Lloyd agreed with Lords Slynn and Clyde.[42] Lord Hutton agreed with Lords Slynn and Clyde.[43] Lord Millet gave a short concurring speech expressly dealing with the vicarious liability point but also saying he was in a large measure of agreement with Lords Slynn and Clyde.[44]

7.23 Lord Slynn rejected the argument that to impose a duty of care would contradict the finding that there was no claim for breach of statutory duty[45] on the basis that that argument had been rejected by the House of Lords in *Barrett v Enfield*.[46] Accordingly, he was of the view an LA does owe a direct duty of care in the performance of its statutory functions. While Lord Slynn did contemplate that there would be some statutory functions which involved weighing competing public interests, or which had been dictated by considerations in respect of which Parliament could not have intended for the courts to substitute their views for the views of ministers or officials and that the courts would hold the exercise of such functions to be non-justiciable, he plainly did not regard the typical case of error in relation to the identification of special educational needs as raising such issues. He commented that it would rarely be necessary to invoke a direct duty of care against an LA and seems in the end simply to have refused to strike out this aspect of the case because it was closely intertwined with the vicarious liability case.[47]

7.24 Whether Lord Slynn's views are the ratio of the House of Lords is not easy to discern. Although all their Lordships indicated some agreement with his speech, it was always conjoined with some agreement with the speeches of others who had left the question open.[48]

---

[36] [1995] 2 AC 633.
[37] [1995] 2 AC 633, at 760H–762H and 770B–770D.
[38] [2001] 2 AC 619 at 657G–658E.
[39] [2001] 2 AC 619 at 668D–668H.
[40] [2001] 2 AC 619 676A–676D.
[41] [2001] 2 AC 619 at 665C.
[42] [2001] 2 AC 619 at 665D.
[43] [2001] 2 AC 619 at 676G.
[44] [2001] 2 AC 619 at 676H–677E.
[45] Cf Staughton LJ in *M v Newham LBC* [1995] 2 AC 633 at 672H–673D.
[46] [2001] 2 AC 550.
[47] [2001] 2 AC 619 at 662D.
[48] See above at para **7.22**.

Post-*Phelps* cases

Vicarious liability

7.25 The circumstances in which an LA may be vicariously liable for the negligence of its employees in connection with its duties in relation to children with SEN were considered in *Carty v Croydon London Borough Council*.[49] In that case, the Court of Appeal accepted that an education officer could owe a common law duty of care to children with special educational needs.

7.26 Dyson LJ gave the leading judgment. Seemingly running issues of the existence of duty of care and the standard to be applied in determining breach together, he said that in the field of special education there was a spectrum at one end of which lay decisions which are heavily influenced by policy and which come close to being non-justiciable. The court was unlikely to find negligence proved in relation to such decisions, unless the decision was one which no reasonable education authority could have made. At the other end of the spectrum were decisions involving pure professional judgment and expertise in relation to individual children, to which the *Bolam* test would apply.[50] Dyson LJ was attracted to the idea that there should be only two potential areas of inquiry where the question arises where a public authority is liable for negligence in the performance of its statutory functions: whether the decision is justiciable at all and then application of threefold test in *Caparo v Dickman* as to whether it is fair, just and reasonable to impose a duty.[51]

7.27 Dyson LJ noted that there may be aspects of the role of an education officer which involve consultation or advice in respect of policy matters and which may be non-justiciable.[52] He further noted that a claim for damages for the careless performance of a statutory duty would not lie so, on the facts of that case, the mere fact that an education officer failed to make a formal re-assessment of the claimant's needs in accordance with the requirements of regulation 9 of the Education (Special Educational Needs) Regulations 1983 would not give rise to a private law claim for breach of statutory duty or negligence.[53] However, where an education officer in the performance of his or her statutory functions entered into relationships with or assumed responsibilities towards a child, he or she might owe a duty to the child. Whether or not the education officer did owe such a duty would depend on an application of the threefold test in *Caparo v Dickman*,[54] that is whether it was fair, just and reasonable to impose a duty of care. The question was not whether the decisions made were so unreasonable as to fall outside the ambit of the authority's statutory discretion. However, given the difficulty of the decisions that had to be reached in the special educational needs context, the

---

49   [2005] EWCA Civ 19.
50   [2005] EWCA Civ 19, para 26.
51   [2005] EWCA Civ 19, para 28.
52   [2005] EWCA Civ 19, para 42.
53   [2005] EWCA Civ 19, para 42.
54   [1990] 2 AC 605.

court would usually only hold that there was a duty of care to avoid decisions that were plainly and obviously wrong.[55]

7.28 Dyson LJ rejected an argument that a duty should not be imposed because an education officer was not a 'professional' person of the sort contemplated in *Phelps* and *Barrett v Enfield Borough Council*[56] but rather performed an administrative function akin to that of a civil servant. The phrase 'professional person' was not, he held, a term of art.[57] Dyson LJ considered that what Sir Thomas Bingham MR said of social workers in *M (A Minor) and Another v Newham London Borough Council and others*[58] applied with equal force to education forces namely:

'Those who engage professionally in social work bring to their task skill and expertise, the product partly of training and partly of experience, which ordinary uninstructed members of the public are bound to lack. I have no doubt that they should be regarded as members of a skilled profession. Their task is one of immense difficulty, and frequently they are exposed to unjust criticism; but both those things may, to a greater or lesser extent, be said of other professionals also.'

7.29 Dyson LJ went on to note that an education officer would often be responsible for resolving disputes between parents and teachers or educational psychologists or the other consultees involved in the making of statements of SEN and would often be responsible for determining when further information was needed. These tasks could only be performed effectively by somebody with the appropriate skill and experience. The fact that there was no particular qualification required to become an education officer and no professional body regulating education officers did not mean that they should not have been considered to be exercising a professional function in the relevant sense.[59]

7.30 The court further rejected arguments that education officers should enjoy a blanket immunity from suit because claims made against them when a child attained majority would often be historic and that there were adequate alternative remedies to an action for damages in the form of the statutory appeals process.[60] On the facts however, the claimant failed to establish that the education officer involved in his case was negligent.

7.31 Mummery LJ agreed with Dyson LJ but sounded a warning in relation to establishing a duty of care. At paragraph 83 of the judgment, he expressed a concern that:

'it is all too easy, as apparently happened in some aspects of the presentation of this case at trial, to slip into the fallacy that an education officer owes a duty of care to a child because: (a) under the 1981 Act the local education authority has

---

[55] [2005] EWCA Civ 19, para 43.
[56] [2001] 2 AC 550.
[57] [2005] EWCA Civ 19, para 45.
[58] [1995] 2 AC 633.
[59] [2005] EWCA Civ 19, paras 45–46.
[60] [2005] EWCA Civ 19, paras 51–52.

duties and discretions in relation to children with special educational needs, and (b) the education officer is employed by the authority to perform functions relevant to the performance of the statutory duties and discretions. This approach would produce a kind of circular vicarious liability in reverse: an education officer, through whom a LA performs its statutory functions, might, by use of the tort of negligence, be made personally liable for the failings of the authority. As, employer, the authority would then be vicariously liable for the tort of negligence committed by the education officer in the course of his employment. As Gibbs J pointed out the result would be to introduce by the back door an action for breach of statutory duty in a case where, as here, it was agreed that no cause of action for breach of statutory duty was created by the relevant legislation.'

7.32   He went on to emphasise[61] that the duty of care was owed on account of the special relationship that existed between the professional engaged by the authority and the child with special educational needs towards whom that professional had undertaken specific educational responsibilities.

7.33   So far as the question of breach was concerned, the Judge had concluded that the defendant had not been negligent. The Court of Appeal upheld the judge's conclusion. The claimant first alleged that the education officer and/or the LA directly had been negligent for failing to formally re-assess the claimant's needs following a breakdown in his placement at St Nicholas' school and in failing to amend the statement of SEN to name an appropriate placement. The failure to re-assess was a breach of the authority's duties under the statute but that did not suffice; and the defendant was not negligent in placing the claimant at a second school, Cyril Burt. The education officer had taken the decision on placement only after a careful assessment of the claimant's needs and the conclusion that he had not been negligent in doing so was unassailable.[62] The claimant then alleged that the education officers and/or the defendant were negligent in failing to re-assess the claimant while he was at Cyril Burt school. While Cyril Burt school was not the most appropriate setting for the claimant, it was not an inappropriate placement and was reasonably suitable to meet the claimant's needs at the time. There were no viable alternatives in the Borough. The authority could have considered an out of borough placement but there were various practical difficulties and the authority considered that the claimant was making progress at Cyril Burt. The judge concluded that it would have made no difference had the defendants undertaken a statutory re-assessment as they required to do, and the Court of Appeal upheld his conclusions.[63]

7.34   It is submitted that the question whether an education officer owes a duty of care in any particular case will require a detailed assessment of the particular facts, in particular as to the relationship that in fact existed between the education officer and the particular child. An education officer may have responsibility for special educational needs across a large geographical area and have greater or lesser involvement with any particular child depending on that

[61]   [2005] EWCA Civ 19, paras 84-85.
[62]   [2005] EWCA Civ 19, paras 55-63.
[63]   [2005] EWCA Civ 19, paras 64-79.

child's needs and information and communications with the parents and school: whether an education officer's functions are akin to those of a social worker or an administrator may, it is submitted, depend on the particular facts.

7.35 It does not appear to have been argued that imposition of a duty of care might have any adverse effect on the discharge by an education officer of their public functions but it submitted that the courts should proceed cautiously. An education officer may be responsible for managing or at least spending a budget that needs to cater for many children with SEN in a particular area, not all of whom will have statements, and has a duty not to incur unreasonable public expenditure or use finite resources inefficiently. If an education officer can be fixed with a duty of care to a particular child where they are found to have assumed responsibility for a particular child, that might risk skewing the judgment of an education officer in favour of making more generous provision for that child than is compatible with the duty owed to children with SEN generally. The indication that the duty is likely to be limited to avoiding decisions that are plainly and obviously wrong limits the risk of any such skew in decision-making. The expression of that limitation also brings out a notable feature of the approach the courts have taken in analysing duty of care in a public context in that there is a tendency to assimilate what might be thought to be a test of the standard for establishing breach and question of the scope of the duty of care.

7.36 Conceptually, limiting the scope of a duty of care such that it is a duty to avoid only decisions that are plainly and obviously wrong may appeal on pragmatic grounds but may be problematic. First, if the relationship between a claimant and an education officer is of the sort to warrant the imposition of a duty of care, should it avail the defendant to show that although a course of action may have fallen below what could reasonably be expected, it did not plainly and obviously fall below what could be expected? Secondly, what becomes the standard to apply in determining breach? In *Carty* Dyson LJ did not expressly identify the standard that he was applying in upholding the judge's conclusion that the defendant had not been negligent. In view of the conclusion that the placements impugned were reasonably suitable to meet the claimant's needs and that the claimant had kept its decisions under review (albeit without formally re-assessing), the qualification that a duty was likely to be imposed only to avoid a decision that was plainly and obviously wrong did not arise. But ordinarily the question to ask is whether the person who owed the duty of care acted unreasonably in failing to fulfil the duty: it sounds odd that the question should now become whether the person acted unreasonably in failing to avoid a decision or course of action that was plainly and obviously wrong. Conceptually, Dyson LJ's suggested qualification of the duty of care appears to invite assimilating the standard of breach to the scope of the duty of care.

7.37 A second question that arises is whether, and if so what, functions of an education officer are subject to the *Bolam* test. Dyson LJ did not expressly refer to that test or compare the actions taken to what would have been sanctioned by a responsible body of professional opinion, although plainly the expert evidence given as to the suitability of the placement was critical. It appears that the judge at first instance did consider that the defendants had been 'shown to have approached the claimant's case throughout in a manner which would be regarded as acceptable by a significant body of educational opinion'.[64] It is submitted that whether *Bolam* applies or not is likely to depend on the nature of the alleged negligence: a court may well need expert evidence on the question whether a decision as to placement was appropriate and it seems right that this should attract the *Bolam* test. If the alleged failures were more administrative in nature, a court may well not require such evidence and may consider itself able to reach its own judgment.

7.38   An example of a case in which a class of employee was held not to owe a duty of care by dint of performing the functions of a profession is *Marr v Lambeth County Council*.[65] Amongst many other allegations, the claimant alleged that the council was vicariously liable for the alleged negligence of officers of the council's Educational Front Line Service. The claimant had been permanently excluded from mainstream school but no place was immediately available at the PRU. The claimant was put on the waiting list for the PRU but his mother was told that she had to find an alternative school placement. In May 1996, the claimant was removed from the waiting list for the PRU because a place was said to have become available at the London Nautical School. In fact, that place remained available for only a day or so before it was filled by somebody else on the waiting list for that school. The claimant was never put back on the waiting list for the PRU.[66] Between April 1996 and June 1997, the council provided the claimant's mother with information about vacancies in schools in the borough but for various reasons, none were taken up. The claimant alleged that the defendant's employees were negligent in withdrawing the claimant from the PRU waiting list and failing to reinstate it and in failing to ascertain whether the claimant had re-entered mainstream education and act on the fact that he had not. That required the claimant to establish that there was a relationship of proximity between the members of staff of the Council's Educational Front Line Service who were to inform the claimant's mother of vacancies at the PRU, and who were the gatekeepers of the PRU.[67]

7.39   Ouseley J rejected that as an impossible claim. The officers had no professional qualifications or skills; were not advising the claimant or his mother on any steps in particular which they should take or schools to which they should apply; provided no substantive educational advice; and undertook no special obligation towards the claimant nor held themselves out as having any particular skill or obligation to the claimant for his education. They were merely fulfilling the task of providing information about vacancies and reminding the claimant's mother that she had to take steps to secure a place at

---

[64]   Paragraph 112 of the judgment, quoted at [2005] EWCA Civ 19, para 65.
[65]   [2006] EWHC 1175.
[66]   [2006] EWHC 1175, paras 11–13 and 210-216.
[67]   [2006] EWHC 1175, paras 368-360.

school for the claimant.[68] In that regard, they were acting towards the claimant just as they would act for others, though in fact they were probably called upon to contact the claimant's mother more frequently than would have been the norm. Ouseley J considered the removal of the claimant's name form the waiting list for PRU 'extraordinary', given that even if there was a place at the London Nautical School there would have been other pupils going for that place who may have been more likely to get it; but the remedy for the removal of the claimant from the PRU waiting list would have been an action for judicial review.[69]

7.40 When it comes to determining whether or not there has been a breach of any duty of care owed on the basis of the exercise of professional skill in the educational context, it will be important to understand what are the relevant skills or expertise in question. A classroom teacher, headteacher or SENCO will have a different expertise from an educational psychologist. So too, an educational psychologist may not obviously be the judge of the failure of school staff to consult them unless they were to give evidence that the general run of teachers would have brought an Educational Psychologist in at a particular stage, based on their experience of the condition of those whom they saw as Educational Psychologists.[70]

7.41 The post-*Phelps* case-law also illustrates the importance of remembering that the issue of breach has to be considered with reference to the standards and practices in place at the relevant time which may be different from what is regarded as acceptable or unacceptable at the time of judgment: see eg *Smith v London Borough of Havering*.[71] Many cases of educational negligence relate to decisions that were taken about a child's education many years before a claim is brought. That said, it should also be remembered that the practice in question must be capable of withstanding logical analysis.[72] In determining what is reasonable professional practice, the setting within which that professional practice takes place will be a relevant factor. So for example in considering whether or not a LA educational psychologist has acted reasonably, one must consider their actions in the LA context.[73] It is submitted that that may be relevant where, for example, the question arises whether a particular diagnostic test ought to have been undertaken: it may be that it would not be reasonable to expect an educational psychologist working with the limited resources available to a LA to undertake certain forms of assessment that a private educational psychologist who is not so fettered as to resources would undertake as a matter of course.

---

[68] [2006] EWHC 1175, para 360.

[69] [2006] EWHC 1175, para 361.

[70] See para 309 of the judgment in *Marr v Lambeth London Borough Council* [2006] EWHC 1175.

[71] [2004] EWHC 599, at para 67.

[72] A qualification of the *Bolam* test introduced by the House of Lords in *Bolitho v City and Hackney Health Authority* [1998] AC 232.

[73] See eg para 149 of the judgment in *Crowley (by his Mother and Litigation Friend Patricia Crowley) v Surrey County Council and Others* [2008] EWHC 1102.

Direct duty of care

7.42 Whether the LA owed a direct duty of care was revisited by Stanley Burnton J at the substantive trial of *Keating v Bromley London Borough*.[74] The case was unusual because, following the conjoined appeals in *X v Bedfordshire*, the direct duty of care alleged in that case had been ruled by the House of Lords not to be maintainable as a matter of law. Nevertheless, the trial in *Keating* was delayed until after the House of Lords decision in *Phelps* and following that decision, the plaintiff was allowed to amend his pleadings to reintroduce allegations that the LA owed him a duty of care. The court held[75] that the matter was res judicata between the parties as a result of the House of Lords decision in *X v Bedfordshire*, that the subsequent decision of the House of Lords in *Phelps* could be a special circumstance which exceptionally would have the effect as an exception to the principle of res judicata, but that it was not in this case. The court held that the effect of *Phelps* was not that the earlier House of Lords decision in *Keating v Bromley* was wrong, but that there might be exceptions to the general exclusion of a direct duty of care laid down in *X v Bedfordshire*. Accordingly, it was held that there was no direct duty of care owed in that case. For good measure the court held[76] that even if the matter was not strictly res judicata, no duty of care should be held to exist because the question whether a duty of care was owed involved considerations of changing public policy perceptions and the case fell to be judged on the perception of public policy near to the time of the events in question. Judged on that basis, the House of Lords decision in *X v Bedfordshire* represented the best evidence of what the perceived requirements of fairness, justice and reasonableness would have required at the time.

7.43 In *Carty*, Dyson LJ said[77] that 'where justiciable claims are made in relation to the management by LAs of children who have special educational needs or who have been take into care, the inquiry is likely to focus on the potential vicarious liability for the conduct of the employees who make the decisions complained of.' Dyson LJ noted that Lord Slynn did not rule out the possibility of direct liability in *Phelps* but otherwise said no more since on the facts of that case there was no prospect of establishing direct liability if vicarious liability was not proved. As is set out at paras **7.62–7.66** below subsequent authorities seem more willing than was formerly the case to hold that a public authority owes a direct duty of care in the performance of its statutory functions unless imposition of such a duty would conflict with performance of those functions.

7.44 While there may be, in some circumstances, a direct duty of care in relation to the performance by the LA of functions in relation to identification of SEN, it is unlikely to cover all areas where a mistake occurs in the SEN field. Where, for example, a particular special educational need was not discovered

---

[74]   [2003] EWHC 1070, [2003] ELR 590.
[75]   [2003] EWHC 1070, [2003] ELR 590, at para 137.
[76]   [2003] EWHC 1070, [2003] ELR 590, at para 138.
[77]   See at para 33.

because the child had a rare condition that could only have been identified by particularly esoteric expertise or expensive testing (but could have been identified quite easily by the relevant expert or test) and a LA had taken a policy decision not to incur expense doing that particularly rarefied or expensive testing because it wished to spend the money on another competing need, then there may be no direct duty of care.[78] That, it is submitted, would be precisely the sort of competing public interest case that Lord Slynn was contemplating in his speech in *Phelps*.

7.45 It may be that it will not often matter whether a direct duty of care is owed by the LA in relation to the performance of its functions with regard to SEN. In many cases it should be possible to identify a particular individual who has been at fault and for whom the LA is vicariously responsible and whose fault has caused the damage. It will not, however, be possible in all cases readily to do this; it may be that a series of mistakes are made by different professionals, none of which can be characterised as negligent but which, taken together, are serious and cause damage.

The exercise of public law discretion in fulfilment of a pre-existing private law duty

7.46 In *Connor v Surrey County Council*[79] it was uncontroversial that Surrey owed the claimant a private law duty of care in its capacity as her employer but the question arose whether fulfilment of that private law duty of care could require Surrey to exercise a public law discretion in a particular way. Laws LJ emphasised that the decision in that case very much turned on its facts; but his general discussion of the case-law cited is of interest.

7.47 The claimant was the headteacher of a maintained school and an employee of the LA. It was common ground that the LA owed the claimant a duty of care to take reasonable steps to safeguard her health, including her mental health, in the course of her employment with them.

7.48 In 2003, a number of Muslim activists with an agenda to promote certain religious issues and interests (which were not found to be reflective of the interests of the wider Muslim community) were elected to the school's governing body as parent governors. The claimant was an ex officio member of the governing body. The new governors pursued an aggressive campaign in furtherance of their agenda including making demands for documents and

---

[78] Budgetary and educational policy considerations appear to have been matters relied on by HH Judge Marr-Johnson, sitting as a Deputy High Court Judge, in *Gammon v East Sussex* [2006] EWHC 477 at paras 41–43 in holding that a claim in negligence against the council for failing to place a child with SEN in a special school was not justiciable and hence no direct duty of care was owed by the council. He further held that even if there had been a direct duty of care the council was not in breach of it and that the claimant had been right to abandon any attempt to establish negligence on the part of any individual education officer for which the council was vicariously liable.

[79] [2010] EWCA Civ 286.

information, making allegations of anti-Muslim feeling on the part of certain members of staff and making complaints about the attitude of the claimant herself. Governance at the school deteriorated and staff reported that this was having an impact on their work at the school.

7.49 In 2004, a review of governance took place. M (a governor) challenged the review and listed issues of concern with the chair of governors, the claimant, the school secretary and the LA. At the LA's suggestion, a mediation took place but to little effect. From at least 2004, there was evidence that the claimant's mental health was at imminent risk.[80] In May 2005, the governing body decided to use its power to relieve M of his governorship. M complained of institutional racism and circulated a petition of no confidence in the claimant. The petition was described by Laws LJ as a disgraceful document 'full of bile and malice'[81] and there was evidence to suggest that some parents had been intimidated into signing it. The LA made a bland response and commissioned an independent investigation into the allegation of racism. In July 2005, the claimant emailed the council expressing her astonishment that she was expected to continue to work with certain members of the governing body. The GMB union unanimously resolved to request the LA to dissolve the governing body and investigate the circulation of the petition. Instead, over the claimant's protests, the LA expanded the scope of the investigation to explore the responsiveness of the school to the needs of the community. The investigation dismissed the allegations of racism but upheld the complaint that the school had not been responsive to the community and concluded that the headteacher had shown cultural and religious insensitivities. In September 2005, the claimant was signed off work with clinical depression and never returned.

7.50 The claimant claimed damages for psychiatric injury. The High Court found that negligence had been established. The LA had been in breach of the duty of care owed to the claimant because they had disregarded the health and welfare of the claimant and her staff in delaying the establishment of an interim executive board and in deciding to set up an independent investigation into M's complaints. Essentially, the LA had put its concern to avoid offending M and his associates (who were not in fact representative of the local Islamic community) above its duties to the claimant and her staff. The LA should have issued a formal warning no later than February 2005 to enable an interim executive board to be set up by May 2005.

7.51 Before the Court of Appeal, the LA argued that the failure to establish an interim executive board by May 2005 and the decision to set up an investigation into the complaint M had made lay wholly within the authority's public law functions and that the decisions were not therefore justiciable in a private law claim for damages for personal injury. The Court of Appeal dismissed the appeal.

---

[80] [2010] EWCA Civ 286, para 72.
[81] [2010] EWCA Civ 286, para 39.

7.52 Laws LJ recognised that 'the scope of a pre-existing private law duty, whose edges are not fixed ('fair, just and reasonable') may be affected by the bite of public law responsibilities'.[82] Laws LJ concluded that where the only or primary means of fulfilling the pre-existing private law duty of care would consist in the exercise of a public law discretion, the law would in an appropriate case require the duty-ower to exercise that discretion but only if that might be done consistently with the duty-ower's full performance of his public law obligations.[83] Laws LJ considered it a premise of this approach that in the particular case the only or primary means of fulfilling the pre-existing duty of care consisted in the exercise of the public law power: that implied the availability of 'a concrete choice of action, unmuddied by the nuance of policy, which serves the duty'[84].

7.53 A private law duty of care could not require an authority to act inconsistently with its public law duties. The standard tests of legality, rationality and fairness had to be met and if the case was one in which the action's severity had to be measured against its effectiveness then it had to be proportionate to the statutory purpose. The effect of the *Padfield* principle that a power must be exercised only for the purpose(s) for which it was conferred was to require that there be no inconsistency between the private law aim and the public law purpose.[85]

7.54 Laws LJ rejected the argument that the LA's director of school's decision as to how to respond to M's complaint was subject to the *Bolam* test for breach. The business of responding to such complaints required no specialised learning 'though no doubt it needed mature judgment and some understanding, and not only at the surface, of the complaints' context' but the court did not require expert evidence to decide whether her decisions were negligently taken.[86]

7.55 In the instant case, the establishment of an interim executive committee would have been justified on the relevant statutory grounds because there had been a serious breakdown in the way the school was managed or governed which was prejudicing or likely to prejudice the standards of performance of pupils at the school. The LA's duty to correct that position marched alongside the LA's private law duty to the claimant on the facts of the present case.

7.56 As for the investigation, Laws and Sedley LJJ noted that the decision to investigate M's complaints was made under the authority's general statutory powers. It therefore had a very broad discretion whether to commission an investigation or not; and while there were factors pro and con, there had been no public law imperative which should have prevented the authority from fulfilling its duty of care to the claimant by declining to set up an investigation.

---

[82] [2010] EWCA Civ 286, para 105.
[83] [2010] EWCA Civ 286, para 106.
[84] [2010] EWCA Civ 286, para 106.
[85] [2010] EWCA Civ 286, paras 106-108.
[86] [2010] EWCA Civ 286, para 67.

The LA had therefore been obliged to decline. Thomas LJ disagreed that the LA were in breach in relation to the decision to investigate M's complaints.

7.57 It should be noted that Laws LJ expressed the view that the case was an unusual one. Damages for negligence consisting in the use or non-use of public law powers must rarely be available: the conclusions as to the Interim Executive Board and the inquiry into M's complaints were only justified by 'their specific place in the whole extraordinary history of events...' He went on to stress that nothing in the case remotely resembled 'a vade mecum for others in the future to build private law claims out of what may be sensitive and difficult decisions, including policy decisions, of public authorities'.

7.58 Sedley LJ said:[87]

> 'The need for the authority to act decisively much sooner than it did arose equally from its public law and its private law duties. Although, as Laws LJ made clear, it is the latter that give rise to this claim, it is because the former offered no obstacle that the deputy judge was entitled to find in the claimant's favour. What might have been the proper outcome had the two things pulled in opposite directions is a question for another day and another claim.'

7.59 While Laws LJ stressed that the case was exceptional, the principles he articulated are broad principles and it is not obvious that the facts of that case are as exceptional as Laws LJ maintained, considered in relation to the principles he articulated. In particular, although Laws LJ maintained that it was a premise of the decision that the LA was faced with a 'concrete choice of action, unmuddied by the nuance of the policy', it is difficult to see how a decision whether or not to establish an Interim Executive Board can be so described; let alone a decision based on the exercise of general statutory functions as to how to respond to a complaint. It is not clear what is meant by 'a concrete choice of action'. The LA's private law duty to the claimant was to avoid placing the claimant at unreasonable risk of harm including psychological harm, but that might have been fulfilled in a wide range of ways: a more robust public declaration of support; an investigation into the circumstances surrounding the circulation of the petition of no confidence in the headteacher; perhaps even behind-the-scenes support. So far as fulfilment of the private law duty is concerned, it is therefore difficult to see that it was indeed a 'concrete choice'.

7.60 It is submitted that it is difficult to see that an LA should be obliged to exercise a public law discretion in one particular way in fulfilment of a private law duty unless that is the only way of fulfilling the private law duty and if in addition it is not inconsistent with the performance of the authority's public law duties. Even then, it may be doubted whether the fulfilment of a private law duty of care should become a determining factor rather than one amongst others; but, in essence, that is what the Court of Appeal suggests it would be. A public authority will often have a broad discretion such that numerous possible

---

87   At para 124.

actions would be lawful in public law terms but involve different trade-offs and it is not clear that the fulfilment of a private law duty, itself cast in broad terms, should have peremptory force to require one particular course of action.

7.61 This is not to suggest that the decision was necessarily wrong on its facts. Perhaps the key to the decision is Sedley LJ's reference to 'the need for the authority to act decisively much sooner than it did' rather than the specific respects in which the LA were found to have been negligent. The authority might have so acted in a number of ways and it is submitted that the court did not need to find specifically that it had to establish an Interim Executive Board and that it had to decline an investigation to fulfil its private law duty: it would have been enough to find that the authority had not taken any of the actions open to it.

The current status of X v Bedfordshire

7.62 In *JD and others v East Berkshire Community Health and others*[88] the Court of Appeal gave a narrow reading to *X v Bedfordshire*. The context was very different from the education field as the Court of Appeal was concerned with whether duties of care were owed to the victim of alleged child abuse and his parents by various public authorities. In each case the allegations of child abuse had proved unfounded and the parents claimed damages for psychiatric harm alleged to have been caused by the false accusations and their consequences. In one of the cases, *K v Dewsbury Healthcare NHS Trust*,[89] the child also brought a claim. The Court of Appeal held that no duty of care was owed to the parents but that a duty of care was owed to the child.[90] More generally, the Court of Appeal held that:[91]

(a) *Phelps* had cast doubt on the proposition that an LA owed no duty of care to children when exercising powers and discretions under the Education Act 1981;

(b) much of the reasoning of Lord Browne-Wilkinson in *X v Bedfordshire* to justify holding that there was no duty of care in relation to the child abuse cases had been undermined by subsequent decisions;

(c) *X v Bedfordshire* should be taken to have decided simply that a decision by a LA whether or not to take a child into care was not reviewable by way of a claim in negligence.

---

88 [2003] EWCA Civ 1151, [2003] 3 FCR 1.
89 [2003] EWCA Civ 1151, [2003] 3 FCR 1.
90 [2003] EWCA Civ 1151, [2003] 3 FCR 1, at paras 83–85. Reliance was placed on the duties under Arts 3 and 8 of the Convention and the duty of care was said to apply to victims both post- and pre-October 2000.
91 [2003] EWCA Civ 1151, [2003] 3 FCR 1, at para 49.

7.63   The Court of Appeal's decision in relation to the parents' claims was appealed to the House of Lords.[92] The House of Lords, by a 4 – 1 majority, upheld the decision of the Court of Appeal. Lord Bingham, who dissented, noted that some had questioned the Court of Appeal's bold approach to the status of *X v Bedfordshire* but neither party sought to maintain the full breadth of the decision, though they did rely on much of the reasoning supporting the decision in that case.[93] Lord Bingham said[94] that it 'could not now be plausibly argued that a common law duty of care may not be owed by a publicly-employed healthcare professional to a child with whom the professional is dealing'. Lord Nicholls, with whom Lord Steyn agreed, said[95] that the law had moved on since *X v Bedfordshire*: the proposition that it was not just and equitable to impose a common law duty on LAs in respect of their performance of their statutory duties to protect children was stated too broadly and such duties might now be owed. Neither Lord Rodger nor Lord Brown suggested that the concession that the doctors owed a duty of care to the children in relation to the investigation of child abuse was not properly made. None of their Lordships commented expressly on the narrow reading of *X* offered by the Court of Appeal. However in *Trent Strategic Health Authority v Jain*[96] the House of Lords while holding that a public authority when vested with powers for the protection of a particular class of persons owed no duty of care where imposition of such a duty might inhibit or conflict with the exercise of those powers for the benefit of the protected class[97] regarded *X v Bedfordshire* as now questionable in so far as it held no duty of care was to owed to the child. In doing so it relied[98] on the analysis of the CA in *JD v East Berkshire Community NHS Trust*.

7.64   In *Connor*, Laws LJ gave a somewhat different analysis of the status of the authorities from that given by Lord Philips in *JD and others* (which does not appear to have been referred to in *Connor*). Laws LJ began by analysing the decision in *X v Bedfordshire* from which he drew a broader principle than the Court of Appeal had drawn in *D and others*. *X v Bedfordshire* he held located the limit of the principle that 'a public bodies' actions or omissions which are authorised by Parliament generally cannot, though they cause injury, sound in damages recoverable by private law action.'[99] That immunity extended only to the choice of policy or the exercise of discretion which the statute distinctly allowed: it did not extend to the choice of means of operations to implement the policy or the manner in which the policy was to be implemented.[100] Furthermore, the immunity would not apply to a decision so unreasonable that it could not be said to have been taken under the statute (though that did not

---

[92]   [2005] UKHL 23.
[93]   [2005] UKHL 23 at para 22.
[94]   [2005] UKHL 23 at para 30.
[95]   [2005] UKHL 23 at para 82.
[96]   [2009] UKHL 4.
[97]   At para 28.
[98]   See at paras 22,23 and 25.
[99]   [2010] EWCA Civ 286, para 82.
[100]   [2010] EWCA Civ 286, paras 82–83.

mean that a duty of care would be owed in all such cases).[101] Laws LJ noted that the policy/operations distinction was subject to criticism by Lord Hoffmann in *Stovin v Wise*.[102] Lord Hoffmann's two main reservations were that the distinction could be elusive in practice and that even where the distinction was clear cut, and the discretion had been exercise irrationally, that did not mean that there was necessarily a duty of care. As to the first reservation, Laws LJ considered that while there might be decisions that involved both policy and operations, the question would then be whether the policy element was sufficient 'to engage the requirement of immunity which is owed to Parliament's authority'. As to the second reservation, Laws LJ considered that Lord Browne-Wilkinson's formulation had anyway left open the possibility of cases where there was no duty of care despite irrationality.[103]

7.65 Laws LJ saw the decision in *Barrett v Enfield* as representing a departure from an analysis based on the authority of Parliament towards an analysis based on a test of justiciability that looked to the competence of the court. Laws LJ saw this as a more pragmatic, flexible approach than that taken in *X v Bedfordshire* and considered that *Phelps v Hillingdon* provided further support for that approach.[104] Laws LJ considered that all of the cases cited comprised a discussion of what is fair, just and reasonable and that 'though there seems to be something of a shift from the sharp-edged rule of immunity for policy decisions found in *X* towards the looser spectrum from strategic to specific decision-making found in *Barrett* and later authorities, the corpus is a principled whole'.[105]

7.66 Laws LJ's review of the authorities and of the shift in the nature of the court's analysis is convincing; but the shift he identifies makes doubtful the claim that this case-law can be read as a principled whole. While it may be argued that the focus on justiciability by reference to the competence of the court is a more nuanced interpretation of Parliament's intention than the more hard-edged formulation in *X v Bedfordshire*, there do appear to be different principles working to different practical effect. It is one thing to say that the courts cannot impose a private law liability in damages as a matter of constitutional principle and quite another to say that they cannot do so as a matter of institutional competence: plainly, the former has the potential to apply to a much wider category of cases than the latter. The matter appears deserving of authoritative treatment by the Supreme Court.

Article 6 of the European Convention on Human Rights

7.67 As we have seen in *X v Bedfordshire*,[106] the House of Lords held that an LA did not owe a duty of care when exercising its statutory functions to

---

[101] [2010] EWCA Civ 286, para 84.
[102] [1996] AC 923.
[103] Laws LJ discussion of *Stovin v Wise* is at paras 86–91 of the judgment.
[104] [2009] UKHL 4, paras 92–96.
[105] [2009] UKHL 4, para 102.
[106] [1995] 2 AC 633.

prevent children being abused. When these cases reached the European Court of Human Rights (ECtHR), it held that the LA had failed to protect the victims from inhuman and degrading treatment contrary to Article 3 of the ECHR and that there had also been a breach of Article 13 because the victims had not been afforded any remedy for the damage as a result of the failure of the LA to protect them: see *Z and others v United Kingdom*.[107] The court went on to state[108] that there had been no breach of Article 6 by the House of Lords holding that there was no duty of care owed.

7.68 The decision of the ECtHR in *Z and others v UK* and *TP and KM v United Kingdom*[109] provided welcome clarification of the question whether it was possible, consistently with Article 6 of the ECHR, for a public body to have what had been described,[110] inaccurately,[111] as a blanket immunity from liability in negligence in relation to certain fields of activity.

7.69 The difficulty stemmed from the European Court's decision in *Osman v United Kingdom*.[112] In that case, the ECtHR upheld a claim that the Osmans' rights under Article 6 of the ECHR had been infringed when the Court of Appeal struck out the claim in negligence against the police. In doing so the Court of Appeal[113] did no more than apply settled law[114] that the police did not owe a duty of care in the prevention and pursuit of crime. To a common lawyer there was nothing odd about this. If, applying the established law, there was no duty of care then there was no right to enforce, and providing the Osmans had access to a court for consideration fairly of the applicable law on duty of care (which they had) no question of breach of Article 6 could arise. Put another way, a common lawyer would regard Article 6 as the territory of procedural fairness in the determination of what substantive rights existed, not as having a substantive content in laying down for signatories to the ECHR what their domestic laws should be.

7.70 However, what the ECtHR had said in *Osman* was that:

> '139. ... the court considers that the applicants must be taken to have had a right, derived from the law of negligence, to seek an adjudication on the admissibility and merits of an arguable claim, that they were in a relationship of proximity to the police, that the harm caused was foreseeable and in the circumstances it was fair, just and reasonable not to apply the exclusionary rule in the *Hill* case. In the view of the court the assertion of that right by the applicants is in itself sufficient to ensure the applicability of Art 6(1) of the Convention.'

---

[107] [2001] 2 FLR 612, 10 May 2001.
[108] [2001] 2 FLR 612, 10 May 2001, at para 104.
[109] (2002) 34 EHRR 2.
[110] *Osman v United Kingdom* (2000) 29 EHRR 245 at para 151.
[111] *Barrett v Enfield* per Lord Browne-Wilkinson [2001] 2 AC 550 at 559–560.
[112] (2000) 29 EHRR 245.
[113] *Osman v Ferguson* [1993] 4 All ER 344.
[114] *Hill v Chief Constable of West Yorkshire* [1989] AC 53.

7.71 The decision in *Osman* did not command universal support in England and the House of Lords referred to it with concern in *Barrett v Enfield*[115] where the decision was described as 'extremely difficult to understand' leading to a 'very unsatisfactory state of affairs' with the expression of a hope that 'the law under Art 6 be further interpreted'.[116] Lord Browne-Wilkinson made clear[117] that to refer to an immunity having been conferred by the courts when they hold in any given class that it is not fair, just and reasonable to impose a duty of care was to misunderstand what the court was doing in so holding. Rather than conferring any immunity the courts were simply holding there was no liability in negligence at all.

7.72 Nevertheless, despite the concern with which *Osman* was viewed it was apparent that the House of Lords was influenced by it in deciding in *Barrett v Enfield* that it was not appropriate to strike out a claim against an LA which was alleged to be negligent in relation to a child who had been placed in care.[118] The alleged negligence included a failure to arrange for the child's adoption or provide him with appropriate and properly monitored placements. The House of Lords held that the public policy considerations, which meant that it would not be fair, just and reasonable to impose a duty of care on an LA when deciding whether to take a child into care, did not have the same force when the child was already in care.

7.73 *Osman* was also pressed in argument in *Phelps v Hillingdon LBC*,[119] but in the light of their Lordships' conclusions on vicarious liability[120] it received little attention in the speeches. Lord Slynn stated that it was unnecessary for him to consider the judgment.[121] Lord Clyde expressed the view that in determining whether a duty of care was owed, more than broad policy considerations were in play and it was necessary to look at the particular facts and circumstances of a particular case and cited *Osman* in support of that.[122] As a majority of the House of Lords approved Lord Clyde's speech and there is here no conflict with what Lord Slynn said (who simply found it unnecessary to deal with the point rather than expressly leaving it open), it appears to be the position that, under the approach adopted in *Phelps*, it would not have been possible to determine that in a defined category of case no duty of care was owed. It is submitted, however, for reasons which appear below, that that is not the current position.

---

[115] [2001] 2 AC 550 at 558–560.
[116] In *JD and others v East Berkshire Community Health* [2003] EWCA Civ 1151, [2003] 3 FCR 1 the Court of Appeal stated at para 14 that the decision in *Osman* had 'perplexed common law judges and jurists'.
[117] [2001] 2 AC 550 at 559.
[118] This seems to have been a ground of the decision of Lord Browne-Wilkinson at 560B–560C and his speech was agreed to by Lords Nolan and Steyn. Lord Slynn did not refer to *Osman* and Lord Hutton expressly stated he found it unnecessary to discuss its implications: see 590D.
[119] [2001] 2 AC 619.
[120] See the discussion at paras **7.18** and **7.19** above.
[121] [2001] 2 AC 619 at 665B.
[122] [2001] 2 AC 619, at 672A–672B.

7.74 It was argued by the applicants in *Z and others v UK* that:

(a) they had an arguable case in negligence based on proximity and foreseeability of damage relying on *Osman*;[123]

(b) there was a serious dispute as to the existence of any exclusionary principle and Article 6 was applicable;

(c) the exclusionary rule amounted in practical effect to an immunity and acted as a restriction on access to the court;[124]

(d) the application of a blanket rule constituted a disproportionate restriction on the applicants' right of access to the court.[125]

7.75 The court rejected the applicants' case and held that:[126]

> 'The applicants, and the Commission in its report, relied on the *Osman* case (cited above) as indicating that the exclusion of liability in negligence, in that case concerning the acts or omissions of the police in the investigation and prevention of crime, acted as a restriction on access to court. The Court considers that its reasoning in the *Osman* judgment was based on an understanding of the law of negligence (see, in particular, paras 138 and 139 of the *Osman* judgment) which has to be reviewed in the light of the clarifications subsequently made by the domestic courts and notably by the House of Lords. The Court is satisfied that the law of negligence as developed in the domestic courts since the case of *Caparo plc v Dickman and others*[127] (cited above, para 58) and as recently analysed in the case of *Barrett v London Borough of Enfield*[128] (loc cit) includes the fair, just and reasonable criterion as an intrinsic element of the duty of care and that the ruling concerning that element in this case does not disclose the operation of an immunity. In the present case, the Court is led to the conclusion that the inability of the applicants to sue the LA flowed not from an immunity but from the applicable principles governing the substantive right of action in domestic law. There was no restriction on access to court of the kind contemplated in the *Ashingdane*[129] judgment ...'

7.76 It is to be noted that Lord Browne-Wilkinson's speech in *Barrett v Enfield* was quoted by the court[130] and relied on in distinguishing *Osman*.

---

[123] Application No 29392/95, [2001] 2 FLR 612, at para 81.
[124] Application No 29392/95, [2001] 2 FLR 612, at para 82.
[125] Application No 29392/95, [2001] 2 FLR 612, at para 83.
[126] Application No 29392/95, [2001] 2 FLR 612d, at para 100.
[127] [1990] 2 AC 605.
[128] [1999] 3 WLR 79.
[129] [2001] 2 FLR 612 at para 93: 'Where the individual's access is limited either by operation of law or in fact, the court will examine whether the limitation imposed impaired the essence of the right and in particular whether it pursued a legitimate aim and there was a reasonable relationship of proportionality between the means employed and the aim sought to be achieved ... If the restriction is compatible with these principles, no violation of Art 6 will arise.'
[130] [2001] 2 FLR 612 at para 65.

Further, the ECtHR made clear[131] that Article 6 did not in itself guarantee any particular content for civil rights and obligations in national law, nor was it enough to bring into play that the non-existence of a cause of action under domestic law might be described as having the same effect as an immunity in the sense of not enabling the applicant to sue for a given category of harm.

7.77 In *Fogarty v United Kingdom*[132] the ECtHR held that the immunity against employment claims conferred on foreign States by section 16(1) of the State Immunity Act 1978 were to be seen not as qualifying a substantive right but as a procedural bar preventing a claimant from bringing a claim for victimisation and discrimination under the SDA 1975.[133] It accordingly proceeded on the basis that Article 6 of the ECHR was engaged, although it held that there had been no violation because the restriction on access reflected generally recognised rules of International law and was not disproportionate.[134]

7.78 These issues were revisited in *Matthews v Ministry of Defence.*[135] In that case, the claimant had served in the Navy and issued a claim against the Ministry of Defence (MOD) for damages for personal injuries alleging breach of statutory duty and negligence in exposing him to asbestos during the course of his service. The MOD denied the claim in reliance upon section 10 of the Crown Proceedings Act 1947 which exempted it from liability in tort for injuries suffered by servicemen as a consequence of events which took place before 1987. A certificate was issued by the Secretary of State under section 10(1)(b) stating that in so far as the injury in question was due to anything suffered by the claimant during service, it would be treated as attributable to service for the purposes of any pension entitlement. At first instance it was held that section 10 was incompatible with the right to a fair trial in Article 6(1) of the ECHR. The Court of Appeal reversed that decision and the House of Lords upheld the Court of Appeal.

7.79 The Lords held that no relevant substantive right existed in domestic law for the claimant to sue the Crown; that Article 6 was not concerned with whether or not a person should have a substantive right to sue in tort; that Article 6 applied only to the determination of rights which could be said, on at least arguable grounds, to be recognised under national law and did not guarantee any particular content for such rights; and that the section 10 certificate did not operate as a procedural bar. It was on this basis that it distinguished the case of *Fogarty v United Kingdom*[136] which had been strongly relied upon by the claimant in argument.

---

[131] [2001] 2 FLR 612, at paras 87 and 98.
[132] (2001) 34 EHRR 302.
[133] (2001) 34 EHRR 302, at para 26.
[134] (2001) 34 EHRR 302, at paras 36–39.
[135] [2003] UKHL 4, [2003] 1 AC 1163.
[136] (2001) 34 EHRR 302; see in *Matthews v MOD* at paras 18, 52, 71, 78, 139 and 143.

7.80 In *JD and others v East Berkshire Community Health and others*,[137] the Court of Appeal, while referring to the difficulty of drawing the line between substantive and procedural entitlements under domestic law, held in the cases before it that there was no difficulty. They were concerned with whether it was fair, just and reasonable to recognise a duty of care on facts alleged by the appellant and that exercise did not contravene Article 6 of the ECHR.[138] In the House of Lords, Lord Bingham described the criticisms made of *Osman* by Lord Browne-Wilkinson in *Barrett v Enfield London Borough Council* as 'compelling'.[139] Their lordships did not otherwise allude to the matter.

7.81 In *Brooks v Metropolitan Police Commissioner*,[140] the claimant was present at the killing of his friend Stephen Lawrence and was himself abused and attacked. He brought an action against the police claiming that he suffered personal injury in the form of exacerbation of or aggravation of the post traumatic stress disorder that was induced by the attack as a result of the negligence of the police officers investigating and that such injury was of a reasonably foreseeable type. The judge struck out the action. The Court of Appeal proceeded on the basis that a claim should only be struck out in absolutely clear cases and allowed his appeal. The Court of Appeal considered that the police arguably owed the claimant a common law duty to:

(a) take reasonable steps to assess whether the claimant was a victim of crime and then to accord him reasonably appropriate protection, support, assistance and treatment if he was so assessed;

(b) take reasonable steps to afford the claimant the protection, assistance and support commonly afforded to a key eye-witness to a serious crime of violence; and

(c) afford reasonable weight to the account that the claimant gave and to act upon it accordingly, that those causes of action were sustainable in law.

7.82 The Commissioner relied on the decision in *Hill v Chief Constable of West Yorkshire*[141] as authority for the proposition that the police owed no such duties. While none of their Lordships were willing to endorse the full breadth of the decision in *Hill*, they allowed the Commissioner's appeal. At paragraph 27 of the judgment, Lord Steyn, with whom Lord Nicholls, Rodger and Steyn agreed noted that there had been developments which affected the reasoning of the decision in *Hill*. Referring to the decision in *Z and others v UK*, he said that in light of that decision 'it would be best for the principle in *Hill* to be reformulated in terms of absence of duty of care rather than a

---

137 [2003] EWCA Civ 1151, [2003] 3 FCR 1.
138 [2003] EWCA Civ 1151, [2003] 3 FCR 1, at para 22.
139 [2005] 2 FLR 284, para 25.
140 [2005] UKHL 24.
141 [1989] AC 53

blanket immunity'. The issue of duty of care was again addressed in accordance with the *Caparo* approach, which both parties agreed was the correct approach.

7.83 Under section 2(1)(a) of the HRA 1998, a court or tribunal must take account of any judgment of the ECtHR in determining a question which has arisen in connection with a Convention right. That section was considered by the House of Lords in *Alconbury*.[142] Lord Slynn made clear that under the HRA 1998 the courts were not bound by decisions of the European Court but that in the absence of special circumstances they should follow any clear and constant jurisprudence of the European Court.[143] That test was qualified somewhat by Lord Neuberger in *Manchester City Council v Pinnock*.[144] He held that a clear and constant line of decisions of the ECtHR should be followed if the effect of that line was not inconsistent with some fundamental substantive or procedural aspect of domestic law and the reasoning deployed did not overlook or misunderstand some argument or point of principle. It is submitted that this approach is likely to govern the future approach of the courts to Convention jurisprudence.

7.84 While *Z and others v UK* may not yet have become a clear and constant jurisprudence,[145] it would be very surprising if future courts did not follow the approach it sets out, particularly in the light of the same approach having been adopted by the House of Lords in *Matthews v MOD*[146] and the interpretation adopted in *Matthews* of the European Court's decision in *Fogarty*. It is submitted, therefore, that future courts will not regard themselves as bound to adopt an *Osman*-type approach simply because a majority of the House of Lords in *Phelps v Hillingdon LBC*[147] seem to have adopted that approach.

7.85 It is submitted that the decisions in *Z and others*, *Matthews v MOD* and *JD v East Berkshire Community Health and others* mean that it will not now be held to be a breach of Article 6 for the courts, having considered whether it is fair, just and reasonable to impose a duty of care in a previous given category of case, to hold that it would not be appropriate for a duty of care to be held to exist in a subsequent case in the same category. While an arbitrary removal of the court's jurisdiction to determine a whole range of civil claims may not be lawful,[148] there seems no reason why the courts cannot continue to hold that in given categories of case it is not fair, just and reasonable to hold that a duty of care exists. Such an approach permits the principled development of the law of negligence, rather than requiring each individual case to consider afresh both

---

[142] *R (Alconbury Developments Ltd) v Secretary of State for the Environment, Transport and the Regions* [2001] UKHL 23, [2001] 2 WLR 1389.

[143] See Lord Slynn of Hadley at para 26.

[144] [2010] UKSC 45 at para 48.

[145] Not least because of the decision in *Fogarty v UK* (2001) 34 EHRR 302.

[146] [2003] UKHL 4, [2003] 1 AC 1163.

[147] [2001] 2 AC 619.

[148] See para 87.

whether a duty of care is in principle justified, and whether it was breached on the facts. It avoids the law degenerating into a myriad of single instances.

Examples of the courts' approach when faced with claims of negligence after *X v Bedfordshire*

7.86   The courts have not been astute to find on the evidence that there has been a breach of a duty of care when, as a matter of law, such a duty is owed. We have seen that in the *Phelps* case, Garland J upheld the claim of negligence and the House of Lords affirmed that decision on appeal. That, however, has been the exception rather than the rule in cases which have reached a full trial. While each case must turn on its own facts, in view of the recent nature of this head of liability, and the paucity of the case-law, it is useful to see how the courts have approached the cases that have come before them.

7.87   As a result of the House of Lords decision in *X v Bedfordshire*, the conjoined appeal of *Christmas v Hampshire*[149] went to trial. The trial of the substantive issues in the case came before Ian Kennedy J, who found, on the facts, that neither the headteacher nor the advisory service had breached their duty of care.[150] The judge attached weight to the fact that after the plaintiff's parents had sent him to an independent school with experience of pupils with SEN (More House), there was nothing to suggest that that school thought, or was advised, that a radical change of approach was needed. He stated:[151]

> 'If I conclude that the defendant Council's advisory teachers failed the plaintiff, it must, on the evidence that I have heard, follow that More House in its turn failed him. While it is perfectly possible that a series of teachers and schools missed what was, at this time, a fairly well-known difficulty, the improbability of that explanation increases with each opportunity for a review.'

7.88   In *Liennard v Slough BC*,[152] the plaintiff contended that his teachers had negligently failed to assess his learning difficulties and had, in consequence, negligently failed to refer him for specialist advice and assessment by a remedial teacher or educational psychologist. The court dismissed the claim, holding, and applying the *Bolam* test, that the teachers could reasonably believe at the time that the plaintiff suffered from a discipline problem rather than had special educational needs.[153] The pupil had demonstrated ability and potential in every subject although he appeared to have had behavioural problems.

7.89   In *Button v Norfolk County Council*,[154] the claimant alleged that the County Council had been negligent in the provision of her education. She had been referred in 1990 to a member of the school's psychological services and a

---

[149]   [1998] ELR 1.
[150]   *Christmas v Hampshire County Council* [1998] ELR 1.
[151]   *Christmas v Hampshire County Council* [1998] ELR 1, at 27B.
[152]   [2002] ELR 527.
[153]   [2002] ELR 527, at paras 115 and 166.
[154]   [2003] All ER (D) 211.

report had been written. It was copied, inter alia, to the council's divisional educational psychologist and it was contended that his review of the report fell well short of the standard required and that he should have recognised that the claimant needed formal assessment by an educational psychologist. The court rejected the claim, holding that there was no reason at the time for thinking that an educational psychologist would add anything of significance to what the report had said. The school report was sensible and the divisional educational psychologist had no reason to overrule its approach. In addition, the claim originally pleaded against him was held to lack the particularity required for an allegation of professional negligence.

7.90   When *Keating v Bromley London Borough*[155] eventually went to trial the claim was also dismissed. Little of the discussion of the evidence in that case is of general relevance, although it is to be noted that a complaint of delay in producing a psychologist's report was excused on the basis of the heavy workload of such psychologists and the national shortage of such professionals.[156] The council was held not to have failed to devote appropriate resources to its educational psychology service even assuming that a failure to do so might give rise to a liability in negligence.[157]

7.91   The decisions in *Carty v Croydon, Marr v Lambeth* and *Gammon v East Sussex* cited above at paras **7.25, 7.38** and **7.44** respectively are further examples of the difficulty of establishing breach of a duty of care. In *Marr v Lambeth*, in which there were numerous allegations of negligence on the part of a number of schools and LA officials, Ouseley J noted that 'it is not difficult with the benefit of hindsight to look back at [the claimant's] education and conclude that something must have gone seriously wrong at a number of stages for a boy to be permanently excluded at 13 ½ years old, to be then without education for over a year and to emerge from the education system functionally illiterate'. Nonetheless, the claim failed and indeed Ouseley J considered there was force in the suggestion that the claim was a claim for a general breach of statutory duty in disguise.

Procedure to be adopted in cases alleging educational negligence

7.92   In *DN (By his Father and Litigation Friend RN) v London Borough of Greenwich*[158] the Court of Appeal confirmed that in a professional negligence case, the evidence of the professional defendant as to why he considers that his conduct did not fall below the standard of care reasonably to be expected of him, was admissible. Such a defendant might give that evidence by reference to the professional literature that was reasonably available to him as a busy practitioner or by reference to the reasonable limits of his professional experience or by way of rebuttal as one professional man against another of the criticisms made of him by the claimant's expert. Nonetheless, that case

---

[155]   [2003] EWHC 1070, [2003] ELR 590, Stanley Burnton J.
[156]   [2003] EWHC 1070, [2003] ELR 590, at paras 188–189.
[157]   [2003] EWHC 1070, [2003] ELR 590, at para 189.
[158]   [2004] EWCA Civ 1659.

underscores the risks to a defendant of not securing independent expert witness in support as well as that of the defendant himself: as the Court of Appeal noted, the defendant's own evidence may lack the objectivity to be accorded to the evidence of an independent report.[159]

7.93 The Court of Appeal also gave procedural guidance for educational negligence cases in the following terms:[160]

(a) a case management order must specify the disciplines in which expert evidence is being permitted;

(b) such an order should impose similar requirements as to the identification of learned articles, textbook entries and research studies, as are now commonly made in clinical negligence cases;

(c) if an expert refers to research evidence in his report, he must identify it in the report, so that it will be available to be considered by the other side without delay, and not merely four days before the trial starts;

(d) the timetable laid down in a case management order for experts to discuss issues and to deliver a report is there to be obeyed and not ignored;

(e) an expert witness must not be permitted to depart substantially from his written report unless the trial judge is satisfied that no injustice will result in the circumstances of the particular case;

(f) a trial judge must not, without good reason, adopt a differential approach towards the evidence-in-chief of different categories of witness (the trial judge in that case had rigidly refused to allow the defendant educational psychologist as a witness of fact to expand upon his witness statement but had allowed the claimant's expert to expand at length on his report); and

(g) constraints imposed by the public funding regime must not unreasonably inhibit the performance by the claimant's solicitors of their obligation to ensure that the defendants are not disadvantaged by any disobedience on their part of pre-trial orders as to the disclosure of documents or the meeting of experts.

---

[159] [2004] EWCA Civ 1659, para 26.
[160] [2004] EWCA Civ 1659, para 92.

DUTIES OF CARE OUTSIDE THE SPECIAL EDUCATIONAL NEEDS FIELD

7.94 Cases in which the courts have had to rule outside the SEN field on whether a duty of care was owed in relation to the educational well being of a child are rare. Consideration is given below to a number of areas where the point might arise.

Poor teaching

7.95 The courts have not yet had to rule on whether there is a duty of care to avoid poor teaching causing poor exam results. Following *Z and others v UK*, it is now open to the courts to rule that it is not fair, just and reasonable to impose a duty of care in those circumstances. The current guidance we presently have from the House of Lords in *Phelps* is that while a minority of their Lordships were prepared to find that a duty of care was owed, whether directly by the LA or vicariously through its teachers,[161] they were also going to be astute to avoid the mounting of generalised educational malpractice claims. While Lord Nicholls was not prepared to rule out a duty of care, he gave a clear hint that it would be in a rare case that the courts would countenance a generalised claim that a child had not received an adequate education at school.[162] It remains to be seen what turn the law takes on this issue now that the courts are free to determine it as a matter of principle rather than on the facts of each case that comes before them.

7.96 Although it was a claim in contract rather than tort, the case of *Abromava v Oxford Institute of Legal Practice*[163] was in essence a claim about negligent teaching and/or guidance. The case concerned a claim by a student who failed her LPC. OXILP did not dispute that by reason of section 13 of the Supply of Goods and Services Act 1982 the contract between the claimant and OXILP included an implied term requiring OXILP to exercise reasonable care and skill in providing services. OXILP did however deny two further implied terms on which the claimant sought to rely: that it would exercise reasonable care and skill in, or in relation to: (i) the giving of guidance to the claimant concerning the taking of written examinations, and (ii) the giving of feedback to the claimant if and when she failed an examination, including a written unseen paper. The claimant complained that she did not receive adequate tuition in exam techniques nor adequate feedback on performance in mock exams. Further, she claimed that the practice of requiring students to mark some mock exam papers (rather than staff) was negligent. OXILP not only denied that it had failed to meet the standard of care and skill expected but that

---

[161] [2001] 2 AC 619. See Lord Nicholls of Birkenhead at 667C–668C. Only Lord Jauncey of Tullichettle agreed with his speech. Lord Nicholls gave an example of a teacher teaching the wrong syllabus for an external examination leading to provable financial loss. An example of that happening at an independent school was reported in *The Daily Telegraph* for 7 June 2001, but there is no reported case of litigation on the point.

[162] [2001] 2 AC 619 at 804H–805C.

[163] [2011] EWHC 613.

the question whether it did so was non-justiciable because it would involve the court evaluating academic judgments, which it was ill-equipped to do.[164]

7.97 Burnett J. considered that a claim brought in contract in reliance upon section 13 of the Supply of Goods and Services Act 1982 was for practical purposes to be approached in the same way as a claim for negligence. He agreed that the court was not well placed to evaluate academic judgments but he did not consider that this claim required it to do so: the court simply had to ascertain whether educational services had been provided without negligence.[165] The *Bolam* test would apply in answering that question.[166] On the facts, the claimant's allegations that the service OXILP had provided was negligent were comprehensively rejected.

School inspections

7.98 In *Gallagher v Berwood School and others*[167] it was sought to allege that the Secretary of State owed a duty of care when inspecting the school under what was section 77 of the Education Act 1944. The point came before the court by way of an application to amend the Statement of Claim to join the Secretary of State to existing proceedings. In that case it was alleged that a child at a boarding school had suffered serious physical abuse which had a marked effect on his psychological development. Jackson J refused to permit the amendment. He held that there was no duty of care:

(a) on the ground that there was no proximity between the plaintiff and the Secretary of State;

(b) on the basis that the Secretary of State had exercised a statutory discretion and there was no plea that he acted outside that discretion; and

(c) on the basis that it was not fair, just and reasonable to impose such a duty.

The Court of Appeal upheld him on the first two grounds.[168] It did not say that he was wrong on the third ground, merely that, in reliance on the current view based on *Barrett v Enfield*,[169] it was difficult to determine that point in the absence of all the facts being found.[170]

7.99 School inspections are now a matter for Her Majesty's Inspectorate of Schools pursuant to Part 1 of the Education Act 2005. Section 5(5) of that Act sets out that it shall be the general duty of the Chief Inspector to report on the

---

[164] The defendant cited observations of Lord Woolf MR in *Clark v University of Lincolnshire and Humberside* [2000] 3 All ER 752 in support of this proposition.

[165] Paragraph 58.

[166] Paragraph 61.

[167] (Unreported) 9 February 1999, Jackson J and 7 October 1999 for the Court of Appeal.

[168] At 7B–7E.

[169] [2001] 2 AC 550.

[170] See at 5A–B and 7C–7E.

quality of the education provided at the school, how far the education provided in the school meets the needs of the range of pupils at the school, the educational standards achieved in the school, the quality of the leadership in and management of the school, including whether the financial resources made available to the school are managed effectively, the spiritual, moral, social and cultural development of the pupils at the school, the contribution made by the school to the well-being of those pupils, and the contribution made by the school to community cohesion. These duties do not extend to investigating physical abuse at the school and it is unlikely that the courts would hold there was a duty of care in relation to this provision where there had previously been none under section 77 of the Education Act 1944. Proximity between the Inspector and the child would be difficult to establish and it is difficult to see it is fair, just and reasonable to impose a duty of care in this context in relation to physical abuse, having regard to the other agencies that would have specific child protection responsibilities.

The duty to provide sufficient schools

7.100 The LA is under a duty pursuant to section 14 of the Education Act 1996 to provide sufficient schools for its area, in number, character and equipment, and to provide for all pupils the opportunity of appropriate education (ie education which offers such variety of instruction and training as may be desirable in view of the pupils' different ages, abilities and aptitudes and the different periods for which they may be expected to remain at school), including practical instruction and training appropriate to their needs. This is the kind of area in which attempts to establish a duty of care would, it is submitted, fail at the first hurdle; the authority's exercise of its discretion is so dependent on policy considerations that it is unlikely to be considered justiciable at all. The question was considered by the courts prior to the decision in *X v Bedfordshire*.

7.101 In *Meade v Haringey*,[171] an action was brought against an LA seeking injunctive and declaratory relief for breach of section 8 of the Education Act 1944 (the predecessor of section 14 of the EA 1996), when strike action by, inter alia, school caretakers led to schools being closed for some weeks. The Chief Education Officer, following notification of the strike action by the trade union, instructed headteachers not to attempt to open schools. In considering whether, if the LA had failed in its duty to keep open the schools, the parents had a remedy in the courts, Lord Denning MR found that the right to complain to the Secretary of State (pursuant to section 99 of the 1944 Act) did not preclude other remedies. Relying on cases in which damages had been recovered, e g where children were injured by defective premises, he found that damages might be recoverable. He stated:[172]

> 'that where a public authority so conducts itself, by act or omission, as to frustrate or hinder the policy and objects of the Act, it is acting ultra vires, and ... any

---

[171] [1979] 1 WLR 637.
[172] [1979] 1 WLR 637 at 647C.

person who is particularly damnified thereby can bring an action in the courts for damages or an injunction, whichever be the most appropriate.'

7.102　However, this case has not since been followed. In *R v Mid-Glamorgan County Council ex parte Greig*[173] an action was brought against the LA which, it was alleged, had failed to provide residential schooling for a child whose special educational needs demanded such provision. Simon Brown J found that *Meade* was not authority for the proposition that damages were in principle recoverable for a breach of section 8 of the 1944 Act. In the cases relied on in *Meade* damages were not sought (except in the personal injury cases to which special considerations applied) nor, in fact were they sought in *Meade* itself. Further, the decision was reached without the benefit of certain authority to the contrary.

7.103　In any event, Simon Brown J considered that the essential objection to the damages claim was the want of any good cause of action. It was only in certain exceptional and well-recognised circumstances that damages could be claimed for such a breach, eg where the authority's conduct involved the commission of a recognised tort, which was not so in the case before him.

7.104　In *R v Inner London Education Authority ex parte Ali*,[174] actions for damages for breach of section 8 of the Education Act 1944 were brought against the education authority in respect of a failure to provide sufficient places for primary school children in Tower Hamlets. Woolf LJ also declined to adopt the obiter dictum of Lord Denning in *Meade*, approving the comments of Simon Brown J in *Greig*.[175] He found that the duty under section 8 was a broad and general duty, or 'target duty' and, having regard to this, that it was intended to enure for the benefit of the public in general, and not intended to give the individual litigant a cause of action.

7.105　It is submitted that the position remains unchanged by the decision in *X v Bedfordshire* not least because of the consideration in that case of *Meade v Haringey* in the context of breach of statutory duty.[176] In *Thurkettle v Suffolk County Council*,[177] a pupil contended that the LA that had placed him at an unsuitable school in another LA was in breach of a duty of care provided by section 8 of the Education Act 1944. He alleged that following his placement at a special school he had been bullied, sexually assaulted and inappropriately punished at the school by staff and students and, as a result, had suffered psychological damage. The action was struck out on the basis that there was no duty of care owed by either the LA or the relevant educational professionals who recommended the placement.

---

[173]　(Unreported) 20 April 1988.
[174]　(1990) LG Rev 852.
[175]　(1990) LG Rev 852, at 854.
[176]　[1995] 2 AC 633 at 768B–770A.
[177]　(Unreported) 15 June 1998, Day J.

7.106 An LA has been held not to owe a duty of care in relation to sexual abuse of pupils committed by staff employed at an independent school. Such assaults were held not to be foreseeable, there was not a sufficient relationship of proximity nor was it just and reasonable to impose a duty of care.[178]

School admissions

7.107 It is unlikely that any action for damages could be brought arising out of the exercise of discretion by the LA or governing body pursuant to section 86 of the SSFA 1998. The discretion under section 86 expressly depends on prejudice to the provision of efficient education or the efficient use of resources, which are classic policy considerations. In relation to section 9 of the EA 1996, the LA is required to do no more than have regard to a general principle, and the prospects would be even less good. Factors similar to those referred to in *X* suggesting that it would not, in any event, be just and reasonable to impose a duty of care, are also present. Potential conflicts arise, since the preferences of all parents must be considered, and where a particular school is a popular choice, it will inevitably be necessary to disappoint some. Further, as in the SEN field, there is a detailed statutory appeals process for parents to pursue. The House of Lords declined to impose a duty of care in relation to the naming of an appropriate school for a child with SEN in *X*, and it is submitted that the two situations are not too far removed from one another.

7.108 The underlying considerations of cost to LAs and to communities militate strongly against the imposition of a duty. In particular, this of all areas would be likely to lead to vexatious or hopeless applications.

Discrimination[179]

7.109 A pupil who claims to have been subject to an act of discrimination on the grounds of disability, gender reassignment, pregnancy and maternity, race, religion or belief, sex or sexual orientation may bring civil proceedings against the appropriate body by virtue of section 114(1) of the Equality Act 2010. A county court has jurisdiction to determine such a claim and has power to grant any remedy which could be granted by the High Court in proceedings in tort, which of course includes damages.[180] An award of damages may include compensation for injured feelings, whether or not it includes compensation on any other basis.[181] The county court must not make an award of damages unless it first considers whether to make any other disposal.[182] The same provisions apply in relation to acts of discrimination on the part of institutions

---

[178] *P v Harrow LBC* [1993] 1 FLR 723, Potter J. In the light of the decision of the Court of Appeal in *JD and others v East Berkshire Community Health and others* [2003] EWCA Civ 1151, [2003] 3 FCR 1, this case may now be decided differently.

[179] See, generally, Chapter 3 for discrimination in the education field.

[180] Equality Act 2010, s 119(1) and (2).

[181] Equality Act 2010, s 119(4).

[182] Equality Act 2010, s 119(6).

of further and higher education or on the part of general qualification bodies but the relevant protected characteristics are age, disability, gender reassignment, pregnancy and maternity, race, religion or belief, sex and sexual orientation.[183]

7.110 One example in the context of sex discrimination would be a female pupil denied the opportunity to attend a single-sex selective school who would have been afforded that opportunity had she been male. Where, in mitigation of loss, fees at an independent school are incurred, these would, in principle, seem recoverable. It might also be argued that the school actually attended offered a lower standard of education and that losses were caused by poorer exam results than would otherwise have been obtained. Such speculative losses would be much more difficult to establish.

Duty to provide free school transport

7.111 The distinction between the exercise of the discretion and its implementation in practice is pertinent here.[184] As to the latter, problems in the actual provision of free school transport have been discussed in Chapter 1. There could, in addition, be circumstances in which the authority was in breach of its obligation to provide non-stressful transport, such that the pupil was unable to benefit from the educational provision. It is possible in these circumstances and the related case where the transport actually provided is unsafe and causes physical or recognised psychiatric injury, that an action for negligence or for breach of statutory duty would lie.

7.112 As to failure to provide any school transport, any action would, in principle, lie against the LA in relation to its duties under section 508B and 508C of the EA 1996. It would be necessary to demonstrate both that it was irrational not to provide free transport in a particular instance, and that there was a discernible policy that financial recompense should be available for such a failure. It is submitted that it is likely that there would be a duty of care to provide free school transport, or an action for breach of statutory duty, where the LA is at fault in considering that the school is within walking distance by the nearest available route. This is akin to the limited duty of care in relation to SEN with its close parallel to medical negligence.

Discipline and exclusions

7.113 The questions of general discipline and exclusions should be considered separately.

---

183   By reason of the Equality Act 2010, ss 4, 90 and 95.
184   For this distinction see *X v Bedfordshire* [1995] 2 AC 633 at 735F–735H.

Discipline

7.114 An action for damages might lie in relation to a failure to maintain proper discipline in a school, leading to physical harm to a pupil or staff,[185] or to disruption of classes and a consequent fall in the standard of education provided. There would be a number of potential defendants who should be sued as joint tortfeasors. First, a headteacher may be in breach of his common law duty of care for the educational well-being of the pupils, either in the exercise of his responsibilities under section 61(4) of the SSFA 1998, or perhaps, in his failure to exclude a specific pupil. The governing body also has responsibilities in relation to discipline in the school, pursuant to section 61 of the SSFA, upon which an action might be based. However, it would be an extension of liability to find that the governing body owed a common law duty of care for the educational well-being of the pupils.

7.115 The LA would be vicariously liable for any breach by the headteacher. An LA might also be found to be under a direct duty of care in relation to its power under section 62 of the SSFA 1998 to take such steps as it considers are required to prevent the breakdown or continuing breakdown of discipline in a school. The authority may take steps if, in its opinion, the behaviour of pupils at the school, or action taken by them or their parents, is such that the education of any pupils at the school is, or is likely to become, severely prejudiced. This involves practical rather than policy judgements, and an LA that decided, despite being of the view that the circumstances set out above were satisfied, not to take any steps, or to take wholly inadequate steps, might well be found to have acted so unreasonably as to be outside the ambit of its discretion. It is submitted that the requirements of foreseeability and proximity would then be readily satisfied, given the express account to be taken of likely prejudice to the education of the pupils. Would it then be just and reasonable to impose a duty? The discretion differs from those under consideration in *X* because, in particular, there is no parental participation or right of appeal. On the other hand, there would be the prospect of large numbers of pupils within the school in question bringing proceedings. Establishing any recoverable loss is likely to be difficult; any claim based on a loss of employment prospects would be highly speculative.

---

[185] In Scotland the possibility of such an action was recognised in *McLeod v Aberdeen City Council* (1999) GWD 23–1115. An auxiliary at a school for children with special needs sued her employers in respect of injuries she had suffered when she and a teacher physically removed a disruptive pupil. At a procedural hearing she was permitted to aver that the pupil should have been excluded from the school prior to the incident on the basis that it was reasonably foreseeable the assault would happen. In *Webster v The Ridgeway Foundation School* [2010] EWHC 157 the court rejected the claimant's contentions that the school was in breach of a duty of care by failing to exclude a particular pupil at a particular stage on the facts, although implicitly accepted in principle that such a failure could found an action in negligence: see paras 143–173.

Exclusion

7.116   An action might lie in relation to the wrongful exclusion of a pupil, for instance one excluded permanently who suffers detriment as a result, or one who loses the opportunity to take a public examination. The power to exclude is the headteacher's, and any action would be based on a breach of the common law duty of care. Disregard of the detailed statutory guidance would be relevant to whether the headteacher had failed to exercise the requisite standard of care. It might also be possible to bring an action against a governing body having powers under the Articles of government to hear appeals or direct that the pupil be reinstated and failing so to direct.

7.117   Possible heads of damages would include psychological injury suffered by a wrongly excluded pupil, or the more speculative future loss of earnings, based on the pupil as he or she might have been but for the wrongful exclusion. *Phelps* signals some of the difficulties in assessing such losses. Contributory negligence could well play a considerable part in any such action.

PROXIMITY AND FORESEEABILITY

7.118   It does not follow that, in all cases where an LA exercises statutory functions, damage to particular plaintiffs will be foreseeable or that there will be a relationship of proximity. In *Surrey CC v M*[186] the Court of Appeal held that an LA was not sufficiently proximate to a person who was abused by a child housed by another authority in a flat across the road. There the victim was within the wide category of members of the public, rather than an exceptional category of risk. In *Palmer v Tees HA*[187] a former patient of a health authority who was still undergoing outpatient treatment committed sexual abuse and the murder of a child. It was held that the health authority was not sufficiently proximate to the child or his mother and an action for negligence was struck out.

7.119   In *Gallagher v Berwood School and others,*[188] as we have seen, Jackson J held that proximity could not be established between the Secretary of State and a child abused at school.[189] That point was not said, either in the Notice of Appeal to the Court of Appeal, nor in the accompanying skeleton argument, to have been wrongly decided.[190] When an attempt was made to raise the matter in the Court of Appeal, it was held that the judge was right on the issue of proximity.[191]

---

[186]   [2001] EWCA Civ 691, (2001) *The Independent,* 11 June.
[187]   (2000) 2 LGLR 69.
[188]   (Unreported) Transcripts 9 February 1999, Jackson J and 7 October 1999 for the Court of Appeal.
[189]   See Transcript at 35E.
[190]   See Transcript at 6C.
[191]   See Transcript at 6C–6G.

7.120 A relationship of proximity between an LA and the pupils with SEN it placed at an independent school was held not to exist when the pupils were sexually abused by staff at the independent school: *P v Harrow.*[192]

BREACH OF STATUTORY DUTY

7.121 Lord Browne-Wilkinson[193] in *X v Bedfordshire* dealt with the question of whether there was a cause of action for breach of statutory duty.[194] In conformity with the Court of Appeal, he held that there was not. He was influenced, in relation to the Education Act 1981, by the extensive rights of appeal given at every stage to the parent and held, in the light of these, that Parliament cannot have possibly intended that there be, in addition, a right to sue for damages.[195] In relation to the claim based on breach of section 8 of the Education Act 1944, he interpreted previous authority as merely enabling public law rights to be brought by private action (before the modern development of judicial review) and not being soundly based in so far as it suggested that a private law claim for damages might lie.

7.122 A further attempt to bring a claim for breach of statutory duty in reliance upon sections 33 and 36 of the Education Act 1944 was made in *Holtom v Barnet LBC*[196] and dismissed having regard to *X v Bedfordshire.*

7.123 In the light of *X v Bedfordshire*, it is submitted that it is very unlikely that duties of the LA outside the SEN field will be held to give rise to claims for breach of statutory duty.

DAMAGES UNDER THE HUMAN RIGHTS ACT 1998[197]

7.124 By virtue of section 8(1) of the Human Rights Act 1998 (HRA 1998), the court may grant such relief within its powers as it considers appropriate

---

[192] [1993] 1 FLR 723. As observed at para **7.106** above this case might now be decided differently.
[193] Lord Jauncey delivered a short concurring speech. Lords Lane and Ackner simply agreed. Lord Nolan also delivered a short speech agreeing in large measure with Lord Browne-Wilkinson (all of his conclusions and the whole of his reasoning save that in relation to the abuse cases he added some reasoning of his own).
[194] The issue arose, in relation to the education cases, in the *Bromley* case only. In the *Dorset* case the Court of Appeal had dismissed the case brought for breach of statutory duty and there was no appeal on the point, and in the *Hampshire* case no case for breach of statutory duty was brought. In the abuse cases, the case on breach of statutory duty was dismissed at 747C–748E. In that context, his starting point was that the legislation was for the establishment of an administrative system designed to promote the social welfare of the community with sensitive questions on how to strike the balance between protecting the child from harm and disrupting the relationship with the parent.
[195] See at 769G–769H.
[196] [1999] ELR 255, CA.
[197] See, for general discussion of this topic, Scorey and Eike *Human Rights Damages Principles and Practice* (Sweet and Maxwell, 2002), Fairgrieve *State Liability in Tort – A Comparative Study* (Oxford University Press, 2003) at paras 3.3.2, Grosz, Beatson and Duffy *Human Rights,*

where it finds that an act, or proposed act, of a public authority would be unlawful under the HRA 1998. No award of damages is to be made unless, taking into account all the circumstances of the case, including any other order made, and the consequences of any decision made by the court, the court is satisfied that the award is necessary to afford just satisfaction to the person in whose favour an award is made.[198] In determining whether to award damages, or the amount of the award, the court must take into account the principles applied by the ECtHR in relation to the award of compensation under Article 41 of the ECHR.[199]

7.125 Many commentators have referred to the difficulty in identifying the principles upon which the ECtHR acts when awarding damages.[200] Compensation is only awarded under Article 41 if it is necessary and that imports a discretion.[201] The court has frequently said that compensation is awarded on an 'equitable basis', but the court has yet to define what it means by that phrase. The Law Commission[202] suggested that the following factors were taken into account by the Strasbourg Court when it assessed damages:

(a)   a finding of a violation may constitute just satisfaction;

(b)   the degree of loss suffered must be sufficient to justify an award of damages;

(c)   the seriousness of the violation will be taken into account;

(d)   the conduct of the respondent will be taken into account. This can include both the conduct in the particular case giving rise to the claim and the record of previous violations by the State;

(e)   the conduct of the applicant will be taken into account.

The jurisprudence of the European Court of Human Rights

7.126 There are many cases where the court has held that the finding of a violation is, in itself, just satisfaction. Such cases are often where the applicant lacks general merit because he was involved in criminal conduct. An example is

---

The 1998 Act and the European Convention (Sweet and Maxwell, 2000) at paras 6-16–6-21 and Clayton and Tomlinson *The Law of Human Rights* (2nd Edn, Oxford University Press, 2009) at paras 21.13–21.90.

[198]   HRA 1998, s 8(3).

[199]   HRA 1998, s 8(4).

[200]   See, for example, Grosz, Beatson and Duffy *Human Rights, The 1998 Act and the European Convention* (Sweet and Maxwell, 1999) at paras 6–20 and Clayton and Tomlinson *The Law of Human Rights* (op cit) at paras 21–30. See also, *Anufrijeva and others v Southwark and others* [2003] EWCA Civ 1406, [2003] All ER (D) 288 (Oct) at para 58.

[201]   *Guzzardi v Italy* (1980) 3 EHRR 333 at para 114.

[202]   *Damages under the Human Rights Act 1998* (October 2000) at para 4.44. This paragraph was cited with apparent approval by Sullivan J in *R (on the application of Bernard) v Enfield LB* [2002] EWHC 2282 (Admin), (2002) 5 CCL Rep 577 at para 35.

McCann v United Kingdom,[203] where the court thought it inappropriate to award compensation to three terrorist suspects who had intended to plant a bomb in Gibraltar.

7.127 Reported cases of the ECtHR in the education field where there has been any discussion of the question of remedy are rare.[204]

7.128 In *Campbell and Cosans v UK*,[205] the court held that the LA's refusal to exempt Mrs Campbell's and Mrs Cosans' children from corporal punishment violated the second sentence of Article 2 of the First Protocol. It further held that the LA's refusal to allow Mrs Cosans' son to return to school because he would not submit to corporal punishment, which suspension lasted nearly a year, was a breach of the first sentence of Article 2 of the First Protocol. When it came back to deal with questions of just satisfaction, it held that those findings were sufficient just satisfaction for any non-pecuniary loss suffered by Mrs Cosans and Mrs Campbell.[206]

7.129 Mrs Campbell also submitted an unquantified claim in respect of the cost of obtaining private education for her children. She did not submit any supporting evidence[207] and, following a report in a newspaper that her son was attending an independent school which used corporal punishment, she refused to name the school involved. She did not deny the truth of the report. It is, perhaps, not surprising that the court refused in those circumstances to make any award on this part of the claim. Not only was there a lack of proof, there was an obvious lack of factual merit in the applicant's conduct in claiming for the cost of education at a private school which adopted the same practice as to corporal punishment of which she complained in the state school.

7.130 Jeffrey Cosans claimed £25,000 as 'moral damage'.[208] He claimed that his suspension from school had prevented him from taking certain examinations and from continuing study and training at further education establishments or night school, with the result that he was denied the opportunity of acquiring a skill for the future. He further stated that since his suspension he had, except for a brief period, been unemployed and had had to rely on his parents and social security for financial support. He claimed that the suspension had caused him considerable embarrassment at the time and, being a matter of common knowledge, had had adverse effects on his employment opportunities and prospects.

---

[203] (1995) 21 EHRR 97.

[204] In *Belgian Linguistic Case (No 2)* (1979) 1 EHRR 252 at 336, the ECtHR reserved to the applicants the right to apply for just satisfaction in respect of the breach they found and there is no further report of what followed.

[205] (1982) Series A No 48. The report on liability is (1982) 4 EHRR 293. The decision on just satisfaction is dated 22 March 1983.

[206] Paragraphs 10(b) and 20.

[207] See at para 11.

[208] See at para 23.

7.131   The European Court awarded Jeffrey Cosans £3,000. It took into account[209] that the incident that led to his suspension was a breach of the school's disciplinary rules. It also took into account that the suspension was disproportionate and in breach of Article 2 of the First Protocol. The ECtHR accepted he must have suffered some non-pecuniary loss. In addition, to the initial mental anxiety, it held that he must have felt himself at a disadvantage as compared with others in his age group. It was further held that his failure to complete his schooling deprived him of some opportunity to develop his intellectual potential.

7.132   The material damage claim was held not to lend itself to a process of calculation.[210] The court concluded that, while the suspension may well have contributed to the material difficulties Jeffrey Cosans had encountered, it could not be regarded as the principal cause of those difficulties. Reliance was placed upon the fact that, had he completed his education, he would probably have obtained only limited qualifications, his failure to pursue to the full opportunities of training or to register at all times with the local employment exchange, as well as his receipt of state benefits.

7.133   In *Valsamis v Greece*,[211] the ECtHR held that there had been a breach of Article 2 of the First Protocol, taken with Articles 13 and 9 of the ECHR, when a Jehovah's Witness, contrary to her religious beliefs, was required to attend a school parade to celebrate the outbreak of war between Greece and fascist Italy. The pupil had refused to attend the parade and was punished by one day's suspension from school. The court, while satisfied that the applicants had sustained non-pecuniary damage, held that its finding of violation was sufficient just satisfaction in relation to the non-pecuniary damage.[212] This was a case where it is difficult to see serious damage was caused by the violation of the ECHR, having regard to the nature and duration of the punishment inflicted. Therefore it is probably an example of the second category identified by the Law Commission: namely, where the degree of loss suffered was probably not sufficient to justify an award.

7.134   Where there is loss of sufficient seriousness to justify an award, it has to be shown that the Convention breach caused the loss[213] although sometimes this will be presumed without specific proof.[214] The principle, if an award is to be made, is *restitutio in integrum*, so that the claimant is put so far as possible in the position in which he would have been had there been no breach of his Convention rights.[215] Compensation can be awarded for both pecuniary and

---

[209]   At para 26.

[210]   (1982) Series A No 48.

[211]   (1997) 24 EHRR 294.

[212]   (1997) 24 EHRR 294, at paras 51–53. The court did make substantial award in respect of costs and expenses assessed on an equitable basis: see at paras 54–56.

[213]   See, for example, *Airey v Ireland* (1981) 3 EHRR 592 at para 12.

[214]   *Pine Valley Developments Ltd v Ireland* (1993) 16 EHRR 379 at para 17.

[215]   *Pine Valley Developments Ltd v Ireland* (1993) 16 EHRR 379, at para 20. See *Anufrijeva and others v Southwark and others* [2003] EWCA Civ 1406, [2003] All ER (D) 288 (Oct) at para 59.

non-pecuniary damage. The former can include loss of opportunity,[216] the latter compensation for feelings of distress, anxiety and humiliation caused by the breach of the ECHR.[217]

7.135 In *DH and others v Czech Republic*[218] the court found, by a majority, that the Czech Republic was in breach of A2P1 in conjunction with Article 14. The applicants were Roma children who had been placed in schools for children with mental disabilities where a more basic curriculum was followed than was followed in ordinary schools. The decision to place a child in such a school was taken by the headteacher on the basis of results of tests to measure a child's intellect carried out in an educational psychology and child guidance centre and required the consent of the child's parent or guardian. The applicants' parents had in fact consented to the placements and in each case a decision was made in accordance with the procedure. The written decision as to placement informed the applicants' parents of the right to appeal but none chose to exercise that right. A subsequent letter informed the applicants of the possibility of applying to transfer to ordinary schools. Four of the applicants were successful in aptitude tests for ordinary school and thereafter attended such schools. All but four of the applicants asked the education authority to revoke the decision on placement otherwise than through the appeal mechanism. The authority refused.

7.136 More than half of all children placed in special schools were Roma children; more than half of Roma children in the Czech republic attended such schools; a Roma child was 27 times more likely to be placed in a special school than a non-Roma child. The applicants complained to the European Court of a violation of Article 14 ECHR in conjunction with A2P1. The Grand Chamber found, by a majority, that there had been such a violation. The court considered that the system did not have adequate procedural safeguards in place and although the practice was intended to address the difficulties faced by the Czech Republic in providing schooling for Roma children, the effect was that such children received an education which compounded their difficulties and compromised their subsequent personal development.[219]

7.137 The court did not examine the individual cases to determine how the particular individuals before it had been affected by the system that was in place, reasoning that since the legislation as applied at the material time had a disproportionately prejudicial effect on the Roma community and the applicants as members of that community necessarily suffered the same discriminatory treatment.[220] The applicants did not claim pecuniary damage but each claimed 22,000 euros for non-pecuniary damage including

---

[216] *Weekes v United Kingdom* (1988) 10 EHRR 293 at para 13. The court is not consistent on this and often says it will not speculate what would have happened had a hearing not been in breach of Art 6: see, for example, *Saunders v United Kingdom* (1996) 23 EHRR 313 at para 86.

[217] *Gaskin v United Kingdom* (1989) 12 EHRR 36 at para 58.

[218] (2007) 23 BHRC 526.

[219] (2007) 23 BHRC 526, paras 207–208.

[220] (2007) 23 BHRC 526, para 209.

'educational, psychological and emotional harm and compensation for the anxiety, frustration and humiliation they had suffered as a result of their discriminatory placement in special schools'.[221]

7.138 The court considered that it could not speculate on what the outcome of the situation would have been if the applicants had not been placed in special schools. In view of the fact that the court had refused to consider the facts of each individual case that is unsurprising but it perhaps highlights a flaw in that approach. However, the court considered that it was clear that they had sustained non-pecuniary damage, in particular as a result of the humiliation and frustration caused by the indirect discrimination of which they were victims – and that a finding of a violation of the convention did not provide sufficient redress. The court assessed the non-pecuniary damage sustained by each applicant at 4,000 euros.[222]

7.139   *DH* was distinguished in *Orsus and others v Croatia*,[223] in which case the court rejected claims that the applicants, Crotian Roma, had been subject to a breach of Article 3 of the ECHR or A2P1 either alone or in conjunction with Article 14 of the ECHR where Roma children found to lack sufficient or even basic knowledge of the Czech language were placed in separate classes upon their enrolment in regular elementary school. However, the court upheld the applicants' claim that the four years it took the Czech constitutional court itself to rule on the question was a sufficient delay to amount to a violation of Article 6 of the ECHR, in particular in view of what was at stake for the applicants, namely their right to education. Each applicant had claimed 22,000 euros in respect of non-pecuniary damage (although it is not clear from the report whether this was in respect of the violation of Article 6 only or in respect of the other claims). The court awarded 1,300 euros to each applicant in the way of non-pecuniary damages.

7.140   In *Zengin v Turkey*,[224] the court found that there had been a breach of A2P1 where the state had refused to grant the applicants, adherents of Alevis, a distinct form of Islam, a full exemption from religious culture and ethics classes which failed to cover the Alevi faith despite the fact that a large proportion of Turkey's population adhere to that faith. The applicants made no claim for compensation in respect of pecuniary and non-pecuniary damage and the court itself considered that the finding of a violation with regard to A2P1 constituted just satisfaction in itself for the damage they sustained.

7.141   In *Timishev v Russia*,[225] the court found a violation of A2P1 where the applicant's children were refused admission to the school they attended because the applicant, of Checehn ethnicity, had surrendered a migrant's card confirming his status as a forced migrant from Chechnya in exchange for

---

[221]   (2007) 23 BHRC 526, para 213.
[222]   (2007) 23 BHRC 526, para 217.
[223]   [2008] ECHR 15766/03.
[224]   [2007] ECHR 1448/04.
[225]   [2005] ECHR 55762/00.

compensation for property lost in the Chechen republic. The court found that a right to education was indispensable to the furtherance of human rights and played such a fundamental role that a restrictive interpretation of A2P1 would not be consistent with the purpose of that provision. The court said there was 'no doubt that the right to education guaranteed access to elementary education that was of primordial importance for a child's development'.[226] The applicant's children having been denied such access, there had been a violation of A2P1. The applicant claimed EUR 500,000 in respect of the violation of his children's right to education as well as 300,000 EUR in respect of separate violations of A2P4 and A2P4 in conjunction with Article 14 of the ECHR relating to the applicant's own freedom of movement. The court considered that the applicant had suffered non-pecuniary damage 'such as distress and frustration resulting from the actions and decisions of the domestic authorities that have been found to be incompatible with the Convention and its Protocols' which was not sufficiently compensated by the findings of violations but awarded only EUR 5,000 under this head.

7.142 In *Folgero and others v Norway*,[227] the court found, by a majority, that there had been a violation of A2P1 when Norway did not permit the applicants, who were humanists, a full exemption from taking a subject in Christianity, Religion and Philosophy which the court found to have an excessively Christian focus. The state did not take sufficient care to ensure that information and knowledge included in the curriculum was conveyed in an objective, critical and pluralistic manner and the system of partial exemptions in place was inadequate in a number of respects. The applicants sought no compensation for pecuniary damage but claimed an amount in respect of non-pecuniary damage, leaving determination of the amount to the discretion of the court. The court considered that in light of the readiness of Norway to review the impugned subject, a finding of a breach of A2P1 constituted sufficient just satisfaction in the case.[228]

7.143 In *Ponomaryov v Bulgaria*,[229] the court found a violation of Article 14 of the ECHR considered in conjunction with A2P1 when Bulgaria required two Russian boys, who were living in Bulgaria as they were entitled to do by reason of their Russian mother's permanent residence, to pay school fees for secondary education. The boys had been living in Bulgaria since a young age, attended a Bulgarian primary school and spoke fluent Bulgarian. The court emphasised that its task was not to decide whether and to what extent it was permissible for states to charge fees for secondary, or indeed any, education.[230] The court accepted that states may have legitimate reasons for limiting the use of public services by short-term and illegal immigrants who, as a rule, did not contribute to their funding. However, unlike certain other public services that states provided, education was a right that enjoys direct protection under the

---

[226] [2005] ECHR 55762/00, para 64.
[227] (2007) BHRC 227.
[228] (2007) BHRC 227, para 109.
[229] [2011] ECHR 5335/05.
[230] [2011] ECHR 5335/05, para 53.

Convention.[231] Furthermore, education not only directly benefited those using it but also society at large and society had an interest to integrate minorities. The state's margin of appreciation in the domain of education was in inverse proportion to the importance of the type of education at issue for those concerned and societies at large: states had a broader margin of appreciation when university education was at stake than they had in respect of primary education.[232] However, secondary education was of increasing importance in knowledge-based societies and the court would therefore apply stricter scrutiny to the assessment of the proportionality of the measure affecting the applicants in this case. The court did not have to determine whether the Bulgarian state was entitled to deprive any irregularly residing aliens from educational benefits but had to focus on the particular circumstances of the appellants. They were not persons who arrived in the country unlawfully and then sought to claim its public services: they arrived lawfully, inadvertently fell into the situation of aliens lacking permanent residence and no serious steps were being taken to remove them.[233] Nor had they tried to abuse the Bulgarian educational system.[234] In these circumstances, the requirement for them to pay school fees was unjustified discrimination. So far as damages were concerned, there was no evidence that the fees had in fact been paid so damages were not awarded for them but the court considered that the applicants had suffered a certain amount of frustration on account of the discrimination and awarded each of them 2,000 Euros plus tax.[235]

The domestic courts: When damages will be awarded

7.144   So far as the domestic courts are concerned, the principles upon which the domestic courts will act when awarding damages in the educational field for breach of a Convention right have yet to be fully worked out.[236] In many cases, it is to be anticipated that the availability of judicial review will be sufficient to prevent damage occurring and an award will not be necessary for the purposes of just satisfaction. In other cases it is to be anticipated that the emerging law of negligence will make it unnecessary to make an award of damages under the HRA 1998. There will, however, be some cases where no duty of care is owed

---

[231]   [2011] ECHR 5335/05, para 55.

[232]   [2011] ECHR 5335/05, para 56. This observation was applied by the High Court in *R (on the application of Hurley) v Secretary of State for Business, Innovation and Skills* [2012] EWHC 201 in dismissing a claim that an increase in the maximum chargeable tuition fees at university was a violation of A2P1 either alone or in conjunction with Art 14: see para 64 of the judgment.

[233]   [2011] ECHR 5335/05, para 60.

[234]   [2011] ECHR 5335/05, para 61.

[235]   [2011] ECHR 5335/05, paras 71 and 72.

[236]   The issue arose in *A v The Headteacher and Governors of the Lord Grey School* [2003] EWHC 1533, [2003] ELR 517 (Stanley Burnton J), but he held that the defendants were not in breach of Art 2 of the First Protocol. When this case got to the House of Lords the majority held that there had been no breach of Art 2 of the First Protocol. Baroness Hale, who dissented on this issue, held that a declaration was all that was required to vindicate the claimant's rights and damages were not necessary for just satisfaction: see para 83.

and an award of damages is appropriate under the HRA 1998, but early indications are that awards of damages will be exceptional and moderate in size.

7.145 The first question is in what circumstances will the courts award damages under the HRA 1998 at all. The leading case is the unanimous decision of the House of Lords in *R (Greenfield) v Secretary of State for the Home Department.*[237] In that case, the appellant's rights under Article 6 of the ECHR had been violated. A drugs charge under the Prison Rules had been determined by a deputy controller of the prison, who was not an independent tribunal, and the appellant was wrongly denied legal representation of his own choosing which was available to him. The appellant claimed damages under the HRA 1998 in addition to declarations.

7.146 Lord Bingham said that in deciding whether to award damages the court was not strictly bound by the principles applied by the European Court in awarding compensation under Article 41 of the Convention but it must take those principles into account. Lord Bingham's analysis focused on the approach that the Strasbourg court had taken in Article 6 cases and noted that there is a risk of error if Strasbourg decisions given in relation to one Article of the Convention are read across as applicable to another. Notwithstanding that caveat, it is submitted that the principles enunciated in *Greenfield* are broadly applicable to any claim for damages brought under the HRA 1998.

7.147 Lord Bingham expressly approved the following principles set down by the of the Court of Appeal in *Anufrijeva v Southwark London BC*[238] (a case concerning Articles 5 and 8 of the ECHR):

'[52]... The remedy of damages generally plays a less prominent role in actions based on breaches of articles of the [convention] than in actions based on breaches of private law obligations where, more often than no, the only remedy claimed is damages.

[53] Where an infringement of an individual's human rights has occurred, the concern will usually be to bring the infringement to an end and any question of compensation will be of secondary, if any, importance'

7.148 Lord Bingham went on to consider the Strasbourg court's jurisprudence on Article 6 of the ECHR. At paragraph 11, after citing a passage from paragraph 40 of the Strasbourg court's judgment in *Kingsley v UK*[239] he said:

'As appears from the passage just cited, the European Court has ordinarily been willing to depart from its practice of finding a violation of art 6 to be, in itself, just satisfaction under art 41 only where the court finds a causal connection between the violation found and the loss for which an applicant claims to be compensated. Such claim may be for specific heads of loss, such as loss of earnings or profits,

---

[237] [2005] UKHL 14.
[238] [2003] EWCA Civ 1406.
[239] [2002] ECHR 35605/97.

said to be attributable to the violation. The court has described this as pecuniary loss, which appears to represent what English lawyers call special damage. This head does not call for consideration here. It is enough to say that the court has looked for a causal connection, and on the whole been slow to award such compensation.'

7.149 Lord Bingham then analysed a second head of general damages awarded by the Strasbourg court in cases where but for the violation of Article 6 found by the court the outcome of the proceedings would probably have been more favourable to the applicant or that the applicant was deprived of an opportunity to achieve a different result which was not in all the circumstances of the case a valueless opportunity. Lord Bingham considered that in the absence of a clear causal connection, the court's standard response had been to treat the finding of violation without more as just satisfaction but had used varied language to reflect its assessment of the differing levels of probability held to attach to the causal connection that warranted an award of damages in particular cases in 'a field which pre-eminently calls for case by case judgment'.[240]

7.150 A third head of general damages had been awarded in Article 6 cases for anxiety and frustration (however expressed) although the court had been sparing in making such awards.[241]

7.151 On the facts of *Greenfield* the award of damages was not necessary to award just satisfaction and Lord Bingham opined the pursuit of damages should rarely, if ever, be an end in itself in an Article 6 case.[242]

7.152 In *Marcic v Thames Water Utilities*[243] the Court of Appeal was concerned with a breach of Article 8 of the ECHR arising out of the failure of the defendant to carry out the necessary works to prevent the plaintiff's land being adversely affected by sewage discharged from its sewers. The Court of Appeal held that the defendant was liable in nuisance and under Article 8, but that the availability of damages for nuisance at common law was sufficient to afford the plaintiff just satisfaction and no further award of damages under the HRA 1998 was necessary.[244]

7.153 There are a number of cases in which the domestic courts have considered that an award of damages is necessary to afford a claimant just satisfaction. The cases cited below were decided before *Greenfield* but some aspects of the guidance given as to when the courts will award damages remain relevant.[245]

---

[240] [2005] UKHL 14, para 15.
[241] [2005] UKHL 14, para 16.
[242] [2005] UKHL 14, para 30.
[243] [2002] EWCA Civ 64, [2002] 2 WLR 932.
[244] [2002] EWCA Civ 64, [2002] 2 WLR 932 at para 104.
[245] Care should be taken when looking at these earlier authorities not to regard as correct all the statements of principle therein contained as some of those statements have become outdated as a result of the decision in *Greenfield*.

7.154 In *R (on the application of Bernard) v London Borough of Enfield*,[246] Sullivan J was concerned with a failure by an LA to discharge its duty under section 21 of the National Assistance Act 1948 to make arrangements for the provision of suitably adapted accommodation for the second claimant. She was severely disabled and incontinent and was forced to live with her husband (her carer and the first claimant) for 20 months, which was seriously unsuitable and demeaning. It was held that there had been a failure to respect the claimants' rights under Article 8 of the ECHR and the court awarded £2,000 to the husband and £8,000 to the wife. Sullivan J set out the following principles as applicable in that case:

(a) it was necessary to make an award of damages because this was a serious breach of the claimants' rights. They had had to live in deplorable conditions wholly inimical to any normal family life and to the physical and psychological integrity of the wife;[247]

(b) although, as a result of the relief granted by the court, the defendant had belatedly discharged its duties to the claimants in full measure and might have discharged those duties with the offer of less satisfactory accommodation, that affected only the quantum of any award and did not justify the refusal to award the claimants any financial compensation for the 20 months when their Article 8 rights had not been respected;[248]

(c) while in many cases a finding of violation coupled with a mandatory order might constitute just satisfaction, that was not so in this case.[249] The defendant had failed to take reasonable steps to remedy a wrong drawn to its attention, had not acknowledged it was in error, or provided explanation or apology for the failing. It had even threatened eviction. There was nothing to indicate that the defendant's procedures had improved so that similar errors might not occur again.

7.155 In *R (on the application of KB and others) v Mental Health Review Tribunal and Secretary of State for Health*,[250] the court considered what awards of damages were appropriate for patients detained under the Mental Health Act 1983, who had made applications for the review of their detentions to Mental Health Review Tribunals and who had suffered delays in the hearing of those reviews.

---

[246] [2002] EWHC 2282 (Admin), (2002) 5 CCL Rep 577 at para 148. See *Anufrijeva and others v Southwark and others* [2003] EWCA Civ 1406, [2003] All ER (D) 288 (Oct) at paras 77 and 78.

[247] [2002] EWHC 2282 (Admin), (2002) 5 CCL Rep 577, at para 36.

[248] [2002] EWHC 2282 (Admin), (2002) 5 CCL Rep 577, at para 38.

[249] [2002] EWHC 2282 (Admin), (2002) 5 CCL Rep 577, at paras 39–42 and 61.

[250] [2003] EWHC 193 (Admin), [2003] 2 All ER 209, Stanley Burnton J. See *Anufrijeva and others v Southwark and others* [2003] EWCA Civ 1406, [2003] All ER (D) 288 (Oct) at paras 63–65, 72 and 73.

7.156 Further guidance on the applicable principles was set out by Silber J in *R (on the application of N) v Secretary of State for the Home Department.*[251] Again, the context was far removed from the education field. The case concerned an asylum-seeker whose claim had not been processed properly. His evidence had been sent to the wrong address, resulting in his claim for asylum being dismissed on non-compliance grounds, removal directions were set for him to return to Libya despite the Home Office knowing that failed asylum-seekers who were returned to Libya were at risk of serious ill-treatment and his appeal was delayed. Following judicial review proceedings his claim was considered substantively and he was granted refugee status. In the meantime he had suffered loss of benefits and a deterioration in his mental health. He claimed a breach of Articles 3 and 8 of the ECHR. Silber J dismissed the claim under Article 3 but upheld the claim under Article 8. In relation to the claim for damages he held:

(a) the defendant was not liable in damages under the HRA 1998 simply because the ECHR had been breached and irrespective of any question of fault or foreseeability;[252]

(b) he could be liable where:[253]

   (i) he was, or ought to have been, aware that the claimant was suffering or was at risk of the harm in question necessary to engage Articles 3 and 8. The test of 'real and immediate risk' applied in *Osman v United Kingdom*[254] was too high when the defendant was in part responsible for the acts or omissions;[255]
   (ii) he did not take the steps reasonably open to him to protect the claimant from that;
   (iii) those measures could have a real prospect of altering or mitigating the harm: *E v United Kingdom.*[256]

7.157 On the facts, Silber J held that the Secretary of State was liable for breach of the Convention and under the Human Rights Act 1998. He granted a declaration to that effect. He further held that damages were not to be awarded as a matter of right and suggested[257] a five-fold test:

(1) whether the court had power and jurisdiction to award damages;

(2) whether damages ought to be awarded bearing in mind the need to take into account the principles applied by the European Court in relation to the award of compensation under Article 41 of the ECHR;

---

[251] [2003] EWHC 207, (2003) *The Times*, 7 March. Reversed in *Anufrijeva*, ibid.
[252] [2003] EWHC 207 at para 130.
[253] [2003] EWHC 207, at paras 137 and 148.
[254] (2000) 29 EHRR 245.
[255] [2003] EWHC 207 at para 139.
[256] (2003) 36 EHRR 31.
[257] [2003] EWHC 207 at para 179.

(3)   whether damages ought to be awarded in the light of another remedy granted to the claimant;

(4)   whether an award was necessary after taking into account the consequences of awarding damages;

(5)   whether, taking into account all other factors, it was just and appropriate to award damages. This factor could include a discount for failure to mitigate loss.[258] He held on the facts this five-fold test was satisfied and stated that damages would be assessed at a further hearing.

7.158   These issues were considered by the Court of Appeal in *Anufrijeva and others v Southwark and others*.[259] In addition to *Anufrijeva*, the Court of Appeal had before it appeals from the decision of Silber J in *N v Secretary of State for the Home Department* and from Richards J in *M v Secretary of State for the Home Department*. Although they did not have appeals before them from the decisions of Stanley Burnton J in *R (KB and others) v Mental Health Review Tribunal*[260] or from Sullivan J in *Bernard*, both decisions were expressly approved.[261] The Court of Appeal dismissed the appeals in *Anufrijeva* and *M* but allowed the appeal from the decision of Silber J in *N*.

7.159   The Court of Appeal first[262] contrasted an award of damages under the HRA 1998 with an award of private law damages in a claim in contract or tort and made the following observations:

(a)   an award of damages under the HRA 1998 was confined to the class of unlawful acts of public authorities identified by section 6(1);

(b)   the court had a discretion as to whether to make an award; it must be 'just and appropriate' to do so;

(c)   the award under the HRA 1998 had to be necessary to achieve 'just satisfaction'. That contrasted with the invariable entitlement under private law for a claimant to be restored to the position he would have been in if he had not suffered the injury of which complaint was made. The concept of 'necessary to afford just satisfaction' provided a link to the Strasbourg approach under Article 41 of the ECHR;

---

[258]   [2003] EWHC 207, at para 202.
[259]   [2003] EWCA Civ 1406.
[260]   [2003] EWHC 193 (Admin).
[261]   *R (KB) v Mental Health Review Tribunal* was 'commended' at para 63 and discussed further at paras 64, 65, 72 and 73. *Bernard* was referred to at paras 65 and 77 and approved at para 78, although the award there was said to be at the top end of permissible awards. This suggests that similar awards in the future will be rare.
[262]   [2003] EWCA Civ 1406 at para 55.

(d)   the court was required to take into account in determining whether damages were payable and the amount of damages the different principles applied by the ECtHR in awarding compensation;

(e)   exemplary damages were not awarded.

7.160   The Court of Appeal stressed[263] that in considering whether to award damages, and if so, how much, a balance had to be struck between the interests of the victim and the interests of the public as a whole. An analogy with the approach in Canada and South Africa, which had similar human rights instruments, was appropriate and the appropriate remedy had to be judged on the individual facts of the case, both from the standpoint of the victim and the wider public which had an interest in the continued funding of public service. The Court of Appeal went on to say that damages were not an automatic entitlement but a remedy of last resort.

7.161   The court observed[264] that it was obliged by section 8(4) of the HRA 1998 to take account of the principles applied by the ECtHR and that the award of damages under the HRA 1998 should be no less liberal. The Court of Appeal then analysed[265] the Strasbourg principles. After referring to the difficulty in identifying clear and coherent principles from that jurisprudence, they identified the following basic principles:

(a)   the fundamental principle was *resitutio in integrum*;[266]

(b)   where significant pecuniary loss had been suffered, this was usually to be assessed and awarded;[267]

(c)   when breach of a Convention right caused consequences which were not capable of being computed in terms of financial loss, the appropriate principles turned on the nature of the convention right infringed. The Court distinguished[268] between breach of Article 5 and breach of Article 8. In relation to breach of Article 5, the court approved the statement of principle of Stanley Burnton J[269] that the feelings of frustration and distress caused by delay should be significant. In relation to claims for maladministration involving a breach of Article 8, the court should adopt a broad-brush approach. The court should examine whether the other remedies granted to the successful claimant were sufficient to vindicate the right that had been infringed, taking into account the claimant's own responsibility for what had occurred. That task should be done without a close examination of the authorities or an extensive and

---

263   [2003] EWCA Civ 1406, at para 56.
264   [2003] EWCA Civ 1406, at para 57.
265   [2003] EWCA Civ 1406, at paras 57–70.
266   [2003] EWCA Civ 1406, at para 59.
267   [2003] EWCA Civ 1406 at para 59.
268   [2003] EWCA Civ 1406, at para 65.
269   [2003] EWCA Civ 1406, at para 73.

prolonged examination of the facts and, in many cases, would be capable of being ascertained by an examination of the correspondence and the witness statements.

(d) in determining whether damages should be awarded, the approach was an 'equitable' one.[270] Reference should be made to the character and conduct of the parties and the scale and manner of the violation.[271]

7.162 The statement of principles to be applied in deciding when to award damages leaves some questions unanswered. It does not give any guidance on when the other remedies granted to a successful claimant are to be regarded as sufficient to vindicate the right that has been infringed. Moreover, the suggestion that a broad-brush approach should be adopted without close examination of the authorities will inhibit development of coherent principles at appellate court level. That development will be further inhibited by what the Court of Appeal stated on quantum and the procedure that should be adopted to claim damages for breach of the HRA 1998. In *Greenfield*, Lord Bingham did not comment on the approach set out in *Anufrijeva* except to the limited extent set out above.

The domestic courts: approach to quantum

7.163 In *Greenfield*, Lord Bingham rejected the appellant's submission that courts in England and Wales should apply a domestic scale of damages when exercising their power to award damages under section 8 of the HRA 1998. The appellant had suggested that awards under section 8 should not be on the low side as compared with tortious awards; that English courts should be free to depart from the scale of damages awarded by the European court and that English awards by appropriate courts or bodies should provide the appropriate comparator; and that in calculating awards for anxiety and frustration, the scales of damages awarded by English courts and tribunals in discrimination cases provided an appropriate comparison.[272]

7.164 Lord Bingham concluded that this approach should not be followed. He held that while judges in England were not inflexibly bound by the level of award made by the Strasbourg court, they should not aim to be significantly more or less generous than the court might be expected to be in a case where it would be willing to make an award at all.[273]

7.165 Lord Bingham advanced three main reasons for rejecting the appellant's approach:

---

[270] [2003] EWCA Civ 1406, at para 66.
[271] [2003] EWCA Civ 1406, at paras 66 and 67.
[272] [2005] UKHL 14, para 18. The appellant had relied on the cases of *R (on the application of Bernard) v London Borough of Enfield* [2002] EWHC 2282 (Admin) and *R (on the application of KB and others) v Mental Health Review Tribunal* and *Secretary of State for Health* [2003] EWHC 193 (Admin).
[273] [2005] UKHL 14, para 19.

'First, the 1998 Act is not a tort statute. Its objects are different and broader. Even in a case where a finding of violation is not judged to afford the applicant just satisfaction, such a finding will be an important part of his remedy and an important vindication of the right he has asserted. Damages need not ordinarily be awarded to encourage high standards of compliance by member states, since they are already bound in international law to perform their duties under the Convention in good faith, although it may be different if there is felt to be a need to encourage compliance by individual officials or classes of official. Secondly, the purpose of incorporating the Convention in domestic law through the 1998 Act was not to give victims better remedies at home than they could recover in Strasbourg but to give them the same remedies without the delay and expense of resort to Strasbourg. This intention was clearly expressed in the White Paper 'Rights Brought Home: The Human Rights Bill' (Cm 3782, 1 October 1997), para 2.6:

"The Bill provides that, in considering an award of damages on Convention grounds, the courts are to take into account the principles applied by the European Court of Human Rights in awarding compensation, so that people will be able to receive compensation from a domestic court equivalent to what they would have received in Strasbourg."

Thirdly, s 8(4) requires a domestic court to take into account the principles applied by the European Court under art 41 not only in determining whether to award damages but also in determining the amount of an award. There could be no clearer indication that courts in this country should look to Strasbourg and not to domestic precedents. The Appellant contended that the levels of Strasbourg awards are not "principles" applied by the Court, but this is a legalistic distinction which is contradicted by the White Paper and the language of s 8 and has no place in a decision on the quantum of an award, to which principle has little application. The Court routinely describes its awards as equitable, which I take to mean that they are not precisely calculated but are judged by the Court to be fair in the individual case. Judges in England and Wales must also make a similar judgment in the case before them.'

7.166 In light of that decision, the approach to quantum adopted by Sullivan J in *R (on the application of Bernard) v Enfield London Borough Council*, Stanley Burnton LJ in *R (on the application of KB) v Mental Health Review Tribunal* [2003] 2 All ER 209 and of Lord Woolf CJ in *Anufrijeva v Southwark London Borough Council* (2003) 15 BHRC 526 can no longer be relied upon insofar as those cases endorsed an assessment of damages by reference to the damages that might be awarded for a comparable claim in tort.

7.167 However, it is noteworthy that even applying a tortious approach to the assessment of damages, the awards made by the court were modest. In *KB*, the court made awards ranging from nothing (where it considered the delay was short and the claimant would not have been released) to £4,000 (where it considered the claimant would have been released three months earlier than he was). While this case is far removed from the education context, it shows that the level of awards is not high. It is difficult to see that the victim of a school expulsion is likely to get higher awards than a mental health patient deprived of his liberty.

7.168 In *R (Mambakasa) v Secretary of State for the Home Department*,[274] Richards J held that there had been no breach of Article 8 in relation to the processing of that claimant's and his family's claims for refugee status and entry clearance and therefore the issue of damages did not arise. He did, however, give it some consideration and, in general, adopted the approach of Sullivan J in *Bernard*.[275] He further indicated that had he found a breach of Article 8, he would have regarded it as appropriate to make an award but, on the facts of that case, it would have been in the region of £1,000 to £2,000 and that £12,000 would have been much too high.

7.169 As to the procedure that should be adopted in relation to claims for damages for breach of the HRA 1998, in *Anufrijeva* the Court of Appeal held:[276]

(a) the courts should look critically at any attempt to recover damages under the HRA 1998 for maladministration by any procedure other than judicial review;

(b) although a claim for damages alone could not be brought by way of an application for judicial review, such claims should still be brought in the Administrative Court by an ordinary claim;

(c) before giving permission for judicial review. the Administrative Court should require the claimant to explain why it would not be more appropriate to use any available internal complaint procedure or proceed by making a claim to the PCA or LGO;

(d) if there was a legitimate claim for other relief, permission should, if appropriate, be limited to that relief and consideration given to deferring permission for the damages claim adjourning or staying that claim until use had been made of ADR or remitting the claim to a district judge or master if it cannot be dismissed summarily on the grounds that in any event an award of damages was not required to achieve just satisfaction;

(e) claims should be dealt with summarily by reading the relevant evidence. The citing of more than three authorities should be justified and the hearing should be limited to half a day, except in exceptional circumstances.

7.170 These principles are clearly designed to limit damages claims for breach of the HRA 1998 in the courts. That is clearly the case with applications for judicial review where the claimant must show why some other mechanism was not first resorted to in order to deal with the damages claim. While there is no similar restriction in terms to an ordinary claim in the Administrative Court for damages, no doubt the courts will seek to discourage claims for damages which

---

[274] [2003] EWHC 319 (Admin). Affirmed in *Anufrijeva*, [2003] EWCA Civ 1406.
[275] [2003] EWHC 319 (Admin), at para 130.
[276] [2003] EWCA Civ 1406, at para 81.

do not require permission to be brought by exercising their powers as to disallow costs where the equivalent to the damages claimed could have been obtained (for example, from the Ombudsman) without recourse to the courts.

The domestic courts: approach to determining a violation of A2P1

7.171   The principles set out above as to when damages will be awarded and how damages will be quantified are, it is submitted, of general application where a claim is made for damages under the HRA 1998. But the domestic courts have also had occasion to consider the approach to be taken in determining whether or not there has been a violation of A2P1, the right under the Convention system that is obviously most pertinent to education. The matter has received attention from the House of Lords in in *Ali v Headteacher and Governors of Lord Grey School*,[277] *R (Begum) v Denbigh High School*[278] and most recently *A v Essex County Council*.[279]

7.172   *Ali's* case concerned an unlawful exclusion from school. The claimant was alleged to have been involved in arson at the school. The school determined that the claimant should not attend while the matter was investigated by the police but did not follow the statutory procedures for exclusion. The school provided work for the claimant to undertake at home and eventually referred him to the LA for the LA to provide alternative education. On 6 June, the maximum aggregate time for temporary exclusion (45 days) was exceeded but the school did not take steps permanently to exclude the claimant. The police investigation was discontinued for want of evidence and the school indicated that the claimant could return when it received notice of discontinuation. Upon receipt of notice of discontinuation, the school wrote to the claimant's parents inviting them to a meeting at the end of the summer term on 13 July to discuss the claimant's return. At around this time, the LA offered the claimant a place at the PRU although the claimant did not take that place up. The claimant's parents did not attend the meeting on 13 July and the headteacher wrote to inform them that, as a result, the claimant would be removed from the school roll. When term began in early September, the claimant's parents made no attempt to get in touch with the school and in mid-September the claimant was removed from the school roll. It appears that the claimant and his parents were unaware that he had been removed from the roll at that stage. In mid-October, the claimant's parents contacted the LA in relation to finding the claimant a place at school; in November, the claimant's father asked the school to reinstate the claimant but by that stage there was not a place available and so the request was refused.

7.173   At first instance, Stanley Burnton J concluded that the claimant's exclusion had been unlawful under domestic law from the period 8 March–13 July because it did not comply with the mandatory requirements of domestic law, but it was sensible and reasonable and involved no violation of A2P1. The

---

[277]   [2006] UKHL 14.
[278]   [2006] UKHL 15.
[279]   [2010] UKSC 33.

school was not responsible for the lack of suitable education between 13 July and 20 July because the family had declined the LA's offer of tuition during that period. As for the subsequent autumn term, the cause of the applicant not receiving a suitable education was more difficult to ascertain but it was the LA's duty to provide suitable education to the claimant; there were educational facilities available to fulfil that duty; and he could have enforced that duty. The decisions to exclude the claimant and remove him from the school roll were unlawful but they did not give rise to a breach of A2P1.

7.174 The Court of Appeal agreed that for the period until 7 June there was no breach of A2P1 because the claimant had been provided with suitable alternative education. However, from 7 June to 13 July, the claimant had been denied his right to education notwithstanding the school's offer to send work home. The fact that the school had sent work home would be relevant only to the question of damages. From 14 July onwards, the Court of Appeal considered that the unlawful exclusion of the claimant amounted to a denial of the claimant's education that had been complete and prolonged. The fact that the LA had a duty to make alternative education available, and that the claimant could have enforced that duty, did not relieve the school of the consequences of its failure to discharge its primary duty to educate the claimant by unlawfully excluding him.

7.175 The House of Lords, by a majority, upheld the school's appeal against the Court of Appeal's decision and dismissed the claim for damages for violation of A2P1.

7.176 Counsel for both parties agreed that the exclusion had in fact been unlawful under domestic law from 8 March 2001 onwards: the majority of the House of Lords reluctantly agreed.[280] However, the majority considered that that did not suffice to establish a violation of A2P1.

7.177 Lord Bingham, with whom Lords Nicholls, Scott and Hoffmann agreed, considered that the guarantee of an education under A2P1 was a deliberately weak one. The underlying premise of A2P1 was that all existing member states of the Council of Europe had, and all future member states would have, an established system of state education. A2P1 aimed to secure fair and non-discriminatory access to that system for those within the state's jurisdiction. But there was no right to education of a particular kind or quality other than that prevailing in the state. There was no Convention guarantee of compliance with domestic law nor of education at or by a particular institution. The test was a highly pragmatic one to be applied to the specific facts of the case: 'have the authorities of the state acted so as to deny to a pupil effective access to such educational facilities as the state provides for such pupils?'.[281] On the facts, the court's attention had to focus on the school, as the only public authority against which a claim had been brought, and the school

---

[280] See Lord Bingham at paras 21–22.
[281] Lord Bingham at para 24.

had not acted in violation of A2P1. The school had invited the claimant's parents to collect work for him, which they did not do; it had referred the claimant to the LA's access panel which referred him to the PRU but he declined to take up a place; the school arranged a meeting with the claimant's parents to arrange for his re-admission but they failed to attend and the removal from the school roll had not in fact had any causal effect or legal consequence.

7.178 Lord Hoffmann, with whom Lords Nicholls, Bingham and Scott agreed, delivered a separate concurring opinion. At paragraph 56 he said that A2P1 did not 'guarantee access to any particular educational institution the domestic system does provide: see *Simpson v United Kingdom*.[282] Nor was there a right to remain at any particular institution. Everyone was no doubt entitled to be educated to a minimum standard (*R (Holub) v Secretary of State for the Home Department*),[283] but the right under Article 2 extended no further. The fact that the claimant was required to attend a PRU rather than the school would not establish a breach of the Convention before the Strasbourg court: and so there could not have been an infringement of a Convention right giving rise to a claim under the HRA 1998. The correct approach in considering whether there was a claim for damages under the HRA 1998 was first to ask whether there had been a denial of a Convention right. In the case of A2P1 that required 'a systemic failure of the educational system which resulted in the respondent not having access to a minimum level of education … It is only if a denial of a Convention right is established that one examines domestic law in order to discover which public authority, if any, is liable under s 6'. The question whether there is any material difference of approach between Lord Bingham and Lord Hoffmann is considered below in the discussion of *A v Essex County Council*.

7.179 Baroness Hale dissented. Baroness Hale agreed that it was not the object of A2P1 to prescribe any particular syllabus or curriculum but, as Lord Bingham had said, to guarantee fair and non-discriminatory access to the educational system established in the particular member state.[284] But she considered that the claimant had been denied that. First, the school had unlawfully excluded him for no good reason. Secondly, insofar as the LA had a fall-back responsibility to provide alternative suitable education, a place at the PRU was not a substitute for ordinary access to the full national curriculum at an ordinary school.[285] Baroness Hale considered that there was no violation of A2P1 until 13 July, until which point the actions taken were consistent with a rational system of school management and discipline, but thereafter the school was in violation of A2P1. However, it was not necessary to award damages to afford just satisfaction to the claimant for the violation.

---

[282] (1989) 64 DR 188.
[283] [2001] 1 WLR 1369, [2001] ELR 401.
[284] [2006] UKHL 14, para 79.
[285] [2006] UKHL 14, paras 80–81.

7.180 The decision of the Strasbourg Court on Ali's application to that court is considered at paras **7.204–7.210** below.

7.181 *R (Begum (By her litigation friend, Rahman)) v Headteacher and Governors of Denbigh High School*[286] raised issues under Article 9 of the ECHR and A2P1. The claimant, a Muslim female, was a pupil at a mixed community school which was predominantly Muslim. The school permitted Muslim female pupils to wear the shalwar kameeze if they did not wish to wear the traditional school uniform. The school's policy on uniforms had been developed in consultation with the imams of the three local mosques, amongst others. The claimant wore the shalwar kameeze for two years without objection. In September 2002, the claimant and her brother went to the school indicating that she wished to wear the jilbab on the basis of her understanding of Islamic requirements of dress for mature women. The shalwar kameeze was said to reveal too much of her arms and the skirt was not long enough. The school refused to allow her to attend school otherwise than wearing the approved uniform. The claimant claimed that she had been excluded from the school and began judicial review proceedings. In December 2002, the school and Luton education authority took independent advice as to whether the school's dress code offended against Islamic requirements and were told that it did not. The school continued to encourage her to return but she did not do so. In or around October 2003, the school governors met to consider the matter and upheld the decision to require that the claimant adhere to the school's policy on uniform. The governing body wrote to the claimant indicating that she should return or seek a place at another school. The claimant applied to one other school at which she could wear the jilbab but it was full; she did not apply to two other schools at which the jilbab was permitted. In September 2004, she accepted a place at a different local school which permitted her to wear the jilbab. In the meantime, the school had continued to seek to persuade her to return.

7.182 At first instance, the administrative court held that the claimant had not been excluded; that if she had been excluded it was because of her refusal to adhere to the school's uniform policy and not her religious beliefs as such and therefore there was no breach of Article 9(1) of the ECHR; if there had been a limitation of Article 9(1) of the ECHR it was prescribed by law, pursued a legitimate aim and was proportionate; and there had been no breach of her right to education under A2P1.

7.183 The Court of Appeal held that the school had unlawfully excluded the claimant, unlawfully denied her the right to manifest her religious beliefs and unlawfully denied her access to suitable and appropriate education. The Court of Appeal considered that the fact that the school had not undertaken a human rights based proportionality assessment in reaching its decision not to allow the claimant to wear the jilbab itself sufficed to establish a breach of the HRA 1998. The school would have to re-take the decision in the proper fashion: it may be that on re-taking the decision the school would reach the same

---

[286] [2006] UKHL 15, [2006] ELR 273.

conclusion and that decision might be within the range of proportional responses open to it. The House of Lords allowed the school's appeal.

7.184 Lord Bingham noted that the Strasbourg court has not been 'at all ready to find an interference with the right to manifest religious belief in practice or observance where a person has voluntarily accepted an employment or role which does not accommodate that practice or observance and there are other means open to the person to practise or observe his or her religion without undue hardship or inconvenience.'[287] On the facts, the claimant had chosen to attend the school, which was not her catchment school, notwithstanding the school's uniform policy which was clearly stated. The claimant's elder sister had worn the uniform without objection as had the claimant for her first two years. While it was open to the claimant to modify her beliefs, she did so against a background of free and informed consent to attending the school. There was no evidence that it would have been unduly difficult for the claimant to attend one of the other local schools at which the jilbab was permitted. Therefore, Lord Bingham concluded that there had been no interference with Article 9.[288] However, he went on to consider the question of justification.

7.185 On the issue of justification, Lord Bingham first clarified that the Court of Appeal was wrong to conclude that because the school had not itself gone through a structured process of asking whether or not the application of its uniform policy would constitute an interference with a Convention right and then asking whether such interference would be proportionate, there had been a violation. The purpose of the HRA 1998 was not to enlarge the rights or remedies of those in the UK whose Convention rights had been violated but only to enable them to be asserted and enforced in the domestic courts. The focus at Strasbourg had never been on whether a challenged decision or action was the consequence of a defective decision-making process but whether, in fact, the applicant's Convention rights had been violated.[289] Asking whether, in fact, an individual's rights had been violated required the court itself to embark on an assessment whether or not the act or decision was proportionate: it could not be suggested that an action was disproportionate (on the basis that it had not been properly reasoned) but that it might on reconsideration be maintained.[290] What mattered was the practical outcome, not the process of decision-making that led to it.[291] On the facts, the school's approach was justified as proportionate. It had taken great pains to devise a uniform that accorded with Muslim beliefs but in an inclusive, unthreatening and uncompetitive way. The rules were acceptable to mainstream Muslim opinion and acceding to the request for the introduction of jilbab could have had adverse repercussions.[292]

---

[287] [2006] UKHL 15, para 23.
[288] [2006] UKHL 15, para 25.
[289] [2006] UKHL 15, para 29.
[290] [2006] UKHL 15, para 30.
[291] [2006] UKHL 15, para 31.
[292] The school's particular concern appeared to be the impact on community cohesion and the risk

7.186 Lord Hoffmann gave a separate concurring opinion. There had been no interference with Article 9(1): there was nothing to stop the claimant from going to school where religion did not require a jilbab or where she was allowed to wear one.[293] There was nothing to suggest it would have been difficult to do so but even if it had put the claimant to some inconvenience, there was an expectation of accommodation, compromise and if necessary sacrifice in the manifestation of religious beliefs.[294] Like Lord Bingham, Lord Hoffmann emphasised that Article 9 was concerned with the substance of the action or decision taken by a public authority and not the process by which the action or decision was reached.[295]

7.187 Lord Scott agreed with Lords Bingham and Hoffmann. Lord Nicholls agreed with Lord Bingham and Lord Hoffmann on the issue of justification but was unsure about the question whether there had been an interference with Article 9(1) in the first place. He indicated that he would prefer that in a case such as *Begum* the school should be called upon to explain and justify its decision.[296] It seems therefore, that although he clearly preferred for the school to justify its stance, he did not hold as a matter of law that they had interfered with Ms Begum's Article 9 rights. Baroness Hale considered there had been an interference with the claimant's Article 9 rights but this is difficult to reconcile with the Strasbourg jurisprudence to which the majority referred.[297]

7.188 As to A2P1, Lord Bingham considered the two-year interruption in the claimant's education to be regrettable but held that was the result of the claimant's unwillingness to comply with a rule to which the school was entitled to adhere and of her failure to secure prompt admission to a school where her religious convictions could be accommodated.[298] Lord Hoffmann cited *Ali*'s case said that the right was 'infringed only if the claimant is unable to obtain education from the system as a whole'.[299]

7.189 A2P1 was given further consideration by the Supreme Court in *A v Essex County Council*.[300]

7.190 A was autistic, had a severe learning disability and a severe communication disorder. From the age of six he attended a community special day school for children with severe learning difficulties. As he approached the age of 12 his behaviour deteriorated. In January 2002, at a meeting attended by the school and the LA, his parents were informed that the school could not cope with him and asked that they not bring him into school until a five day

---

that permitting a more restrictive form of dress could lead to an element of religious competition and coercion into adopting that more restrictive dress.
[293] Paragraph 50.
[294] [2006] UKHL 15, para 54.
[295] [2006] UKHL 15, para 68.
[296] Paragraph 41.
[297] [2006] UKHL 15, paras 93–94.
[298] [2006] UKHL 15, para 36.
[299] [2006] UKHL 15, para 69.
[300] [2010] UKSC 33.

medical assessment in a residential setting had been carried out. It was hoped that the assessment would take place in April or May but in the event it did not take place until September. That assessment recommended placement in a residential school. Between October and December, the LA searched for a place for A but without success. In February 2003, the LA found a place although it did not become available until July. A then took up his place at the school and his behaviour and health improved.

7.191   During the period from January 2002–July 2003, A was not in school. During that interim period, A was provided with some work and speech and language therapy. However, it appears to have been accepted by the court that the interim provision was pretty minimal and unlikely to have satisfied Essex's duties under domestic law.

7.192   A issued proceedings against the LA in relation to the period between January 2002 and July 2003 claiming damages under the Human Rights Act 1998 for breach of A's right to education under A2P1 of the ECHR. The High Court granted the LA's application to dismiss A's claim on the basis that it had no real prospect of success and refused A's application to extend time to bring a claim under the HRA 1998. The Court of Appeal dismissed A's appeal.

7.193   The Supreme Court dismissed A's appeal by a 4 to 1 majority. Three of the Justices, Lord Philips, Lord Kerr and Baroness Hale considered that A would have had an arguable claim against Essex under A2P1 but only Baroness Hale would have allowed an extension of time to bring the claim. Lords Clarke and Brown did not consider there to be an arguable breach of A2P1 at all. Each justice gave a separate judgment and no judgment was fully endorsed by that of another Justice. As the judgments are not, with respect, models of clarity it is difficult to extract a clear ratio or clear guidance for future cases. Indeed, there appeared to be some difference of opinion amongst their Lordships as to how the appellant's case had been put.[301]

7.194   Their lordships appeared to agree that the starting point for analysis was the judgment of Lord Bingham in *Ali*. However, each took a different approach in developing that analysis to apply to the very different legal and factual context that arose in *A*.

7.195   It is clear that the majority of their lordships rejected the contention that A2P1 imposes any absolute positive obligation to provide effective education for children who have special educational needs.[302] Nor would the mere fact that the education provided to A was not in accordance with domestic law be sufficient to establish a breach of A2P1.[303]

---

[301]   Compare e g Lord Phillips at para 89 and Lady Hale at para 95.

[302]   Lord Philips rejected this submission in terms at para 75; see also Lord Clarke at paras 15 and 19 and Lord Brown at para 128.

[303]   [2010] UKSC 33, paras 55, 84–87, 124. See also Baroness Hale at para 108.

7.196 However, the majority of their lordships considered that it could be arguable (depending on facts that were not before them) that A's rights under A2P1 had been violated during the 18 month interim period before a suitable residential placement was provided to him.

7.197 Lord Kerr considered that a failure to supply education during the reasonable period of time required to investigate what was required to meet an individual child's needs would not give rise to a violation of A2P1.[304] Lord Kerr rejected A's contention that he was entitled under A2P1 to the particular form of education specified in the statement of special educational needs. However, Lord Kerr appears to have taken Lord Hoffmann's speech in *Ali* as authority for the proposition that A was entitled to the basic minimum of education available under the domestic system and 'what that basic minimum involves must be assessed by reference (at least in part) to A's special needs'.[305] Lord Kerr considered that A was 'entitled to a minimum education geared to his particular condition'.[306] That was subject to the need for a reasonable period to investigate A's needs. A calculated refusal to provide education or a failure to take steps to provide education when the relevant authority is aware that a pupil is not receiving it could constitute a breach of A2P1 but so too could a completely ineffectual attempt to provide education[307] and so in A's case the questions arose whether the entire period of A's absence from school could have been accounted for on the basis that that was the period reasonably required to investigate A's needs and identify a school at which they could be met and whether, in the meantime, interim steps could have been taken to mitigate the harm A suffered during his absence from education.[308]

7.198 Lady Hale agreed that there was a triable issue in relation to A2P1. Lady Hale did not consider it necessary to decide whether A2P1 guaranteed a child an absolute minimum standard of education or not but considered that the Strasbourg authorities left the question open.[309] The question was whether there was a triable case that the appellant was unjustifiably denied access to the education which our system provided for children like him ie children with special educational needs. The mere fact the appellant was not provided with the education he was entitled to under domestic law was not sufficient to establish a breach but the questions arose whether enough had been done to prevent the appellant's placement from breaking down; whether it should have taken so long to assess his needs and find an appropriate placement; and whether he should have been left without an alternative while the assessment was taking place.[310]

---

[304] [2010] UKSC 33, para 153.
[305] [2010] UKSC 33, para 157.
[306] [2010] UKSC 33, para 158.
[307] [2010] UKSC 33, para 161.
[308] [2010] UKSC 33, paras 162–164.
[309] [2010] UKSC 33, paras 96–99.
[310] [2010] UKSC 33, para 108.

7.199   Lord Phillips held there was no obligation under A2P1 for states to provide a minimum level of education. What was required was access without discrimination to the education system that existed in the state.[311] Accordingly there was no positive obligation to provide effective education for children who had special educational needs.[312] A failure to provide what was required by domestic law did not of itself amount to a breach of A2P1.[313]

7.200   Lords Clarke and Brown did not consider there to be an arguable breach of Article 2. However, it is notable that at paragraph 45 of his judgment, Lord Clarke said that if the question 'was A deprived of an effective education during the relevant period' was answered only by reference to what he was provided with between January 2002 and July 2003 then 'it could be answered in the affirmative'. It was because A ultimately got the provision that he needed that there had been no violation of A2P1. That raises the question what Lord Clarke's view would have been had a claim been brought under A2P1 *before* an appropriate placement had been identified and secured.

7.201   In the course of their judgments, each of the Justices considered the question whether there was any possible tension between the approach laid out by Lord Bingham in *Ali* and that laid out by Lord Hoffmann. Lords Clarke,[314] Brown,[315] Kerr[316] did not consider there to be a tension when the judgments of Lord Bingham and Lord Hoffmann were considered as a whole. Lord Philips suggested that Lord Hoffmann's observation as to a need for a 'systemic failure' was not an observation of general application but made in the context of a case where a child was excluded not from the education system as a whole but from a particular institution within it.[317] Lord Clarke thought that reference had to be 'viewed in the context of the education system provided' but likewise did not appear to consider there to be a need for a failure that is systemic in the sense of applying across the whole system.[318] Lord Kerr considered that there could be a denial of education even without systemic default in the usual sense.[319]

7.202   Lady Hale considered that there was a possible tension between Lord Bingham's reference to 'such educational facilities as the state provides for such pupils' and Lord Hoffmann's reference to 'the basic minimum of education available under the domestic system' and to 'a systemic failure of the educational system which resulted in the respondent not having access to a minimum level of education' in *Ali*. In the context of A's case there was a possible tension between what the state provided for 'such pupils' ie pupils with special educational needs and 'the basic minimum'. The effect of excluding

---

[311]   [2010] UKSC 33, para 75.
[312]   [2010] UKSC 33, para 81.
[313]   [2010] UKSC 33, para 85.
[314]   At paras 12–14.
[315]   [2010] UKSC 33, para 129.
[316]   [2010] UKSC 33, para 157.
[317]   [2010] UKSC 33, para 91.
[318]   [2010] UKSC 33, para 16.
[319]   [2010] UKSC 33, para 161.

pupils with special educational needs from education could be much more serious than for other children and could have catastrophic long term effects.[320]

7.203 Taking those comments together, it seems clear that the majority of the Justices did not consider there to be any difference in substance between the formulations of Lord Bingham and Lord Hoffmann in *Ali*; but Lord Hoffmann's reference to 'systemic failure' is not to be taken as a requirement for establishing a denial of the right under A2P1.

Subsequent Strasbourg authority

7.204 The *Ali* case discussed above was taken to Strasbourg.[321] The Strasbourg Court dismissed the claim. Although the court did not analyse the arguments raised by the parties in any detail, the court's approach confirmed the importance of characterising the educational system to which it was said the claimant has been denied access.

7.205 At paragraphs 51–54 of the judgment, the court re-affirmed its jurisprudence on A2P1 as set out in the *Belgian Linguistics Case*. The core of the right was the right of access to educational institutions existing at a given time. That right might be subject to limitations. The regulation of educational institutions might vary in time and place 'according to the needs and resources of the community and the distinctive features of different levels of education'. As such, states enjoyed a margin of appreciation. In order to ensure that any restrictions did not impair the very essence of the right and impair its effectiveness, the court had to satisfy itself that they were foreseeable for those affected and pursued a legitimate aim, though there was no prescribed list of such aims. There had to be proportionality between the aim pursued and the means employed.

7.206 The court expressly reaffirmed that A2P1 did not necessarily entail a right of access to education at a particular educational institution nor did it exclude recourse to disciplinary measures such as suspension or expulsion.

7.207 In analysing whether there had been a violation of A2P1 on the particular facts of *Ali*, the court began by characterising what was the relevant system of education in place in the UK. It was access to that system that had to be guaranteed. At paragraph 55, the court said 'In the United Kingdom, all maintained schools have a duty to provide education in accordance with the national curriculum to every child of compulsory school age on their register. Article 2 of the First Protocol therefore requires that the United Kingdom guarantee to every child of compulsory school age within its jurisdiction, like the applicant in the present case, access to an educational institution or facility which will provide an education in accordance with the national curriculum'.

---

[320] [2010] UKSC 33, para 101.
[321] [2011] ECHR 40385/06, [2011] All ER (D) 96.

7.208 In determining whether an exclusion resulted in a denial of the right to education, the court had to consider whether a fair balance was struck between the exclusion and the justification given for that measure. The court would therefore have regard to such factors as 'the procedural safeguards in place to challenge the exclusion and to avoid arbitrariness; the duration of the exclusion; the extent of the cooperation shown by the pupil or his parents with respect to attempts to re-integrate him; the efforts of the school authorities to minimise the effects of exclusion and, in particular, the adequacy of alternative education provided by the school during the period of the exclusion; and the extent to which the rights of any third parties were engaged'.

7.209 The court accepted that the fact that the exclusion was not wholly in accordance with domestic law was not determinative. On the facts, the exclusion had been for the minimum period necessary and the fact that the applicant was not reintegrated following the cessation of the criminal investigation was the fault of his parents and not of the school. As to the provision of alternative education in the interim, the court said:

> 'While the alternative education did not cover the full national curriculum, the court accepts that it was adequate in view of the fact that the period of exclusion was at al times considered temporary pending the outcome of the criminal investigation. Article 2 of the first protocol does not require schools in the United Kingdom to offer alternative education covering the full national curriculum to all pupils who have been temporarily excluded from school. However, the situation might well be different if a pupil of compulsory school age were to be permanently excluded from one school and were not able to subsequently secure full-time education in line with the national curriculum at another school'.

7.210 The approach of the court on the issue of interim provision supports the view of the majority in *A v Essex*, that a failure to make suitable interim provision for a pupil with special educational needs pending a suitable placement could amount to a violation of A2P1 before the Strasbourg Court: while the domestic SEN regime cannot be characterised as straightforwardly as the system of mainstream provision was characterised by the court, it is plain that the UK system at least purports to ensure that all children with SEN have those needs met either in school or by appropriate alternative provision. The fact that certain other Convention states may not provide this would not preclude the court from concluding that the UK was in breach if it failed.

PHYSICAL WELL-BEING

7.211 The physical safety of pupils is well protected both by the common law and by statutory regulation.

Common law duty of care

7.212 At common law it has long been established that schools and teachers owe a duty to take reasonable care for the health and safety of pupils in their charge. The duty extends to other school or LA employees, such as playground supervisors, as well as pupils. The proper defendant will be the LA or the governing body, as well as any individual alleged to have been negligent. In considering whether the duty has been breached it may be relevant to have regard to section 1 of the Compensation Act 2006 which provides that a court considering a claim for negligence or breach of statutory duty 'may', in determining whether the defendant should have taken particular steps to meet the standard of care (whether by taking precautions against a risk or otherwise) have regard to whether such a requirement might prevent a desirable activity from being undertaken at all, to some extent or in a particular way or discourage persons from undertaking functions in relation to that activity. In practice, section 1 does not appear to add anything to the factors that would anyway have been considered under the common law and the explanatory memorandum makes clear that it is not intended to do so.

7.213 In *Woodland v Essex County Council*,[322] the Court of Appeal, by a majority, upheld the decision of Langstaff J to strike out a claim that an LA owed a non-delegable duty of care in the capacity *loco parentis* to ensure that reasonable care was taken to secure the claimant's safety in the course of a swimming lesson. The claimant was a pupil at a school maintained by Essex. She sustained serious brain damage at a swimming lesson held in a pool run by another LA with the assistance of an independent contractor engaged by that LA and the contractor's staff. The allegation that Essex owed a non-delegable duty for her safety was struck out.[323]

7.214 Tomlinson LJ (with whom Kitchin LJ agreed) expressed dissatisfaction that the question whether such a duty was owed had been determined as a preliminary issue in circumstances where the factual position was not entirely clear (for example, it was not entirely clear which of the various potential defendants had liability insurance and to what extent, or whether or not there were school staff present at the swimming pool). Nonetheless, he agreed with the judge's decision to strike out that part of the claim. To recognise that a school owed a non-delegable duty in these circumstances would be a significant extension of the common law for which there was no strong policy rationale. Indeed, given that a reasonably careful parent would be willing to entrust their child to a public swimming pool under the supervision of a reasonably carefully chosen lifeguard and in the presence of a reasonably careful swimming teacher, to argue that the school should be responsible for any failure of the lifeguard to exercise due care would have gone well beyond any duty a parent owed.[324] Furthermore, as a matter of policy, Tomlinson LJ considered that, taking the

---

[322] [2012] EWCA Civ 239.

[323] A claim that Essex owed a duty to take reasonable care to ensure that the independent contractor it had engaged to run the lesson was careful and competent so that her employees were suitably qualified and experienced persons could proceed to trial. A claim that Essex was vicariousaly liable for the acts of its independent contractors was struck out and no appeal was brought against the decision to strike that aspect of the claim out.

[324] Paragraph 40, in which Tomlinson LJ quotes with approval passages from the judgment of Langstaff J; to that effect.

liability insurance of the independent contractor and lifeguard into account, and the other duties in play there was no strong reason of policy in support of finding there to be a non-delegable duty.[325] The imposition of a duty would be likely to have had a chilling effect on the willingness of education authorities to provide valuable educational experiences for pupils.[326]

7.215 Laws LJ dissented. Laws LJ accept that there were situations in which a school would owe a non-delegable duty of care to a pupil by analogy with the circumstances in which a hospital may owe such a duty to a patient. Broadly speaking, in the case of both a hospital and a school, the institution had '[accepted] responsibility to take care of a group of persons who are particularly vulnerable or dependent'.[327] However, that did not give rise to a non-delegable duty in all circumstances. Instead Laws LJ considered that 'A school or hospital owes a non-delegable duty to see that care is taken for the safety of a child or patient who is: (a) generally in its care, and (b) is receiving a service which is part of the institution's mainstream function of education or tending to the sick.'[328] Applying that test in the *Woodland* case, the judge could not have concluded that the claim was bound to fail.

7.216 Tomlinson LJ noted that the control Laws LJ sought to impose to narrow the circumstances in which a school would owe a non-delegable duty applying the 'acceptance of responsibility for the vulnerable or dependent' basis for such a duty might not in fact act as much of a control. Tomlinson LJ considered that Laws LJ's formulation '[would] leave an educational authority liable without more for the negligence of the zoo-keeper's staff ... [were] a child bitten by an animal in consequence of such negligence whilst on a class outing to a zoo as part of a school's regular schedule of important educational visits. That result [would] follow unless, which I doubt, the trip could can be regarded as not part of the school's mainstream function of education.' Given the increasing breadth of the curriculum and the importance attached to extra-curricular activities, it is submitted that Tomlinson LJ was right to be concerned that the 'mainstream function of education' may prove a somewhat elastic concept.

7.217 The usual principles of the law of negligence apply in ascertaining the existence and scope of the duty of care. It has been held that the duty to take reasonable care may in appropriate circumstances, include a duty to take positive steps to protect the pupil from physical harm: see *Hippolyte v London Borough of Bexley*,[329] which concerned action taken by a teacher in respect of a pupil suffering an asthma attack. Steyn LJ (as he then was) said:

---

[325] Paragraph 35.
[326] Paragraph 57.
[327] Paragraph 25.
[328] Paragraph 30.
[329] [1995] PIQR 309; see also DfEE Circular 14/96 'Supporting Pupils with Medical Needs in School' for guidance on appropriate procedures.

'... it has long been recognised that there is a special relationship between a teacher and a pupil which may potentially give rise to a duty on a teacher to take positive steps to protect the pupil from physical harm. See *Rich v London County Council* [1953] 2 All ER 376; *Beaumont v Surrey County Council* (1968) 12 SJ 704; *Van Oppen v Clerk to Bedford Charity Trustees* [1990] 1 WLR 261B–261D and page 263F–263G.

Such duties to take affirmative action may arise when the requirements of foreseeability and proximity, as well as the requirement that it is reasonable and just to impose a particular duty, as explained in *Caparo Industries Plc v Dickman* [1990] 2 AC 605, are satisfied. But such a duty may also arise if the case falls within what Lord Goff of Chieveley in *Spring v Guardian Assurance Plc* [1994] 3 WLR 354 at page 369A described as the "wide scope of the principle in *Hedley Byrne*".[330] It is not difficult to visualise circumstances in which a school may by conduct assume a relevant responsibility on which the parent and pupil then rely. Duties of affirmative action may be generated in such circumstances. In short, school children, whatever their ages, are in principle, within the protective pale of a teacher for whom an education authority is responsible.'

7.218 *Van Oppen v Clerk to the Bedford Charity Trustees*[331] concerned a pupil who was injured during the course of a rugby match at school. The Court of Appeal was concerned with the failure of the school to ensure that the pupil was covered by accident insurance. In deciding that the school was under no duty in this regard, Balcombe LJ stated[332] that the duties imposed on the school must bear a fair and reasonable relationship to the activities carried on at the school and[333] that it would not be fair or reasonable to impose on the school a wider duty than is imposed on parents.

7.219 The standard of care expected of teachers, who are considered to be in loco parentis, is that of 'careful parents'.[334] It may be that the standard of the careful parent will be modified having regard to the fact that a teacher, unlike a parent, is responsible for a whole class of pupils: see *Lyes v Middlesex County Council*.[335]

7.220 What is reasonable in the circumstances will depend on a number of factors, including the age of the child[336] and the nature of the activity. A school does not have to take precautions against every foreseeable risk, merely precautions against risks which are reasonably likely to happen. Accordingly, in *Gough v Upshire Primary School*[337] a school was held not to be negligent when a boy fell 12 feet from a bannister at the top of the stairs to the floor below. It was unclear whether he had fallen when he started to slide down the bannister

---

[330] *Hedley Byrne and Co v Heller and Partners* [1964] AC 465.
[331] [1990] 1 WLR 235.
[332] [1990] 1 WLR 235, at p 261B.
[333] [1990] 1 WLR 235, at p 261D.
[334] See *Williams v Eady* (1893) 10 TLR 41; *Rich v London County Council* [1953] 2 All ER 376 and *Martin v Middlesborough Corporation* (1965) 63 LGR 385.
[335] (1962) 61 LGR 443. See also *Beaumont v Surrey County Council* (1968) 66 LGR 580 at 585.
[336] *Jeffery v London County Council* (1954) 52 LGR 521.
[337] [2002] ELR 169.

or when he climbed on it. However, the bannister and stairway, which had been in place since 1936, complied with the relevant building regulations, and there had been no previous incidents reported. Some time after the accident happened studs were placed on the bannister. Although it was foreseeable that a child would seek to slide down a bannister in the circumstances where proper instruction was given not to pursue this activity together with the lack of any previous incident, the school did not have to do more.

7.221 Accidents in the playground, even if caused by an uneven playground, will not necessarily lead to liability of the LA. In *Barrie v Cardiff City Council*[338] a six year-old girl was injured when she tripped over edging at a height of 15mm in the playground. At first instance, the court had held the LA liable but the decision was reversed by the Court of Appeal. Following,[339] with some modification, the dictum of Cumming-Bruce LJ in *Littler v Liverpool Corporation*,[340] the Court of Appeal held that the playground was not to be criticised by the standards of the bowling green. A school was held not liable in negligence when a child broke his arm playing with a swing during a school sports day in *Simonds v Isle of Wight Council*.[341] The child had been returned to the care of the parent and the school was held to be under no duty to immobilise the swings.

7.222 Accidents in the playground outside school hours may still engage the responsibility of the school. In *Kearn-Price v Kent County Council*,[342] the claimant was injured when a football hit him in the eye five minutes before the school day began. It was held to be neither just nor reasonable to exclude a duty of care in those circumstances and, on the facts, the school was in breach of its duty as it had not taken sufficient steps to enforce its ban on the use of full-size leather footballs in the playground.

7.223 It is accepted that it may be proper and desirable to allow children to participate in certain inherently risky activities; the duty on the school is to take all reasonable care to guard against those risks. At first instance, in *Van Oppen v Clerk to the Bedford Charity Trustees*,[343] the school was found not to be in breach of its duty of care so far as the conduct of the rugby match was concerned; the standard of supervision was high, the refereeing vigilant and proper emphasis was placed on discipline.[344] The decision in *Smoldon v Whitworth*[345] went the opposite way. In that case the Court of Appeal upheld a finding that the referee of a colts rugby match was in breach of a duty of care in failing to take reasonable care to prevent scrums collapsing. Many scrums had collapsed already during the game, and it was well known that this could

---

[338] [2001] EWCA Civ 703, [2001] All ER (D) 375 (May).
[339] [2001] EWCA Civ 703, [2001] All ER (D) 375 (May), at paras 22–23.
[340] [1968] 2 All ER 343 at 345.
[341] [2003] All ER (D) 156.
[342] [2002] EWCA Civ 1539, [2003] ELR 17.
[343] [1989] 1 All ER 273.
[344] This aspect of the decision was not subject of the appeal to the Court of Appeal.
[345] [1997] ELR 249.

cause neck or spinal injuries. The then rules of the colts game contained provisions designed to prevent scrums collapsing which the referee was found, on the facts, not to have enforced. The court drew a distinction between this failing, and oversights or errors of judgment that might easily be made during the course of a fast-moving game.[346]

7.224 In *MM v Newlands Manor School and Another*[347] the claimant, who attended Shoreham College Sussex, was injured in the course of an under-15 rugby match as a result of a tackle by a pupil of Newlands Manor School who was over 15 at the relevant time. Rule 5 of the Junior Rugby Guidelines of the England Rugby Football Schools' Union did not impose an absolute prohibition on playing older players but provided that players should not normally be allowed to play other than in their own junior age grouping. The master in charge of team selection at Newlands Manor School was in breach of a duty of care owed to the claimant by failing to take reasonable care in applying rule 5 of the Guidelines to the tackler: indeed he admitted that he did not even know the age of the tackler. The physical disparity between the tackler and the claimant was not as such problematic: had such a physical disparity existed between the claimant and another boy of his age it would have been acceptable for both to play. However, the Court of Appeal considered that the tackler was the size and weight that he was because he was more mature; and that to bring such boys down an age group must be to increase the risk of injury because of that difference in size and weight due to maturity. The Court of Appeal further accepted as a matter of causation that the superior size, weight and maturity of the tackler had contributed to the claimant being injured, the very risk against which rule 5 guarded.

7.225 In *Scout Association v Barnes*,[348] the Court of Appeal upheld (by a majority) the decision of the trial judge that a scout leader had been negligent in deciding that the boys at a scout meeting would play a game called 'Objects in the Dark', which in essence was a game called 'Grab' played in the dark. Smith and Ward LJJ (the latter with some reluctance) held that the judge had been entitled to conclude that the foreseeable increased risk of the game played in the dark outweighed the additional excitement or value of the game. Jackson LJ did not consider that the judge had given adequate attention to the social value of the activity, which had been properly supervised, structure and played on many occasions before without mishap such that it could not possibly be said that there had been a failure to exercise reasonable care by the scout leader and his assistants.[349]

---

[346] For an example see *Fowles v Bedfordshire County Council* [1996] ELR 51, in which the plaintiff suffered spinal injuries in the activities room of a council-owned youth house while performing gymnastics; the council was held to have been negligent in failing to give a warning or notice, or to control potentially dangerous unsupervised use of mats for gymnastics.
[347] [2007] EWCA Civ 21.
[348] [2010] EWCA Civ 1476.
[349] [2010] EWCA Civ 1476, para 32.

7.226 It is clear that the liability of schools and teachers extends beyond the classroom. The school remains responsible for the safety of its pupils during break times and lunch times, and a duty of care is owed by any non-teaching staff employed to supervise pupils at such times. An example of a school being liable during break times is *J v North Lincolnshire County Council*.[350] There, a nine year-old boy who suffered from global development delay, left school during a break and without permission. He was injured when hit by a car some 1000 metres from the school. The court held that where the school accepted the care of a child who would be at risk if left alone beside a highway and the child was injured as a result of being where he should not have been, then the onus was on the school to show how it was he came to be where he should not have been and that that was through no fault of their own.[351] As the school was unable to show this it was held to be in breach of duty.

7.227 In *Palmer v Cornwall County Council*,[352] a school was in breach of its duty of care where there was only one dinner lady supervisor at lunchtime responsible for over 150 pupils in years 7 and 8 as well as a similar number in years 9 and 10 at which she would cast a glance from time to time. The school was liable for the injury sustained when a year 9 pupil threw a rock at a seagull which bounced and hit the claimant in the eye. So far as causation was concerned, Waller LJ noted that since the purpose of appropriate supervision was to deter children from taking part in dangerous activities and to stop dangerous activities if they do occur, a court should not be too ready to accept that a dangerous activity would have happened anyway.[353]

7.228 The system of supervision during breaks must be adequate, both in theory and in practice. In *Nwabudike v Southwark London Borough Council*,[354] a primary school pupil ran out of the playground during the lunch break into the path of a car, and it was held that the duty of the school was to take all reasonable and adequate steps to prevent children leaving the school premises at a time when they should have been in school; it was required to ensure that proper safeguards were in place and implemented. The school in that case was found to have fulfilled its duty. Account was taken, inter alia, of its record of similar incidents.[355]

7.229 As appears from *Kearn-Price v Kent County Council*[356] the school's responsibility also extends to the beginning and end of the school day. Younger children will need some form of supervision until they are collected by their parents, and appropriate action should be taken if children are not collected. The Children Act 1989, section 3(5) authorises anyone not having parental responsibility (as defined by section 3(1)) but having care of a child, which it is

---

[350] [2000] ELR 245.
[351] [2000] ELR 245, at para 18.
[352] [2009] EWCA Civ 456
[353] Paragraph 23.
[354] [1997] ELR 35.
[355] See also *Pettican v Enfield London Borough Council* (1970) *The Times*, 22 October.
[356] [2002] EWCA Civ 1539, [2003] ELR 17.

submitted, may include a teacher, to do what is reasonable in all the circumstances for 'safeguarding or promoting the child's welfare'. In *Barnes v Hampshire County Council*[357] it was held to be negligent to release a class of five year-olds from school five minutes before the official end of the school day when their parents would be there to collect them.

7.230 Where the school or LA provides school transport, it remains under a duty to take reasonable care of the children during the journey, and, presumably, when they are boarding and alighting from buses. Supervision during the journey may be required (see *Shrimpton v Hertfordshire County Council Ltd*)[358] and again the standard of care is that of the reasonable parent.[359] This may be satisfied by supervision by older children or prefects: *Jacques v Oxfordshire County Council.*[360]

7.231 The steps necessary to satisfy the duty will depend on the circumstances. For instance, where LAs provide taxi transport for children with SEN, they may need to carry out checks on drivers, or provide escorts. In *Myton v Woods,*[361] an authority that made arrangements for a taxi firm to escort a child with SEN was found to have acted in accordance with its statutory duties and its duty of care at common law to provide suitable arrangements. It was found not to be vicariously liable for the negligence of the taxi driver in dropping the child off in a lay-by, contrary to detailed instructions, so that he needed to cross a busy road unassisted and was injured in doing so.

School trips

7.232 The duty of care also extends to school trips of all kinds. Whatever the activity involved, the principle remains unchanged: those responsible are under a duty to take reasonable care to safeguard the health and safety of the pupils. More dangerous activities may demand a greater degree of supervision, but there is nothing wrong in principle in schools taking children on adventure activity holidays, skiing holidays and the like, where their parents consent. Indeed, such experiences are seen as a valuable part of a child's education in its broadest sense. Always, those in charge must ask what degree of care and supervision would be exercised by a careful parent. Note, though, that a school does not generally owe a non-delegable duty of care: provided it has fulfilled its duty to take reasonable care in the identification of suitable activities and appropriate providers it will not generally be liable if a third party provider fails itself to take reasonable care: see *Woodlands v Essex.*[362]

---

[357] [1969] 3 All ER 746.
[358] (1911) 104 LT 145.
[359] *Ellis v Sayers Confectioners Ltd* (1963) 61 LGR 299.
[360] (1967) 66 LGR 440.
[361] (1980) 79 LGR 28.
[362] Discussed above at paras **7.213–7.216.**

7.233   An example of the duties of teachers in this context is provided by the Court of Appeal decision in *Woodbridge School v Chittock*.363 In that case a boy had been severely reprimanded for skiing off piste and was threatened with confiscation of his ski pass. The threat was not implemented on an assurance that the action would not be repeated. The boy then skied on a piste above the standard for which he was competent and was injured. It was held, applying *Bolam*, and reversing the High Court, that the teachers had not acted negligently. The reaction of the teacher in charge to the off-piste incident was within the generous ambit the law allowed, but in any event, the failure to remove the ski pass or to require the boy to submit to supervised skiing had not caused the accident.

7.234   A further example is provided by the decision of Owen J in *Wilkin Shaw (administratrix of the Estate of Charlotte Shaw (Deceased) v Fuller and another*.364 This was a claim for personal injury. The claimant sought to claim damages for a chronic grief reaction and severe PTSD she suffered as a result of the death of her daughter and for damages for loss to her daughter's estate. The claim was against her daughter's school and the teacher in charge of a training expedition for the Ten Tors Expedition on Dartmoor in the course of which her daughter drowned while crossing a stream at a time when she and her group were subject only to 'remote supervision'. No member of staff was with the claimant and her group at the time of accident, two members of staff having been delayed by a navigational error. The claimant and her group had been told to proceed to a particular tor and not to cross a particular stream which was in heavy flood. A scoutmaster who was on the moor with another group approached the group and advised of a place where he considered it was in fact safe to cross the stream. The group tried to do so and in the course of crossing the claimant dropped her bag and was swept away as she tried to retrieve it. The case does not raise any novel legal principle, but was dismissed on its facts. Not only had the teacher in charge not been negligent, even if he had been negligent, the chain of causation had been broken by the intervention of the scout master on whose advice they tried to cross.365

7.235   The Activity Centres (Young Persons' Safety) Act 1995, which was introduced following the Lyme Bay tragedy, requires providers of facilities for adventure holidays to be licensed. The Adventure Activities Licensing Regulations 2004,366 which govern the licensing regime, apply also to LAs providing such facilities. Detailed guidance to schools, LAs, governing bodies and teachers on ensuring, so far as reasonably practicable, the safety of pupils attending outdoor activity centres is to be found in DFE Circular 22/94 'Safety in Outdoor Activity Centres: Guidance'. The circular covers such matters as the need to be satisfied that a centre has good safety provision before entering any contract, the selection of participants and the need for parental consent, as

---

363   [2002] EWCA Civ 915, [2002] ELR 735. The Court of Appeal set out the governing principles at paras 18 and 19.
364   [2012] EWHC 1777.
365   See further para **7.257** below.
366   SI 2004/1309.

well as the conduct of the trip itself. It is noted that a teacher may discharge his or her common law duty of care to pupils by temporarily entrusting their safety to a member of the centre's staff for the duration of the specific hazardous activity.[367]

Responsibility for acts of third parties

7.236 There are circumstances in the educational context in which a school or LA may be held liable for the acts of third parties, most often a school's pupils. The general approach to the question when a duty may be imposed on a person for the acts of a third party was considered by the Court of Appeal in *Selwood v Durham County Council and others*.[368] The claimant was a social worker involved with the daughter of a man, GB, who was involved in family court proceedings and suffering from mental illness. GB's daughter was under the care of the local CAMHS team run by the Tees, Esk and Wear Valley NHS Foundation Trust. GB was in the care of their Community Mental Health Team. GB was also under the care of a consultant psychiatrist at a hospital operated by the Northumberland, Tyne and Wear NHS Foundation Trust. GB indicated to staff of the NHS Trusts that he was having fantasies about killing somebody involved in his case. At a case review which the claimant had offered to attend, GB was asked by the consultant psychiatrist whether the claimant could attend and he had said he would kill her on the spot if he saw her. This information was not passed on to Durham County Council or the claimant. The claimant attended a case review meeting with GB at which he attacked her and grievously injured her.

7.237 The council and the two NHS Trusts worked (or purported to work) closely together (the community mental health team was staffed by employees of both the NHS Trust and social services). They had undertaken to adopt a multi-agency approach to delivering services, recorded in a policy document 'Working together in the delivery of services to adults and children.'

7.238 The claimant brought a claim in negligence against the council and both NHS Trusts. The NHS Trusts applied to strike out the claim on the basis that they did not owe the claimant any duty of care in relation to the acts of GB. The judge struck out the claim. The Court of Appeal reversed his decision.

7.239 So far as general principles are concerned, Smith LJ noted that where a claimant seeks to establish that a school or LA was responsible for the acts of a third party (not being an employee), the claimant will need to establish 'something more' than foreseeability and proximity. That 'something more' need not necessarily be an assumption of responsibility towards the claimant on the part of the putative tortfeasor. It will suffice if the tripartite test of foreseeability, proximity and fairness, justice and reasonableness is satisfied.[369] However, on the facts, the Court of Appeal (unlike the trial judge) considered

---

[367] See at para 49 of the Circular.
[368] [2012] EWCA Civ 979.
[369] Paragraph 50.

that there had been an assumption of responsibility. An assumption of responsibility, they held, did not require something positive to have been said or done to indicate such an assumption.[370] On the facts, it would have been open for the trial judge to conclude that the NHS Trusts had assumed responsibility to do what was reasonable in the circumstances to reduce or avoid a foreseeable risk of harm to which a social worker was exposed in the course of their joint operations. The protocol on multi-agency working and evidence as to how the working arrangements operated in practice would be relevant in considering whether that argument was made good.[371] Furthermore, in considering whether public policy favoured the imposition of a duty of care, the judge had paid insufficient regard to the particular position of the claimant who was not simply a member of the public at large but one of a small team of professionals to whom the duty might be assumed.[372]

7.240 Although that case concerned the relationship between an LA and NHS Trusts, the importance of multi-agency working will be familiar to those working in schools perhaps especially where child protection, special educational needs and pupils with serious behavioural difficulties are concerned. While the court was merely concerned with the question whether the matter should go for trial rather than the question whether the NHS Trusts owed a duty of care was in fact owed in the circumstances of that case, the case is a reminder of the importance that there be multi-agency working in practice as well as on paper.

7.241 There is, as yet, little case-law showing the approach of the courts when faced with actions for negligence based on bullying. While the courts have recognised a duty of care, they have not been astute to find it to have been breached.

7.242 In *Bradford-Smart v West Sussex County Council*,[373] the claimant alleged that she had been bullied both outside and on the way to and from school (using public transport) and within the school. At trial, the judge accepted, in relation to two years, that there had been some name calling and uncouth behaviour on the bus, but concluded, on the evidence before him, that in his view there had not been the targeted and persistent action required to amount to bullying. He further held that there was no evidence that the school knew about it. In relation to the third year, the trial judge held that child had been seriously bullied at home and on the bus going to and from school and that threats were made as to what would happen in school, but that the class teacher prevented bullying in school. She had not failed to take appropriate action, and had done all she could as a class teacher and did not fall short of what a class teacher exercising ordinary skill and care should do. Those factual findings were held unassailable by the Court of Appeal.[374] The Court of

---

[370] Paragraph 52.
[371] Paragraph 52.
[372] Paragraph 54.
[373] [2002] EWCA Civ 7, [2002] ELR 139.
[374] [2002] EWCA Civ 7, [2002] ELR 139, at para 19.

Appeal did, however, disagree with the restricted basis upon which the trial judge had held a duty of care arose. He had held that the duty went no further than to prevent the bullying actually happening inside the school. The Court of Appeal held that the school could not directly protect its pupils all the time because, in relation to a day school, its charge would usually end at the school gates.[375] However, a school could be liable if it failed to take action against known bullies in relation to their conduct outside school, although this would not be generally the case.[376] On the evidence, the Court of Appeal held that even with this broader duty, the judge would have been right in holding there was no breach of duty by the school as the teacher was careful and acted in accordance with a responsible body of professional opinion.[377]

7.243 More generally, in *Bradford-Smart*,[378] the Court of Appeal stated that it was necessary to identify with some precision any breach of duty found and to consider whether the steps proposed would have been effective in preventing bullying. It was also necessary to show that the breach of duty had caused the injury and not simply that the bullying had caused the injury and that would often be difficult to prove.

7.244 In *Faulkner v Enfield London Borough Council*,[379] two sisters suffered an assault at school as a result of which neither of them attended the school again, save that the first claimant attended to take her GCSEs. They claimed they had been bullied prior to the assault and alleged that the defendants were in breach of their duty of care in failing to prevent the assault or by making the school safe. The court held that the defendants had taken reasonable care and there was nothing they could have done to prevent the assault. The action was accordingly dismissed.[380]

7.245 In *Beaumont v Surrey County Council*,[381] it was held that it was part of a headteacher's duty, considering the known propensities of children aged from 11 to 18 years old, to take reasonable steps to prevent injury from inanimate objects, other pupils, or a combination of the two. The negligence in that case consisted in leaving a piece of potentially dangerous strong elastic lying on top of a waste bin.

7.246 In *Webster v The Ridgeway Foundation School*,[382] Nicol J accepted that the school had a duty to take reasonable care to see that the claimant was reasonably safe during school hours and for a reasonable period after the end

---

375 [2002] EWCA Civ 7, [2002] ELR 139, at para 32.
376 [2002] EWCA Civ 7, [2002] ELR 139, at para 34. The decision of Brooke J in *R v London Borough of Newham ex parte X* [1995] ELR 303 at 306–307 was expressly endorsed.
377 [2002] EWCA Civ 7, [2002] ELR 139, at para 36.
378 [2002] EWCA Civ 7, [2002] ELR 139, para 37.
379 [2003] ELR 426.
380 For an example of an action based on bullying failing on the application of *Bolam* principles, see *Newby v Shotton Hall Comprehensive School Governors* Recorder Goose QC, 5 July 2002, Hartlepool County Court (unreported).
381 (1968) 66 LGR 580.
382 [2010] EWHC 157

of the school day when he was still on school premises. That extended to a duty to protect a pupil from persons who were not themselves part of the school community.[383] The claimant had arranged to fight another pupil after school at the school tennis courts, part of a very large school site. Associates of that other pupil, including some adults, who were not themselves pupils at the school arrived and attacked the claimant. One attacked him with a claw hammer which left him with lasting brain damage. On the facts, Nicol J rejected each of the putative breaches of duty put forward by the claimant. The school was not in breach of its duty of care because it had not constructed a perimeter fence at the date of the attack: there was no requirement to construct a perimeter fence under the Education (School Premises) Regulations 1999[384] and there were significant financial and planning obstacles to the construction of a fence at the relevant time. Nor was the school in breach of duty by failing to have a member of staff on duty at the tennis court at the relevant time: the school's judgment as to the allocation of teacher supervision at the end of the day was within the range of reasonable responses open to it. Whether the school had adhered to its security policy was a relevant factor in considering whether or not the school was in breach of duty but it was not determinative and, on the facts, did not require a staff presence at the tennis courts after school. The school's general approach to discipline was not in breach of duty: amongst other things, it was not negligent in failing to restrict the use of mobile phones more than it did and it was not negligent in not excluding a particular pupil before the events in question.

7.247 In *S v London Borough of Redbridge*,[385] the female claimant, who was 13 years old at the relevant time, was assaulted by a group of boys. In the course of the assault, the split in the claimant's skirt was opened. The headteacher concluded, and the court accepted that it was reasonable for the headteacher to conclude, that the incident was one of horseplay and not indecent assault. The court held that there had been no breach of a duty of care where the headteacher had failed directly to inform the victim's parents of the incident. The court found that the headteacher had told the pupil that she should inform her parents. In the circumstances, where the pupil had herself reported the matter to the headteacher, that decision was one consistent with a reasonable body of professional opinion. The court further rejected an argument that the school had been negligent in failing to refer the claimant for counselling or other professional help: the incident as reported was not sufficiently serious to require such a referral and the claimant had not exhibited any continuing signs of unhappiness in the weeks following the incident.

Duties to staff

7.248 The LA responsible for a maintained school will owe members of staff a duty of care arising from the employment relationship that subsists between the authority and its employees. Likewise, the governing body of a foundation

---

[383] [2010] EWHC 157, para 118.
[384] See para **7.264** below.
[385] [2005] EWHC 150.

school or an independent school would owe such a duty. As the focus of this work is education law and not employment law, we do not attempt a general survey of the duty of care owed by an employer to an employee.

7.249 In *Alexis v London Borough of Newham*,[386] the court dismissed a claim for negligence in which it was alleged that the defendant was in breach of duty by failing to take reasonable steps to prevent conduct on the part of pupils that might result in injury to other pupils or teaching staff, in particular by failing to adhere to its policy of locking classrooms to minimise the risk of injury being caused by mischievous or malicious behaviour.

7.250 The claimant was a teacher at the school. There was tension between the claimant and a pupil who was otherwise considered to be responsible by staff. The claimant had not made a report of any tension between her and the pupil in question. On a day when the claimant was not at the school, the claimant's class was being taught by a second teacher. The second teacher gave the pupil a key to the claimant's classroom in order for her to collect coursework folders from the classroom. The pupil put cleaning fluid in the claimant's water bottle. The next day, the claimant drank from the bottle and became physically ill. The event exacerbated an existing anxiety disorder from which the claimant suffered.

7.251 The judge accepted that it was foreseeable that if unsupervised pupils got up to mischief a situation might arise where there was a risk of injury to teachers and it was foreseeable that within the school population there were likely to be emotionally and behaviourally disturbed children who might pose a physical threat to teachers.[387] It was not foreseeable in general terms that any pupil might seek to poison a teacher, nor that that the pupil in particular would seek to poison the particular teacher in question. The pupil had not deliberately sought to injure the claimant but had indulged in a prank the consequences of which she had not fully anticipated. What happened was within the same type of behaviour which was reasonably foreseeable, even if the particular form it took was not.[388] The school owed the claimant a duty to take such precautions as were reasonable in all the circumstances to minimise the risk of a pupil's mischievous or malicious behaviour causing injury.[389] However, on the facts, there had been no breach of that duty. While the school may have maintained an informal policy of keeping classrooms locked and not giving pupils the keys, it admitted exceptions at the discretion of class teachers.[390] With the possible exception of the claimant herself, none of the teachers had reason to suspect the malefactor of being likely to do what she did and so her colleague was not negligent in giving the malefactor and another pupil the keys to the claimant's classroom in order for them to make the short trip there and back to pick up

---

[386] [2009] EWHC 1323.
[387] Paragraph 99.
[388] Paragraphs 99–100.
[389] Paragraph 103.
[390] Paragraph 108.

some work.[391] Likewise, it was not negligent that the teacher taking the claimant's class was teaching them in her own classroom and not the claimant's classroom.[392]

7.252   *Vahidi v Fairstead House School Trust Ltd*[393] was a stress at work case in an educational context. The case raises no point of general principle, but on the facts following the claimant's initial bout of mental illness, it was held that the respondent school had not been in breach of duty by failing to suggest that the claimant seek further medical help (which at the time would have been intrusive and suggested that the school did not believe her when she said that she was seeing her doctor) or sending her home when she had indicated a willingness to work (which the claimant would have perceived as hostile and would have been the sort of conduct that might have triggered a relapse). The facts might be contrasted with the well known leading case on stress at work, *Barber v Somerset*,[394] that also arose in an educational context albeit in that case Lord Walker expressed the view that such comparison is not often fruitful.[395]

7.253   *Connor v Surrey County Council*, discussed above in detail at para **7.46**ff was an example of a case in which the LA's duty to take reasonable steps to protect the mental health of the headteacher of a maintained school required the authority to exercise its public law functions, in particular by taking steps to establish an interim executive board to replace a dysfunctional governing body and refusing to investigate a spurious complaint that it made been made to it about aspects of the running of the school.

CAUSATION

7.254   It must be remembered that it is not enough to establish that there existed a duty of care and that the defendant was in breach of that duty: the claimant must establish that the defendant caused the harm giving rise to the damages claimed. For example, in *Webster v The Ridgeway Foundation School*,[396] Nicol J held that even if the school had been in breach of certain duties as alleged, this did not cause the claimant's loss. For example, in relation to the claim that the school was in breach by leaving the tennis court unattended after school, the claimant's evidence was that he and the pupil he fought arranged to meet there precisely because it was on the site but unsupervised; and had they not met there, there were numerous other locations on the school site where they could have met unobserved.[397] If the policy on

---

[391]   Paragraphs 109–111.
[392]   Paragraph 112.
[393]   [2005] EWCA Civ 765.
[394]   [2004] UKHL 13.
[395]   [2004] UKHL 13, para 69.
[396]   Discussed above at para **7.246**.
[397]   [2010] EWHC 157, paras 139–142.

mobile phones had been stricter it is likely that it would have been ignored by the individuals involved in the incident who would have called for outside support surreptitiously.[398]

7.255 Furthermore, the claimant cannot succeed where breach of a duty to take care against one risk of injury has allowed events to unfold that have led the claimant to suffer injury of a different kind. In *Webster v The Ridgeway Foundation*, Nicol J considered that while a punch is an assault whether it is wielded by another pupil or an outsider, on the facts of that case they should be regarded as injuries of a different type. What steps it is reasonable to expect a school to take to prevent an assault by another pupil may not necessarily be appropriate or reasonable in relation to assault by an outsider.[399] That might be contrasted with decision in *Alexis*, in which he did not appear to consider injury inflicted by poisoning with whiteboard cleaner fluid (which was not a reasonably foreseeable type of injury) to be an injury of a different type from that one might reasonably foresee a pupil inflicting on a teacher, albeit it was not necessary for him to consider this point in the context of causation and damages in view of his findings on breach. This demonstrates the importance of identifying the scope of the duty of care.

7.256 In *DN (by his Father and Litigation Friend RN) v London Borough of Greenwich*,[400] the Court of Appeal set out the approach to take to causation in cases where it is alleged that as a result of the negligence of an educational psychologist or other professional the claimant was not placed in an appropriate school environment. It was to be taken as a starting premise that the claimant would have been placed in a more appropriate school with his parents' agreement. The question was then what, on the balance of probabilities, would have been the better outcome if he had had more suitable schooling within that scenario.[401] But it was for the claimant to establish a 51 per cent likelihood that there would indeed have been a better outcome: the claimant was not entitled to be compensated for the loss of the chance that the outcome would have been more satisfactory if he could not establish on the balance of probabilities that it would be so.[402] The judge had therefore been wrong to approach the issue of causation by holding that the defendant's negligence had caused the claimant to lose the opportunity to improve his social skills, manage his behavioural difficulties and gain some educational opportunities. The judge also erred in failing to make a finding as to whether the claimant's tendency to set fires would on the balance of probabilities have arisen even if he had gone to an appropriate school. In giving guidance for the assessment of quantum, the Court of Appeal considered that in light of the many uncertainties as to how that particular claimant's life would have developed even in the absence of the defendant's negligence, the evidence could only justify a small award for loss of earning capacity, no more than that

---

[398] [2010] EWHC 157, para 147.
[399] [2010] EWHC 157, para 194.
[400] [2004] EWCA Civ 1659.
[401] [2004] EWCA Civ 1659, para 70.
[402] [2004] EWCA Civ 1659, para 72.

awarded in wrongful birth cases.[403] In *Devon County Council v Clarke*,[404] the Court of Appeal rejected the LA's submission that in order to establish that an educational psychologist's breach of duty had caused the claimant loss the claimant had to establish that there would have been a 'measurable difference' relating to the claimant's literacy and numeracy skills.

7.257 Finally, it should be remembered that the chain of causation between the negligent act and the loss sustained can be broken by a *novus actus interveniens*. Although it was not necessary to dispose of the case, in *Wilkin-Shaw v Fuller*, discussed above at para **7.234**, Owen J held that the chain of causation between the allegedly negligent acts and omissions and the death of the claimant's daughter had been broken. The claimant's daughter died while crossing a stream that her group had been told not to cross. They did so after a well meaning scoutmaster who was working with another group suggested a place where it would be safe to cross. While it was foreseeable that the group might seek or take advice if they encountered an adult working with other groups on the moor it was not reasonably foreseeable that such adult would give bad advice thereby putting the group at risk.[405] Owen J did not elaborate on this point in detail – he did not need to do so for the purposes of his judgment – but this conclusion might be doubted.

Statutory regulation

Occupiers' Liability Acts

7.258 The Occupiers' Liability Act 1957 regulates the duty owed by persons having occupation or control of premises, to their visitors:

> 'to take such care as in all the circumstances of the case is reasonable to see that the visitor will be reasonably safe in using premises for the purposes for which he is invited or permitted by the occupier to be there.'[406]

If more than one person is in control of the premises, there may be more than one occupier, as in *Wheat v Lacon (E) & Co Ltd*,[407] where the House of Lords held that both the manager and the owner of a public house were occupiers. Both the governing body of a school and the LA may similarly be considered to be occupiers. Liability under the Act may fall on both, although responsibility for the relevant part of the school premises may fall only on one.

7.259 A lawful visitor is anyone with an express or implied licence to be on the premises, which obviously includes pupils, parents, guardians, teachers and so on. 'The premises' includes both the inside and the outside of the school; see,

---

[403]   [2004] EWCA Civ 1659, paras 77–78.
[404]   [2005] EWCA Civ 266, [2005] 1 FCR 752.
[405]   [2012] EWHC 1777 at 137.
[406]   Occupiers' Liability Act 1957, s 2(2).
[407]   [1966] 1 All ER 582.

eg *Murphy v Bradford Metropolitan Council*,[408] in which the authority was held liable for injuries sustained by a teacher who slipped on frozen snow on a path leading into the school.

7.260 Among the factors relevant in determining the standard of care owed is that 'an occupier must be prepared for children to be less careful than adults'.[409] Additionally, if it is reasonable to assume, for instance, that pupils will be accompanied by their parents, account may be taken of that fact.[410] Age will also be material in determining whether the occupier's liability is avoided by the giving of a warning. If a proper warning which can reasonably be acted upon is given, but a visitor nonetheless voluntarily accepts the risk, then the occupier will not be held liable.[411] However, where the premises in question are school premises, bearing in mind the capacity of children to consent, as well as their tendency to mischief, it may be considered unlikely that a mere warning would be adequate.[412]

7.261 In *Sutton v Syston Rugby Football Club Ltd*[413] the Court of Appeal considered the standard of inspection required of a rugby pitch by a rugby club before a training session. The claimant was injured playing touch rugby when he fell and gashed his knee on a plastic object found to have been a broken off part of a cricket boundary marker. The Club admitted that it owed a duty of care under the Occupiers Liability Act 1957 to take such care as was reasonable in all the circumstances to ensure that visitors would be safe in using the Club's premises. The Club further admitted that there should have been a general inspection of the pitch before the training session began and that no such inspection had taken place. But the Club contended that a quick walk across the pitch to check for such obvious obstructions as broken glass or dog excrement was all that was required. A more detailed inspection such as would have identified a broken stub that did not obtrude above the surface of the grass was not required. The Court of Appeal agreed with the trial judge that before a game or training session, a pitch should be walked over 'at a reasonable walking pace by the coach or match organiser (or someone on their behalf)' and that would satisfy the duty of care.[414] The Court of Appeal did not agree with the trial judge that more attention would be needed at the touch down ends.[415] The Court considered section 1 of the Compensation Act 2006

---

[408] [1992] PIQR P68.
[409] Occupiers' Liability Act 1957, s 2(3)(a).
[410] See *Bates v Parker* [1953] 1 All ER 768.
[411] Occupiers' Liability Act 1957, s 2(5).
[412] In *Tomlinson v Congleton Borough Council* [2003] UKHL 47, [2003] 3 WLR 705, Lord Hoffmann stated, at para 45, that it would be rare for an occupier of land to owe a duty to prevent people from risks which were inherent in activities that they freely chose, although he accepted, at para 46, there was such a duty in relation to children because there was no genuine or informed choice by such persons. Lord Nicholls agreed with his speech and Lord Hobhouse (at para 81) expressed similar views. Lords Hutton and Scott delivered concurring speeches.
[413] [2011] EWCA Civ 1182.
[414] [2011] EWCA Civ 1182, para 13.
[415] [2011] EWCA Civ 1182, para 11.

but did not consider that it made any difference to the case. Overturning the trial judge, the Court of Appeal concluded that on the facts of the case an inspection of the sort required would have been unlikely to have revealed the stub.

7.262 In *Hufton v Somerset County Council*,[416] the Court of Appeal upheld the decision of the trial judge dismissing a claim under the Occupiers Liability Act 1957 in which it was alleged that the defendant did not have a proper system in place for preventing an assembly hall floor on which the claimant slipped from getting wet or clearing up the floor if it did become wet. Following a risk assessment some years before after a member of staff had fallen on the wooden floor when it was wet, the school had fitted barrier matting inside the entranceway to the assembly hall and rubber matting outside the entranceway. Prefects were posted on the door to prevent access during wet weather and a sign would be placed by the fire exit doors, albeit on days when there was a change in the weather there might be a bit of a gap between the rain and the sign being put up. Pupils knew they shouldn't go into the assembly hall and staff were vigilant in dealing with breaches. The patch of water on which the claimant slipped was small, it was not raining at the start of the morning break during which the claimant slipped, her accident occurred about half way through the break and the school was not required to have a system in place such that that water would have been spotted and mopped up during the brief period between its arrival and the claimant's fall.

7.263 The Occupiers' Liability Act 1984 imposes a duty of care in respect of persons other than visitors.[417]

The Education (School Premises) Regulations 1999

7.264 Section 542 of the Education Act 1996[418] imposes on LAs a duty to secure that the premises conform to the standards prescribed by the regulations made under the section. The Education (School Premises) Regulations 1999[419] prescribe in some detail the minimum standards with which school premises must conform. If a pupil is injured as a result of a failure to comply with the regulations, the LA may be liable for breach of statutory duty: see *Reffell v Surrey County Council*.[420]

---

[416] [2011] EWCA Civ 789.
[417] For recent judicial discussion of this Act see *Tomlinson v Congleton Borough Council* [2003] UKHL 47, [2003] 3 WLR 705.
[418] As amended by the SSFA 1998, Sch 30, paras 57 and 158 and Sch 31.
[419] SI 1999/2. These regulations were amended by SI 2012/1943 to insert a new reg 1A that made them apply expressly to all schools maintained by LAs in Wales.
[420] [1964] 1 All ER 743. See also *Ching v Surrey County Council* [1910] 1 KB 736 and *Morris v Carnarvon County Council* [1910] 1 KB 858.

The Health and Safety at Work Etc Act 1974

7.265 The Health and Safety at Work Etc Act 1974 is also of relevance to the school as a working environment. The Act imposes duties on employers to ensure, so far as is reasonably practicable, the health, safety and welfare at work of their employees, and to conduct their undertakings in such a way as to ensure, so far as is reasonably practicable, that persons not in their employment who may be affected thereby are not exposed to risks to their health or safety.[421] Teachers (as employees) are protected as, it seems likely, are pupils (as persons other than employees).

7.266 Section 4 of the 1974 Act imposes a duty on all persons, having regard to any extent control of premises, to ensure, so far as reasonably practicable, that the premises, means of access and any plant or substance, are safe and without risks to health. Both the LA and the governing body may fall within the scope of this section. It has been held that the duty under section 4 extends to children at an indoor play centre.[422]

7.267 Pupils will also benefit from the duty imposed by section 7 on teachers and others working in the school to take reasonable care for the health and safety of themselves and of others who may be affected by their acts or omissions at work.

7.268 Section 47(1) of the Health and Safety at Work Etc Act 1974 provides that it is not to be construed as conferring a right of action in any civil proceedings in respect of any failure to comply with any duty imposed by sections 2–7. However, that is without prejudice to any right of action which exists apart from the Act. Further, section 47(2) provides that breach of a duty imposed by health and safety regulations shall, so far as it causes damage, be actionable unless the regulations provide otherwise.

Measure of damages for negligence and related torts

7.269 The damages recoverable for injuries caused by breaches of any of the above duties will be assessed according to the usual principles for the assessment of damages in tort, ie the plaintiff is to be restored to the position he or she would have been in had the tort not been committed.[423] For cases involving negligence in the assessment and provision for children with SEN, the assessment of damages can be extremely difficult.[424] Special damages, the quantifiable financial losses incurred to date, would generally be easily

---

[421] Health and Safety at Work Etc Act 1974, ss 2 and 3.

[422] *Moualem v Carlisle City Council* [1995] ELR 22.

[423] See e g *Livingstone v Rawyards Coal Company* (1880) 5 App Cas 25 at 39 per Lord Blackburn. The general rules on the measure of damages and the recovery of interest thereon in relation to personal injury are beyond the scope of this book.

[424] *Phelps v Hillingdon* [2001] 2 AC 619 at 657 per Lord Slynn. The House of Lords, although it accepted that there was much room for debate as to quantum, considered that no better approach had been suggested than that adopted by the trial judge and therefore refused to interfere with his award: see [2001] 2 AC 619 at 657 per Lord Slynn.

established, for instance, the cost of tuition fees or alternative educational provision. In *Phelps*,[425] Garland J awarded £3,750 for future costs of tuition, enrolment fees and books and £2,806.50 for past loss under this head.

7.270 In principle a claim for past loss of earnings will lie, although in *Phelps* the claim was dismissed because, for much of the time, the plaintiff had been signed off as unfit to work and there was insufficient evidence for any finding as to her fitness for, or attempts to find, work before she was signed off.[426]

7.271 There can, in principle, be an award for future loss of earnings, based on the assumption that given proper treatment the individual would have achieved greater academic success and, consequently, entered better paid employment. In *Phelps*[427] the judge was alive to the impossibility of accurately evaluating such speculative losses. It is likely that the approach he adopted, namely awarding a reasonably modest lump sum, in line with the approach taken in *Blamire v South Cumbria Health Authority*,[428] will be common. In *Phelps* the amount of the award under this head was £25,000. In *Liennard*,[429] Henriques J indicated he would, had he found negligence, have awarded £20,000. In *Devon County Council v Clarke*[430] the Court of Appeal accepted that an award of £25,000 for past and future loss of earnings was within the permissible range of award where there had been a failure to diagnose the claimant's dyslexia. In *DN (by his Litigation Friend RN) v London Borough of Greenwich*[431] the Court of Appeal considered the uncertainties of the case so great that an award larger than that given in *Phelps* would not be appropriate; and indeed given that the likelihood that the claimant would eve have been capable of gainful employment was problematical, the evidence would only justify an award for loss of earnings much smaller than that in the *Phelps* case.[432]

7.272 As for general damages, a number of heads should be considered. First, in cases of personal injury there may be an award for pain and suffering and loss of amenity. The courts apply a 'going rate' for different types of injuries.[433] This might include an award for loss of congenial employment, as in *Phelps*,[434] where the total award for general damages, including the element for loss of congenial employment, was £12,500. In *Liennard*,[435] Henriques J stated that he would have awarded £15,000 under this head had the claimant succeeded. The Judicial College guidelines for moderate psychological damage (for which one

---

[425] [1998] ELR 38 at 64D.
[426] [1998] ELR 38, at 64E.
[427] [1998] ELR 38, at 64F–64G.
[428] [1993] PIQR Q1.
[429] [2002] ELR 527.
[430] [2005] EWCA Civ 266
[431] [2004] EWCA Civ 1659
[432] [2004] EWCA Civ 1659, para 77
[433] See, eg Kemp & Kemp *The Quantum of Damages* (Sweet and Maxwell, 1975) for examples of the appropriate level of award.
[434] [1998] ELR 38 at 64, Garland J.
[435] [2002] ELR 527.

factor is the injured person's ability to cope with life and work) is an award of £4,200 to £13,650, and for moderately severe damage, £13,650 to £39,150.[436]

7.273 So far as actual personal injury is concerned, in *Skipper v Calerdale Metropolitan Borough Council and the Governors of Crossley Heath School*,[437] the Court of Appeal accepted that general damages can include damages for frustration, loss of self-confidence and loss of self-esteem. Latham LJ (with whom Hallet LJ and Sir Igor Judge P agreed) considered *Phelps* to be authority for the proposition that 'if it can be shown that a claimant's disability has a real effect on his or her ability to cope with school and work, or has otherwise interfered significantly with his enjoyment of life, that will be a loss of amenity which can properly sound in damages' though he confessed to finding the dividing line between such heads of damage and distress and upset which cannot found a claim somewhat elusive.[438] It appears that it is not necessary to suffer psychological damage amounting to an identifiable mental illness. In *Christmas v Hampshire* the judge stated[439] that he would have been prepared to award a sum to reflect the prospect that the plaintiff's problems in the form of specific learning difficulty could have been ameliorated by the timely taking of appropriate action, ie there was no need for actual psychiatric injury. In *Devon County Council v Clarke*,[440] the judge awarded £10,000 general damages for a three year period during which the claimant's dyslexia was not ameliorated: the council did not appeal against the award. In *DN*, the Court of Appeal considered that on the facts of that case justice would have been done if the total award (including loss of earnings and general damages) had been similar to that awarded in wrongful birth cases but noted that further guidance from the House of Lords would be useful to establish judicial policy in such cases.

7.274 In relation to poor teaching, the courts are likely to be reluctant to impose liability directly on individual teachers, and the difficulty of establishing a relevant loss may be important. However, it would be arguable that seriously deficient teaching leading to exam failure in a subject such as English or Mathematics, with consequent impact on employment prospects, did lead to such a loss.

Contributory negligence

7.275 It is likely that in many cases the contributory negligence of the child concerned may be an issue. It is for the defendant to establish contributory negligence, but the standard of care to be applied is 'the degree of care which may reasonably be expected of a person in the plaintiff's situation'.[441] Where children are concerned, a finding of contributory negligence should be made

---

[436] The Judicial College *Guidelines for the Assessment of General Damages in Personal Injury Cases, 11th Edition* (OUP, 2012).
[437] [2006] EWCA Civ 238.
[438] [2006] EWCA Civ 238, at para 27.
[439] [1998] ELR 1 at 27E–27F. The remarks were obiter as the claim was dismissed.
[440] [2005] EWCA Civ 266.
[441] *Lynch v Nurdin* (1841) 1 QB 29 at 36.

only where the child is of an age at which he or she can reasonably be expected to take precautions for his or her own safety.[442] The question then is, what could be expected of an ordinary child of the plaintiff's age, being neither a 'paragon of prudence' nor 'scatter-brained'?[443]

7.276 It will be difficult to establish contributory negligence in cases where the defendant's own negligence consists in leaving temptation in a child's path, in the form of something that a pupil might foreseeably injure him or herself with if he or she interfered with it, as, for instance, in the *Beaumont* case. This is the very situation that the plaintiff should have guarded against.[444]

Joint tortfeasors

7.277 No special problems are raised in this field by the possibility of there being more than one potential defendant for the damage caused (eg a teacher and an LA). In such cases, if both potential defendants are of financial standing the prudent course is to sue both as joint tortfeasors and leave them to sort out between themselves all questions of contribution.

Limitation

7.278 The general limitation period for an action in tort is six years from the date on which the cause of action accrues.[445] The general limitation period for an action for negligence nuisance or breach of duty where the damages claimed consist of, or include, damages for personal injury, is three years subject to a discretion vested in the court to extend time.[446] For children there is an extended limitation period of six years from the date they ceased to be under a disability.[447]

7.279 Claims for educational negligence arising out of a failure to diagnose and ameliorate dyslexia will usually include damages for personal injury. This issue was considered by the Court of Appeal in *Robinson v St Helens Metropolitan Borough Council*.[448] There must be, however, some emotional or physical damage caused by the failure to ameliorate the relevant condition by appropriate teaching.[449]

---

[442] *Gough v Thorne* [1966] 3 All ER 398, per Lord Denning MR at 399.

[443] *Gough v Thorne* [1966] 3 All ER 398, at 400, per Salmon LJ.

[444] See *Yachuk v Oliver Blais Co Ltd* [1949] AC 386.

[445] Limitation Act 1980, s 2.

[446] Limitation Act 1980, s 11. For discussion see A Dugdale *Clerk and Lindsell on Torts* (Sweet and Maxwell, 18th edn) at Chapter 33.

[447] Limitation Act 1980, s 38(2), discussed in A Dugdale *Clerk and Lindsell on Torts* (Sweet and Maxwell, 18th edn) at Chapter 33.

[448] [2002] EWCA Civ 1099, [2002] ELR 681.

[449] [2002] EWCA Civ 1099, [2002] ELR 681 at, 21–24, 37–38. If the claim is for economic loss alone, then the action is not one of personal injury.

7.280 In *Adams (FC) v Bracknell Forest Borough Council*,[450] the House of Lords held that an action for negligence against a local education authority for failing to identify and ameliorate a congenital defect which could have been mitigated by early diagnosis and appropriate treatment or educational provision, with resulting detriment to the claimant's level of educational attainment and employability, was a claim for personal injury. The inability to read and write (in the case of dyslexia) would be treated as an untreated injury originally proceeding from other causes. As such, section 11 of the Limitation Act 1980 will apply for limitation purposes.

7.281 By virtue of section 11(4) of the Limitation Act 1980, the general rule is that an action for negligence in respect of personal injuries should not be brought after the expiration of three years from the date on which the cause of action accrued or (if later) the date of knowledge of the person injured. Note that following the decision of the House of Lords in *A v Hoare and other appeals*,[451] that section will apply to an action for intentional trespass, for example in the context of allegations of sexual abuse. Section 14 elaborates further on the definition of the date of knowledge. Section 28(1) and (6) of the Limitation Act 1980 provides that if a cause of action accrued while a person was under a disability then the action might be brought within three years from the date when he ceased to be under a disability. The cause of action accrues when the damage is first suffered.[452] Accordingly, it is likely, in the education context, to accrue while the potential claimants are under a disability.

7.282 It is possible that the claimants in a personal injury case will contend that time started to run from the date of knowledge and that this is later than the date of injury, applying the tests in section 14 of the Limitation Act 1980. Under section 14, the date of knowledge is when the claimant first had knowledge of the following facts:

(a) that the injury in question was significant;[453]

(b) that the injury was attributable in whole or in part to the act or omission which is alleged to constitute negligence, nuisance or breach of duty;

(c) the identity of the defendant;

(d) if it is alleged that the act or omission was that of a person other than the defendant, the identity of that person and the additional facts supporting the bringing of an action against the defendant.

---

[450] [2004] UKHL 29.
[451] [2008] UKHL 6.
[452] *Cartledge v Jopling* [1963] AC 758.
[453] Section 14(2) provides that an injury is significant if the person whose date of knowledge is in question would reasonably have considered it sufficiently serious to justify his instituting proceedings for damages against a defendant who did not dispute liability and was able to satisfy a judgment

7.283 Knowledge that any acts or omissions did, or did not, as a matter of law involve negligence, nuisance or breach of duty is irrelevant.[454]

7.284 Under section 14(3), a claimant's knowledge includes knowledge which he might reasonably have been expected to acquire from facts observable or ascertainable by him or from facts ascertainable by him with the help of medical or other appropriate expert advice which it is reasonable for him to seek; but a person shall not be fixed with knowledge of a fact ascertainable only with the help of expert advice so long as he has taken all reasonable steps to obtain (and, where appropriate, to act on) that advice.

7.285 As to the question when knowledge of an injury will be significant, in *A v Hoare and other appeals*,[455] Lord Hoffmann said:[456]

> 'Section 14(2) is a test for what counts as a significant injury. The material to which that test applies is generally "subjective" in the sense that it is applied to what the claimant knows of his injury rather than the injury as it actually was. Even then, his knowledge may have to be supplemented with imputed "objective" knowledge under section 14(3). But the test itself is an entirely impersonal standard: not whether the claimant himself would have considered the injury sufficiently serious to justify proceedings but whether he would "reasonably" have done so. You ask what the claimant knew about the injury he had suffered, you add any knowledge about the injury which may be imputed to him under section 14(3) and then you ask whether a reasonable person with that knowledge would have considered the injury sufficiently serious to justify his instituting proceedings for damages against a defendant who did not dispute liability and was able to satisfy a judgment'.

One does not therefore consider whether someone with the claimant's intelligence would have been reasonable if he did not regard the injury as sufficiently serious.

7.286 As to section 14(1)(c) of the Limitation Act 1980, which relates to the identity of the defendants, a claimant will not be fixed with knowledge which he might reasonably have been expected to ascertain with the help of a solicitor if the solicitor acting reasonably on his behalf would not have acquired it.[457] He is, however, equipped with knowledge that a reasonably competent legal representative ought to have acquired.[458]

7.287 The issue of constructive knowledge under section 14(3) was given extensive attention by the House of Lords in *Adams (FC) v Bracknell Forest*

---

[454] Section 14(1) proviso, *Dobbie v Medway Health Authority* [1994] 1 WLR 1234; *Robinson v St Helens MBC* [2002] ELR 681 at para 28; *Meherali v Hampshire County Council* [2003] ELR 338 at para 27.

[455] [2008] UKHL 6.

[456] At para 34.

[457] *Nash v Eli Lilly* [1991] 2 Med LR 169.

[458] *Henderson v Temple Pier Co* [1998] 1 WLR 1540.

Borough Council.[459] The majority of the House of Lords held that the test for constructive knowledge was not subjective.[460] The claimant had to be assumed to be a person who had suffered the injury to which the proceedings related and not some other person, but his particular characteristics or intelligence were irrelevant.[461] So, in that case, if untreated dyslexia would reasonably inhibit a claimant from seeking advice then that is a factor which must be taken into account.

7.288 On the facts of *Adams* there was no evidential foundation to support an assumption that a person with untreated dyslexia was likely to be unable to speak about the matter to his doctor. There was no reason why the normal expectation that a person suffering from a significant injury would be curious about its origins should not also apply to dyslexia.[462] As Lord Scott said 'My own, non-expert, inclination would be to think that a person of average intelligence (Mr Adams was rated as above average intelligence) who knew himself to be illiterate, knew that his illiteracy was at the back of problems such as stress, depression etc and who consulted a doctor about those problems, could reasonably be expected to inform the doctor about the illiteracy. Expert evidence to the contrary could lead to a different conclusion...'.[463]

7.289 *Adams* was applied in *Smith v Hampshire County Council.*[464] In that case, there was expert evidence to the effect that if undiagnosed dyslexics are treated as being of low ability at school, they would be inhibited from challenging the conclusion that they were of low ability unless and until somebody of comparable or higher authority to those educating them informed them that they were suffering from a specific condition which it was possible to do something about. However, the Court of Appeal upheld the Judge's finding that the claimant in that case did not himself suffer from that inhibition. In any event, the claimant had been advised to seek an assessment for dyslexia well before he did so, albeit the advice had not been given by an educational psychologist.

7.290 If the primary limitation period has expired, the question of the exercise of discretion under section 33 of the Limitation Act 1980 arises. The burden is on the claimants to show that it is equitable to disapply the limitation period. In exercising the discretion, section 33(3) directs the courts to have regard to all the circumstances of the case and, in particular, six factors:

---

[459] [2004] UKHL 29.
[460] Baroness Hale took a somewhat different approach. At para 91 she indicated that she did not wish to rule out the possibility that personal characteristics may be relevant to what knowledge can be imputed to a person under s 14(3): a factor or attribute which is connected with the ability of a claimant to discover facts which are relevant to an action should be taken into account but a factor which has no discernible ability effect upon his ability to discover relevant facts should be disregarded.
[461] See especially Lord Hoffmann at paras 45 and 47.
[462] See Lord Hoffmann at paras 50 and 51.
[463] [2004] UKHL 29, para 72.
[464] [2007] EWCA Civ 246.

(a)   the length and the reasons for the delay;

(b)   the extent to which as a result of the delay the evidence adduced, or likely to be adduced, by either the plaintiff or defendant is likely to be less cogent;

(c)   the conduct of the defendants after the cause of action arose, including the extent to which they responded to requests reasonably made by the plaintiff for information or inspection for the purposes of ascertaining facts which were, or might be, relevant to the plaintiff's cause of action against the defendant;

(d)   the duration of the plaintiff's disability arising after the date of the accrual of the cause of action;

(e)   the extent to which the plaintiff has acted promptly once he knew that the act or omission of the defendants might be capable of giving rise to an action for damages;

(f)   the steps taken by the plaintiff to obtain medical, legal or other expert advice and the nature of any such advice he may have received.

All the circumstances of the case include the merits of the case.[465]

7.291   The exercise of the discretion in an educational negligence case was considered by the Court of Appeal in *Robinson v St Helens*.[466] They held that the courts should be slow to exercise their discretion[467] in favour of a plaintiff in the absence of cogent medical evidence showing a serious effect on the claimant's health or enjoyment of life and employability. The likely amount of an award was an important factor, especially if the case would take considerable time to try. In *Adams*, the House of Lords approved those observations.[468] The issue was also considered in *Smith v Hampshire County Council*,[469] in which Longmore LJ underscored the difficulty of having a fair trial in circumstances where LA records have been destroyed in the course of time.[470]

7.292   As to the exercise of discretion in cases of sexual abuse, Lord Brown made the following observations in *A v Hoare*.[471] First, insofar as future claims might be expected to be brought against employers on the basis of vicarious liability rather than systematic negligence in failing to prevent the acts of abuse,

---

[465]   *Davis v Jacobs* [1999] Lloyds Rep Med 72, CA.

[466]   [2002] ELR 681 at para 33.

[467]   For examples of discretions not being exercised in favour of plaintiffs, see *Sullivan v Devon*, His Honour Judge Zucker QC (unreported) 27 September 2002 and *Meherali v Hampshire County Council* [2002] EWHC 2655, [2003] ELR 338, His Honour Judge Zucker QC.

[468]   See Lord Hoffmann at para 55.

[469]   [2007] EWCA Civ 246.

[470]   See especially para 35.

[471]   At paras 85–88.

they would probably involve narrower factual disputes than hitherto which would bear significantly upon the possibility of having a fair trial. Secondly, a substantially greater number of allegations were now likely to be made many years after the event than before. By no means everyone who brought a late claim for damages of sexual abuse could expect the section 33 discretion to be exercised in his favour. He gave by way of example cases in which a fair trial would be simply impossible where a complaint was first made long after the events complained of and the defendant did not have a fair opportunity to investigate it. Thirdly, Lord Brown noted that the test under section 14(2) referred to the justifiability of bringing proceedings against a defendant able to satisfy a judgment. The question could arise how the section 33 discretion should be exercised where suddenly, after many years, the defendant becomes rich. Lord Brown suggested that it would be unfortunate if people felt obliged (often at public expense) to bring proceedings for sexual abuse against indigent defendants simply with a view to their possible future enforcement.

7.293 Discrimination cases under section 114 of the Equality Act 2010 have a limitation period of six months by virtue of section 118 of the Equality Act 2010, with again, a discretion to extend time if the county court considers that it is just and equitable to do so under section 118(1). By section 118(3) the time limit is nine months if the claim relates to the acts of a qualifying institution under section 11 of the Higher Education Act 2004 and a complaint relating to the act is referred under the student complaints scheme before the end of the period of six months starting with the date of the act.

7.294 Where the cause of action is based on alleged breach of a public law duty or power vested in the proposed defendant, is it necessary to move for judicial review before bringing an action for damages? It is submitted that it is not. This was not done in *X v Bedfordshire*[472] or *Phelps v Hillingdon*,[473] and where private law rights are in issue the courts do permit collateral challenge to decisions of public law bodies.[474]

LAW REFORM AND CONCLUSION

7.295 Brief mention should be made of the Law Commission's Paper 'Administrative Redress: Public Bodies and the Citizen', presented to Parliament in 2010, and of the Consultation that preceded it. The Law Commission concluded that, in light of difficulty obtaining quantitative data on the current compensation position of public bodies, it was not practical to proceed with the reform of state liability at the current time.[475] The

---

[472] [1995] 2 AC 633.
[473] [1998] ELR 38 (Garland J), affirmed [2001] 2 AC 619.
[474] See for general discussion of this topic De Smith, Woolf and Jowell *Judicial Review of Administrative Action* (op cit) at paras 5.049–5.056.
[475] Law Com No 322, para 1.6.

Government itself had expressed opposition to the proposals set out by the Law Commission in its consultation paper on the subject in 2008.[476]

7.296 The Law Commission saw the courts as having only a residual role in providing redress for individuals aggrieved by administrative action, in circumstances where internal mechanisms for redress (e g complaints), external non-court avenues of redress (such as tribunals and public inquiries), and ombudsmen were not able to provide adequate redress.

7.297 As to the subject with which this Chapter is concerned, the award of damages by the court, the Law Commission proposed reform in both the public law and private law spheres.

7.298 As to public law, the Law Commission proposed that damages should be available in a claim for judicial review where a claimant could establish 'serious fault'[477] on the part of the defendant public body and where the underlying statutory or common law regime conferred some sort of benefit on the claimant of a similar nature to the harm suffered. The award of damages would remain discretionary.[478]

7.299 As to private law proceedings, the Law Commission recommended that when public bodies are acting in a 'truly public' manner,[479] the claimant should be required to establish the same elements – serious fault and conferral of a benefit – as the proposed action in public law proceedings.[480]

7.300 The Law Commission further proposed that the tort of misfeasance in public office be abolished and that the tort of breach of statutory duty be

---

[476] Law Com No 322, para 1.3.

[477] Conduct would involve serious fault if it fell far below the standard expected in the circumstances, having regard to factors including: (1) the risk or likelihood of harm involved in the conduct of the public body, (2) the seriousness of the harm caused, (3) the knowledge of the public body at the time that the harm occurred that its conduct could cause harm, and whether it knew or should have known about vulnerable potential victims, (4) the cost and practicality of avoiding the harm, (5) the social utility of the activity in which the public body was engaged when it caused the harm; this would include factors such as preventing an undue administrative burden on the public body, (6) the extent and duration of departures from well-established good practice, (7) the extent to which senior administrators had made possible or facilitated the failure or failures in question. Law Com Consultation Paper No 187, paras 4.145–4.146.

[478] Law Com Consultation Paper No 187, para 4.96.

[479] A public body would be acting in a truly public manner if the contested action was conducted in the exercise of a statutory power or the prerogative: Law Com Consultation Paper No 187, paras 4.103 and 4.110–4.131. The provisional test proposed was in the following terms: 'An act or omission of the public body is to be regarded as "truly public" if: (a) the body exercised, or failed to exercise, a special statutory power, or (b) the body breached a special statutory duty, or (c) the body exercised, or failed to exercise, a prerogative power. A "special statutory power" is a power that allows the public body to act in a way not open to private individuals. A "special statutory duty" is a statutory duty placed on the public body that is specific to it and is not placed on private individuals.'

[480] Law Com Consultation Paper No 187, para 4.99.

abolished except in certain contexts eg health and safety.[481] The Law Commission also proposed conferring a discretion on the courts to abandon the usual rules on joint and several liability in the context of truly public cases such that in an appropriate case the court could apportion liability between the public body and any private party that was also at fault.[482]

7.301 The Law Commission's proposals were subject to a range of criticism but the Law Commission's final report, while recognising the force of certain criticisms, maintained that its proposals could be modified to good effect. However, as the Law Commission recognised, there is no real prospect of its proposals being brought forward at this stage.

---

[481] Law Com Consultation Paper No 187, para 4.105.
[482] Law Com Consultation Paper No 187, paras 4.190–4.195.

Chapter 8

UNIVERSITY STUDENTS

INTRODUCTION

8.1 Litigation by students against universities has increased markedly. In broad terms, disputes tend to fall into one of two categories. In the first category, students may be claiming that a decision to refuse a degree, to fail a student or to require him or her to leave the university is in some way legally flawed. The student will often be contending that the institution has misconstrued its own regulations or failed to follow its own procedures or has acted in a way that is procedurally unfair or irrational. The aim of the student in this type of litigation is, generally, to have the university's decision quashed or set aside. To achieve that, the student will, usually, approach the independent complaints scheme and possibly thereafter seek judicial review of the institution's decision. In the second category of cases, the student may be claiming damages. He or she will usually be contending that, in some way, the university has breached the express or implied terms of the contract between them and the university, for example, by failing to provide adequate supervision or teaching. The aim of the student in this type of essentially private law litigation is, generally, to obtain compensation, for example, the fees paid or money wasted in pursuing the course.

8.2 There are two other areas of concern, the first is the extent to which the Human Rights Act 1998 (HRA 1998) applies to the various activities of universities. These claims are usually brought by way of judicial review for either a public law remedy or damages under the HRA 1998. Another area of increasingly frequent litigation concerns access by students to grants or loans from central or local government.

8.3 This Chapter sets out the legal framework of universities and the basis in law of their relationships with their students. The chapter then considers private law claims against universities and judicial review. It then examines the independent student complaints scheme and the role of the Visitor. Next, it addresses the applicability and potential impact of the HRA 1998 to student-university disputes. Finally, the law relating to grants and loans is considered, where, usually, the student will be seeking judicial review of the decision of the relevant local authority (LA) or regulations made by a government department.

THE ORIGINS OF UNIVERSITIES

8.4 Universities in the United Kingdom differ in their legal origin. Formerly, universities and colleges tended to be legal corporations created by royal charter issued under the royal prerogative. One of the consequences of this method of creation is that chartered universities have a Visitor which used to have 'sole and exclusive jurisdiction over the internal arrangements and dealings ... within the institution'.[1] Disputes between students and universities went to the Visitor not the courts, although the courts had a limited supervisory function over the actions of the Visitor. In 2004 this system was replaced by the establishment of the Office of the Independent Adjudicator.[2] A small number of the older institutions were set up by Act of Parliament rather than created by charter.

8.5 The modern institutions of higher education have emerged by a different legal route. Higher education corporations will normally have been incorporated and designated as eligible to receive higher education funding.[3] The institutions will be carried on in accordance with instruments and articles of government.[4] Some institutions are in fact companies (usually companies limited by guarantee). These, too, may be designated as eligible to receive higher education funding and their articles of association must incorporate instruments and articles of government.[5] The Privy Council may by order specify that an institution of higher education may award degrees, diplomas or certificates.[6] Higher education corporations may, in certain circumstances, be able to incorporate the word 'university' in their title provided that the consent of the Privy Council is obtained.[7] Such higher education corporations are, therefore, ordinary statutory corporations with legal personality and the ability to enter into contracts within their powers.[8] It is disputes involving these higher education corporations that tend to come directly before the courts.

8.6 In June 2011, the government published a white paper[9] which proposed significant changes to higher education, including changes to regulation and funding of universities and the encouragement of private market in higher education through increasing the number of private degree-awarding institutions. However, the promised Higher Education Bill was not brought forward in the Queen's Speech in 2012, and is unlikely to be published before 2015.

---

[1] *Thomson v University of London* (1864) 33 LJ (Ch) 625 at 634.
[2] See at para **8.37** and following below.
[3] Education Reform Act 1988, ss 121, 124 and 129.
[4] Education Reform Act 1988, ss 124A and 129A.
[5] Education Reform Act 1988, ss 129 and 129B.
[6] Further and Higher Education Act 1992, s 76.
[7] Further and Higher Education Act 1992, at s 77.
[8] See *Clark v University of Lincolnshire and Humberside* [2000] 1 WLR 1988 at para 11.
[9] 'Students at the Heart of the System' (Cm 8122).

THE NATURE OF THE STUDENT-UNIVERSITY RELATIONSHIP

8.7 The relationship between a student and the university is a hybrid one, governed partly by contract and partly by the principles of public law enforceable by way of judicial review. First, the arrangements between a student and a university will usually involve the creation of a contract between them.[10] The precise terms of the contract may be difficult to identify. The student may have signed a document, often on matriculation, indicating that the university's statutes and regulations form part of the terms of the contract. In any event, an obligation to comply with the statutes and regulations will usually be implied so far as the student and the university are concerned. In addition, the university prospectus or handbook may, in certain circumstances, be incorporated and form part of the contract.

8.8 On one occasion, the courts held that the prospectus outlining the syllabus for a course could form part of the contract between the student and the university.[11] Consequently, there could, in principle, be a breach of contract if the course failed to correspond to the syllabus. The courts indicated, however, that it would, in practice, be difficult to establish such a breach as the institution had to decide how to teach the course and, so long as the course was taught, the fact that the emphasis differed from that which the student expected would not usually amount to a breach of contract.[12] The courts have also held that the contract between the student and the university includes an obligation to provide proper tuition and may include an implied term under which the university warrants that it has adequate staff and facilities to provide tuition.[13]

8.9 There may even be an earlier and different contract made before the student actually enrols. The Court of Appeal has held that a person who had been made an unconditional offer of a place at a polytechnic and had accepted that place, had a contract under which the polytechnic was obliged to enrol the student on his arrival at the institution. There was, therefore, a breach of contract when the polytechnic subsequently refused to honour the offer.[14]

8.10 A university is also a public body amenable in principle to judicial review. Students may be seeking to have a decision of the institution quashed or set aside because of misinterpretation by the institution of its regulations, or because of a procedural error or some other failure to act in accordance with one of the recognised principles of public law. These issues are capable of being dealt with by way of judicial review, as long as other remedies, such as approaching the independent student complaints scheme, have been exhausted or do not in the circumstances provide an adequate alternative remedy. There

---

[10] [2000] 1 WLR 1988 at para 12; *Herring v Templeman* [1973] 3 All ER 569 at 584–585.
[11] *D'Mello v Loughborough College of Technology* (1970) *The Times*, 17 June.
[12] *D'Mello v Loughborough College of Technology* (1970) *The Times*, 17 June.
[13] *Sammy v Birbeck College* (1964) *The Times*, 3 November, although in this case the court did not find that the obligation was breached.
[14] *Moran v University College, Salford (No 2)* [1994] ELR 187.

have been a number of cases where students have been permitted to bring claims for judicial review[15] and the courts have, on occasions, quashed the decisions of university bodies, such as a board of examiners and an academic board, because they had failed to adhere to their own regulations.[16]

8.11   The procedure for judicial review is fundamentally different from that used in ordinary private law disputes. There are a number of practical advantages, particularly from the institution's point of view, in dealing with student grievances by way of judicial review rather than a contract claim. First, the student needs permission to proceed with the claim for judicial review and must demonstrate an arguable case that the institution has made some error of law. Frequently cases fail at this hurdle. Secondly, claims for judicial review must be brought promptly and in any event within three months of the date when the grounds of challenge first arose (usually the date of the contested decision). Thirdly, if permission is granted and the matter goes to a full court hearing, evidence is usually by way of witness statements only. Cross-examination is not usually ordered in judicial review cases. In contractual claims, by contrast, there will be a series of stages, involving disclosure of documents held by the university or its individual employees and the full hearing with witnesses giving evidence and being cross-examined. A contract action, therefore, is likely to involve greater cost and greater disruption than a judicial review claim.

8.12   The courts draw a distinction between contractual claims and public law claims capable of being pursued by judicial review; contractual claims are seen as falling outside the ambit of judicial review.[17] The question inevitably arose whether a student who was challenging a decision claiming that it involved a breach of the university rules could only bring a claim for judicial review, or, alternatively, if a contractual claim could be brought, whether judicial review was an available remedy.[18] The Court of Appeal recognised that, in effect, the student-university relationship is a hybrid one. Claims that the university has acted in breach of its own regulations can, and usually should, be brought by way of judicial review. However, the rules still form part of the contract between the student and the university and claims can be brought for breach of contract and do not have to be brought by way of judicial review.[19] The main practical difference is that there is a far longer time-limit (six years) for bringing a contract claim (as compared with an obligation to act promptly and in any event within three months in a judicial review claim). The Court of Appeal held, however, that courts could ensure that the method of proceeding did not involve an abuse of process. If a claim which would normally be brought by

---

[15]   See, e g *R v Liverpool John Moores University ex parte Hayes* [1998] ELR 261; *R v University of the West of England ex parte M* [2001] ELR 77.

[16]   *R v Board of Governors of Sheffield Hallam University ex parte R* [1995] ELR 267; *R v Manchester Metropolitan University ex parte Nolan* [1994] ELR 380.

[17]   This is still true of claims by academic staff alleging a breach of the contract of employment: see *R (on the application of Evans) v University of Cambridge* [2003] ELR 8.

[18]   *Clark v University of Lincolnshire and Humberside* [2000] 1 WLR 1988.

[19]   *Clark v University of Lincolnshire and Humberside* [2000] 1 WLR 1988, at paras 12–13 and 32.

way of judicial review were brought by way of a contract claim, and if there were unjustified delay in bringing proceedings (even if they were brought within the six-year time-limit for private law contractual claims), the courts could strike out the claim as an abuse of process.[20]

CONTRACT CLAIMS

8.13 As indicated at para **8.7** above, there will usually be some sort of 'contract of matriculation' between the student and the university. The precise terms of this contract will vary. Some universities may require students to sign a form on matriculation and that form may state that the student agrees to be bound by the terms of the university's regulations. It may be that nothing is expressly agreed and in those circumstances it is likely that a contract based on the prospectus or student handbook or other similar document issued to students at, or prior to enrolment, will form the basis of the contract. It may be that such documents, together with the university regulations, comprise the entire contract.

Specific obligations

8.14 The contract may create specific obligations on the university, for example requiring the appointment of a supervisor or enabling students (particularly post-graduate students) to see their supervisor once a fortnight. From time to time, universities do fail to comply with these obligations and claims for damages arise where a student has failed a course and seeks to contend that the failure was caused by the failure to provide the agreed level of supervision. Where this did not happen, a student could allege that there had been a breach of a specific provision in the contract or that the university had not acted with reasonable skill.[21] University staff are well advised to keep some documentary record of when supervisions were held, or why they were cancelled (eg if at the request of the student and what reason was given). Challenges to purely academic decisions, such as what mark or level of degree to award or whether to require a student to repeat a year or withdraw from a course due to poor academic performance, are not matters upon which the courts will adjudicate and any claim for breach of contract which challenges such academic judgment will be struck out.[22]

---

[20] *Clark v University of Lincolnshire and Humberside* [2000] 1 WLR 1988, at paras 14–18 and 34–36. See also *Moroney v Anglo-European College of Chiropractic* [2008] EWHC 2633 (QB), [2009] ELR 111 at paras 32–36.

[21] In *Haddad v The University of Bradford* [2011] EWCA Civ 821, Elias LJ suggested at paragraph 4 that insufficient supervision or inadequate provision of material would arguably not be justiciable. However, the case was a renewed permission application and the matter was not argued, so the weight to be afforded to this dictum is limited.

[22] See *Clark v University of Lincolnshire and Humberside* [2000] 1 WLR 1988 at paras 6–8; *Van Mallaert v Oxford University* [2006] EWHC 1565 (QB), [2006] ELR 617 at para 23; *Moroney v Anglo-European College of Chiropractic* [2008] EWHC 2633 (QB), [2009] ELR 111 at paras 19 and 26.

Implied obligations

8.15   The courts may also hold that there are implied terms in the contract. The courts have held that there may be an implied term in the contract to provide proper tuition,[23] and have implied a term that the university is to exercise reasonable skill and care in the provision of tuition.[24] It is, however, likely to be very difficult in practice for a student to establish a failure to demonstrate reasonable skill. It is not impossible, however, to imagine cases where a member of staff was consistently absent or consistently failed to give lectures or mark work and that may amount to a failure to provide appropriate tuition. It is easier to imagine such cases arising in relation to postgraduate studies. The Court of Appeal has held that it is unlikely that a power such as the power to require a student to withdraw from a course would be implied rather than explicit within the university regulations.[25]

8.16   Another potential source of litigation is where a decision has been made not to uphold an offer to a student to enrol at the university or a decision not to offer a particular course of study. A university which accepts a person for a course may find that that constitutes a contract under which the university is obliged to enrol that student or to offer that course. Failure to enrol the student or to offer that course (for whatever reason) may amount to a breach of contract. This arose in the *Moran* case[26] discussed above where an offer of an unconditional place was made in error and accepted by the student, who did not know that an error had been made. The subsequent refusal to honour the offer of a place amounted to a breach of contract.

Loss or damage

8.17   Even if a student can show a breach of a term, he or she will still have to establish that the breach caused loss or damage. If the student failed to meet the requisite standards for a degree, and it was said that that was due to the university's failure to provide proper tuition or supervision, the student would face very great difficulty in establishing that he or she would have obtained the degree if there had been proper tuition. A student may possibly be able to claim that he or she was not provided with the supervision or course contracted for and therefore should be able to recover lost fees.

---

[23]   See para **8.8** above.

[24]   *Abramova v Oxford Institute of Legal Practice* [2011] EWHC 613 (QB) at para 9, based on s 13 of the Supply of Goods and Service Act 1982. The court held at paras 59–61 that the approach to a claim brought in contract in reliance upon s 13 of the 1982 Act is for practical purposes the same as for one brought in negligence – the term will be satisfied where university or its lecturers have exercised 'the ordinary skill of an ordinary competent man exercising that particular art'.

[25]   *Oxford Brookes University v McKoy* [2009] EWCA Civ 1561 at para 35 per Sir David Keene.

[26]   See [1994] ELR 187.

JUDICIAL REVIEW CASES

8.18 In broad terms, the role of the court in judicial review cases is supervisory. Its task is to ensure that the university has correctly interpreted the relevant regulations, has acted in accordance with those regulations and has acted in accordance with the usual principles of public law that any public body must observe. These principles include ensuring that the public body has regard to all relevant considerations and has acted in accordance with the procedural requirements contained in its own rules and those laid down by the general law on procedural fairness and natural justice. Provided that the relevant university body has properly directed itself as to the relevant rules, and has observed the relevant procedures, the actual decision on the merits is for the university body, not the courts, and the courts will not review the merits of the decision.

8.19 The types of decisions taken by university bodies vary enormously and a great many may be subject to judicial review.[27] Among the decisions taken are the following three broad categories. First, the university will take academic decisions, for example deciding whether a student should pass or fail or be given a degree or not. Secondly, there will be cases involving academic discipline. Here, a student may be accused of cheating in an examination or other form of assessment. Thirdly, there may be instances of discipline unconnected with any academic matter, such as harassing another student or damaging university property.

8.20 The starting point for the university in each case is to consider the university regulations to determine the scope of the university's powers and to determine which university body has power to deal with a particular matter and what procedures it must follow. Thus, in one case, the question arose whether or not a university was entitled, on a proper construction of its rules, to exclude a student from a course in social work where she was unable to obtain a social work placement.[28] The court construed the relevant regulations in order to 'give the words a sensible meaning in their context' and held that the university had the power to remove the student from the course.[29]

8.21 More usually, the claim is that the university has failed to act in accordance with its own regulations, rather than that it does not have the power to act. Failure to do so is a recognised ground of judicial review and is likely to lead to the setting aside or quashing of a decision not reached in accordance with the regulations. On one occasion, for example, a university's rules provided that a student could not be expelled for academic reasons relating to poor

---

[27] For example, in *R (Odusami) v University of East London* [2011] EWHC 1256 (Admin), a student challenged the decision of the university's board of governors to annul the results of elections held in March 2010 for the major offices of the university's students' union, including the office of president. The matter was justiciable, but the challenge was not successful.

[28] *R v University of West of England ex parte M* [2001] ELR 77.

[29] *R v University of West of England ex parte M* [2001] ELR 77, at paras 22–31.

performance unless 'adequate prior warning and advice' had been given. No warning had been given and, consequently, the decision to expel was unlawful and was quashed.[30]

8.22 Many challenges are based on breaches of procedure. The university rules will often lay down precise procedures for certain types of decision. It is common, for example, for rules to specify that disciplinary matters will be dealt with by a particular committee, that the student will be given notice in advance of the allegations and that at the hearing before the committee the university representative will put forward the university's case and call any relevant witnesses. The student will then put forward his or her case and call any witnesses. The rules will often provide that the student may be accompanied by a friend or student union representative. In addition to following its own detailed rules, universities will also need to observe the general principles of procedural fairness and natural justice to ensure that each student has a fair hearing. The precise content of those rules will differ depending on the type of decision in issue, and the particular facts of the case.[31]

Challenges to academic decisions

8.23 In a purely academic decision, a board of examiners will be deciding whether to pass a student or grant or refuse a degree, or a particular class of degree. Matters of purely academic assessment, such as whether a mark is right or wrong, or outside the range of academic convention, are not matters upon which the courts will adjudicate.[32] Similarly, the choice of examiners will not normally be a matter suitable for judicial review.[33] Nor will the courts grant mandatory orders requiring the university to award a degree or a particular class of degree.[34]

8.24 The procedural rules by which such matters are considered do, however, give rise to justiciable issues and, if the rules are not observed, then the decision of the examiners may be quashed and the matter remitted to them for reconsideration in accordance with the correct procedures.[35] The courts will normally require the board to have regard to any relevant considerations,

---

[30] *R v Sheffield Hallam University ex parte R* [1995] ELR 267.
[31] See generally *R v Chelsea College of Art and Design ex parte Nash* [2000] ELR 686 and *R (Leung) v Imperial College of Science, Technology and Medicine* [2002] ELR 653. See also Lewis 'Procedural Fairness and University Students: England and Canada Compared' [1985] *Dalhousie Law Review* 313.
[32] See *Clark v University of Lincolnshire and Humberside* [2000] 1 WLR 1988 at paras 6–8; *R v University of Cambridge ex parte Persaud* [2001] ELR 64.
[33] *R v Cranfield University ex parte Bashir* [1999] ELR 317; *R v Committee of the Lords of the Judicial Committee of the Privy Council acting for the Visitor of the University of London ex parte Vijayatunga* [1990] 2 QB 444 at 459.
[34] See dicta in *R v Liverpool John Moores University ex parte Hayes* [1998] ELR 261 at 279C–E.
[35] As was done in *Clark v University of Lincolnshire and Humberside* [2000] 1 WLR 1988 at para 9 (there the claim was framed in contract but could, and preferably should, have been brought by way of a claim for judicial review of the decision of the academic board).

including mitigation,[36] although the weight to be attached to such mitigating factors is a matter for the board. Most universities' rules do provide for consideration of mitigating circumstances, usually through the student putting forward written or documentary evidence (ie a written mitigation statement or medical certificates) so that the board can consider whether the student has underperformed and should be awarded a higher mark.

8.25 University rules do not, generally, permit the student to attend an examiners' meeting and make oral representations. The courts do not generally consider that the rules of natural justice or procedural fairness require a student to have an oral hearing in such circumstances and the university regulations may permit the exclusion of students from examiners' meetings, giving them an opportunity to make their representations on mitigation in writing.[37]

8.26 The court has emphasised that procedural fairness in this context generally requires the decision-maker to have regard to any representations that the student wishes to make unless, exceptionally, the material relied upon is plainly irrelevant or the representations are made for an improper purpose, and even then it is usually prudent to consider the representations.[38] Material is not generally to be excluded because of concerns over confidentiality; it may be possible in some cases to anonymise allegations, but where the submissions that a student wishes to make necessarily involve identifying an individual (as in a case where a student claimed harassment by her tutor had affected her academic performance), concerns over confidentiality could not justify refusing to allow the material to be placed before the examiners.[39] Further, the student should normally be informed of any additional material that the university is proposing to put before the relevant committee.[40]

Challenges to decisions concerning discipline

8.27 University regulations commonly require that a person be notified of an allegation of plagiarism or cheating as soon as the possibility of such a charge is known and for there to be a hearing before a particular type of body (such as a disciplinary panel) with the student knowing what the allegation is and having the opportunity to make representations. A right to know the charge, and have the opportunity of commenting upon it will usually be required by the common law rules of natural justice, even if the regulations are silent on

---

[36] *R v Aston University Senate ex parte Roffey* [1969] 2 QB 538 at 554. See also *R (Burgess) v South Bank University* [2001] ELR 300; university appeal committee acted unfairly in rejecting appeal where mitigating material had not been considered by the examiners through no fault of the student.

[37] See, eg *Brighton Corporation v Parry* (1972) LGR 576 and see dictum of Sedley J in *R v Manchester Metropolitan University ex parte Nolan* [1994] ELR 380 at 393C–393E.

[38] *R v Chelsea College ex parte Nash* [2000] ELR 686.

[39] *R v Chelsea College ex parte Nash* [2000] ELR 686.

[40] *R v Chelsea College ex parte Nash* [2000] ELR 686. The courts do not generally require the disclosure of the material forming the basis of the academic judgment itself, such as academic assessments: see *R v University of Cambridge ex parte Persaud* [2001] ELR 64.

this point. There have been cases where members of the academic staff have decided not to notify the student but to hold an informal oral examination to probe into the facts and then report the outcome to the board of examiners, or simply for the board to discuss the matter, without the student ever being given the chance to respond into the allegations. Such a departure from the rules would almost inevitably lead to the decision of the board of examiners being quashed.

8.28 Cases involving academic discipline will not simply involve matters of purely academic assessment. There will usually be factual questions to determine, such as whether or not a student cheated in an examination. Such matters will often involve questions as to the credibility of the student and any witnesses. Such cases may, therefore, require some form of oral hearing where the relevant university officers and the student each have the opportunity of putting forward their own case and calling and questioning their own and the other's witnesses. This may be done before the body that will ultimately take the decision. It may be that the rules will provide for an oral hearing before a disciplinary panel which will report to the board of examiners or other body. In either case, it is crucial that an adequate opportunity is given to the student to put forward his or her case before the fact-finding body.[41] This will involve the student being given adequate notice in advance of the substance of the allegations made against the student and being provided with relevant documentation in sufficient time to enable the student to be able to respond to that material at the hearing. Claims that material is confidential are unlikely to justify non-disclosure to the student of material that the university officers intend to place before the disciplinary panel.[42]

8.29 If the hearing takes place before a disciplinary panel or investigative body which is different from the ultimate decision-making body, then it is important that the report or minutes of the disciplinary panel or investigative body sets out its findings of fact fully and also records all relevant material, including, for example, mitigating factors advanced on behalf of the student. If it does not do this, then the ultimate decision-making body will not be in possession of all the relevant facts when it comes to make its final judgment and the body may fail to have regard to relevant considerations, or there may be a failure to follow a fair procedure which may lead to the final decision being quashed, as happened in *ex parte Nolan*.[43] If the charges are upheld, the

---

[41]   See *ex parte Nolan* [1994] ELR 380. In *Ceylon University v Fernando* [1960] 1 WLR 233, the Privy Council ruled that fairness required a fair opportunity for the student in that case to challenge the evidence put forward by the university but, absent a request to cross-examine, failure to inform the student that he was entitled to cross-examine was not a breach of natural justice. It is doubtful whether that ruling correctly reflects the current law relating to natural justice and the decision was subject to powerful criticism by Professor de Smith in (1960) 23 MLR 428. Usually, however, university rules provide expressly for the right to question witnesses.

[42]   See *R v Chelsea College of Art and Design ex parte Nash* [2000] ELR 686.

[43]   [1994] ELR 380.

decision on penalty is one for the university authorities and the courts will not generally intervene unless the penalty is manifestly unreasonable.[44]

8.30 Disciplinary cases unconnected with academic matters will also be likely to attract some sort of oral hearing, either because the university regulations require that, or because a penalty is being imposed and the issues involved raise questions of fact and witness credibility which usually require an oral hearing. Current judicial attitudes towards disciplinary hearings suggest that the rules of procedural fairness require a university to follow a procedure where the student is notified of the allegations in advance, and there is a hearing where the relevant university officers put forward the case against the student and the student has the opportunity to question witnesses called by the university and to call witnesses on his or her own behalf. This type of procedure may not always be easy, particularly in cases involving alleged harassment of another student, but the court has indicated that it is not acceptable for a university to exclude a student from material parts of a disciplinary hearing even when allegedly vulnerable complainants were giving evidence about alleged sexual and other harassment.[45]

8.31 One aspect of the disciplinary procedure has been standardised – the issuing of the final decision. Under the Rules of the Office of the Independent Adjudicator (OIA), with which most higher educational institutions are required to comply, an institution must issue a Completion of Procedures letter to a student promptly after any of its internal complaints procedures have been completed.[46] The Completion of Procedures letter fixes the date on which the student completes the institution's internal complaints procedure and must advise the student of the possibility of and timescale for bringing a complaint to the OIA. The OIA has issued Guidance on what the Completion of Procedures letter should contain:[47]

(a) a summary of the complaint or appeal the student has made to the university;

(b) the title of the regulations/procedures which were applied;

(c) a summary of the issues considered at the final stage of the internal complaints procedures;

(d) the final decision taken by the university;

(e) the reasons for that decision.

---

[44] *R v Cambridge University ex parte Begg* [1999] ELR 404.
[45] *R (Carnell) v Regents Park College* [2008] EWHC 739 (Admin), [2008] ELR 268 at para 16.
[46] OIA Rules (1 February 2012), para 4.3. The Rules are available at http://www.oiahe.org.uk/media/1258/oia-rules.pdf.
[47] OIA *Guidance Note regarding Completion of Procedures Letters* (September 2011), section 2. The Guidance is available at http://www.oiahe.org.uk/media/38488/completion_of_procedures_ letter_ guidance_september_2011.pdf.

8.32 Some universities have created an ombudsman to carry out an investigation of complaints as an alternative to (or additional method of) resolving such matters by a disciplinary hearing. Nevertheless, if disciplinary sanctions are to be imposed, the university must follow its own regulations properly and must ensure that the student receives a fair hearing. The disciplinary committee will, therefore, need to maintain a balance between ensuring that the accused student has the opportunity to challenge the evidence but that any questioning of witnesses (particularly a person alleged to have been the subject of harassment) is limited to relevant matters and does not extend into the intrusive and irrelevant. The disciplinary committee will also have to produce a reasoned decision in a Completion of Procedures letter.

8.33 Universities also have to ensure that the decision-making body is impartial and that there is no danger of bias, that is, no danger that a fair-minded and informed observer would conclude that there was a real possibility that the decision-making body was biased in favour of, or against, one of the parties.[48] If a disciplinary allegation (whether academic or non-academic) involves an allegation arising from some direct and personal conflict with a member of the academic staff, that member ought not to sit on the decision-making body.[49] The better course of action is for that person to stand down. In purely academic decisions, however, the fact that a person has taught or examined a student is obviously not the sort of matter giving rise to a real possibility of bias and does not generally require the member of staff not to sit on the decision-making body.

8.34 There may, however, be instances where there is a degree of personal animosity between a student and a member of staff. Depending on the facts, it is, broadly speaking, unlikely that a court would find that a decision was unlawful if that member of staff sat on the board of examiners that determines whether or not to award the student a pass or a fail.[50] It may even be that it is necessary for the member of staff to sit if he or she is the only person competent to assess a particular subject. There may be instances, however, where the degree of animosity, or the nature of the staff member's involvement with the student, make it wise, even if not legally necessary, for the staff member to stand down. In the context of academic disciplinary decision, the courts have held that the fact that the university officer presenting the case for the university comes from the same faculty as the chairman of the disciplinary panel does not give rise to any risk of the possibility of bias.

---

[48]   See *Porter v Magill* [2002] 2 WLR 37 at para 103.

[49]   *R (Clarke) v Cardiff University* [2009] EWHC 2148 (Admin) (two staff members accused by the claimant of upsetting her before an examination should not have participated in the decision-making of the subsequent Extenuating Circumstances Committee).

[50]   See, e g *R v Liverpool John Moores University ex parte Hayes* [1998] ELR 261 (member of staff alleged to have humiliated a student in public); *R v Cranfield University ex parte Bashir* [1999] ELR 317 (disagreement over what constituted originality in a thesis did not constitute bias).

Bringing a judicial review claim – alternative remedy

8.35 In all cases where a student wishes to challenge the outcome of a disciplinary process, the student must first make a complaint to the independent adjudicator of student complaints – currently the OIA – before bringing judicial review proceedings. It is a key principle of judicial review that, before approaching the court, the claimant must have exhausted all alternative remedies. The courts have held that the OIA complaints system is an effective alternative remedy[51] and, in one instance, refused permission on a fairly strong claim because the claimant failed to take his complaint to the OIA before launching proceedings.[52]

8.36 The OIA does not have jurisdiction over certain types of complaints, including complaints concerning admissions.[53] In *R v University College London ex p Idriss*,[54] Sullivan J expressed grave doubts as to whether a straightforward decision to refuse admission would be susceptible to judicial review. There is, however, no principled reason why a refusal to admit a student which was not in accordance with a university's published procedures or was wholly unreasonable could not be challenged by judicial review. What is clear is that any aspect of the admission decision which is a matter of academic judgment is not judicially reviewable.[55] The courts have also accepted that there is no requirement for universities to give reasons for refusing admission to applicants.[56]

INDEPENDENT ADJUDICATION OF STUDENT COMPLAINTS

8.37 In 2004, the adjudication of student complaints was transformed by the establishment of an independent body corporate to operate a student complaints system.[57] This was achieved through the Higher Education Act 2004 (HEA 2004), which empowers the Secretary of State to designate a

---

51 *R (Carnell) v Regent's Park College* [2008] EWHC 739 (Admin), [2008] ELR 268; *R (Peng Hu Shi) v King's College London* [2008] EWHC 857 (Admin), [2008] ELR 414.
52 In *Carnell*, the claim concerned alleged procedural unfairness in disciplinary proceedings in which the claimant was accused of harassment of other students, including sexual harassment, and both the judge who considered the claim on the papers and the judge who heard the oral application for permission had misgivings about the exclusion of the claimant from material parts of the proceedings before the disciplinary committee. Despite this, and despite the fact that the OIA had, by the time the oral application was considered, refused jurisdiction over the claimant's complaint, the court refused permission, holding that an alternative remedy had existed when the claim was brought and that the claimant had lost that remedy through his own initial choice to bypass the OIA.
53 OIA Rules (1 February 2012), para 3.1.
54 [1999] EdCR 462.
55 [1999] EdCR 462. See also the cases cited at para **8.23** above.
56 *R v University College London ex p Idriss* [1999] EdCR 462.
57 HEA 2004, s 13.

body corporate as the 'designated operator' of an independent student complaints system in England[58] and empowers the Welsh Assembly to designate in relation to Wales.[59]

8.38   The Office of the Independent Adjudicator (OIA) has been designated in both England and Wales. It is a company limited by guarantee, the members of which are the Association of Heads of University Administration, the Committee of University Chairs, GuildHE, Higher Education Wales, the National Union of Students and Universities UK.[60] The OIA's property and affairs are controlled by a 15 member Board of Directors, which is also responsible for appointing and removing the Independent Adjudicator.[61] The OIA is a registered charity in England and Wales.

8.39   The Independent Adjudicator in not an officer of the company, but acts independently of the Board in operating the complaints scheme.[62] It is the Independent Adjudicator who is responsible for recruiting, appointing, training, managing and removing staff to operate the complaints scheme.[63]

8.40   The OIA is not permitted to require complainants to pay a fee for the operation of the scheme.[64] Instead, the scheme is funded by each HEI being required to pay an annual subscription, based on a published scale.[65] The total subscriptions are not permitted to exceed the amount incurred by the OIA in providing the scheme.[66] The Court of Appeal has held that the organisational and funding structure of the OIA could not lead a fair-minded and informed observer to say that there was a real possibility that either the OIA or the Independent Adjudicator lacked independence from higher educational institutions.[67]

The complaints scheme

8.41   The OIA is required to operate a complaints scheme which meets the requirements set out in the HEA 2004.[68] The scheme must provide that every qualifying complaint made about a qualifying institution is capable of being referred for review by an individual who is independent of the parties and

---

58   HEA 2004, s 13(1).
59   HEA 2004, s 13(2).
60   See the website of the OIA http://www.oiahe.org.uk/about-us.aspx.
61   OIA Rules (1 February 2012), para 10. The Rules are available at http://www.oiahe.org.uk/media/1258/oia-rules.pdf.
62   OIA Rules, para 8.
63   OIA Rules, para 11.8.
64   HEA 2004, s 13 and Sch 2, para 8.
65   OIA Rules, para 12.2.
66   HEA 2004, s 13 and Sch 2, para 9
67   *R (Sandhar) v Officer of the Independent Adjudicator* [2011] EWCA Civ 1614, [2012] ELR 160. See also *Budd v Office of the Independent Adjudicator* [2010] EWHC 1056 (Admin), [2010] ELR 579.
68   HEA 2004, s 14 and Sch 3.

suitable to review the complaint.[69] 'Qualifying institutions' include all types of universities; constituent colleges, schools, halls or other institutions of a university; an institution conducted by a higher education corporation and any designated institution as defined by section 72(3) of the Further and Higher Education Act 1992.[70]

8.42 A 'qualifying complaint' is defined as a complaint about an act or omission of a qualifying institution which is made by a person as a student or former student of that institution or as a student or former student of another institution undertaking a course of study or programme of research leading to an award by a qualifying institution.[71] However, matters of academic judgment are specifically excluded from the ambit of a qualifying complaint.[72] 'Academic judgment' is not defined in the HEA 2004. The OIA describes 'academic judgment' as 'a judgment that is made about a matter where only the opinion of an academic expert will suffice', although the OIA acknowledges that the interpretation of the term will ultimately be for the courts.[73] The OIA will treat a judgment about assessment, a degree classification, fitness to practise, research methodology or course content/outcomes as normally ones of academic judgment. The OIA has advised institutions that the fairness of procedures, the facts of the case, misrepresentation, the manner of communication, bias, an opinion expressed outside the area of an academic's competence, the way evidence is considered and maladministration in relation to these matters are all issues where academic judgment is not involved.

8.43 The HEA 2004 also permits the designated operator to extend the scheme to non-qualifying institutions,[74] such as private degree-awarding bodies. The OIA has extended the complaints scheme, and a non-qualifying institution may apply to the Board of the OIA to join the scheme.[75] A complaint brought by a student from a non-qualifying institution which has joined the scheme would therefore fall within the jurisdiction of the OIA.

8.44 The governing bodies of every qualifying institution are required to comply with any obligation imposed on them by the scheme for reviewing qualifying complaints.[76] The OIA has formulated Rules with which the procedures and regulations of all qualifying institutions must comply. All non-qualifying institutions which join the complaints scheme are also required to adhere to the Rules. The key obligations imposed by the Rules are that the final decision of any internal complaints procedure must be communicated

---

[69] HEA 2004, s 13 and Sch 2, paras 3–4.
[70] HEA 2004, s 11.
[71] HEA 2004, s 12(1).
[72] HEA 2004, s 12(2).
[73] See http://www.oiahe.org.uk/glossary.aspx#academic.
[74] HEA 2004, s 13 and Sch 2, para 10.
[75] OIA Rules, para 8. See also the OIA's 'Protocol Relating to the Admission of Non-Qualifying Institutions to the Scheme', available at http://www.oiahe.org.uk/media/35819/protocol_for_nqis.pdf.
[76] HEA 2004, s 15.

promptly by the issuing of a Completions of Procedures Letter,[77] and that the institution comply with any formal decision of and recommendations made by the OIA.[78]

8.45 The OIA generally requires that the complainant first complete the internal complaints or appeals procedure of the institution, and that any subsequent complaint be made within three months of the issue by the institution of a Completion of Procedures Letter.[79] The OIA will not normally consider a complaint where the substantive events complained about occurred more than three years before it receives the complaint.[80]

8.46 When a complaint is made, the OIA is required to determine, as soon as reasonably practicable, the extent to which the complaint is justified.[81] The OIA has devised a two stage process in dealing with complaints. The first concerns eligibility, and entails a determination as to whether the complaint is a qualifying complaint and the allocation of the complaint to a case handler.[82] The reviewer[83] may also reject the complaint if it is frivolous or vexatious.[84] The second stage concerns the determination of the complaint, and may involve the reviewer asking for further information, allowing the institution to respond to the complaint and allowing the student to comment on the response. The reviewer is not bound by legal rules of evidence, nor by previous decisions of the OIA.[85]

8.47 In determining whether the complaint is justified, paragraph 7.3 of the Rules states that the reviewer may consider whether or not the higher educational institution properly applied its regulations and followed its procedures, and whether or not the decision was reasonable in all the circumstances.[86] The OIA has a broad discretion to be flexible in how it reviews the complaint and in deciding on the form, nature and extent of its investigation in each case.[87] As a matter of general policy, the OIA only asks the question set out in paragraph 7.3 of the Rules, rather than undertaking a full merits review. The Court of Appeal has held that this policy is lawful, so long as the OIA is prepared to make exceptions to the policy in appropriate

---

[77] OIA Rules (1 February 2012), para 4.3. See also para **8.31** above.
[78] OIA Rules, para 7.5.
[79] OIA Rules, rules 4.2–4.3.
[80] OIA Rules, para 4.5.
[81] HEA 2004, s 13 and Sch 2, para 5.
[82] OIA Rules, para 5.3.
[83] 'Reviewer' is defined in the HEA 2004, Sch 2, para 14 as 'the Independent Adjudicator or the Deputy Adjudicator or such other person to whom the review of a complaint has been delegated'.
[84] OIA Rules, para 5.4.
[85] OIA Rules, para 6.6.
[86] OIA Rules, para 7.3.
[87] *R (Maxwell) v Office of the Independent Adjudicator* [2011] EWCA Civ 1236 at para 23(6) per Mummery LJ.

cases and it gives proper consideration to representations by or on behalf of a complainant as to why it should take a different approach in an individual case.[88]

8.48 The Court of Appeal has observed that it is not the function of the OIA to determine the legal rights and obligations of the parties involved, or to conduct a full investigation into the underlying facts.[89] Those are matters for judicial processes in the ordinary courts and tribunals, access to which is not affected by the operations of the OIA. Accordingly, even though the OIA can consider complaints concerning sex, race or disability discrimination, the OIA will generally not make a finding that a university has discriminated against a student.[90] Instead, the reviewer will refer to the law and guidance on discrimination to form an opinion as to good practice and to decide whether the university has acted fairly. Students who bring a complaint to the OIA about sex, race or disability discrimination are allowed an additional three months over the usual period within which to institute proceedings in the County Court,[91] but must be mindful of the fact that the time limit starts running when the original incident occurred and not from the time of the OIA's determination.

8.49 The OIA's determination is normally based on a review of documentation or other information. The OIA Rules provide that the reviewer will not hold an oral hearing unless it is considered necessary to do so.[92] If the case-handler considers that a hearing might be necessary or a student requests a hearing, the complaint will be referred to the Deputy Adjudicator for consideration. The Court of Appeal has warned against the 'judicialisation' of the OIA process, remarking that it would not be in the interests of students generally if the OIA were to perform the same fact-finding functions and make the same decisions on liability as the ordinary courts and tribunals.[93]

8.50 Where a complaint is found to be justified, either in whole or in part, the OIA aims to put the student in the position he/she would have been had the act or omission by the higher educational institution (HEI) not occurred. The OIA may make recommendations to the HEI, including:[94]

---

[88]   *R (Siborurema) v Office of the Independent Adjudicator* [2007] EWCA Civ 1365, [2008] ELR 209 at para 76 per Richards LJ. It is notable that later decisions have moved away from using the phrase 'full merits review' as though this marked a fixed threshold in the OIA's investigative process. Instead, the Court of Appeal has emphasised that the OIA will make a continuous assessment of whether any more information is needed in order to make a decision on a particular complaint: see *R (Sandhar) v Officer of the Independent Adjudicator* [2011] EWCA Civ 1614, [2012] ELR 160 at para 39.

[89]   *Siborurema*, paras 69–70 per Moore-Bick LJ.

[90]   This approach was sanctioned by the Court of Appeal in *R (Maxwell) v Office of the Independent Adjudicator for Higher Education* [2011] EWCA Civ 1236, [2012] PTSR 884.

[91]   Equality Act 2010, s 118(2)–(3) provides for a time limit of nine months (the general time limit being six months).

[92]   OIA Rules, para 6.2.

[93]   *R (Maxwell) v Office of the Independent Adjudicator* [2011] EWCA Civ 1236 at para 37 per Mummery LJ.

[94]   OIA Rules, para 7.4.

(a) that the complaint should be referred back to the HEI for a fresh determination because its internal procedures have not been properly followed in a material way;

(b) that the complaint would be better considered in another forum;

(c) that compensation should be paid to the complainant, including, at the reviewer's discretion, an amount for inconvenience and distress;

(d) that the HEI should take a course of action that the reviewer considers to be fair in the circumstances;

(e) that the HEI should change the way it handles complaints;

(f) that the HEI should change its internal procedures or regulations.

8.51 The HEI is required to comply with the OIA's recommendation[95] and must, if requested, report to the reviewer on compliance.[96] Non-compliance is considered to be a serious matter which will be reported by the Independent Adjudicator to the OIA Board, which will publish any non-compliance in its Annual Report. The OIA's decision is not binding on the student, and the student may pursue any other available remedy. Decisions of the OIA are subject to judicial review, which is discussed in more detail below.

Judicial review of the OIA's decisions

8.52 In *R (Siborurema) v Office of the Independent Adjudicator,*[97] the Court of Appeal considered whether the OIA was amendable to judicial review. The Independent Adjudicator had, in evidence to the court, stated that the efforts of the OIA to serve students and HEIs cheaply and efficiently 'would be hindered significantly if decisions made under the Scheme were to be subject to judicial review'.[98] That was rejected by the Court of Appeal, which had no difficulty in concluding that the statutory basis of the OIA and the functions it performs meant it was amenable to judicial review.[99] The court also found that the aspiration to be an informal substitute for court proceedings was not inconsistent with the presence of supervision by way of judicial review.[100]

8.53 Accordingly, although the HEA 2004 leaves OIA with a broad discretion, its decisions may be challenged where there have been breaches of the rules of natural justice, by way of bias or relevant procedural injustice, or where there has been such scant or inappropriate consideration of a complaint

---

[95]   HEA 2004, s 15(1).
[96]   OIA Rules, para 7.6.
[97]   [2007] EWCA Civ 1365, [2008] ELR 209.
[98]   [2007] EWCA Civ 1365, [2008] ELR 209 at para 18.
[99]   [2007] EWCA Civ 1365, [2008] ELR 209 at para 49 per Pill LJ, para 69 per Moore Bick LJ and para 73 per Richards LJ.
[100] [2007] EWCA Civ 1365, [2008] ELR 209 at para 50 per Pill LJ and para 74 per Richards LJ.

that what had occurred could not fairly be described as a review.[101] The courts have indicated that an appropriate degree of deference to the expertise of the OIA in handling complaints should be shown. The OIA is expected to follow rational and fair procedures and to give adequate reasons for its decisions and recommendations.[102] The reasons must deal adequately with the principal issues and, where a decision-letter raises an issue, it must give reasons for the conclusion reached on that issue.[103] If the reasoning is seriously inadequate, the court may quash the decision and remit it to the OIA for re-determination.[104] However, a 'degree of benevolence' will be afforded to the assessment of the way in which the decision letter is expressed.[105]

8.54 The Court of Appeal in *Siborurema* also considered the question of whether the OIA was required by the HEA 2004 to conduct a full merits review, an 'enquiry de novo', into qualifying complaints. The court held unanimously that, although the OIA has the power to conduct its own investigation into the facts underlying the complaint and to undertake a full merits review, there is no requirement in either the HEA 2004 or the OIA Rules for the reviewer to do so in every case.[106] The High Court held, without much analysis, that this is Article 6 compliant.[107]

8.55 Later decisions have attempted to move away from the dichotomy between a 'review' and a 'full merits review'.[108] Instead, the courts have sought to characterise the OIA's investigative process as a continuum, stating that the OIA performs its task properly if it continues its investigation until it is confident it has all the material necessary to make a decision in the individual complaint.[109] This approach overlooks the core of the reasoning in *Siborurema* and *Maxwell*: there is a significant difference of focus and therefore of analysis between the OIA investigating whether the HEI properly applied its procedures and regulations and acted reasonably (ie a 'review') and the OIA investigating afresh the student's underlying complaint in order to substitute its view for that of the university (ie a 'full merit review').

---

[101] [2007] EWCA Civ 1365, [2008] ELR 209 at para 55.

[102] [2007] EWCA Civ 1365, [2008] ELR 209 at para 56. See also *R (Maxwell) v Office of the Independent Adjudicator* [2011] EWCA Civ 1236 at para 23(7).

[103] *R (Cardao-Pito) v Office of the Independent Adjudicator* [2012] EWHC 203 (Admin), [2012] ELR 231 at paras 26 and 29.

[104] As happened in *Cardao-Pito*.

[105] *R (Carnell) v Regent's Park College* [2008] EWHC 739 (Admin), [2008] ELR 268.

[106] *R (Siborurema) v Office of the Independent Adjudicator* [2007] EWCA Civ 1365, [2008] ELR 209 at para 79 per Richards LJ; *R (Arratoon) v Office of the Independent Adjudicator* [2008] EWHC 3125 (Admin), [2009] ELR 186 at paras 69 and 82.

[107] *R (Cardao-Pito) v Office of the Independent Adjudicator* [2012] EWHC 203 (Admin), [2012] ELR 231 at para 99.

[108] *Budd v Office of the Independent Adjudicator* [2010] EWHC 1056 (Admin), [2010] ELR 579 at para 73, endorsed by the Longmore LJ in *R (Sandhar) v Officer of the Independent Adjudicator* [2011] EWCA Civ 1614, [2012] ELR 160 at para 39.

[109] *Budd v Office of the Independent Adjudicator* [2010] EWHC 1056 (Admin), [2010] ELR 579 at para 73, endorsed by the Longmore LJ in *R (Sandhar) v Officer of the Independent Adjudicator* [2011] EWCA Civ 1614, [2012] ELR 160 at para 39.

Organisational requirements imposed on the designated operator

8.56 The OIA, as the designated operator, may not make any changes to a provision of the complaints scheme unless it has first consulted interested parties about the proposed change and notified the Secretary of State or the Assembly of the proposed change.[110] 'Interested party' is not defined in the HEA 2004, but may include the Secretary of State, all qualifying institutions and those non-qualifying institutions which have joined the scheme, and the National Union of Students.

8.57 The OIA is required to produce an annual report on the scheme and its operation,[111] and to publish the report as it sees fit. The annual report must include information about:[112]

(a)   complaints referred under the scheme;

(b)   the decisions and recommendations made by reviewers;

(c)   the extent to which recommendations made by reviewers have been followed; and

(d)   the way in which the operator has used the fees (if any) paid in connection with the scheme.

Should the Secretary of State or the Assembly require any information about the OIA, the complaints scheme or its operation, then the OIA is required to provide that information.

THE UNIVERSITY VISITOR

8.58 Universities created by royal charter and have a university Visitor. The charter will name the Visitor or, if no person is named as the Visitor, the Queen is the Visitor and she usually acts through the Lord Chancellor. University colleges established by benefactors[113] also have a Visitor, which may be the founder's kin or nominee or may be the Crown.[114] The Visitor's jurisdiction does not exist in respect of universities created by statute or universities which are designated higher education corporations entitled to use the word 'university' in their title.

8.59 The basis for the visitatorial jurisdiction lies in the confluence of charity and property law in the 1300s. The jurisdiction is incidental to the creation of an eleemosynary charitable corporation (ie a corporation founded for the

---

[110]   HEA 2004, s 14 and Sch 3, para 4.

[111]   HEA 2004, s 14 and Sch 3, para 6(1).

[112]   HEA 2004, s 14 and Sch 3, para 6(2).

[113]   This includes the colleges of Oxford and Cambridge which, unlike the universities themselves, are eleemosynary corporations.

[114]   *Green v Rutherford* (1750) 27 ER 1144 at 1149.

purpose of distributing a founder's bounty),[115] which includes eleemosynary corporations founded to promote and support learning. The founder of an eleemosynary corporation is entitled to reserve to himself or to the Visitor the exclusive right to adjudicate upon the internal laws of the foundation that he has established. This supervision includes ensuring that the statutes of the foundation are properly interpreted, applied and observed. Thus, where a university or college is established by royal charter, the Sovereign, as founder, is entitled to appoint a Visitor with exclusive power to determine the way in which the internal laws of the university or college are to be interpreted and applied.

8.60 The scope of the Visitor's jurisdiction in relation to universities and colleges was, therefore, wide-ranging. It was also powerful, as the exclusivity of the Visitor's jurisdiction was held to oust the jurisdiction of the court, even if the dispute could be characterised as one involving public law, contract or tort.[116]

8.61 The visitatorial jurisdiction in relation to universities and colleges has, however, been significantly curtailed by statute. Section 20 of the HEA 2004 excludes the Visitor's jurisdiction in relation to all complaints by students,[117] former students[118] or applicants for admission as students.[119] Section 46 excludes the Visitor's jurisdiction in relation to staff disputes concerning:

(a) the appointment or employment of a staff member or the termination of the appointment or employment;[120]

(b) any other dispute between a member of staff and the qualifying institution[121] in respect of which proceedings could be brought before any court or tribunal;[122] and

---

[115] *Thomas v Bradford University* [1987] AC 795 at 827C per Lord Ackner.

[116] *Thomas v Bradford University* [1987] AC 795, especially at 814H–815C and 820F–821F per Lord Griffiths and 826H–828C per Lord Ackner. See also *Labinjo v University of Salford* [2005] ELR 1 at para 32 per Lord Falconer.

[117] HEA 2004, s 20(3)(a). Such complaints now fall within the jurisdiction of the OIA, once the university's internal complaints procedure has been exhausted.

[118] HEA 2004, s 20(3)(b). Such complaints also fall within the jurisdiction of the OIA, once the university's internal complaints procedure has been exhausted.

[119] HEA 2004, s 20(2). Once an applicant has exhausted the university's internal complaints procedure, a decision concerning admission can only be challenged by judicial review, although the scope for bringing such challenges is limited. See *R v University College London ex p Idriss* [1999] Ed CR 462 and para **8.36** above.

[120] HEA 2004, s 46(1)(a). This replaces and broadens the exclusion to the Visitor's jurisdiction made under the Education Reform Act 1988, s 206(1), discussed in *Labinjo v University of Salford* [2005] ELR 1.

[121] 'Qualifying institution' is defined in the HEA 2004. s 11. See para **8.41** above.

[122] HEA 2004, s 46(1)(b). In determining whether a dispute falls within this exclusion, s 46(3) requires that it is to be assumed that the Visitor does not have jurisdiction to determine the dispute.

(c)   any dispute as to the application of the statutes or other internal laws of
      the institution in relation to a matter falling within the areas just set
      out.[123]

8.62   The Visitor thus has a limited residual jurisdiction to deal with
complaints of individual members of a university or college (such as members
of council, for example) which are not raised by students and which are
unconnected with employment and are not otherwise justiciable. This extends
to any matters that in substance involve a dispute as to how the regulations of a
university are to be interpreted and applied and how the discretions conferred
by the university's internal rules are exercised, but which are not excluded by
statute. These could include issues of academic judgment (though not
stemming from a student complaint), appointment to membership of council,
elections to office within an institution or matters concerning the institution's
responsibilities to its student union.[124]

8.63   The Visitor is not bound to adopt any particular form of procedure and,
provided he or she acts fairly, the Visitor can decide how appeals should be
pursued.[125] The Visitor is subject to judicial review to ensure that he or she acts
fairly[126] and complies with the HRA 1998. The courts do not, at present, review
decisions as to correctness of the Visitor's interpretation of the internal
regulations.[127] The extent to which the Visitor's jurisdiction is itself compatible
with the HRA 1998 is considered at para **8.72** below.

UNIVERSITIES AND THE HUMAN RIGHTS ACT 1998

8.64   It seems likely that universities will be regarded by domestic courts as a
standard or pure 'public authority' rather than merely a 'hybrid' or functional
public authority within the meaning of section 6 of the HRA 1998.[128] As
discussed at paras **8.4–8.6** above, universities are either chartered universities
created by Royal Charter or are incorporated under statutory powers. They are
also subject to control or influence, to an extent, by other public authorities,

---

[123]   HEA 2004, s 46(1)(c).
[124]   Nicola Hart 'I'm Not Dead Yet – The University Visitor' *Universities Legal Briefing* (April
        2006).
[125]   *R v Committee of the Lords of the Judicial Committee of the Privy Council acting for the Visitor
        of the University of London ex parte Vijayatunga* [1988] 2 QB 322.
[126]   *R (Varma) v HRH The Duke of Kent* [2004] EWHC 1705 (Admin), [2004] ELR 616 at para 14.
[127]   *R v Hull University Visitor ex parte Page* [1993] AC 682; *R v Brunel University ex parte Jemchi*
        [2003] ELR 125. The significant reduction in the jurisdiction of the Visitor makes it likely that
        the limited scope of judicial review of the Visitor's decisions will remain.
[128]   In *Copland v United Kingdom* (2007) 45 EHRR 37 (ECtHR), (2007) 25 BHRC 216 at paras 31
        and 39, the government accepted that a college which was a further education corporation
        under the Further and Higher Education Act 1992, s 17 was a public body. See, generally,
        Clayton and Tomlinson *The Law of Human Rights* (2nd edn, OUP, 2009) Chapter 5 and
        para 19.10. The only possible exceptions are private universities such as the University of
        Buckingham.

including the DfES.[129] Furthermore, it has been suggested by the Court of Appeal that the fact that a body is amenable to judicial review is indicative of the fact that it is a public authority.[130] As discussed above, it is clear that universities are amenable to judicial review.[131] The result of this is that universities, when exercising both public functions such as providing education and private functions, such as employing individual members of staff, must act compatibly with the Convention rights incorporated into domestic law by the HRA 1998.[132]

The applicability of Article 2 of the First Protocol to further education

8.65   Article 2 of the First Protocol provides:

> 'No person shall be denied the right to education. In the exercise of any functions which it assumes in relation to education and to teaching, the state shall respect the rights of parents to ensure such education and teaching in conformity with their own religious and philosophical convictions.'

In *Sahin v Turkey*,[133] the Grand Chamber held that the guarantees of Article 2 of the First Protocol apply to existing institutions of higher education within the member states of the Council of Europe, commenting:

> 'Although that article does not impose a duty on the Contracting States to set up institutions of higher education, any State so doing will be under an obligation to afford an effective right of access to them. In a democratic society, the right to education, which is indispensable to the furtherance of human rights, plays such a fundamental role that a restrictive interpretation of the first sentence of art 2 of Protocol No. 1 would not be consistent with the aim or purpose of that provision.'

8.66   In light of this strong statement of the Grand Chamber, it is likely that the domestic courts will be cautious in following the various earlier authorities doubting whether Article 2 of the First Protocol entitled an individual to access to university,[134] which were based on Strasbourg decisions pre-dating *Sahin*.[135]

---

[129]   See *Poplar Housing and Regeneration Community Association Ltd v Donaghue* [2001] 3 WLR 183 and *R (on the application of Heather) v Leonard Cheshire Foundation and Another* [2002] 2 All ER 936.

[130]   *Poplar Housing and Regeneration Community Association Ltd v Donaghue* [2001] 3 WLR 183, at para 65.

[131]   See para **8.19** above.

[132]   HRA 1998, s 6.

[133]   (2005) 41 EHRR 8 (GC) at para 137.

[134]   For example, *R (Y) v Birmingham City Council* [2001] LGR 218 and *R (Mitchell) v Coventry University and the Secretary of State for Education* [2001] ELR 594 (boy refused funding to attend full-time vocational dance course).

[135]   Domestic courts are obliged to 'take into account' the Strasbourg jurisprudence (see the HRA 1998, s 2). The jurisprudence concerning s 2 is confused, with the courts seemingly moving away from the 'mirror principle' established in *R (Ullah) v Special Adjudicator* [2004] UKHL 26; [2004] 2 AC 323 that the courts should, in the absence of some special circumstances, follow any clear jurisprudence of the Strasbourg court. In *Cadder v Her Majesty's Advocate*

8.67 The jurisprudence of the ECtHR since 2005 exhibits a conscious strengthening of Article 2 of the First Protocol as an individual right of access to education rather than simply requiring regulation by the state of a general education system.[136] The individual right can now be relied on to challenge the Convention compatibility of individual suspension or expulsion decisions from higher educational institutions.[137] The court has reiterated that the right to education does not in principle exclude proper recourse to disciplinary measures, including suspension or expulsion from an educational institution, in order to ensure compliance with its internal rules.[138] However, those rules and their application must be proportionate and must not conflict with other rights enshrined in the Convention or its Protocols.[139]

8.68 In *Ali v Head Teacher and Governors of Lord Grey School*,[140] which pre-dated most of the Strasbourg case-law discussed above, Lord Bingham characterised Article 2 of the First Protocol as 'deliberately' weak, and not affording a Convention objection to the expulsion of a pupil from an educational institution on disciplinary grounds.[141] Lord Hoffmann held that that a breach of Article 2 of the First Protocol could only be made out where there was a systemic failure of the educational system which resulted in the respondent not having access to a minimum level of education.[142] When the matter came before the ECtHR in *Ali v United Kingdom*,[143] it took a different approach. It did not require that the applicant show a 'systemic failure' or suggest that the applicant could not challenge his exclusion, but instead subjected the validity of the individual exclusion to a rigorous proportionality analysis in order to determine whether it was Convention compliant.[144]

[2010] 1 WLR 2601, the Supreme Court reiterated the obligation to follow a Grand Chamber decision, but in *Manchester City Council v Pinnock* [2011] 2 AC 104 and *In Re Caughey* [2011] 2 WLR 1279, the Supreme Court contemplated the possibility of departing from a decision of the Grand Chamber.

[136]   See *Sahin v Turkey* (2005) 41 EHRR 8 (GC); *Timishev v Russia* (2007) 44 EHRR 37 (ECtHR); *Arac v Turkey* (unreported) 23 September 2008 (ECtHR), *DH v Czech Republic* (2007) 47 EHRR 3 (GC); *Temel v Turkey* (unreported) 3 March 2009 (ECtHR). This is an important development, given that the inclusion of the right in the ECHR was controversial and, as a result, the right was more limited than that found in other international instruments: see Clayton and Tomlinson *The Law of Human Rights* (op cit) at paras 19.02–19.04.

[137]   See, for example. *Temel v Turkey* (unreported) 3 March 2009 (ECtHR), in which the ECtHR found a violation of Article 2, Protocol 1 arising from the suspension of students at various faculties attached to Afyon Kocatepe University, Turkey, for between one and two terms because they petitioned the University Rector requesting that Kurdish language classes be introduced as an optional module.

[138]   See the Grand Chamber decision in *Sahin v Turkey* (2005) 41 EHRR 8 (GC) at para 156.

[139]   *Temel v Turkey*, para 45; *Sahin v Turkey* paras 154–155.

[140]   [2006] UKHL 14, [2006] 2 AC 363.

[141]   [2006] UKHL 14, [2006] 2 AC 363, para 24.

[142]   [2006] UKHL 14, [2006] 2 AC 363, para 61.

[143]   (2011) 30 BHRC 44.

[144]   (2011) 30 BHRC 44, paras 53 and 56–61.

Article 6 of the ECHR: does it apply in the University context?

8.69 Article 6 of the ECHR is concerned with the right to a fair trial and provides:

> 'In the determination of his civil rights and obligations ... everyone is entitled to a fair and public hearing within a reasonable time by an independent and impartial tribunal established by law ...'

Article 6 of the ECHR thus only applies to determinations of civil rights and obligations. In *Emine Arac v Turkey*,[145] the ECtHR moved away from its previous case-law and explicitly recognised that the right of access to higher education is a right of a civil nature. *Arac* was endorsed and extended by the Grand Chamber in *Orsus v Croatia*,[146] which characterised the court as having 'abandoned' the previous case-law of the Commission, exemplified by *Simpson v United Kingdom*.[147]

8.70 The domestic courts have, thus far, not been willing to adopt the approach in *Arac*. In *R (LG) v Board of Governors of Tom Hood School*,[148] the High Court found that *Arac* was dependent on the applicant's rights under the Turkish Constitution and rejected the contention that a hearing concerning exclusion from school determined a civil right. This approach was endorsed by the Court of Appeal in a permission hearing.[149] The court observed that English law was clear that the general right to education does not extend to education in any particular institution, citing *Simpson v United Kingdom*.[150]

8.71 Matters may well be clearer in the sphere of higher education given that, once a student has been admitted to a university, he or she is in a contractual relationship with the university and contractual rights are undoubtedly civil rights for Article 6 purposes. However, it is only decisions that are 'determinative' of a civil right that give rise to the full panoply of fair trial rights protected by Article 6 of the ECHR.[151] Decisions to expel a student are likely to be regarded as determinative, although decisions imposing lesser punishments, such as suspensions, may well not be regarded as determinative of a civil right.[152] Decisions not to award degrees are not determinative of a student's civil rights.[153]

---

[145] (Unreported) 23 September 2008 (ECtHR) at paras 18–25.

[146] (2010) 52 EHRR 300 (GC), (2010) 28 BHRC 558 at para 104.

[147] *Simpson v United Kingdom* (1989) 64 DR 188.

[148] [2009] EWHC 369 (Admin) at paras 18–28.

[149] [2010] EWCA Civ 142, [2010] ELR 291.

[150] (1989) 64 DR 188.

[151] 'Determinative' means 'directly decisive', see Clayton and Tomlinson (op cit) at paras 11.20–11.22 and 11.329–11.334 and the cases cited therein.

[152] See *Le Compte v Belgium* (1981) 4 EHRR 1 (ECtHR) and *Ghosh v GMC* [2001] UKPC 29, [2001] 1 WLR 1915.

[153] See *Re Croskery's Application for Judicial Review* [2010] NIQB 129, [2011] NIJB 234, where Treacy J held that the determination of the applicant's degree classification did not engage Art 6.

Article 6 of the ECHR and universities with the visitatorial jurisdiction

8.72 Before the statutory exclusions of the visitatorial jurisdiction were promulgated, the breadth of the Visitor's jurisdiction, coupled with the very low level of review by the High Court on judicial review,[154] appeared to be in breach of the requirement of independence and impartiality in Article 6, given the fact that the Visitor was closely integrated with the institution.[155] The statutory limitation of the visitatorial jurisdiction has largely removed the urgency from these concerns, although it is plain that whatever residual jurisdiction is exercised by the Visitor may not be HRA compliant. Some of these problems can be resolved by the Visitors themselves. Visitors can, and sometimes do, hold oral hearings and sometimes sit in public. There is no reason why a Visitor cannot provide the full panoply of procedural rights to an individual who has brought a case before him or her, including an oral hearing,[156] to which, by virtue of Article 6 of the ECHR, an individual is now entitled. This oral hearing should include an opportunity for the individual to put his or her case and call witnesses. The individual subject to the adverse decision should also have the right to challenge the university's case, usually by way of cross-examination of witnesses called to support the university's case.[157] There is also a requirement that an individual is entitled to a hearing within a reasonable time. Concern has been expressed that visitatorial hearings are often delayed until the Visitor, who is usually a busy member of the senior judiciary, is available.[158] Such delays will need to be minimised to comply with this requirement. However, Visitors are not able to address certain difficulties caused by their jurisdiction.

8.73 The first issue of concern is whether a Visitor can be regarded as 'established by law'. Whilst the contrary view has been argued,[159] it seems likely that the visitatorial jurisdiction will be regarded as 'established by law'. Lord Griffiths in *Thomas v University of Bradford*[160] noted that the common law recognised the power of the founder to appoint a Visitor.[161] It is suggested that this basis for the jurisdiction, together with the substantial body of

---

[154] See *R v Hull University Visitor ex parte Page* [1993] AC 682; see *Jemchi v The Visitor, Brunel University* [2001] EWCA Civ 1208 at para 6 per Sedley LJ.

[155] Beloff and Bamforth, 'The University Visitor, Academic Judgment, and the European Convention on Human Rights' [2002] *Judicial Review* 221 at paras 7–9. Beloff and Bamforth concluded that there was a need for parliamentary intervention for the visitor's jurisdiction to be made compatible with Art 6 of the ECHR.

[156] Examples of hearings before visitors where there was an oral hearing include: *Thomas v University of Bradford (No 2)* [1992] 1 All ER 96; *Peace v University of Aston (No 2)* [1991] 2 All ER 469.

[157] See, generally, Clayton and Tomlinson (op cit) at paras 11.204–11.211.

[158] See T Kaye 'Academic judgment, the University Visitor and Human Rights Act 1998' (1999) 11 *Education and the Law* 165 at 178.

[159] See Beloff and Bamforth (op cit) at para 41.

[160] [1987] AC 795.

[161] Ibid at 814H–815A, see also *R v Hull University Visitor ex parte Page* [1993] AC 682 at 700. See also the case-law on the meaning of the analogous concept of 'in accordance with the law' discussed below.

case-law detailing the powers and functions of the Visitor is sufficient legal underpinning to enable the jurisdiction to be described as 'established by law'. A Visitor is sufficiently 'independent and impartial'. Visitors are often senior members of the judiciary and have been described as 'independent persons of the highest judicial eminence'.[162]

Article 6 of the ECHR and universities without visitatorial jurisdiction

8.74 Similar issues will arise in relation to disciplinary hearings in universities that do not have a visitatorial jurisdiction. The disciplinary proceedings of these universities vary, but now that Article 6 of the ECHR has been incorporated into domestic law they will all need to comply with its requirements. The High Court has been prepared to scrutinise such decisions of university tribunals more fully than those of Visitors and such decisions have, in the past, been required to comply with the rules of natural justice which, at least in the view of one High Court judge, are identical to the requirements of Article 6 of the ECHR.[163] This more exacting scrutiny is likely to make such decisions less vulnerable to challenge under Article 6 of the ECHR, although each case is likely to turn on its own particular facts.

The right to respect for private life: Article 8 of the ECHR

8.75 Article 8 of the ECHR[164] protects a wide variety of interests. In relation to universities, at present, there has been very little case-law in this field.[165] However, there is substantial scope for litigation in this area because actions of universities regularly interfere with students', and sometimes employees', rights to respect for private life. Areas where future litigation is likely include access and use of personal information[166] and monitoring of internet and email usage.

8.76 Universities hold substantial amounts of personal data on students. The mere collection and storage of personal data relating to the private life of an individual falls within the application of Article 8(1)[167] and may amount to a

---

[162] *Thomas* at 824G–824H.
[163] *R v Cambridge University ex parte Begg* [1999] ELR 404 at 412C.
[164] Article 8 of the ECHR provides: '1. Everyone has the right to respect for his private and family life, his home and his correspondence. 2. There shall be no interference by a public authority with the exercise of this right except such as is in accordance with the law and is necessary in a democratic society in the interests of national security, public safety or the economic well-being of the country, for the prevention of disorder or crime, for the protection of health or morals, or for the protection of the rights and freedoms of others.'
[165] See *Copland v United Kingdom* (2007) 45 EHRR 37 (ECtHR), (2007) 25 BHRC 216 (college monitoring staff member's telephone, e-mail and internet usage); *Jones v University of Warwick* [2003] 3 All ER 760 (insurance company of university carrying out covert surveillance to provide evidence in personal injury litigation), and *R (on the application of M) v University of West of England* [2001] ELR 458 (disclosure of anonymised personal information) discussed below.
[166] See, generally, P Coppel *Information Rights* (Hart Publishing, 2nd Edn, 2010).
[167] *Amann v Switzerland* (2000) 30 EHRR 843 (ECtHR) at para 65.

breach if there is no lawful justification for collecting and storing the data.[168] Disclosure of personal information to third parties is, prima facie, an interference with a student's right to respect for private life.[169] To survive scrutiny, any such disclosure must be 'in accordance with the law' and be proportionate to a legitimate aim. For the interference to be 'in accordance with the law' it must have a legal basis and also be reasonably precise and accessible.

8.77 Sufficient legal basis is likely to be found if the university can point to a contractual provision, either with its staff, or with the student, broadly underpinning the action, although in order to rely on the provision it is likely that the university will need to draw the staff member or student's attention to that contractual provision.[170] Universities should, therefore, make explicit any possible interference with the student's right to respect for private life when drafting prospectuses, regulations and rules. Universities should have clear published policies on how and when personal data will be used and to whom it may be supplied.

8.78 Equally, IT policies should authorise monitoring and be widely published and inform students and staff as to the extent of the e-mail and internet monitoring carried out by the university and the likely sanctions if students or staff are found to have breached the policy.[171] This is particularly important in relation to staff, as in *Copland v United Kingdom*, the ECtHR rejected the government's contention that, in the absence of an explicit policy or regulation, it was lawful for a college to monitor a staff member's telephone, e-mail and internet usage because the college, as a statutory body, had the power to do anything necessary and expedient for the purpose of enabling it to provide further and higher education, including the power to take reasonable control of its facilities.[172]

8.79 Any disclosure or monitoring must be proportionate to achieve a 'legitimate aim'. A university is unlikely to have difficulty establishing that it has a legitimate aim in supplying personal data or monitoring e-mail/internet usage. Depending on the circumstances, such disclosure may further the potential legitimate aims of protecting national security, the prevention of disorder or crime and the protection of rights and freedoms of others, although

---

[168] See *Copland v United Kingdom* (2007) 45 EHRR 37 (ECtHR), (2007) 25 BHRC 216 at paras 43–44.

[169] *Department of Health v Information Commissioner and Pro-Life Alliance*, Information Tribunal, 15 October 2009 at 71–72; *Amann v Switzerland* (2000) 30 EHRR 843(ECtHR). See, generally, P Coppel *Information Rights* (Hart Publishing, 2nd Edn, 2010) at para 24-015.

[170] See the discussion in Clayton and Tomlinson *The Law of Human Rights* (op cit) at para 12.81.

[171] See, generally, the Telecommunications (Lawful Business Practice) (Interception of Communications) Regulations 2000, SI 2000/2699.

[172] (2007) 45 EHRR 37 (ECtHR), (2007) 25 BHRC 216 at paras 34 and 47. This remains an important ruling, given that the Investigatory Powers Tribunal has held that the Regulation of Investigatory Powers Act 2000 does not apply to the surveillance of employees for employment purposes: *C v The Police* [2006] 1 Pol LR 151.

disclosure for commercial gain may well fall foul of Article 8 of the ECHR.[173] Equally, monitoring e-mail and internet usage can potentially be justified on the grounds of protection of morals, prevention of crime and disorder and the protection of rights and freedoms of others. When considering whether a particular interference with a student or employee's private life is proportionate, a court will consider whether the legitimate aim could be achieved by less intrusive means. Thus, policies on disclosure and monitoring must be narrowly tailored to achieve the legitimate aim.

8.80 One example of litigation concerning universities disclosing personal data is the Court of Appeal decision in *R (M) v University of the West of England*.[174] The Court of Appeal concluded that the disclosure of anonymised personal data relating to the appellant's background (including the fact that her child had twice been placed on a child protection register) to various institutions to see if they would take someone with that background on social work placement was permissible. The Court of Appeal concluded that by applying for a social work course at the university and putting herself in the position of requiring the university to seek places for her, the appellant surrendered 'an absolute right to privacy in respect of material that was reasonably relevant to such endeavours on the university's part on her behalf'.[175] While the characterisation of the right of privacy as absolute, when it is a qualified right, is somewhat strange, the general pragmatic approach taken by the Court of Appeal has much to commend it.

8.81 It seems unlikely, at least for the foreseeable future, that more generalised claims relating to the right to develop one's personality through education, either as an argument for admission to a particular institution or as an argument against expulsion from an institution, will succeed.[176]

The right to freedom of thought, conscience and religion: Article 9 of the ECHR

8.82 The ECtHR has dealt with a number of cases concerning the right to religious freedom in the context higher education.[177] In *Sahin v Turkey*, the majority of the Grand Chamber upheld a ban on the wearing of Islamic

---

[173] See *R (Robertson) v Wakefield Metropolitan Council and Secretary of State for the Home Department* [2002] 2 WLR 889.

[174] [2001] ELR 458.

[175] [2001] ELR 458, Buxton LJ at para 23.

[176] See, by analogy, *R v Head Teacher of Alperton Community School ex parte B* [2001] EWHC Admin 229, [2001] ELR 359, Newman J at first instance at para 67, discussing the scope of *Niemetz v Germany* (1992) 16 EHRR 97 (the point was not discussed in detail by the Court of Appeal [2002] EWCA Civ 693, [2002] ELR 556).

[177] See, for example, *Sahin v Turkey* (2005) 41 EHRR 8 (GC), *Kurtulmus v Turkey* (unreported) 24 January 2006 (ECtHR) and *Karduman v Turkey* (1990) 74 DR 93. In relation to secondary education, see *Dogru v France* (2008) 49 EHRR 179 (ECtHR), [2009] ELR 77 and *Dahlab v Switzerland* (unreported) 15 February 2001 (ECtHR).

headscarves by students attending higher education institutions.[178] In *Kurtulmus v Turkey*,[179] the court held to be inadmissible a complaint by an associate-professor at a university who was deemed to have resigned from her post by repeatedly breaching a regulation prohibiting the wearing of a headscarf.[180] This approach has a long heritage – in 1990 the European Commission upheld a ban on wearing headscarves on a university identity photograph because the individual voluntarily attended the university.[181]

8.83 There is a line of Strasbourg authority holding that an employer's working practices cannot constitute an interference with an employee's religious convictions where the employee is free to resign.[182] The domestic courts have followed this authority,[183] The ECtHR has also held that rules or laws of general applicability which interfere with an individual's right to freedom of religion are permissible.[184]

8.84 Given the narrowness of the jurisprudence in this area, it is likely that Article 9 will have a limited impact in the university field. One possible area of dispute could relate to conflicts between teaching or exams and religious festivals. While many universities are sensitive to such issues and attempt to accommodate students of various religious faiths, it is unlikely, given the jurisprudence discussed above, that a failure to so accommodate will give rise to a successful claim.

The right to freedom of expression and Article 10 of the ECHR[185]

8.85 The right to freedom of speech in universities was given statutory protection prior to the incorporation of the ECHR by the HRA 1998.

---

[178] (2005) 41 EHRR 8 (GC). In a persuasive dissent, Judge Tulkins at para 3 noted that none of the other member states banned religious symbols in universities (as opposed to schools).

[179] (Unreported) 24 January 2006 (ECtHR).

[180] In *Dahlab v Switzerland* (unreported) 15 February 2001 (ECtHR), the court upheld a prohibition on secondary school teachers wearing headscarves in the classroom, finding it was justified as it ensured that children were taught in a religiously neutral attitude.

[181] *Karduman v Turkey* (1990) 74 DR 93.

[182] Ending with *Stedman v United Kingdom* (1997) 23 EHRR CD 168 (dismissal of an employee who refused to work on Sundays). See generally Clayton and Tomlinson (op cit) at paras 14.62–14.66, 14.100 and 14.103. The authors cogently criticise this approach for removing much of the substance from Art 9 rights.

[183] *Copsey v WBB Devon Clays Ltd* [2005] EWCA Civ 932, [2005] ICR 1789 (dismissal of an employee who refused to comply with a new shift rota requiring work on Sundays). See also *R (Begum) v Governing Body of Denbigh High School* [2006] UKHL 15, [2007] 1 AC 100.

[184] See generally Clayton and Tomlinson (op cit) at para 14.76. Again, the domestic courts have adopted a similar approach; see eg *R v Taylor* [2002] 1 Cr App R 37 (prosecution of a Rastafarian for possession of cannabis did not violate Art 9 of the ECHR because the legislation was of general application).

[185] Article 10 of the ECHR provides: '1. Everyone has the right to freedom of expression. This right shall include freedom to hold opinions and to receive and impart information and ideas without interference by public authority and regardless of frontiers. This Article shall not prevent states from requiring the licensing of broadcasting, television or cinema enterprises. 2. The exercise of these freedoms, since it carries with it duties and responsibilities, may be subject to such formalities, conditions, restrictions or penalties as are prescribed by law and are

Section 43(1) of the Education (No 2) Act 1986 requires every 'individual and body of persons concerned in the government of any establishment to which this section applies'[186] to take:

'such steps as are reasonably practicable to ensure that freedom of speech within the law is secured for members, students and employees of the establishment and for visiting speakers.'

That duty includes a duty to ensure, so far as reasonably practicable, that the use of any premises is not denied to any individual or body of persons on any ground connected with:

(a) the beliefs or views of that individual or of any member of that body; or

(b) the policy or objects of that body.[187]

8.86 The University is also required to issue and keep up to date a Code of Practice on, inter alia, conduct and procedures to be followed by members, students and employees in connection with the organisation of meetings and other activities.[188]

8.87 Sedley J (as he then was) commented that the principal purpose of section 43 of the Education (No 2) Act 1986 is:

'to prevent the banning from campuses of speakers whose views might be unacceptable to a majority, or even a vocal minority, of either the student body or the teaching body or both or, come to that, of the governing body. But its breadth is, in subs (1) somewhat larger and seeks the securing of freedom of speech in all respects.'[189]

The Divisional Court concluded that when performing its duty under section 43, the university concerned should not take into account any risk of public disorder outside the confines of the university by persons not within the university's control.[190] However, the university is entitled, when deciding whether to permit a particular speaker or the conditions under which a speaker is to be permitted to speak, to take into account the risk of disorder on university premises and among university members.[191]

---

necessary in a democratic society, in the interests of national security, territorial integrity or public safety, for the prevention of disorder or crime, for the protection of health or morals, for the protection of the reputation or rights of others, for preventing the disclosure of information received in confidence, or for maintaining the authority or impartiality of the judiciary.'

[186] By virtue of the Education (No 2) Act 1988, s 43(5) the section applies to universities, institutions other than universities in the higher education sector and any establishment of higher or further education which is maintained by an LEA.

[187] Education (No 2) Act 1986, s 43(2).

[188] Education (No 2) Act 1986, s 43(3).

[189] *R v UCL ex parte Riniker* [1995] ELR 213 at 216B.

[190] *R v University of Liverpool ex parte Caesar-Gordon* [1991] 1 QB 124 at 132.

[191] *R v University of Liverpool ex parte Caesar-Gordon* [1991] 1 QB 124.

8.88   Section 43 now has to be read in a way that is compatible with Article 10 of the ECHR. It seems unlikely that anything will turn on the reference in section 43 to 'freedom of speech' rather than 'freedom of expression'. Domestic courts will be obliged to give an expansive definition to the phrase 'freedom of speech' to include, inter alia, expressive conduct.[192] The incorporation of Article 10 of the ECHR is likely to have some impact on the interpretation of section 43 of the Education (No 2) Act 1986.

8.89   It is suggested that universities need to be careful when considering how to react to extremist speech. In general, freedom of expression includes speech that shocks, offends or disturbs.[193] Universities, understandably, may wish to restrict such speech, given its offensive nature and the impact it may have on other students. The case-law of the European Commission and the ECtHR has tended to permit states a substantial margin of appreciation in relation to racist speech, permitting states to prohibit it or to impose sanctions against those who express objectionable views.[194]

8.90   One area not covered by section 43 of the Education (No 2) Act 1986, is the speaker who wishes to speak on university premises but has not been invited so to speak. English law has traditionally accorded landowners, including universities, the absolute power to determine whether individuals can enter their land. As such, domestic English law does not differentiate between an individual's back garden and, for example, a square in a university.[195] In *Appleby v United Kingdom*,[196] the ECtHR concluded that, on the particular facts of the case, campaigners wishing to collect signatures in a private shopping mall which dominated a town centre could be lawfully excluded from doing so in the precincts of the shopping mall. However, a university square, unlike a shopping mall, is property dedicated to the public use and, as such, is more likely to require the university to take steps to promote freedom of expression, subject to reasonable time, manner and place restrictions.[197] Further, the landowners of university property are public authorities within the meaning of the HRA 1998 and, as such, are obliged, unlike the private landowner of a shopping mall, not to act incompatibly with Article 10 of the ECHR.

---

[192]   Such an interpretation, it is submitted, is required by the jurisprudence of the European Court of Human Rights. See, eg the concurring opinion of Judge Jambrek in *Grigoriades v Greece* (1997) 27 EHRR 464 (ECtHR) where the judge drew on the US flag-burning cases, including *Texas v Johnson* 491 US 397 (1989), where the US Supreme Court concluded that expressive conduct such as burning the US flag was speech protected by the First Amendment to the US Constitution.

[193]   See, for example, *Jersild v Denmark* (1994) 19 EHRR 1 (ECtHR) (the conviction of a journalist for aiding and abetting racist insults in a television programme was disproportionate).

[194]   See generally, Nicol, Millar and Sharland *Media Law and Human Rights* (Blackstone Press, 1st Edn, 2001) at Chapter 7.

[195]   See *CIN Properties v Rawlins* [1995] 2 EGLR 130.

[196]   (2003) 37 EHRR 783 (ECtHR).

[197]   See, by analogy, *State v Schmid* 423 A2d 615 (1980) (Supreme Court of New Jersey held that the university violated the defendant's rights to freedom of speech by evicting him from university premises for distributing political material on campus).

8.91 Both students and staff, unlike school children, are generally permitted to wear what they choose, so it is rare that issues relating to dress codes will arise. However, restrictions on dress, particularly relating to the display of political messages during formal occasions, such as graduation ceremonies, may give rise to problems. University restrictions on expressive conduct at such ceremonies, provided that they are content-neutral and published in advance, will probably survive scrutiny because the university will be able to argue that such an interference with the individual's right to freedom of expression is proportionate to the legitimate aim of protecting the rights of others. The university will be able to contend that the limitation is proportionate provided that it applies only to certain limited occasions, and students have the opportunity to express their views in a wide variety of ways at other times. Thus, a university could, for example, legitimately ban all wearing of badges or other statements of political opinions during a graduation ceremony. However, if the university sought to exclude just one type of political expression, such as badges signifying opposition to a war, there is a real risk that such restrictions would fall foul of Article 10 of the ECHR read with Article 14 of the ECHR.

8.92 Academic freedom is protected, in addition to section 43 of the Education (No 2) Act 1986 and Article 10 of the ECHR, by section 202(2)(a) of the Education Reform Act 1988 under which institutions' governance arrangements must have regard to the need:

> 'to ensure that academic staff have freedom within the law to question and test received wisdom, and to put forward new ideas and controversial or unpopular opinions, without placing themselves in jeopardy of losing their jobs or privileges they may have at their institutions.'

8.93 Sanctions against academics including, but not limited to dismissal, for publication of controversial research or expression of controversial views in academic literature will engage Article 10 of the ECHR. Guidance will no doubt be gained from US case-law in this area. In *Levin v Karleston*, an academic's arguments that black people were less intelligent on average than white people were held to be protected speech.[198] The court concluded that the setting up of an investigative committee created a 'chilling effect' on his right to speak freely about his research.[199] A similar approach is likely to be adopted by domestic courts.

Article 14 discrimination

8.94 Article 14 of the ECHR provides:

> 'The enjoyment of the rights and freedoms set forth in this Convention shall be secured without discrimination on any ground such as sex, race, colour, language,

---

[198] 966 F 2d 85 (1992).
[199] 966 F 2d 85 (1992). The importance of avoiding a chilling effect on speech has been recognised by the House of Lords in, inter alia, *Derbyshire County Council v Times Newspapers Ltd* [1993] AC 534.

religion, political or other opinion, national or social origin, association with a national minority, property, birth or other status.'

Article 14 of the ECHR is not a free-standing prohibition against discrimination, but prevents a state from being discriminatory in the way it guarantees the free-standing rights set out in the Convention. To rely on Article 14 of the ECHR, an individual does not need to show that there has been a breach of a substantive right such as for Article 2 of the First Protocol, but merely that the complaint of discrimination falls within the ambit[200] of Article 2 of the First Protocol.

8.95 Generally, the court will not go on to consider Article 14 where a separate breach has been found of the substantive Article on which the Article 14 claim rests, unless inequality of treatment in the enjoyment of the right in question is 'a fundamental aspect of the case'.[201] Unfortunately, the ECtHR has not articulated a clear approach as to when discrimination is 'fundamental'.[202]

8.96 In the sphere of education, the Grand Chamber considered Article 14 and Article 2 of the First Protocol and found there to be a breach of Article 14 in the context of the assignment of Roma children to Roma-only classes where a curriculum was taught that was significantly reduced in volume and in scope compared to the officially prescribed curriculum.[203]

8.97 At present, there is limited guidance from domestic courts as to how they will approach this issue, although it is likely that they will not adopt a liberal and generous approach given the generally conservative approach to construing Convention issues. Thus, potential arguments relating to, for example, discrimination on the grounds of social origin, in relation to access to university, are likely to fail.

UNIVERSITIES AND THE EQUALITY ACT 2010

8.98 This matter is dealt with in Chapter 3.

STUDENT LOANS AND GRANTS

8.99 Provision for financial assistance for students is primarily controlled through regulations promulgated by the Secretary of State in England and the Welsh Ministers in Wales under section 22 of the Teaching and Higher Education Act 1998. The regulations essentially provide that eligible students

---

[200] 'Ambit' has been given a generous interpretation, see the concurring opinion of Judge Bratza in *Zarb Adami v Malta* (2007) 44 EHRR 3, where he comments that 'even the most tenuous link' will suffice.

[201] See *Chassagnou v France* (1999) 29 EHRR 615 (ECtHR), (1999) 7 BHRC 151 at para 89.

[202] See generally, Clayton and Tomlinson *The Law of Human Rights* (op cit) at para 17.151.

[203] *Orsus v Croatia* (2010) 52 EHRR 300 (GC), (2010) 28 BHRC 558.

may receive a grant for fees and may be eligible for a student loan to assist with living costs and, in certain circumstances, a disability allowance equal to the amount of the additional expenditure that they have to incur in respect of attendance on the course by reason of a disability.[204] Eligible students include students who are settled in the UK (that is, ordinarily resident in the UK and not subject to any restrictions on their ability to remain in the UK) and they must be ordinarily resident in the UK on the first day of the academic year of the course and have been ordinarily resident in the UK for the preceding three years.[205]

8.100 As a result of a challenge to the previous regulations which led to a preliminary ruling by the European Court of Justice (ECJ),[206] EU nationals and their family members are eligible for assistance with both fees and maintenance if they are attending or undertaking a designated course and have been ordinarily resident in the territory comprising the European Economic Area and Switzerland throughout the three years preceding the first day of the first academic year of the course.[207]

8.101 The Higher Education Funding Council for England (HEFCE) is a statutory corporation established under section 62 of the Further and Higher Education Act 1992 in order to distribute public funds, by way of grant, loans, or other payments, to support the provision of education and the undertaking of research by higher education institutions.[208] The HEFCE may impose terms and conditions on the provision of funding, and is empowered to require the repayment, in whole or in part, of sums paid to a higher education institution if any of its terms and conditions are not complied with.[209] The failure to comply with a term or condition is not a precedent fact, and so a court reviewing a decision by the HEFCE to require repayment is not required to conduct an objective factual inquiry into whether there has been such a failure.[210]

---

[204] See the Education (Student Support) Regulations 2011, SI 2011/1986 in England and the Assembly Learning Grants and Loans (Higher Education) (Wales) (No 2) Regulations 2011, SI 2011/886 in Wales.

[205] In England, reg 4 and para 1 of Pt 2 of Sch 1 to SI 2011/1986, and in Wales, reg 4 and para 1 of Pt 2 of Sch 1 to SI 2011/886.

[206] Case C-209/03 *R (Bidar) v London Borough of Ealing and the Secretary of State for Home Department* [2005] QB 812, [2005] ECR I-2119.

[207] Education (Student Support) Regulations 2011, reg 4 and para 9 of Pt 2 of Sch 1.

[208] Further and Higher Education Act 1992, s 65(1).

[209] Further and Higher Education Act 1992, s 65(4).

[210] *R (Queen Mary, University of London) v Higher Education Funding Council for England* [2008] EWHC 1472 (Admin), [2008] ELR 540 at para 22 per Burnett J.

Chapter 9

INDEPENDENT SCHOOLS

INTRODUCTION

9.1 'Independent schools' (also commonly referred to as 'private schools' or 'public schools')[1] may be run by limited companies, by registered charities,[2] or by individuals. They are ordinarily thought of as schools which are fee-charging and which are owned and operated by private organisations. However, the Education Act 1996 (EA 1996) provides a statutory definition which is somewhat wider in its scope. By virtue of section 463(1) of the EA 1996,[3] an independent school is any school at which full-time education is provided for five or more pupils of compulsory school age, or at least one pupil of compulsory school age for whom a statement of SEN is maintained or who is a looked-after child within the meaning of section 22 of the Children Act 1989, and which is neither a school nor a special school maintained by an LA.[4]

9.2 Academy schools and free schools, governed by the Academies Act 2010, are thus independent schools, even though they are publicly funded, non-fee paying and operated by charities. These schools will be discussed in a separate section below.[5]

9.3 The Education and Skills Act 2008 (ESA 2008) also creates a new category of 'independent educational institution', to which the regulatory regime for independent schools in England is extended.[6] An 'independent educational institution' is an institution other than an independent school which provides part-time education for one or more persons of compulsory school age,[7] and would be an independent school but for the fact that the

---

[1] Although there is no statutory definition of a public school, the Public Schools Act 1868 applies only to Charterhouse, Eton, Harrow, Rugby, Shrewsbury, Westminster and Winchester.

[2] In order to retain charitable status, such schools have to demonstrate that they provide a wider public benefit, beyond that to their own pupils, and have to provide 'more than a token benefit' to the poor. It is for the charity trustees of the school concerned to address and assess how their obligations might best be fulfilled in the context of their own particular circumstances: *Independent Schools Council v Charity Commission for England and Wales; A-G v Charity Commission for England and Wales* [2011] UKUT 421 (TCC), [2012] Ch 214.

[3] As amended by the EA 2002, s 172, and adopted by the ESA 2008, ss 92 and 168.

[4] It is immaterial that a school also provides full-time education for pupils under or over compulsory school age: EA 1996, s 463(2).

[5] From para **9.52** below.

[6] ESA 2008, s 92(1).

[7] Defined in the EA 1996, s 8. A person begins to be of compulsory school age when she attains the age of five, if she attains that age on a prescribed day (currently 31 March, 31 August and

students are part-time rather than full time. The ESA 2008 will define 'part-time' in section 92(2), but this provision is not yet in force and no date has yet been appointed for it to come into force.

THE REGULATION OF INDEPENDENT SCHOOLS

Registration of independent schools

9.4   The Education Act 2002 (EA 2002), Part 10 currently sets out the regime for the regulation of independent schools[8] in England and Wales. From a date yet to be appointed, Part 10 will only apply to Wales[9] and the regime in England will be set out in Part 4 of the ESA 2008.[10] Some of the provisions of the ESA 2008 are already in force, meaning that the regimes are running in parallel.

9.5   The starting point for the regimes in both England and Wales is that it is an offence for a person to 'conduct' an independent school which is not a 'registered school'.[11] The concept of 'conduct' is not defined in either the EA 2002 or the ESA 2008,[12] so it is not immediately clear whether the proprietor[13] or the headteacher or both may be guilty of the offence.[14] However, as the EA 2002 and the ESA 2008 place the relevant obligations in relation to registration

---

31 December), and otherwise at the beginning of the prescribed day next following his attaining that age. A person ceases to be of compulsory school age at the end of the day which is the school leaving date for any calendar year: (1) if he attains the age of 16 after that day but before the beginning of the school year next following, (2) if he attains that age on that day, or (3) (unless head (1) above applies) if that day is the school leaving date next following his attaining that age.

8   As defined in the EA 1996, s 463 (as amended). See para **9.1** above.

9   EA 2002, s 156A, inserted by ESA 2008 s 179(1), Sch 1 paras 13 and 15.

10   It is unclear why a separate regime for regulating independent schools was thought necessary for England, particularly as the regime had been revised in the EA 2002. The driving force behind the implementation of the ESA 2008 was the decision to put a duty on all young people in England to participate in education or training until the age of 18, with corresponding duties on local educational authorities and employers to enable and support participation. This arose out of the findings in the Leitch Report *Prosperity for All in the Global Economy – World Class Skills* (December 2006), which focussed on raising skill levels. The Leitch Report does not mention independent schools, and whatever amendments may have been necessary to bring into being 'independent educational institutions' did not require tinkering with the regime in the EA 2002.

11   EA 2002, s 159(1). A person guilty of such an offence is liable on summary conviction to a fine up to level 5 on the standard scale or up to six months' imprisonment or both: EA 2002, s 159(2). When the ESA 2008 comes into force, s 96(1) will make it an offence to conduct and unregistered educational institution, punishable on summary conviction to a fine up to level 5 of the standard scale or imprisonment for a term not exceeding 51 weeks, or both.

12   Nor was it defined in the comparable provision under the EA 1996, see s 466(1) of that Act.

13   By virtue of the EA 2002, s 212(3)(h) and the ESA 2008,s 168 the provisions of Pt 10 of the EA 2002 and Pt 4 of the ESA 2008 are to be construed as if those provisions were contained in the EA 1996. Accordingly, the definition of 'proprietor' provided by the EA 1996, s 579 (ie the person or body of persons responsible for the management of the school) applies.

14   Similarly, the ESA 2008 will not, once it is in force, define 'conduct'.

on the proprietor of an independent school,[15] and as the ordinary meaning of conduct is 'direct or manage', it is likely that it is intended to be the proprietor who bears the potential liability under this section. It may be that in certain circumstances the headteacher (and even other staff) could be guilty of aiding and abetting an offence committed by a proprietor.[16]

9.6 If the proprietor of an independent school is a body corporate, any offence under Part 10 of the EA 2002 or Part 4 of the ESA 2008 which is proved to have been committed with the consent or connivance of, or to be attributable to the neglect of, any director, manager, secretary or similar officer of the body corporate, will give rise to guilt on the part of that person as well as the body corporate.[17]

9.7 A 'registered school' is a school which is entered in the register of independent schools in England or Wales as the case may be.[18] The register of independent schools in England is kept by the Secretary of State[19] and the register of independent schools in Wales is currently kept by the National Assembly for Wales.[20]

9.8 In order to become registered, the proprietor[21] of an independent school must make an application to the registration authority.[22] Where the independent school is located in England, the registration authority is the Secretary of State[23] and where the independent school is located in Wales, the registration authority is currently the National Assembly for Wales.[24]

9.9 An application must be made in the prescribed manner[25] and it must contain the prescribed information.[26] In England, these matters have been prescribed by the Education (Independent Educational Provision in England) (Provision of Information) Regulations 2010,[27] and in Wales by the

---

[15] EA 2002, s 160; ESA 2008, s 98. Both these sections are currently in force.
[16] For a discussion of aiding and abetting offences, see *Archbold* (2011 Edn), paras 18.10–18.19.
[17] EA 2002, s 168B. ESA 2008, s 135.
[18] EA 2002, s 171. ESA 2008, s 138(1).
[19] EA 2002, s 158(2). This provision will be replaced by ESA 2008, s 95 with the register being redesignated the 'register of independent educational institutions'. Section 140(1) of the transitional provisions in the ESA 2008 provides that the existing register of independent schools in England kept under the EA 2002 will become the 'register of independent educational institutions', so there will not be any need for an independent school in England which is already registered to apply for a fresh registration under the ESA 2008, although such a school will be subject to the ESA 2008 regime in other respects.
[20] EA 2002, s 158(3). 'The Welsh Ministers' will become the registration authority for Wales.
[21] That is, the person or body of persons responsible for the management of the school; EA 1996, s 579.
[22] EA 2002, s 160(1). ESA 2008, s 98(1).
[23] EA 2002, s 160(1).
[24] EA 2002, s 171. This section has been amended by Education and Skills Act 2008, s 169(1), Sch 1, paras 13, 17(b) to substitute 'the Welsh Ministers' as the registration authority for Wales. However, this amendment is yet to come into force.
[25] EA 2002, s 160(1)(b). ESA 2008, s 98(2)(b).
[26] EA 2002, s 160(1)(a). ESA 2008, s 98(2)(a).
[27] SI 2010/2919, which came into force on 1 January 2011. The regs do not apply to schools

Independent Schools (Provision of Information) (Wales) Regulations 2003.[28] Every application for registration must be made in writing[29] and must state the first date on which the school intends to admit students.[30] The application must provide the information specified in Part 2 of the Schedule to the Regulations.[31] This information includes details about the proprietor[32] and the chair of any governing body;[33] the address or addresses of the school and details of its premises and accommodation;[34] details of the students to be admitted to the school;[35] details of whether the school will provide accommodation for students;[36] details of the education to be provided at the school;[37] the school's policies on bullying, safeguarding the welfare of students, promoting the health and safety of students on activities outside the school, and promoting good behaviour amongst students;[38] the school's complaints procedure;[39] and the religious ethos of the school, if any.[40]

9.10 In Wales, the application must also contain a copy of the school's health and safety risk assessment[41] and a copy of the certificate issued by the Criminal Records Bureau confirming the proprietor's suitability to work with children.[42] In both England and Wales, the application must contain a certificate signed by

---

established as city technology colleges or a city college for the technology of the arts before 26 July 2002, and only partly apply to Academies; reg 1(2).

28 SI 2003/3230, which came into force on 1 January 2004.
29 SI 2010/2919 (England), reg 3(a); SI 2003/3230 (Wales), reg 3(a).
30 SI 2010/2919 (England), reg 3(b) ; SI 2003/3230 (Wales), reg 3(b).
31 SI 2010/2919 (England), reg 3(c); SI 2003/3230 (Wales), reg 3(c).
32 SI 2010/2919 (England), Sch, paras 2(1) and (2); SI 2003/3230 (Wales), Sch, paras 2(1) and (2).
33 SI 2010/2919 (England), Sch, para 2(4); SI 2003/3230 (Wales), Sch, para 2(4).
34 SI 2010/2919 (England), Sch, paras 2(3), 3(8) and 3(15); SI 2003/3230 (Wales), Sch, paras 2(3), 3(8), 3(1) and 3(14).
35 SI 2010/2919 (England), Sch, paras 3(2)–(4) and 3(6); SI 2003/3230 (Wales), Sch, paras 3(1)–(3), 3(5) and 3(7).
36 SI 2010/2919 (England), Sch, paras 3(5), 3(8) and 3(13); SI 2003/3230 (Wales), Sch, paras 3(4), 3(8) and 3(12).
37 SI 2010/2919 (England), Sch, paras 3(7) and 3(9); SI 2003/3230 (Wales), Sch, paras 3(6) and 3(9).
38 SI 2010/2919 (England), Sch, paras 3(10) and (11). These paragraphs refer to Sch paras 7, 9, 10 and 12 of the Education (Independent School Standards) (England) Regulations 2010, SI 2010/1997, which require certain written policies to be in place and set out how schools can meet certain standards. SI 2003/3230 (Wales), Sch, para 3(10), which refers to the written policies required by the Independent Schools Standards (Regulations) Wales 2003, SI 2003/3234. As to independent school standards, see further para **9.11** below.
39 SI 2010/2919 (England), Sch, para 3(12), as required by the Education (Independent School Standards) (England) Regulations 2010, reg 3 and Sch, para 25. SI 2003/3230 (Wales), Sch, para 3(11), as required by the Independent Schools Standards (Regulations) Wales 2003, reg 3 and Sch, para 7. As to independent school standards, see further para **9.11** below.
40 SI 2010/2919 (England), Sch, para 3(14); SI 2003/3230 (Wales), Sch, para 3(13).
41 SI 2003/3230, Sch, para 3(17). That is, the risk assessment required under the Management of Health and Safety at Work Regulations 1999, SI 1999/3242 in so far as it relates to the obligations under the Fire Precautions (Workplace) Regulations 1997, SI 1997/1840, Part II: SI 2003/1934, Sch 1, para 3(15).
42 SI 2003/3230, Sch, para 3(16).

the proprietor of the school that, to the best of his or her knowledge and belief, the statements made in the application are accurate.[43]

9.11 Where the proprietor of an independent school makes an application for registration, the registration authority is required to notify[44] the Chief Inspector,[45] who is in turn required to inspect the school and report back to the registration authority on the extent to which the school meets, and is likely to be able to continue to meet, the 'independent school standards'.[46] In England, the 'independent school standards' are prescribed by the Education (Independent School Standards) (England) Regulations 2010,[47] and in Wales by the Independent Schools Standards (Regulations) Wales 2003.[48] These regulations relate to:

(a) the quality of the education provided by a school;[49]

(b) the spiritual, moral, social and cultural development of students at a school;[50]

(c) the welfare, health and safety of students;[51]

(d) the suitability of proprietors and staff;[52]

(e) the premises of, and accommodation at, a school;[53]

(f) the provision of information to parents of students, parents of prospective students, the Chief Inspector or the Secretary of State;[54] and

(g) the manner in which a school handles complaints.[55]

---

[43] SI 2010/2919 (England), reg 3(d); SI 2003/3230 (Wales), reg 3(d).

[44] EA 2002, s 160(3). ESA 2008, s 98(4).

[45] That is, Her Majesty's Chief Inspector of Education, Children Services and Skills in England (ESA 2008, s 138(1)) or the Chief Inspector of Education and Training in Wales (EA 2002, s 171).

[46] EA 2002, s 160(4). ESA 2008, s 99(1).

[47] SI 2010/1997.

[48] SI 2003/3234.

[49] SI 2010/1997 (England), reg 3 and Sch 1, paras 1–4. These standards do not apply to Academy schools in England. SI 2003/3234 (Wales), reg 3 and Sch, para 1.

[50] SI 2010/1997 (England), reg 3 and Sch 1, para 5; SI 2003/3234 (Wales), reg 3 and Sch, para 2.

[51] SI 2010/1997 (England), reg 3 and Sch 1, paras 6–17, some of which does not apply to city technology colleges or city colleges for the technology of the arts in England. SI 2003/3234 (Wales), reg 3 and Sch, para 3.

[52] SI 2010/1997 (England), reg 3 and Sch 1, paras 18–22; SI 2003/3234 (Wales), reg 3 and Sch, para 4.

[53] SI 2010/1997 (England), reg 3 and Sch 1, para 23; SI 2003/3234 (Wales), reg 3 and Sch, para 5.

[54] SI 2010/1997 (England), reg 3 and Sch 1, para 24, some of which does not apply to Academy schools, city technology colleges or city colleges for the technology of the arts in England. SI 2003/3234 (Wales), reg 3 and Sch, para 6.

[55] SI 2010/1997 (England), reg 3 and Sch 1, para 25; SI 2003/3234 (Wales), reg 3 and Sch, para 7.

9.12 Once an independent school which is applying for registration has been inspected by the Chief Inspector, then the registration authority is required to determine whether the independent school standards are met, and are likely to continue to be met, in relation to that school.[56] In making this determination, the registration authority is required to take into account the report of the Chief Inspector and any other evidence relating to the independent school standards.[57] If the registration authority determines that the independent school standards are met, and are likely to continue to be met, then it is under a duty to enter the school in the register.[58] The registration authority does not have any power to enter a school in the register in any other circumstances.

9.13 Neither the EA 2002 nor the ESA 2008 prescribes any particular procedure for the registration authority to follow when making its determination. However, in the light of the consequence of an adverse determination for the proprietor of an independent school, which is, in effect, a prohibition on running the school, it is likely that the courts will impose a duty to act fairly on the registration authority in this context. Although the requirements of fairness vary from case to case, there are strong arguments that a proprietor should be informed of at least the gist of the evidence before the registration authority and should have an opportunity to comment on it before a determination is made.[59] It is also arguable that, because the decision of the registration authority as to whether to register an independent school will be directly decisive of the proprietor's ability to engage in the commercial activity of running such a school, Article 6 of the European Convention on Human Rights (ECHR) will be engaged.[60] However, when considering whether the procedure followed by the registration authority when making its determination is Article 6-compliant, it is necessary to consider the decision-making process as a whole, including the availability of judicial review, paying particular regard to the context in which the decision is being taken.[61] In the light of the regulatory nature of the registration authority's function, it is likely

---

[56] ESA 2008, s 99(2) (England); EA 2002, s 161(1) (Wales).
[57] ESA 2008, s 99(2) (England); EA 2002, s 161(1) (Wales).
[58] ESA 2008, s 99 (4) (England); EA 2002, s 161(3) (Wales).
[59] See *R v Secretary of State for the Home Department ex parte Doody* [1994] 1 AC 531, 560D–560G per Lord Mustill.
[60] The jurisprudence on what constitutes a 'civil right' within the meaning of Art 6 was reviewed in *R (Alconbury Developments Limited) v Secretary of State for the Environment, Transport and the Regions* [2001] UKHL 23, [2001] 2 WLR 1389, 1413H–1415F per Lord Hoffmann and in *Runa Begum v Tower Hamlets London Borough Council* [2003] UKHL 5, [2003] 2 AC 430 paras 78–94 per Lord Millett. See also *Benthem v Netherlands* (1985) 8 EHRR 1, *Pudas v Sweden* (1987) 10 EHRR 380 and *Tre Traktörer Aktiebolag v Sweden* (1989) 13 EHRR 309. It should be noted, however, that in these latter cases the ECtHR was concerned with the situation where a licence to carry on a commercial activity had been granted then revoked, rather than the decision to grant a licence in the first place.
[61] *R (Alconbury Developments Limited) v Secretary of State for the Environment, Transport and the Regions* [2001] UKHL 23, [2001] 2 WLR 1389 (HL); *Runa Begum v Tower Hamlets LBC* [2003] UKHL 5, [2003] 2 WLR 388 (HL). As to the availability of judicial review as a means of challenging the registration authority's decision not to register an independent school, see further para **9.15** below.

that in most cases a procedure similar to that outlined above, combined with the availability of judicial review, would constitute compliance with Article 6.

9.14 Unlike the situation with regard to other determinations of the registration authority,[62] there is no statutory right of appeal in the EA 2002 against a refusal by the registration authority to enter a school on the register. The ESA 2008 does afford such a statutory right of appeal,[63] but at the time of writing the relevant provision has not come into force,[64] nor has a day been appointed for its coming into force.[65] An anomalous and highly unsatisfactory situation will arise if section 125 of the ESA 2008 is brought into force without concomitant amendment of the EA 2002, in that potential proprietors of independent schools in England would be afforded a right to appeal against a refusal to register, whilst those in Wales would not.

9.15 At the time of writing, the only route for challenging a refusal to register is through judicial review. As a public body exercising a public function under statute, a registration authority will be susceptible to judicial review in this context. The proprietor of an independent school which has been refused registration would almost certainly have a sufficient interest in the determination to make a claim for judicial review.

9.16 However, the effectiveness of judicial review as a means of challenge in these circumstances may be limited. First, neither the EA 2002 nor the ESA 2008 impose any duty on the registration authority to provide reasons for its determination.[66] Absent a general common law duty to give reasons, it must be questionable whether the courts will impose upon registration authorities a duty to give reasons in this particular context.[67] The situation is slightly different where the registration authority refuses to register a school despite a positive recommendation by the Chief-Inspector. In those circumstances, the registration authority will have to give cogent reasons for rejecting the recommendation.[68]

9.17 Secondly, in practical terms, any challenge to the non-registration of an independent school will be directed at the determination by the registration authority that the independent school standards are not met (or will not continue to be met) in relation to the relevant school. The independent school

---

[62] As to situations where an appeal lies from a decision of the registration authority, see further para **9.40** below.

[63] ESA 2008, s 125(1).

[64] Apart from for the purposes of making regulations, see the Education and Skills Act 2008 (Commencement No 3) Order 2009, SI 2009/1513, Art 2(2).

[65] Under ESA 2008, s 173(4).

[66] Pursuant to the EA 2002, s 161(2) and ESA 2008, s 99(3), the only obligation on the registration authority is to notify the proprietor of the institution of any determination made by it in relation to the school.

[67] For a discussion of the circumstances in which the courts will impose a duty to give reasons, see *R v Higher Education Funding Council, ex parte Institute of Dental Surgery* [1994] 1 WLR 242 (Div Ct); *R (Hasan) v Secretary of State for Trade and Industry* [2008] EWCA Civ 1312.

[68] Cf *R (Bradley) v Work and Pensions Secretary* [2008] EWCA Civ 36, [2009] QB 114 at para 72.

standards import somewhat amorphous concepts,[69] and therefore consideration of whether they are met will necessarily involve the exercise of a value
judgment. Decisions which involve the exercise of a value judgment can be
difficult to challenge on perversity grounds[70] and accordingly, claimants may
find it extremely difficult to impugn a determination of the registration
authority on this basis.[71]

9.18 It is debatable whether a decision to refuse to register an independent
school amounts to an interference with the proprietor's peaceful enjoyment of
his possessions within the meaning of Article 1 of the First Protocol to the
ECHR, such as to require the courts to apply an enhanced level of scrutiny on
an application for judicial review.[72] It could be argued that as registration is a
necessary condition for carrying on the business of an independent school, the
refusal of registration can, in principle, amount to a measure of control on the
use of the proprietor's possessions, but it may be difficult to identify the
possessions which have been adversely affected.[73] In any event, it is likely that in
most cases, any control will be justified under the second paragraph of Article 1
of the First Protocol as being in the general interest.[74]

9.19 Thirdly, it may be that the thrust of a challenge is, in fact, directed at the
Chief Inspector's report; for example, on the grounds that he conducted an
inadequate inspection or reached a conclusion without having any evidence to
support it. The difficulty with a direct challenge to the Chief Inspector's report
is that the report does not itself directly affect any rights or interests, nor does it
involve the final determination of the question to which it is addressed.[75] On
the other hand, an adverse report is, as a matter of fact, likely to have serious

---

[69] See further para **9.11** above.

[70] That is, a challenge based on the contention that the decision was so unreasonable that no
reasonable decision-maker, properly applying himself to the matter to be decided, could have
reached it: *Associated Provincial Picture Houses v Wednesbury Corporation* [1948] 1 KB 223.

[71] See, for example, *R v Secretary of State for Education, ex parte Avon County Council (No 2)*
(1990) 88 LGR 737, 742–743 per Nicholls LJ in relation to the reluctance of the court to
intervene on irrationality grounds in the context of a school closure and see generally
Chapter 2.

[72] As to the enhanced level of scrutiny in cases where an executive decision interferes with an
individual's human rights, see *R (Daly) v Secretary of State for the Home Department* [2001]
2 AC 532, 546C–548D per Lord Steyn.

[73] Cf *Tre Traktörer Aktiebolag v Sweden* (1989) 13 EHRR 309 at paras 53–55. In
Anheuser-Busch Inc v Portugal (2007) 45 EHRR 36, the Grand Chamber held that an
application for registration of a trade mark was a possession, although the marketable
economic value of the application itself played a significant role in the Grand Chamber's
assessment. Unless it can be shown that an application for registration has marketable
economic value, it is difficult to see how any economic interests connected with the running of
a school could be affected if, prior to the date of the decision, the proprietor was not actually
running the school. See also *R (Amvac Chemical UK Ltd) v Department for the Environment,
Food and Rural Affairs* [2003] EWHC 1011 (Admin) at paras 87–97 per Crane J.

[74] For a discussion of justification under Art 1 of the First Protocol, see Clayton and Tomlinson,
The Law of Human Rights (2nd edn, OUP, 2009) at paras 18.36–18.43 and 18.112–18.130.

[75] *Council of Civil Service Unions v Minister for the Civil Service* [1985] AC 374, 408F–409B per
Lord Diplock. See also *R v Secretary of State for Education and the North East London
Education Association ex parte M* [1996] ELR 162, 203D–203F per Simon Brown LJ, where it

repercussions for a proprietor.[76] It is suggested that, as the report is an integral, and indeed mandatory, part of the process leading up to the decision, the better view is that any challenge should be made to the registration authority's decision rather than to the report itself.[77]

9.20 There are difficulties in making good a challenge to the registration authority's decision on the basis that the report was in some way deficient. As has been set out above, the registration authority is under a duty to take into account the Chief Inspector's report when making its determination;[78] therefore, it is unlikely that it could be said that, unless the report could be subjected to a compelling attack which demolished it as a worthwhile document,[79] the registration authority took into account an irrelevant consideration. Depending on the circumstances of a particular case, however, it may be that if the report omits to mention an important matter (and that matter was not addressed in any of the other evidence before the registration authority),[80] the registration authority's decision might be challenged on the basis that it had failed to take into account a relevant consideration when making its determination.[81]

9.21 It is feasible that, in certain circumstances, the registration of an independent school may be the subject of challenge, although the issue of whether the potential claimant has a sufficient interest in the determination is likely to be crucial. In any event, such a challenge may face difficulties similar to those set out above.

---

was doubted that the report of an education association to the Secretary of State could be the subject of a direct challenge, notwithstanding the fact that the report was the basis for the Secretary of State's decision to close a school.

[76] This was the basis for the imposition of a duty to act fairly on the Board of Trade Inspectors in *Re Pergamon Press* [1971] Ch 388 at 399D–399H per Lord Denning MR.

[77] For a discussion of the circumstances where a report may be the subject of a direct challenge by way of judicial review, see Lewis, *Judicial Remedies in Public Law* (4th Edn, 2009), paras 4.029–4.033.

[78] EA 2002, s 161(1)(a).

[79] *R v Secretary of State for Education and the North East London Education Association, ex parte M* [1996] ELR 162, 205G–H per Simon Brown LJ, where it was stated that nothing short of bad faith or a fundamental error would suffice for this purpose.

[80] One of the circumstances which would be likely to be relevant to the grant of relief in such a case would be whether the claimant had been given the opportunity to draw the omission to the attention of the registration authority, but had failed to do so.

[81] In the context of town and country planning, where a planning inspector provides a report to the Secretary of State for the purposes of the latter making a decision on a planning appeal, the decision of the Secretary of State may be challenged on the basis that the inspector's report did not refer to an important matter with the result that the Secretary of State was wholly unaware of it or on the basis that such a matter was put in a wholly wrong way with the consequence that the Secretary of State was never provided with the true picture: *East Hampshire District Council v Secretary of State for the Environment* [1979] JPL 533 (Lord Denning MR, Lord Justice Eveleigh and Sir Stanley Rees).

Monitoring of registered independent schools

9.22   The registration authority may at any time require the Chief Inspector to inspect any registered independent school, either by himself, by one or more registered inspectors or by a body approved by the registration authority for this purpose.[82] The inspection is to relate to the independent school standards which are specified by the registration authority either in relation to the particular school or in relation to a category of school into which the school falls.[83] The person who conducts the inspection is required to make a report to the registration authority on the extent to which the school meets the standard or standards to which the inspection relates.[84]

9.23   Unlike a report made for the purposes of determining whether an independent school should be registered, the EA 2002 makes specific provision for the publication of the report of an inspection of a registered independent school, if the registration authority so requires.[85] Although the Act confers privilege on such a report for the purposes of a claim for libel,[86] it is likely that a claim for judicial review may lie against the decision to require the publication of such a report. The publication of such a report, if it contained unfavourable conclusions about a school, could have a detrimental effect on the school by leading to serious factual consequences such as the loss of business. Again, however, it is likely that any challenge would have to be directed towards the decision to require publication of the report rather than towards the report itself.[87]

9.24   The EA 2002 also enables the making of regulations which may require the proprietor of an independent school to provide the registration authority with such information relating to the school as may be prescribed.[88] Regulations have been made for both England[89] and Wales.[90] The regulations envisage two different stages when a proprietor may have to provide information. The first concerns an initial return in writing to be delivered to the

---

[82]   EA 2002, ss 162A(1) and 163(1). The EA 2002 currently contains two sets of broadly similar provision, one relating to England and one to Wales. The ESA 2008 will consolidate those provisions into one – s 163 – through a process of repeal and amendment which will come into force on a date yet to be appointed.

[83]   EA 2002, at ss 162A(2) and 163(2).

[84]   EA 2002, at ss 162A(3)(a) and 163(3)(a).

[85]   EA 2002, at ss 162A(3)(b) and 163(3)(b).

[86]   EA 2002, s 163(4) (in relation to Wales) and the Education and Inspections Act 2006, s 151 in relation to England.

[87]   As to the appropriate challenge, see further para **9.20** above. It is unlikely that an interim injunction could be obtained to restrain publication in the light of the decision in *R v Advertising Authority ex parte Vernons* [1993] 2 All ER 202, Laws J.

[88]   EA 2002, s 168(1).

[89]   Education (Independent Educational Provision in England) (Provision of Information) Regulations 2010, SI 2010/2919. These regulations do not apply to schools established as city technology colleges or a city college for the technology of the arts before 26 July 2002, and only partly apply to Academies; reg 1(2).

[90]   Independent Schools (Provision of Information) (Wales) Regulations 2003, SI 2003/3230.

registration authority within three months of the admission of students to the school.[91] This return must include details of:

(a)   the fees charged by the school;[92]

(b)   the number of pupils;[93]

(c)   whether the school will provide accommodation;[94]

(d)   in England, whether the school is specially organised to make special educational provision for students;[95] and in Wales, the number of pupils at the school who have special educational needs;[96]

(e)   in Wales, the number of pupils at the school who are looked after by a LA;[97]

(f)   in Wales, details concerning the teachers and other persons employed by the school.[98]

The return must also contain a certificate from the proprietor of the school stating that, to the best of his knowledge and belief, the statements made in the application are accurate.[99]

9.25   Secondly, in every school year the proprietor of an independent school must deliver to the registration authority an annual return in writing within one month of being requested to do so by the registration authority.[100] The annual return must be made up to the date specified by the registration authority[101] and it must include much of the same information required in an application for registration and in the initial return made within three months of the admission of pupils.[102] It must also include details of:

---

[91]   SI 2010/2919 (England), reg 4; SI 2003/3230 (Wales), reg 4. In Wales, the requirement to provide an initial return arises automatically, whereas in England it only arises following a request from the Secretary of State.

[92]   SI 2010/2919 (England), reg 6(a) and Sch, para 8; SI 2003/3230 (Wales), reg 4 and Sch, para 8.

[93]   SI 2010/2919 (England), reg 4 and Sch, para 3(2)–(3) requires the maximum number of students and their age ranges; SI 2003/3230 (Wales) reg 4 and Sch, para 4(1) requires the number of pupils in each year group.

[94]   SI 2010/2919 (England), reg 4 and Sch, para 3(5). In Wales, the number of pupils for whom the school is providing boarding accommodation and the ages of the youngest and oldest boarding pupils are required: SI 2003/3230 (Wales), reg 4 and Sch, para 4(2).

[95]   SI 2010/2919 (England), reg 4 and Sch, para 3(6).

[96]   SI 2003/3230 (Wales), reg 4 and Sch, para 5.

[97]   SI 2003/3230 (Wales), reg 4 and Sch, para 5A.

[98]   SI 2003/3230 (Wales), reg 4 and Sch, paras 6–7.

[99]   SI 2010/2919 (England), reg 4(2)(c); SI 2003/3230 (Wales), re 4(b). The English regs use the word 'made' instead of 'signed', in order to facilitate the electronic submission of reports. The Welsh regs require the certificate to be signed.

[100]   SI 2010/2919 (England), reg 5; SI 2003/3230 (Wales), reg 5.

[101]   SI 2010/2919 (England), reg 5(2)(b); SI 2003/3230 (Wales), reg 5(2)(b).

[102]   SI 2010/2919 (England), reg 5(2)(c) and Pt 4 of Sch; SI 2003/3230 (Wales), reg 5(2)(c) and Pt 4

(a) individuals who have commenced or ceased employment at the school;[103]

(b) in Wales, the number pupils who have been provided with accommodation at the school;[104]

(c) the number and gender demographic of pupils who are and who are not pursuing courses for examinations;[105]

(d) any changes in the premises of, or accommodation at, the school;[106] and

(e) any changes in the membership of the people or body named as the proprietor of the school.[107]

The annual return must also contain a certificate from the proprietor of the school stating that, to the best of his knowledge and belief, the statements made in the application are accurate.[108]

9.26 The registration authority may remove a school from the register if it is satisfied that its proprietor has failed to comply with a requirement to provide information.[109] There is a disparity between England and Wales as to the process of removal and the way in which such removal can be challenged. In England, the registration authority is required to notify the proprietor of the school of the decision to remove it from the register.[110] The proprietor then has the right to appeal the decision to the First-tier Tribunal,[111] and the decision to remove the school from the register does not have effect until the appeal has been disposed of.[112] On appeal, the Tribunal may either confirm the decision or direct that it is on no effect. There are no restrictions on the matters to which the Tribunal may or may not have regard when deciding how to dispose of an appeal. In the circumstances, it is suggested that the Tribunal should approach the matter *de novo* and reach a fresh decision on the merits, rather than merely reviewing the decision of the registration body. Such an approach would almost certainly ensure that the decision-making process is Article 6-compliant.[113]

---

of Sch. As to the information required in an application for registration, see further paras **9.9–9.10** above and as to the information required in an initial return within three months of the admission of pupils, see further para **9.25** above.

[103] SI 2010/2919 (England), reg 5(2)(c) and Sch, para 11; SI 2003/3230 (Wales), reg 5(2)(c) and Sch, para 10.

[104] SI 2003/3230 (Wales), reg 5(2)(c) and Sch, para 11.

[105] SI 2010/2919 (England), reg 5(2)(c) and Sch, para 13; SI 2003/3230 (Wales), reg 5(2)(c) and Sch, para 12.

[106] SI 2010/2919 (England), reg 5(2)(c) and Sch, para 14; SI 2003/3230 (Wales), reg 5(2)(c) and Sch, para 13.

[107] SI 2010/2919 (England), reg 5(2)(c) and Sch, para 15; SI 2003/3230 (Wales), reg 5(2)(c) and Sch, para 14.

[108] SI 2010/2919 (England), reg 5(d); SI 2003/3230 (Wales), reg 5(d).

[109] SI 2010/2919 (England), reg 6; SI 2003/3230 (Wales), reg 6.

[110] ESA 2008, s 123(5) and SI 2010/2919, reg 6(2).

[111] That is, the First-tier Tribunal, Health, Education and Social Care Chamber.

[112] ESA 2008, s 128 (which came into force on 1 January 2011) and SI 2010/2919, reg 6(3).

[113] As to compliance with Art 6, see further para **9.13** above.

9.27 In Wales, there is no specific requirement for the registration authority to notify the proprietor of the school of the decision to remove it from the register, although there is an obvious practical need to do so. The decision to remove a school from the register cannot be challenged by way of appeal. However, the registration authority must exercise its discretion lawfully and any unlawful exercise of its discretion will be susceptible to challenge by way of an application for judicial review. Similarly, as a decision to remove a school from the register in this context will almost inevitably have a detrimental effect on the proprietor, it is likely that the courts will impose a duty on the registration authority to act fairly and a failure to comply with any such duty will also be susceptible to a challenge by way of judicial review.[114]

9.28 In Wales, it is an offence for a proprietor of an independent school to fail to comply with a requirement under the Independent Schools (Provision of Information) (Wales) Regulations 2003 to provide information, an offence which is punishable with a fine not exceeding level 5 on the standard scale.[115]

9.29 Proprietors of independent schools are under a further freestanding duty under section 35 of the Safeguarding Vulnerable Groups Act 2006 to provide information to the Independent Safeguarding Authority ('ISA'), which maintains a list of individuals barred from working with children. The duty requires 'employers' who provide 'regulated activities', such as the provision of education to children,[116] to refer information to the ISA when they have removed an individual from any post in the school because the proprietor thinks that individual has engaged in relevant conduct or posed a risk of harm to children. The duty also arises where the individual leaves their post in circumstances where they would or might otherwise have been removed because they harmed, or posed a risk of harm, to a child or vulnerable adult.

9.30 In Wales, additional duties arise the where a proprietor of an independent school has ceased to use the services of a teacher registered with the General Teaching Council for Wales,[117] on the grounds of misconduct, professional incompetence or conviction of a relevant offence[118] which is not covered by the Safeguarding Vulnerable Groups Act 2006. The proprietor is under a duty[119] to report this in writing to the relevant Committee of the Council for Wales.[120] The report must include a statement of the reasons for

---

[114] As to the duty to act fairly, see further para **9.13** above.

[115] SI 2003/3230 (Wales), reg 8. A similar provision was contained in the previous English regulations, SI 2003/1934, reg 10, but was repealed by the 2010 regulations. The Explanatory Note to the 2010 regulations does not explain why the offence has been removed.

[116] Safeguarding Vulnerable Groups Act 2006, s 5 and Sch 4, Pt 1.

[117] Under the Education (Supply of Information) (Wales) Regulations 2009, SI 2009/1301.

[118] Within the meaning of para 8 of Sch 2 to the Teaching and Higher Education Act 1998, which amounts to a criminal offence that has 'material relevance' to the teacher's fitness to be a registered teacher.

[119] SI 2009/1301, reg 4.

[120] An Investigating Committee, a Professional Competence Committee or a Professional Conduct Committee established under the General Teaching Council for Wales (Disciplinary Functions) Regulations 2001, see SI 2009/1301, reg 3.

ceasing to use the person's services;[121] relevant records;[122] relevant letters, warnings or notices issued to the person;[123] any relevant statements, representations or evidence submitted by the person;[124] any letter advising of the person's intention to cease to provide services;[125] and any other document or information which the proprietor considers is relevant to the exercise of the Committee's functions in relation to prohibiting individuals from teaching or working with children.[126]

Changes to the registered details of an independent school

9.31   The entry for an independent school in the register shall include the name and address of the school, the name of the proprietor of the school, the age range of pupils, the maximum number of pupils, whether the school is for male or female pupils or both, whether the school provides accommodation for pupils, and whether the school admits children with SEN.[127]

9.32   If there is a 'material change' in relation to the school, then an application in writing needs to be made to the registration authority for the approval of that change.[128] For this purpose, a material change is a change of proprietor, a change of address or a change in any one or more of the age range of pupils, the maximum number of pupils, whether the school is for male or female pupils or both, whether the school provides accommodation for pupils and whether the school admits children with SEN.[129]

9.33   Where the registration authority receives an application for approval of a material change, it is required to approve the change if it is satisfied that the independent school standards will continue to be met in relation to the school.[130] If the registration authority is not so satisfied, then it is required to refuse approval.[131] When deciding whether or not it is satisfied that the independent school standards will continue to be met, the registration authority must take into account any report which it has required the Chief Inspector to make and any other evidence relating to the independent school standards.[132] The registration authority has the power (although not a duty) to require the Chief Inspector to inspect the school and report on the extent to

---

[121]   SI 2009/1301, reg 4 and Sch, para 1.
[122]   SI 2009/1301, reg 4 and Sch, paras 2–3.
[123]   SI 2009/1301, reg 4 and Sch, para 4.
[124]   SI 2009/1301, reg 4 and Sch, para 5.
[125]   SI 2009/1301, reg 4 and Sch, para 6.
[126]   SI 2009/1301, reg 4 and Sch, para 7.
[127]   EA 2002, s 161(4). ESA 2008, s 98(3).
[128]   EA 2002, s 162(3). In England, the ESA 2008, ss 101–105 will deal with material change to registered details. At the time of writing, these provisions had come into force only for the purpose of making regulations (which is yet to occur). They will be brought into force for other purposes on a day yet to be appointed.
[129]   EA 2002, s 162(2).
[130]   EA 2002, s 162(6)(a) and (7).
[131]   EA 2002, s 162(6)(b).
[132]   EA 2002, s 162(7).

which, if the material change is made, any of the independent school standards specified by the registration authority are likely to continue to be met.[133]

9.34 If there is a material change in relation to the school which has not been approved by the registration authority (or by the First-tier Tribunal on an appeal),[134] then the registration authority has the power to remove the school from the register.[135] The Act does not provide for a right of appeal against a decision to remove a school from the register in this context; however, the registration authority will have to exercise its discretion lawfully and any unlawful exercise of its discretion will be susceptible to challenge by way of judicial review. Similarly, as a decision to remove a school from the register in this context will almost inevitably have a detrimental effect on the proprietor, it is likely that the courts will impose a duty on the registration authority to act fairly and a failure to comply with any such duty will also be susceptible to a challenge by way of judicial review.[136] Care should be taken to distinguish between a complaint about a decision to remove a school from the register and the underlying decision not to approve a material change. In the latter case, the underlying decision should be challenged by way of an appeal under the Act.[137]

Failure by independent school to meet independent school standards

9.35 Where the registration authority is satisfied, after taking into account the report of an inspection of a registered school[138] or any other evidence,[139] that any one or more of the independent school standards is or are not being met, then only two courses of action are open to it.[140] The first course of action is only open to the registration authority if it determines that there is a risk of serious harm to the welfare of pupils at the school. In such a case, it may decide to remove the school from the register.[141]

9.36 The second course of action must be taken by the registration authority if it does not take the first course of action. This involves serving a notice on the proprietor of the school, identifying the relevant independent school standards and requiring the proprietor to submit an action plan by a specified

---

[133] EA 2002, s 162(4).
[134] As to an appeal against a decision not to approve a material change, see further para **9.40** below.
[135] EA 2002, s 161(1).
[136] As to the duty to act fairly, see further para **9.13** above.
[137] As to an appeal against a decision not to approve a material change, see further para **9.40** below.
[138] That is, a report made pursuant to the EA 2002, s 163: s 165(1)(a).
[139] EA 2002, s 165(1)(a).
[140] In England, the ESA 2008, ss 114–118 will deal with failure to meet standards. At the time of writing, these provisions had come into force only for the purpose of making regulations (which is yet to occur). They will be brought into force for other purposes on a day yet to be appointed.
[141] EA 2002, at s 165(2). The decision may only be a decision to remove the school from the register on a date after the expiry of the period for instituting an appeal against the decision.

date.[142] An action plan must specify the steps which will be taken to meet the relevant standards and the time by which each step will be taken.[143] Where the proprietor of a school submits an action plan, the registration authority may reject it or approve it (with or without modifications).[144]

9.37 Where a proprietor fails to submit an action plan by the specified date, or where an action plan has been submitted but rejected, then the registration authority may determine that the school is to be removed from the register or it may make an order restricting aspects of the running of the school.[145] Similarly, where an action plan has been approved, but a step specified in it has not been taken by the specified date, then the registration authority may: specify a later date by which the step must be taken, determine that the school is to be removed from the register, or make an order restricting aspects of the running of the school.[146]

9.38 The order which may be made by a registration authority is an order requiring the proprietor of the school to do one or more of the following:

(a) cease using any part of the school premises for all purposes or for purposes specified in the order;

(b) close any part of the school's operation;

(c) cease to admit new pupils or new pupils of a particular description.[147]

The proprietor may apply to the registration authority to have the order varied or revoked, but the registration authority may only do so if it is satisfied that it is appropriate to do so because of any change of circumstance.[148] It is a criminal offence for a proprietor to fail to comply with an order and, where there is such a failure, the registration authority may determine that the school is to be removed from the register.[149]

9.39 The proprietor has a right of appeal to the First-tier Tribunal against a determination under section 165 of the EA 2002 to remove the school from the register, against an order, and against a refusal to vary or revoke an order.[150]

---

[142] EA 2002, s 165(3).

[143] EA 2002, s 165(4).

[144] EA 2002, s 165(5).

[145] EA 2002, s 165(6). As to orders, see further para **9.42** below.

[146] EA 2002, s 165(7). As to orders, see further para **9.42** below.

[147] EA 2002, s 165(8).

[148] EA 2002, s 165(10).

[149] EA 2002, s 165(9).

[150] As to appeals to the First-tier Tribunal (previously the Care Standards Tribunal), see further para **9.40** below.

Appeals to the First-tier Tribunal

9.40 An appeal lies to the First-tier Tribunal ('the Tribunal')[151] against a refusal to approve a material change,[152] a determination to remove a school from the register because any one or more of the independent school standards is or are not being met,[153] an order,[154] and a refusal to revoke or vary an order.[155] Any appeal must be made within the period of 28 days beginning with the day on which the relevant notice is served on the proprietor.[156] The procedure for appeals is governed by the Tribunal Procedure (First-tier Tribunal)(Health, Education and Social Care Chamber) Rules 2008.[157]

9.41 The EA 2002 gives the Tribunal very broad powers where an appeal is made to it.[158] Further, apart from in the case of an appeal against a refusal by the registration authority to vary an order,[159] there are no restrictions on the matters to which the Tribunal may or may not have regard when deciding how to dispose of an appeal. The Tribunal should approach the matter *de novo* and reach a fresh decision on the merits, rather than merely reviewing the decision of the registration body.[160] The burden of proof rests on the Secretary of State to show that the decision under appeal was appropriate both in law and based on the facts.[161] This approach almost certainly ensures that the decision-making process, in so far as it related to appealable decisions, is Article 6-compliant.[162]

---

[151] In England, the ESA 2008, s 125 will deal with such appeals to the First-tier Tribunal. At the time of writing, these provisions had come into force only for the purpose of making regulations (which is yet to occur). They will be brought into force for other purposes on a day yet to be appointed.

[152] A decision pursuant to the EA 2002, s 162(6)(b): s 166(1)(a).

[153] A decision pursuant to the EA 2002, s 165(2), (6)(a), (7)(c) or (9)(b): s 166(1)(b).

[154] An order made pursuant to the EA 2002, s 165(8): s 166(1)(c).

[155] A decision pursuant to the EA 2002, s 165(10)(b): s 166(1)(d).

[156] EA 2002, s 166(2). This is a similar formulation to that used in, for example, the Employment Rights Act 1996, s 111(2), and it is suggested that a similar approach to the calculation of the relevant period should be adopted as is adopted under that Act. This would mean that the correct method for determining the final day of the period is to take the day immediately before the date on which the notice was given to the proprietor and then go forward 28 days: *Pruden v Cunard Ellerman Ltd* [1993] IRLR 317 (EAT). As to the rules for calculating time, see rule 11 of the Tribunal Procedure (First-tier Tribunal) (Health, Education and Social Care Chamber) Rules 2008.

[157] SI 2008/2699. See in particular Pts 2 and 3 of the Rules.

[158] EA 2002, s 167.

[159] In which case the Tribunal may only vary or revoke the order if it is appropriate to do so because there has been a change of circumstance after the making of the order: EA 2002, s 167(7)(b).

[160] In *Thomas Francis Academy v Secretary of State* [2007] EWCST 939(IS) (11 January 2008), the First-tier Tribunal held that that a section 166 appeal is a full merits appeal and that it may consider post-decision facts and material, even if that necessitated the Secretary of State conducting a further inspection of the school.

[161] *Thomas Francis Academy v Secretary of State* [2007] EWCST 939(IS) (11 January 2008), para 17.

[162] As to compliance with Art 6, see further para **9.13** above.

9.42 The legislation provides for the Tribunal to have the power to make an interim order where there is a risk of harm to the pupils at a school.[163] Where a proprietor has appealed against a decision of the registration authority to remove the school from the register on the grounds that any one or more of the independent schools standards is or are not being met and there is a risk of serious harm to the welfare of pupils at the school,[164] the Tribunal has a power, where it considers that there is a risk of serious harm occurring to the welfare of pupils before the determination, to order that the school is to be treated as if it were not registered pending the resolution of the appeal.[165] The Tribunal can exercise this power on its own motion, even if the Secretary of State no longer pursues an application an order.[166] Special procedural provisions govern applications for such orders.[167]

9.43 A decision of the Tribunal can be appealed to the Upper Tribunal on a point of law.[168] Permission to appeal is required, either from the First-tier Tribunal[169] or, if that is refused, from the Upper Tribunal.[170] On receiving an application for permission to appeal, the First-tier Tribunal is required to consider whether to review the decision.[171] A review entails determining whether the decision contains an error of law.[172] If the Tribunal decides not to review the decision, or reviews the decision and decides to take no action in relation it, the Tribunal must go on to consider whether to give permission to appeal.

9.44 Upon refusal, in whole or in part, of permission to appeal, the applicant can approach the Upper Tribunal directly for such permission.[173] Where the Upper Tribunal refuses permission to appeal, in whole or in part, without a hearing, the applicant may apply for the decision to be reconsidered at a hearing.[174] If the Upper Tribunal grants permission to appeal, it can determine the appeal with or without holding a hearing.[175] It is likely that, in determining

---

[163] EA 2002, s 166(5).
[164] A decision under the EA 2002, s 165(2).
[165] EA 2002, s 166(5).
[166] *Jewish Senior Boys' School, Salford (Keser Torah) v Secretary of State for Children, Schools and Families* [2008] EWCST 1317(JS) (08 September 2008) at paras 19 24.
[167] Tribunal Procedure (First-tier Tribunal) (Health, Education and Social Care Chamber) Rules 2008, rule 22.
[168] Tribunals, Courts and Enforcement Act 2007, s 11.
[169] Tribunal Procedure (First-tier Tribunal) (Health, Education and Social Care Chamber) Rules 2008, rule 46.
[170] Tribunal Procedure (Upper Tribunal) Rules 2008, SI 2698/2008, rule 21.
[171] Tribunal Procedure (First-tier Tribunal) (Health, Education and Social Care Chamber) Rules 2008, rule 47.
[172] Tribunal Procedure (First-tier Tribunal) (Health, Education and Social Care Chamber) Rules 2008, rule 49.
[173] Tribunal Procedure (Upper Tribunal) Rules 2008, rule 21.
[174] Tribunal Procedure (Upper Tribunal) Rules 2008, rule 22(3)–(4).
[175] Tribunal Procedure (Upper Tribunal) Rules 2008, rule 34.

the appeal, the Upper Tribunal will apply similar principles to those which have been developed in relation to appeals on a point of law from the SENDIST.[176]

Other provisions regulating independent schools

9.45 In England, an independent school can be named in a statement of SEN and the former requirement for approval by the Secretary of State of a placement of a child with SEN in an independent school has been abolished.[177] However, that requirement remains in place in Wales, where a statemented child cannot be educated in an independent school unless that school has been approved by the Welsh Ministers as suitable for the admission of children with SEN.[178] A Welsh LA intending to place a statemented child in an independent school in England will require the consent of the Welsh Ministers, but an English LA can place a statemented child in a school in Wales, whether or not it is approved by the Welsh Ministers, provided the English LA is satisfied the school is suitable for the child.

9.46 The Children Act 1989 contains various provisions relating to the protection of the welfare of children at independent boarding schools.[179] For example, the proprietor of an independent school which provides accommodation for any child has a duty to safeguard and promote the welfare of any child for whom accommodation is provided[180] and the Secretary of State has a power to cause such a school to be inspected at any time.[181]

THE RELATIONSHIP BETWEEN PARENTS AND INDEPENDENT SCHOOLS

9.47 The relationship between an independent school and the parents of a pupil at the school will usually be governed by a contract.[182] Since, in most cases[183], an independent school is not a public body and its rights and obligations in relation to the parents are governed by contract rather than underpinned by statute, the decisions of an independent school in relation to a

---

[176] As to the principles applied in relation to appeals from the SENDIST, see further Chapter 4 above.

[177] ESA 2008, s 146, amending the EA 1996, s 347(5). For the rationale behind the amendment, see the Guidance issued by the Department for Children, Schools and Families 'Section 146 of the Education Act 2008 – placement of pupils in independent schools and NMSSs' (June 2009).

[178] EA 1996, s 347(5). The Welsh Assembly Government wished to undertake consultation with interested parties in Wales before implementing similar proposals to abolish the requirement in Wales. For cross-border issues between England see further Chapter 4.

[179] See the Children Act 1989, ss 80, 87, 87A, 87B, 87C and 87D.

[180] Children Act 1989, at s 87(1).

[181] Children Act 1989, at s 80(1)(l).

[182] However, if the parents do not pay a fee to the school, the absence of consideration may mean that no contract exists.

[183] Academies although independent schools probably are amenable to judicial review. That was the case in relation to City Technology Colleges which were in many respects similar: see *R v Governors of Haberdashers' Aske's Hatcham College Trust ex parte T* [1995] ELR 350, Dyson J.

pupil are unlikely to be susceptible to judicial review[184] and they can only be challenged in the courts if they amount to a breach of contract.

9.48 There is one aspect of the contractual relationship between the school and the parent where the public law statutory framework applicable to other schools may be relevant: a contractually implied obligation of fairness. The Court of Appeal has recognised a 'basic symmetry in essentials' between a contractually implied obligation of fairness and that derived from statute or general public law.[185] However, the question ultimately remains whether, in the circumstances, the parent 'has had a fair deal of the kind that he bargained for'.[186]

9.49 Absent any quantifiable loss on the part of the parent, the utility of a claim for breach of contract is likely to be limited. First, such contracts often confer upon schools wide-ranging discretions as to how they deal with matters such as discipline and exclusion. Although, depending on the facts of a particular case, the Unfair Contract Terms Act 1977[187] and the Unfair Terms in Consumer Contract Regulations 1999[188] may apply to a contract between a parent and an independent school, the absence of any general duty on a contracting party to exercise its contractual rights reasonably or in good faith[189] is likely to mean that it will be difficult to assert that any particular exercise of a school's discretion under the contract constitutes a breach of contract. Secondly, the courts are likely to be reluctant to order specific performance of the contract.[190]

THE RELATIONSHIP BETWEEN CHILDREN AND INDEPENDENT SCHOOLS

9.50 Unless a pupil is party to any contract between his or her parents and the independent school, he or she is unlikely to be in a position to enforce any

---

[184] *R v Fernhill Manor School, ex parte A* [1994] ELR 67, Brooke J and *R v Incorporated Froebel Institute ex parte L* [1999] ELR 488, Tucker J. Cf *R v Cobham Hall School ex parte S* [1998] ELR 389, where it was held by Dyson J that a decision of an independent school in relation to an assisted place was amenable to judicial review.

[185] *Gray v Marlborough College* [2006] ELR 516, Auld LJ at paras 41 and 57. See also *E v Merchant Taylors' School* [2009] EWCA Civ 1050, where the existence of a duty to act fairly was assumed.

[186] *Calvin v Carr* [1980] AC 574, Lord Wilberforce at 594, cited in *Gray* at para 57.

[187] For a further discussion of the Unfair Contract Terms Act 1977, see *Chitty on Contracts* (Sweet & Maxwell, 30th Edn, 2008), paras 14.059–14.113.

[188] SI 1999/2083. For a further discussion of the Unfair Terms in Consumer Contract Regulations 1999, see *Chitty on Contracts* (Sweet and Maxwell, 30th Edn, 2008), paras 15.001–15.076.

[189] *Interfoto Picture Library Ltd v Stilletto Visual Programmes Ltd* [1989] QB 433, 439D–F per Bingham LJ. However, this general position may be changing: see the implication of an implied term in *Paragon Finance Plc v Nash* [2002] 1 WLR 685, 701D–703A per Dyson LJ. For further discussion of the role of good faith in contract, see *Chitty on Contracts* (Sweet & Maxwell, 28th Edn, 1999), paras 1.019–1.024.

[190] *R v Incorporated Froebel Institute ex parte L* [1999] ELR 488 Tucker J.

contractual rights against the school.[191] However, an independent school is likely to have the same potential liabilities in tort as a maintained school.[192]

9.51 The Equality Act 2010 applies to Independent Schools. The relevant provisions are discussed in the Discrimination Chapter.

ACADEMIES AND FREE SCHOOLS

9.52 Academies are hybrids. They are publicly funded schools, but are independent of LA control. As Academies are not maintained by LAs, they fall within the definition of 'independent schools',[193] even though they are funded by central government. Successive governments have promoted this de-coupling of state schools from LAs and, as of 1 April 2012, there were 1776 Academies open in England.[194] By contrast, the Welsh Assembly is yet to permit Academies to be opened in Wales.

9.53 Free Schools are a sub-set of Academy schools, based on the Charter School system in the United States. They require evidence of parental demand in order to be established. The first free schools opened in September 2011.

9.54 The Academies Act 2010 (AA 2010) provides a statutory basis, for the first time, for all primary, secondary and special schools in England to seek to convert to an Academy school,[195] as well as for new primary, secondary and special Academy schools to be created. The Act also includes a permissive provision that could in future be used to allow Academy schools to be established in Wales.[196]

9.55 Three types of educational institution fall within the ambit of 'Academies':

(a) **an Academy school**,[197] which is either:

    (i) an independent school with a balanced and broadly based curriculum satisfying the requirements of section 78 of the EA 2002,

---

[191] This is subject to the right of a third party to enforce a contractual term, under the Contracts (Rights of Third Parties) Act 1999, s 1. This may, in certain circumstances, give the pupil a right to enforce a term of the contract, for example an express or implied term to take reasonable care of the pupil. For further discussion of this Act, see *Chitty on Contracts* (op cit) paras 18-043–18-120.

[192] As to the liabilities in tort of a maintained school, see further Chapter 7.

[193] EA 1996, s 463.

[194] Department for Education website http://www.education.gov.uk/schools/leadership/typesofschools/ Academies/b0069811/open-Academies-and-Academy-projects-in-development (last accessed 7 April 2012).

[195] Previously, EA 1996, s 482 had empowered the Secretary of State to enter into arrangements for the establishment, maintenance and carrying on of city technology colleges and city colleges for the technology of the arts.

[196] AA 2010, s 18.

[197] AA 2010, s 1A.

provide education for pupils of different abilities, who are drawn wholly or mainly from the area in which the school is situated; or

(ii) an independent school specially organised to make special educational provision for pupils with special educational needs;

(b) **a 16 to 19 Academy**,[198] which is an educational institution principally concerned with providing full-time or part-time education (including vocational, social, physical and recreational training) to people over compulsory school age but under 19;

(c) **an alternative provision Academy**,[199] which is an educational institution principally concerned with providing full-time or part-time education for children of different abilities, who are drawn wholly or mainly from the area in which the school is situated, who by reason of illness, exclusion from school or otherwise may not receive suitable education[200] for any period.

9.56 Academies have freedoms that maintained schools do not: they can set their own pay and conditions for staff, change the lengths of terms and school days and choose how to deliver the curriculum. Academies are also designed to benefit from sponsorship. The government has encouraged a wide range of sponsors for Academies, including high performing schools, universities, individuals, businesses, charities and faith bodies.

9.57 There are two routes by which an Academy can be created: through the Secretary of State entering into 'Academy arrangements' in order to create a new Academy, or though the Secretary of State making an 'Academy order' to convert an existing school into an Academy.

Academy arrangements

9.58 Section 1 of the AA 2010 empowers the Secretary of State to enter into two different types of Academy arrangements. The first is an 'Academy agreement',[201] which is an agreement between the Secretary of State and another party[202] that imposes obligations on both parties to the agreement. The

---

[198] AA 2010, s 1B.

[199] AA 2010, s 1C.

[200] Defined in AA 2010, s 1C(2) as 'efficient education suitable to the child's age, ability and aptitude and to any special education needs the child may have.'

[201] AA 2010, s 1(3).

[202] Although the primary legislation never uses the term 'sponsor' when referring to the 'other party', the Teachers' Pensions Regulations 2010, SI 2010/990, Sch 2, para 2 defines the phrase 'sponsor of a proposed Academy' to mean 'any person who approaches the Secretary of State expressing an interest in establishing and maintaining an Academy with a view to creating a charitable company limited by guarantee and which company it is proposed will then enter into an' Academy arrangement.

second is an 'arrangement for Academy financial assistance',[203] through which the Secretary of State provides financial assistance pursuant to section 14 of the EA 2002.

9.59 It would appear that the only difference between the two forms of arrangement is that an Academy agreement requires the parties to enter into a contract, whereas the arrangement for financial assistance does not. In both instances, the other party is required to give the undertakings set out in section 1(5) of the AA 2010:[204]

(a) to establish and maintain an educational institution in England which meets the requirements of an Academy school,[205] a 16 to 19 Academy[206] or an alternative provision Academy;[207] and

(b) to carry on, or provide for the carrying on, of the institution.

9.60 The AA 2010 also dictates that Academy arrangements must include terms designed to secure that Academies are non-fee paying[208] and that they abide by certain obligations in relation to SEN.[209] At the time of writing, the model Academy arrangements published by the Secretary of State also require Academies to follow the law and guidance on admissions and exclusions as if they were maintained schools, but this is not necessitated by the AA 2010.

9.61 Before deciding whether to enter into Academy arrangements in relation to a new school,[210] the Secretary of State must take into account the impact of establishing the additional school on maintained schools, Academies, institutions within the further educational sector and alternative provision in the area where the additional school will be situated.[211]

9.62 The proposed other party to the Academy arrangements is required to consult such persons as it thinks appropriate on the question of whether the arrangements should be entered into.[212] The AA 2010 does not specify any particular consultees, but it is suggested that the relevant LA and any other educational institutions in the area should be consulted.

---

[203] AA 2010, s 1(4).

[204] As amended by the Education Act 2011, s 53(2).

[205] AA 2010, s 1A, see para **9.55** above.

[206] AA 2010, s 1B, see para **9.55** above.

[207] AA 2010, s 1C, see para **9.55** above.

[208] AA 2010, s 1(9). However, exceptions can be specified in the Academy arrangement in relation to charges for education provision at the school.

[209] AA 2010, s 1(8). These obligations are defined as those imposed on governing bodies of maintained schools by Chapter 1 of Part 4 of EA 1996 and regulations made under any provisions of that Chapter.

[210] AA 2010, s 9(3)(a) defines a 'new school' as a school that does not replace one or more maintained schools, Academies or sixth form colleges that have been or are to be discontinued

[211] AA 2010, s 9(2).

[212] AA 2010, s 10(1).

9.63 Payments under an Academy agreement may be in respect of capital or current expenditure. Where current expenditure is concerned, the agreement must provide for payments to continue for at least seven years,[213] or to continue indefinitely, but be terminable by the Secretary of State giving at least seven years' written notice.[214] The Government's stated aim is that Academies receive the same level of per-pupil funding as they would receive from the LA as a maintained school, plus additions to cover the services that are no longer provided for them by the LA.[215] The Academy then has a choice as to how to obtain such services, including retaining the services of the LA.

9.64 Payments for current expenditure are subject to the other requirements of the agreement being fulfilled.[216] Accordingly, the AA 2010 makes it clear that funding to an Academy provider under an Academy agreement may be suspended or terminated if the provider is failing to meet the undertakings stipulated in the Academy agreement.

9.65 If an Academy agreement makes provision for payments in respect of capital expenditure, the agreement may provide for the repayment to the Secretary of State, in circumstances specified in the agreement, of sums determined in accordance with the agreement.[217]

9.66 In the event of the Secretary of State terminating the Academy agreement, the other party may be indemnified for expenditure incurred in carrying out the undertakings under the agreement, or otherwise in consequence of the termination of the agreement.[218]

9.67 Previously, the Secretary of State was empowered to require the Young Person's Learning Agency for England (an arm's length body) to enter into Academy arrangements in order to carry out some of the government's duties under such arrangements; in particular the provision of funding.[219] This Agency was abolished by the Education Act 2011[220] and its functions transferred to the Department for Education, which has set up a new executive agency – the Education Funding Agency – to carry out those functions.

---

[213] AA 2010, s 2(2)(a)

[214] AA 2010, s 2(2)(b).

[215] Such as school transport, SEN support, occupational health and safety, human resources and legal services.

[216] AA 2010, s 2(2).

[217] AA 2010, s 2 (3).

[218] AA 2010, s 3(4).

[219] Apprenticeship, Skills, Children and Learning Act 2009, s 77ff.

[220] Section 66 and Schs 16–17.

9.68 For each academic year,[221] the Secretary of State is required to prepare and publish a report setting out the number of Academy arrangements entered into during the year.[222] The Secretary of State is required to lay the report before Parliament.[223]

Academy orders

9.69 An Academy order in respect of a maintained school 'is an order for the purpose of enabling the school to be converted into an Academy'.[224] The Academy order converts the maintained school into an Academy by ordering that, on the 'conversion date',[225] the school shall be converted to an Academy and the Academy shall open as provided for in Academy arrangements entered into in relation to the school.[226] Every Academy order thus also entails the Secretary of State entering into Academy arrangements in relation to the school.

9.70 The description of the process as 'conversion' is something of a misnomer: the Academy order in fact closes the maintained school and replaces it with an Academy.[227] The decision to become an Academy thus cannot be reversed once the Academy order has been implemented.

9.71 Despite being styled 'orders', Academy orders are not required to be made by statutory instrument[228] and are therefore not subject to Parliamentary approval.

9.72 There are two instances in which the Secretary of State may make an Academy order in respect of a school: where an existing maintained school makes an application for such an order;[229] or where an existing maintained school is eligible for intervention within the meaning of section of the 59 EIA 2006.[230]

9.73 Where an existing maintained school in England[231] wishes to apply to the Secretary of State for an Academy order to be made in respect of the school,[232] the application has to be made by the governing body of the school.[233] In relation to a federated governing body, the Secretary of State can

---

[221] Defined in AA 2010, s 11(5) as 'a period of 12 months beginning on 1 August'.
[222] AA 2010, s 11(1)(a).
[223] AA 2010, s 11(4).
[224] AA 2010, s 4(2).
[225] AA 2010, s 6(2). This is the date on which the educational institution that replaces the school opens as an Academy.
[226] AA 2010, s 4(3).
[227] AA 2010, ss 6(2) and 6(9). See further para **9.85** below.
[228] AA 2010, s 4(6).
[229] AA 2010, s 4(1)(a).
[230] AA 2010, s 4(1)(b).
[231] AA 2010, s 4(1).
[232] AA 2010, s 4(1)(a).
[233] AA 2010, s 4(1)(a).

prescribe by regulation the number and type of members who can apply for an Academy order in respect of one of the federated schools.[234]

9.74 The governing body of a maintained school is empowered to form, or participate in forming, a company to enter into Academy arrangements.[235] The governing body is able to do 'anything which appears to them to be necessary or expedient in connection with a proposal that Academy arrangements be entered into with a company formed (or proposed to be formed) by them',[236] including incurring expenditure.[237] There is thus no requirement that the school find an external sponsor in order to become an Academy, although the option is available.

9.75 The school's governing body is required to undertake consultation as to whether the conversion to an Academy should take place.[238] However, this consultation requirement is seriously flawed.[239] Section 5(2) of the AA 2010 provides that the consultation 'may take place before **or after** an Academy order, or an application for an Academy order, has been made in respect of the school' (emphasis added). This flies in the face of the well-established common law requirements of a proper consultation: that consultation must be undertaken at a time when proposals are still at a formative stage and that the product of consultation must conscientiously be taken into account when the ultimate decision is taken.[240] It is difficult to see how these requirements can be fulfilled by a consultation undertaken after an application for an Academy order has been made (after the governing body had taken the decision to apply), let alone after the order itself has been made.[241]

9.76 Section 5 is also vague as to whom the governing body should consult. It requires only that the views of such persons as the person carrying out the consultation thinks appropriate should be sought.[242] It is suggested that, at a minimum, the views of the LA, the teaching staff, the parents of children at the school and, if possible, the children themselves, should be sought.

9.77 In the case of a foundation or voluntary school that has a foundation, the governing body is required to consult the foundation before making an

---

[234] AA 2010, s 3(6). At the time of writing, no such regulations had been made.
[235] Children, Schools and Families Act 2010, s 5(1)(a).
[236] Children, Schools and Families Act 2010, s 5(1)(b).
[237] Children, Schools and Families Act 2010, s 5(3)(a).
[238] AA 2010, s 5(1).
[239] This flaw was re-enacted when the AA 2010, s 5 was replaced by the EA 2011, s 56.
[240] See, for example, *R v North and East Devon Health Authority, ex parte Coughlan* [2001] QB 213 at 108, citing *R v Brent London Borough Council, ex parte Gunning* (1985) 84 LGR 168.
[241] By contrast, the EIA 2006, s 16 requires significant consultation to take place *before* proposals for discontinuing a maintained school are published. This includes consultation with the registered parents of registered pupils at the school, the relevant LA and any other relevant people. The AA 2010, s 6(9) specifically disapplies these consultation requirements, even though the effect of an Academy order is the discontinuance of a maintained school.
[242] AA 2010, s 5(5).

application for an Academy order.[243] Furthermore, the application may only be made with the consent of the trustees of the school,[244] and the person or persons by whom the foundation governors are appointed.[245]

9.78 A limited requirement for consultation is imposed on the Secretary of State. Before an Academy order is made in relation to a foundation school: he is required to consult the trustees of the foundation and, where appropriate, the relevant religious body.[246] The Secretary of State is not required to consult the LA, the teaching staff or the parents or pupils of a school applying to become an Academy, although it would clearly be prudent to do so.

9.79 Where the proposed Academy will provide education for pupils of a wider range of ages than the existing maintained school, the Academy is considered to be a new school.[247] Accordingly, before making an Academy order in such a circumstance, the Secretary of State is required to take into account the impact of establishing the new school on maintained schools, Academies, institutions within the further educational sector and alternative provision in the area where the additional school will be situated.[248]

9.80 In relation to the second category of Academy orders – those concerning 'failing schools'[249] – the government has made it clear that it will seek to address the difficulties of those schools by converting them to Academies.[250] This policy extends to low performing infant and primary schools and weak special schools. The government's aim is to partner such failing schools with a sponsor or an outstanding school when making the Academy order. Whilst this process may take place at the behest of the school and/or the LA, the Secretary of State has the power unilaterally to make an Academy order in respect of a failing school.[251] In such an instance, the consultation required by section 5 of the AA 2010 may be carried out by the proposed party to the Academy arrangements, rather than by the governing body of the school.[252]

9.81 The AA 2010 is silent as to the factors that the Secretary of State should consider when deciding whether to make an Academy order (apart from where the order creates a new school).[253] Nor has an official policy document been produced setting out such factors. Instead. the Department for Education

---

[243] AA 2010, s 3(3).
[244] AA 2010, s 3(4)(a).
[245] AA 2010, s 3(4)(b).
[246] AA 2010, ss 4(1A) and 4(8)–(9).
[247] AA 2010, s 9(1)(b).
[248] AA 2010, s 9(2).
[249] Ie, schools eligible for intervention within the meaning of the EIA 2006, s 59.
[250] *The Importance of Teaching: The Schools White Paper 2010* (November 2010), para 5.15.
[251] The White Paper made it plain that the Secretary of State would be more likely to exercise the power unilaterally than had previously been the case. see para 5.15.
[252] AA 2010, s 5(3).
[253] See para **9.79** above.

(DfE) states on its website that only schools that are 'performing well' will be eligible to convert to Academies.[254] Such performance is said to be determined considering:

(a)   the school's last three years of exam results and its general performance trend;

(b)   comparisons, both locally and nationally, with exam performance in similar schools;

(c)   the most recent Ofsted inspection report;

(d)   financial management of the school, including any deficits;

(e)   any additional evidence which the school feels is significant in proving its performance.

9.82   For schools that do not collect such data, such as infant schools, the DfE's website states that the Secretary of State will take into account:

(a)   the school's last two Ofsted inspection grades, with focus particularly on judgments for overall effectiveness, capacity to improve and leadership and management;

(b)   any available data on pupil attainment and progress; and

(c)   any additional evidence which the school feels is significant in proving its performance.

9.83   When the Secretary of State makes an Academy order (by whatever route), he is required to provide a copy of it to the relevant LA,[255] the governing body and headteacher of the relevant school[256] and, in the case of a foundation or voluntary school that has a foundation, the trustees of the school, the person or persons by whom the foundation governors are appointed, and, in the case of a school which has a religious character, the appropriate religious body.[257] There is no duty to give reasons where the Secretary of State decides he will make the order.

9.84   If the Secretary of State decides not to make an Academy order, then he must provide the reasons for his decision to the relevant LA,[258] the governing

---

[254] http://www.education.gov.uk/schools/leadership/typesofschools/Academies/a0068038/
       expansion-of-the-programme-to-all-schools-that-are-performing-well-faqs (last accessed 9
       April 2012).
[255] AA 2010, s 4(4)(b).
[256] AA 2010, s 4(4)(a).
[257] AA 2010, s 4(4)(c).
[258] AA 2010, s 4(5)(b).

body and headteacher of the relevant school[259] and, in the case of a foundation or voluntary school that has a foundation, the trustees of the school, the person or persons by whom the foundation governors are appointed, and, in the case of a school which has a religious character, the appropriate religious body.[260]

9.85 The effect of an Academy order is to discontinue[261] (ie close) the maintained school and replace it with an Academy school. The order requires the LA to cease to maintain the school[262] on the date on which the educational institution that replaces the school opens as an Academy.[263]

9.86 The making of an Academy order triggers an obligation on the LA that maintained the previous school to calculate whether that school has a surplus;[264] ie whether the amount available to the school's governing body by way of delegated budget has not yet been spent.[265] If a surplus does exist, the LA must calculate the amount of the surplus[266] and must pay that sum to the proprietor of the Academy.[267] If the school is a federated school, the questions of whether the school has a surplus, and, if so, the amount of the surplus, are to be determined in accordance with regulations.[268]

9.87 The EA 2011 softened the break between Academies and LAs by making it possible for LAs to provide financial or other assistance in respect of Academies,[269] including by making payments in respect of some (but not all) of the expenses of maintaining the Academy,[270] providing premises, goods or services for the Academy,[271] or making premises, goods or services available to be used for the purposes of the Academy.[272]

9.88 In addition to making an Academy order, the Secretary of State also has the power to make a 'transfer scheme' in relation to property, rights and liabilities which are held for the purposes of the school by the LA or the governing body.[273] This power is available regardless of the route by which the Academy order was made. Such a scheme may transfer property, rights and

---

[259] AA 2010, s 4(5)(a).

[260] AA 2010, s 4(5)(c).

[261] AA 2010, s 6(9). This impliedly recognises that the Academy order discontinues the maintained school, as it disapplies the EA 2006, ss 15–17. See also *ML v Tonbridge Grammar School* and *SB v West Bridgford Academy* (unreported) 1 August 2012 at paras 10–13.

[262] AA 2010, s 6(2).

[263] AA 2010, s 6(2).

[264] AA 2010, s 7(2).

[265] AA 2010, s 7(6).

[266] AA 2010, s 7(2).

[267] AA 2010, s 7(3). This process is governed by the Academy Conversions (Transfer of School Surpluses) Regulations 2010, SI 2010/1938.

[268] AA 2010, s 7(9). At the time of writing, no such regulations had been promulgated.

[269] EA 2011, s 58.

[270] AA 2010, s 6(2A)(a).

[271] AA 2010, s 6(2A)(b).

[272] AA 2010, s 6(2A)(c).

[273] AA 2010, s 8(2).

liabilities to a person concerned with the running of the Academy.[274] The Secretary of State may also make a separate transfer scheme in relation to freehold or leasehold interests in land.[275]

9.89 The requirement to provide education for pupils of different abilities which generally applies to Academies, does not apply where a selective school is replaced by an Academy.[276] If the previous maintained school was selective or had a religious character, then those characteristics will be preserved in the replacement Academy.[277]

Free schools

9.90 The term 'free schools' does not appear in the AA 2010. The entire free school initiative has been developed and promoted through guidance and policy documents. The DfE website describes free schools as schools 'set up in response to real demand within a local area for a greater variety of schools'.[278] A proposer for a free school is required to provide evidence of parental demand for such a school, for example in the form of a petition or declaration from interested parents, as well as a 'clear and compelling business case'.

9.91 The legislative framework for free schools is found in sections 9–10 of the AA 2010 concerning the establishment of 'new schools'. Free schools are, therefore, Academies and are created through Academy arrangements. In determining whether to permit a free school to be established, the Secretary of State must take into account the impact of establishing the additional school on maintained schools, Academies, institutions within the further educational sector and alternative provision in the area where the additional school will be situated.[279]

9.92 Guidance on the DfE website states that the Secretary of State will consider the following criteria when assessing whether to permit the establishment of a free school:[280]

(a)   the age range of the Free School;

(b)   overall cost and value for money;

(c)   equality issues under section 149 of the Equality Act 2010;

(d)   the standards of schools in the local area;

---

[274]   AA 2010, s 8(4).

[275]   AA 2010, Sch 1.

[276]   AA 2010, s 6(3).

[277]   AA 2010, ss 6(7)–6(8).

[278]   http://www.education.gov.uk/schools/leadership/typesofschools/freeschools/b0061428/free-schools/what (last accessed 9 April 2012).

[279]   AA 2010, s 9(2).

[280]   http://dera.ioe.ac.uk/12492/1/how%20to%20apply%20guidance%20-%20alternative%20provision.pdf (last accessed 9 April 2012)

(e)   the level of deprivation in the community the school will serve;

(f)   the need for more school places in the area;

(g)   the type of provider;

(h)   the recent track record of the provider, including on education;

(i)   the balance between secular and faith schools.

Charitable status of Academies

9.93 All Academies are automatically charities. The proprietor of an Academy is required to be a company limited by guarantee, whose registered office is situated in England and Wales, and whose object is expressed in its articles or memoranda of association as a charitable purpose[281] – generally, the advancement of education. The sponsor or 'other party' to Academy arrangements is therefore often referred to as an 'Academy trust'.

9.94 Academies are exempt charities[282] and are regulated by the Secretary of State, rather than having to register with the Charities Commission.[283]

Multi-Academy arrangements

9.95 The government has indicated strong support for multi-Academy arrangements.[284] There are three ways in which it envisages Academies being formed into chains:

(a)   **The Multi-Academy Trust Model** (also known as 'brands'): this is where several Academies are created using one Academy arrangement. Although there is only one company acting as the 'other party', each Academy might have its own governing body with limited powers.

(b)   **Umbrella Trust Model** (also known as 'chains'): this is where each Academy is established through its own Academy arrangements, but is affiliated to an umbrella trust that is completely separate from the agreements with the Secretary of State. The umbrella trust is established and populated by the member Academies according to pre-determined objects.

---

[281]   AA 2010, s 12.

[282]   Charities Act 2011, s 22 and Sch 3, para 8.

[283]   This was not the position when Academies were introduced. Initially, they had to register with the Charities Commission, which was strongly opposed to Academies being made exempt charities.

[284]   See *The Importance of Teaching: The Schools White Paper 2010* (November 2010), para 16 of the Executive Summary and para 5.4.

(c) **The Collaborative Partnership Model**: this is where each Academy exists as a separate entity, but a management agreement is put in place to bring the Academies into working partnership for specific purposes.

Academies and independent school standards

9.96 Where an Academy is created by an Academy order, the relevant independent school standards[285] will be deemed to be met in relation to the new Academy on the date that it commences.[286] This means that the Academy will not need to be inspected by Ofsted prior to opening or being registered as an independent school.

9.97 Where an Academy is a new school, it will be subject to an initial independent school registration inspection,[287] and is required to be entered on the independent schools register. The initial registration inspection does not include inspection of the curriculum or of teaching and learning.[288]

9.98 Thereafter, the independent school standards apply to Academies in broadly the same way that they apply to other independent schools.[289] Accordingly, Academies are required to meet prescribed standards in relation to:

(a) the spiritual, moral, social and cultural development of students at a school;[290]

(b) the welfare, health and safety of students;[291]

(c) the suitability of proprietors and staff;[292]

---

[285] The independent school standards as defined in the EA 2002, s 157(2) and the Education (Independent School Standards) (England) Regulations 2010, SI 2010/1997. See further para **9.11** above.

[286] AA 2010, ss 6(5)–6(6).

[287] Education (Independent Educational Provision in England) (Provision of Information) Regulations 2010, SI 2010/2919, reg 2(b).

[288] SI 2010/2919, reg 2(b), which disapplies paras 3(6)–3(12) of Pt 2 of the Schedule.

[289] There are three exceptions. SI 2010/1997, reg 3 disapplies Pt 1, concerning the requirement for a written policy on the curriculum, supported by appropriate plans and schemes of work; and two paras in Pt 6 requiring the provision of information concerning the particulars of the school's academic performance during the preceding school year, including the results of any public examinations and the number of staff at the school, including temporary staff, and a summary of their qualifications.

[290] Education (Independent School Standards) (England) Regulations 2010 SI 2010/1997, reg 3 and Sch 1, para 5.

[291] Education (Independent School Standards) (England) Regulations 2010 SI 2010/1997, reg 3 and Sch 1, paras 6–17.

[292] Education (Independent School Standards) (England) Regulations 2010 SI 2010/1997, reg 3 and Sch 1, paras 18–22.

(d)   the premises of, and accommodation at, a school;[293]

(e)   the provision of information to parents of students, parents of prospective students, the Chief Inspector or the Secretary of State;[294] and

(f)   the manner in which a school handles complaints.[295]

9.99   All Academies are subject to inspection by the Chief Inspector at regular intervals.[296] The Chief Inspector's report is required to cover:

(a)   the achievement of pupils at the school;[297]

(b)   the quality of teaching in the school;[298]

(c)   the quality of the leadership in and management of the school;[299]

(d)   the behaviour and safety of pupils at the school;[300]

(e)   the spiritual, moral, social and cultural development of pupils at the school;[301]

(f)   the extent to which the education provided at the school meets the needs of the range of pupils at the school, and in particular the needs of pupils who have a disability for the purposes of the Equality Act 2010, and pupils who have special educational needs.[302]

Under section 165(1)(b) of the EA 2002,[303] the Chief Inspector's report concerning an Academy could amount to evidence that the Academy is not meeting the requirements of the independent school standards, thereby triggering the duties on the registration authority to take action in relation to Academies on the independent schools register to ensure that the standards are met.[304]

---

[293]   Education (Independent School Standards) (England) Regulations 2010 SI 2010/1997, reg 3 and Sch 1, para 23.

[294]   Education (Independent School Standards) (England) Regulations 2010 SI 2010/1997, reg 3 and Sch 1, para 24, apart from paras 24(1)(h), and 24(1)(b) insofar as it relates to the information referred to in paras 24(3)(b), (c), (f) and (h).

[295]   Education (Independent School Standards) (England) Regulations 2010 SI 2010/1997, reg 3 and Sch 1, para 25.

[296]   EA 2005, s 5(2).

[297]   EA 2005, s 5A(a).

[298]   EA 2005, s 5A(b).

[299]   EA 2005, s 5A(c).

[300]   EA 2005, s 5A(d).

[301]   EA 2005, s 5B(a).

[302]   EA 2005, s 5B(b).

[303]   And, when it comes into force, ESA 2008, s 114.

[304]   See paras **9.35–9.44** above.

9.100 Academies are not required to file initial returns or annual returns,[305] so they are not at risk of removal from the register for failure to provide such information.[306]

Challenging decisions concerning Academies and free schools

9.101 The Secretary of State's decision whether or not to enter into Academy arrangements or to make an Academy order is challengeable on normal judicial review grounds. However, the requirements of the public procurement regime do not to apply to the establishment of Academies.[307]

9.102 Although Academies are independent schools, the nature of their establishment, their funding through public money and the statutory requirements imposed on them all point to Academies being public law bodies, some of whose decisions are amenable to judicial review. The High Court held in *R v Haberdashers' Aske's Hatcham College Trust (Governors), ex p T*[308] that city technology colleges were amenable to judicial review because their existence and their essential characteristics derived from the exercise by government of statutory power. Precisely the same legal analysis applies to Academies. The source of the power to create Academies is derived from statute, the contract establishing them is underpinned by statute and the nature and functions of Academies in relation to admission, exclusion and special educational needs provision have public law consequences. Accordingly, such decisions are challengeable by way of judicial review as long as the parent/child concerned does not have an alternative remedy to challenge the decision.

---

[305] SI 2010/2919, reg 2(b), which disapplies regs 4 and 5. On initial returns and annual returns, see paras **9.24–9.25** above.

[306] See para **9.26** above.

[307] *R (Chandler) v Secretary of State for Children, Schools and Families* [2009] EWCA Civ 1011, [2010] LGR 1.

[308] [1995] ELR 350.

Chapter 10

HUMAN RIGHTS

CONVENTION RIGHTS RELEVANT TO THE EDUCATION FIELD

10.1 Convention rights can be relevant in a variety of areas in the education field. In this book where a convention right is relevant to a particular area, such as school transport, it is dealt with there. There is, however, a general corpus of Convention jurisprudence on Article 2 of the First Protocol which is relevant to a variety of different subject areas covered in this book and it is this topic which is dealt with here. This Chapter does not purport to be a comprehensive review of the jurisprudence of the ECHR, but merely to set out some of the general principles that can be derived from the case-law on Article 2 of the First Protocol to the ECHR. Other convention rights which may be relevant in the education field, such as Articles 9 and 14, are dealt with in more detail elsewhere.

Article 2 of the First Protocol and the UK's reservation

10.2 Article 2 of the First Protocol to the European Convention on Human Rights provides:

> 'No person shall be denied the right to education. In the exercise of any functions which it assumes in relation to education and teaching, the State shall respect the right of parents to ensure such education and teaching in conformity with their own religious and philosophical convictions.'

The UK has entered a reservation in respect of the second sentence of Article 2. It provides that:

> '... in view of certain provisions of the Education Acts in force in the United Kingdom, the principle affirmed in the second sentence of Art 2 is accepted by the United Kingdom only so far as it is compatible with the provision of efficient instruction and training and the avoidance of unreasonable public expenditure.'

10.3 The reservation reflects what is now section 9 of the Education Act 1996:

> 'pupils are to be educated in accordance with the wishes of their parents so far as that is compatible with the provision of efficient instruction and training and the avoidance of unreasonable public expenditure.'

Article 2 of the First Protocol accordingly has effect subject to this reservation.

10.4 In the *Belgian Linguistic Case*,[1] a challenge was brought by French-speaking parents in Belgium who complained that certain provisions of the Belgian laws governing the use of languages in education violated Article 2 in that they were denied public support and recognition of French-speaking schools in certain areas of Belgium officially designated as Flemish and, therefore, as unilingual for the purposes of education. The parents wanted their children to be educated in French and alleged that the effect of the language laws was to abrogate the right to education guaranteed by Article 2 and was discriminatory.

10.5 The court held that the first sentence of Article 2:

(a) enshrined a 'right' (despite its negative formulation);

(b) did not require atates to establish at their own expense, or to subsidise, education of any particular type or at any particular level;

(c) merely guaranteed to individuals the right, in principle, to avail themselves of the means of instruction existing at a given time;

(d) included:

    (i)   a right of access to educational institutions existing at a given time;
    (ii) the right to be educated in the national language, or one of the national languages;
    (iii) the right to obtain official recognition of the studies completed; and
    (iv) implied such particular rights as were necessary to make the right to education 'effective' and meaningful.

10.6 The other right expressly articulated in Article 2 of the First Protocol is that contained in the second sentence, ie the right of parents to respect for their religious and philosophical convictions in the education and teaching of their children. The scope and content of that right was considered in *Kjeldsen, Busk Madsen & Pedersen v Denmark*,[2] *Campbell and Cosans v UK*,[3] *Valsamis v Greece*,[4] *Lautsi v Italy*,[5] *Temel v Turkey*,[6] *Orsus v Croatia*,[7] and *Ali v United Kingdom*.[8]

---

[1]   Judgment of 23 July 1968, Series A. No 6, (1979–80) 1 EHRR 252.
[2]   Judgment of 7 Dec 1976, Series A, No 23 (1979–80) 1 EHRR 711.
[3]   Judgment of 25 Feb 1982, Series A, No 48 (1982) 4 EHRR 293.
[4]   Judgment of 18 Dec 1996, (1997) 24 EHRR 294.
[5]   *Lautsi v Italy* – 30814/06 [2009] ECHR 1901 (03 November 2009).
[6]   [2009] ECHR 36458/02.
[7]   (2010) 28 BHRC 558.
[8]   [2011] ECHR 40385/06 (11 January 2011).

10.7 In those cases the court has held that:

(a) Article 2 of the First Protocol constitutes a whole which is dominated by its first sentence, enshrining the right of everyone to education. The right to respect for religious and philosophical convictions is an adjunct of the fundamental right to education, and the second sentence, therefore, has to be read together with the first. As the court explained in *Kjeldsen*, parents are primarily responsible for the education and teaching of their children, and it is in the discharge of that 'natural duty' that the right of parents to require the state to respect their religious and philosophical convictions arises;[9]

(b) the two sentences of Article 2 also have to be read, not only in the light of each other, but in the light of other provisions of the Convention, in particular, Articles 8, 9 and 10, guaranteeing the right to respect for private and family life, to freedom of thought, conscience and religion, and the freedom to receive and impart information and ideas;[10]

(c) the verb 'respect' in the second sentence of Article 2 means more than merely 'acknowledge' or 'take into account'. In addition to a primarily negative undertaking, it implies some positive obligation on the part of the State;[11]

(d) this positive obligation to respect parents' religious and philosophical convictions is of broad application. It applies to all schools, state and private.[12]

10.8 In *Kjeldsen*, the Danish Government argued that the second sentence of Article 2 did not apply to state schools where attendance was not obligatory, relying on the availability of private schools to which the state paid very substantial subsidies, and the possibility of parents educating their children at home.[13] The existence of such alternatives, it was argued, meant that parents were not being forced to send their children to state schools. The court rejected this argument, holding that the mere existence of private schools, even though they were subsidised by the state, did not relieve the state of its obligation under the second sentence of Article 2 to ensure respect for parents' religious and philosophical convictions in state teaching.

10.9 In *Orsus v Croatia*[14] the applicants complained that their teaching in Roma only classes and the subsequent length of time it had taken to litigate their rights in the domestic courts in Croatia violated their rights under Articles 6 and Article 2 of the First Protocol of the Convention read with

---

9   *Kjeldsen*, paras 50 and 52; *Campbell & Cosans*, para 40.
10 *Kjeldsen*, para 52.
11 *Kjeldsen*, para 52; *Valsamis*, para 25.
12 *Campbell & Cosans*, para 37; *Valsamis*, para 27.
13 *Kjeldsen*, para 50.
14 (2010) 28 BHRC 558.

Article 14. The Grand Chamber held, unanimously that there had been a breach of Article 6 and, by a majority, of Article 2 of the First Protocol read with Article 14. They did not reach a conclusion on Article 2 of the First Protocol read alone. The measures taken were disproportionate because, inter alia, the children were placed in Roma classes on the basis of inadequate grasp of the Croatian language without any proper testing of their language ability, the curriculum followed in the Roma only classes was not as extensive as that for pupils attending the general classes, and no other group that had difficulty with the Croatian language was treated in a like manner.

10.10 In *Lautsi*,[15] the applicant complained about the presence of a crucifix on the wall of the classroom in the state school her children were educated in. She considered that was contrary to the principle of secularism by which she wished to bring up her children. She contended before the European Court of Human Rights that there had been a breach of Article 9 of the Convention and Article 2 of the First Protocol thereto.

10.11 The court reached the following conclusions:

(a)   It rejected the government's argument that the obligation to display (or the fact of displaying) the crucifix was justified by the positive moral message of the Christian faith, which transcended secular constitutional values, the role of religion in Italian history and the deep roots of religion in the country's tradition. The Italian Government had attributed to the crucifix a neutral and secular meaning with reference to Italian history and tradition, which were closely bound up with Christianity, and had submitted that the crucifix was not only a religious symbol but one which could equally represent other values. However, while the court accepted that the symbol of the crucifix has a number of different meanings, it found that the religious meaning was predominant among them.

(b)   The court considered that the presence of the crucifix in classrooms went beyond the use of symbols in specific historical contexts.

(c)   Ms Lautsi's convictions were sufficiently serious and consistent for the compulsory presence of the crucifix to be capable of being understood by her as being incompatible with them. She saw the display of the crucifix as a sign that the state took the side of Catholicism. That was the meaning officially accepted in the Catholic Church, which attributed to the crucifix a fundamental message. Consequently, the applicant's apprehension that the symbol conflicted with her convictions and infringed her children's right not to profess Catholicism was not arbitrary.

(d)   Ms Lautsi's convictions also concerned the impact of the display of the crucifix on her children. The court agreed with Ms Lautsi that it was impossible not to notice crucifixes in the classrooms, and found that in the

---

[15]   Unreported. Application No. 30814/06, 3.11.2009.

context of public education they were necessarily perceived as an integral part of the school environment and might therefore be considered 'powerful external symbols'.[16]

(e) The presence of the crucifix mighty easily be interpreted by pupils of all ages as a religious sign, and they would feel that they had been brought up in a school environment marked by a particular religion. What might be encouraging for some religious pupils might be emotionally disturbing for pupils of other religions or those who professed no religion. That risk was particularly strong among pupils belonging to religious minorities. Negative freedom of religion was not restricted to the absence of religious services or religious education. It extended to practices and symbols expressing, in particular or in general, a belief, a religion or atheism. That negative right deserved special protection if it was the state which expressed a belief and dissenters were placed in a situation from which they could not extract themselves unless they made disproportionate efforts and acts of sacrifice.

(f) The display of one or more religious symbols could not be justified either by the wishes of other parents who wanted to see a religious form of education in conformity with their convictions or, as the Italian Government submitted, by the need for a compromise with political parties of Christian inspiration. Respect for parents' convictions with regard to education had to take into account respect for the convictions of other parents. The state had a duty to uphold confessional neutrality in public education, where school attendance was compulsory regardless of religion, and which had to seek to inculcate in pupils the habit of critical thought.

(g) The court was unable to see how the display in state-school classrooms of a symbol that it was reasonable to associate with Catholicism (the majority religion in Italy) could serve the educational pluralism which was essential for the preservation of 'democratic society' within the Convention meaning of that term (noting that the Italian Constitutional Court took the same view in its case-law).

10.12 By a decision of 18 March 2011 the Grand Chamber by 15 votes to 2 overturned the decision of the court. The Grand Chamber held that could be seen from the court's case-law that the obligation on the member states of the Council of Europe to respect the religious and philosophical convictions of parents bound them 'in the exercise' of all the 'functions' which they assumed in relation to education and teaching. That included the organisation of the school environment where domestic law attributed that function to the public authorities. The decision whether crucifixes should be present in state-school classrooms formed part of the functions assumed by the Italian State and, accordingly, fell within the scope of Article 2 of Protocol No 1. That provision

---

[16]   See *Dahlab v Switzerland* (Dec), no 42393/98, ECHR 2001-V.

conferred on the state the obligation, in the exercise of the functions they assumed in relation to education and teaching, to respect the right of parents to ensure the education and teaching of their children in conformity with their own religious and philosophical convictions.

10.13   The Grand Chamber went on to hold that, while the crucifix was above all a religious symbol, there was no evidence that the display of such a symbol on classroom walls might have an influence on pupils. Furthermore, whilst it was nonetheless understandable that the first applicant might see in the display of crucifixes in the classrooms of the state school formerly attended by her children a lack of respect on the state's part for her right to ensure their education and teaching in conformity with her own philosophical convictions, her subjective perception was not sufficient to establish a breach of Article 2 of Protocol No. 1.

10.14   The Italian Government submitted that the presence of crucifixes in state school classrooms at the then current time corresponded to a tradition which they considered it important to perpetuate. They added that, beyond its religious meaning, the crucifix symbolised the principles and values which formed the foundation of democracy and western civilisation, and that its presence in classrooms was justifiable on that account. With regard to the first point, the court took the view that, while the decision whether or not to perpetuate a tradition fell in principle within the margin of appreciation of the member states of the Council of Europe, the reference to a tradition could not relieve them of their obligation to respect the rights and freedoms enshrined in the Convention and its Protocols. Regarding the second point, noting that the Italian Consiglio di Stato and the Court of Cassation had diverging views on the meaning of the crucifix and that the Constitutional Court had not given a ruling, the court considered that it was not for it to take a position regarding a domestic debate among domestic courts.

10.15   The Grand Chamber nonetheless considered that the state enjoyed a margin of appreciation in its efforts to reconcile the exercise of the functions they assumed in relation to education and teaching with respect for the right of parents to ensure such education and teaching in conformity with their own religious and philosophical convictions. The court therefore concluded that it had a duty in principle to respect the states' decisions in those matters, including the place they accorded to religion, provided that those decisions did not lead to a form of indoctrination. Accordingly, the decision whether crucifixes should be present in classrooms was, in principle, a matter falling within the margin of appreciation of the state, particularly where there was no European consensus. That margin of appreciation, however, went hand in hand with supervision by the court, whose task was to satisfy itself that the choice did not amount to a form of indoctrination.

10.16   In that connection it observed that by prescribing the presence of crucifixes in state school classrooms the Italian regulations conferred on the country's majority religion preponderant visibility in the school environment.

In the court's view, that was not in itself sufficient, however, to denote a process of indoctrination on Italy's part and establish a breach of the requirements of Article 2 of Protocol No. 1. It observed that a crucifix on a wall was an essentially passive symbol whose influence on pupils was not comparable to that of didactic speech or participation in religious activities.

10.17 The court also considered that the effects of the greater visibility which the presence of the crucifix gave to Christianity in schools needed to be further placed in perspective by consideration of the following points: the presence of crucifixes was not associated with compulsory teaching about Christianity; according to the Government, Italy opened up the school environment to other religions (pupils were authorised to wear symbols or apparel having a religious connotation; non-majority religious practices were taken into account; optional religious education could be organised in schools for all recognised religious creeds; the end of Ramadan was often celebrated in schools, and so on). There was nothing to suggest that the authorities were intolerant of pupils who believed in other religions, were non-believers or who held non-religious philosophical convictions. In addition, the applicants had not asserted that the presence of the crucifix in classrooms had encouraged the development of teaching practices with a proselytising tendency. Lastly, the court noted that Ms Lautsi had retained in full her right as a parent to enlighten and advise her children and to guide them on a path in line with her own philosophical convictions.

10.18 The court concluded that, in deciding to keep crucifixes in the classrooms of the state school attended by Ms Lautsi's children, the authorities had acted within the limits of the margin of appreciation left to Italy in the context of its obligation to respect, in the exercise of the functions it assumed in relation to education and teaching, the right of parents to ensure such education and teaching in conformity with their own religious and philosophical convictions. Accordingly, there had been no violation of Article 2 of Protocol No. 1 in respect of the first applicant. The court further considered that no separate issue arose under Article 9.

10.19 *Ali v United Kingdom*[17] concerned a pupil who had been excluded from school in breach of the relevant domestic law principles. It was submitted on behalf of the pupil that the resulting absence of the pupil from school meant that there had been a breach of Article 2 of the First Protocol of the Convention. As appears below, the claim had been litigated in the United Kingdom against the headteacher and governors up to the House of Lords where the applicant had lost. The applicant also lost in the European Court of Human Rights. The court held:

(a)   Article 2 of Protocol 1 guaranteed a right of access to educational institutions existing at a given time. That right had to be effective which

---

[17]   [2011] ECHR 40385/06. This case is discussed at paras **7.204–7.210**.

meant it was necessary that the individual should be able to profit for his education by getting official recognition of the studies he had completed.[18]

(b)   The right to education was not absolute. It could be subject to limitations provided these did not injure the substance of the right.[19] There was no exhaustive list of permissible legitimate aims for such limitations but they must be foreseeable and there must be a reasonable relationship of proportionality between the means employed and the aim sought to be achieved.[20]

(c)   The right did not necessarily entail a right of access to a particular educational institution[21] nor did it exclude the recourse to disciplinary measures such as suspension or exclusion from an educational institution in order to ensure compliance with its internal rules.[22]

10.20   Applying those principles, the court held there had been no breach of Article 2. Although the applicant had not been technically excluded for disciplinary reasons or to ensure compliance with the school's internal rules, the court held that his exclusion was in pursuit of a legitimate aim because it was justified to suspend a pupil pending a criminal investigation. The court also held that that suspension, though in breach of the relevant domestic law principles, was foreseeable and that a fair balance was struck between the exclusion and the justification given, the pupil was only temporarily excluded until the end of the criminal investigation, attempts were made to reintegrate him to the school thereafter which he and his parents did not take up and he was offered adequate alternative education. Accordingly it has held his exclusion was a proportionate response to a legitimate aim.

10.21   As can be seen from the above, the obligation in the second sentence of Article 2 of the First Protocol also applies to the exercise of each and every function that the state undertakes in the sphere of education and teaching. Thus it applies not only to the content of the curriculum and the manner of its teaching, but to other functions assumed by the state, such as the organisation and financing of public education, and matters relating to internal administration, such as discipline.[23] Even functions which are, strictly speaking, 'ancillary' to the provision of education and teaching, such as administrative matters, are therefore covered by the wide-ranging obligation to respect parents' religious and philosophical convictions. Nor is it permissible to

---

[18]   Paragraph 51.
[19]   Paragraph 52.
[20]   Paragraph 53.
[21]   For a case where the court held there was a breach of Art 2 of the first protocol where the applicants were temporarily excluded from a particular institution, but not education generally, see *Temel v Turkey* [2009] ECHR 36458/02.
[22]   Paragraph 54.
[23]   *Kjeldsen*, para 50, *Campbell & Cosans*, para 33, *Valsamis*, para 27.

interpret the scope of the obligation narrowly by distinguishing, for example, between religious instruction and other subjects. It applies 'throughout the entire state education programme'.[24]

10.22 The court in these cases has taken an overtly teleological approach to interpreting the second sentence of Article 2. The aim of that provision, as the court saw it in *Kjeldsen* and *Lautsi*, was to safeguard the possibility of pluralism in education, a possibility it regarded as essential for the preservation of the 'democratic society' as conceived by the Convention. The state, in fulfilling the functions assumed by it in relation to education and teaching, must take care that it conveys information or knowledge in an objective, critical and pluralistic manner. It is forbidden from pursuing an aim of indoctrination that might be considered as not respecting parents' religious or philosophical convictions[25]. 'That is the limit that must not be exceeded.'[26] The court has considered such an interpretation to be consistent with the general spirit of the Convention, as an instrument designed to maintain and promote the ideals and values of a democratic society.

10.23 As for the meaning of 'philosophical convictions', the court has held that in its ordinary meaning the word 'convictions', taken on its own, is not synonymous with the words 'opinions' and 'ideas', such as are found in Article 10, guaranteeing freedom of expression, but is more akin to the term 'beliefs' in Article 9, guaranteeing freedom of thought, conscience and religion. It denotes views that attain a certain level of cogency, seriousness, cohesion and importance.[27] The adjective 'philosophical' has been said to be incapable of exhaustive definition, and a term on the significance of which little can be gleaned from the travaux préparatoires.

10.24 In the court's view, the expression 'philosophical convictions' denotes such convictions as are worthy of respect in a democratic society and are not incompatible with human dignity, and which do not conflict with the fundamental right of the child to education.[28]

10.25 However, there are limits to what the obligation contained in the second sentence of Article 2 requires of the state. Just as there is no obligation under the first sentence to establish or to subsidise education of any particular type or at any particular level, so under the second sentence it has been held by the Commission that there is no obligation on the state to subsidise any particular

---

24   *Kjeldsen*, para 51, *Valsamis*, para 27.
25   For a striking example of the importance attached to the principle, see *X v UK* No 8010/77, Decision 1.3.79, 16 DR 1010, in which a teacher complained that forbidding him to wear religious and anti-abortion stickers on his clothes and brief case was contrary to his right to freedom of expression guaranteed by Art 10. The Commission declared his application inadmissible, finding the interference to be justified on the basis that teachers in non-denominational schools should have regard to the rights of parents to respect for their religious and philosophical convictions in the education of their children.
26   *Kjeldsen*, para 53.
27   *Campbell & Cosans*, para 36, *Valsamis*, para 25.
28   *Campbell & Cosans*, para 36.

form of education in order to respect the religious and philosophical beliefs of parents.[29] It is sufficient for the state to show respect for those convictions within the existing and developing system of education.

10.26 The court has acknowledged that the setting and planning of the curriculum are matters which fall, in principle, within states' competence, and that the second sentence of Article 2 does not prevent states from imparting through teaching or education information or knowledge of a directly or indirectly religious or philosophical kind.[30] Nor does it permit parents to object to the integration of such teaching or education in the school curriculum, because otherwise, all institutionalised teaching would run the risk of proving impracticable.[31]

10.27 The court and Commission have also made clear that the second sentence of Article 2 does not guarantee an absolute right to have children educated in accordance with parents' philosophical convictions, but a right to respect for those convictions. Allowing parents to educate their children at home, but requiring them to co-operate in the assessment of their children's educational standards by an education authority in order to ensure that certain standards of literacy and numeracy are being attained, does not constitute a lack of respect for the parents' rights under the second sentence of Article 2.[32]

10.28 Most of the domestic case-law on Article 2 of the First Protocol has arisen from cases where by reason of exclusion or otherwise, but not a failure to provide transport a pupil has been out of school: see *A v Head teacher and Governors of Lord Grey School*,[33] *R (Begum) v Head Teacher and Governors of Denbigh High School*,[34] *Re JR17 (Northern Ireland)*[35] and *A v Essex County Council*.[36] This case-law is discussed in Chapter 7.[37]

---

[29] *X v UK*, No 7782/77, Decision 2.5.78, 14 DR 179 at 180; *W and KL v Sweden*, No 10476/83, Decision 11.12.85, DR 143 at 148-9 (Art 2 of the First Protocol neither required the state to make a grant to alternative private schools such as Steiner schools, nor to provide financial assistance to the pupils; its obligation under that Article was fulfilled by permitting establishment of the school).

[30] See, eg *X, Y & Z v Federal Republic of Germany*, No 9411/81, Decision 15.7.82, DR 224 (complaint that school curricula imposed on children an ideology based on science to which they did not subscribe declared inadmissible; the state offered a choice of secondary schools, each with a different educational orientation).

[31] *Kjeldsen*, para 53.

[32] *Family H v UK*, No 10233/83, Decision 6.3.84, 37 DR 105.

[33] [2005] UKHL 14.

[34] [2006] UKHL 15.

[35] [2010] UKSC 27.

[36] [2010] UKSC 33.

[37] See paragraphs **7.171–7.203**.

INDEX

References are to paragraph numbers.